Research Anthology on Game Design, Development, Usage, and Social Impact

Information Resources Management Association
USA

Volume III

Published in the United States of America by
  IGI Global
  Information Science Reference (an imprint of IGI Global)
  701 E. Chocolate Avenue
  Hershey PA, USA 17033
  Tel: 717-533-8845
  Fax: 717-533-8661
  E-mail: cust@igi-global.com
  Web site: http://www.igi-global.com

Library of Congress Cataloging-in-Publication Data

Names: Information Resources Management Association, editor.
Title: Research anthology on game design, development, usage, and social
  impact / Information Resources Management Association, editor.
Description: Hershey, PA : Information Science Reference, [2023] | Includes
  bibliographical references and index. | Summary: "Videogames have risen
  in popularity in recent decades and continue to entertain many all over
  the world. As game design and development becomes more accessible to
  those outside of the industry, their uses and impacts are further
  expanded. Games have been developed for medical, educational, business,
  and many more applications. While games have many beneficial
  applications, many challenges exist in current development processes as
  well as some of their impacts on society. It is essential to investigate
  the current trends in the design and development of games as well as the
  opportunities and challenges presented in their usage and social impact.
  The Research Anthology on Game Design, Development, Usage, and Social
  Impact discusses the emerging developments, opportunities, and
  challenges that are found within the design, development, usage, and
  impact of gaming. It presents a comprehensive collection of the recent
  research, theories, case studies, and more within the area. Covering
  topics such as academic game creation, gaming experience, and violence
  in gaming, this major reference work is a dynamic resource for game
  developers, instructional designers, educators and administrators of
  both K-12 and higher education, students of higher education,
  librarians, government officials, business leaders and executives,
  researchers, and academicians"-- Provided by publisher.
Identifiers: LCCN 2022040888 (print) | LCCN 2022040889 (ebook) | ISBN
  9781668475898 (h/c) | ISBN 9781668475904 (eISBN)
Subjects: LCSH: Video games--Design--Research. | Video games--Social
  aspects--Research.
Classification: LCC GV1469.3 .R47 2023 (print) | LCC GV1469.3 (ebook) |
  DDC 794.8/3--dc23/eng/20220930
LC record available at https://lccn.loc.gov/2022040888
LC ebook record available at https://lccn.loc.gov/2022040889

British Cataloguing in Publication Data
A Cataloguing in Publication record for this book is available from the British Library.

The views expressed in this book are those of the authors, but not necessarily of the publisher.

For electronic access to this publication, please contact: eresources@igi-global.com.

List of Contributors

Abida, Fatma Choura / *Institute of Computer Science of Tunis, Tunisia* 105

Adnan, Mohd Muttaqin Bin Mohd / *Taylor's University, Malaysia* 1140

Ahmad, Faizan / *Research Center for Human-Computer Interaction (RC-HCI), COMSATS University Islamabad (CUI), Lahore, Pakistan* 1411

Ahmad, Mifrah / *Deakin University, Australia* 872

Ahmed, Zeeshan / *Institute of Software, Chinese Academy of Sciences, Beijing, China* 1411

Alhasanat, Mahmoud B. / *Al-Hussein Bin Talal University, Maan, Jordan* 1321

Ali, Raian / *Bournemouth University, Poole, UK* 144

Al-Rawashdeh, Baker / *Mutah University, Mutah, Jordan* 1321

Alshamaileh, Mohammed / *Mutah University, Mutah, Jordan* 1321

Altarawneh, Ghada / *Mutah University, Karak, Jordan* 1321

Ampatzidou, Cristina / *University of Groningen, Faculty of Spatial Sciences, Groningen, Netherlands* 482

Andrews, Sharon / *University of Houston-Clear Lake, USA* 307

Anning-Dorson, Thomas / *Wits Business School, University of the Witwatersrand, South Africa* 1836

Antonova, Albena / *Sofia University, Bulgaria* 1346

Ashraf, Mujeeba / *Institute of Applied Psychology, University of the Punjab, Lahore, Pakistan* . 1781

Atiker, Baris / *Bahcesehir University, Turkey* 121

Atsikpasi, Pinelopi / *University of the Aegean, Department of Primary Education, Rhodes, Greece* 1621

Austin, Hailey J. / *University of Dundee, UK* 1435

Bacos, Catherine A. / *University of Nevada, Las Vegas, USA* 774

Baek, Joeun / *Boise State University, USA* 433

Bao, Wenrui / *Baoji University of Arts and Sciences, China* 680

Barnes, Steven / *University of Bolton, UK* 732, 994

Barral, Laure Vidaud / *Université Grenoble Alpes, France & IRSTEA, France & ETNA, France* 212

Bartolucci, Marco / *Università degli Studi di Perugia, Perugia, Italy* 1923

Batini, Federico / *Università degli Studi di Perugia, Perugia, Italy* 1923

Batista, Arthur V. / *Universidade Federal de Santa Catarina, Brazil* 456

Ben Saad, Sihem / *Carthage Business School, Université Tunis Carthage, Tunisia* 105

Ben Yahia, Ali / *LIGUE, Tunis, Tunisia* 105

Bielefeldt, Talbot / *Independent Researcher, USA* 914

Birchfield, David / *SmalLab Learning, USA* 1097

Blight, Michael G / *North Central College, USA* 1304

Blignaut, A. Seugnet / *TELIT, North-West University, South Africa* 240

Botha-Ravyse, Chrisna R. / *TELIT, North-West University, South Africa* 240

Bradbury, Robert E. / *University of Houston-Clear Lake, USA* 307

Bradley, Melvin / *Mental Health Independent Support Team, UK* 994

Buckingham, Christopher / *University of Southampton, UK* 198

Buckley, Patrick / *University of Limerick, Limerick, Ireland* 1852

Bueno, Bruna S. / *Universidade Federal de Santa Catarina, Brazil* 456

Cabras, Cristina / *University of Cagliari, Cagliari, Italy* 1735

Çadırcı, Tugce Ozansoy / *Yıldız Technical University, Turkey* 1495

Calado, Felipe Matheus / *Universidade Católica de Pernambuco, Brazil* 286

Campbell, Laurie O / *University of Central Florida, Orlando, USA* 716

Canady, Fawn / *Sonoma State University, USA* 891

Candemir, Tülay / *Pamukkale University, Turkey* 1581

Candemir, Tülin / *Akdeniz University, Turkey* 1581

Çat, Arzu Kalafat / *Abant Izzet Baysal University, Turkey* 1978

Ceniza, Angie Monterde / *University of San Carlos, Philippines* 785

Chen, Kenneth / *Drexel University, USA* 1222

Choi, Youngkeun / *Sangmyung University, Seoul, Korea* 1031, 1043

Conceição, Karolini R. / *Universidade Federal de Santa Catarina, Brazil* 456

Cordero-Brito, Staling / *Universidad de Salamanca, Salamanca, Spain* 691

Crawford, Caroline M. / *University of Houston-Clear Lake, USA* 307

Cubadda, Maria Laura / *University of Cagliari, Cagliari, Italy* 1735

Cunha, Ana Rafaela / *School of Health, Polytechnic of Porto, Portugal* 1263

DaCosta, Boaventura / *Solers Research Group, USA* 1055, 1470

Daniel, Jr., Emory S. / *Appalachian State University, USA* 1304

de Voogt, Alex / *Drew University, Madison, USA* 1321

Deliyannis, Ioannis / *Ionian University, Department of Audiovisual Arts, Corfu, Greece* 1621

Djaouti, Damien / *LIRDEF, University of Montpellier, Montpellier, France* 617

Dodero, Juan Manuel / *Escuela Superior de Ingeniería, University of Cadiz, Spain* 839

Donald, Iain / *Abertay University, UK* 1435

Donga, João / *LabRP, School of Allied Health Technologies, Polytechnic of Porto, Portugal* 187

Dores, Artemisa / *Polytechnic of Porto, Portugal* 84

Drivet, Alessio / *Geogebra Institute of Turin, Italy* 967

Dubbels, Brock Randall / *McMaster University, Canada* 258

Dunn, Robert Andrew / *East Tennessee State University, Johnson City, USA* 1938

Durán-Yañez, Esteban A. / *Tecnológico Nacional de México IT Aguascalientes, Mexico* 944

Egert, Christopher A. / *Rochester Institute of Technology, USA* 1358

Eren, P. Erhan / *Middle East Technical University, Turkey* 31

Faris, Hossam / *The University of Jordan, Amman, Jordan* 1321

Fernandes, Farley / *UNIDCOM IADE, Portugal & Universidade da Beira Interior, Portugal* 286

Filho, Marisardo Bezerra de Medeiros / *Universidade Federal de Pernambuco, Brazil* 286

Fiuza, Patricia J. / *Universidade Federal de Santa Catarina, Brazil* 456

Fokides, Emmanuel / *University of the Aegean, Department of Primary Education, Rhodes,
Greece* 1621

Franzwa, Christopher / *Rowan University, USA* 914

Gao, Linxia / *Wuhan Business University, China* 1795

Geary, Conor / *University of Limerick, Limerick, Ireland* 1852

Gezgin, Deniz Mertkan / *Trakya University, Edirne, Turkey* 662

Ghavifekr, Simin / *Faculty of Education, University of Malaya, Kuala Lumpur, Malaysia* 391

Gillberg, David / *Insert Coin, Sweden* 557

Gladston, Angelin / *Anna University, Chennai, India* 1085

Goh, See Kwong / *Taylor's University, Malaysia* 1140

Goli, Mahendar / *Madanapalle Institute of Technology and Science, India* 1516

Gomes, Paulo Veloso / *LabRP, School of Allied Health Technologies, Polytechnic of Porto,*
Portugal 187

Gómez de Merodio, Milagros Huerta / *University of Cadiz, Spain* 839

Gomide, Joao Victor Boechat / *Universidade FUMEC, Brazil* 585

Goode, Kaila / *Oklahoma State University, USA* 62

Goyal, Pramod Kumar / *Department of Training and Technical Education, Government of*
Delhi, India 814

Griffiths, Mark D. / *International Gaming Research Unit, Psychology Division, Nottingham*
Trent University, Nottingham, UK 662

Guadagno, Rosanna / *Stanford University, Stanford, USA* 1938

Gugerell, Katharina / *University of Groningen, Faculty of Spatial Sciences, Groningen,*
Netherlands 482

Gungor, Aysegul Sagkaya / *Isik University, Turkey* 1495

Gunter, Glenda A / *The University of Central Florida, Orlando, USA* 716

Gupta, Diali / *University of Calgary, Canada* 1387

Gutica, Mirela / *British Columbia Institute of Technology, Canada* 411

Hallewell, Madeline J. / *University of Nottingham, UK* 323

Hamutoğlu, Nazire Burçin / *Kırşehir Ahi Evran University, Kırşehir, Turkey* 662

Hassanat, Ahmad B. / *Mutah University, Karak, Jordan* 1321

Hawi, Nazir / *INTA Institute for Technology Addiction, Notre Dame University-Louaize,*
Lebanon 1704

Head, Danielle L. / *University of Nevada, Las Vegas, USA* 774

Helmefalk, Miralem / *Linnaeus University, Sweden* 530, 1870

Himang, Celbert Mirasol / *Cebu Technological University, Philippines* 785

Himang, Melanie M. / *Cebu Technological University, Philippines* 785

Hong, Seong Choul / *Kyonggi University, Seoul, South Korea* 1721

Hosseini, Mahmood / *Bournemouth University, Poole, UK* 144

Jahan, Kauser / *Rowan University, USA* 914

Janssen, Marijn / *Delft University of Technology, The Netherlands* 1956

Jiang, Nan / *Taylor's University, Malaysia* 1140

Joensuu, Kosti / *University of Lapland, Rovaniemi, Finland* 1423

Johnson, Mina C. / *Arizona State University, USA & Embodied Games, USA* 1097

Jousselme, Anne-Laure / *NATO STO Centre for Maritime Research and Experimentation,*
Italy 212

Kaimara, Polyxeni / *Ionian University, Department of Audiovisual Arts, Corfu, Greece* 1621

Kappas, Arvid / *Department of Psychology and Methods, Jacobs University Bremen, Bremen,*
Germany 1480

Kaur, Manmeet / *Taylor's University, Malaysia* 1140

Kenny, Robert F / *Florida Gulf Coast University, Fort Myers, USA* 716

Kermanidis, Katia Lida / *Ionian University, Department of Informatics, Corfu, Greece* 341

Khatri, Preety / *Institute of Management Studies Noida, India* 14

Kim, Beaumie / *University of Calgary, Canada* 1387

Kit, Cheah Wen / *Universiti Sains Malaysia, Malaysia* 1238

Kleiman, Fernando / *Delft University of Technology, The Netherlands* 1956

Kosa, Mehmet / *Tilburg University, The Netherlands* 31

Kosmas, Panagiotis / *Center for the Advancement of Research and Development in Educational
Technology, Cyprus & School of Education, University of Nicosia, Cyprus* 507

Krach, S. Kathleen / *Florida State University, Tallahassee, USA* 774

Krumhuber, Eva G. / *Department of Experimental Psychology, University College London,
London, UK* 1480

Laferriere, Jeffrey R. / *Lebanon Valley College, Annville, USA* 774

Lage de Oliveira, Pedro Henrique Roscoe / *Minas Gerais State University, Brazil* 585

Lamb, Nathan / *Rowan University, USA* 914

Lemos, Robson R. / *Universidade Federal de Santa Catarina, Brazil* 456

Liu, Liqiong / *Wuhan Business University, China* 1795

Loh, Christian S. / *Southern Illinois University, USA* 1818

López-Luévano, César A. / *Universidad Politécnica de Aguascalientes, Mexico* 944

Lundqvist, Siw / *Linnéuniversitetet, Kalmar, Sweden* 1870

Mackessy, Thomas / *University of Limerick, Limerick, Ireland* 1852

Mansur, Samira S. / *Universidade Federal de Santa Catarina, Brazil* 456

Maravalhas, Vanessa / *School of Health, Polytechnic of Porto, Portugal* 1263

Marcusson, Leif / *Linnéuniversitetet, Kalmar, Sweden* 1870

Marques, António / *School of Health, Polytechnic Institute of Porto, Portugal* 1263

Martins, Helena / *Lusófona University, Portugal* 84

Mast, Fred W. / *University of Bern, Switzerland* 1198

Mattioli, Francesco / *Università degli Studi di Perugia, Perugia, Italy* 1923

McBride, Tom / *Beloit College, USA* 633

McCreery, Michael P. / *University of Nevada, Las Vegas, USA* 774

Megowan-Romanowicz, Colleen / *American Modeling Teachers Association, USA* 1097

Mei, Quanjun / *Wuhan Business University, China* 1795

Meijer, Sebastiaan / *KTH Royal Institute of Technology, Sweden* 1956

Mena, Juanjo / *Facultad de Educación, Universidad de Salamanca, Salamanca, Spain &
Institute of Psychology and Education, Kazan Federal University, Kazan, Russia* 691

Min, Ellen / *Timberline High School, USA* 433

Misra, Richa / *Jaipuria Institute of Management, Noida, India* 1678

Moseley, Alex / *University of Leicester, Leicester, UK* 1908

Muneeb, Sara / *Research Center for Human-Computer Interaction (RC-HCI), COMSATS
University Islamabad (CUI), Lahore, Pakistan* 1411

Murdoch, Ryan / *The Glasgow School of Art, UK* 599

Nagelhout, Ed / *University of Nevada, Las Vegas, USA* 891

Nagle, Eoghan / *University of Limerick, Limerick, Ireland* 1852

Naveen V. / *Anna University, Chennai, India* 1085

Neha B. / *Anna University, Chennai, India* 1085

Neves, André Menezes Marques / *Universidade Federal de Pernambuco, Brazil* 286

Noonan, Seamus / *University of Limerick, Limerick, Ireland* 1852
Notargiacomo, Pollyana / *Mackenzie Presbyterian University, Brazil* 1121
Ntokos, Konstantinos / *Solent University of Southampton, UK* 169
Núñez, José Mª Portela / *University of Cadiz, Spain* 839
Núñez, Nestor Mora / *University of Cadiz, Spain* 839
Ocampo, Lanndon / *Cebu Technological University, Philippines* 785
Ofosu-Ampong, Kingsley / *Business School, University of Ghana, Ghana* 1836
Palmquist, Adam / *School of Informatics, University of Skövde, Sweden* 557
Park, Hyekyeong / *Sancheong Middle School, South Korea* 433
Patel, Harshada / *University of Nottingham, UK* 323
Pereira, Poliana F. / *Universidade Federal de Santa Catarina, Brazil* 456
Perreault, Gregory P. / *Appalachian State University, USA* 1304, 1661
Perreault, Mildred F. / *East Tennessee State University, USA* 1661
Petrina, Stephen / *University of British Columbia, Canada* 411
Phalp, Keith / *Bournemouth University, Poole, UK* 144
Phelps, Andrew M. / *University of Canterbury, New Zealand & American University, USA* 1358
Philippou, Andrea / *Center for the Advancement of Research and Development in Educational
   Technology, Cyprus* 507
Pinet, Francois / *Université Clermont Auvergne, France & IRSTEA, France & UR TSCF,
   Clermont-Ferrand, France* 212
Pinto, Mário / *ESMAD, Polytechnic Institute of Porto, Portugal* 1
Plerou, Antonia / *Ionian University, Department of Informatics, Corfu, Greece* 1621
Portela, Carlos Filipe / *University of Minho, Portugal* 1
Prasath, Surya V. B. / *Cincinnati Children's Hospital Medical Center, Cincinnati, USA* 1321
Prescott, Julie / *University of Bolton, UK* 732
Preuß, Anna Katharina / *Johannes Gutenberg University of Mainz, Mainz, Germany* 1558
Psomos, Panagiotis / *University of the Aegean, Greece* 507
Queiros, Ricardo Alexandre Peixoto de / *ESMAD, Polytechnic Institute of Porto, Portugal* 1
Ravyse, Werner Siegfried / *TELIT, North-West University, South Africa* 240
Rodríguez-Díaz, Mario A. / *Tecnológico Nacional de México IT Aguascalientes, Mexico* 944
Rudolph, Cristiane Meneghelli / *Universidade Federal de Santa Catarina, Brazil* 456
Ryynänen, Sanna / *University of Lapland, Rovaniemi, Finland* 1423
Sá, Vítor J. / *LabRP, Polytechnic of Porto, Portugal & Centro ALGORITMI. Universidade
   Católica Portuguesa, Portugal* 187
Saeedi-Hosseiny, Marzieh S. / *Rowan University, USA* 914
Samaha, Maya / *INTA Institute for Technology Addiction, Notre Dame University-Louaize,
   Lebanon* 1704
Samur, Yavuz / *Bahçeşehir University, Istanbul, Turkey* 662
Schiffer, Sheldon / *Georgia State University, USA* 365
Sechi, Cristina / *University of Cagliari, Cagliari, Italy* 1735
Seok, Soonhwa / *Korea University, South Korea* 1055, 1470
Sepetci, Tülin / *Abant İzzet Baysal University, Turkey* 1581
Shahri, Alimohammad / *Bournemouth University, Poole, UK* 144
Silva de Miranda, Carlos Alberto / *Minas Gerais State University, Brazil* 585
Simões, Alberto / *Polytechnic Institute of Cávado and Ave, Portugal* 1
Simões-Silva, Vitor / *School of Health, Polytechnic of Porto, Portugal* 1263

Singh, Nidhi / *Jaipuria Institute of Management, Noida, India* 1678
Singh, Pawan / *Indira Gandhi National Tribal University, Amarkantak, India* 814
Singh, Sonali / *Jaipuria Institute of Management, Noida, India* 1678
Siqueira da Silva, Isabel Cristina / *UniRitter, Brazil* 1891
Soares, Maria Inês / *School of Health, Polytechnic of Porto, Portugal* 1263
Söğüt, Fatih / *Kırklareli University, Turkey* 1457
Spöhrer, Markus / *University of Konstanz, Germany* 644
Sun, Shengtao / *Rowan University, USA* 914
Swiderska, Aleksandra / *Department of Psychology, Warsaw University, Warsaw, Poland* 1480
Tacnet, Jean-Marc / *Université Grenoble Alpes, France & IRSTEA, France & ETNA, France* 212
Tang, Ying / *Rowan University, USA* 914
Tarawneh, Ahmad S. / *Eotvos Lorand University ELTE, Budapest, Hungary* 1321
Taylor, Jacqui / *Bournemouth University, Poole, UK* 144
Topal, Murat / *Sakarya University, Sakarya, Turkey* 662
Turgut, Hasan / *Ondokuz Mayıs University, Turkey* 1640
Turner, Jason James / *Asia Pacific University of Technology and Innovation, Malaysia* 1140
Uysal, Ahmet / *Stanford University, Stanford, USA* 31
Vasinda, Sheri / *Oklahoma State University, USA* 62
Vemuri, Vishnu Vandana / *Anurag University, India* 1516
Walder Marin, Werner / *Mackenzie Presbyterian University, Brazil* 1121
Wanick, Vanissa / *University of Southampton, UK* 198
Weber, Stefan / *University of Bern, Switzerland* 1198
Weibel, David / *University of Bern, Switzerland* 1198
Westerberg, Charles / *Beloit College, USA* 633
Wilkin, Terri L. / *American Public University System, USA* 1285
William, Linda / *Temasek Polytechnic, Singapore* 1162
Williams, Andrew / *University of Bolton, UK* 994
Williams, Russell Blair / *Zayed University, Dubai, UAE* 1183, 1538
Wong, Seng Yue / *Centre for the Initiation of Talent and Industrial Training (CITra), University of Malaya, Kuala Lumpur, Malaysia* 391
Yang, Ruan / *Temasek Polytechnic, Singapore* 1162
Yayla, Neslihan / *Ondokuz Mayıs University, Turkey* 1640, 1756
Ye, Pinghao / *Wuhan Business University, China* 1795
Zhou, Ting / *Fort Hays State University, USA* 1818
Zolkepli, Izzal Asnira / *Universiti Sains Malaysia, Malaysia* 1238

Table of Contents

Preface...xxiv

Section 1
Fundamental Concepts and Theories

Chapter 1
A Primer on Gamification Standardization.. 1
    Ricardo Alexandre Peixoto de Queiros, ESMAD, Polytechnic Institute of Porto, Portugal
    Mário Pinto, ESMAD, Polytechnic Institute of Porto, Portugal
    Alberto Simões, Polytechnic Institute of Cávado and Ave, Portugal
    Carlos Filipe Portela, University of Minho, Portugal

Chapter 2
The Gaming Experience With AI 14
    Preety Khatri, Institute of Management Studies Noida, India

Chapter 3
Acceptance of Virtual Reality Games: A Multi-Theory Approach 31
    Mehmet Kosa, Tilburg University, The Netherlands
    Ahmet Uysal, Stanford University, Stanford, USA
    P. Erhan Eren, Middle East Technical University, Turkey

Chapter 4
Videogames and Sensory Theory: Enchantment in the 21st Century.................................. 62
    Kaila Goode, Oklahoma State University, USA
    Sheri Vasinda, Oklahoma State University, USA

Chapter 5
Fun and Games: How to Actually Create a Gamified Approach to Health Education and Promotion 84
    Helena Martins, Lusófona University, Portugal
    Artemisa Dores, Polytechnic of Porto, Portugal

Chapter 6
Towards Better Understanding of Children's Relationships With Online Games and Advergames .. 105
    Ali Ben Yahia, LIGUE, Tunis, Tunisia
    Sihem Ben Saad, Carthage Business School, Université Tunis Carthage, Tunisia
    Fatma Choura Abida, Institute of Computer Science of Tunis, Tunisia

Section 2
Development and Design Methodologies

Chapter 7

Augmented Reality Games 121

    Baris Atiker, Bahcesehir University, Turkey

Chapter 8

How to Engineer Gamification: The Consensus, the Best Practice and the Grey Areas 144

    Alimohammad Shahri, Bournemouth University, Poole, UK
    Mahmood Hosseini, Bournemouth University, Poole, UK
    Keith Phalp, Bournemouth University, Poole, UK
    Jacqui Taylor, Bournemouth University, Poole, UK
    Raian Ali, Bournemouth University, Poole, UK

Chapter 9

Techniques on Multiplatform Movement and Interaction Systems in a Virtual Reality Context for
Games 169

    Konstantinos Ntokos, Solent University of Southampton, UK

Chapter 10

Software Requirements Definition Processes in Gamification Development for Immersive
Environments 187

    Paulo Veloso Gomes, LabRP, School of Allied Health Technologies, Polytechnic of Porto,
        Portugal
    João Donga, LabRP, School of Allied Health Technologies, Polytechnic of Porto, Portugal
    Vítor J. Sá, LabRP, Polytechnic of Porto, Portugal & Centro ALGORITMI. Universidade
        Católica Portuguesa, Portugal

Chapter 11

Crowdfunding Serious Games: Towards a Framework 198

    Christopher Buckingham, University of Southampton, UK
    Vanissa Wanick, University of Southampton, UK

Chapter 12

Combining UML Profiles to Design Serious Games Dedicated to Trace Information in Decision
Processes 212

    Laure Vidaud Barral, Université Grenoble Alpes, France & IRSTEA, France & ETNA,
        France
    Francois Pinet, Université Clermont Auvergne, France & IRSTEA, France & UR TSCF,
        Clermont-Ferrand, France
    Jean-Marc Tacnet, Université Grenoble Alpes, France & IRSTEA, France & ETNA, France
    Anne-Laure Jousselme, NATO STO Centre for Maritime Research and Experimentation,
        Italy

Chapter 13
Codebook Co-Development to Understand Fidelity and Initiate Artificial Intelligence in Serious
Games 240

Werner Siegfried Ravyse, TELIT, North-West University, South Africa
A. Seugnet Blignaut, TELIT, North-West University, South Africa
Chrisna R. Botha-Ravyse, TELIT, North-West University, South Africa

Chapter 14
Requirements-Based Design of Serious Games and Learning Software: An Introduction to the
Vegas Effect 258

Brock Randall Dubbels, McMaster University, Canada

Chapter 15
An ARM Framework for F2P Mobile Games... 286

Marisardo Bezerra de Medeiros Filho, Universidade Federal de Pernambuco, Brazil
Farley Fernandes, UNIDCOM IADE, Portugal & Universidade da Beira Interior, Portugal
Felipe Matheus Calado, Universidade Católica de Pernambuco, Brazil
André Menezes Marques Neves, Universidade Federal de Pernambuco, Brazil

Chapter 16
Fiero and Flow in Online Competitive Gaming: The Gaming Engagement Framework 307

Sharon Andrews, University of Houston-Clear Lake, USA
Robert E. Bradbury, University of Houston-Clear Lake, USA
Caroline M. Crawford, University of Houston-Clear Lake, USA

Chapter 17
Persona-Scenarios in Game Development: Communication Tensions Between Hearing Aid Users
and Communication Partners... 323

Harshada Patel, University of Nottingham, UK
Madeline J. Hallewell, University of Nottingham, UK

Chapter 18
Identifying Latent Semantics in Action Games for Player Modeling... 341

Katia Lida Kermanidis, Ionian University, Department of Informatics, Corfu, Greece

Chapter 19
Multi-Disciplinary Paths to Actor-Centric Non-Player Character Emotion Models........................ 365

Sheldon Schiffer, Georgia State University, USA

Chapter 20
User Experience Design of History Game: An Analysis Review and Evaluation Study for
Malaysia Context 391

Seng Yue Wong, Centre for the Initiation of Talent and Industrial Training (CITra),
*   University of Malaya, Kuala Lumpur, Malaysia*
Simin Ghavifekr, Faculty of Education, University of Malaya, Kuala Lumpur, Malaysia

Chapter 21
Emotional Agents in Educational Game Design: Heroes of Math Island..411
    Mirela Gutica, British Columbia Institute of Technology, Canada
    Stephen Petrina, University of British Columbia, Canada

Chapter 22
Designing a Minecraft Simulation Game for Learning a Language Through Knowledge Co-
Construction...433
    Joeun Baek, Boise State University, USA
    Hyekyeong Park, Sancheong Middle School, South Korea
    Ellen Min, Timberline High School, USA

Chapter 23
Design of a Web3D Serious Game for Human Anatomy Education: A Web3D Game for Human
Anatomy Education..456
    Robson R. Lemos, Universidade Federal de Santa Catarina, Brazil
    Cristiane Meneghelli Rudolph, Universidade Federal de Santa Catarina, Brazil
    Arthur V. Batista, Universidade Federal de Santa Catarina, Brazil
    Karolini R. Conceição, Universidade Federal de Santa Catarina, Brazil
    Poliana F. Pereira, Universidade Federal de Santa Catarina, Brazil
    Bruna S. Bueno, Universidade Federal de Santa Catarina, Brazil
    Patricia J. Fiuza, Universidade Federal de Santa Catarina, Brazil
    Samira S. Mansur, Universidade Federal de Santa Catarina, Brazil

Chapter 24
Mapping Game Mechanics for Learning in a Serious Game for the Energy Transition 482
    Cristina Ampatzidou, University of Groningen, Faculty of Spatial Sciences, Groningen,
        Netherlands
    Katharina Gugerell, University of Groningen, Faculty of Spatial Sciences, Groningen,
        Netherlands

Chapter 25
Towards the Development of a Game for Computational Thinking: Identifying Students' Needs
and Interests 507
    Panagiotis Kosmas, Center for the Advancement of Research and Development in
        Educational Technology, Cyprus & School of Education, University of Nicosia, Cyprus
    Andrea Philippou, Center for the Advancement of Research and Development in Educational
        Technology, Cyprus
    Panagiotis Psomos, University of the Aegean, Greece

Chapter 26
What Can Gamification Learn From Sensory Marketing? In the Context of Servicescapes 530
    Miralem Helmefalk, Linnaeus University, Sweden

Chapter 27
Eye of the Beholder: Analyzing a Gamification Design Through a Servicescape Lens......................557
Adam Palmquist, School of Informatics, University of Skövde, Sweden
David Gillberg, Insert Coin, Sweden

Section 3
Tools and Technologies

Chapter 28
Applied Alternative Tools and Methods in the Replacement of the Game Design Document 585
Pedro Henrique Roscoe Lage de Oliveira, Minas Gerais State University, Brazil
Carlos Alberto Silva de Miranda, Minas Gerais State University, Brazil
Joao Victor Boechat Gomide, Universidade FUMEC, Brazil

Chapter 29
Serious Games, Meditation, Brain-Computer Interfacing, and Virtual Reality (VR): Empowering
Players to Discover Their Minds...599
Ryan Murdoch, The Glasgow School of Art, UK

Chapter 30
DICE: A Generic Model for the Design Process of Serious Games...617
Damien Djaouti, LIRDEF, University of Montpellier, Montpellier, France

Chapter 31
How to Track Progress: Progressive Tracking Games...633
Charles Westerberg, Beloit College, USA
Tom McBride, Beloit College, USA

Chapter 32
Playing With Auditory Environments in Audio Games: Snake 3D...644
Markus Spöhrer, University of Konstanz, Germany

Chapter 33
The Development of the Online Player Type Scale: Construct Validity and Reliability Testing 662
Nazire Burçin Hamutoğlu, Kırşehir Ahi Evran University, Kırşehir, Turkey
Murat Topal, Sakarya University, Sakarya, Turkey
Yavuz Samur, Bahçeşehir University, Istanbul, Turkey
Deniz Mertkan Gezgin, Trakya University, Edirne, Turkey
Mark D. Griffiths, International Gaming Research Unit, Psychology Division, Nottingham
  Trent University, Nottingham, UK

Chapter 34
The Application of Intelligent Algorithms in the Animation Design of 3D Graphics Engines 680
Wenrui Bao, Baoji University of Arts and Sciences, China

Chapter 35
Gamification and Its Application in the Social Environment: A Tool for Shaping Behaviour...........691
  Staling Cordero-Brito, Universidad de Salamanca, Salamanca, Spain
  Juanjo Mena, Facultad de Educación, Universidad de Salamanca, Salamanca, Spain &
    Institute of Psychology and Education, Kazan Federal University, Kazan, Russia

Chapter 36
Evaluating Social Change Games: Employing the RETAIN Model...716
  Laurie O Campbell, University of Central Florida, Orlando, USA
  Glenda A Gunter, The University of Central Florida, Orlando, USA
  Robert F Kenny, Florida Gulf Coast University, Fort Myers, USA

Chapter 37
Therapeutic Gaming for Adolescent Anxiety: Development and Evaluation of a Mobile
Intervention 732
  Steven Barnes, University of Bolton, UK
  Julie Prescott, University of Bolton, UK

Chapter 38
Can Video Games Be Used as a Stealth Assessment of Aggression? A Criterion-Related Validity
Study 774
  Michael P. McCreery, University of Nevada, Las Vegas, USA
  S. Kathleen Krach, Florida State University, Tallahassee, USA
  Catherine A. Bacos, University of Nevada, Las Vegas, USA
  Jeffrey R. Laferriere, Lebanon Valley College, Annville, USA
  Danielle L. Head, University of Nevada, Las Vegas, USA

Chapter 39
Using an Extended Technology Acceptance Model for Online Strategic Video Games: A Case of
Multiplayer Online Battle Arena (MOBA) 785
  Melanie M. Himang, Cebu Technological University, Philippines
  Celbert Mirasol Himang, Cebu Technological University, Philippines
  Angie Monterde Ceniza, University of San Carlos, Philippines
  Lanndon Ocampo, Cebu Technological University, Philippines

Chapter 40
Two-Stage Non-Cooperative Game Model for Vertical Handoffs in Heterogeneous Wireless
Networks 814
  Pramod Kumar Goyal, Department of Training and Technical Education, Government of
    Delhi, India
  Pawan Singh, Indira Gandhi National Tribal University, Amarkantak, India

Chapter 41
Flip-Game Engineering and Technology Methodology 839
    Milagros Huerta Gómez de Merodio, University of Cadiz, Spain
    Juan Manuel Dodero, Escuela Superior de Ingeniería, University of Cadiz, Spain
    Nestor Mora Núñez, University of Cadiz, Spain
    José Mª Portela Núñez, University of Cadiz, Spain

Chapter 42
Educational Games as Software Through the Lens of Designing Process 872
    Mifrah Ahmad, Deakin University, Australia

Chapter 43
Game Design as Literacy-First Activity: Digital Tools With/In Literacy Instruction 891
    Fawn Canady, Sonoma State University, USA
    Ed Nagelhout, University of Nevada, Las Vegas, USA

Chapter 44
Sustain City: Effective Serious Game Design in Promoting Science and Engineering Education 914
    Ying Tang, Rowan University, USA
    Christopher Franzwa, Rowan University, USA
    Talbot Bielefeldt, Independent Researcher, USA
    Kauser Jahan, Rowan University, USA
    Marzieh S. Saeedi-Hosseiny, Rowan University, USA
    Nathan Lamb, Rowan University, USA
    Shengtao Sun, Rowan University, USA

Chapter 45
Towards a Role-Playing Game Procedural Dungeon Generation Strategy to Help Developing
Working Skills 944
    Esteban A. Durán-Yañez, Tecnológico Nacional de México IT Aguascalientes, Mexico
    Mario A. Rodríguez-Díaz, Tecnológico Nacional de México IT Aguascalientes, Mexico
    César A. López-Luévano, Universidad Politécnica de Aguascalientes, Mexico

Section 4
Utilization and Applications

Chapter 46
Probability and Game 967
    Alessio Drivet, Geogebra Institute of Turin, Italy

Chapter 47
"Piece of Mind" and "Wellbeing Town": Engaging Service Users in the Development of a
Wellbeing Game... 994
    Steven Barnes, University of Bolton, UK
    Melvin Bradley, Mental Health Independent Support Team, UK
    Andrew Williams, University of Bolton, UK

Chapter 48
A Study of the Antecedents of Game Engagement and the Moderating Effect of the Self-Identity
of Collaboration 1031
    Youngkeun Choi, Sangmyung University, Seoul, Korea

Chapter 49
A Study of the Moderating Effect of Social Distance on the Relationship Between Motivators and
Game Engagement 1043
    Youngkeun Choi, Sangmyung University, Seoul, Korea

Chapter 50
Developing a Clearer Understanding of Genre and Mobile Gameplay 1055
    Boaventura DaCosta, Solers Research Group, USA
    Soonhwa Seok, Korea University, South Korea

Chapter 51
Detection of Hands for Hand-Controlled Skyfall Game in Real Time Using CNN 1085
    Neha B., Anna University, Chennai, India
    Naveen V., Anna University, Chennai, India
    Angelin Gladston, Anna University, Chennai, India

Chapter 52
If the Gear Fits, Spin It Again! Embodied Education, Design Components, and In-Play
Assessments 1097
    Mina C. Johnson, Arizona State University, USA & Embodied Games, USA
    David Birchfield, SmalLab Learning, USA
    Colleen Megowan-Romanowicz, American Modeling Teachers Association, USA

Chapter 53
Creativity and Digital Games: A Study of Developing Creativity Through Digital Games 1121
    Werner Walder Marin, Mackenzie Presbyterian University, Brazil
    Pollyana Notargiacomo, Mackenzie Presbyterian University, Brazil

Chapter 54
Development of Habitual Behaviour in Online Social Gaming: Understanding the Moderating
Role of Network Externality 1140
    Nan Jiang, Taylor's University, Malaysia
    Manmeet Kaur, Taylor's University, Malaysia
    Mohd Muttaqin Bin Mohd Adnan, Taylor's University, Malaysia
    Jason James Turner, Asia Pacific University of Technology and Innovation, Malaysia
    See Kwong Goh, Taylor's University, Malaysia

Chapter 55
Using Sentiment Analytics to Understand Learner Experiences in Serious Games........................ 1162
    Linda William, Temasek Polytechnic, Singapore
    Ruan Yang, Temasek Polytechnic, Singapore

Chapter 56
The Social Facilitation of Performance, Emotions, and Motivation in a High Challenge Video
Game: Playing People and Playing Game Characters 1183
    Russell Blair Williams, Zayed University, Dubai, UAE

Chapter 57
Experiencing Presence in a Gaming Activity Improves Mood After a Negative Mood Induction .. 1198
    Stefan Weber, University of Bern, Switzerland
    Fred W. Mast, University of Bern, Switzerland
    David Weibel, University of Bern, Switzerland

Chapter 58
The Fallacies of MDA for Novice Designers: Overusing Mechanics and Underusing Aesthetics... 1222
    Kenneth Chen, Drexel University, USA

Chapter 59
The Role of Narrative Elements in Gamification Towards Value Co-Creation: A Case of Mobile
App Users in Malaysia 1238
    Cheah Wen Kit, Universiti Sains Malaysia, Malaysia
    Izzal Asnira Zolkepli, Universiti Sains Malaysia, Malaysia

Chapter 60
The Use of Gamification in Social Phobia.. 1263
    Vitor Simões-Silva, School of Health, Polytechnic of Porto, Portugal
    Vanessa Maravalhas, School of Health, Polytechnic of Porto, Portugal
    Ana Rafaela Cunha, School of Health, Polytechnic of Porto, Portugal
    Maria Inês Soares, School of Health, Polytechnic of Porto, Portugal
    António Marques, School of Health, Polytechnic Institute of Porto, Portugal

Chapter 61
Online Simulations and Gamification: A Case Study Across an Emergency and Disaster
Management Program... 1285
    Terri L. Wilkin, American Public University System, USA

Chapter 62
Is the News Cycle "Real"? A Case Study of Media "Phandom" and Agenda Setting in Persona 5. 1304
    Emory S. Daniel, Jr., Appalachian State University, USA
    Gregory P. Perreault, Appalachian State University, USA
    Michael G Blight, North Central College, USA

Chapter 63
On Computerizing the Ancient Game of Ṭāb 1321
    Ahmad B. Hassanat, Mutah University, Karak, Jordan
    Ghada Altarawneh, Mutah University, Karak, Jordan
    Ahmad S. Tarawneh, Eotvos Lorand University ELTE, Budapest, Hungary
    Hossam Faris, The University of Jordan, Amman, Jordan
    Mahmoud B. Alhasanat, Al-Hussein Bin Talal University, Maan, Jordan
    Alex de Voogt, Drew University, Madison, USA
    Baker Al-Rawashdeh, Mutah University, Mutah, Jordan
    Mohammed Alshamaileh, Mutah University, Mutah, Jordan
    Surya V. B. Prasath, Cincinnati Children's Hospital Medical Center, Cincinnati, USA

Section 5
Organizational and Social Implications

Chapter 64
Institutions as Designers of Better Social Games 1346
    Albena Antonova, Sofia University, Bulgaria

Chapter 65
Balancing Entertainment and Educational Objectives in Academic Game Creation 1358
    Christopher A. Egert, Rochester Institute of Technology, USA
    Andrew M. Phelps, University of Canterbury, New Zealand & American University, USA

Chapter 66
The Minecraft Aesthetics: Interactions for Reflective Practices 1387
    Diali Gupta, University of Calgary, Canada
    Beaumie Kim, University of Calgary, Canada

Chapter 67
Effect of Gaming Mode Upon the Players' Cognitive Performance During Brain Games Play: An
Exploratory Research 1411
    Faizan Ahmad, Research Center for Human-Computer Interaction (RC-HCI), COMSATS
        University Islamabad (CUI), Lahore, Pakistan
    Zeeshan Ahmed, Institute of Software, Chinese Academy of Sciences, Beijing, China
    Sara Muneeb, Research Center for Human-Computer Interaction (RC-HCI), COMSATS
        University Islamabad (CUI), Lahore, Pakistan

Chapter 68
The Significance of the Hermeneutics of Play for Gamification: The Limits of Virtual and Real
Gamification 1423
    Kosti Joensuu, University of Lapland, Rovaniemi, Finland
    Sanna Ryynänen, University of Lapland, Rovaniemi, Finland

Chapter 69
Playing With the Dead: Transmedia Narratives and the Walking Dead Games 1435
Iain Donald, Abertay University, UK
Hailey J. Austin, University of Dundee, UK

Chapter 70
Digital Games and Orientalism: A Look at Arab and Muslim Representation in Popular Digital
Games 1457
Fatih Söğüt, Kırklareli University, Turkey

Chapter 71
The Cyber Awareness of Online Video Game Players: An Examination of Their Online Safety
Practices and Exposure to Threats 1470
Soonhwa Seok, Korea University, Seoul, South Korea
Boaventura DaCosta, Solers Research Group, FL, USA

Chapter 72
Behavioral and Physiological Responses to Computers in the Ultimatum Game 1480
Aleksandra Swiderska, Department of Psychology, Warsaw University, Warsaw, Poland
Eva G. Krumhuber, Department of Experimental Psychology, University College London,
*   London, UK*
Arvid Kappas, Department of Psychology and Methods, Jacobs University Bremen, Bremen,
*   Germany*

Chapter 73
Gap Between Mobile and Online Advergames: The Possible Effects of the Optimal Gaming
Experience-Flow 1495
Tugce Ozansoy Çadırcı, Yıldız Technical University, Turkey
Aysegul Sagkaya Gungor, Isik University, Turkey

Chapter 74
Users' In-Game Purchase Intention: The Effects of Flow Experience and Satisfaction 1516
Mahendar Goli, Madanapalle Institute of Technology and Science, India
Vishnu Vandana Vemuri, Anurag University, India

Chapter 75
The Social Facilitation of Performance, Engagement and Affect in a Complex Videogame:
Opponent Identity 1538
Russell Blair Williams, Zayed University, Dubai, UAE

Chapter 76
The Impact of Personality and Motivation on Immersion in Simulation Games 1558
Anna Katharina Preuß, Johannes Gutenberg University of Mainz, Mainz, Germany

Chapter 77
Anxiety of the Avatar: Relation of Character Design to Reception in Transmediatic Games.......... 1581
Tülin Sepetci, Abant İzzet Baysal University, Turkey
Tülin Candemir, Akdeniz University, Turkey
Tülay Candemir, Pamukkale University, Turkey

Chapter 78
Serious Games Effect Analysis On Player's Characteristics.. 1621
Polyxeni Kaimara, Ionian University, Department of Audiovisual Arts, Corfu, Greece
Emmanuel Fokides, University of the Aegean, Department of Primary Education, Rhodes,
* Greece*
Antonia Plerou, Ionian University, Department of Informatics, Corfu, Greece
Pinelopi Atsikpasi, University of the Aegean, Department of Primary Education, Rhodes,
* Greece*
Ioannis Deliyannis, Ionian University, Department of Audiovisual Arts, Corfu, Greece

Chapter 79
Ottomentality as Technology of Self: How Do Mobile Games Aestheticize the Entrepreneurial
Self? 1640
Hasan Turgut, Ondokuz Mayıs University, Turkey
Neslihan Yayla, Ondokuz Mayıs University, Turkey

Chapter 80
Mobile Gaming Strategic Communication and Fear of Missing Out (FoMO) in Fan Culture: A
Case Study of Final Fantasy Brave Exvius 1661
Mildred F. Perreault, East Tennessee State University, USA
Gregory P. Perreault, Appalachian State University, USA

Chapter 81
Assessing Behavioral Patterns for Online Gaming Addiction: A Study Among Indian Youth........ 1678
Richa Misra, Jaipuria Institute of Management, Noida, India
Sonali Singh, Jaipuria Institute of Management, Noida, India
Nidhi Singh, Jaipuria Institute of Management, Noida, India

Chapter 82
Internet Gaming Disorder and Its Relationships With Student Engagement and Academic
Performance 1704
Maya Samaha, INTA Institute for Technology Addiction, Notre Dame University-Louaize,
* Lebanon*
Nazir Hawi, INTA Institute for Technology Addiction, Notre Dame University-Louaize,
* Lebanon*

Chapter 83
News Presentation and the Third-Person Effect of Violent Video Games 1721
Seong Choul Hong, Kyonggi University, Seoul, South Korea

Chapter 84
Relationships Among Violent and Non-Violent Video Games, Anxiety, Self-Esteem, and
Aggression in Female and Male Gamers 1735
    Cristina Cabras, University of Cagliari, Cagliari, Italy
    Maria Laura Cubadda, University of Cagliari, Cagliari, Italy
    Cristina Sechi, University of Cagliari, Cagliari, Italy

Chapter 85
Homo Aestheticus' Search for Violence: An Examination on the Aestheticization and Reception
of Violence in Digital Games 1756
    Neslihan Yayla, Ondokuz Mayıs University, Turkey

Chapter 86
Violent Video Games and Their Relation to Aggressive Behaviour in Late Childhood in Pakistan 1781
    Mujeeba Ashraf, Institute of Applied Psychology, University of the Punjab, Lahore, Pakistan

Chapter 87
Factors Affecting Woman's Continuance Intention for Mobile Games 1795
    Pinghao Ye, Wuhan Business University, China
    Liqiong Liu, Wuhan Business University, China
    Linxia Gao, Wuhan Business University, China
    Quanjun Mei, Wuhan Business University, China

Chapter 88
The Effects of Fully and Partially In-Game Guidance on Players' Declarative and Procedural
Knowledge With a Disaster Preparedness Serious Game 1818
    Ting Zhou, Fort Hays State University, USA
    Christian S. Loh, Southern Illinois University, USA

Section 6
Critical Issues and Challenges

Chapter 89
Gamification Research: Preliminary Insights Into Dominant Issues, Theories, Domains, and
Methodologies 1836
    Kingsley Ofosu-Ampong, Business School, University of Ghana, Ghana
    Thomas Anning-Dorson, Wits Business School, University of the Witwatersrand, South
        Africa

Chapter 90
An Empirical Study of Gamification Frameworks 1852
    Patrick Buckley, University of Limerick, Limerick, Ireland
    Seamus Noonan, University of Limerick, Limerick, Ireland
    Conor Geary, University of Limerick, Limerick, Ireland
    Thomas Mackessy, University of Limerick, Limerick, Ireland
    Eoghan Nagle, University of Limerick, Limerick, Ireland

Chapter 91
The Role of Mechanics in Gamification: An Interdisciplinary Perspective 1870
 Miralem Helmefalk, Linnéuniversitetet, Kalmar, Sweden
 Siw Lundqvist, Linnéuniversitetet, Kalmar, Sweden
 Leif Marcusson, Linnéuniversitetet, Kalmar, Sweden

Chapter 92
The Convergence Between Challenge-Based Learning and Game Design Thinking
Methodologies: Exploring Creativity and Innovation in the Game Development Process 1891
 Isabel Cristina Siqueira da Silva, UniRitter, Brazil

Chapter 93
Real-Life Contexts in Learning Games: Towards a New Typology 1908
 Alex Moseley, University of Leicester, Leicester, UK

Chapter 94
Do Board Games Make People Smarter? Two Initial Exploratory Studies 1923
 Marco Bartolucci, Università degli Studi di Perugia, Perugia, Italy
 Francesco Mattioli, Università degli Studi di Perugia, Perugia, Italy
 Federico Batini, Università degli Studi di Perugia, Perugia, Italy

Chapter 95
Who Are You Online? A Study of Gender, Race, and Gaming Experience and Context on Avatar
Self-Representation 1938
 Robert Andrew Dunn, East Tennessee State University, Johnson City, USA
 Rosanna Guadagno, Stanford University, Stanford, USA

Chapter 96
A Systematic Literature Review on the Use of Games for Attitude Change: Searching for Factors
Influencing Civil Servants' Attitudes 1956
 Fernando Kleiman, Delft University of Technology, The Netherlands
 Sebastiaan Meijer, KTH Royal Institute of Technology, Sweden
 Marijn Janssen, Delft University of Technology, The Netherlands

Chapter 97
Digital Games and Violence 1978
 Arzu Kalafat Çat, Abant Izzet Baysal University, Turkey

Index xxvii

Preface

Gaming has gained popularity in recent years as more areas of society discover the benefits and opportunities it offers in various sectors. More research is emerging in this area in designing and developing games in order to increase the utility across sectors, and technology is being developed to increase both utility and enjoyment from these games. Recently, the practice of gamification has been applied to education, the medical field, business, and more. However, games, specifically online and video games, often face criticism for a perceived negative impact on society.

It is critical to understand the best practices, challenges, and strategies of gaming design and development to ensure games are utilized appropriately. Research on the social impact of games is also of importance so that a complete view is gained of both the positive and negative attributes of gaming in society.

Staying informed of the most up-to-date research trends and findings is of the utmost importance. That is why IGI Global is pleased to offer this four-volume reference collection of reprinted IGI Global book chapters and journal articles that have been handpicked by senior editorial staff. This collection will shed light on critical issues related to the trends, techniques, and uses of various applications by providing both broad and detailed perspectives on cutting-edge theories and developments. This collection is designed to act as a single reference source on conceptual, methodological, technical, and managerial issues, as well as to provide insight into emerging trends and future opportunities within the field.

The *Research Anthology on Game Design, Development, Usage, and Social Impact* is organized into six distinct sections that provide comprehensive coverage of important topics. The sections are:

1. Fundamental Concepts and Theories;
2. Development and Design Methodologies;
3. Tools and Technologies;
4. Utilization and Applications;
5. Organizational and Social Implications; and
6. Critical Issues and Challenges.

The following paragraphs provide a summary of what to expect from this invaluable reference tool.

Section 1, "Fundamental Concepts and Theories," serves as a foundation for this extensive reference tool by addressing crucial theories essential to understanding the concepts and uses of games and game design in multidisciplinary settings. Opening this reference book is the chapter "A Primer on Gamification Standardization" by Prof. Carlos Filipe Portela from the University of Minho, Portugal; Prof. Alberto Simões of Polytechnic Institute of Cávado and Ave, Portugal; and Profs. Ricardo Alexandre Peixoto de Queiros and Mário Pinto from ESMAD, Polytechnic Institute of Porto, Portugal, which presents a systematic study on gamification standardization aiming to characterize the status of the field, namely describing existing frameworks, languages, services, and platforms. This section ends with "Towards Better Understanding of Children's Relationships With Online Games and Advergames" by Dr. Ali Ben Yahia from LIGUE, Tunis, Tunisia; Prof. Sihem Ben Saad of Carthage Business School, Université Tunis Carthage, Tunisia; and Prof. Fatma Choura Abida from Institute of Computer Science of Tunis, Tunisia, which favors an in-depth understanding of the child's relation with online games and advergames through an exploratory qualitative approach.

Section 2, "Development and Design Methodologies," presents in-depth coverage of the design and development of games for their use in different applications. This section starts with "Augmented Reality Games" by Prof. Baris Atiker from Bahcesehir University, Turkey, which evaluates how augmented reality games interpret gaming concepts and principles through field research methods, new applications, and studies that deal with gamification, presence, immersion, and game transfer phenomena. This section ends with "Eye of the Beholder: Analyzing a Gamification Design Through a Servicescape Lens" by Prof. Adam Palmquist from the School of Informatics, University of Skövde, Sweden and Dr. David Gillberg of Insert Coin, Sweden, which uses the theories from environmental psychology and the servicescape methods to construct a lens to suggest improvements in gamification design for a learning management system used in higher education.

Section 3, "Tools and Technologies," explores the various tools and technologies used within game design. This section begins with "Applied Alternative Tools and Methods in the Replacement of the Game Design Document" by Profs. Pedro Henrique Roscoe Lage de Oliveira and Carlos Alberto Silva de Miranda from Minas Gerais State University, Brazil and Prof. Joao Victor Boechat Gomide from the Universidade FUMEC, Brazil, which proposes alternatives to replace or optimize the use of the game design document (GDD). This section ends with "Towards a Role-Playing Game Procedural Dungeon Generation Strategy to Help Developing Working Skills" by Profs. Esteban A. Durán-Yañez and Mario A. Rodríguez-Díaz from Tecnológico Nacional de México IT Aguascalientes, Mexico and Prof. César A. López-Luévano from the Universidad Politécnica de Aguascalientes, Mexico, which describes the insights towards a proposal to integrate a procedural content generation strategy in a computer role-playing usable and accessible learning video game for gaining replayability to encourage engagement and motivation in learners.

Section 4, "Utilization and Applications," describes how gaming is used and applied in diverse industries for various applications. The opening chapter in this section, "Probability and Game," by Prof. Alessio Drivet from Geogebra Institute of Turin, Italy, emphasizes not only the theoretical aspects but above all the certainty that you always play "against the dealer" with an expected loss assessable for the various games. This section ends with "On Computerizing the Ancient Game of Ṭāb" by Profs. Ahmad B. Hassanat, Ghada Altarawneh, Baker Al-Rawashdeh, and Mohammed Alshamaileh from Mutah University, Jordan; Prof. Ahmad S. Tarawneh from Eotvos Lorand University ELTE, Hungary; Prof. Hossam Faris of The University of Jordan, Jordan; Prof. Mahmoud B. Alhasanat from Al-Hussein Bin Talal University, Jordan; Prof. Alex de Voogt of Drew University, USA; and Dr. Surya V. B. Prasath from Cincinnati Children's Hospital Medical Center, USA, which develops three versions of the game tab—human versus human, human versus computer, and computer versus computer—and employs a genetic algorithm (GA) to help the computer to choose the 'best' move to play.

Section 5, "Organizational and Social Implications," includes chapters discussing the impact of gaming on society. The chapter "Institutions as Designers of Better Social Games" by Prof. Albena Antonova from Sofia University, Bulgaria, discusses how institutions can transform into designers of new types of rules and social arrangements that will be more just and efficient for all within social games. The closing chapter, "The Effects of Fully and Partially In-Game Guidance on Players' Declarative and Procedural Knowledge With a Disaster Preparedness Serious Game," by Prof. Ting Zhou from Fort Hays State University, USA and Prof. Christian S. Loh of Southern Illinois University, USA, investigates the effects of players' gaming frequency, prior knowledge, and in-game guidance received on their declarative and procedural knowledge in a disaster preparedness serious game.

Section 6, "Critical Issues and Challenges," presents coverage of academic and research perspectives on the challenges and issues of games and gaming design. Starting this section is "Gamification Research: Preliminary Insights Into Dominant Issues, Theories, Domains, and Methodologies" by Prof. Kingsley Ofosu-Ampong from the University of Ghana, Ghana and Prof. Thomas Anning-Dorson of the University of the Witwatersrand, South Africa, which explains the idea of game design elements in information systems and provides real-world examples of gamified systems outcomes from developing countries. This section ends with "Digital Games and Violence" by Prof. Arzu Kalafat Çat from Abant Izzet Baysal University, Turkey, which discusses violent elements in digital games within the framework of relevant theoretical approaches through three games that children play most.

Although the primary organization of the content in this multi-volume work is based on its six sections, offering a progression of coverage of the important concepts, methodologies, technologies, applications, social issues, and emerging trends, the reader can also identify specific content by utilizing the extensive indexing system listed at the end of each volume. As a comprehensive collection of research on the latest findings related to games and gaming design, the *Research Anthology on Game Design, Development, Usage, and Social Impact* provides game developers, instructional designers, educators and administrators of both K-12 and higher education, students of higher education, librarians, government officials, business leaders and executives, researchers, and academicians with a complete understanding of the applications and impacts of games and gaming design. Given the vast number of issues concerning usage, failure, success, strategies, and applications of gaming design and development, the *Research Anthology on Game Design, Development, Usage, and Social Impact* encompasses the most pertinent research on the applications, impacts, uses, and development of games.

Chapter 47
"Piece of Mind" and
"Wellbeing Town":
Engaging Service Users in the Development of a Wellbeing Game

Steven Barnes

https://orcid.org/0000-0002-5114-2178
University of Bolton, UK

Melvin Bradley
Mental Health Independent Support Team, UK

Andrew Williams
University of Bolton, UK

ABSTRACT

The long-term implications of COVID-19 for wellbeing are predicted to be both significant and enduring. Data from previous epidemics indicates long-term detrimental effects are more pronounced among particular demographics, including individuals with pre-existing mental health conditions. The Mental Health Independent Support Team (MhIST) is a charitable organisation offering a range of free-at-the-point-of-contact services via self-referral for a range of mental health and wellbeing concerns, both with and without diagnosis. Since March 2020, the organisation noted significant rises in demand for services. Serious games and their active involvement in eliciting rapid positive behavioural change is associated with their emergence as a key learning tool, with effects transferable to the real world. While a growing number of gamified interventions exist for a range of mental health diagnoses, their presence in the domain of positive psychology is more limited. The chapter reports two studies conducted to enhance the development of an educational game for adult wellbeing.

DOI: 10.4018/978-1-6684-7589-8.ch047

INTRODUCTION

Outline

The following chapter will comprise of a synopsis of two empirical studies conducted in conjunction with the Mental Health Independent Support Team (MhIST) in Bolton, UK, to develop a serious game for adult wellbeing. In the following chapter proposal, contextual information is provided, along with an overview of the two studies; (1) a potential end-user survey to establish interest and preferences/requirements among the demographic prior to the development of two prototype games and (2) a user-feedback study conducted on these two prototypes to establish their acceptability and to outline directions for further development.

Wellbeing During the Covid-19 Pandemic

At the end of March 2020, the United Kingdom (UK) government initiated the first of a series of 'lockdown' restrictions aimed at decelerating the spread of COVID-19. These restrictions have been associated with detrimental implications for social connectedness and with increasing feelings of social isolation (White & van der Boor, 2020), which are established factors in promoting positive wellbeing (Jetten, Haslam, Haslam, Dingle & Jones, 2014; Al Issa & Jaleel, 2021). Contrastingly, the ability to perceive kindness, feelings of connectedness with community and essential worker status have been found to be associated with better mental health and well-being outcomes during lockdown (White & van der Boor, 2020).

Beyond the immediate and short-term future, the long-term implications of COVID-19 for wellbeing are predicted to be both significant and enduring (Hotopf, Bullmore, O'Connor & Holmes, 2020). However, it is as yet unclear who will be affected, how effects will manifest, and to what extent. Extant data from previous epidemics however has indicated that specific long-term detrimental effects are more pronounced among particular demographics (Cheung, Chau & Yip, 2008; Mak, Chu, Pan, Yiu & Chan, 2009), for instance increased risk of suicide in older adults following severe acute respiratory syndrome (SARS) (Yip, Cheung, Chau & Law, 2010). Early data from COVID-19 investigations indicate that self-harm and thoughts of suicide and self-harm were more prevalent among women, Black, Asian and minority ethnic groups, people experiencing socioeconomic disadvantage, and individuals with pre-existing mental health conditions (Lob, Steptoe & Fancourt, 2020).

The Mental Health Independent Support Team (MhIST) is a user-led charitable organisation located in Bolton, United Kingdom, offering a range of free at the point of contact groups and services via self-referral (including self-help groups, advocacy services, and talking therapies) to people with a range of mental health and wellbeing concerns, both with and without formal diagnosis. Service users present to the charity with a range of mental health needs at varying degrees of symptom severity. Of service-users providing feedback data (N=100) via an online survey in February 2020, 62.5% of service users were female, 36.4% male, and 1.1% did not state their gender. 19.3% of respondents were aged 18-29 years, 14.8% were aged 30-44, 46.6% were aged 45-59, and 19.3% were aged 60+ years. 48% reported having a long-term illness, and 29% of respondents reported themselves as having a disability.

Since the onset of the COVID restrictions at the end of March 2020, the organisation noted a rise in demand for services – increasing from approximately 1,500 referrals in the year to end of March 2020, to over 2,500 by December 2020. The severity of symptom presentation among service users was also noted to have deteriorated during this time. The organisation utilises a range of online facilities encompassing both the digitalisation of pre-COVID amenities via cloud-based video conferencing systems, as well as a range of new innovations designed to respond to changing demand amid the decreased availability face-to-face services.

Digital Games for Adult Wellbeing

First noted by Abt (1970), serious games are video games (VGs) designed with a primary purpose other than entertainment, usually to educate or inform the player (Djaouti et al., 2011). The intrinsic and extrinsic motivational systems employed by serious games engage users in learning opportunities with immediate feedback. The reinforcement ability of TGs and their active involvement in eliciting rapid positive behavioural change has been linked to their emergence as a key learning tool (Gentile & Gentile, 2008), capable of producing significant improvements across a diverse range of psychological conditions (Baranowski et al., 2013, Tárrega et al., 2015; Giner-Bartolomé et al., 2015; Rica et al., 2020), maintained beyond the virtual environment in which the game exists and operates (Bindoff et al., 2016).

Additionally, the reduced cognitive-load of games, and the comparatively fewer barriers to engagement (such as perceived probability of stigma) afforded by their use, in turn positively influences the probability of help-seeking behaviours (Wiljer *et* al., 2020; Vallury et al., 2015). Using a computerised intervention for just one day per week has shown to have a positive effect on outcomes and attrition rates, with research reporting a 23% reduction in drop-out rates compared to conventional treatments (Scherer et al., 2017), and improvements to end-of-treatment outcomes (King, Currie & Petersen, 2012). There is therefore a clear capability for immersive games to make meaningful inroads to improving access to, and engagement with, psychological wellbeing protocols.

The importance of the needs and experience of the player however must not be overlooked in the design of gamified interventions (Fitzgerald & Ratcliffe, 2020). Previous literature has suggested that games designed for older adult players must cater to the requirements of the demographic in order to maintain engagement (Salmon et al., 2017), specifically indicating that while the need for challenge remains important, games for older adults ought to be easily accessible and intuitive to use. The concept of 'flow' first outlined by Csikzentmihalyi (1975) posits that the capacity of a game to create feelings of enjoyment and captivation can be linked to the successful completion of tasks which lie at edge of the player's present abilities (Csikzentmihalyi, 1990; Belchior, Marsiske, Sisco, Yam & Mann, 2012).

Mechanically, previous research suggests that older adults prefer puzzle-based games above other genres (Charlier et al., 2012) and that their preference for fantasy-based games is low compared to younger demographics (Blocker, Wright & Boot, 2014). Adult gamers also reported less enjoyment and greater negative attitudes towards online multiplayer gaming (Nap, de Kort & Ijsselsteijn, 2009). Structurally, user-preference studies indicate that games are enhanced for older players by enhancing the colour palette and luminance contrasts on display, reducing use of text and the complexity of background imagery, and minimising the number of individual steps required to complete in-game tasks (Gamberini et al., 2006). As gaming may be less familiar to older adults, Gerling et al. (2012) suggest that game-designers can reduce the demands gameplay may place on cognitive functions by simplifying and homogenising the rules and physical operations required. This catalogue of preferences, which differ from those of younger players, underline the need to involve potential adult users in the design of gamified interventions to ensure end products best suit their needs (Havukainen, Laine, Martikainen & Sutinen, 2020).

In addition to structural and usability requirements, the notion of game-based learning may also be less familiar to older adults, with the potential value of using games as a learning tool being less apparent (Charlier, Ott, Remmele & Whitton, 2012). Whether adults use serious games may be dependent on their judgment of the benefits of their engagement (Salmon et al., 2017). In this regard, a taxonomy of gameplay motivations among older adults has been developed (de Schutter and Malliet, 2014), suggesting 'context' (passing time or substituting for less-desirable real-world activities), and 'content' (learning and the enjoyment of gameplay) are key considerations when designing games for this audience. Further investigation is however warranted to ensure that these factors generalise across populations with differing mental health presentations.

MAIN FOCUS OF THE CHAPTER

The 'Five Ways to Wellbeing' framework (Aked, Marks, Cordon & Thompson, 2008) was developed to promote wellbeing among the general population, and consists of five methods for improving wellbeing in daily life (Hone, Jarden, Duncan & Schofield, 2015):

1. 'connect': emphasising the importance of social relationships (Chu, Saucier & Hafner, 2010);
2. 'be active': emphasises the benefits of regular exercise (Caddick & Smith, 2014);
3. 'take notice': emphasises awareness of personal emotions, sensations, and reflections (Galante, Galante, Bekkers & Gallacher, 2014);
4. 'keep learning': focuses on the importance of learning and achievement in driving self-efficacy and self-esteem (Randelin, Saaranen, Naumanen & Louhevaara, 2012);
5. 'give': emphasises selfless and meaningful behaviours (Quinn, Clare & Woods, 2010).

This conceptual framework is widely used in the promotion of wellbeing (Abdallah, Main, Pople & Rees, 2014). While a growing number of virtual interventions now exist in response to a range of mental health diagnoses, the availability of digital programmes in the domain of positive psychology is more limited. The Mental Health Foundation of New Zealand developed the web-based 'The Wellbeing Game', which raised user-awareness of ways to improve their wellbeing (Green, 2013), as well as reducing stress compared to non-players (Keeman, Näswall, Malinen & Kuntz, 2017). However, the game is now no longer available. The present research therefore aimed to address this gap in provision by designing an educational game for adult wellbeing, with the involvement of service users to ensure that the game best met their needs and preferences.

The present chapter reports the findings of two studies conducted with volunteering service-users from MhIST and the general public, in order to enhance the development of an educational game for adult wellbeing: (1) a potential end-user survey to establish interest and preferences/requirements among the demographic prior to the development of two prototype games and (2) a user-feedback study conducted on these two prototypes to establish their acceptability and to outline directions for further development.

STUDY ONE

Aims

In the first stage of the development process, existing service users of the MhIST charity were polled. The intentions of this initial survey were twofold: (1) firstly to ascertain the acceptability of a gamified intervention for adult wellbeing; (2) to establish any preferences and requirements among the demographic (including familiarity with, and access to, technology), before choices regarding game-conceptualisation, platform selection, and the development of prototype games could begin.

Method

Design

Initial demographic research took the form of self-report measures administered via anonymous online survey. While the data obtained from the survey was quantitative, the opportunity for participants to provide additional qualitative feedback was provided, in order to enhance the effectiveness of the feedback in developing prototype interventions (Laver, George, Thomas, Deutsch, & Crotty, 2015). Self-report survey was chosen as the method of data collection owing to its advantages for speed of data collection and accessibility for the respondents (Healey, Baron & Ilieva, 2002), of particular importance in light of the restrictions created by the COVID-19 pandemic.

Participants

Participants were recruited on a self-selecting volunteer basis via a mailing list sent by the MhIST charity, containing participant information for the study and directing interested parties to an online survey link hosted by Qualtrics. Upon following this link, participants were provided with a full overview of the study aims and intentions and were instructed that their consent was implied by the completion of the questionnaire, but that they may withdraw by a stated date. Before proceeding, participants generated a unique identification code and were instructed to make note of this, should they wish to withdraw later. Contact details of the lead researcher were also provided for this purpose, or should participants have any concerns or questions.

A total of 41 respondents completed the questionnaire initially. One later chose to exercise their right to withdraw, leaving a final *N* of 40. Of these, 12 were male (30.0%), 27 were female (67.5%) and 1 declined to provide their gender (2.5%). Ages of the participants were spread widely, including seven (17.5%) participants aged between 20-29 years, five aged 30-39 (12.5%), seven aged 40-49 (17.5%), twelve aged 50-59 (30.0%), six aged 60-69 (15.0%) and two aged 70-79 (5.0%). One respondent declined to provide their age (2.5%).

Materials and Procedure

Participants were asked a series of demographic questions relating to gender, age, the average hours a week they spent playing video games (including an option for if they did not engage with videogaming at all), the duration of an average play session (if relevant), and if they would be interested in a gamified intervention for adult wellbeing. If respondents answered 'yes' to the latter of these questions, they were then directed to complete the rest of the survey – respondents stating they were not interested in a gamified wellbeing intervention were directed to the end of the survey and thanked for their participation.

Participants continuing through the survey were then asked about their preferences towards a range of potential game features, including ease of use, clarity of health information, availability on a range of platforms, customisability and replayability. Responses were collected on a six-point Likert scale ranging from 0 ('not at all important') to 5 ('extremely important'). Finally, respondents were asked to complete the 10-item eHealth Literacy Scale (eHEALS) (Norman & Skinner, 2006), which measures perceived ability in using technology for the acquisition of legitimate health information. The first two items of the scale measure the respondent's perception of information on the Internet generally and are measured along a five-point Likert scale ranging from 1 ('not useful at all') to 5 ('very useful') and 1 ('not important at all') to 5 ('very important') respectively.

The remaining eight items measure the respondent's perceived capacity to source, evaluate and engage with Internet-based health information. Responses are collected along a five-point Likert scale ranging from 1 ('strongly disagree') to 5 ('strongly agree'). A total score for the eHEALS can be calculated by summing the responses to the eight individual capacity items, with the minimum possible score being 8 indicating low perceived eHealth literacy, and maximum possible score being 40 indicating high perceived eHealth literacy. The psychometric assessment of the eHEALS scale conducted by Norman and Skinner (2006) demonstrated the scale has high internal consistency ($\alpha=.86$), although test-retest reliability was lower with a Pearson coefficient of 0.467. A full version of the survey can be found in *Appendix 1*.

Results

Descriptive Statistics

The aim of the present study was first to ascertain the acceptability of a gamified intervention for adult wellbeing, before proceeding to establish any preferences and requirements among the demographic (including familiarity with, and access to, technology). As previously stated, 40 respondents provided data via anonymous online survey.

General acceptability and interest in using a gamified intervention for wellbeing was good – 22 participants (55.0%) responded that they would 'definitely' be interested in such a game, with a further 15 participants indicating that they 'might' be interested (37.5%). Only 2 participants indicated that they would not be interested in such a game (5.0%). One participant did not provide a response (2.5%). Acceptability was good across the age ranges, although while younger participants were more likely to respond with definite interest, older participants were more likely to respond with 'maybe'.

The amount of time that respondents spent playing videogames in an average week ranged between 0 hours and 21 hours (M=4.29, SD=6.39). Of note however, 17 respondents (42.5%) reported spending zero hours per week playing videogames, despite their potential interest in a gamified wellbeing intervention. For respondents who did report playing games, the average time that they indicated they would be likely to spend playing a game for wellbeing was 10-30 minutes.

In terms of specific features, mechanics and platform choices, participants were asked their preference towards a number of potential choices. The findings can be found in *Table 1* below:

Table 1. Respondent preferences

Item	M(SD) (N Respondents)
How important would ease of use be for you?	4.11 (.91) (37)
How important would detailed health information be for you?	3.22 (1.24) (36)
How important would simple health information be for you?	3.53 (.94) (36)
How important would it be to have contact details for mental health services?	3.57 (1.41) (37)
How important would it be to have ways to track your wellbeing?	3.76 (1.23) (37)
How important would it be for the game to be available on a mobile device?	3.86 (1.38) (37)
How important would it be for the game to be available on a desktop computer?	2.70 (1.53) (33)
How important would it be for the game to be available online via a web-browser?	2.57 (1.61) (35)
How important would it be for the game to be customisable (e.g. change character appearance, game-settings, game-environment)?	2.94 (1.48) (34)
How important would it be to have an option to replay previously completed levels and tasks?	3.22 (1.36) (37)
How important would it be to have an option to save and export your data?	3.29 (1.34) (35)

The data provided by respondents differed notably over some of the items (e.g.), indicating the diversity of needs and preferences and the difficulty therefore of providing gamified interventions for the demographic. The highest rated items were for ease of use, availability on a mobile device and having ways to track wellbeing over time. The lowest rated items were for availability online via a web-browser, availability via a desktop computer and customisability. Participants responded with notable consistency regarding the need for the game to be easy to use, with all responses ranging between 3 and 5.

The need for a digital wellbeing intervention to be easily navigable was confirmed by eHEALS data. Respondent electronic health literacy scores indicated that while the sample overall demonstrated an average perceived ability to use the Internet for health-related purposes (M=28.57, SD=5.27), a notable proportion of the respondents reported low confidence with 19 respondents scoring below the mean, and 9 participants scoring ≤25.

Further Analysis

The data was then assessed for normality to determine its suitability for further analysis. While Shapiro-Wilk testing found respondent age ($p=.659$) and eHEALS score ($p=.356$) to be normally distributed, the number of hours spent playing videogames on an average week was not ($p<.001$), likely a product of the large number of respondents ($N=17$) who reported a score of 0.

Gender groups were well represented across the age range of the respondents ($F(1,37)=.104, p=.749$), and no significant differences emerged between gender groups for the average number of hours spent playing video games ($F(1,37)=.181, p=.178$) or for eHEALS scores ($F(1,37)=.004, p=.948$).

No significant relationship emerged between eHEALS score and the average number of hours participants reported spending playing videogames in a given week ($r_s=-.234, p=.162$). A significant negative relationship between age and eHEALS score was noted, whereby older respondents reported feeling increasingly less confident with using technology for health-related activities ($r=-.335, p=.043$). Age also significantly correlated with the average number of hours spent playing videogames per week, whereby older adults were less likely to spend time playing video games than younger respondents ($r_s=-.564, p<.001$). As previous MhIST data indicated that 46.6% of participants were aged 45-59 and 19.3% of participants were aged $\geq$60 years, these findings were considered noteworthy when designing and conceptualising a game for wellbeing.

Additional Feedback

At the end of the survey, participants were provided with the opportunity to submit additional feedback if they wished to do so. A total of seventeen participants provided some form of additional feedback, which ranged in depth and detail. As this feedback pertained to just one item on the survey and was only answered by a subsection of respondents, this was not considered to be sufficient for any formal analysis procedure. Comments did however follow a discernible pattern, including a reiterated need for accessibility and for the game to be easy to use, prompts and reminders to engage with the game and the need for a game to be relatable to real-life wellbeing (e.g. by encouraging real-world activity or interaction with others).

A sample of the comments from this item can be found in *Table 2*.

Table 2. Example responses from the additional feedback item.

Response
"Accessibility feature is simple graphic colour sceam font aize"
"Sometimes thier is to much information overload."   "Selecting various aspects of wellbeing you need to work towards."   "Anything that gives daily support so the game helps mind reciver on low days or low periods"   "meditation that was available as part of level in the evening or levels with prompts to do things at certain times?"   "Anything that gives daily support so the game helps mind reciver on low days or low periods"   "Mental health facts popping up on loading screens, local/online multiplayer options, a "get help now" button, extra mini games/activities eg 10 minutes of yoga or some guided meditation, reminders to come off the game and do some productive mental health techniques rg going for a walk or spending time with friends and family, in-game purchases eg links to mental health gifts such as wellbess diaries, compliment pens or positive notes etcccc I have lots of ideas for things like this lol"   "Id like challenges that could be transferred to real life situations with tasks and rewards"   "support interaction"

* Responses are as provided by participants and are quoted directly.

PROTOTYPE DEVELOPMENT

'Piece of Mind' and 'Wellbeing Town'

Following on from the analysis of the above data, two prototypes were developed by students on the MA Games Development at the Centre for Games Design at the University of Bolton as part of their programme assessment, under the supervision of the module teaching team. The prototypes were intended to be working demonstrations of the game-concepts, offering players an insight into the intended direction, structure and aims of the game, incorporating the present findings and best practice in games design to embed the Five Ways to Wellbeing. The prototypes were designed with basic principles of motivational psychology in mind, in order to increase player motivation, including the use of reinforcement techniques, challenge and flow and competition.

For ease of distribution in the user-review study, both games were programmed initially to operate on desktop computer. Although the two prototype games differed in terms of the scenarios and mechanics used, they both retained the reliance on these motivational strategies, as well as placing the Five Ways to Wellbeing framework at the centre of player activity. An overview of these games can be found in the following section.

'Piece of Mind'

'Piece of Mind' segments the components of the Five Ways to Wellbeing into a series of simply designed individual tasks for players to complete, each specialising in and focusing on a specific aspect of the framework. The game operates around an in-game sticker-book, which operates simultaneously as a central point for navigating between individual tasks as well as a means for the player to keep track of their progress. Individual tasks include clearing the sky of clouds to 'take notice' of an image in the background.

Additional items are also placed in the background of individual tasks in order to enhance the game's capacity to promote taking notice. The successful detection of these additional items is rewarded with a specific sticker, encouraging players to revisit tasks if additional items have not yet been detected, and enhancing the depth and replayability of the game. An example screenshot of the game along with a screenshot of the in-game sticker book can be found in *Figure 1* and *Figure 2*.

'Wellbeing Town'

By contrast, 'Wellbeing Town' does not separate the individual components of the Five Ways to Wellbeing framework into independent tasks, but instead combines these into a more complex 'open-world' role-playing game. Players take control of an in-game avatar and are tasked with navigating a small forest and neighbouring village environment inhabited by a small number of non-playable characters (NPCs). Tasks relating to the Five Ways to Wellbeing are provided by the NPCs and stored in an in-game journal, which acts as a central repository for task-reminders and rewards collected during gameplay.

The tasks themselves include 'connecting' with the NPCs, 'learning' about the game environment and its various characters and plants, and collection of items from the forest which the player can then 'give' to the non-playable characters, either for reward or to further the storyline. An example screenshot of the in-game world and of the in-game journal can be found in *Figure 3* and *Figure 4*.

Figure 1. Example screenshot of 'Piece of Mind'.

Figure 2. In-game sticker book.

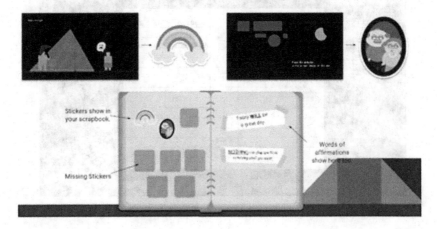

Following the development of these two prototypes, a user-evaluation of the games was conducted to assess their acceptability, ease of use, and to allow users to contribute to the further development of the games.

Figure 3. Example screenshot of 'Wellbeing Town'.

Figure 4. In-game journal.

STUDY TWO

Aims

In the second stage of the project following on from the user-survey and the development of the two prototype games, potential users were offered the opportunity to provide preliminary feedback, to ascertain the acceptability of the games and to assist with directions for further development.

Method

Design

As previously, anonymous online self-report surveys were deployed as the method of data collection owing to its advantages for speed of data collection and accessibility for the respondents (Healey, Baron & Ilieva, 2002). While the majority of the survey items were quantitative, respondents were again provided with the opportunity to submit additional feedback or thoughts in a qualitative item.

Participants

Participants were recruited on a self-selecting volunteer basis via a mailing list sent by the MhIST charity, containing participant information for the study and directing interested parties to an online survey link hosted by Qualtrics. In addition to MhIST users, access to the feedback survey was widened to the general public accessing any kind of service to improve their wellbeing, with the study hosted online via social networks. Upon following the survey link, participants were provided with a full overview of the study aims and intentions and were instructed that their consent was implied by the completion of the questionnaire, but that they may withdraw by a stated date. Before proceeding, participants generated a unique identification code and were instructed to make note of this, should they wish to withdraw later. Contact details of the lead researcher were also provided for this purpose, or should participants have any concerns or questions.

Overall 60 responses were received, of which 28 were for 'Piece of Mind' and 32 for 'Wellbeing Town'. A total with 20 participants provided feedback for both games, and 20 participants provided feedback for only one of the games. Of the 40 participants, 23 were male (57.5%) and 17 were female (42.5%). Ages of the participants were again widely spread, with three participants (7.5%) aged between 20-29 years, four aged 30-39 (10.0%), 14 aged 40-49 (35.0%), 12 aged 50-59 (30.0%), three aged 60-69 (7.5%) and four aged 70-79 years (10.0%).

Materials and Procedure

The two prototypes were hosted online on their own individual pages via itch.io – a website used by indie game developers to host, sell and download games. Additionally, a dedicated page on the MhIST website was created in order to direct potential participants to the itch.io pages. For users accessing the MhIST centre, a group of dedicated PCs were set up to enable visitors to review the games. While the two prototypes were surveyed separately, the structure, layout and items of the two surveys were kept identical in order to allow for comparison and consistency. For respondents from the general public, the itch.io and survey links were distributed online via social networks.

For MhIST respondents, service-users engaged with MhIST who had already provided their consent to receiving MhIST communications via email or text were contacted and informed about the development of the two games, that these were available to download and trial on PC, and that an opportunity to provide feedback would be provided via anonymous online survey. Members of the general public were recruited via marketing the research online.

The links to the itch.io pages were provided in the text/email and participants were recruited on a self-selecting volunteer basis. Visitors to the MhIST centre in Bolton were also asked if they would like to participate. Participants were informed that there was no requirement to take part, that they may trial either one of the games or both, and that their engagement with the research had no implications for their eligibility to continue to receive existing services. For online reviewers, survey links were distributed one week after the links to the games were shared. For reviews conducted by visitors to the MhIST centre, participants were allowed to play the prototype games for as long as they wished before reviewing commenced via the surveys.

Upon following the link to either of the online surveys, participants were initially asked to create an anonymous online code, so that their response could be identified should they later wish to withdraw, as with the previous study. Participants were then asked their age in years, gender, and the number of hours they spent playing video games in an average week. Participants were then asked ten questions scored on a Likert scale of 1 to 5, where '1' equalled 'strongly disagree' and 5 equalled 'strongly agree'. Items related to the ease with which the participant felt they could use the game, the quality of wellbeing information provided, the effects (or anticipated effects) of use of the game on player wellbeing and the motivational qualities of the game. This items could be totalled to provide an overall score for the game reviewed. An additional item was provided to enable participants to provide any further feedback they wished to provide. A full copy of the survey can be found in *Appendix 2*.

Results

Descriptive Statistics

The aim of the second study was to offer potential end-users of the games the opportunity to provide feedback, to ascertain the acceptability of the games and to assist with directions for further development.

Of the 40 participants, respondents spent an average of 3.87 hours videogaming in an average week (SD=5.69). Again, a large number of participants (N=19) indicated that they did not spend any time playing videogames usually.

Data was initially assessed for normality to determine suitability for further analysis using Shapiro-Wilk tests. While overall scores for 'Piece of Mind' were normally distributed (p=.663), the scores for 'Wellbeing Town' were not (p<.001). One outlier was detected in the data but was left in order to reflect the views of the respondents more accurately. Additionally, while age was normally distributed (p=.100), the number of hours which participants spent playing video games in an average week was not (p<.001), again likely due to the large number of participants reporting a score of '0'.

Scores from the quantitative items on the feedback survey were then assessed. A breakdown of the average scores by item can be found in *Table 3*.

Overall, 'Wellbeing Town' (M=38.59, SD=6.19) significantly outperformed 'Piece of Mind' (M=32.39, SD=4.44) (Z=-4.983, p<.001). No significant differences emerged for the game 'Piece of Mind' between gender groups ($t(24)$=.269, p=.790) or between age groups ($F(5,28)$=1.418, p=.257). Regarding 'Wellbeing Town', again no significant differences emerged between gender groups ($t(30)$=-1.056, p=.299) or between age groups ($F(5,32)$=1.399, p=.257). While these findings indicate that the games were reviewed with equal favour across these demographics, the small numbers of participants ought to be noted.

Table 3. Responses by item

Item	'Piece of Mind' M(SD)	'Wellbeing Town' M(SD)
Q1: The menus and in-game tasks were easy to navigate.	3.93 (.77)	2.97 (.82)
Q2: The game made it clear to me what I was expected to do.	4.07 (.81)	3.03 (.93)
Q3: I was able to understand the game and how to use it without assistance.	4.25 (.80)	3.06 (1.05)
Q4: The types of activities in the game were appropriate.	2.96 (.84)	4.13 (.75)
Q5: Playing the game would help me to understand ways to improve my wellbeing.	3.11 (.74)	4.66 (.90)
Q6: Playing the game would help to improve my wellbeing.	2.64 (.87)	4.22 (.87)
Q7: The game contained enough variety of activities.	3.36 (.83)	3.94 (.84)
Q8: The activities in the game were enjoyable and rewarding.	2.82 (.72)	4.16 (.72)
Q9: The activities in the game were sufficiently challenging to keep my interest.	2.50 (.88)	4.13 (.83)
Q10: I would be motivated to play this game often to help improve my wellbeing.	2.75 (.89)	4.31 (1.12)

Players were more positive about the simpler design of 'Piece of Mind' when considering the ease with which they could navigate the game, clarity of task explanation and being able to use the game without assistance. However despite its more complex design, 'Wellbeing Town' outperformed 'Piece of Mind' across most of the items on the questionnaire, particularly with regards to items relating to effect on improving wellbeing, enjoyment, challenge and future use.

Additional Feedback

At the end of the survey, participants were provided with the opportunity to submit additional feedback if they wished to do so. A total of 33 items of feedback were obtained, 12 relating to 'Piece of Mind' and 21 relating to 'Wellbeing Town'. Feedback for 'Piece of Mind' generally focused on the need for additional challenge and task-variety, as players noted that once they had played the demonstrations available, they would have preferred to have been more challenged with a wider variety of tasks:

If it was more challenging I would probably play this. Did teach me some things so could be useful.

The game was simple to use but not interesting or challenging enough. It would be better to have more activities and be more challenging then it would be rewarding to complete and make you want to use it again.

This game seemed a little to childish for use with adults. Although there's some good information on wellbeing, the games were too easy and simple so I don't think adults would play this for long.

More variety and make the games harder. I like the idea but this is too simple.

Feedback for 'Wellbeing Town' was generally positive and referred to the game's 'relaxing' nature. Unlike 'Piece of Mind', which used a more simplistic and visual representation of the Five Ways to Wellbeing framework, respondents for 'Wellbeing Town' noted that they felt the game had been informative about ways to improve wellbeing. Respondents also commented on the variety of tasks available and the opportunity to freely navigate the in-game environment as they wished. In terms of suggestions for future improvement, feedback here complimented the quantitative survey in identifying the need for clear instructions and guidance, particularly when approaching the game for the first time. Participants also made suggestions for how the game might be further expanded:

The activities are more varied and you can do things in your own way which i liked. it was also good to just be able to free roam in the world without being forced to do things. could use some better instructions to make it clearer but once i knew how to use it it was fine.

I really like this game i just wish it was longer and more developed. i would definitely use something like this to stay calm and to learn ways to make myself feel better. i really like how the game gives you advice without forcing you to do things.

More variety of activities needed and make it a little easier to use at the start. Once I understood what I was meant to do it was interesting and I would have liked there to be more for me to do. I would definitely consider using this as I was starting to enjoy it and learn about things I could do to make my wellbeing better which is really valuable. For someone who does not play video games or know much about them I enjoyed this a lot more than I thought I would.

Would be good to see a few more activities in this game and to see how it develops, maybe with some quests or adventures to do outside of the village to keep it interesting and to make players practice what they learn about wellbeing.

Feedback for this game was not only obtained in greater number, but was also generally more expansive and detailed, perhaps reflecting the extent to which the game had captured the attention of the audience.

Discussion

The present chapter has reported the findings of two studies conducted in order to enhance the development of an educational game for adult wellbeing. Firstly, a potential end-user survey was presented with the aim of establishing interest and preferences/requirements among the demographic. Subsequently, the development of two prototype games was outlined followed by a user-feedback study conducted to establish their acceptability and to outline directions for further development.

Findings from the first study revealed that the general acceptability and interest in using a game designed to improve wellbeing was good. Previous research has indicated good acceptability for gamified interventions for health purposes, including for smoking cessation (Raiff, Jarvis & Rapoza, 2012) and for exercise promotion (Nawaz, Skjæret, Lægdheim Helbostad, Vereijken, Boulton & Svanaes, 2016) including for exercise as a means of improving wellbeing (Cruz, Kugel, Hewitt & Salamat, 2018). While videogaming as an activity might be associated with younger audiences, older adults are increasingly active in using technology (Duggan, 2015) and are increasingly engaged in gaming. Despite this, respondents in our study typically reported playing videogames relatively infrequently, with a large number of respondents reporting that they did not play videogames at all, increasing with age. Furthermore, eHEALS scores revealed that a notable number of respondents in the current study scored relatively lowly in terms of digital health literacy, both regardless of their current exposure to videogaming and increasingly with age. This serves to highlight the diverse needs of older demographics, for instance the need for any gamified intervention to be easily accessible and simple to use and navigate.

Additionally, respondents were keen to be able to record their progress in the game to enable them to track the progress in their wellbeing over time. While gaming has been shown to satisfy adult individual needs for useful health outcomes (Kaufman, 2017), the use of health tracking systems requires users to be able to navigate to, access and understand the data produced (Yang & Silverman, 2014; Ginossar et al., 2017). As previously mentioned, scores for electronic health literacy were low in our sample. Therefore, the design and implementation of health tracking systems must consider usability and accessibility for end-users in order for this data to be meaningful. Research in the field suggests that use of plain language, simplicity in design and affording the opportunity to review material is of value in increasing the impact of health data in digital applications (Broderick, Devine, Langhans, Lemerise, Lier & Harris, 2013).

Finally respondents also indicated a preference in free-response feedback for prompts and reminders to use the game on a regular basis. Due to time constraints, we were unfortunately not able to include this feature in the prototype games, hence at this stage it is not possible to ascertain the extent or manner in which our respondents would have responded. Literature does however confirm that alerts and reminders can positively drive engagement with health applications (Consolvo et al., 2008) providing these find an appropriate balance between persistency and not being too obtrusive (Holtz & Whitten, 2009; Anhøj & Møldrup, 2004), and respect the privacy of the user (Curioso, 2009).

Participants also reported a preference for in-game activities to be relatable to real-world wellbeing, e.g. by encouraging real-world activity. Adult Learning Theory proposes that older adults in particular seek to learn information which has a practical application to their everyday life (Knowles, 1980; Seah, Kaufman, Sauvé & Zhang, 2018) and are accepting of technological means of doing so when their benefits outweigh any effort required to adapt and use them (McLaughlin, Gandy, Allaire & Whitlock, 2012; Melenhorst, Rogers & Bouwhuis, 2006; de Schutter and Malliet, 2014). Models of acceptance of technology also confirm that perceived usefulness and the ease with which a technology can be used and implemented are significant predictors of its adoption (Davis, Bagozzi & Warshaw, 1989).

Findings from the second study also reinforced those of the pre-development survey. Respondents again indicated a relatively low amount of time spent playing videogames in an average week, with a large proportion of the demographic not playing videogames at all. While this does not necessarily imply a lack of interest among older players (interest in the option for a game for wellbeing was good), these findings are a reminder of the need for accessibility and simple and intuitive design in a demographic which may be either inexperienced with the mechanics and design attributes of videogames, possess lower electronic health literacy, or both (Gamberini et al., 2006; Gerling et al., 2012). To this end, our prototype game 'Piece of Mind' received positive user feedback in terms of how accessible and intuitive its simplistic design was.

Despite the preference for the simplistic design of 'Piece of Mind' however, it quickly became apparent that 'Wellbeing Town' was more favourably reviewed overall. While respondents acknowledged the benefits of a game which could be easily navigated and where task-requirements were clearly established, 'Piece of Mind' was rated as less enjoyable and rewarding. Despite there being an established need for serious games to be accessible, there is nonetheless a need for them to be challenging, thought provoking, provide a good variety of in-game tasks and objectives, and to be enjoyable. (Csikzentmihalyi, 1990; Belchior, Marsiske, Sisco, Yam & Mann, 2012). Participants frequently cited the non-linearity of 'Wellbeing Town' and the freedom to complete the game in the manner they wished (or to deviate from the game storyline and explore the environment at will) as a positive feature. These findings are in keeping with theories of motivation such as Self-Determination Theory, which point to autonomy and markers of competency as proponents of intrinsic drive and the manner in which games can achieve them (Ryan & Deci, 2000, Ryan, Deci & Przybylski, 2006). In extending either of the two prototypes outlined in this chapter, this is a vital consideration to ensure the games' sustained reach.

Limitations

While the present findings hold value in providing further insight into the needs and requirements of adults when developing a serious game for wellbeing, they are not without limitation. Firstly, while we attempted to ensure that all respondents were offered a fair amount of time to engage with the prototype games before reviewing, we were unable to control for the precise amount of time players spent engaging with the games before review. Consequently, it is likely that players engaged with the games for differing amounts of time. Furthermore, while the relaxing of COVID-19 restrictions enabled some data toward the end of the second study to be collected at the MhIST centre, ongoing restrictions meant that the vast majority of data was collected online. Given the lower electronic health literacy reported by the demographic in the first study, this presented a number of challenges. Unsurprisingly, some participants experienced difficulties in accessing and running the games independently, therefore limiting the data they could provide in review. Nonetheless, while this negatively affected the number of participants able to take part in the active review of the prototypes, the interest and acceptability for a game for wellbeing remained. This therefore serves as a reminder of the need to make serious and informative games accessible and easy to use.

Additionally, the present findings must be considered in relation to the relatively small sample sizes, which may leave some analyses underpowered. Furthermore, while some participants were recruited from the general public, a large number of responses, including all participants in the first study, were drawn from users of the MhIST charity in Bolton, UK. Consequently, while the present findings appear to complement as well as build on the existing literature, it is likely that our findings do not fully represent adults who nonetheless may benefit from a digitised intervention for adult wellbeing. For example, given the voluntary nature of recruitment and the active nature of participation in the second study (participants were required to play the games before review), it is possible that the present sample is more representative of adults actively involved in their health and wellbeing. As lower wellbeing is associated with higher avoidance (Briki, 2018), the present sample is less likely to encompass the needs and requirements of adults with more significant wellbeing intervention needs.

As the games reviewed in the present chapter were prototypes, they were consequently not at a sophisticated enough stage of development for more complex analytical features such as detailed remote data capturing, or social features such as online multiplayer modes to be included. It is therefore currently not possible to ascertain how acceptable these features may have been to users, or the extent to which they might drive continued engagement. Data capturing methods which automatically detect psychological events and respond by prompting the user or passing data to a professional may represent an opportunity to proactively drive engagement with therapeutic tools. This potentially preventative or early-intervention technique is in contrast to the typically reactive 'disease oriented' approach which is characteristic of the medical model (Riva, Banos, Botella, Wiederhold & Gaggioli, 2012). However, understanding the factors which drive user-acceptability or may arouse user suspicion are critical in ensuring the adoption of remote data collection protocols (LaMonica, Davenport, Roberts & Hickie (2021). With regard to social interaction, the benefits of gaming for loneliness, depression and social support are noted in the literature, and are particularly associated with existing enjoyment of relationships and quality of play in an online community or guild (Zhang & Kaufman, 2016). Furthermore, many adult players develop meaningful online relationships in online play (Zhang & Kaufman, 2017). Of note, these were both features which participants in our first study reported to be of value in using a game for wellbeing, and as such would be a development priority in future iterations of the games.

Finally, in order to appropriately assess the extent to which the game achieved its aims in educating users regarding the Five Ways to Wellbeing Framework, further evaluation is required to assess changes to wellbeing and acquisition of the educational content. While the present findings provide valuable insight into the acceptability of two prototype games and suggestions for further development, further investigation and iterative development is required via controlled trials to determine the game's efficacy in improving user wellbeing, capacity to encourage longitudinal engagement, and the extent to which user-feedback is addressed in future versions of the games.

CONCLUSION

In this chapter we have presented the findings of two studies conducted with volunteering service-users from MhIST and the general public to develop two prototype videogames for adult wellbeing. Findings determined that adults were receptive towards the development of a game to improve their wellbeing and offered insight into their preferences. Prototype reviews revealed the need for clarity in design and accessibility which recognises the lower electronic health literacy of the population and the lack of gaming experience among a number of respondents. However, while acceptability of a game for wellbeing is good, such interventions are not without their challenges.

Previous literature suggests that the design of videogames must consider the needs of the demographic in order to maintain play (Salmon et al., 2017). While the present findings indicate that a desire to engage with digital interventions for wellbeing exists among our respondents, and that the general acceptability of a gamified intervention is good, there is a need to consider the specific needs of the demographic (for instance in relation to digital health literacy) when designing serious and informative games. Sustained engagement is of significant importance in ensuring that the valuable learning material contained within such interventions is delivered effectively (HEFCE, 2015; Wiles et al., 2015; Cartwright-Hatton, 2004), particularly in a demographic where the potential value of using games as a learning tool may be less apparent (Charlier, Ott, Remmele & Whitton, 2012). It is therefore imperative that developers of games for health and wellbeing understand the interests and abilities of their target players to create games with low barrier to entry and recognition of prior experience of videogaming (or lack thereof), while preserving the essence and challenge of what makes gaming engaging and entertaining.

FUNDING STATEMENT

This research received no specific grant from any funding agency in the public, commercial, or not-for-profit sectors.

ACKNOWLEDGMENT

The authors would like to thank the following students for their contribution to the project in developing the games:

- Robin Armstrong-Wood
- Kyle Blenkinship
- Patrick Davies
- Tanya Madeva
- Callum Pogson
- Robert Valache
- Chloe Webb-Adam

We would also like to extend our thanks to Col Harding and Rebecca Mayhew of the Centre for Games Design at the University of Bolton, for the input and guidance they provided to students during development.

REFERENCES

Abdallah, S., Main, G., Pople, L., & Rees, G. (2014). *Ways to Well-being: Exploring the links between children's activities and their subjective well-being*. The Children's Society. https://www.york.ac.uk/inst/spru/research/pdf/SCways.pdf

Abt, C. (1970). *Serious games*. Viking Press.

Aked, J., Marks, N., Cordon, C., & Thompson, S. (2008). *Five Ways to Wellbeing: A report presented to the Foresight Project on communicating the evidence base for improving people's well-being*. New Economics Foundation.

Al Issa, H.-E., & Jaleel, E. M. (2021). Social isolation and psychological wellbeing: Lessons from Covid-19. *Management Science Letters*, *11*(2), 609–618. doi:10.5267/j.msl.2020.9.006

Anhøj, J., & Møldrup, C. (2004). Feasibility of collecting diary data from asthma patients through mobile phones and SMS (short message service): Response rate analysis and focus group evaluation from a pilot study. *Journal of Medical Internet Research*, *6*(4), e42. doi:10.2196/jmir.6.4.e42 PMID:15631966

Baranowski, T., Buday, R., Thompson, D., Lyons, E. J., Shirong-Lu, A., & Baranowski, J. (2013). Developing games for health behaviour change: Getting started. *Games for Health*, *2*(4), 183–190. doi:10.1089/g4h.2013.0048 PMID:24443708

Belchior, P., Marsiske, M., Sisco, S., Yam, A., & Mann, W. (2012). Older adults' engagement with a video game training program. *Activities, Adaptation and Aging*, *36*(4), 269–279. doi:10.1080/01924788.2012.702307 PMID:23504652

Bindoff, I., de Salas, K., Peterson, G., Ling, T., Lewis, I., Wells, L., Gee, P., & Ferguson, S. G. (2016). Quittr: The Design of a Video Game to Support Smoking Cessation. *JMIR Serious Games, 4*(2), e:19. doi:10.2196/games.6258

Blocker, K. A., Wright, T. J., & Boot, W. R. (2014). Gaming preferences of aging populations. *Gerontechnology (Valkenswaard)*, *12*(3), 174–184. doi:10.4017/gt.2014.12.3.008.00 PMID:29033699

Briki, W. (2017). Trait self-control: Why people with a higher approach (avoidance) temperament can experience higher (lower) subjective wellbeing. *Personality and Individual Differences, 120*(1), 112–117. doi:10.1016/j.paid.2017.08.039

Broderick, J., Devine, T., Langhans, E., Lemerise, A. J., Lier, S., & Harris, L. (2013). Designing health literate mobile apps. *NAM Perspectives*. Retrieved from: http://www.iom.edu/Global/Perspectives/2014/HealthLiterateApps.aspx

Caddick, N., & Smith, B. (2014). The impact of sport and physical activity on the well-being of combat veterans: A systematic review. *Psychology of Sport and Exercise, 15*(1), 9–18. doi:10.1016/j.psychsport.2013.09.011

Cartwright-Hatton, S., Roberts, C., Chitsabesan, P., Fothergill, C., & Harrington, R. (2004). Systematic review of the efficacy of cognitive behaviour therapies for childhood and adolescent anxiety disorders. *British Journal of Clinical Psychology, 43*(4), 421–436. doi:10.1348/0144665042388928 PMID:15530212

Charlier, N., Ott, M., Remmele, B., & Whitton, N. (2012). Not just for children: game-based learning for older adults. *6th European Conference on Game Based Learning (ECGBL 2012)*, 102-108.

Cheung, Y. T., Chau, P. H., & Yip, P. S. F. (2008). A revisit on older adults' suicides and severe acute respiratory syndrome (SARS) epidemic in Hong Kong. *International Journal of Geriatric Psychiatry, 23*(12), 1231–1238. doi:10.1002/gps.2056 PMID:18500689

Chu, P. S., Saucier, D. A., & Hafner, E. (2010). Meta-analysis of the relationships between social support and well-being in children and adolescents. *Journal of Social and Clinical Psychology, 29*(6), 624–645. doi:10.1521/jscp.2010.29.6.624

Consolvo, S., Klasnja, P., McDonald, D. W., Avrahami, D., Froehlich, J., LeGrand, L., Libby, R., Mosher, K., & Landay, J. A. (2008). Flowers or a robot army? Encouraging awareness & activity with personal, mobile displays. In *Proceedings of the 10th international conference on Ubiquitous computing* (pp. 54-63). 10.1145/1409635.1409644

Cruz, M., Kugel, J. D., Hewitt, L., & Salamat, A. (2018). Perceptions of Older Adults on the Use of an Interactive Video Game in Promoting Health and Well-Being. *The Open Journal of Occupational Therapy, 6*(3). Advance online publication. doi:10.15453/2168-6408.1490

Csikzentmihalyi, M. (1975). *Beyond Boredom and Anxiety*. Jossey-Bass.

Csikzentmihalyi, M. (1990). *Flow: The Psychology of the Optimal Experience*. Harper & Row.

Curioso, W. H., Quistberg, D. A., Cabello, R., Gozzer, E., Garcia, P. J., Holmes, K. K., & Kurth, A. E. (2009). "It's time for your life": How should we remind patients to take medicines using short text messages? *AMIA ... Annual Symposium Proceedings - AMIA Symposium. AMIA Symposium, 2009*, 129. PMID:21633523

Davis, F. D., Bagozzi, R., & Warshaw, P. R. (1989). User Acceptance of Computer Technology: A Comparison of Two Theoretical Models. *Management Science, 35*(8), 982–1003. doi:10.1287/mnsc.35.8.982

Djaouti, D., Alvarez, J., Jessel, J. P., & Rampnoux, O. (2011). *Origins of Serious Games*. Springer. doi:10.1007/978-1-4471-2161-9_3

Fitzgerald, M., & Ratcliffe, G. (2020). Serious Games, Gamification, and Serious Mental Illness: A Scoping Review. *Psychiatric Services (Washington, D.C.)*, *71*(2), 170–183. doi:10.1176/appi.ps.201800567 PMID:31640521

Galante, J., Galante, I., Bekkers, M.-J., & Gallacher, J. (2014). Effect of kindness-based meditation on health and well-being: A systematic review and meta-analysis. *Journal of Consulting and Clinical Psychology*, *82*(6), 1101–1114. doi:10.1037/a0037249 PMID:24979314

Gamberini, L., Alcaniz, M., Barresi, M., Fabregat, M., Ibanez, D., & Prontu, L. (2006). Cognition, technology and games for the elderly: An introduction to ELDERGAMES Project. *PsychNology*, *4*, 285–308.

Gentile, D. A., & Gentile, J. R. (2008). Violent video games as exemplary teachers: A conceptual analysis. *Journal of Youth and Adolescence*, *37*(2), 127–141. doi:10.100710964-007-9206-2

Gerling, K. M., Schulte, F. P., Smeddinck, J., & Masuch, M. (2012). Game design for older adults: effects of age-related changes on structural elements of digital games. *The International Conference on Entertainment Computing (ICEC '12)*, 235-242. 10.1007/978-3-642-33542-6_20

Giner-Bartolomé, C., Fagundo, A. B., Sánchez, I., Jiménez-Murcia, S., Santamaría, J. J., Ladouceur, R., Menchón, J. M., & Fernández-Aranda, F. (2015). Can an intervention based on a serious videogame prior to cognitive behavioural therapy be helpful in bulimia nervosa? A clinical case study. *Frontiers in Psychology*, *6*, 982. doi:10.3389/fpsyg.2015.00982 PMID:26236261

Ginossar, T., Fawad Ali Shah, S., West, A. J., Bentley, J. M., Caburnay, C. A., Kreuter, M. W., & Kinney, A. Y. (2017). Content, Usability, and Utilization of Plain Language in Breast Cancer Mobile Phone Apps: A Systematic Analysis. *JMIR mHealth and uHealth*, *5*(3), e20. doi:10.2196/mhealth.7073 PMID:28288954

Green, J. (2013). *Evaluation of the 2012 Wellbeing Game*. Canterbury District Health Board.

Havukainen, M., Laine, T. H., Martikainen, T., & Sutinen, E. (2020). A Case Study on Co-designing Digital Games with Older Adults and Children: Game Elements, Assets, and Challenges. *The Computer Games Journal*, *9*(2), 163–188. doi:10.100740869-020-00100-w

Healey, N. M., Baron, S., & Ilieva, J. (2002). Online surveys in marketing research. *International Journal of Market Research*, *44*(3), 361–376. doi:10.1177/147078530204400303

Higher Education Funding Council for England (HEFCE). (2015). *Understanding provision for students with mental health problems and intensive support needs*. Retrieved from: http://www.hefce.ac.uk/media/HEFCE,2014/Content/Pubs/Independentresearch/2015/Understanding,provision,for,students,with,mental,health,problems/HEFCE2015_mh.pdf

Holtz, B., & Whitten, P. (2009). Managing asthma with mobile phones: A feasibility study. *Telemedicine Journal and e-Health*, *15*(9), 907–909. doi:10.1089/tmj.2009.0048 PMID:19919198

Hone, L. C., Jarden, A., Duncan, S., & Schofield, G. M. (2015). Flourishing in New Zealand Workers: Associations With Lifestyle Behaviors, Physical Health, Psychosocial, and Work-Related Indicators. *Journal of Occupational and Environmental Medicine*, *57*(9), 973–983. doi:10.1097/JOM.0000000000000508 PMID:26340286

Hotopf, M., Bullmore, E., O'Connor, R. C., & Holmes, E. A. (2020). The scope of mental health research during the COVID-19 pandemic and its aftermath. *The British Journal of Psychiatry*, *217*(4), 540–542. doi:10.1192/bjp.2020.125 PMID:32493516

Jetten, J., Haslam, C., Haslam, S. A., Dingle, G., & Jones, J. M. (2014). How groups affect our health and well-being: The path from theory to policy. *Social Issues and Policy Review*, *8*(1), 103–130. doi:10.1111ipr.12003

Kaufman, D. (2017). The promise of digital games for older adults. *Open Access Journal of Gerontology & Geriatric Medicine*, *1*(5).

Keeman, A., Näswall, K., Malinen, S., & Kuntz, J. (2017). Employee wellbeing: Evaluating a wellbeing intervention in two settings. *Frontiers in Psychology*, *8*, 505. doi:10.3389/fpsyg.2017.00505 PMID:28421021

King, G., Currie, M., & Petersen, P. (2012). Child and parent engagement in the mental health intervention process: A motivational framework. *Child and Adolescent Mental Health*, *19*(1), 2–8. doi:10.1111/camh.12015 PMID:32878365

Knowles, M. S. (1980). *The modern practice of adult education: From pedagogy to andragogy*. Englewood Cliffs, NJ: Prentice Hall.

LaMonica, H. M., Davenport, T. A., Roberts, A. E., & Hickie, I. B. (2021). Understanding Technology Preferences and Requirements for Health Information Technologies Designed to Improve and Maintain the Mental Health and Well-Being of Older Adults: Participatory Design Study. *JMIR Aging*, *4*(1), e21461. doi:10.2196/21461 PMID:33404509

Laver, K. E., George, S., Thomas, S., Deutsch, J. E., & Crotty, M. (2015). Virtual reality for stroke rehabilitation. *Cochrane Database of Systematic Reviews*, *12*(2). Advance online publication. doi:10.1002/14651858. CD008349.pub3 PMID:25927099

Lob, E., Steptoe, A., & Fancourt, D. (2020). Abuse, self-harm and suicidal ideation in the UK during the COVID-19 pandemic. *The British Journal of Psychiatry*, *217*(4), 543–546. doi:10.1192/bjp.2020.130 PMID:32654678

Mak, I. W. C., Chu, C. M., Pan, P. C., Yiu, M. G. C., & Chan, V. L. (2009). Long-term psychiatric morbidities among SARS survivors. *General Hospital Psychiatry*, *31*(4), 318–326. doi:10.1016/j.genhosppsych.2009.03.001 PMID:19555791

McLaughlin, A., Gandy, M., Allaire, J., & Whitlock, L. (2012). Putting fun into video games for older adults. *Ergonomics in Design*, *20*(2), 13–22. doi:10.1177/1064804611435654

Melenhorst, A. S., Rogers, W. A., & Bouwhuis, D. G. (2006). Older adults' motivated choice for technological innovation: Evidence for benefit-driven selectivity. *Psychology and Aging*, *21*(1), 190–195. doi:10.1037/0882-7974.21.1.190 PMID:16594804

Nap, H. H., de Kort, Y. A. W., & Ijsselsteijn, W. A. (2009). Senior gamers: Preferences, motivations, and needs. *Gerontechnology (Valkenswaard)*, *8*(4), 247–262. doi:10.4017/gt.2009.08.04.003.00

Nawaz, A., Skjæret, N., Lægdheim Helbostad, J., Vereijken, B., Boulton, E., & Svanaes, D. (2015). Usability and acceptability of balance exergames in older adults: A scoping review. *Health Informatics Journal*, *22*(4), 911–931. doi:10.1177/1460458215598638 PMID:26303810

Norman, C. D., & Skinner, H. A. (2006). eHEALS: the eHealth literacy scale. *Journal of Medical Internet Research, 8*(4), e:27. doi:10.2196/jmir.8.4.e27

Quinn, C., Clare, L., & Woods, R. T. (2010). The impact of motivations and meanings on the wellbeing of caregivers of people with dementia: A systematic review. *International Psychogeriatrics*, *22*(1), 43–55. doi:10.1017/S1041610209990810 PMID:19772684

Raiff, B. R., Jarvis, B. P., & Rapoza, D. (2012). Prevalence of Video Game Use, Cigarette Smoking, and Acceptability of a Video Game–Based Smoking Cessation Intervention Among Online Adults. *Nicotine & Tobacco Research: Official Journal of the Society for Research on Nicotine and Tobacco*, *14*(12), 1453–1457. doi:10.1093/ntr/nts079 PMID:22422929

Randelin, M., Saaranen, T., Naumanen, P., & Louhevaara, V. (2012). The developed hypothetical model for promoting sustainable well-being at work by learning: A systematic literature review. *Theoretical Issues in Ergonomics Science*, *14*(5), 417–454. doi:10.1080/1463922X.2011.648669

Rica., R. L., Shimojo, G. L., Gomes, M. C. S. S., Alonso, A. C., Pitta, R. M., Santa-Rosa, F- A-, Pontes Junior, F. L., Ceschini, F., Gobbo, S., Bergamin, M., & Bocalini, D. S. (2021). Effects of a Kinect-based physical training program on body composition, functional fitness and depression in institutionalized older adults. Epidemiology, *Clinical Practice and Health, 20*(3), 195-200. doi:10.1111/ggi.13857

Riva, G., Banos, R., Botella, C., Wiederhold, B. K., & Gaggioli, A. (2012). Positive Technology: Using Interactive Technologies to Promote Positive Functioning. *Cyberpsychology, Behavior, and Social Networking*, *15*(2), 69–77. doi:10.1089/cyber.2011.0139 PMID:22149077

Ryan, R. M., & Deci, E. L. (2000). Self-determination theory and the facilitation of intrinsic motivation, social development, and well-being. *The American Psychologist*, *55*(1), 68–78. doi:10.1037/0003-066X.55.1.68 PMID:11392867

Ryan, R. M., Scott Rigby, C., & Przybylski, A. (2006). The Motivational Pull of Video Games: A Self-Determination Theory Approach. *Motivation and Emotion*, *30*(4), 344–360. doi:10.100711031-006-9051-8

Salmon, J. P., Dolan, S. M., Drake, R. S., Wilson, G. C., Klein, R. M., & Eskes, G. A. (2017). A survey of video game preferences in adults: Building better games for older adults. *Entertainment Computing*, *21*, 45–64. doi:10.1016/j.entcom.2017.04.006

Scherer, E. A., Ben-Zeev, D., Li, Z., & Kane, J. M. (2017). Analyzing mHealth engagement: Joint models for intensively collected user engagement data. *JMIR mHealth and uHealth*, *5*(1), e1. doi:10.2196/mhealth.6474 PMID:28082257

Seah, E. T.-W., Kaufman, D., Sauvé, L., & Zhang, F. (2018). Play, learn, connect: Older adults' experience with a multiplayer, educational, digital Bingo game. *Journal of Educational Computing Research*, *56*(5), 675–700. doi:10.1177/0735633117722329

Tárrega, S., Castro-Carreras, L., Fernández-Aranda, F., Granero, R., Giner-Bartolomé, C., Aymamí, N., Gómez-Peña, M., Santamaría, J. J., Forcano, L., Steward, T., Menchón, J. M., & Jiménez-Murcia, S. (2015). A serious videogame as an additional therapy tool for training emotional regulation and impulsivity control in severe gambling disorder. *Frontiers in Psychology, 6*, 1721. doi:10.3389/fpsyg.2015.01721 PMID:26617550

Vallury, K. D., Jones, M., & Oosterbroek, C. (2015). Computerized cognitive behaviour therapy for anxiety and depression in rural areas: a systematic review. *Journal of Medical Internet Research, 17*(6), e:139. doi:10.2196/jmir.4145

White, R. G., & van der Boor, C. (2020). Impact of the COVID-19 pandemic and initial period of lockdown on the mental health and well-being of adults in the UK. *BJPsych Open, 6*(5, e90), 1–4. doi:10.1192/bjo.2020.79 PMID:32799958

Wiles, N., Thomas, L., Abel, A., Barnes, M., Carroll, F., Ridgway, N., Sherlock, S., Turner, N., Button, K., Odondi, L., Metcalfe, C., Owen-Smith, A., Campbell, J., Garland, A., Hollinghurst, S., Jerrom, B., Kessler, D., Kuyken, W., Morrison, J., ... Lewis, G. (2014). Clinical effectiveness and cost-effectiveness of cognitive behavioural therapy as an adjunct to pharmacotherapy for treatment-resistant depression in primary care: The CoBalT randomised controlled trial. *Health Technology Assessment, 18*(31), 1–167. doi:10.3310/hta18310 PMID:24824481

Wiljer, D., Shi, J., Lo, B., Sanches, M., Hollenberg, E., Johnson, A., Abi-Jaoudé, A., Chaim, G., Cleverley, K., Henderson, J., Isaranuwatchai, W., Levinson, A., Robb, J., Wong, H. W., & Voineskos, A. (2020). Effects of a Mobile and Web App (Thought Spot) on Mental Health Help-Seeking Among College and University Students: Randomized Controlled Trial. *Journal of Medical Internet Research, 22*(10), e20790. doi:10.2196/20790 PMID:33124984

Yang, Y. T., & Silverman, R. D. (2014, February). Mobile health applications: The patchwork of legal and liability issues suggests strategies to improve oversight. *Health Affairs, 33*(2), 222–227. doi:10.1377/hlthaff.2013.0958 PMID:24493764

Yip, P. S. F., Cheung, Y. T., Chau, P. H., & Law, Y. W. (2010). The impact of epidemic outbreak the case of Severe Acute Respiratory Syndrome (SARS) and suicide among older adults in Hong Kong. *Crisis, 31*(2), 86–92. doi:10.1027/0227-5910/a000015 PMID:20418214

Zhang, F., & Kaufman, D. (2016). Can Playing Massive Multiplayer Online Role Playing Games (MMORPGs) Improve Older Adults' Socio-Psychological Wellbeing? In S. Zvacek, M. Restivo, J. Uhomoibhi, & M. Helfert (Eds.), *Computer Supported Education. CSEDU 2015. Communications in Computer and Information Science, 583*. Springer. doi:10.1007/978-3-319-29585-5_29

Zhang, F., & Kaufman, D. (2017). Massively Multiplayer Online Role-Playing Games (MMORPGs) and Socio-Emotional Wellbeing. *Computers in Human Behavior, 73*, 451–458. doi:10.1016/j.chb.2017.04.008

This research was previously published in Digital Innovations for Mental Health Support; pages 151-186, copyright year 2022 by Medical Information Science Reference (an imprint of IGI Global).

APPENDIX 1

Copy of User-Preferences Survey (Study One)

Please begin the survey by creating a code for yourself. This is so you can be identified later if you wish to withdraw (see below). You will create this code using your year of birth, your initials, and the date on which you complete the questionnaire, for example:

Year of Birth: 1972
Name: John Smith
Date when John Completed the Questionnaire: 15 November 2020
Code: 1972JS15112020

1. What is your age: _____
2. How would you describe your gender?
    a. Male
    b. Female
    c. Non-binary
    d. Other
3. How many hours per week on average would you say you play video games?
4. Would you be interested in using an informative game designed to improve your wellbeing?
    a. Yes
    b. Maybe
    c. No

If you answered no to question 4 here, please scroll to the bottom of the survey now and click 'submit'. Otherwise, please continue.

5. How many hours per week do you think you would use a game to improve wellbeing?
6. When playing, for how long would you like an individual play session to be in minutes?
7. Rank in order of importance (1-5, where 1 is 'not at all important', and 5 is 'very important'):
    a. Ease of use
    b. Detailed health information (e.g. ...)
    c. Simple health information (e.g. ...)
    d. Info regarding how to contact other services
    e. Ways to track your wellbeing (e.g. charts)
    f. Available on mobile device
    g. Available online
    h. Customisable in-game avatar
    i. Option to replay already completed levels/mini-games.
    j. Option to export your in-game data to send to doctor/external agency.

eHEALS

Next, this scale will ask for your opinion and experiences using the Internet for health information. For each statement, please state which response best reflects your opinion and experience right now.

8. How useful do you feel the Internet is in helping you in making decisions about your health?
    a. Not useful at all
    b. Not useful
    c. Unsure
    d. Useful
    e. Very useful
9. How important is it for you to be able to access health resources on the Internet?
    a. Not important at all
    b. Not important
    c. Unsure
    d. Important
    e. Very important
10. I know what health resources are available on the Internet.
    a. Strongly disagree
    b. Disagree
    c. Undecided
    d. Agree
    e. Strongly agree
11. I know where to find helpful health resources on the Internet.
    a. Strongly disagree
    b. Disagree
    c. Undecided
    d. Agree
    e. Strongly agree
12. I know how to find helpful health resources on the Internet.
    a. Strongly disagree
    b. Disagree
    c. Undecided
    d. Agree
    e. Strongly agree
13. I know how to use the Internet to answer questions about my health.
    a. Strongly disagree
    b. Disagree
    c. Undecided
    d. Agree
    e. Strongly agree

14. I know how to use the health information I find on the Internet to help me.
    a. Strongly disagree
    b. Disagree
    c. Undecided
    d. Agree
    e. Strongly agree
15. I have the skills I need to evaluate the health resources I find on the Internet.
    a. Strongly disagree
    b. Disagree
    c. Undecided
    d. Agree
    e. Strongly agree
16. I can tell high quality health resources from low quality health resources on the Internet.
    a. Strongly disagree
    b. Disagree
    c. Undecided
    d. Agree
    e. Strongly agree
17. I feel confident in using information from the Internet to make health decision.
    a. Strongly disagree
    b. Disagree
    c. Undecided
    d. Agree
    e. Strongly agree

APPENDIX 2

Copy of User-Feedback Survey (Study Two)

MhIST Adult Wellbeing Game: Concept Games - User Review ('Wellbeing Town')

Introduction and Participant Information

Figure 5.

Thank you for your interest in this research.

This study forms the secondary stages of a wider project, whereby we aim to develop a mobile videogame for adult wellbeing. Following on from feedback obtained from MhIST clients recently, two prototype games have been developed in a collaborative partnership between MhIST, and the Psychology Department and Centre for Games Design at the University of Bolton.

Before completing this survey, you will have been asked to trial the prototype version of the game:

'Wellbeing Town'

The following survey will ask you a number of questions to ascertain your perception of the game and your suggestions for future improvements. The survey takes approximately 20-30mins to complete.

You will begin the survey by creating a code for yourself. This is so you can be identified later if you wish to withdraw (see below). You will create this code using your year of birth, your initials, and the date on which you complete the questionnaire, for example:

Year of Birth: 1972
Name: John Smith
Date when John completed the questionnaire: 15 November 2020
Code: 1972JS15112020

Your consent to take part in this survey is implied by you completing the questionnaire. If you wish to withdraw at any point, you can do so by closing the questionnaire. Any data collected will not be used unless you fully complete the survey. If you wish to withdraw at a later date, you may do so up until 31 March 2021. Please email S.Barnes@bolton.ac.uk quoting the code you created as detailed above.

If you are happy to take part, please proceed to the next page.

Create a unique identification code

Code-Entry

Please begin the survey by creating a code for yourself. This is so you can be identified later if you wish to withdraw (see below). You will create this code using your year of birth, your initials, and the date on which you complete the questionnaire, for example:

Year of Birth: 1972
Name: John Smith
Date when John completed the questionnaire: 15 November 2020
Code: 1972JS15112020

Demographic Information

Q1

Table 4. What is your age in years?

Please select your age in years.	010	20	30	40	50	60	70	80	90	100

Q2

How would you describe your gender?

- Male
- Female
- Non-binary / third gender
- Prefer not to say

Q3

On average, how many hours a week do you normally spend playing video-games (on any device)?
GAME TITLE: NOTE TO PARTICIPANT
G2-NOTE
The following questions relate to the concept game "Wellbeing Town".

Figure 6.

Wellbeing Town: Evaluation Questions

WT-Q1

The menus and in-game tasks were easy to navigate.

- Strongly disagree
- Somewhat disagree
- Neither agree nor disagree
- Somewhat agree
- Strongly agree

WT-Q2

The game made it clear to me what I was expected to do.

- Strongly disagree
- Somewhat disagree
- Neither agree nor disagree
- Somewhat agree
- Strongly agree

WT-Q3

I was able to understand the game and how to use it without assistance.

- Strongly disagree
- Somewhat disagree
- Neither agree nor disagree
- Somewhat agree
- Strongly agree

WT-Q4

The types of activities in the game were appropriate.

- Strongly disagree
- Somewhat disagree
- Neither agree nor disagree
- Somewhat agree
- Strongly agree

WT-Q5

Playing the game would help me to understand ways to improve my wellbeing.

- Strongly disagree
- Somewhat disagree
- Neither agree nor disagree
- Somewhat agree
- Strongly agree

WT-Q6

Playing the game would help to improve my wellbeing.

- Strongly disagree
- Somewhat disagree
- Neither agree nor disagree
- Somewhat agree
- Strongly agree

WT-Q7

The game contained enough variety of activities.

- Strongly disagree
- Somewhat disagree
- Neither agree nor disagree
- Somewhat agree
- Strongly agree

WT-Q8

The activities in the game were enjoyable and rewarding.

- Strongly disagree
- Somewhat disagree
- Neither agree nor disagree
- Somewhat agree
- Strongly agree

WT-Q9

The activities in the game were sufficiently challenging to keep my interest.

- Strongly disagree
- Somewhat disagree
- Neither agree nor disagree
- Somewhat agree
- Strongly agree

WT-Q10

I would be motivated to play this game often to help improve my wellbeing.

- Strongly disagree
- Somewhat disagree
- Neither agree nor disagree
- Somewhat agree
- Strongly agree

WT-OTHER

Do you have any further comments or suggestions regarding the game 'Wellbeing Town'?

MhIST Adult Wellbeing Game: Concept Games - User Review ('Piece of Mind')

Introduction and Participant Information

Figure 7.

Thank you for your interest in this research.

This study forms the secondary stages of a wider project, whereby we aim to develop a mobile videogame for adult wellbeing. Following on from feedback obtained from MhIST clients recently, two prototype games have been developed in a collaborative partnership between MhIST, and the Psychology Department and Centre for Games Design at the University of Bolton.

Before completing this survey, you will have been asked to trial the prototype game:

'Piece of Mind'

The following survey will ask you a number of questions to ascertain your perception of the game and your suggestions for future improvements. The survey takes approximately 20-30mins to complete.

You will begin the survey by creating a code for yourself. This is so you can be identified later if you wish to withdraw (see below). You will create this code using your year of birth, your initials, and the date on which you complete the questionnaire, for example:

Year of Birth: 1972
Name: John Smith
Date when John completed the questionnaire: 15 November 2020
Code: 1972JS15112020

Your consent to take part in this survey is implied by you completing the questionnaire. If you wish to withdraw at any point, you can do so by closing the questionnaire. Any data collected will not be used unless you fully complete the survey. If you wish to withdraw at a later date, you may do so up until 31 March 2021. Please email S.Barnes@bolton.ac.uk quoting the code you created as detailed above.

If you are happy to take part, please proceed to the next page.

Create a unique identification code

Code-Entry

Please begin the survey by creating a code for yourself. This is so you can be identified later if you wish to withdraw (see below). You will create this code using your year of birth, your initials, and the date on which you complete the questionnaire, for example:

Year of Birth: 1972
Name: John Smith
Date when John Completed the Questionnaire: 15 November 2020
Code: 1972JS15112020

Demographic Information

Q1

Table 5. What is your age in years?

Please select your age in years.	010	20	30	40	50	60	70	80	90	100

Q2

How would you describe your gender?

- Male
- Female
- Non-binary / third gender
- Prefer not to say

Q3

On average, how many hours a week do you normally spend playing video-games (on any device)?

GAME 1: NOTE TO PARTICIPANT

G1-NOTE

The following questions relate to the concept game "Piece of Mind".

Please complete this section if you trialled this game, otherwise please skip to the next page.

Figure 8.

Piece of Mind: Evaluation Questions

PoM-Q1

The menus and in-game tasks were easy to navigate.

- Strongly disagree
- Somewhat disagree
- Neither agree nor disagree
- Somewhat agree
- Strongly agree

PoM-Q2

The game made it clear to me what I was expected to do.

- Strongly disagree
- Somewhat disagree
- Neither agree nor disagree
- Somewhat agree
- Strongly agree

PoM-Q3

I was able to understand the game and how to use it without assistance.

- Strongly disagree
- Somewhat disagree
- Neither agree nor disagree
- Somewhat agree
- Strongly agree

PoM-Q4

The types of activities in the game were appropriate.

- Strongly disagree
- Somewhat disagree
- Neither agree nor disagree
- Somewhat agree
- Strongly agree

PoM-Q5

Playing the game would help me to understand ways to improve my wellbeing.

- Strongly disagree
- Somewhat disagree
- Neither agree nor disagree
- Somewhat agree
- Strongly agree

PoM-Q6

Playing the game would help to improve my wellbeing.

- Strongly disagree
- Somewhat disagree
- Neither agree nor disagree
- Somewhat agree
- Strongly agree

PoM-Q7

The game contained enough variety of activities.

- Strongly disagree
- Somewhat disagree
- Neither agree nor disagree
- Somewhat agree
- Strongly agree

PoM-Q8

The activities in the game were enjoyable and rewarding.

- Strongly disagree
- Somewhat disagree
- Neither agree nor disagree
- Somewhat agree
- Strongly agree

PoM-Q9

The activities in the game were sufficiently challenging to keep my interest.

- Strongly disagree
- Somewhat disagree
- Neither agree nor disagree
- Somewhat agree
- Strongly agree

PoM-Q10

I would be motivated to play this game often to help improve my wellbeing.

- Strongly disagree
- Somewhat disagree
- Neither agree nor disagree
- Somewhat agree
- Strongly agree

PoM-OTHER

Do you have any further comments or suggestions regarding the game 'Piece of Mind'?

Chapter 48
A Study of the Antecedents of Game Engagement and the Moderating Effect of the Self-Identity of Collaboration

Youngkeun Choi
ⓘ https://orcid.org/0000-0002-8842-9826
Sangmyung University, Seoul, Korea

ABSTRACT

The purpose of the present study was to examine the relationships between motivation factors and game engagement and explore the moderating effect of self-identity on those relationships. For this, the present study collected data from 228 college students in South Korean through a survey method and used hierarchical multiple regression analyses. In the results, first, the more competition, challenge, or social interaction participants pursue in gameplay, the more they are engaged in a game. Second, a positive relationship between social interaction and game engagement is stronger for participants in high rather than low in interdependent self-view. However, interdependent self-view was found to have no significance in the relationship between other motivators and game engagement. This study is the first one to examine the integral model of motivation factors of game engagement by including the moderating effect of self-identity.

1. INTRODUCTION

Video games are a multi-billion-dollar industry worldwide. Gamers provide endless entertainment and escape through a series of game types, ever-increasing graphics, and the ability to compete and collaborate with players around the world through online consoles and advanced computer games. However, the World Health Organization (WHO) recently asserted that the increasing time people spend gaming should be monitored and evaluated as it may constitute a risk factor for developing internet game disorder (WHO, 2018).

DOI: 10.4018/978-1-6684-7589-8.ch048

Recently, psychological research to review video games has undergone significant changes. Until very recently, the dominance of research on video games has focused its attention on research to identify the potential negative impacts of the game. The specific focus of these research programs includes the relationship between games and increased aggression, social isolation and overuse (Grüsser, Thalemann, & Griffiths, 2007). Recently, however, many researchers have focused on mediation to tailor games or relieve pain for educational or health-related interventions, taking advantage of the exciting appeal of video games (Sardia, Idria, & Fernández-Alemán, 2017). Increasingly, mediation-centered researchers have shown that games can have a positive impact on psychological and physical well-being. Both focused and interventional intensive studies share a different but exploratory approach. The methods and theories used will assess the degree to which a video game does not have a positive, negative, or affective effect on a given outcome in a given set of circumstances. Less well-known and less widely researched is the mechanism underlying these positive and negative connections.

Especially, massively multiplayer online role-playing games (MMORPGs) are the virtual successor of the tabletop games that saw their rise in the 20th century with Dungeons and Dragons. Modern MMORPGs are adventures through fantasy worlds and blends advanced graphics, endless achievements and options of collaboration and competitive gameplay. This game allows players to create and fancy virtual identities in the online fantasy world. Here, outside of the realistic social structure, you can play a new role that you choose. MMORPG also allows players to communicate with other players in a virtual environment through an online identity that allows them to share quests, talk with themselves or characters, and build online relationships and social capital (Trepte, Reinecke, & Juechems, 2012; Naidoo, Coleman, & Guyo, 2019). Gamers spend countless hours in this game, and many games require commissions and subscriptions, and time and spirited energy gamers occasionally make significant financial investments, not when they contribute to MMORPG games on a weekly basis (Jang, & Byon, 2019). Each game has specific mechanisms, ideas, and roles that players can take. As these games become more popular and expanding in functionality, more and more gamers are testing their skills in MMORPGs (Proffitt, Glegg, Levac, & Lange, 2019).

Despite a growing practical importance, there is a lack of quantitative studies on motivational factors that affect participants' engagement in MMORPGs. This article explores people's motivations to participate in MMORPG. For this, the article is structured as follows. The next section presents the theoretical framework and background for the hypotheses. This study adopts the lens of psychological motivation in engagement in MMORPGs (Lindenberg, 2001; Lee, Ko, & Lee, 2019). And, theories on the development of the self-identity as well as the relationship between the self and objects of consumption suggest that the sharing of an object will be associated with closer perceived social distances (Belk, 1988). Belk's (1988) work on the extended-self established the idea that people expand their concept of who they are to include their possessions and objects they consume. This study applies ideas on the extended self to MMORPG. And, the subsequent section then outlines data and methods, followed by the results. The article concludes with a discussion on implications and directions for future research.

2. THEORETICAL BACKGROUND AND HYPOTHESIS DEVELOPMENT

2.1. Game Engagement

The term "engagement" was investigated in a number of different disciplines, such as sociology, political science, psychology, and organizational behavior. In the marketing discipline, fewer studies were devoted to the terms "consumer engagement," and "customer engagement" before 2005 (Bordie et al., 2011). Customer engagement is defined as "a psychological state that occurs by virtue of interactive, co-creative customer experiences with a focal/ object (e.g., video game) in focal service relationships" (Bordie et al., 2011). Adults and children across demographic levels play games in their leisure time. They use different types of technologies to achieve the optimal entertainment experience. Many scholars emphasize the importance of engagement in the virtual environment (Wasko & Faraj, 2005).

Game engagement was proposed as a topic that is worthy of further study (Brockmyer et al., 2009). This study is answering that call by examining gamer's engagement in a different genre and how that impacts games purchase intention. The ultimate goal of marketers and game developers is to engage gamers in the game. For example, Warcraft III designs the game in a way to encourage gamers to co-create meaningful story (Buchanan-Oliver & Seo, 2012). However, game developers did not fully look at the difference between gamer psychological factors and motivation. Further, Yee (2006) argues that females prefer social, relationship, and teamwork games, whereas males prefer advancement, mechanics, and competition games. The author continues arguing that even male players socialized as much as female players, but they socialized very differently. Thus, understanding these differences will increase gamer engagement into the game.

2.2. Hypothesis Development

Sherry et al. (2006) argued that competition is an important motivation that can be obtained from video games. Competition in video games refers to competing and proving that a gamer is more skilled than his/her peers. Also, gamers play games competitively to enjoy the game itself. Researchers in the past have proven that male have higher competitiveness than female. However, if that is entirely true, we will not see a competitive female at any professional sport (Jenson & De Castell, 2010). Women and men have different motivation to compete at play games. The power of competition come from establishing a relative position in peer group's hierarchy. For example, gamers play to establish his position among his new friends. He will engage in the game and try to be good at it to impress his friends. Also, he might buy the game to practice at his personal time. Competition is the most important reason for people to play games with some genre such as sport and fighter (Sherry et al., 2006). Moreover, game can increase people's level of competitiveness which means that they will be more competitive in other social activities, and that winning becomes an important social goal for them (Greenberg et al., 2010). Competition is different from a challenge where the competition is against the player's personal best or the game itself (Lucas and Sherry, 2004). Thus, gamers, who are motivated by competition, will have be more engaged in the game and will purchase video game more.

H1: Gamers' competition motivation has a positive relationship with their game engagement.

Challenge refers to being good at the activity that the person is doing (unlike competition where the competition is against other players). The game challenge can range from learning new language to lose weight. People challenge themselves to be better in certain activities. In the video game context, gamers challenge themselves to pass levels and advance in the game. Female may shy away from "masculine" games to avoid direct competition with them. However, they play these games to challenge themselves which they will feel more control (Lucas & Sherry, 2004). Challenge was one of the principal motivation that was identified early in playing video game (Myers, 1990). Gamers' flow state will be the balance between the game's challenge and the skills they have. If the game is more challenging than their skills, they will leave the game soon and have anxiety. Also, if the game does not challenge the gamer's skills, they will be bored, and they will leave the game. The ideal position is when the challenge in the game is close to the gamers skills. In that situation, gamers will reach flow state and will enjoy the game (Hoffman & Novak, 2009). Gamers at this level are engaged into the game. Thus, gamers' challenge motivation would predict their level of video game engagement (presence-flow-psychological absorption) and their purchase intention of video game.

H2: Gamers' challenge motivation has a positive relationship with their game engagement.

People seek social recognition and status within a society. People want to belong to a group as Maslow explain in the hierarchy of needs. The second level of Maslow' pyramid is the need to belong (Maslow, 1943). People can belong to a particular group by interacting with that group. So, people interact with a group of people to determine the compatibility that can occur between them and that group or individuals. Also, people seek social capital. That capital can substitute financial capital in some cases. For example, a person with high social capital might not need high financial capital (Duclos, Wan, & Jiang, 2013). In the video game context, gamers are motivated to interact with other gamers to gain social capital. Also, social interaction can be one of the main reasons that many gamers got to play games. For example, game console brought friends together and sleepovers. Many gamers use games to interact with friends and learn about the personality of others (Sherry et al., 2006). That motivation would predicate their level of engagement and their purchase intention.

H3: Gamers' social interaction motivation has a positive relationship with their game engagement.

Previous work has used the terms independent and interdependent to describe how individuals derive their self-identity (Markus & Kitayama, 1991). Interdependent individuals and groups tend to put an emphasis on the needs of collaboration with others and fit in with a harmonious group, whereas people from independent cultures tend to value expressing unique inner attributes (Markus & Kitayama, 1991). The more an individual is dependent on the group, the more they will attend to the group cues for development of their own self-identity (Triandis, 1989). Independent and interdependent self-views have been found to be associated with abstract and concrete representations, respectively. Spassova and Lee (2013) saw that when asked to describe future events, those with independent self-views responded with more abstract descriptions and with a perception that that even was even farther in the future than did those who were interdependent. This may suggest that those described as having higher levels of interdependent self-views are more sensitive to environmental cues and have a propensity to see things in more concrete ways. An in-group boundary is the extent to which an individual sees others as being part of their own social group. The definitions of such boundaries keep adjusting along with situational factors, i.e., things such as common fates, common outside threats, and proximity (Triandis, 1989). So, even though someone with an interdependent self-view does not just indiscriminately subordinate themselves to the needs or goals of others (Markus & Kitayama, 1991), to them other people would represent a much more important role and be more of a focal point of one's own actions. Given the more central nature of the in-group for an interdependent-self, inclusion may be a more discerning process and the subjective boundary of an individual's in-group may on average be narrower for the interdependent selves than for those with independent selves (Triandis, 1989). However, although individuals with strongly interdependent self-views may be much more selective about in-group membership, they are also much more sensitive to social cues. Therefore, those with an interdependent self-view would be more sensitive to social cues for perceptions of social distances (such cues are expected to be more present in a MMORPG context). Also, MMORPG reflects more of an exchange-relationship as opposed to a communal-relationship (Trepte, Reinecke, & Juechems, 2012), so the exchange would lack the richly detailed information that collectivists might need to expand their in-group boundary. However, in the context of MMORPG, the relationships between the gamers need not exhibit interpersonal trust as would exchange defined as sharing or gifting.

Therefore, people with a high level of interdependent view can have a high level of trust in those participating in the MMORPG platform. These people can show enhanced participants' behavior during the MMORPG play. In other words, the competition defined as a motivator in the game engagement may not be achieved by the participant alone, so it is necessary to trust that those who participate in the MMORPG platform will be competent. Therefore, the higher the level of interdependent self-view, the more participants will engage in MMORPG because they think that other people will participate in MMORPG as they consider competition as important.

And, the challenge defined as a motivator in the MMORPG play will not be achievable if other participants are involved in fraud, so trust in those involved in the MMORPG platform will be needed. Therefore, the higher the level of interdependent self-view, the more participants will engage in MMORPG because they will participate in the MMORPG play so that others will do the honest plays.

Finally, the social interaction defined as a motivator in the MMORPG play will be achieved by the participants' play interactively, so it is necessary to trust that those who participate in the MMORPG platform will think the same way. Therefore, the higher the level of interdependent self-view, the more participants will engage in MMORPG because they think that other people will participate in MMORPG as they consider social capital as important. Therefore, this study hypothesizes that interdependent self-view is a major moderator for the relationship between three predictors and game engagement:

H4: Interdependent self-view positively influences the relationship between competition and game engagement.

H5: Interdependent self-view positively influences the relationship between challenge and engagement in game engagement.

H6: Interdependent self-view positively influences the relationship between social interaction and engagement in game engagement.

3. METHODOLOGY

3.1. Sample

The sample for this study consists of 228 college students with previous experience engaging in MMORPG. The sample consists of undergraduate and graduate students in programs related to business, social science and engineering in Korea. The criteria for participation in the study includes past engagement in MMORPG and a minimum age of 18 years. Though the sample is considered as one of convenience, college students represent a significant subset of major participant segment that is the focus of MMORPG marketers.

3.2. Data Collection and Instrumentation

The objective of the study was to identify the factors of psychological behaviors related to game engagement based on empirical analysis. These factors can be identified by measuring the participants' perceptions of MMORPG platforms. The survey research method is very useful in collecting data from a large number of individuals in a relatively short period of time and at a lower cost. Hence, for the current study, the questionnaire survey was used for data collection. All participants received a paper-and-pencil questionnaire with an accompanying letter that explained the purpose of the survey, emphasized voluntary participation, and guaranteed confidently. Participants were asked to fill out the questionnaire and put it back into an envelope that was collected by the researcher.

The questionnaire employed psychometric measurement (Nunnally, 1978). This study measured each construct with four or five items that were all on a 5-point Likert scale. Gamers' motivation scale was developed by Lucas and Sherry (2004). The scale measured three video game uses and gratifications: competition with reliability of 0.86 (e.g., "I got upset when I lose to my friend"); challenge with reliability of 0.79 (e.g., "I feel prude when I master an aspect a game"); social interaction with reliability of 0.81 (e.g., "I play with someone because I cannot play by myself"). Interdependent self-view was measured using twelve items from the Singelis Interdependent Self-view Construal Scale (Singelis, 1994). Game engagement employs nineteen items (Brockmyer et al., 2009)). For example, "I lose track of time."

4. ANALYSIS RESULT

4.1. Verification of Reliability and Validity

The validity of variables was verified through the principal components method and factor analysis with the varimax method. The criteria for determining the number of factors is defined as a 1.0 eigen value. I applied factors for analysis only if the factor loading was greater than 0.5 (factor loading represents the correlation scale between a factor and other variables). The reliability of variables was judged by internal consistency as assessed by Cronbach's alpha. I used surveys and regarded each as one measure only if their Cronbach's alpha values were 0.7 or higher.

4.2. Common Method Bias

As with all self-reported data, there is the potential for the occurrence of common method variance (CMV) (MacKenzie & Podsakoff, 2012; Podsakoff et al., 2003). To alleviate and assess the magnitude of common method bias, I adopted several procedural and statistical remedies that Podsakoff et al. (2003) suggest. First, during the survey, respondents were guaranteed of anonymity and confidentiality to reduce the evaluation apprehension. Further, we paid careful attention to the wording of the items, and developed our questionnaire carefully to reduce the item ambiguity. These procedures would make them less likely to edit their responses to be more socially desirable, acquiescent, and consistent with how they think the researcher wants them to respond when answering the questionnaire (Podsakoff et al., 2003; Tourangeau, Rips, & Rasinski, 2000). Second, I conducted a Harman's one-factor test on all of the items. A principle component factor analysis revealed that the first factor only explained 34.1 percent of the variance. Thus, no single factor emerged, nor did one factor account for most of variance. Furthermore, the measurement model was reassessed with the addition of a latent common method variance factor (Podsakoff et al., 2003). All indicator variables in the measurement model were loaded on this factor. Addition of the common variance factor did not improve the fit over the measurement model without that factor with all indicators still remaining significant. These results do suggest that common method variance is not of great concern in this study.

4.3. Relationship Between Variables

Table 1 summarizes the Pearson correlation test results between variables and reports the degree of multi-collinearity between independent variables. The minimum tolerance of 0.818 and the maximum variance inflation factor of 1.222 show that the statistical significance of the data analysis was not compromised by multi-collinearity.

Table 1. Variables' correlation coefficient

	1	2	3	4
Competition	1			
Challenge	.029	1		
Social interaction	.029	.088	1	
Interdependent self-view	.018	.104	.027	1
Game engagement	.042*	.021*	.041**	.036*

$*p < .05, **p < .01$

4.4. Hypothesis Testing

This study used hierarchical multiple regression analyses of SPSS 24.0 with three-steps to test the hypotheses. In the first step, demographic variables were controlled. Motivation factors were entered in the second step. In the final step the multiplicative interaction terms between motivation factors and interdependent self-view were entered to directly test the current hypothesis about the moderating effect.

Table 2 shows the results. First, only sex among the control variables has a positive relationship with game engagement. This means that men are more likely to be engaged in game than women. Second, to analyze the relationship between motivation factors and game engagement, the model 2 in Table 2 shows that the all of motivation factors have statistical significances with game engagement. Competition is positively related with game engagement ($\beta = .047$, $p < .01$). Challenge has a positive relationship with game engagement ($\beta = .032$, $p < .01$). Social interaction shows a positive association with game engagement ($\beta = .068$, $p < .01$). Therefore, hypotheses 1, 2, 3 are supported.

Table 2. Analysis 1

	Game Engagement		
	Model 1	**Model 2**	**Model 3**
Sex	.055*	.049*	.043*
Age	-.022	-.019	-.018
Competition		.047**	.039**
Challenge		.032**	.027**
Social interaction		.069**	.051**
Interdependent self-view			.015*
Competition * Interdependent self-view			.110
Challenge * Interdependent self-view			.031
Social interaction * Interdependent self-view			.025**
Adj. R^2	.105	.167	.181
F	4.681**	9.982**	13.881**

*$p < .05$, **$p < .01$

Figure 1. Interaction effect

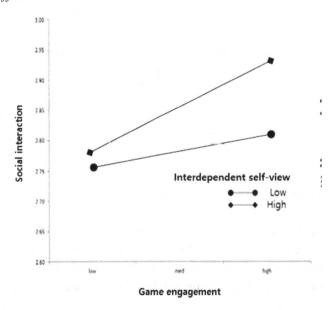

Lastly, the model 3, consisting of moderators, shows the interactions between motivation factors and interdependent self-view on game engagement. Interdependent self-view was found to have a positive effect on the relationship between social interaction and game engagement ($\beta = .025$, $p < .05$). Interdependent self-view was found to have no significance on the relationship between other motivators and game engagement. Based on these results, when participants in MMORPG have higher interdependent self-view, social interaction has a stronger impact on their engagement in game, which is expected in H6 (see Figure 1).

5. CONCLUSION

5.1. Discussion

The purpose of the present study was to examine the relationships between motivation factors and game engagement and explore the moderating effect of self-identity on that relationship. The results show that the more completion, challenge or social interaction participants pursue in game play, the more they are engaged in game. And in the results, positive relationship between social interaction and game engagement is stronger for participants in game platform high rather than low in interdependent self-view. However, interdependent self-view was found to have no significance on the relationship between other motivators and game engagement. This study suggests that people with a high level of interdependent view can have a high level of trust in those participating in the MMORPG play. Based on this suggestion, this study anticipates that these people can show enhanced participants' behavior during the game play. Therefore, the results show that the higher the level of interdependent self-view, the more participants are engaged in game play because they think that other people participate in MMORPG as they consider social capital as important. And, this study anticipates that the higher the level of interdependent self-view the participants in MMORPG have, the more they will be engaged in game play because they will participate in the game play so that others will be competent or do the honest play. However, the results that competition and challenge that participants expect in MMORPG platforms do not depend on participants' interdependent self-view. In other words, unlike social interaction, competition and challenge cannot be increased through the trust among the people participating in the MMORPG platform, but is pursued by the individual needs of the participants.

5.2. Research Contributions and Practical Implications

For research contribution, first, this study is the first one to examine the integral model of motivation factors of engagement in game platform. Despite a growing practical importance, there are few quantitative studies on motivational factors that affect participants' attitudes and intentions towards game. However, this study focused on the motivations of participants directly and especially, proposed a model that integrates motivation factors rather than identifying fragmentary factors. Although these motivation factors may not coexist or even show conflicts, this study showed that these motivators can coexist in the game play. This study shows that people who participate in game play pursue individual needs related to game than social purpose. Second, this study is the first one to investigate the moderating effect of self-identity in game play. Especially, this study shows that since the social interaction defined as a motivator in the MMORPG play is achieved by the participants' play interactively, it is necessary to trust that those who participate in the MMORPG platform think the same way. Therefore, the higher the level of interdependent self-view, the more participants will engage in MMORPG because they think that other people will participate in MMORPG as they consider social capital as important. Therefore, this study extends the scope of the game study by suggesting the study of the factors of the moderating effect on the relationship between motivation factors and game engagement.

For practical implications, first, the results of this study show that individual factors such as competition and challenge are important to enhance game participation, but also social factor such as social interaction is important. Therefore, game platform managers need to make the participants in game perceive that they can not only perceive competition and challenge but the social interaction. For example, it would be a good idea to allow various forms of communication (e.g., text, pictures, voice, video, etc.) between game participants. Second, the results of this study show that the self-identity of the participants enhances the impact of motivation factors such as social interaction on game participation, but does not affect other factors such as economic benefits on game participation. Therefore, game platform managers need to be aware of their propensity through play records of participants. For example, participants who show a lot of social interaction behaviors on the game platform will have an interdependent self-view that trusts other participants, so it will be necessary to recommend participants with the high level of social interaction to increase their game engagement.

5.3. Limitations and Future Research Directions

By this research results, the present study could have several insights into the motivation of participants in game. However, it should also acknowledge the following limitations in this research. First, the present study collected the responses from university students in South Korea. There may exist some nation cultural issues in the research context. Future studies should re-test this in other countries in order to assure this results' reliability. Second, as the variables were all measured at the same time, it cannot be sure that their relationships are constant. Although the survey questions occurred in reverse order of the analysis model to prevent additional issues, the existence of causal relationships between variables is a possibility. Therefore, future studies need to consider longitudinal studies. Finally, this study uses completion, challenge, and social interaction as motivation factors and explore self-identity as a moderator. However, considering the characteristics of game, future studies may find other motivators and other moderating factors. For example, as other motivation factors, diversion, fantasy, arousal may be considered. In addition, the social distance felt by the participants of the platform can be considered as a moderating factor.

REFERENCES

Belk, R. (1988). Possessions and the extended self. *The Journal of Consumer Research, 15*(2), 139–168. doi:10.1086/209154

Brockmyer, J. H., Fox, C. M., Curtiss, K. A., McBroom, E. B., Kimberly, M., & Pidruzny, J. N. (2009). The development of the Game Engagement Questionnaire: A measure of engagement in video game-playing. *Journal of Experimental Social Psychology, 45*(4), 624–634. doi:10.1016/j.jesp.2009.02.016

Brodie, R. J., Ilic, A., Juric, B., & Hollebeek, L. (2011). Consumer engagement in a virtual brand community: An exploratory analysis. *Journal of Business Research, 66*(1), 105–114. doi:10.1016/j.jbusres.2011.07.029

Buchanan-Oliver, M., & Seo, Y. (2012). Play as co-created narrative in computer game consumption: The hero's journey in Warcraft III. *Journal of Consumer Behaviour, 11*(6), 423–431. doi:10.1002/cb.392

Duclos, R., Wan, E. W., & Jiang, Y. (2013). Show me the honey! Effects of social exclusion on financial risk-taking. *The Journal of Consumer Research, 40*(1), 122–135. doi:10.1086/668900

Greenberg, B. S., Sherry, J., Lachlan, K., Lucas, K., & Holmstrom, A. (2010). Orientations to Video Games Among Gender and Age Groups. *Simulation & Gaming, 41*(2), 238–259. doi:10.1177/1046878108319930

Grüsser, S. M., Thalemann, R., & Griffiths, M. D. (2007). Excessive computer game playing: Evidence for addiction and aggression? *Cyberpsychology & Behavior, 10*(2), 290–292. doi:10.1089/cpb.2006.9956 PMID:17474848

Hoffman, D., & Novak, T. (2009). Flow online: Lessons learned and future prospects. *Journal of Interactive Marketing, 23*(1), 23–34. doi:10.1016/j.intmar.2008.10.003

Jang, W. & Byon, K. (2019). Antecedents and consequence associated with esports gameplay. *International Journal of Sports Marketing and Sponsorship*. doi:10.1108/IJSMS-01-2019-0013

Jenson, J., & De Castell, S. (2010). Gender, simulation, and gaming: Research review and redirections. *Simulation & Gaming, 41*(1), 51–71. doi:10.1177/1046878109353473

Lee, J., Ko, D., & Lee, H. (2019). Loneliness, regulatory focus, inter-personal competence, and online game addiction. *Internet Research, 29*(2), 381–394. doi:10.1108/IntR-01-2018-0020

Lindenberg, S. (2001). Intrinsic motivation in a new light. *Kyklos, 54*(2–3), 317–342. doi:10.1111/1467-6435.00156

Lucas, K., & Sherry, J. L. (2004). Sex differences in video game play: A communication-based explanation. *Communication Research, 31*(5), 499–523. doi:10.1177/0093650204267930

MacKenzie, S. B., & Podsakoff, P. M. (2012). Common method bias in marketing: Causes, mechanisms, and procedural remedies. *Journal of Retailing, 88*(4), 542–555. doi:10.1016/j.jretai.2012.08.001

Markus, H., & Kitayama, S. (1991). Culture and the self: Implications for cognition, emotion, and motivation. *Psychological Review, 98*(2), 224–253. doi:10.1037/0033-295X.98.2.224

Maslow, A. H. (1943). A theory of human motivation. *Psychological Review, 50*(4), 370–396. doi:10.1037/h0054346

Myers, D. (1990). A Q-study of game player aesthetics. *Simulation & Gaming, 21*(4), 375–396. doi:10.1177/104687819002100403

Naidoo, R., Coleman, K. & Guyo, C. (2019). Exploring gender discursive struggles about social inclusion in an online gaming community. *Information Technology & People*. doi:10.1108/ITP-04-2019-0163

Nunnally, J. (1978). *Psychometric methods*. New York: McGraw-Hill.

Podsakoff, P. M., MacKensie, S. B., Lee, J.-Y., & Podsakoff, N. P. (2003). Common method biases in behavioral research: A critical review of the literature and recommended remedies. *The Journal of Applied Psychology*, *88*(5), 879–903. doi:10.1037/0021-9010.88.5.879 PMID:14516251

Proffitt, R., Glegg, S., Levac, D., & Lange, B. (2019). End-user involvement in rehabilitation virtual reality implementation research. *Journal of Enabling Technologies*, *13*(2), 92–100. doi:10.1108/JET-10-2018-0050

Sardi, L., Idri, A., & Fernández-Alemán, J. L. (2017). A systematic review of gamification in e-Health. *Journal of Biomedical Informatics*, *71*, 31–48. doi:10.1016/j.jbi.2017.05.011 PMID:28536062

Sherry, J. L., Lucas, K., Greenberg, B. S., & Lachlan, K. (2006). Video game uses and gratifications as predictors of use and game preference. *Paper presented at the Playing video games: Motives, responses, and consequences*. Academic Press.

Spassova, G., & Lee, A. Y. (2013). Looking into the future: A match between self-view and temporal distance. *The Journal of Consumer Research*, *40*(1), 159–171. doi:10.1086/669145

Trepte, S., Reinecke, L., & Juechems, K. (2012). The social side of gaming: How playing online computer games creates online and offline social support. *Computers in Human Behavior*, *28*(3), 832–839. doi:10.1016/j.chb.2011.12.003

Triandis, H. (1989). The self and social behavior in differing cultural contexts. *Psychological Review*, *96*(3), 506–520. doi:10.1037/0033-295X.96.3.506

Wasko, M. M., & Faraj, S. (2005). Why should I share? Examining social capital and knowledge contribution in electronic networks of practice. *Management Information Systems Quarterly*, *29*(1), 35–57. doi:10.2307/25148667

World Health Organization (WHO). (2018). Gaming disorder. Retrieved from http://www.who.int/features/qa/gaming-disorder/en/

Yee, N. (2006). Motivations for play in online games. *Cyberpsychology & Behavior*, *9*(6), 772–775. doi:10.1089/cpb.2006.9.772 PMID:17201605

This research was previously published in the International Journal of e-Collaboration (IJeC), 16(2); pages 1-11, copyright year 2020 by IGI Publishing (an imprint of IGI Global).

Chapter 49
A Study of the Moderating Effect of Social Distance on the Relationship Between Motivators and Game Engagement

Youngkeun Choi

https://orcid.org/0000-0002-8842-9826

Sangmyung University, Seoul, Korea

ABSTRACT

The purpose of the present study was to examine the relationships between motivation factors and game engagement and explore the moderating effect of perceived social distance on those relationships. For this, the present study collected data from 228 college students in South Korean through a survey method and used hierarchical multiple regression analyses with three-steps to test the hypotheses. In the results, first, the more fantasy, diversion, or arousal participants pursue in gameplay, the more they are engaged in the game. Second, the positive relationship between arousal and game engagement is stronger for participants in high rather than low in social exclusion. However, social exclusion was found to have no significance in the relationship between other motivators and game engagement. For research contribution, this study is the first one to examine the integral model of motivation factors of engagement in the game platform and to investigate the moderating effect of perceived social distance in gameplay.

1. INTRODUCTION

The video game (hereafter, games) industry is booming, surpassing the movie industry in terms of both annual sales and global revenues in the entertainment category (Prena, & Sherry, 2018). Games are among the fastest and most exciting type of mass media. While academic research on game content and users has increased significantly over the past quarter-century, there are many research gaps (Seo et al.,

DOI: 10.4018/978-1-6684-7589-8.ch049

2019). Far more research has focused on other entertainment categories, such as consumers' attitudes toward and patronage of cinema, music concerts, and television (Marchand & Hennig-Thurau, 2013). Thus, marketing academician contributions lags far behind the actual video game industry practices.

Most of these researches of video games focus on the relationship between games and increasing aggression, social isolation, and overuse (Gru¨sser, Thalemann, & Griffiths, 2007). Recently, however, many researchers have focused on game adjustment or pain relief for education or health interventions by exploiting the new appeal of video games (Sardia, Idria, & Fernández-Alemán, 2017). Gradually, mediation-centered researchers have shown that games can have a positive impact on psychological and physical well-being (Bessiere, Seay, & Kiesler, 2007). Essential research and intensive interventional studies share a different but exploratory approach. The methods and theories used will evaluate the degree to which video games do not have positive, adverse, or emotional effects on a given outcome in a given situation (Katsarov et al., 2019). These well-known and less widely researched mechanisms of these positive and negative connections.

In particular, the massively multiplayer online role-playing game (MMORPG) is a virtual heir to the desktop game that rises in the 20th century with Dungeon and Dragons (Harviainen, & Rapp, 2018). Modern MMORPGs are adventures through fantasy worlds and combine advanced graphics, endless achievements, and collaborative and competitive gameplay options (Lee et al., 2018). This game allows players to create a virtual identity and make it high in the online fantasy world (Jin et al., 2017). Outside a realistic social structure, you can play a new role in your choice. MMORPGs also allow players to communicate with other players in a virtual environment through an online identity that enables them to share quests, talk to themselves or characters, and build online relationships and social capital (Trepte, Reinecke, & Juechems, 2012). As this game becomes popular and expanding in functionality, more gamers are testing their skills in MMORPGs (Harviainen, & Rapp, 2018).

Despite the increasing importance of practicality, there is a lack of quantitative research on the motivators that influence the participation of MMORPGs participants. This article explores people's motivations to participate in MMORPGs. For this, the paper is structured as follows. The next section presents the theoretical framework and background for the hypotheses. This study adopts the lens of psychological motivation in engagement in MMORPGs (Lindenberg, 2001). Also, theories on the development of the social exclusion as well as the relationship between the self and objects of consumption suggest that the sharing of an object will be associated with closer perceived social distances (Belk, 1988). Belk's (1988) work on the extended-self established the idea that people expand their concept of who they are to include their possessions and objects they consume. This study applies ideas on the extended self to MMORPGs. Also, the subsequent section then outlines data and methods, followed by the results. The article concludes with a discussion on implications and directions for future research.

2. THEORETICAL BACKGROUND AND HYPOTHESIS DEVELOPMENT

2.1 Game Engagement

The term "engagement" has been investigated in a variety of fields such as sociology, political science, psychology, and organizational behavior. Marketing discipline has reduced research on the terms "consumer engagement" and "customer engagement" before 2005 (Bordie et al., 2011). Customer engagement is defined as "the psychological state that occurs through co-creative customer experience, interacting with a focus/audience (e.g., video game) in a focus service relationship" (Bordie et al., 2011; Moliner et al., 2019). Adults and children play games in their spare time, but use different types of technology to get the best entertainment experience. Many scholars emphasize the importance of participation in virtual environments (Wasko & Faraj, 2005; Walker & Venker, 2019).

The game engagement has been proposed as a topic appropriate for future research (Brockmyer et al., 2009; Shu & Liu, 2019). This study is answering that call by examining gamer's engagement in a different genre and how that impact games purchase intention. The ultimate goal of marketers and game developers is to engage players in the game. For example, Warcraft III designs the game in a way to encourage gamers to co-create meaningful story (Buchanan-Oliver & Seo, 2012). However, game developers did not thoroughly look at the difference between gamer psychological factors and motivation. Also, Yee (2006) argues that women prefer social, relationship, and teamwork games, while men prefer promotion, machines, and competitive games. The author continues supporting that even male players socialized as much as female players, but they socialized very differently. Thus, understanding these differences will increase gamer engagement in the game.

2.2 Hypothesis Development

In history, humans tried to fly and swim deep in the ocean. There is a small group of people who attempted to do things that not everybody can do, such as the Wright brothers, who built a successful airplane. People also want to be zombies and be things that they cannot be in real life. Movies and early generations of video game allow people to imagine things that they are not such as flying, being a ghost, and being animals. However, games today enable gamers to be somebody else and somewhere else. For example, players can create their ideal physical avatar in a game and pretend to be that avatar. Also, people in simulation games (i.e., AeroWings, Pilotwings Resort) can fly airplane even though they are not pilots (Prena, & Sherry, 2018). Games give gamers some fantasy of being something else such as being a professional NFL player, a pilot, and even opposite sex (Greenberg et al., 2010; Sherry et al., 2006). Gamers' level of fantasy would predict their level of engagement.

H1: Gamers' fantasy motivation has a positive relationship with game engagement

Escapism (i.e., diversion) refers to avoiding real-life problems by engaging in playing games and other types of activities (Li, Liau, & Khoo, 2011; Riedel, & Mulcahy, 2019). People differ in their escapism level. Some people prefer to take extended breaks to escape their lives while others prefer to take short breaks to escape. Moreover, there is a significant difference between male and female gamers regarding their game escapism (Yee, 2006). Thus, gamers' escape level predicts their level of engagement (Frostling-Henningsson, 2009). Moreover, entertainment is viewed as an opportunity to escape from the boredom of everyday life to a fantasy world of exciting and attractive characters. Selnow (1984) argues that people play games to escape life. The author found that escapism is significantly correlated with game engagement. Thus, gamers' motivation to escape would predict gamers' level of engagement.

H2: Gamers' diversion motivation has a positive relationship with game engagement

Gamers play games for arousal and companionship (Bae et al., 2019). The level of excitement that players are trying to reach is the gamer's arousal level. Also, games stimulate emotions as a result of high graphics and high overall of the game. Arousal was one of people's motivation to play games on arcade games (Griffiths, 1991). The level of arousal can be a high motivation to play games. Many games are fun to play in. For example, one player would say, "I got crazy when I am playing a video game, sometimes. I am jumping up and down." (Sherry et al., 2006). Gamers' excitement would impact their level of engagement. For example, if they have a high level of excitement, they might reach psychological absorption. On the other hand, if the gamer is not so excited about the game, he might not be interested in the game. Thus, the level of gamers' excitement would predict the gamers' engagement.

H3: Gamers' arousal motivation has a positive relationship with game engagement

It has been proposed that a need to belong, which means a need to form and maintain at least a minimum quantity of interpersonal relationships, is innately prepared among human beings (Baumeister & Learly, 1995). This kind of characteristic can vary among individuals, and much work has been done to develop an excellent way to measure interpersonal differences (Lakin, Chartrand, & Arkin, 2008). Such interpersonal differences with regards to the need to establish human connections may be trait-based, as with interdependent self-view above, or it may be a result of one's immediate environment. One environmentally-based construct that deals with a person's sensitivity to social connections is social exclusion (Lakin et al., 2008; Scorgie & Forlin, 2019). Social exclusion is not so much an individual trait as it is a situational response that comes from some form of rejection or prohibition to joining a social group of some kind (Lakin et al. 2008). When people experience social exclusion, they may seek to reduce social distances by way of mimicry (Lakin et al. 2008) and behavioral synchrony (Miles, Lumsden, Richardson, & Macrae, 2011). Research has shown that exclusion increases people's desire to enter into new social interactions and that people who are socially excluded are more interested in working and playing with others (Maner, DeWall, Baumeister, & Schaller 2007). Social exclusion also increases the tendency for the excluded to see new social connections in a positive and optimistic way (Mead, Baumeister, Stillman, Rawn, & Vohs, 2011). Individuals also show higher levels of mimicry after experiencing social rejection (Mead, Baumeister, Stillman, Rawn, & Vohs, 2011).

Therefore, people have an increased desire for social closeness after experiencing some social exclusion (Lakin, Chartrand, & Arkin 2008). These people can show enhanced participants' behavior during MMORPGs play. First, games give gamers some fantasy of being something else such as being a professional NFL player, a pilot, and even opposite sex (Greenberg et al., 2010; Sherry et al., 2006). Social networking services and similar service design used elsewhere can be seen to especially promote relatedness (Hamari & Koivisto, 2015), which is a significant determinant for motivated use such as a fantasy. Thus, fantasy defined as a motivator in MMORPGs play may not be achieved by the participant alone, so it is necessary to have sharing-related activities with those who participate in the MMORPGs play. Therefore, because people who feel more loneliness from more social exclusion, the more satisfaction they will get from the fantasy based on sharing-related activities in MMORPGs play than any others, which will make them more engaged in game.

Second gamers' diversion motivation level predicts their level of engagement (Frostling-Henningsson, 2009). Diversion from escape activities can be an incentive for active participation and the most reliable indicator of the possibility of working together online (Hars & Ou, 2001). Therefore, because people who feel more loneliness from social exclusion, the more satisfaction they will get from the diversion by working together in MMORPG play than any others, which will make them more engaged in game.

Finally, arousal was one of people's motivation to play games (Griffiths, 1991). Arousal defined as a motivator in MMORPGs play may be achieved by the play of many participants, so it is necessary to have collaborative activities with those who participate in the MMORPGs play. Therefore, because people who feel more loneliness from social exclusion, the more satisfaction they will get from the arousal based on collaborative activities in MMORPG play than any others, which will make them more engaged in game. Therefore, this study hypothesizes that social exclusion is a significant moderator for the relationship between three predictors and engagement in game

H4: Social exclusion positively moderates the relationship between fantasy and engagement in game.
H5: Social exclusion positively moderates the relationship between diversion and engagement in game.
H6: Social exclusion positively moderates the relationship between arousal and engagement in game.

3. METHODOLOGY

3.1 Sample

The survey research method is very useful in collecting data from a large number of individuals in a relatively short period of time and at better cost. Hence, for the current study, the questionnaire survey was chosen for data collection. This study is based on responses from Korean users plying MMORPG. Out of 256 responses collected, 228 (89.1 percent) responses were usable for analysis. The sample for this study consists of 228 college students with previous experience engaging in MMORPGs. The sample consists of undergraduate and graduate students in programs related to business, social science, and engineering in Korea. The criteria for participation in the study include past engagement in MMORPGs and a minimum age of 18 years. Though the sample is considered as one of convenience, college students represent a significant subset of major participant segment that is the focus of MMORPGs marketers.

3.2 Data Collection and Instrumentation

The objective of the study was to identify the factors of psychological behaviors related to game engagement based on empirical analysis. These factors can be identified by measuring the participants' perceptions of MMORPG platforms. The survey research method is very useful in collecting data from a large number of individuals in a relatively short period and at a lower cost. Hence, for the current study, the questionnaire survey was used for data collection. All participants received a paper-and-pencil questionnaire with an accompanying letter that explained the purpose of the study, emphasized voluntary participation, and guaranteed confidently. Participants were asked to fill out the survey and put it back into an envelope that was collected by the researcher.

The questionnaire employed psychometric measurement (Nunnally, 1978). This study measured each construct with five items that were all on a 5-point Likert scale. Gamers' motivation scale was developed by Lucas and Sherry (2004). The scale measured three video game uses and gratifications. Fantasy has four questionnaires with reliability of 0.88 (e.g., "I enjoy the excitement of assuming an alter ego in a game"). Diversion has four questionnaires with reliability of 0.89 (e.g., "I play video game instead of other things I should be doing") and Arousal has four questionnaires with reliability of 0.85 (e.g., "I play video game because they stimulate my emotions"). Social exclusion was measured using three questionnaires from the scale developed by Mead et al. (2011). For example, "I felt excluded." Game engagement employs nineteen items (Brockmyer et al., 2009). For example, "I lose track of time."

4. ANALYSIS RESULT

4.1 Verification of Reliability and Validity

The validity of variables was verified through the principal components method and factor analysis with the varimax method. The criteria for determining the number of factors is defined as a 1.0 eigenvalue. This study applied factors for analysis only if the factor loading was more significant than 0.5 (factor loading represents the correlation scale between a factor and other variables). The reliability of variables was judged by internal consistency as assessed by Cronbach's alpha. This study used surveys and regarded each as one measure only if their Cronbach's alpha values were 0.7 or higher.

4.2 Common Method Bias

As with all self-reported data, there is the potential for the occurrence of common method variance (CMV) (MacKenzie & Podsakoff, 2012; Podsakoff et al., 2003). To alleviate and assess the magnitude of common method bias, this study adopted several procedural and statistical remedies that Podsakoff et al. (2003) suggest. First, during the survey, respondents were guaranteed anonymity and confidentiality to reduce the evaluation apprehension. Further, we paid careful attention to the wording of the items and developed our questionnaire carefully to lessen the item ambiguity. These procedures would make them less likely to edit their responses to be more socially desirable, acquiescent, and consistent with how they think the researcher wants them to respond when answering the questionnaire (Podsakoff et al., 2003; Tourangeau, Rips, & Rasinski, 2000). Second, this study conducted a Harman's one-factor test on all of the items. A principal components factor analysis revealed that the first factor only explained 34.1 percent of the variance. Thus, no single factor emerged, nor did one factor account for most of the variance and the measurement model was reassessed with the addition of a latent common method variance factor (Podsakoff et al., 2003). All indicator variables in the measurement model were loaded on this factor. Addition of the common variance factor did not improve the fit over the measurement model without that factor with all indicators remaining significant. These results do suggest that common method variance is not of great concern in this study.

4.3 Relationship Between Variables

Table 1 summarizes the Pearson correlation test results between variables and reports the degree of multi-collinearity between independent variables. The minimum tolerance of 0.823 and the maximum variance inflation factor of 1.215 show that the statistical significance of the data analysis was not compromised by multi-collinearity.

Table 1. Variables' correlation coefficient

	1	**2**	**3**	**4**
Fantasy	1			
Diversion	.018	1		
Arousal	.025	.029	1	
Social exclusion	.011	.015	.051	1
Game engagement	.013*	.032*	.061**	.052*

*$p < .05$, **$p < .01$

4.4 Hypothesis Testing

This study used hierarchical multiple regression analyses of SPSS 24.0 with three-steps to test the hypotheses. In the first step, demographic variables were controlled. Motivation factors were entered in the second step. In the final step, the multiplicative interaction terms between motivation factors and interdependent self-view were entered to test the current hypothesis about the moderating effect directly. Table 2 shows the results. First, only sex among the control variables has a positive relationship with game engagement. It means that men are more likely to be engaged in a game than women. Second, to analyze the relationship between motivation factors and game engagement, model 2 in Table 2 shows that all of the motivation factors have statistical significances with game engagement. Fantasy is positively related with game engagement ($\beta = .071$, $p < .01$). Diversion has a positive relationship with game engagement ($\beta = .042$, $p < .01$). Arousal shows a positive association with game engagement ($\beta = .039$, $p < .01$). Therefore, hypotheses 1, 2, 3 are supported.

Table 2. Analysis 1

	Game engagement		
	Model 1	**Model 2**	**Model 3**
Sex	.044*	.039*	.033*
Age	-.012	-.009	-.006
Fantasy		.071**	.059**
Diversion		.042**	.037**
Arousal		.039**	.019**
Social exclusion			.024*
Fantasy * Social exclusion			.101
Diversion * Social exclusion			.013
Arousal * Social exclusion			.028*
Adj. R^2	.104	.161	.179
F	4.677**	9.971**	13.873**

*$p < .05$, **$p < .01$

Lastly, model 3, consisting of moderators, shows the interactions between motivation factors and interdependent self-view on game engagement. Social exclusion was found to have a positive effect on the relationship between arousal and game engagement ($\beta = .028$, $p < .05$). Social exclusion was found to have no significance in the relationship between other motivators and game engagement. Based on these results, when participants in MMORPGs have higher social exclusion, arousal has a stronger impact on their engagement in game, which is expected in H6 (see Figure 1).

Figure 1. Interaction effect

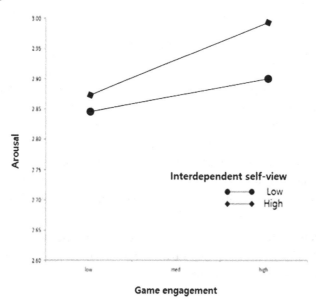

5. CONCLUSION

5.1 Discussion

The purpose of this study was to investigate the relationship between motivation and game participation and explore the effect of self-identity interventions in that relationship. Results show that the more fantasy, mood change, or excited participants pursue gameplay, the more they participate in the game. Also, in the results, a positive relationship between arousal and game engagement is stronger for participants in the MMORPGs platform high rather than low in social exclusion. However, social exclusion proved to be meaningless in the relationship between different motives and participation in the game. The study suggests that people who feel lonely due to social exclusion will participate more in games because they will gain more satisfaction from the excitement based on the collaborative activities of MMORPGs play than others. Based on this proposal, the study expects these people to show improved player behavior during gameplay. Thus, the results show that the higher the level of social exclusion participants experience, the more satisfaction they get from their excitement than anything else, the more they participate in gameplay. The study also predicts that MMORPGs participants will participate in gameplay more because the higher the level of social exclusion they are aware of, the more satisfied they will be compared to fantasy or diversion. However, the fantasies and mood swings that participants expect from the MMORPGs platform do not rely on participants' social exclusion. In other words, unlike excitement, fantasy, and mood swings cannot be increased through the loneliness of participants on the MMORPGs platform, but are pursued by the individual needs of the participants.

5.2 Research Contributions and Practical Implications

For research contribution, first, this study is the first one to examine the integral model of motivation factors of engagement in the game platform. Despite growing practical importance, there are few quantitative studies on motivational factors that affect participants' attitudes and intentions towards the game. However, this study focused on the motivations of participants directly and especially, proposed a model that integrates motivation factors rather than identifying fragmentary factors. Although these motivation factors may not coexist or even show conflicts, this study showed that these motivators could coexist in the gameplay. This study shows that people who participate in gameplay pursue individual needs related to the game than social purpose. Second, this study is the first one to investigate the moderating effect of perceived social distance in gameplay. Mainly, this study shows that because people who feel more loneliness from social exclusion, the more satisfaction they will get from the arousal based on collaborative activities in MMORPGs play than any others, which will make them more engaged in game. Therefore, this study extends the scope of the game study by suggesting the study of the factors of the moderating effect on the relationship between motivation factors and game engagement.

For practical implications, first, the results of this study show that functional factors such as fantasy and diversion are essential to enhance game participation, but also emotional factor such as social interaction is essential. Therefore, game platform managers need to make the participants in game perceive that they can not only see fantasy and diversion but the arousal. For example, it would be a good idea to provide various forms of enjoyment (e.g., sound, light, storytelling, background music, etc.). Second, the results of this study show that the perceived social exclusion of the participants enhances the impact of motivation factors such as arousal on game participation, but does not affect other factors on game participation. Therefore, game platform managers need to be aware of their propensity through play records of participants. For example, when some players who show a lot of social exclusion behaviors, it is necessary to recommend them with the dramatic game situation.

5.3 Limitations and Future Research Directions

By this research results, the present study could have several insights into the motivation of participants in game. However, it should also acknowledge the following limitations of this research. First, the present study collected the responses from university students in South Korea. There may exist some nation cultural issues in the research context. Future studies should re-test this in other countries to assure these results' reliability. And, to examine how different Western and Eastern tastes in MMORPGs can be, future study needs to compare the research findings with research conducted on Western MMORPG players may be valuable. Second, as the variables were all measured at the same time, it cannot be sure that their relationships are constant. Although the survey questions occurred in reverse order of the analysis model to prevent additional issues, the existence of causal relationships between variables is a possibility. Therefore, future studies need to consider longitudinal studies. Finally, this study used fantasy, diversion, and arousal as motivation factors and explored self-identity as a moderator. However, considering the characteristics of the game, future studies may find other motivators and other moderating factors. For example, as other motivation factors, completion, challenge, or social interaction may be considered. Also, the social identity perceived by the participants of the platform can be considered as a moderating factor.

REFERENCES

Bae, J., Kim, S., Kim, K., & Koo, D. (2019). Affective value of game items: A mood management and selective exposure approach. *Internet Research*, *29*(2), 315–328. doi:10.1108/INTR-12-2017-0477

Baumeister, R., & Leary, M. (1995). The need to belong: Desire for interpersonal attachments as a fundamental human motivation. *Psychological Bulletin*, *117*(3), 497–529. doi:10.1037/0033-2909.117.3.497 PMID:7777651

Belk, R. (1988). Possessions and the extended self. *The Journal of Consumer Research*, *15*(2), 139–168. doi:10.1086/209154

Bessiere, K., Seay, A. F., & Kiesler, S. (2007). The ideal elf: Identity exploration in world of warcraft. *Cyberpsychology & Behavior*, *10*(4), 530–535. doi:10.1089/cpb.2007.9994 PMID:17711361

Brockmyer, J. H., Fox, C. M., Curtiss, K. A., McBroom, E. B., Kimberly, M., & Pidruzny, J. N. (2009). The development of the Game Engagement Questionnaire: A measure of engagement in video game-playing. *Journal of Experimental Social Psychology*, *45*(4), 624–634. doi:10.1016/j.jesp.2009.02.016

Buchanan Oliver, M., & Seo, Y. (2012). Play as co-created narrative in computer game consumption: The hero's journey in Warcraft III. *Journal of Consumer Behaviour*, *11*(6), 423–431. doi:10.1002/cb.392

Frostling-Henningsson, M. (2009). First-person shooter games as a way of connecting to people:"Brothers in blood. *Cyberpsychology & Behavior*, *12*(5), 557–562. doi:10.1089/cpb.2008.0345 PMID:19817566

Greenberg, B. S., Sherry, J., Lachlan, K., Lucas, K., & Holmstrom, A. (2010). Orientations to Video Games Among Gender and Age Groups. *Simulation & Gaming*, *41*(2), 238–259. doi:10.1177/1046878108319930

Griffiths, M. (1991). The observational study of adolescent gambling in UK amusement arcades. *Journal of Community & Applied Social Psychology*, *1*(4), 309–320. doi:10.1002/casp.2450010406

Gru¨sser, S. M., Thalemann, R., & Griffiths, M. D. (2007). Excessive computer game playing: Evidence for addiction and aggression? *Cyberpsychology & Behavior*, *10*(2), 290–292. doi:10.1089/cpb.2006.9956 PMID:17474848

Hars, A., & Ou, S. (2001). Working for Free? - Motivations of Participating in Open Source Projects. *Proceedings of the 34th Hawaii International Conference on System Sciences*. IEEE. 10.1109/HICSS.2001.927045

Harviainen, J., & Rapp, A. (2018). Multiplayer online role-playing as information retrieval and system use: An ethnographic study. *The Journal of Documentation*, *74*(3), 624–640.

Hoffman, D., & Novak, T. (2009). Flow online: Lessons learned and future prospects. *Journal of Interactive Marketing*, *23*(1), 23–34. doi:10.1016/j.intmar.2008.10.003

Jin, W., Sun, Y., Wang, N., & Zhang, X. (2017). Why users purchase virtual products in MMORPG? An integrative perspective of social presence and user engagement. *Internet Research*, *27*(2), 408–427. doi:10.1108/IntR-04-2016-0091

Katsarov, J., Christen, M., Mauerhofer, R., Schmocker, D., & Tanner, C. (2019). Training Moral Sensitivity Through Video Games: A Review of Suitable Game Mechanisms. *Games and Culture*, *14*(4), 344–366. doi:10.1177/1555412017719344

Lakin, J., Chartrand, T., & Arkin, R. (2008). I am too just like you nonconscious mimicry as an automatic behavioral response to social exclusion. *Psychological Science*, *19*(8), 816–822. doi:10.1111/j.1467-9280.2008.02162.x PMID:18816290

Lee, Y., Hsieh, Y., Hsiao, C., & Lin, C. (2018). From virtual worlds to reality. *Information Technology & People*, *31*(2), 557–577. doi:10.1108/ITP-05-2017-0156

Li, D., Liau, A., & Khoo, A. (2011). Examining the influence of actual-ideal self-discrepancies, depression, and escapism, on pathological gaming among massively multiplayer online adolescent gamers. *Cyberpsychology, Behavior, and Social Networking*, *14*(9), 535–539. doi:10.1089/cyber.2010.0463 PMID:21332374

Lindenberg, S. (2001). Intrinsic motivation in a new light. *Kyklos*, *54*(2–3), 317–342. doi:10.1111/1467-6435.00156

Lucas, K., & Sherry, J. L. (2004). Sex differences in video game play: A communication-based explanation. *Communication Research*, *31*(5), 499–523. doi:10.1177/0093650204267930

MacKenzie, S. B., & Podsakoff, P. M. (2012). Common method bias in marketing: Causes, mechanisms, and procedural remedies. *Journal of Retailing*, *88*(4), 542–555. doi:10.1016/j.jretai.2012.08.001

Maner, J. K., DeWall, C. N., Baumeister, R. F., & Schaller, M. (2007). Does social exclusion motivate interpersonal reconnection? Resolving the "porcupine problem." *Journal of Personality and Social Psychology*, *92*(1), 42–55. doi:10.1037/0022-3514.92.1.42 PMID:17201541

Marchand, A., & Hennig-Thurau, T. (2013). Value Creation in the Video Game Industry: Industry Economics, Consumer Benefits, and Research Opportunities. *Journal of Interactive Marketing*, *27*(3), 141–157. doi:10.1016/j.intmar.2013.05.001

Mead, N. L., Baumeister, R. F., Stillman, T. F., Rawn, C. D., & Vohs, K. D. (2011). Social exclusion causes people to spend and consume strategically in the service of affiliation. *The Journal of Consumer Research*, *37*(5), 902–919. doi:10.1086/656667

Miles, L., Lumsden, J., Richardson, M., & Macrae, C. (2011). Do birds of a feather move together? Group membership and behavioral synchrony. *Experimental Brain Research*, *211*(3-4), 495–503. doi:10.100700221-011-2641-z PMID:21448575

Moliner-Tena, M., Monferrer-Tirado, D., & Estrada-Guillén, M. (2019). Customer engagement, non-transactional behaviors and experience in services. *International Journal of Bank Marketing*, *37*(3), 730–754. doi:10.1108/IJBM-04-2018-0107

Nunnally, J. (1978). *Psychometric methods*. New York: McGraw-Hill.

Podsakoff, P. M., MacKensie, S. B., Lee, J.-Y., & Podsakoff, N. P. (2003). Common method biases in behavioral research: A critical review of the literature and recommended remedies. *The Journal of Applied Psychology*, *88*(5), 879–903. doi:10.1037/0021-9010.88.5.879 PMID:14516251

Prena, K., & Sherry, J. (2018). Parental perspectives on video game genre preferences and motivations of children with Down syndrome. *Journal of Enabling Technologies*, *12*(1), 1–9. doi:10.1108/JET-08-2017-0034

Riedel, A., & Mulcahy, R. (2019). Does more sense make sense? An empirical test of high and low interactive retail technology. *Journal of Services Marketing*, *33*(3), 331–343. doi:10.1108/JSM-12-2017-0435

Sardi, L., Idri, A., & Fernández-Alemán, J. L. (2017). A systematic review of gamification in e-Health. *Journal of Biomedical Informatics*, *71*, 31–48. doi:10.1016/j.jbi.2017.05.011 PMID:28536062

Scorgie, K., & Forlin, C. (2019). Social Inclusion and Belonging: Affirming Validation, Agency and Voice. In Promoting Social Inclusion: Co-Creating Environments that Foster Equity and Belonging (pp. 3-15). Emerald Publishing Limited.

Selnow, G. W. (1984). Playing videogames: The electronic friend. *Journal of Communication*, *34*(2), 148–156. doi:10.1111/j.1460-2466.1984.tb02166.x

Seo, Y., Dolan, R., & Buchanan-Oliver, M. (2019). Playing games: Advancing research on online and mobile gaming consumption. *Internet Research*, *29*(2), 289–292. doi:10.1108/INTR-04-2019-542

Sherry, J. L., Lucas, K., Greenberg, B. S., & Lachlan, K. (2006). Video game uses and gratifications as predictors of use and game preference. *Paper presented at the Playing video games: Motives, responses, and consequences*. Academic Press.

Shu, L., & Liu, M. (2019). Student engagement in game-based learning: A literature review from 2008 to 2018. *Journal of Educational Multimedia and Hypermedia*, *28*(2), 193–215.

Trepte, S., Reinecke, L., & Juechems, K. (2012). The social side of gaming: How playing online computer games creates online and offline social support. *Computers in Human Behavior*, *28*(3), 832–839. doi:10.1016/j.chb.2011.12.003

Walker, G., & Venker, W. J. (2019). Social and Emotional Learning in the age of virtual play: Technology, empathy, and learning. *Journal of Research in Innovative Teaching & Learning*, *12*(2), 116–132. doi:10.1108/JRIT-03-2019-0046

Wasko, M. M., & Faraj, S. (2005). Why should I share? Examining social capital and knowledge contribution in electronic networks of practice. *Management Information Systems Quarterly*, *29*(1), 35–57. doi:10.2307/25148667

Yee, N. (2006). Motivations for play in online games. *Cyberpsychology & Behavior*, *9*(6), 772–775. doi:10.1089/cpb.2006.9.772 PMID:17201605

This research was previously published in the International Journal of Gaming and Computer-Mediated Simulations (IJGCMS), 11(3); pages 1-14, copyright year 2019 by IGI Publishing (an imprint of IGI Global).

Chapter 50
Developing a Clearer Understanding of Genre and Mobile Gameplay

Boaventura DaCosta

ⓘ https://orcid.org/0000-0003-0692-2172

Solers Research Group, USA

Soonhwa Seok

Korea University, South Korea

ABSTRACT

This chapter presents a study that explored the mobile game-genre preferences of 1,950 South Korean students. The findings help create a clearer picture of the mobile gameplayer, revealing that mobile gameplay is more of a situational activity than a social replacement, often played during periods of interruption or idle time and lasting for short intervals. Action, arcade, sports, adventure, puzzle, board, simulation, and strategy were among the most popular genres played. Statistically significant relationships were found between genre and age and gender, with the younger and older students as well as males and females favoring different genres. For example, puzzle games were popular among the older females, whereas action games were preferred by the younger males. Significant relationships were also found between genre and academic grades and level, with differences found for genre preferences between high- and low-performing as well as vocational high school and college students.

INTRODUCTION

Generally speaking, the educational value of video games has been met with debate, with inconsistent findings across studies (Egenfeldt-Nielsen, 2006). An underlying factor has been the studies themselves (Perrotta, Featherstone, Aston, & Houghton, 2013). That is, investigations have (a) varied in their aims, from studying the impact of video games on learning outcomes to types of learning and kinds of games; (b) focused on various domains, such as civics and society, computer science, language, and math (Per-

DOI: 10.4018/978-1-6684-7589-8.ch050

rotta et al., 2013); (c) used different theories and frameworks, involving behaviorism, cognitivism, and/ or constructivism (Egenfeldt-Nielsen, 2006); and (d) suffered from methodological flaws and limitations (Perrotta et al., 2013), to include bias, weak assessments, short exposure times, and lack of control groups (Egenfeldt-Nielsen, 2006). Altogether, these factors have contributed to difficulty in offering thorough, reliable, and tangible evidence for the educational potential of video games (Perrotta et al., 2013).

Nevertheless, interest in the educational value of video games continues to grow (Cogoi, Sangiorgi, & Shahin, 2006). This is in part because these games are seen as more flexible than other media, naturally lending themselves to adaptive learning (del Blanco, Marchiori, Torrente, Martínez-Ortiz, & Fernández-Manjón, 2013), and contributing to active learning in the areas of critical thinking, knowledge construction, collaboration, and information and communication technology use (Ellis, Heppell, Kirriemuir, Krotoski, & McFarlane, 2006). Furthermore, because video games offer instant feedback, it has been proposed that ambient information can foster an immersive state, stimulating game interest (Mitchell & Savill-Smith, 2004) and boosting exploration and experimentation (Kirriemuir, 2002), in turn, supporting authentic learning by letting students practice in a realistic, safe, and risk-free environment (del Blanco et al., 2013). This could help teach decision-making through increasingly difficult challenges adjusted to a student's aptitude (Gentile & Gentile, 2008). Consequently, video games could be used to offer activities that are paced to students' knowledge and skills, providing differentiated instruction (Paraskeva, Mysirlaki, & Papagianni, 2010).

Mobile Games

Mobile-based video games (hereafter "mobile games") are particularly interesting because of their anytime-, anywhere-, and on-any-device characteristics. A considerable body of research has focused on the technical capabilities of emerging mobile devices (e.g., Bell et al., 2006; Cheok, Sreekumar, Lei, & Thang, 2006; Göth, Häss, & Schwabe, 2004; Grant et al., 2007; Licoppe & Inada, 2006; Matyas et al., 2008; Naismith, Lonsdale, Vavoula, & Sharples, 2004; Schmitz, 2014; Owen et al., 2008; Sedano, Laine, Vinni, & Sutinen, 2007). For example, global positioning system (GPS) capabilities have been used to augment reality, obscuring the boundaries between the virtual and the real world by embedding learning in authentic environments, creating a blended experience (de Freitas & Griffiths, 2008; Huizenga, Admiraal, Akkerman, & ten Dam, 2009; Montola, 2011). This allows students to interact with virtual objects in the real world, taking learning out of the traditional classroom setting (Grant et al., 2007; Huizenga et al., 2009; Roschelle & Pea, 2002). (See DaCosta, Seok, & Kinsell, 2015, 2018, for a discussion of mobile games in the context of integrating learning with aspects of the physical world.)

Given the general attraction of mobile devices, there is also research to suggest that these games appeal to a much broader audience, and are played by people of all ages (Grimes, Kantroo, & Grinter, 2010). Additionally, although video games have traditionally been viewed as a male-dominated activity, females are now thought to play mobile games as much as males (Information Solutions Group, 2011, 2013). This trend may be the result of the increased popularity of social media (Information Solutions Group, 2011) or SOCIAL games (e.g., Information Solutions Group, 2011; Kirriemuir & McFarlane, 2004), because those who play these games are said to use their devices for group purposes (e.g., Information Solutions Group, 2011). Another explanation stems from the belief that mobile games are commonly viewed as an unplanned action, played to kill brief periods of time (Bouça, 2012; Kallio, Mäyrä, & Kaipainen, 2011; Moore & Rutter, 2004) – while waiting (Information Solutions Group, 2013; Kallio et al., 2011) to relax (Kallio et al., 2011), or out of boredom (Kirriemuir & McFarlane, 2004; Moore &

Rutter, 2004). That is, these games are seen as a casual activity, and, as a result, are often associated with certain genres, to include BOARD, CARD, DICE (Gackenbach & Bown, 2011), CONNECT THE DOTS (Chesham, Wyss, Müri, Mosimann, & Nef, 2017), PUZZLE (DaCosta & Seok, 2017a; Gackenbach & Bown, 2011), and PROBLEM-SOLVING (DaCosta & Seok, 2017a), all of which include various game mechanics, such as tile matching.

Genre

Although these genres are commonly connected with casual gameplay, there is little consensus when it comes to game genre (Lee et al., 2007), with some contending the topic is a "mess" (Arsenault, 2009). Numerous attempts at codifying video games have been made. One of the earliest efforts was that of Crawford (1984), who defined five major regions of games: BOARD, CARD, ATHLETIC, CHILDREN'S, and COMPUTER. He viewed computer games as two broad categories: SKILL and ACTION, further comprising the subgroupings of COMBAT, MAZE, SPORTS, PADDLE, RACE, and MISCELLANEOUS games; and STRATEGY, made up of the subgroupings: ADVENTURE, D&D (*Dungeons & Dragons®*), WARGAMES, GAMES OF CHANGE, EDUCATIONAL, and INTERPERSONAL games. Wolf (2000) defined over 40 genres based on gameplay and interactivity, but excluded other elements, such as mood and theme (Clarke, Lee, & Clark, 2017; Lee, Karlova, Clarke, Thornton, & Perti, 2014). King and Krzywinska (2002) attempted to define games using three modifiers (a) GENRE as a broad category or type based on player mechanics and goals of the game; (b) MODE as the way game content is presented to the player; and (c) MILIEU as the game's narrative content. Further, Whalen (2004) proposed that most games can be placed into three classifications: MASSIVE games that are networked, allowing for a huge number of players; MOBILE games that are intended for small screens and short play times; and REAL games, the most obscure of the three, that morphs MASSIVE and REAL, "requir[ing] players to physically relocate themselves as an act of playing the game" (p. 301). Specifically, Whalen (2004) offered *Can You See Me Now?®* and *Human PacMan®* – examples later called out by DaCosta et al. (2015, 2018) as instances of location-based mobile games. Apperley (2006) offered case studies in the context of the four more popular video game genres: SIMULATION games that mimic physical world activities from an entertainment standpoint; STRATEGY games that entail collecting, processing, interpreting, and accessing information; ACTION games that rely on performativity; and ROLE-PLAYING games that involve changes to avatar characteristics. Finally, Elverdam and Aarseth (2007) presented an open-ended model built on the work of Aarseth, Smedstad, and Sunnanå (2003), with the aim of offering a way to accurately classify and identify essential differences among games. Their topology is made up of metacategories (e.g., time, space), each with dimensions (e.g., perspective, mutability), further composing multiple elements.

Efforts such as these have helped to create a better understanding of game genre. However, some still argue that they are insufficient (Lee et al., 2014; Whalen, 2004) due to (a) the difficulty in defining what constitutes genre, (b) overlaps between genres, and (c) the constant state of flux of genres (Wolf, 2000). Efforts to flesh out distinct dimensions have been approached from different perspectives, relying on various theoretical foundations, such as literary film (Lee et al., 2014). Crawford (1984) criticized his own taxonomy because the basis of his division is grounded on historical happenstance rather than on any grand principle. Wolf's (2000) approach has been criticized because it did not account for new genres, to include MASSIVELY MULTIPLAYER ONLINE ROLE-PLAYING GAMES (MMORPGs) (Clearwater, 2011; Whalen, 2004). Categorizations are also commonly based on content (Lee et al., 2007), making game title classifications difficult. Gackenbach and Bown (2011) labeled *The 7th Guest®* and *Myst®* ACTION/ADVENTURE, but admitted that the genre is difficult to define because these games also include puzzles. Wolf (2000) saw these as PUZZLE games, but categorized *The 7th Guest®* as neither ACTION nor ADVENTURE and *Myst®* as only ADVENTURE. He also did not view ACTION as a distinct genre, further illustrating the difficulty in classifying games. These examples also demonstrate that classifications are not necessarily discrete, but continuous, with game titles spanning genres (King, Delfabbro, & Griffiths, 2009; Wolf, 2000). Crawford (1984), for instance, labeled *Pac-Man®* a MAZE game. He also branded *Frogger®* MAZE, although he was the first to admit this was a poor representation of this genre. Recognizing that it defied his own taxonomy, Crawford (1984) classified *Frogger®* as MISCELLANEOUS. Wolf (2000) labeled *Pac-Man®* as primarily a COLLECTING game, and secondarily an ESCAPE and MAZE game (although he also viewed it as an ABSTRACT game), and *Frogger®* a DODGING and OBSTACLE COURSE game, whereas Lucas and Sherry (2004) classified both games as ARCADE. The ongoing release of new titles has also resulted in a wide range of game types (Elliott, Ream, McGinsky, & Dunlap, 2012; Lee et al., 2007), challenging genre boundaries. To demonstrate this point, Clarke et al. (2017) offered *Borderlands 2®*, which has an optional mission mimicking a *Dungeons & Dragons®* (D&D)-style campaign, arguably a MASSIVELY MULTIPLAYER ONLINE ROLE-PLAYING GAME FIRST-PERSON SHOOTER (MMORPGFPS), and DaCosta and Seok (2017a) offered *CrossFire®* and *PlanetSide®* as examples of MASSIVELY MULTIPLAYER ONLINE FIRST-PERSON SHOOTERS (MMOFPS).

Table 1 shows these and other video game genres (and/or game titles) called out in studies. The table is in no way exhaustive. For example, *Time Zone®* is classified in the table as ADVENTURE, although Crawford (1984) stated that the game is a variant of the ADVENTURE theme, and could be seen as a GIANT ADVENTURE (which is not included as a genre in the table). Instead, Table 1 demonstrates the complexity of codifying video games. Take ACTION and ADVENTURE, which by some have been viewed as separate categories (e.g., DaCosta & Seok, 2017a, 2017b; Dobrowolski, Hanusz, Sobczyk, Skorko, & Wiatrow, 2015; Elverdam & Aarseth, 2007; Greenberg, Sherry, Lachlan, Lucas, & Holmstrom, 2010; Kafai, 1998; Lee et al., 2007; Lee et al., 2014; Wolf, 2000), and others as a single genre (e.g., Elliott, Golub, Ream, & Dunlap, 2012; Lucas & Sherry, 2004; Peever, Johnson, & Gardner, 2012), or *Monopoly®*, which has been classified as BOARD (Lucas & Sherry, 2004; Wolf, 2000), MANAGEMENT SIMULATION, and STRATEGY games (Wolf, 2000).

Regrettably, genre in the context of mobile games is no less muddled. While casual gameplay is associated with certain genres, their anywhere-, anytime-, and on any-device nature adds a layer of complexity. As a result, platform may be an important consideration when studying mobile game genre. Thus, King and Krzywinska (2002) noted the importance of platform, recognizing that game titles may be ported across systems, with hardware manufacturers having a possible impact on the types of games published (Clearwater, 2011). Further, Whalen (2004) argued that platform is often ignored in academic efforts to discuss genre, raising questions about the medium of gaming and the role of hardware. This argument was also supported by Clearwater (2011), who noted that hardware is an important consideration and central in helping define the medium itself.

Table 1. Genres and game titles identified in the literature

Genre	Game Title
ABSTRACT (Wolf, 2000)	*Amidar®, Arkanoid®, Ataxx®, Block Out®, Breakout®, Marble Madness®, Pac-Man®, Pipe Dream®, Q*bert®, Qix®, Super Breakout®, Tempest®, Tetris®* (Wolf, 2000)
ACTION (Apperley, 2006; Clarke et al., 2017; DaCosta & Seok, 2017a, 2017b; Eichenbaum et al., 2015; Elverdam & Aarseth, 2007; Kafai, 1998; Lee et al., 2007; Lee et al., 2014; Phan et al., 2012; Scharkow et al., 2015)	*Angry Birds®* (DaCosta & Seok, 2017a); *Grand Theft Auto®, Patapon®* (Clarke et al., 2017); *Sonic the Hedgehog®, Temple Run®* (DaCosta & Seok, 2017a); see FIGHTING, FIRST-PERSON SHOOTER, and SPORTS (Eichenbaum et al., 2015)
ACTION ADVENTURE (Elliott, Golub et al., 2012; Peever et al., 2012; Ventura et al., 2012)	*Grand Theft Auto®* (Elliott, Golub et al., 2012); *Gun®* (Clearwater, 2011); *Legend of Zelda®* (Ventura et al., 2012)
ACTION ROLE-PLAYING (Peever et al., 2012)	-
ACTION/-ADVENTURE (Bilgihan, Cobanoglu, Nusair, Okumus, & Bujisic, 2013; Clarke et al., 2017; Lee et al., 2014; Lucas & Sherry, 2004)	*The 7th Guest®* (Gackenbach & Brown, 2011); *Assassins' Creed®* (Bilgihan et al., 2013); *Catherine®* (Clarke et al., 2017); *Myst®* (Gackenbach & Bown, 2011); *Resident Evil®, Tomb Raider®* (Bilgihan et al., 2013; Lucas & Sherry, 2004)
ADAPTION (Wolf, 2000)	*All American Football®, (Atari) Baseball®, Casino®, Eric's Ultimate Solitaire®, Family Feud®, Hangman®, Hot Shots Tennis®, Jeopardy®, The Joker's Wild®, Ken Uston Blackjack/Poker®, Krull®, Muppet Treasure Island®, Pong®, The Price is Right®, The Simpsons®, Spider-Man®, Spy Vs Spy®, Star Wars®, Sure Shot Pool®, Teenage Mutant Ninja Turtles®, Tic-Tac-Dough®, Tic-Tac-Toe®, Tron®, Virtual Pool®, Wheel of Fortune®, X-Men®* (Wolf, 2000)
ADVENTURE(S) (Crawford, 1984; DaCosta & Seok, 2017a, 2017b; Dobrowolski et al., 2015; Elverdam & Aarseth, 2007; Greenberg et al., 2010; Lee et al., 2007; Scharkow et al., 2015; Wolf, 2000)	*Adventure®* (Crawford, 1984; Wolf, 2000); *Deadline®* (Crawford, 1984); *E.T. The Extraterrestrial®* (Wolf, 2000); *Galahad and the Holy Grail®* (Crawford, 1984); *Haunted House®* (Crawford, 1984; Wolf, 2000); *Krull®, Myst®, Raiders of the Lost Ark®, Spy Vs Spy®* (Wolf, 2000); *Superman®* (Crawford, 1984; Wolf, 2000); *Time Zone®* (Crawford, 1984); *Tomb Raider®* series, *Ultima®* series, *Venture®* (Wolf, 2000); *Wizard and the Princess®* (Crawford, 1984)
ARCADE (Bilgihan et al., 2013; DaCosta & Seok, 2017a, 2017b; Elverdam & Aarseth, 2007; Lucas & Sherry, 2004)	*Angry Birds®* (DaCosta & Seok, 2017a); *Frogger®, Pac-Man®* (Bilgihan et al., 2013; Lucas & Sherry, 2004); *Pinball®* (Lucas & Sherry, 2004); *Sonic the Hedgehog®, Temple Run®* (DaCosta & Seok, 2017a)
ARTIFICIAL LIFE (Wolf, 2000)	*AquaZone®, Babyz®, Catz®, Creatures®, Dogz®, The Little Computer People®, The Sims®* (Wolf, 2000)
ATHLETIC (Crawford, 1984)	
BOARD* and CARD* (Elliott, Golub et al., 2012)	*Solitaire®* (Elliott, Golub et al., 2012)
BOARD* or CARD* (Peever et al., 2012)	-
BOARD* (Crawford, 1984; DaCosta & Seok, 2017a, 2017b; Elverdam & Aarseth, 2007; Greenberg et al., 2010; Wolf, 2000)	*Backgammon®, Battleship®, Clue®, Conquest of the New World®, Fooblitzky®, The Great Wall Street Fortune Hunt®, Jones in the Fast Lane®, Monopoly®, Othello®, Quest for the Rings®, Scrabble®, Stratego®, Video Checkers®, Video Chess®* (Wolf, 2000)
BROWSER (Haagsma et al., 2012)	-
CAPTURING (Wolf, 2000)	*Gopher®, Hole Hunter®, Keystone Kapers®, Surround®, Take the Money and Run®, Texas Chainsaw Massacre®, Tron®* (light cycle) (Wolf, 2000)
CARD* (Crawford, 1984; Wolf, 2000)	*1000 Miles®, Blackjack®, Casino®, Eric's Ultimate Solitaire®, Ken Uston Blackjack/Poker®, Video Poker®* (Wolf, 2000)
CARD*/DICE (Bilgihan et al., 2013; Greenberg et al., 2010; Lucas & Sherry, 2004)	*Solitaire®* (Bilgihan et al., 2013; Lucas & Sherry, 2004); *Vegas Fever 2000®* (Lucas & Sherry, 2004)
CASUAL (Peever et al., 2012)	-
CASUAL ACTION*** (Chesham et al., 2017)	See NO SHOOTING ACTION and FIRST PERSON SHOOTER ACTION (Chesham et al., 2017)
CASUAL PUZZLE*** (Chesham et al., 2017)	See CONNECT-THE-DOTS and TILE-MATCHING (Chesham et al., 2017)
CASUAL SIMULATION*** (Chesham et al., 2017)	See RACING SIMULATION and SPORTS SIMULATION (Chesham et al., 2017)
CASUAL STRATEGY*** (Chesham et al., 2017)	See TOWER DEFENSE (Chesham et al., 2017)
CATCHING (Wolf, 2000)	*Alpha Beam with Ernie®, Big Bird's Egg Catch®, Circus Atari®, Fishing Derby®, Lost Luggage®, Stampede®, Quantum®, Street Racer®* (games 21 through 27) (Wolf, 2000)
CHASE (Wolf, 2000)	See CATCHING, CAPTURING, DRIVING, ESCAPE, FLYING, and RACING (Wolf, 2000)

continues on following page

Table 1. Continued

CHILDREN'S (Crawford, 1984)	-
CLASSIC ARCADE (Greenberg et al., 2010)	-
CLASSIC BOARD* (Bilgihan et al., 2013; Lucas & Sherry, 2004)	*Checkers*® (Lucas & Sherry, 2004); *Monopoly*® (Bilgihan et al., 2013; Lucas & Sherry, 2004)
COLLECTING (Wolf, 2000)	*Amidar*®, *Mouse Trap*®, *Pac-Man*®, *Prop Cycle*®, *Qix*®, *Spy Vs Spy*® (Wolf, 2000)
COMBAT (Crawford, 1984; Wolf, 2000)	*Asteriods*® (Crawford, 1984); *Battletech*® (Wolf, 2000); *Battlezone*® (Crawford, 1984; Wolf, 2000); *Caverns of Mars*®, *Centipede*® (Crawford, 1984); *Combat*® (Wolf, 2000); *CrossFire*® (On-Line Systems; Crawford, 1984); *Dactyl Nightmare*® (Wolf, 2000); *Defender*® (Wolf, 2000); *Galaxian*® (Crawford, 1984); *Missile Command*® (Crawford, 1984); *Outlaws*® (Wolf, 2000); *Red Baron*®, *Space Invaders*®, *Spacewar!*® (Crawford, 1984); *Spy Vs Spy*® (Wolf, 2000); *Star Raiders*® (Crawford, 1984); *Warlords*® (Wolf, 2000); *Yar's Revenge*® (Crawford, 1984)
COMMUNITY (Lee et al., 2007)	-
COMPUTER (Crawford, 1984)	-
CONNECT-THE-DOTS*** (Chesham et al., 2017)	*Flow Free*® (Chesham et al., 2017)
D&D (Crawford, 1984)	*Temple of Apshai*® (Crawford, 1984)
DEMO (Wolf, 2000)	*ADAM Demo Cartridge*®, Dealer Demo (*Bally Astrocade*®), Demonstration Cartridge (*RCA Studio II*®), Music Box Demo (*Coleco ADAM*®) (Wolf, 2000)
DIAGNOSTICS (Wolf, 2000)	Diagnostic Cartridge (Atari 5200®, Atari 7800®), Final Test Cartridge (Coleco ADAM®), Super Controller Test Cartridge (Coleco ADAM®) (Wolf, 2000)
DODGING (Wolf, 2000)	*Dodge 'Em*®, *Freeway*®, *Frogger*®, *Journey Escape*®, *Street Racer*® (Wolf, 2000)
DRIVING (Elliott, Golub et al., 2012; Wolf, 2000)	*Dodge 'Em*®, *Indy 500*®, *Night Driver*®, *Pole Position*®, *Red Planet*®, *Street Racer*® (Wolf, 2000); *Super Mario Kart*® (Elliott, Golub et al., 2012)
DRIVING/RACING (Lee et al., 2014)	
DRIVING/SPORTS (Gackenbach & Bown, 2011)	-
EDUCATION(AL) (Crawford, 1984; DaCosta & Seok, 2017a, 2017b; Peever et al., 2012; Phan et al., 2012; Wolf, 2000)	*Alpha Beam with Ernie*®, *Basic Math*® (Wolf, 2000); *Energy Czar*®, *Hammurabi*®, *Hot Shots Tennis*®, *Lunar Lander*® (Crawford, 1984); *Mario's Early Years! Fun With Numbers*®, *Mario Teaches Typing*®, *Math Blaster: Episode 1: Search of Spot*®, *Math Gran Prix*®, *Morse*®, *Number Games*®, *Playschool Math*® (Wolf, 2000); *Rocky's Boots*®, *Scram*® (Crawford, 1984); *Spelling Games*®, *Word Games*® (Wolf, 2000)
ESCAPE (Wolf, 2000)	*Pac-Man*®, *Maze Craze*®, *Mouse Trap*®, *Ms. Pac-Man*®, *Surround*® (Wolf, 2000)
FANTASY ROLE-PLAYING (Crawford, 1984)	*Ali Baba and the Forty Thieves*® (Crawford, 1984)
FANTASY/ROLE-PLAYING (Bilgihan et al., 2013; Greenberg et al., 2010; Lucas & Sherry, 2004)	*Diablo*® (Lucas & Sherry, 2004); *Final Fantasy*®, *(Legend of) Zelda*® (Bilgihan et al., 2013; Lucas & Sherry, 2004)
FIGHT(ER/ING) (Bilgihan et al., 2013; DaCosta & Seok, 2017a, 2017b; Dobrowolski et al., 2015; Eichenbaum et al., 2015; Granic et al., 2014; Greenberg et al., 2010; Lee et al., 2014; Lucas & Sherry, 2004; Peever et al., 2012; Phan et al., 2012; Ventura et al., 2012; Wolf, 2000)	*America's Army: True Soldiers*® (Clearwater, 2011); *The Avengers*®, *Body Slam*®, *Boxing*® (Wolf, 2000); *Mortal Kombat*® series (Bilgihan et al., 2013; Lucas & Sherry, 2004; Wolf, 2000); *Soul Edge*® (Lucas & Sherry, 2004); *Street Fighter*® (Bilgihan et al., 2013; Ventura et al., 2012); *Street Fighter IV*® (Granic et al., 2014); *Tekken*® series (Lucas & Sherry, 2004; Wolf, 2000); *Wrestle War* (Wolf, 2000)
FIRST-PERSON PUZZLE (Granic et al., 2014)	*Portal 2*® (Granic et al., 2014)
FIRST-PERSON SHOOT(ER/ING) (Dobrowolski et al., 2015; Eichenbaum et al., 2015; Elliott, Golub et al., 2012; Elliott, Ream et al., 2012; Elverdam & Aarseth, 2007; Gackenbach & Bown, 2011; King et al., 2009; Riedel, 2016; Seok & DaCosta, 2012)	*Call of Duty*® (Elliott, Golub et al., 2012; Elliott, Ream et al., 2012); *Counter-Strike*® (Eichenbaum et al., 2015; Jansz & Tanis, 2007); *Doom*® (Jansz & Tanis, 2007); *Halo*® (Clarke et al., 2017; Eichenbaum et al., 2015; Elliott, Golub et al., 2012; Elliott, Ream et al., 2012); *Jedi Knight*® (Whalen, 2004); *JFK Reloaded*® (Clearwater, 2011); *Sudden Attack*® (Seok & DaCosta, 2012)
FIRST PERSON SHOOTER ACTION*** (Chesham et al., 2017)	*Smash Hit*® (Chesham et al., 2017)
FLIGHT (Peever et al., 2012)	-
FLYING (Wolf, 2000)	*A-10 Attack!*®, *Descent*®, *F/A-18 Hornet 3.0*®, *Flight Unlimited*®, *Prop Cycle*®, *Solaris*®, *Starmaster*® (Wolf, 2000)

continues on following page

Table 1. Continued

GAMBLING (Elliott, Golub et al., 2012; Wolf, 2000)	*Blackjack®, Casino®* (Wolf, 2000); *Poker®* (Elliott, Golub et al., 2012); *Slot Machine®, Video Poker®, You Don't Know Jack!®* (Wolf, 2000)
GAMES OF CHANCE (Crawford, 1984)	-
HACK 'N SLASH (Granic et al., 2014)	*DmC: Devil May Cry®* (Granic et al., 2014)
INTERACTIVE MOVIE (Wolf, 2000)	*Dragon's Lair®, Johnny Mnemonic®, Space Ace®, Star Trek: Borg®* (Wolf, 2000)
INTERPERSONAL (Crawford, 1984)	-
KIDS (Greenberg et al., 2010)	-
LIFE SIMULATION (Eichenbaum et al., 2015)	*Habbo®* (Eichenbaum et al., 2015)
MANAGEMENT SIMULATION (Wolf, 2000)	*Aerobiz®, Caesar II®, Civilization®, Monopoly®, M.U.L.E.®, Railroad Tycoon®, SimAnt®, SimCity®, SimFarm®, SimTower®, Spaceward Ho!®* (Wolf, 2000)
MASSIVE (Whalen, 2004)	-
MAZE (Crawford, 1984; Wolf, 2000)	*Descent®, Dig Dug®* (Wolf, 2000); *Dodge 'Em®* (Crawford, 1984); *Doom®* (Wolf, 2000); *Frogger®* (Crawford, 1984); *K. C. Munchkin®, Lode Runner®* (Wolf, 2000); *Maze Craze®* (Crawford, 1984; Wolf, 2000); *Mouskattack®* (Crawford, 1984); *Mouse Trap®* (Wolf, 2000); *Ms. Pac-Man®* (Wolf, 2000); *Pac-Man®* (Crawford, 1984; Wolf, 2000); *Spy Vs Spy®, Take the Money and Run!®, Tunnel Runner®, Tunnels of Doom®* (Wolf, 2000)
MISCELLANEOUS (Crawford, 1984)	*Apple Panic®, Donkey Kong®, Frogger®* (Crawford, 1984)
MOBILE (Whalen, 2004)	-
MULTIPLAYER ONLINE BATTLE ARENA (Clarke et al., 2017; Dobrowolski et al., 2015)	*Castlevania®, Metroid®* (Clarke et al., 2017)
MMORPGFPS (Clarke et al., 2017)	*Borderlands 2®* (Clarke et al., 2017)
MMOFPS (DaCosta & Seok, 2017a)	*CrossFire®, PlanetSide®* (DaCosta & Seok, 2017a)
MMOG (DaCosta & Seok, 2016; DaCosta & Seok, 2017a, 2017b)	*Lord of the Rings Online®* (DaCosta & Seok, 2017a); *Lineage®, RunScape®* (DaCosta & Seok, 2017b); *Star Wars: The Old Republic®* (DaCosta & Seok, 2017a)
MMORPG(s) (Elliott, Golub et al., 2012; Granic et al., 2014; Peever et al., 2012)	*EverQuest®* (Gackenbach & Bown, 2011); *World of Warcraft®* (Elliott, Golub et al., 2012; Granic et al., 2014; Seok & DaCosta, 2012)
MULTI-USER DUNGEON (Seok & DaCosta, 2012)	-
MUSIC (Eichenbaum et al., 2015; Peever et al., 2012; Scharkow et al., 2015)	*Audition Online®* (Eichenbaum et al., 2015)
MUSIC/DANCE (Phan et al., 2012)	-
NO SHOOTING ACTION*** (Chesham et al., 2017)	*Pocket Frog Splash®, Sliders®* (Chesham et al., 2017)
OBSTACLE COURSE (Wolf, 2000)	*Boot Camp®, Clown Downtown®, Freeway®, Frogger®, Pitfall!®, Jungle Hunt®* (Wolf, 2000)
OFFLINE (DaCosta & Seok, 2016; Haagsma et al., 2012)	-
OFFLINE CASUAL (Haagsma et al., 2012)	-
ONLINE (DaCosta & Seok, 2016; Haagsma et al., 2012)	-
OTHER (Elliott, Golub et al., 2012)	*Pac-Man®* (Elliott, Golub et al., 2012)
OTHER ROLE-PLAYING (Elliott, Golub et al., 2012)	*Fallout 3®* (Elliott, Golub et al., 2012)
OTHER SHOOTER (Elliott, Golub et al., 2012)	*Gears of War®* (Elliott, Golub et al., 2012)
OTHER STRATEGY (Elliott, Golub et al., 2012)	*Farmville®* (Elliott, Golub et al., 2012)
PADDLE (Crawford, 1984)	*Avalanche®, Breakout®, Chicken®, Circus Atari®, Pong®, Super Breakout®, Warlords®* (Crawford, 1984)
PARTY (Granic et al., 2014; Peever et al., 2012)	*Mario Party 9®* (Granic et al., 2014)
PENCIL-AND-PAPER (Wolf, 2000)	*3-D Tic-Tac-Toe®, Effacer: Hangman from the 25th Century®, Hangman®, Noughts and Crosses®, Tic-Tac-Toe®* (Wolf, 2000)

continues on following page

Table 1. Continued

PINBALL (Wolf, 2000)	*Arcade Pinball®, Astrocade Pinball®, Electronic Pinball®, Extreme Pinball®, Flipper Game®, Galactic Pinball®, Kirby's Pinball Land®, (Atari) Midnight Magic®, Pachinko!®, Pinball®, Pinball Challenge®, Pinball Dreams®, Pinball Fantasies®, Pinball Jam®, Pinball Quest®, Pinball Wizard®, Power Rangers Pinball®, Pro Pinball®, Real Pinball®, Sonic the Hedgehog Spinball®, Spinball®, Super Pinball: Behind the Mask®, Super Sushi Pinball®, Thunderball!®, True Pinball®, Video Pinball* (Wolf, 2000)
PLATFORM(ER) (Clarke et al., 2017; Dobrowolski et al., 2015; Elliott, Golub et al., 2012; Granic et al., 2014; Peever et al., 2012; Riedel, 2016; Scharkow et al., 2015; Ventura et al., 2012; Wolf, 2000)	*Crazy Climber®, Donkey Kong®, Donkey Kong Jr.®, Lode Runner®* (Wolf, 2000); *Rogue Legacy®, Risk of Rain®* (Clarke et al., 2017); *(Atari) Spider-Man®* (Wolf, 2000); *Super Mario Bros.®* (Elliott, Golub et al., 2012; Granic et al., 2014; Ventura et al., 2012; Whalen, 2004; Wolf, 2000); *Wario Land®, Yoshi's Island®* (Wolf, 2000)
PROBLEM-SOLVING** (DaCosta & Seok, 2017a)	*Angry Birds®, Bejeweled®, Candy Crush Saga®, The Incredible Machine®* (DaCosta & Seok, 2017a); *Sudoku®* (DaCosta & Seok, 2016); *Temple Run®* (DaCosta & Seok, 2017a); *Where's My Water®* (DaCosta & Seok, 2017b); *World of Goo®* (DaCosta & Seok, 2017a)
PROGRAMMING (Wolf, 2000)	*AI Fleet Commander®, AI War®, CoreWar®, Crobots®, Omega®, RARS®* (*Robot Auto Racing Simulator*), *Robot Battle®* (Wolf, 2000)
PUZZLE(S)* (Bilgihan et al., 2013; Clarke et al., 2017; DaCosta & Seok, 2017a, 2017b; Dobrowolski et al., 2015; Eichenbaum et al., 2015; Elliott, Golub et al., 2012; Granic et al., 2014; Greenberg et al., 2010; King et al., 2009; Lee et al., 2014; Lucas & Sherry, 2004; Peever et al., 2012; Scharkow et al., 2015; Ventura et al., 2012; Wolf, 2000)	*The 7th Guest®, Atari Video Cube®* (Wolf, 2000); *Angry Birds®* (DaCosta & Seok, 2017a); *Bejweled®* (Clarke et al., 2017; DaCosta & Seok, 2017a; Eichenbaum et al., 2015; Elliott, Golub et al., 2012; Granic et al., 2014); *Block Out®* (Wolf, 2000); *Candy Crush Saga®* (DaCosta & Seok, 2017a); *Catherine®* (Clarke et al., 2017); *Dice Puzzle®* (Wolf, 2000); *FreeCell®* (Bilgihan et al., 2013; Lucas & Sherry, 2004); *Hearts®* (Eichenbaum et al., 2015); *Hitchhiker's Guide to the Galaxy®* (Wolf, 2000); *The Incredible Machine®* (DaCosta & Seok, 2017a); *Jigsaw®, Myst®* (Wolf, 2000); *Pacxon®* (Eichenbaum et al., 2015); *Portal®* (Clarke et al., 2017); *Rubik's Cube®, Sokoban®* (Wolf, 2000); *Sudoku®* (DaCosta & Seok, 2017b); *Suspended®* (Wolf, 2000); *Temple Run®* (DaCosta & Seok, 2017a); *Tetris®* (Bilgihan et al., 2013; DaCosta & Seok, 2017a; Lucas & Sherry, 2004; Ventura et al., 2012; Wolf, 2000); *Threes®* (DaCosta & Seok, 2017a); *Where's My Water®* (DaCosta & Seok, 2017b); *World of Goo®* (DaCosta & Seok, 2017a)
PUZZLE/CARD* (Phan et al., 2012)	-
PUZZLE/CARD/BOARD* (Gackenbach & Bown, 2011)	-
QUIZ (Wolf, 2000)	*Fax®, Jeopardy®, Name That Tune®, NFL Football Trivia Challenge '94/'95®, Sex Trivia®, Triv-Quiz®, Trivia Whiz®, Trivial Pursuit®, Video Trivia®, Wizz Quiz®, You Don't Know Jack!®* (Wolf, 2000)
QUIZ/TRIVIA (Bilgihan et al., 2013; Greenberg et al., 2010; Lucas & Sherry, 2004)	*Jeopardy®* (Lucas & Sherry, 2004); *Who Wants to be a Millionaire®* (Bilgihan et al., 2013; Lucas & Sherry, 2004)
RACE(R/ING) (Crawford, 1984; DaCosta & Seok, 2017a, 2017b; Dobrowolski et al., 2015; Granic et al., 2014; Peever et al., 2012; Riedel, 2016; Wolf, 2000)	*1000 Miles®, Daytona USA®* (Wolf, 2000); *Dog Daze®, Downhill®* (Crawford, 1984); *High Velocity®, Indy 500®, Mario Kart 64®* (Wolf, 2000); *Match Racer®* (Crawford, 1984); *Math Gran Prix®* (Wolf, 2000); *Need for Speed: Most Wanted®* (Granic et al., 2014); *Night Driver®* (Crawford, 1984); *Pole Position®, Red Planet®, Slot Racers®, Street Racer®, Super GT®* (Wolf, 2000)
RACING SIMULATION*** (Chesham et al., 2017)	*Real Racing 3®* (Chesham et al., 2017)
RACING/SPEED (Bilgihan et al., 2013; Greenberg et al., 2010; Lucas & Sherry, 2004)	*Forza®* (Bilgihan et al., 2013); *Grand Turismo®, Need for Speed®, (Super) Mario Kart®* (Bilgihan et al., 2013; Lucas & Sherry, 2004)
REAL (Whalen, 2004)	*Can You See Me Now®, Human PacMan®* (Whalen, 2004)
REAL-TIME (King et al., 2009)	-
REAL-TIME STRATEGY (Dobrowolski et al., 2015; Eichenbaum et al., 2015; Elliott, Golub et al., 2012; Elverdam & Aarseth, 2007; Peever et al., 2012; Seok & DaCosta, 2012)	*Rakion®* (Eichenbaum et al., 2015); *StarCraft®* (Elliott, Golub et al., 2012; Seok & DaCosta, 2012); *Warcraft III: Reign of Chaos®* (Whalen, 2004)
RHYTHM (Elliott, Golub et al., 2012; Granic et al., 2014)	*Guitar Hero®* (Elliott, Golub et al., 2012); *Guitar Hero 5®* (Granic et al., 2014)
RHYTHM AND DANCE (Wolf, 2000)	*Beatmania®, Bust-a-Groove®, Dance Revolution®, Guitar Freaks®, PaRappa the Rapper®, Pop'n Music®, Samba de Amigo®, Space Channel 5®, Um Jammer Lammy®, Vib-Ribbon®* (Wolf, 2000)
ROGUELIKE (Clarke et al., 2017)	*Rogue®* (Clarke et al., 2017)

continues on following page

Table 1. Continued

ROLE-PLAYING (Apperley, 2006; DaCosta & Seok, 2017a, 2017b; Dobrowolski et al., 2015; Eichenbaum et al., 2015; Elverdam & Aarseth, 2007; Granic et al., 2014; Kafai, 1998; King et al., 2009; Lee et al., 2007; Lee et al., 2014; Peever et al., 2012; Phan et al., 2012; Riedel, 2016; Scharkow et al., 2015; Seok & DaCosta, 2012; Ventura et al., 2012; Wolf, 2000)	*Aion Online*® (Seok & DaCosta, 2012); *Anvil of Dawn*® (Wolf, 2000); *Asheron's Call*® (Whalen, 2004); *Cyphers Online*® (Seok & DaCosta, 2012); *Diablo*®, *Dragon Lore 2*®, *Dungeons & Dragons* series® (Wolf, 2000); *EverQuest*® (Whalen, 2004); *Fallout*® (Wolf, 2000); *Final Fantasy*® (Granic et al., 2014; Whalen, 2004); *Final Fantasy XIII*® (Granic et al., 2014); *Forgotten Realms*® (Whalen, 2004); *Interstate '76*® (Wolf, 2000); *JediMUD*® (Wolf, 2000); *Mabinogi*® (Seok & DaCosta, 2012); *Mageslayer*® (Wolf, 2000); *MappleStory*® (Eichenbaum et al., 2015; Seok & DaCosta, 2012); *Northern Lights*®, *PernMUSH*®, *Phantasy Star*® (Wolf, 2000); *Pokémon*® (Granic et al., 2014;); *RiftMUSH*®, *Rivers of MUD*®, *Sacred Pools*®, *Sunflower*® (Wolf, 2000); *Tierra Americana*® (Seok & DaCosta, 2012); *Ultima series*®, *Unsafe Haven*®, *VikingMUD*® (Wolf, 2000); *World of Warcraft*® (Granic et al., 2014; Seok & DaCosta, 2012; Ventura et al., 2012); *Zodiac*® (Wolf, 2000)
ROLE-PLAYING/STRATEGY (Gackenbach & Bown, 2011)	-
SANDBOX (MULTI) (Granic et al., 2014)	*Minecraft*® (Granic et al., 2014)
SANDBOX (SOLO) (Granic et al., 2014)	*The Sims*® (Granic et al., 2014)
SHOOT'EM UP (Wolf, 2000)	*Asteriods*® (Crawford, 1984; Wolf, 2000); *Berzerk*®, *Centipede*, *Doom*®, *Duckshot*®, *Galaga*®, *Millipede*®, *Missile Command*®, *Robotron: 2084*®, *Space Invaders*® (Wolf, 2000); *Spacewar!*® (Whalen, 2004); *Yar's Revenge*®, *Zaxxon*® (Wolf, 2000)
SHOOT(ER(S)/ING) (Bilgihan et al., 2013; Greenberg et al., 2010; Lee et al., 2007; Lee et al., 2014; Lucas & Sherry, 2004; Peever et al., 2012; Ventura et al., 2012)	*Call of Duty*® (Bilgihan et al., 2013; Ventura et al., 2012); *BioShock*® (Bilgihan et al., 2013); *Duke Nukem*®, *Quake*® (Lucas & Sherry, 2004)
SHOOTER (MULTI) (Granic et al., 2014)	*Halo 4*® (Granic et al., 2014)
SHOOTER (SOLO) (Granic et al., 2014)	*Halo 4*® (Granic et al., 2014)
SIMULATION(S) (Apperley, 2006; Bilgihan et al., 2013; DaCosta & Seok, 2017a, 2017b; Greenberg et al., 2010; Kafai, 1998; Lee et al., 2007; Lee et al., 2014; Lucas & Sherry, 2004; Peever et al., 2012; Phan et al., 2012; Scharkow et al., 2015; Ventura et al., 2012; Wolf, 2000)	*Rollercoaster Tycoon*® (Lucas & Sherry, 2004); *SimCity*® (Bilgihan et al., 2013; Lucas & Sherry, 2004); *The Sims*® (Bilgihan et al., 2013; Ventura et al., 2012); see MANAGEMENT SIMULATION and TRAINING SIMULATION (Wolf, 2000)
SOCIAL** (DaCosta & Seok, 2017a, 2017b; Phan et al., 2012)	*Draw Something*®, *FarmVille 2*® (DaCosta & Seok, 2017a); *Minecraft: Pocket Edition*®, *Words with Friends*® (DaCosta & Seok, 2017b)
SOCIAL MEDIA** (Granic et al., 2014; Ventura et al., 2012)	*FarmVille*® (Granic et al., 2014; Ventura et al., 2012)
SPORT(S) (Bilgihan et al., 2013; Crawford, 1984; DaCosta & Seok, 2017a, 2017b; Eichenbaum et al., 2015; Elverdam & Aarseth, 2007; Granic et al., 2014; Greenberg et al., 2010; Kafai, 1998; Lee et al., 2007; Lee et al., 2014; Lucas & Sherry, 2004; Peever et al., 2012; Scharkow et al., 2015; Seok & DaCosta, 2012; Wolf, 2000)	*9 Innings: Pro Baseball*® (DaCosta & Seok, 2017a; Seok & DaCosta, 2015); *All American Football*®, *(Atari) Baseball*®, *Bowling*®, *Boxing*® (Wolf, 2000); *FIFA*® (Bilgihan et al., 2013; Granic et al., 2014); *Fishing Derby*® (Wolf, 2000); *Golf*®, *Hot Shots Tennis*®, *Human Cannonball*®, *Ice Hockey*®, *Madden Football 97*®, *Miniature Golf*® (Wolf, 2000); *NBA Live*® series (Bilgihan et al., 2013); *NBA Jam*®, *Tony Hawk's Pro Skater*® (Lucas & Sherry, 2004); *NHL 97*® (Wolf, 2000); *Pong*® (Whalen, 2004; Wolf, 2000); *Pro Evaluation Soccer*® series (Bilgihan et al., 2013); *(RealSports) Soccer*®, *Tennis*®, and *Volleyball*®; *SimGolf*®, *Skeet Shoot*®, *Sky Diver*®, *Summer Games*®, *Track & Field*®, *Tsuppori Sumo Wrestling*®, *Video Olympics*®, *World Series Baseball '98*® (Wolf, 2000)
SPORTS GENERAL (Elliott, Golub et al., 2012)	*Wii Fit/Sports*® (Elliott, Golub et al., 2012)
SPORTS OTHER (Elliott, Golub et al., 2012)	*Madden NFL*® (Elliott, Golub et al., 2012)
SPORTS SIMULATION*** (Chesham et al., 2017)	*Virtual Table Tennis HD*® (Chesham et al., 2017)
STRATEGY (Apperley, 2006; Bilgihan et al., 2013; DaCosta & Seok, 2017a, 2017b; Eichenbaum et al., 2015; Granic et al., 2014; Greenberg et al., 2010; Kafai, 1998; Lee et al., 2014; Lucas & Sherry, 2004; Phan et al., 2012; Riedel, 2016; Scharkow et al., 2015; Ventura et al., 2012; Wolf, 2000)	*Ataxx*® (Wolf, 2000); *Checkers*®, *Chess*® (Gackenbach & Bown, 2011; Wolf, 2000); *Civilization*® (Ventura et al., 2012); *Civilization, Age of Empire*®, *Command & Conquer*® (Bilgihan et al., 2013; Lucas & Sherry, 2004); *Monopoly*®, *M.U.L.E.*®, *Othello*®, *Spaceward Ho!*® (Wolf, 2000); *StarCraft II: Wings of Liberty*® (Granic et al., 2014); *Stellar Track*® (Wolf, 2000); See LIFE-SIMULATION, REAL-TIME STRATEGY, and TURN-BASED STRATEGY (Eichenbaum et al., 2015)
SURVIVAL-HORROR (Clarke et al., 2017)	-
TABLE-TOP (Wolf, 2000)	*Battle Pingpong*®, *Electronic Table Soccer!*®, *Parlour Games*®, *Pocket Billiards!*®, *Pong*®, *Sure Shot Pool*®, *Trick Shot*®, *Virtual Pool*® (Wolf, 2000)
TARGET (Wolf, 2000)	*Air-Sea Battle*®, *Carnival*®, *Human Cannonball*®, *Marksman/Trapshooting*®, *Shooting Gallery*®, *Skeet Shoot*®, *Wabbit*® (Wolf, 2000)

continues on following page

Table 1. Continued

TEXT ADVENTURE (Peever et al., 2012; Wolf, 2000)	*A Mind Forever* Voyaging®, *Adventure*® (Whalen, 2004); *The Hitchhiker's Guide to the Galaxy*®, *Leather Goddesses of Phobos*®, *Planetfall*®, *Suspended*® (Wolf, 2000); *Zork*® (Whalen, 2004; Wolf, 2000)
THIRD PERSON (Riedel, 2016)	-
TILE-MATCHING*** (Chesham et al., 2017)	*Bejeweled*® (Chesham et al., 2017)
TOWER DEFENSE*** (Chesham et al., 2017)	*Plants vs. Zombies*® (Chesham et al., 2017)
TRAINING SIMULATION (Wolf, 2000)	*A-10 Attack!*®, *Comanche 3*®, *F/A-18 Hornet 3.0*®, *Flight Unlimited*®, *Police Trainer*®, military and airline flight simulators, driver education simulations (Wolf, 2000)
TRIVIA (DaCosta & Seok, 2017a, 2017b)	-
TURN-BASED STRATEGY (Dobrowolski et al., 2015; Eichenbaum et al., 2015; King et al., 2009; Peever et al., 2012)	-
UTILITY (Wolf, 2000)	*BASIC Programming*®, *Beginning Algebra*®, *Beginning Math*®, *Computer Programmer*®, Diagnostic Cartridge (Atari 5200®), *French Language Translator*®, *Home Finance* [*Analysis*]®, *Mario Teaches Typing*®, *Number Games*®, *Speed Reading*®, *Spelling Games*®, *Touch Typing*®, *Word Games*® (Wolf, 2000)
WARGAMES (Crawford, 1984)	*Computer Ambush*®, *Computer Bismarck*®, *Computer Napoleonics*®, *Eastern Front 1491*®, *Tanktics*® (Crawford, 1984)
WEB BOARDS (Lee et al., 2007)	-

Called out as a casual gamer genre: *(DaCosta & Seok, 2017a, 2017b; Gackenbach & Bown, 2011); **(DaCosta & Seok, 2017a, 2017b); ***(Chesham et al., 2017)

Purpose of the Chapter

Given the perceived importance of platform, this chapter presents a study that explored game genre in the context of mobile gameplay. To gain a stronger understanding of the casual mobile game player, numerous factors were first examined. These included what gaming platforms were most preferred; how often, where, and why mobile games were played; what were the most attractive game characteristics; psychophysical changes experienced during gameplay; and the most popular genres played. Next, the relationships between popular genre and factors commonly studied in educational contexts were examined, including age and gender, as well as academic grading and level.

While much has been reported on video game genre, this chapter is believed to be one of few that explicitly restricts the topic to the mobile platform. It is anticipated that the findings will be of value to educators, practitioners, and researchers interested in the use of mobile games both in an out of the classroom. To ensure scholarly rigor, the great majority of the content comes from a substantive literature review of books as well as print and online academic journals. Considerable effort was made to capture peer-reviewed materials. However, other sources were also used, to include yearly statistical reports on the video game industry.

Further, this chapter identifies games spanning decades, with sources sometimes using different spellings for the same game (e.g., *Pac Man* vs. *Pac-Man*). To ensure consistency, an attempt was made to verify the spelling of each title, with the official game title used. In instances where the games could not be found, the titles were not included in Table 1. For example, Wolf (2000) offered games from the *Daggerfall*® series as an ADVENTURE example. Unable to verify the series other than that from *The Elder Scrolls II*®, the game was not listed in the table. Other instances from Wolf (2000) included *$25,000 Pyramid*® (only *$100,000 Pyramid*® could be found), *Gadget*®, *Ivory Tower*®, *Montana*®, *Password*®, and *OutlawMOO*®. This is not to suggest that these titles do not exist, but rather that we were unable to confirm them at the time of this writing.

METHOD

Participants

The study was conducted at four high schools and six colleges near Seoul, South Korea. Three of the high schools were vocational; the fourth was college preparatory.

Of the 2,465 students who voluntarily participated, 1,950 played mobile games (48 did not complete the questionnaire asking for that information, 438 never played mobile games or did not specify if they played, and 29 did not own or use a mobile phone). Nearly half were 18-20 years of age (47.7%, $n = 931$), followed by those 15-17 (19.2%, $n = 375$) and 21-23 (19.1%, $n = 373$). Most were male (70.4%, $n = 1,373$; female: 29.2%, $n = 569$). More attended high school (63.7%, $n = 1,241$) than college (36.4%, $n = 709$). As for academics, grades were skewed towards the higher performing students, as depicted in Figure 1 and shown in Table 2.

Figure 1. Participants' grades were distributed towards those earning A's and B's

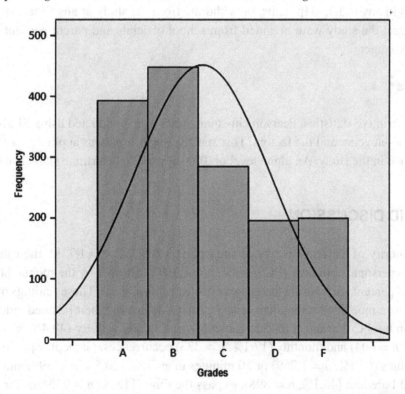

Table 2. Participants' grades

Grades	Freq. (%)
90-100 (A)	393 (20.2%)
80-89 (B)	448 (23.0%)
70-79 (C)	285 (14.6%)
60-69 (D)	196 (10.1%)
50 and less (F)	200 (10.3%)

Materials

A 92-item questionnaire was designed to explore mobile game play in the contexts of game preferences, frequency of play, spending habits, problematic play, personality, and demographics. Part of a larger body of research examining video game play in a rich gaming culture such as South Korea, the findings presented here are based on a subset of the questionnaire items.

Procedure

Volunteer faculty and undergraduate students administered the questionnaire. Students were allowed to answer the items in any order, skip items, or withdraw from the study at any time. All necessary permissions to conduct the study were obtained from school officials and parent consent was sought for students 17 and younger.

Data Analysis

In addition to descriptive statistics, Pearson chi-square tests were conducted using SPSS 24 to examine relationships between genre and the factors. This statistical approach was applied given the categorical variables examined in the study. An alpha level of .05 was used to determine statistical significance.

RESULTS AND DISCUSSION

Although the majority of participants owned smartphones (89.1%, $n = 1,738$), their gaming platform of choice was the personal computer (PC; 59.9%, $n = 1,169$), followed by the mobile phone (34%, $n = 657$), with a small percentage favoring the game console (1.9%, $n = 36$). These findings may suggest that the participants were more avid rather than casual gamers, dedicating their planned video game time to titles available on the PC. For most, mobile gameplay was a daily activity (48.4%, $n = 994$), followed by weekly (31%, $n = 604$) and monthly (17.1%, $n = 333$) occurrences. Gameplay predominantly lasted less than 30 minutes (65.1%, $n = 1,269$) or 30 minutes to an hour (20.5%, $n = 399$) and took place as a means to combat boredom (46.1%, $n = 898$), to pass the time (11.9%, $n = 233$), or for fun (8.4%, $n = 164$); as such, gameplay largely took place in the bedroom (15.5%, $n = 303$), between classes (13.4%, $n = 262$), and on the way to and from school (12.3%, $n = 240$). These findings suggest that mobile gameplay is situational, played during periods of interruption or idle time, lasting in short intervals. That is, to kill brief periods of time (Bouça, 2012; Kallio et al., 2011; Moore & Rutter, 2004), while waiting (Information Solutions Group, 2013; Kallio et al., 2011), or as a way to fight tedium (Kirriemuir & McFarlane, 2004; Moore & Rutter, 2004). However, gameplay at restaurants (.6%, $n = 12$) or the dinner table (.3%, $n = 6$), parks (.5%, $n = 9$), parties (.1%, $n = 2$), and other social events (.3%, $n = 6$) was generally avoided, indicating that these games are not necessarily a social replacement. Moreover, titles were sought that were not boring and fun (19.8%, $n = 387$), but at the same time, free to play (24.4%, $n = 476$), denoting that cost might be a factor in this form of gameplay. Finally, improved mood and feelings of well-being (24.4%, $n = 476$) and mental attention/focus (12.2%, $n = 237$) were reported, with gameplay also serving as a distraction from pain/discomfort (9.2%, $n = 180$). This is a promising finding warranting further careful study.

Genre

Regarding genre, ACTION was the most popular (25.5%, $n = 497$), followed by ARCADE (19%, $n = 370$), SPORTS (12.5%, $n = 243$), ADVENTURE (8%, $n = 158$), PUZZLE (8%, $n = 149$), BOARD (6%, $n = 120$), SIMULATION (5.5%, $n = 107$), and STRATEGY (5%, $n = 95$). These genres, along with those depicted in Figure 2 and shown in Table 3, were chosen based on their standing in studies that examined video games in different contexts and based on their perceived popularity on the mobile platform. For simplicity, subgenres were deliberately avoided. For example, ROLE-PLAYING was included in favor of MMORPGs based on the popularity of video games ported to the mobile platform, such as the *Final Fantasy®* series and *Star Wars: Knights of the Old Republic®*. It is these eight genres that were used in the subsequent analyses of age and gender, as well as academic grading and level.

Table 3. Most popular genres among participants

Genre	Freq. (%)
Action	497 (25.5%)
Adventure	158 (8.1%)
Arcade	370 (19.0%)
Board	120 (6.2%)
Educational	23 (1.2%)
Fighting	63 (3.2%)
Puzzle	149 (7.6%)
Racing	47 (2.4%)
Role-Playing	6 (.3%)
Simulation	107 (5.5%)
Sports	243 (12.5%)
Strategy	95 (4.9%)
Trivia	36 (1.8%)

Figure 2. Action, arcade, sports, adventure, puzzle, board, simulation, and strategy were the most popular genres among the participants

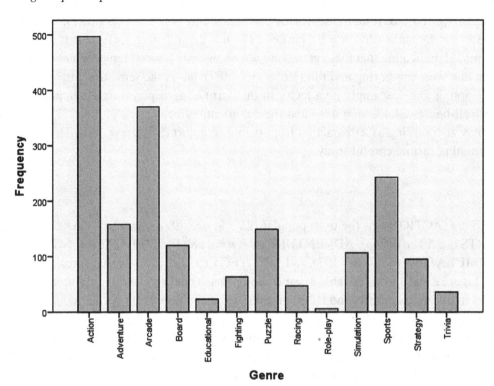

Age and Gender

A statistically significant relationship was found between genre and age, χ^2 (35, $N = 1,736$) = 190.15, $p < .01$, Cramér's V = .148. Largely, the younger age groups (15-20) favored ACTION, ADVENTURE, and ARCADE games. As depicted in Figure 3 and shown in Table 4, ACTION games were overwhelmingly popular among participants aged 15-17 (37%, $n = 126$) and 18-20 (35%, $n = 287$). Games based on the BOARD, PUZZLE, and SIMULATION genres, mostly, were preferred by the older age groups (27 and older), with PUZZLE games, for example, predominate among those 30 and older (28%, $n = 8$). STRATEGY and SPORTS were arguably the exception. Practically speaking, STRATEGY was equally favored by the younger and older age groups, only slightly favored by the younger participants (12.6%, $n = 71$; 27 and older: 12.3%, $n = 6$). SPORTS was also an almost equal favorite among all the groups, with those 27-29 (16%, $n = 9$) ranking it marginally higher, making SPORTS a greater favorite among the older participants (29.9%, $n = 13$; 15-20: 27.4%, $n = 161$).

These findings are aligned with research on gameplay in the context of genre and age. For example, in examining problematic gameplay among a national panel of 902 Dutch residents, aged 14-81, Haagsma, Pieterse, and Peters (2012) found that those older than 60 were predominantly interested in CARD and BOARD games, with the genres much more varied for the younger participants. Further, a study ordered by the Internet Advertising Bureau UK (2014) of gameplay among 4,058 British gamers revealed that more than half (56%) of the females in the sample at least 45 years old and half of those 25-44 cited TRIVIA/WORLD/PUZZLE as their favorite types of games to play; while ACTION/ADVENTURE/

SHOOTER was preferred among 16- to 24-year-old (45%) males and those 25-44 (26%). Scharkow, Festl, Vogelgesang, and Quandt (2015) reported similar findings. In examining relationships between gaming gratification and genre preferences among 4,500 German gamers, the games based on the ACTION and SHOOTER genres were found to be almost exclusively preferred by younger males, whereas PUZZLE and CARD were popular among older female players. Scharkow et al. (2015) also found that the younger gamers in their sample held a stronger preference for most of the genres examined, except for PUZZLE and SIMULATION.

Figure 3. Younger participants favored games based on the action, adventure, and arcade genres, whereas older participants favored the board, puzzle, and simulation genres

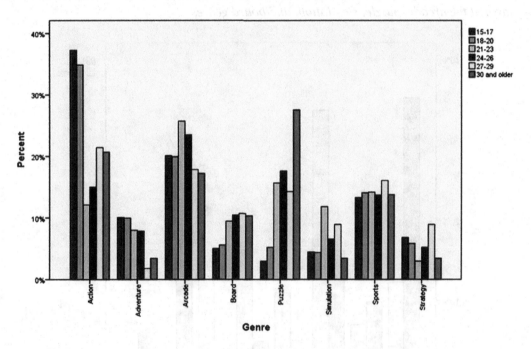

Table 4. Most popular genres by age

Genre	Age					
	15-17	18-20	21-23	24-26	27-29	30 and older
Action	126 (37.3%)	287 (34.9%)	41 (12.1%)	23 (15.0%)	12 (21.4%)	6 (20.7%)
Adventure	34 (10.1%)	82 (10.0%)	27 (8.0%)	12 (7.8%)	1 (1.8%)	1 (3.4%)
Arcade	68 (20.1%)	164 (20.0%)	87 (25.7%)	36 (23.5%)	10 (17.9%)	5 (17.2%)
Board	17 (5.0%)	46 (5.6%)	32 (9.5%)	16 (10.5%)	6 (10.7%)	3 (10.3%)
Puzzle	10 (3.0%)	43 (5.2%)	53 (15.7%)	27 (17.6%)	8 (14.3%)	8 (27.6%)
Simulation	15 (4.4%)	36 (4.4%)	40 (11.8%)	10 (6.5%)	5 (8.9%)	1 (3.4%)
Sports	45 (13.3%)	116 (14.1%)	48 (14.2%)	21 (13.7%)	9 (16.1%)	4 (13.8%)
Strategy	23 (6.8%)	48 (5.8%)	10 (3.0%)	8 (5.2%)	5 (8.9%)	1 (3.4%)

These studies also support the current findings regarding genre and gender, which showed a statistically significant relationship, χ^2 (7, N = 1,733) = 335.63, p < .01, Cramér's V = .440. As depicted in Figure 4 and shown in Table 5, ACTION (35%, n = 431; female: 12%, n = 63) and SPORTS (19%, n = 229; female: 3%, n = 14) games were overwhelmingly popular among males, with distinct differences also found with regard to ADVENTURE (10%, n = 121; female: 7%, n = 36) and STRATEGY (7%, n = 81; female: 3%, n = 14). However, ARCADE (34%, n = 172; male: 16%, n = 198), PUZZLE (17%, n = 88; male: 5%, n = 61), SIMULATION (13%, n = 67; male: 3%, n = 39), and BOARD (11%, n = 56; male: 5%, n = 63) games were favored by females.

Figure 4. Males favored games based on the action, sports, adventure, and strategy genres, whereas females favored the arcade, puzzle, simulation, and board genres

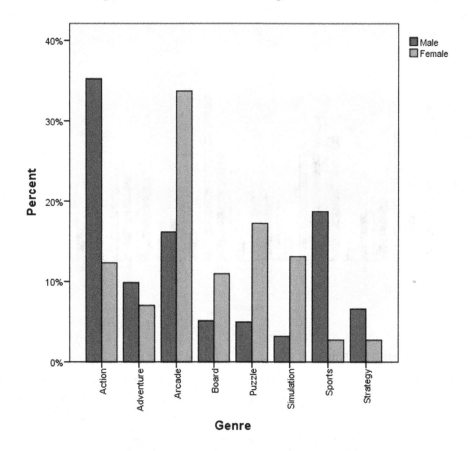

These findings were anticipated, given the literature in this area. For example, in examining the video game behavior of 1,242 U.S. 5th-, 8th-, and 11th-grade public school and undergraduate college students, Greenberg et al. (2010) found that males preferred ACTION, RACING, and SPORTS games, whereas females gravitated towards CLASSIC BOARD and PUZZLES. Similarly, Lucas and Sherry (2004), investigating video game use, frequency of play, and genre preference among 534 young adults, noted that females enjoyed what they called traditional factor games not requiring mental rotation (e.g.,

Table 5. Most popular genres by gender

Genre	Gender	
	Male	Female
Action	431 (35.2%)	63 (12.4%)
Adventure	121 (9.9%)	36 (7.1%)
Arcade	198 (16.2%)	172 (33.7%)
Board	63 (5.2%)	56 (11.0%)
Puzzle	61 (5.0%)	88 (17.3%)
Simulation	39 (3.2%)	67 (13.1%)
Sports	229 (18.7%)	14 (2.7%)
Strategy	81 (6.6%)	14 (2.7%)

PUZZLE, QUIZ/TRIVIA, CARD/DICE), and males preferred to play physical enactment and imagination factor games requiring mental rotation (e.g., FIGHTER, SHOOTER, FANTASY/ROLE-PLAYING, ACTION/ADVENTURE). Haagsma et al. (2012) revealed that the females in their sample preferred BROWSER and OFFLINE CASUAL games, with males mostly interested in OFFLINE. Phan, Jardina, and Hoyle (2012), in surveying gender differences among 341 gamers, reported that males were more interested in ACTION, FIGHTING, ROLE-PLAYING, and STRATEGY games, with females favoring EDUCATIONAL/EDUTAINMENT, MUSIC/DANCE, PUZZLE/CARD, SIMULATION, and SOCIAL games. Roseboom (2015) reported on a DeltaDNA study that surveyed nine million mobile gamers in the free-to-play space, finding that titles in the ACTION (75%; female: 25%) and STRATEGY (68%; female: 32%) genres were predominantly played by males, compared to the PUZZLE genre, which was predominantly played by females (82%; male: 18%). These genres were further decomposed in the DeltaDNA study, showing that males preferred FIRST-PERSON SHOOTER (FPS) (90%; female: 10%), ROLE-PLAYING (78%; female: 22%), BUILDER-STYLE STRATEGY (61%; female: 39%), and FANTASY SPORTS (92%; female: 8%) games, and females favored MATCHING THREE GAMES (78%; male: 22%) and HIDDEN OBJECT (89%; male: 11%). While Yee (2017) reported like findings from a Quantic Foundry motivation study that surveyed 270,000 video game players, asserting that players of MATCH 3 and FAMILY/FARM SIM (69%), and CASUAL PUZZLE (42%) games were likely to be female, compared to those who preferred TACTICAL SHOOTER (4%) and SPORTS (2%).

Academic Grading and Level

As for academics, a statistically significant relationship was found between genre and grading, χ^2 (28, $N = 1,360$) = 84.98, $p < .01$, Cramér's V = .125. Generally speaking, when distinguishing poor- from high-performing students – by using the grade of C as the cutoff – the data depicted in Figure 5 and shown in Table 6 illustrate that games based on the ACTION (C-F: 87.2%, $n = 168$; A-C: 56.3%, $n = 190$) and STRATEGY (C-F: 15.9%, $n = 30.5$; A-C: 12.5%, $n = 42.5$) genres were played by a larger percentage of poor-performing students. By comparison, ARCADE (A-C: 66.2%, $n = 201.5$; C-F: 56.7%, $n = 91.5$), PUZZLE (A-C: 27.3%, $n = 98$; C-F: 16.3%, $n = 31$), SIMULATION (A-C: 18.5%, $n = 65.5$; C-F: 11.0%, $n = 21.5$), and BOARD (A-C: 26.2%, $n = 84$; C-F: 19.1%, $n = 39$) were played by more high-performing students; finally, SPORTS (A-C: 37.0%, $n = 128$; C-F: 37.9%, $n = 74$) and ADVENTURE (A-C: 21.3%, $n = 77$; C-F: 21.0%, $n = 40$) were almost equally distributed, but marginally skewed towards the poor performers.

Figure 5. Games based on the action, strategy, sports, and adventure genres popular among poor-performing students, with arcade, puzzle, simulation, and board favored by high-performing students.

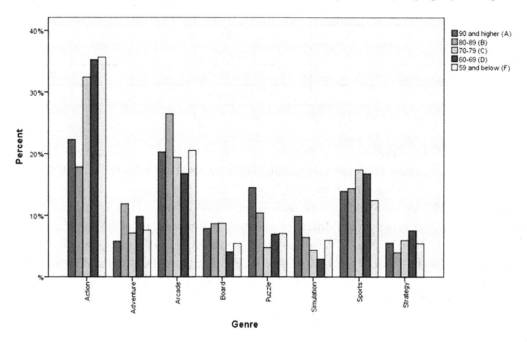

Table 6. *Most popular genres by grade*

Genre	Grades				
	90-100 (A)	80-89 (B)	70-79 (C)	60-69 (D)	59 and below (F)
Action	77 (22.3%)	72 (17.8%)	82 (32.4%)	61 (35.3%)	66 (35.7%)
Adventure	20 (5.8%)	48 (11.9%)	18 (7.1%)	17 (9.8%)	14 (7.6%)
Arcade	70 (20.3%)	107 (26.5%)	49 (19.4%)	29 (16.8%)	38 (20.5%)
Board	27 (7.8%)	35 (8.7%)	22 (8.7%)	7 (4.0%)	10 (5.4%)
Puzzle	50 (14.5%)	42 (10.4%)	12 (4.7%)	12 (6.9%)	13 (7.0%)
Simulation	34 (9.9%)	26 (6.4%)	11 (4.3%)	5 (2.9%)	11 (5.9%)
Sports	48 (13.9%)	58 (14.4%)	44 (17.4%)	29 (16.8%)	23 (12.4%)
Strategy	19 (5.5%)	16 (4.0%)	15 (5.9%)	13 (7.5%)	10 (5.4%)

These findings appear to be aligned with and related to gender. Further analysis revealed that the females (A: 40%, $n = 169$; B: 34%, $n = 145$; male: A: 19%, $n = 175$; B: 28%, $n = 258$) in the study performed better academically than the males (D: 16%, $n = 147$; F: 15.5%, $n = 144$; female: D: 6%, $n = 26$; F: 9%, $n = 39$), as depicted in Figure 6 and shown in Table 7.

Figure 6. Females performed better academically than males

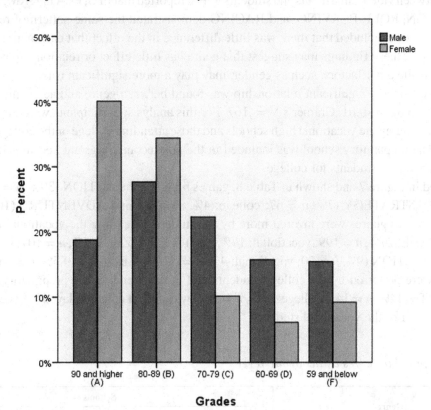

Table 7. Grades by gender

Grades	Gender	
	Male	Female
90-100 (A)	175 (18.8%)	169 (40.0%)
80-89 (B)	258 (27.7%)	145 (34.4%)
70-79 (C)	208 (22.3%)	43 (10.2%)
60-69 (D)	147 (15.8%)	26 (6.2%)
59 and below (F)	144 (15.5%)	39 (9.2%)

Regrettably, little research was found that explicitly examine correlations between genre and grading. In a study investigating the gameplay, personality, and academic performance of 319 students, Ventura, Shute, and Kim (2012) found that of the following genres: FIGHTING, ROLE-PLAYING, ACTION ADVENTURE, PUZZLE, SOCIAL MEDIA, PLATFORMER, STRATEGY, SIMULATIONS, and SHOOTER, only SOCIAL MEDIA and SHOOTER had significant negative correlations with grade point average (GPA). The authors posited that the negative relationships between GPA and SOCIAL MEDIA might be related to accessibility, in that games based on this genre are often played on mobile devices, which they proposed can have negative effects on study time. Finally, Riedel (2016), while examining the association between video game habits and students' GPA, reported that FPS, PLATFORM, STRATEGY, THIRD PERSON, ROLE-PLAYING, and RACING demonstrated the same pattern of results in GPA rank. Riedel (2016) concluded that there was little difference in the effect that each genre had on GPA. Overall, therefore, these findings may suggest that genre has little effect or relationship with academic performance, while other factors, such as gender, may play a more significant role.

Finally, a statistically significant relationship was found between genre and academic level, χ^2 (35, $N = 1,739$) = 243.82, $p < .01$, Cramér's V = .167. For this analysis, participants were divided into two groups: those attending the vocational high schools and those attending college or the college preparatory high school. The preparatory school was included in the postsecondary group because of the school's emphasis on preparing students for college.

As depicted in Figure 7 and shown in Table 8, games based on the ACTION (39%, $n = 384$; college: 15%, $n = 113$), STRATEGY (7%, $n = 67$; college: 4%, $n = 28$), and ADVENTURE (10%, $n = 100$; college: 8%, $n = 58$) genres were favored more by the students attending the vocational high schools, whereas ARCADE (27%, $n = 199$; vocational: 17%, $n = 171$), PUZZLE (14%, $n = 107$; vocational: 4%, $n = 42$), SIMULATION (9%, $n = 70$; vocational: 4%, $n = 37$), and BOARD (9.5%, $n = 71$; vocational: 5%, $n = 49$) were preferred by the college students and those attending the preparatory high school. Finally, SPORTS (14%, $n = 141$; college: 14%, $n = 102$) was almost equally played between the groups, marginally in favor of the vocational students.

Table 8. Most popular genres by academic level

Genre	Schools	
	Vocational	**College**
Action	384 (38.7%)	113 (15.1%)
Adventure	100 (10.1%)	58 (7.8%)
Arcade	171 (17.3%)	199 (26.6%)
Board	49 (4.9%)	71 (9.5%)
Puzzle	42 (4.2%)	107 (14.3%)
Simulation	37 (3.7%)	70 (9.4%)
Sports	141 (14.2%)	102 (13.6%)
Strategy	67 (6.8%)	28 (3.7%)

As with grades, these findings also appear to be aligned with gender, with ACTION, STRATEGY, ADVENTURE, and SPORTS favored by the vocational students, but also by males, and ARCADE, PUZZLE, SIMULATION, and BOARD preferred by the college and preparatory high school students, but also by females. Given these findings, it might be assumed that the vocational students were comprised mostly of males, and the college and preparatory high school mostly of females. Indeed, further analysis revealed this to be the case.

As depicted in Figure 8 and shown in Table 9, the vocational high schools were skewed in favor of males (70.5%, $n = 862$; female: 25%, $n = 126$), and the college and preparatory high school in favor of females (75%, $n = 384$; male: 29.5%, $n = 361$). This makes sense given the locale of the investigation, in that South Korean vocational high schools are typically comprised of male students. As for grades, these findings suggest that gender may play a significant role, warranting further careful study. Unfortunately, the few existing studies on the impact of genre on academic performance have sampled either high school- or college-aged students (e.g., Riedel, 2016; Ventura et al., 2012). At the time of this writing, no studies could be found on correlations between genre and secondary or postsecondary education levels, let alone vocational track institutions.

Figure 7. Games based on the action, strategy, adventure, and sports genres were favored by vocational high school students, whereas the arcade, puzzle, simulation, and board genres were preferred by the college and preparatory high school students

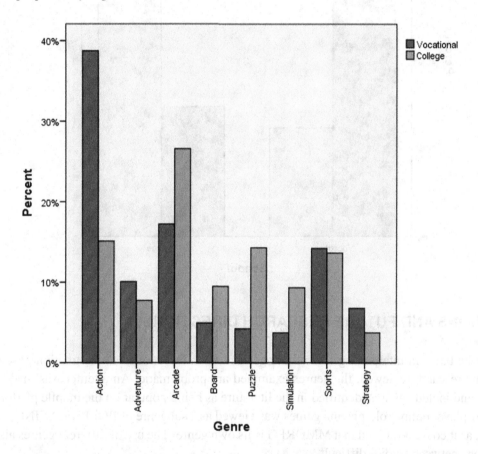

Table 9. School by gender

Type of School	Gender	
	Male	**Female**
Vocational	862 (70.5%)	126 (24.7%)
College & Prep	361 (29.5%)	384 (75.3%)

Figure 8. Vocational high school students were mostly male; college and preparatory high school students were predominantly female

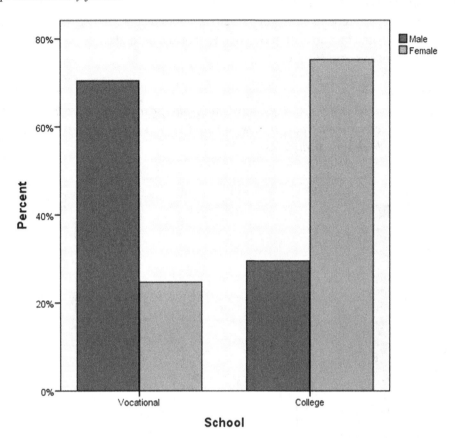

LIMITATIONS AND FUTURE RESEARCH DIRECTIONS

Care must be taken in interpreting these findings, as certain facets of this investigation pose concern. As with the research reviewed, the genres examined are problematic. An attempt was made to avoid subgenres and include genres identified in the literature as being popular on the mobile platform. Massively multiplayer online role-playing games was viewed as a subgenre of ROLE-PLAYING, but this is debatable, as it could be argued that MMORPG is its own genre. The use of different genres also makes comparisons between studies difficult.

According to Clearwater (2011), genre study is a collaborative endeavor needing continuous refinement and is abundantly more robust and diverse than generally assumed. Thus, while the findings in this investigation contribute to an understanding of genre in the context of the mobile platform, more research is needed, and realistically speaking, must be ongoing. This includes other perspectives and the use of sources outside of academia comprising extra-textual materials, such as press coverage, fan activity (e.g., blogs, wikis), and marketing materials (e.g., video game magazines) (Clearwater, 2011).

Self-reported data and social desirability are another concern, as it is conceivable that the participants responded based on what they felt were "social norms" or what they sensed others wanted to hear. The disproportionate number of males vs. females is likewise a worry. This was too expected, in that Korean vocational high schools, which made up a part of the study, are mostly comprised of male students. Nevertheless, with interest in video games supposedly growing among females, future investigations should place greater emphasis on the female gamer. Along these lines, the sample should be expanded for age, given the casual nature and broad popularity of mobile gaming, as well as findings showing that differences exist in genre choice between young and old. Furthermore, although the findings may suggest that platform does not play a significant role as much as other factors, such as gender, because of playability across mobile devices, additional study should address different types of hardware, such as tablets. Finally, South Korea, the location of this study, is seen by many as a mecca of technological innovation. Future investigations, therefore, should include other parts of the world to acquire different viewpoints on mobile game play, including those of players from cultures experiencing certain games and gaming technologies for the first time.

CONCLUSION

This chapter presented the findings of a study exploring game genre in the context of mobile gameplay, based on the argument that platform is often ignored in academic efforts to discuss genre, raising questions about the medium of gaming and the role of hardware. This is particularly important given the unique characteristics of mobile games and mounting interest in their educational value.

The findings confirmed what is generally known about mobile gameplay, that the pastime can be viewed as just that, a situational activity rather than a social replacement, often played during periods of interruption or idle time, and lasting for short intervals. Also aligned with the literature are the findings showing that age and gender are significant factors on genre preference. Specifically, older females found games categorized as PUZZLE to be popular, including titles such as *Bejeweled*® and *Candy Crush Saga*®, while younger males preferred the ACTION genre, playing titles such as *Call of Duty*® and *Grand Theft Auto*®. These preferences are independent of platform. That is, research reveals similar interests between males and females for games played on the PC or console, suggesting that other factors, such as gender, are more significant indicators of genre preferences than game platform. Platform appears to show importance in that, unlike PC- or console-based gaming, mobile games require little investment (i.e., time and/or money), have simple game mechanics (making them easy to learn), and are playable from anywhere and at any time, lending themselves well to certain genres. As to whether platform manufacturers have influenced this trend (King & Krzywinska, 2002), popularizing certain genres, is a subject requiring further study.

As for academics, the findings revealed differences in genre when examined in the context of grading and level. Further investigation, however, showed that genres favored by the poorest performing students were also those predominantly played by males, whereas the genres correlated with the highest performing students were likewise mostly female. Similar findings were found with regard to genre preferences between students attending the vocational high schools vs. college or the college preparatory high school, with the former mostly comprising male students and the latter, female. This adds more weight to the role of gender as a more influential factor on academics than game genres played on the mobile platform.

In summary, while much has been reported on video game genre, this chapter is believed to be one of few to explicitly restrict the topic to the mobile platform. Although more research is needed, platform may not be as an important consideration when studying game genre as believed, instead, other factors may be better suited for subsequent study.

REFERENCES

Aarseth, E., Smedstad, S. M., & Sunnanå, L. (2003). A multi-dimensional typology of games. In M. Copier & J. Raessens (Eds.), *Level up: Digital games research conference proceedings*. Utrecht, The Netherlands: Utrecht University.

Apperley, T. H. (2006). Genre and game studies: Toward a critical approach to video game genres. *Simulation & Gaming, 37*(1), 6–23. doi:10.1177/1046878105282278

Arsenault, D. (2009). Video game genre, evolution and innovation. *Elduamos, 3*(2), 149–176.

Bell, M., Chalmers, M., Barkhuus, L., Hall, M., Sherwood, S., & Tennent, P. Hampshire, M. A. (2006). Interweaving mobile games with everyday life. In *Proceedings of the SIGCHI Conference on Human Factors in Computing System* (pp. 417–426). Montreal, Canada: ACM Press. doi:10.1145/1124772.1124835

Bilgihan, A., Cobanoglu, C., Nusair, K., Okumus, F., & Bujisic, M. (2013). A quantitative study exploring the difference between gaming genre preferences. *The Computer Games Journal, 2*(1), 19–40. doi:10.1007/BF03392334

Bouça, M. (2012). Angry Birds, uncommitted players. In *Proceedings of DiGRA Nordic 2012 Conference: Local and global – Games in culture and society* (pp. 1–13). Tampere, Finland: Digital Games Research Association.

Cheok, A. D., Sreekumar, A., Lei, C., & Thang, L. (2006). Capture the flag: Mixed-reality social gaming with smart phones. *IEEE Pervasive Computing, 5*(2), 62–69. doi:10.1109/MPRV.2006.25

Chesham, A., Wyss, P., Müri, R. M., Mosimann, U. P., & Nef, T. (2017). What older people like to play: Genre preferences and acceptance of casual games. *JMIR Serious Games, 5*(2), e8. doi:10.2196/games.7025 PMID:28420601

Clarke, R. I., Lee, J. H., & Clark, N. (2017). Why video game genres fail: A classificatory analysis. *Games and Culture, 12*(5), 445–465. doi:10.1177/1555412015591900

Clearwater, D. A. (2011). What defines video game genre? Thinking about genre study after the great divide. *Loading, 5*(8), 29–49.

Cogoi, C., Sangiorgi, D., & Shahin, K. (2006). mGBL – Mobile game-based learning: Perspectives and usage in learning and career guidance topics. *eLearning Papers, 1*(1), 1–6.

Crawford, C. (1984). *The art of computer game design*. Berkeley, CA: Osborne/McGraw-Hill. Retrieved from http://www.digitpress.com/library/books/book_art_of_computer_game_design.pdf

DaCosta, B., & Seok, S. (2016, April). *Gamers are more digitally adept? Video games and educating students in the digital information age*. Poster presented at the 2016 annual meeting of the American Educational Research Association, Washington, DC.

DaCosta, B., & Seok, S. (2017a). Factors that explain adolescent and young adult mobile game play, part 1: A quantitative examination of the characteristics describing the casual player. In R. Zheng & M. Gardner (Eds.), *Handbook of research on serious games for educational applications* (pp. 320–339). Hershey, PA: IGI Global; doi:10.4018/978-1-5225-0513-6.ch015

DaCosta, B., & Seok, S. (2017b). Factors that explain adolescent and young adult mobile game play, part 2: A quantitative examination of the casual player in the context of age and gender. In R. Zheng & M. Gardner (Eds.), *Handbook of research on serious games for educational applications* (pp. 340–365). Hershey, PA: IGI Global; doi:10.4018/978-1-5225-0513-6.ch016

DaCosta, B., Seok, S., & Kinsell, C. (2015). Mobile games and learning. In Z. Yan (Ed.), *Encyclopedia of mobile phone behavior* (Vol. 1, pp. 46–60). Hershey, PA: IGI Global; doi:10.4018/978-1-4666-8239-9.ch004

DaCosta, B., Seok, S., & Kinsell, C. (2018). Mobile game-based learning. In M. Khosrow-Pour (Ed.), *Encyclopedia of information science and technology* (4th ed.; vol. 8, pp. 6361–6375). Hershey, PA: IGI Global. doi:10.4018/978-1-5225-2255-3.ch553

de Freitas, S., & Griffiths, M. (2008). The convergence of gaming practices with other media forms: What potential for learning? A review of the literature. *Learning, Media and Technology*, *33*(1), 11–20. doi:10.1080/17439880701868796

del Blanco, A., Marchiori, E. J., Torrente, J., Martínez-Ortiz, I., & Fernández-Manjón, B. (2013). Using e-learning standards in educational video games. *Computer Standards & Interfaces*, *36*(1), 178–187. doi:10.1016/j.csi.2013.06.002

Dobrowolski, P., Hanusz, K., Sobczyk, B., Skorko, M., & Wiatrow, A. (2015). Cognitive enhancement in video game players: The role of video game genre. *Computers in Human Behavior*, *44*(C), 59–63. doi:10.1016/j.chb.2014.11.051

Egenfeldt-Nielsen, S. (2006). Overview of research on the educational use of video games. *Digital Kompetanse*, *1*(3), 184–213.

Eichenbaum, A., Kattner, F., Bradford, D., Gentile, D. A., Choo, H., Hsueh, V., ... Green, C. S. (2015). The role of game genre and the development of Internet gaming disorder in school-aged children. *Journal of Addictive Behaviors, Therapy & Rehabilitation*, *4*(3), 1–7. doi:10.4172/2324-9005.1000141

Elliott, L., Golub, A., Ream, G., & Dunlap, E. (2012). Video game genre as a predictor of problem use. *Cyberpsychology, Behavior, and Social Networking*, *15*(3), 155–161. doi:10.1089/cyber.2011.0387 PMID:22242785

Elliott, L., Ream, G., McGinsky, E., & Dunlap, E. (2012). The contribution of game genre and other use patterns to problem video game play among adult video gamers. *International Journal of Mental Health and Addiction*, *10*(6), 948–969. doi:10.100711469-012-9391-4 PMID:23284310

Ellis, H., Heppell, S., Kirriemuir, J., Krotoski, A., & McFarlane, A. (2006). Unlimited learning. Computer and video games in the learning landscape. London, UK: ELSPA (Entertainment and Leisure Software Publishers Association).

Elverdam, C., & Aarseth, E. (2007). Game classification and game design: Construction through critical analysis. *Games and Culture*, *2*(1), 3–22. doi:10.1177/1555412006286892

Gackenbach, J., & Bown, J. (2011). Mindfulness and video game play: A preliminary inquiry. *Mindfulness*, *2*(2), 114–122. doi:10.100712671-011-0049-2

Gentile, D. A., & Gentile, J. R. (2008). Violent games as exemplary teachers. A conceptual analysis. *Journal of Youth and Adolescence*, *37*(2), 127–141. doi:10.100710964-007-9206-2

Göth, C., Häss, U.-P., & Schwabe, G. (2004). Requirements for mobile learning games shown on a mobile game prototype. In J. Attewell & C. Savill-Smith (Eds.), Mobile learning anytime everywhere – A book of papers from MLEARN 2004 (pp. 95–100). Rome, Italy: Learning and skills development agency. doi:10.5167/uzh-61359

Granic, I., Lobel, A., & Engels, R. C. M. E. (2014). The benefits of playing video games. *The American Psychologist*, *69*(1), 66–78. doi:10.1037/a0034857 PMID:24295515

Grant, L., Daanen, H., Benford, S., Hampshire, A., Drozd, A., & Greenhalgh, C. (2007). *MobiMissions: The game of missions for mobile phones. In Proceedings from the ACM SIGGRAPH 2007 Educators Program*. New York, NY: ACM Press; doi:10.1145/1282040.1282053

Greenberg, B. S., Sherry, J., Lachlan, K., Lucas, K., & Holmstrom, A. (2010). Orientations to video games among gender and age groups. *Simulation & Gaming*, *41*(2), 238–259. doi:10.1177/1046878108319930

Grimes, A., Kantroo, V., & Grinter, R. E. (2010). Let's play! Mobile health games for adults. In *Proceedings of the 12th ACM international conference on ubiquitous computing* (pp. 241–250). Copenhagen, Denmark: ACM. 10.1145/1864349.1864370

Haagsma, M. C., Pieterse, M. E., & Peters, O. (2012). The prevalence of problematic video games in the Netherlands. *Cyberpsychology, Behavior, and Social Networking*, *15*(3), 162–168. doi:10.1089/cyber.2011.0248 PMID:22313358

Huizenga, J., Admiraal, W., Akkerman, S., & ten Dam, G. (2009). Mobile game-based learning in secondary education: Engagement, motivation and learning in a mobile city game. *Journal of Computer Assisted Learning*, *25*(4), 332–344. doi:10.1111/j.1365-2729.2009.00316.x

Information Solutions Group. (2011). *PopCap games mobile phone gaming research*. Retrieved from http://www.infosolutionsgroup.com/popcapmobile2012.pdf

Information Solutions Group. (2013). *PopCap games mobile phone gaming research*. Retrieved from http://www.infosolutionsgroup.com/popcapmobile2013.pdf

Internet Advertising Bureau UK. (2014). Gaming revolution. *IAB*. Retrieved from https://iabuk.net/research/library/gaming-revolution

Jansz, J., & Tanis, M. (2007). Appeal of playing online first person shooter games. *Cyberpsychology & Behavior*, *10*(1), 133–136. doi:10.1089/cpb.2006.9981 PMID:17305460

Kafai, Y. B. (1998). Video game designs by girls and boys: Variability and consistency of gender differences. In H. Jenkins & J. Cassell (Eds.), *From Barbie to Mortal Kombat* (pp. 90–117). Cambridge, MA: MIT Press.

Kallio, K. P., Mäyrä, F., & Kaipainen, K. (2011). At least nine ways to play: Approaching gamer mentalities. *Games and Culture, 6*(4), 327–353. doi:10.1177/1555412010391089

King, D. L., Delfabbro, P., & Griffiths, M. D. (2009). Video game structural characteristics: A new psychological taxonomy. *International Journal of Mental Health and Addiction, 8*(1), 90–106. doi:10.100711469-009-9206-4

King, G., & Krzywinska, T. (2002). Introduction: Cinema/videogames/interfaces. In G. King & T. Krzywinska (Eds.), *ScreenPlay: Cinema/videogames/interfaces* (pp. 1–32). London, UK: Wallflower Press.

Kirriemuir, J. (2002). *The relevance of games and gaming consoles to the higher and further education learning experience.* Techwatch Report TSW 02.01. doi:10.13140/RG.2.2.34765.03044

Kirriemuir, J., & McFarlane, A. (2004). Report 8: Literature review in gaming and learning. *FutureLab.* Retrieved from http://telearn.archives-ouvertes.fr/docs/00/19/04/53/PDF/kirriemuir-j-2004-r8.pdf

Lee, J. H., Karlova, N., Clarke, R. I., Thornton, K., & Perti, A. (2014). Facet analysis of video game genres. In *iConference 2014 Proceedings* (pp. 125–139). doi:10.9776/14057

Lee, M.-S., Ko, Y.-H., Song, H.-S., Kwon, K.-H., Lee, H.-S., Nam, M., & Jung, I.-K. (2007). Characteristics of Internet use in relation to game genre in Korean adolescents. *Cyberpsychology & Behavior, 10*(2), 278–285. doi:10.1089/cpb.2006.9958 PMID:17474846

Licoppe, C., & Inada, Y. (2006). Emergent uses of a multiplayer location-aware mobile game: The interactional consequences of mediated encounters. *Mobilities, 1*(1), 39–61. doi:10.1080/17450100500489221

Lucas, K., & Sherry, J. L. (2004). Sex differences in video game play: A communication-based explanation. *Communication Research, 31*(5), 499–523. doi:10.1177/0093650204267930

Matyas, S., Matyas, C., Schlieder, C., Kiefer, P., Mitarai, H., & Kamata, M. (2008). Designing location-based mobile games with a purpose – Collecting geospatial data with CityExplorer. In *Proceedings of the 2008 International Conference on Advances in Computer Entertainment Technology* (pp. 244–247). Yokohama, Japan: ACME Press. doi:10.1145/1501750.1501806

Mitchell, A., & Savill-Smith, C. (2004). The use of computer and video games for learning: A review of the literature. London, UK: Ultralab: Learning Skills and Development Agency.

Montola, M. (2011). A ludological view on the pervasive mixed-reality game research paradigm. *Personal and Ubiquitous Computing, 15*(1), 3–12. doi:10.100700779-010-0307-7

Moore, K., & Rutter, J. (2004). Understanding consumers' understanding of mobile entertainment. In K. Moore & J. Rutter (Eds.), Proceedings of 2004 mobile entertainment: User-centered perspectives (pp. 49–65). Manchester, UK: Museum of Science & Industry in Manchester.

Naismith, L., Lonsdale, P., Vavoula, G., & Sharples, M. (2004). Report 11: Literature review in mobile technologies and learning. *FutureLab*. Retrieved from https://hal.archives-ouvertes.fr/hal-00190143/document

Owen, M., Frutos, M. B., Zistler, E., Lohr, M., Stratakis, M., Miliarakis, A., ... Spikol, D. (2008). *The COLLAGE project: Guide of good practice for mobile and game-based learning*. Retrieved from http://www.ea.gr/ea/myfiles/File/publications/books/Collage_GGP2008.pdf

Paraskeva, F., Mysirlaki, S., & Papagianni, A. (2010). Multiplayer online games as educational tools: Facing new challenges in learning. *Computers & Education*, *54*(2), 498–505. doi:10.1016/j.compedu.2009.09.001

Peever, N., Johnson, D., & Gardner, J. (2012). Personality & video game genre preferences. In *Proceedings of the 8th Australasian Conference on Interactive Entertainment: Playing the System* (pp. 1–20). Auckland, New Zealand: ACM.

Perrotta, C., Featherstone, G., Aston, H., & Houghton, E. (2013). *Game-based learning: Latest evidence and future directions (NFER Research Programme: Innovation in Education)*. Slough, UK: NFER.

Phan, M. H., Jardina, J. R., & Hoyle, W. S. (2012). Video games: Males prefer violence while females prefer social. *Software Usability Research Laboratory*. Retrieved from http://usabilitynews.org/video-games-males-prefer-violence-while-females-prefer-social/

Riedel, J. K. (2016). *Video game usage and academic success* (Unpublished master's thesis). Texas State University, San Marcos, TX.

Roschelle, J., & Pea, R. (2002). A walk on the WILD side: How wireless handhelds may change computer-supported collaborative learning. *International Journal of Cognitive Technology*, *1*(1), 145–168. doi:10.1075/ijct.1.1.09ros

Roseboom, I. (2015). Gender split in F2P games: Who's playing what. *DeltaDNA*. Retrieved from https://deltadna.com/blog/gender-split-in-f2p-games/

Scharkow, M., Festl, R., Vogelgesang, J., & Quandt, T. (2015). Beyond the "core-gamer": Genre preferences and gratifications in computer games. *Computers in Human Behavior*, *44*(C), 293–298. doi:10.1016/j.chb.2014.11.020

Schmitz, B. (2014). *Mobile games for learning: A pattern-based approach* (Unpublished master's thesis). Open Universiteit in the Netherlands at Welten Institute – Research Centre for Learning, Teaching and Technology (Dutch Research School for Information and Knowledge Systems Dissertation Series No. 2014-45).

Sedano, C. I., Laine, T. H., Vinni, M., & Sutinen, E. (2007). Where is the answer? – The importance of curiosity in pervasive mobile games. In *Proceedings of the 2007 Conference on Future Play* (pp. 46–53). Toronto, Canada: Academic Press. 10.1145/1328202.1328211

Seok, S., & DaCosta, B. (2012). The world's most intense online gaming culture: Addiction and high-engagement prevalence rates among South Korean adolescents and young adults. *Computers in Human Behavior*, *28*(6), 2143–2151. doi:10.1016/j.chb.2012.06.019

Seok, S., & DaCosta, B. (2015). Predicting video game behavior: An investigation of the relationship between personality and mobile game play. *Games and Culture*, *10*(5), 481–501. doi:10.1177/1555412014565640

Ventura, M., Shute, V., & Kim, Y. J. (2012). Video gameplay, personality, and academic performance. *Computers & Education*, *58*(4), 1260–1266. doi:10.1016/j.compedu.2011.11.022

Whalen, Z. (2004). Game/genre: A critique of generic formulas in video games in the context of "the real." *Works and Days, 22*(1&2), 289–303.

Wolf, M. J. P. (2000). Genre and the video game. In M. J. P. Wolf (Ed.), *The medium of the video game* (pp. 113–134). Austin, TX: University of Texas Press.

Yee, N. (2017). Beyond 50/50: Breaking down the percentage of female gamers by genre. *Quantic Foundry*. Retrieved from http://quanticfoundry.com/2017/01/19/female-gamers-by-genre/

ADDITIONAL READING

Apperley, T. H. (2006). Genre and game studies: Toward a critical approach to video game genres. *Simulation & Gaming*, *37*(1), 6–23. doi:10.1177/1046878105282278

Barlett, C. P., Anderson, C. A., & Swing, E. L. (2009). Video game effects – Confirmed, suspected, and speculative: A review of the evidence. *Simulation & Gaming*, *40*(3), 377–403. doi:10.1177/1046878108327539

Clarke, R. I., Lee, J. H., & Clark, N. (2017). Why video game genres fail: A classificatory analysis. *Games and Culture*, *12*(5), 445–465. doi:10.1177/1555412015591900

Clearwater, D. A. (2011). What defines video game genre? Thinking about genre study after the great divide. *Loading*, *5*(8), 29–49.

Crawford, C. (1984). *The art of computer game design*. Berkeley, CA: Osborne/McGraw-Hill; Retrieved from http://www.digitpress.com/library/books/book_art_of_computer_game_design.pdf

DaCosta, B., & Seok, S. (2017a). Factors that explain adolescent and young adult mobile game play, part 1: A quantitative examination of the characteristics describing the casual player. In R. Zheng & M. Gardner (Eds.), *Handbook of research on serious games for educational applications* (pp. 320–339). Hershey, PA: IGI Global; doi:10.4018/978-1-5225-0513-6.ch015

DaCosta, B., & Seok, S. (2017b). Factors that explain adolescent and young adult mobile game play, part 2: A quantitative examination of the casual player in the context of age and gender. In R. Zheng & M. Gardner (Eds.), *Handbook of research on serious games for educational applications* (pp. 340–365). Hershey, PA: IGI Global; doi:10.4018/978-1-5225-0513-6.ch016

DaCosta, B., Seok, S., & Kinsell, C. (2015). Mobile games and learning. In Z. Yan (Ed.), *Encyclopedia of mobile phone behavior* (Vol. 1, pp. 46–60). Hershey, PA: IGI Global; doi:10.4018/978-1-4666-8239-9.ch004

DaCosta, B., Seok, S., & Kinsell, C. (2018). Mobile game-based learning. In M. Khosrow-Pour (Ed.), *Encyclopedia of information science and technology* (4th ed., Vol. VIII, pp. 6361–6375). Hershey, PA: IGI Global; doi:10.4018/978-1-5225-2255-3.ch553

Elverdam, C., & Aarseth, E. (2007). Game classification and game design: Construction through critical analysis. *Games and Culture*, 2(1), 3–22. doi:10.1177/1555412006286892

King, G., & Krzywinska, T. (2002). Introduction: Cinema/videogames/interfaces. In G. King & T. Krzywinska (Eds.), *ScreenPlay: Cinema/videogames/interfaces* (pp. 1–32). London, UK: Wallflower Press.

Whalen, Z. (2004). Game/genre: A critique of generic formulas in video games in the context of "the real". *Works and Days 43/44, 22*(1&2), 289–303.

Wolf, M. J. P. (2000). Genre and the video game. In M. J. P. Wolf (Ed.), *The medium of the video game* (pp. 113–134). Austin, TX: University of Texas Press.

KEY TERMS AND DEFINITIONS

Video Game Genre: A way to classify video games based on elements such as perspective, gameplay, interaction, and objective.

This research was previously published in the Handbook of Research on Immersive Digital Games in Educational Environments; pages 201-231, copyright year 2019 by Information Science Reference (an imprint of IGI Global).

Chapter 51
Detection of Hands for Hand-Controlled Skyfall Game in Real Time Using CNN

Neha B.
Anna University, Chennai, India

Naveen V.
Anna University, Chennai, India

Angelin Gladston
Anna University, Chennai, India

ABSTRACT

With human-computer interaction technology evolving, direct use of the hand as an input device is of wide attraction. Recently, object detection methods using CNN models have significantly improved the accuracy of hand detection. This paper focuses on creating a hand-controlled web-based skyfall game by building a real time hand detection using CNN-based technique. A CNN network, which uses a MobileNet as the feature extractor along with the single shot detector framework, is used to achieve a robust and fast detection of hand location and tracking. Along with detection and tracking of hand, skyfall game has been designed to play using hand in real time with tensor flow framework. This way of designing the game where hand is used as input to control the paddle of skyfall game improved the player interaction and interest towards playing the game. This model of CNN network used egohands dataset for detecting and tracking the hands in real time and produced an average accuracy of 0.9 for open hands and 0.6 for closed hands which in turn improved player and game interactions.

DOI: 10.4018/978-1-6684-7589-8.ch051

INTRODUCTION

Hand detection is an essential step to support many tasks including human computer interaction (HCI) applications. However, the ability to detect, localize and track the hands is crucial in many applications. While egocentric video captures a huge variety of objects, activities, and situations, one specific object is omnipresent in nearly every frame: the hands. Human's hands is used as a main channel of interaction with the physical world, for manipulating objects, sensing the environment, and expressing ourselves to other people. There are several existing approaches to tracking hands in the computer vision domain. Incidentally, many of these approaches are rule based extracting background based on texture and boundary features, distinguishing between hands and background using color histograms and HOG classifiers, making them not very robust. With sufficiently large datasets, neural networks provide opportunity to train models that perform well and address challenges of existing object tracking/detection algorithms — varied/poor lighting, diverse viewpoints and even occlusion. The main drawbacks is that they can be complex, are relatively slow compared to tracking-only algorithms.

In this work, tensorflow framework is used to build the model of hand detection and tracking and puts forward a convolution network model based on tensorflow framework. A vision based hand recognition approach using convolutional neural networks on raw video data has been developed. Furthermore, this entire area of work has been made more approachable by deep learning frameworks such as the tensorflow object detection API that simplify the process of training a model for custom object detection. More importantly, the advent of fast neural network models like ssd, faster r-cnn, rfcn etc make neural networks an attractive candidate for real-time detection and tracking applications.

Using parts of the human body as input for the gaming system has its own advantages. Because the user is always available and the user does not require to carry any secondary device. Results from a real time object detection model could be mapped to the controls of a game. Importantly, appropriating the use of various parts of the human body for gesture based interaction in multiple game environments has been shown to improve user experience and overall engagement (Birk, 2013). Though the idea of using body part as a source providing input is not entirely new, existing approaches which control computer vision, wearables as well as sensors sometimes suffer from current accuracy related challenges. Further, they are not always portable and can impose integrate related issues with respect to other software. Advances in light-weight deep neural networks, specifically models for object detection (Huang, 2017). Enormous works has been carried out, especially on key point extraction (Cao, 2017) in addressing these issues and furthering the goal of using the available body part as input. These models allow us to track the human body with good accuracy using 2D images and with the benefit of easy integration with a range of applications and devices namely desktop, camera, web, mobile as well as interactive systems.

LITERATURE REVIEW

Whether they are made to entertain you, or to educate you, good video games engage you (Birk, 2013). It has been understood that engagement in games can be measured using player experience (PX). Traditionally, PX evaluation has focused on the enjoyment of the game, or the motivation of players; these factors no doubt contribute to engagement, but decisions regarding play environment, namely the choice of game controller affect the player more deeply than that.

Currently, CNNs (Huang, 2017) provide state-of-the-art results for not only image based tasks such as object detection, image segmentation and classification, but also for video based tasks such as activity recognition and action localization as well as gesture recognition. There have been various approaches using CNNs such as fast R-CNN, CNN, 2D CNN, 3D CNN (Huang, 2017) to extract spatio-temporal information from video data. Due to the success of 2D CNNs in static images, video analysis based approaches initially applied 2D CNNs. Video frames are treated as multi-channel inputs to 2D CNNs. A convolutional long short-term memory (LSTM) architecture is proposed in one of the researches. Although 2D CNNs perform pretty well on video analysis tasks (Huang, 2017), they are limited to model temporal information and motion patterns. Therefore 3D CNNs have been proposed which use 3D convolutions and 3D pooling to capture discriminative features along both spatial and temporal dimensions. Different from 2D CNNs, 3D CNNs take a sequence of video frames as inputs. The real-time systems for hand gesture recognition requires to apply detection and classification simultaneously on continuous stream of video.

There are several works addressing detection and classification separately such as applying histogram of oriented gradient (HOG) algorithm together with an SVM classifier, special radar system to detect and segment gestures etc., In some papers, they studied the use of 3D (Cao, 2017) hand poses to recognize first-person dynamic hand actions interacting with 3D objects. Other techniques like data level fusion strategy such as Motion Fused Frames (MFFs), HGR-Net, Key Frames Extraction and Feature Fusion and Long Short-Term Attention for Egocentric Action Recognition are also done.

(Bambach, 2015) CNN-based classification with fast candidate generation based on sampling from a joint model of hand appearance and geometry is used to detect and distinguish hands in first person video. A CNN-based technique for detecting, identifying, and segmenting hands in egocentric videos of multiple people interacting with each other is used. Methods to locate and distinguish between hands in egocentric video using strong appearance models with convolutional neural networks, and introduce a simple candidate region generation approach that outperforms existing techniques at a fraction of the computational cost is done. High-quality bounding boxes can be used to create accurate pixel wise hand regions. (Cao, 2017) Key point extraction method is used with light weight deep neural networks (DNNs) for image detection and pose estimation.

(Borghi, 2018) Frame-by-frame algorithm is used to detect the presence of hands on the steering wheel in real time, in four steps namely image preprocessing, steering wheel homography, steering wheel unrolling and hand detection . Typical points of view is used for detecting hands and tracking hands on moving the steering wheel. Leap motion sensor is used to track the drivers hand and it is captured using a camera. (Li, 2018) A human-computer interaction (HCI) system for entertainment or education via a depth-sensing camera is proposed. The whole system is comprised of three modules: hand detection, hand tracking, and gesture recognition. In this system, specifically, hand detection is based entirely on computer vision and do not use any markers. The Kalman filter and depth data from the Kinect to predict the hand position making the tracking smooth and robust. And the apparent gestural features has been extracted to recognize gestures, which are adaptable and quick.

(Yang, 2018) Hand detection is an essential step to support many tasks including HCI applications. However, detecting various hands robustly under conditions of cluttered backgrounds, motion blur or changing light is still a challenging problem. Recently, object detection methods using CNN models have significantly improved the accuracy of hand detection yet at a high computational expense. (Yang, 2018) A light CNN network, which uses a modified MobileNet (Howard, 2017) as the feature extractor in company with the SSD (Liu, 2016) framework to achieve a robust and fast detection of hand location and orientation. The network generates a set of feature maps of various resolutions to detect hands of different sizes. (Kopuklu, 2019) Hierarchical architecture for the task of real-time hand gesture detection and classification that allows us to integrate offline working models. An offline-trained deep 3D CNN for gesture classification and a light weight, shallow 3D CNN for gesture detection (detector) is also employed.

Compared to the works discussed the work in this paper deviates in the following ways: In this work, a CNN network using Tensorflow detection API is used to figure out the hand location and track. On the basis of SSD framework and MobileNet wrapped under hand trackjs using tensorflow js web model, this system manages to detect and track hands of different sizes. To further introduce real time application that benefits hand detection, skyfall game with hand as game controller input is designed. A more accurate and efficient use of hands as game controller is achieved. This way of designing the game where hand is used as input to control the paddle of skyfall game improved the player interaction and interest towards playing the game. Further design details are given in next section.

EXPERIMENTAL DESIGN

This section presents the overall system design of hand controlled skyfall game in real time using CNN. Design description and details of each module are given in further sections. Figure 1 describes the step by step architecture diagram of hand controlled skyfall game in real time using CNN.

Figure 1. Hand controlled web based skyfall game

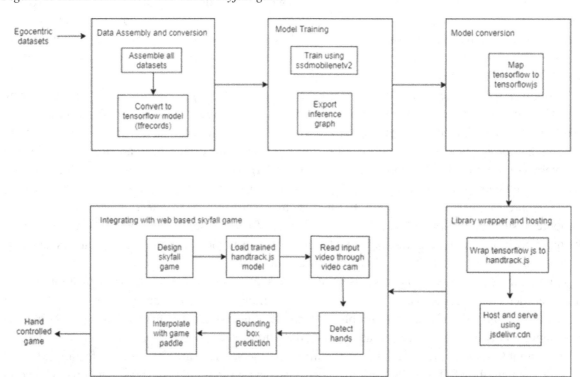

Single shot detector (SSD) is used in hand detection mechanism using CNN. Similarly the Mobilenet architecture is used as a feature extractor in detecting the hands in real time. In data assembly and conversion module, ego hands dataset has been used for hand tracking model. Initial work needs is done to the Egohands dataset to transform it into the format, tfrecord which Tensorflow needs to train a model, thereby converting data to tensorflow model. Convert dataset + csv files to tfrecords. Here, the model is trained so as to detect hands using the Tensorflow Object Detection API. For training the hand detection model, a Single Shot MultiBox Detector is used together with the Mobilenet architecture. Tensorflow's model the `ssd_mobilenet_v1_coco` is used. Once training is completed, results from the trained model was then exported as a saved model.

Followed by model conversion, the saved hand detection model trained in Tensorflow python is converted into the Tensorflow.js webmodel format so that it can be further loaded in the browser using the Tensorflow.js conversion tool. This is carried out for mapping operations in Tensorflow python to their equivalent implementation in Tensorflow.js. Then this is wrapped into handtrack.js and is used in website using script tag. Next module is to integrate web based skyfall game with the trained model so that player could play using his/her hand. This involves following steps such as designing the skyfall game, loading the handtrack.js model, reading input image through video cam, detecting hands and visualizing bounding boxes, and interpolating with the game paddle. All this is done with the handtrack. js with underneath tensorflow.js library.

In data assembly, Ego hands dataset has been used for hand tracking model. Hands in the image is processed from egocentric view. Some initial work needs to be done to the Egohands dataset to transform it into the format, tfrecord which tensorflow needs to train a model converting data to tensorflow model. Convert dataset + csv files to tfrecords. The Ego hands dataset provide a polygon, the white dots around each hand. We need to generate bounding boxes from the polygons, and generate tfrecords to train a tensorflow model.

Once the model is trained to detect hands using the Tensorflow Object Detection API further with neural networks, it is possible to use the process called transfer learning to shorten the amount of time needed to train the entire model. Tensorflow's model the `ssd_mobilenet_v1_coco` model has been used. Once training is completed, the trained inference graph `frozen_inference_graph.pb` is then exported and saved in the `hand_inference_graph` folder. Results from the trained model was then exported as a saved model.

The saved model trained in Tensorflow python is converted into the Tensorflow.js web model format that can be loaded in the browser using the Tensorflow.js conversion tool. This process is mainly around mapping operations in Tensorflow python to their equivalent implementation in Tensorflow.js. A post processing step is striped to achieve better performance. In library wrapper and hosting, the library was modeled after the tensorflow.js. It consists of a main class with methods to load the model, detect hands in an image, and the set of other helpful functions. The source file is then bundled using rollup.js, and published with the web model files. This is wrapped into handtrack.js and is used in website using script tag. As given in figure 2, the handtrack.js model is loaded in website (pong.html).

Integrating With Web Based Skyfall Game

In the process of detecting hands and using it as a game controller in real time website, the general steps are as follows:

- Design the skyfall game using HTML, CSS and javascript.
- Load the frozen_inference_graph.pb trained on the hands dataset as well as the corresponding label map.
- Read in input image.
- Detect hands.
- Visualize detected bounding detection_boxes is done by the draw_box_on_image method.
- Map the detected hands into website to control the game paddle.

EXPERIMENTAL RESULTS

Ego hands dataset is transformed into the format (tfrecord) which Tensorflow needs to train a model converting data to tensorflow model. tfrecords is obtained by combining dataset + csv files. SkyFall is a simple web based single player game. Mouse or hand can be used to control the paddle. The play mechanism of SkyFall is quite simple to follow. There are three types of balls, which fall from the top of the screen in a random order. The three types are white balls, green balls and red balls. The white balls are worth 10 points, green balls are worth 10 points and red balls are worth -10 points. Players earn points by moving a paddle to catch the good balls namely white and green balls and avoid bad balls that are red balls. On loading the game in localhost, handtrack.js model is loaded and game starts. Toggle the control to change from mouse control to hand control and vice versa. Video capturing starts through web camera which is displayed in right corner. On capturing input as frames per second basis, hand is detected and bounding box is generated. Based on the bounding box detection, paddle position is determined and controlled. Paddle position speed is controlled. On left corner, score is being updated based on capturing balls. To stop the game, stop button can be used. As mentioned, underneath, Handtrack.js uses the Tensorflow.js library.

Loading the graph, Reading input image, detecting hands and visualizing bounding boxes is done using handtrack.js with underneath tensorflow js library. In order to change the controller of the game to individual's hands, the mouse controls are replaced with a system that maps the movement of the players hand to the game paddle position. Various steps are used to use hand as game controller in website. Handtrack.js is used to use hand as game controller by including the library URL in a script tag.

<script src="https://cdn.jsdelivr.net/npm/handtrackjs/dist/handtrack.min.js"> </script

Once the above script tag has been added to html page, handtrack.js can be used the handTrack variable. Loading the model: handTrack.load () accepts optional model parameters that allow you control the performance of the model. This method loads a pre trained hand detection model in the web model format also hosted via jsdelivr. As in figure 2, on loading website, handtrack.js model gets loaded.

On toggling the video control, camera feed starts capturing the movement in which hand is detected and tracked thereby controlling the game. In figure 3, Image displays the updation of score points. Sound toggle button can be used. Now tracking shows that the real time video input is being tracked. Toggle video control button can be pressed to go back to mouse control

Figure 2. Loading model in website

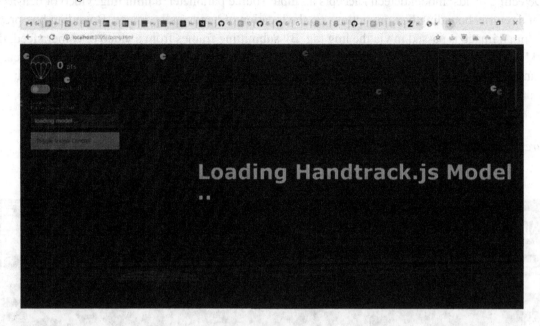

Figure 3. Controls in game

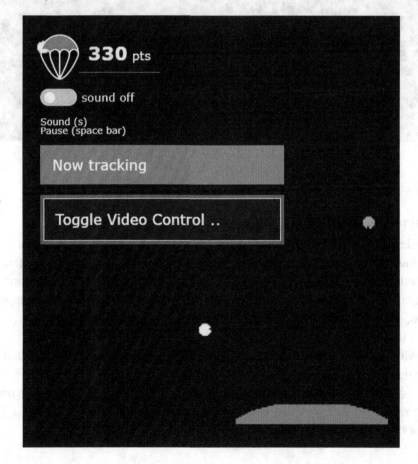

Detecting hands: model.detect() accepts an input source parameter, a html img, video or canvas object and returns bounding box predictions on the location of hands in the image. Bounding box predictions for an image is passed in via the img tag. By submitting frames from a video or camera feed, then "track" hands in each frame. Model.detect takes an input image element (can be an img, video, canvas tag) and returns an array of bounding boxes with class name and confidence level. model.detect(img). then(predictions => { });

Figure 4. Real time capturing of video, detecting hands and controlling the paddle

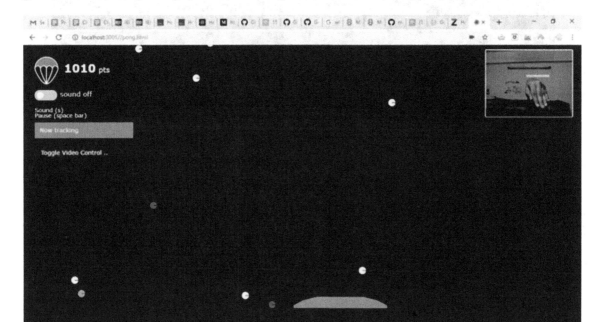

Following methods are used in this hand controlled skyfall game system.

- model.getFPS(): get FPS calculated as number of detections per second.
- model.renderPredictions(predictions, canvas, context, mediasource): draw bounding box (and the input mediasource image) on the specified canvas; predictions are an array of results from the detect() method; canvas is a reference to a html canvas object where the predictions should be rendered, context is the canvas 2D context object, mediasource a reference to the input frame either img, video, or canvas are used in the prediction.
- model.getModelParameters(): returns model parameters.
- model.setModelParameters(modelParams): updates model parameters with modelParams
- dispose(): delete model instance
- startVideo(video): start webcam video stream on given video element. Returns a promise that can be used to validate if user provided video permission.
- stopVideo(video): stop video stream.

After detecting the hands, it is interpolated with game paddle using bounding box coordinates and video width

midval = predictions[0].bbox[0] + (predictions[0].bbox[2] / 2

gamex = document.body.clientWidth * (midval / video.width)

Acceleration is calculated as 0.05 * (window width/10) which is followed by converting the hand position relative to the game video width and setting up the linear velocity for the movement of paddle. Acceleration factor increases the paddle movement speed. As shown in figure 4, top right corner which video capturing captures hand movement. Bounding box is generated and paddle is controlled with respect to the hand position.

Thus the entire hand controlled skyfall game system is implemented in the way as explained above. Hand controlled web based skyfall game has been developed and experimentally evaluated by testing the hand controlled web based skyfall game using web camera in windows i5 7th generation system. The hand detection result has been studied using different hand postures and calculating the accuracy and movement of paddle. The hand detection observed and the discussion on the results obtained are given in the next section.

RESULT ANALYSIS

This section discusses on the experiments carried out and analyzes the performance of the developed hand detection skyfall game system. It has been observed that using hand as input for controlling the game improves the players experience as well as their interest. Hand detection using CNN network produces good results. Prediction results obtained has bounding box coordinates with width and height, class to specify the hands, accuracy score on detecting hand and correlating it with paddle position.

For the experimental evaluation of the game system built, the evaluation parameters namely, accuracy and linear velocity are used. The experiments are conducted and the various values obtained are tabulated. Table 1 shows the accuracy and linear velocity values obtained on detecting and tracking the hand in various positions in controlling the game. Bbox Array(4) has 4 values [x, y, width, height] of bounding box with respect to display. Linear velocity determines the velocity of paddle based on acceleration and position of hand. Accuracy and linear velocity values obtained with respect to various hand positions are observed and the various values are plotted as shown in Figure 5. 98% accuracy is obtained for double palm, palm 1 as well as fist downward. Further 97% accuracy is obtained for cross hand 2.

As shown in Figure 5, it has been observed that system performs well while playing using the downward fist as input which helps us infer that using downward fist as input for controlling the paddle. On an average, this hand detection skyfall game system performs well at all positions of hands. In Figure 5, the accuracy values which determine the performance of the hand detecting system are plotted. This hand detection skyfall game system has achieved the maximum accuracy of 0.982 and a minimum of 0.62. The average accuracy of 0.9 in most of the hand positions is achieved which brings out the strength of the hand detection skyfall game system designed.

Table 1. Various positions of hands with its bounding box position, accuracy and linear velocity

Hand position	Bounding box position	Accuracy	Linear velocity
Palm -1	bbox: Array(4) 0: 366.1618 1: 144.9954 2: 108.6334 3: 242.6223	0.9797	2.5153
Palm - 2	bbox: Array(4) 0: 336.1729 1: 136.1303 2: 95.0379 3: 158.7656	0.95247	4.9555
Fist upward	bbox: Array(4) 0: 369.3460 1: 170.7266 2: 74.1484 3: 142.1547	0.7628	5.1298

In this work, multiplayers could be added so that any number of players could play the game without any inconvenience which makes skyfall game more interactive. While showing a higher detection accuracy, this detector is sometimes fooled by faces or objects of hand-like shapes or colors. Further, it has been found that each camera and lighting condition needed different settings for the model parameters to get good detection. More importantly, this can be improved with additional data and adding more explicit restrictions for hand regions. In future, this work can be extended with additional vocabulary mainly more than one state fist and an open hand. Such can be addressed for better predictions and better control of the game with further optimizations.

Figure 5. Accuracy and linear velocity vs hand position

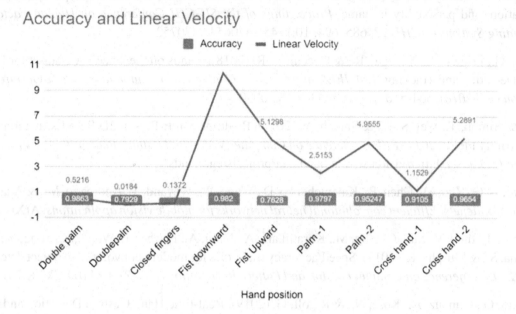

CONCLUSION

In this paper, a CNN network using Tensorflow detection API is used to figure out the hand location and track. On the basis of SSD framework and MobileNet wrapped under hand trackjs using tensorflow js web model, this system manages to detect and track hands of different sizes. To further introduce real time application that benefits hand detection, skyfall game with hand as game controller input is designed. A more accurate and efficient use of hands as game controller is achieved. This way of designing the game where hand is used as input to control the paddle of skyfall game improved the player interaction and interest towards playing the game. In this paper, multiplayers could be added so that any number of players could play the game without any inconvenience which makes skyfall game more interactive. While showing a higher detection accuracy, this detector is sometimes fooled by faces or objects of hand-like shapes or colors. It has been found that each camera and lighting condition needed different settings for the model parameters to get good detection. More importantly, this can be improved with additional data and adding more explicit restrictions for hand regions. In future, additional vocabulary mainly more than one state fist and an open hand can be addressed for better predictions and better control of the game with further optimizations.

REFERENCES

Bambach, S., Lee, S., Crandall, D. J., & Yu, C. (2015). Lending A Hand: Detecting Hands and Recognizing Activities in Complex Egocentric Interactions. ICCV, 1949–1957.

Birk, M., & Mandryk, R. L. (2013). Control your game-self: effects of controller type on enjoyment, motivation, and personality in game. *Proceedings of the SIGCHI Conference on Human Factors in Computing Systems — CHI '13*, 685–694. 10.1145/2470654.2470752

Borghi, G., Frigieri, E., Vezzani, R., & Cucchiara, R. (2018). Hands on the wheel: A Dataset for Driver Hand Detection and Tracking. *13th IEEE International Conference on Automatic Face & Gesture Recognition (FG 2018)*, 564-570. 10.1109/FG.2018.00090

Cao, Z., Simon, T., Wei, S.-E., & Sheikh, Y. (2017). Realtime Multi-Person 2D Pose Estimation using Part Affinity Fields. *2017 IEEE Conference on Computer Vision and Pattern Recognition (CVPR) 2016 Egohands Dataset.* http://vision.soic.indiana.edu/projects/egohands/

Howard, A. G., Zhu, M., Chen, B., Kalenichenko, D., Wang, W., Weyand, T., Andreetto, M., & Adam, H. (2017). *Mobilenets: Efficient convolutional neural networks for mobile vision applications.* ArXiv 2017.

Huang, J., Rathod, V., Sun, C., Zhu, M., Korattikara, A., Fathi, A., Fischer, I., Wojna, Z., Song, Y., Guadarrama, S., & Murphy, K. (2017). Speed/accuracy trade-offs for modern convolutional object detectors. *2017 IEEE Conference on Computer Vision and Pattern Recognition (CVPR).* 10.1109/CVPR.2017.351

Kopuklu, O., Gunduz, A., Kose, N., & Rigoll, G. (2019). Real-time Hand Gesture Detection and Classification Using Convolutional Neural Networks. *14th IEEE International Conference on Automatic Face & Gesture Recognition (FG 2019)*, 1-8. 10.1109/FG.2019.8756576

Li, K., Cheng, J., Zhang, Q., & Liu, J. (2018). Hand Gesture Tracking and Recognition based Human-Computer Interaction System and Its Applications. *IEEE International Conference on Information and Automation (ICIA)*, 667-672. 10.1109/ICInfA.2018.8812508

Liu, W., Anguelov, D., Erhan, D., Szegedy, C., Reed, S., Fu, C. Y., & Berg, A. C. (2016). SSD: Single shot multibox detector. In *European conference on computer vision* (*Vol. 9905*). Springer.

Yang, L. (2018). A Light CNN based Method for Hand Detection and Orientation Estimation. *24th International Conference on Pattern Recognition (ICPR)*, 2050-2055. 10.1109/ICPR.2018.8545493

This research was previously published in the International Journal of Interactive Communication Systems and Technologies (IJICST), 10(2); pages 15-25, copyright year 2020 by IGI Publishing (an imprint of IGI Global).

Chapter 52
If the Gear Fits, Spin It Again!
Embodied Education, Design Components, and In–Play Assessments

Mina C. Johnson
Arizona State University, USA & Embodied Games, USA

David Birchfield
SmaLab Learning, USA

Colleen Megowan-Romanowicz
American Modeling Teachers Association, USA

ABSTRACT

To understand how students learn while engaged in active and embodied science games, two gears games were created. Would students' gear switching skills during the game be correlated with pre- and post-knowledge tests? Twenty-three seventh graders, playing as dyads, used gestures to manipulate virtual gears in the games. The Microsoft Kinect sensor tracked arm-spinning movements. Paper and pencil gear knowledge tests were administered before and after. In Game 1 (the easier one), the in-game switching data was significantly negatively correlated with only pretest gear knowledge. In Game 2 (the harder one), switching was negatively associated with both pre- and posttests. Negative correlations mean that fewer switches were used and that demonstrated better knowledge of mechanical advantage. In-game process data can provide a window onto learner's knowledge. However, the games need to have appropriate sensitivity and map to the learner's ZPD. In ludo (or in-process) data from videogames with high sensitivity may attenuate the need for repetitive traditional knowledge tests.

INTRODUCTION

The use of immersive games as learning tools has become more accepted in classrooms, and their value has been verified (Merchant, Goetz, Cifuentes, Keeney-Kennicutt, & Davis, 2014). This chapter is an update to the 2015 article called, *If the Gear Fits, Spin It*. This chapter version includes a simpler

DOI: 10.4018/978-1-6684-7589-8.ch052

interpretation in the discussion section, more insights on game design, and some updated references to augmented and virtual realities (AR/VR).

While much research supports the assertion that serious games can be more effective in terms of learning (d = 0.29, p < .01) and retention (d =0.36, p < .01), than conventional instruction methods (Wouters, Nimwegen, Oostendorp, & van der Spek, 2013), others have found more limited results in academic domains (Young et al., 2012). The Embodied Games lab has published primarily on mixed reality games and simulations, we have consistently observed that when a comparative class is instructed using game components versus more traditional pedagogies, then the game-based class more often produces better learning outcomes (Johnson-Glenberg, Birchfield, Koziupa, & Tolentino, 2014; Johnson-Glenberg & Megowan-Romanowicz, 2017). The field of STEM and learning games includes domain such as: computer science (Papastergiou, 2009), engineering (Coller & Shernoff, 2009)(Coller & Scott, 2009) and the biological sciences (Lui et al., 2014), to name a few. Coller and Scott (2009) report that the students who were randomly assigned to the videogame-based course showed deeper learning compared to the traditional class students (both groups spent the same amount of time on their course work). A metaanalysis from Young et al. (2012) found evidence for positive effects of videogames on language learning, history, and for exergaming, though they also report *little support for the academic value of videogames in science and math* (Young et al., 2012).

In this reprint of the original article, it is worthy to introduce and explore the concept that not all serious games are created equally. The first author can state unequivocally that she has designed and created games that fall along a spectrum of lame to excellent. Part of the noise in discerning the worth of videogames on STEM learning, and the difficulty in interpreting meta-analyses on games and learning, is that well designed games are lumped together with poorly designed games. In addition, the field still debates the difference between simulations and games. E.g., we opted to call our game-like activities *simulations* in Johnson-Glenberg and Megowan-Romanowicz (2017). Mishra, Anguera, and Gazzaley (2016) succinctly state the obvious.

Scientists are not typically the most proficient video game developers. "Games" developed to accomplish cognitive training goals are frequently limited to the layering on of simple graphic skins and low-level reward to standard cognitive task paradigms. This gamification approach often involves sprinkling game elements on top of low-engaging cognitive tasks, creating slightly less boring exercises, which may be a factor driving the negative findings that have dominated the field. (p. 214.)

It takes a team to create good games, and educators and scientists are not professional game designers. Those of us who trained as learning scientists or educators and wish to create serious games need to pair with professional game designers. In the early days of reviews, it was difficult to find professional grade learning games, but there may be a critical mass now. If the newer meta-analyses were to only include game content that has been designed by small teams of experts, then the field may begin to see more consistent, and positive results on the effects of games for learning. In addition, the field needs more articles that mesh rigorous randomized control trial (RCT) data and quasi-experimental data with clear advice on design for learning. To that end, this article will expand on how gameplay components correlate with traditional knowledge tests, and will end with a set of design guidelines. It is also necessary to understand how some long-held traditions in the entertainment game domain may not translate well into the education game domain. Some of the more established award mechanisms used in entertainment games, e.g., leaderboards and badges, may not be appropriate for classroom environments. A 6-week long study by Hanus and Fox found that the two traditional entertainment game "payoffs" of 1) a public board displaying all scores (called a leaderboard) and 2) the awarding of completion badges might actually hinder learning by negatively affecting intrinsic motivation (Hanus & Fox, 2015).

More research needs to be conducted to understand which components of educational videogames are felicitous to learning. This lab is focused on understanding how embodiment might affect learning during an active STEM game and we continue to develop and explore new methodologies and statistics for mining in-game player data and making sense of the information generated by the learner during gameplay. One gameplay modality that may hold potential for learning is that of embodied learning. "Embodied games" is a category of videogames that incorporates gesture into the act of learning.

Embodiment theory proposes that cognition is deeply rooted in the body's interactions with the environment and that cognition is for action in the world (Wilson, 2002). As evidence, Hauk et al. (2004) describe fMRI experiments that demonstrate that when reading words related to action, areas in the brain are activated in a somatotopic manner. For example, reading "lick" activates motor areas that control the mouth, whereas reading "pick" activates areas that control the hand. This activation is part of a network representing 'meaning' or semantics. The study was done on adults and thus demonstrates that the mappings do not fade once stable comprehension is attained, that is, motor codes are still activated during linguistic comprehension long after the meaning has become stable or automated (Hauk, Johnsrude, & Pulvermüller, 2004). If cognition and the body are deeply and irrevocably connected, then perhaps all cognition, even abstract thought, is embodied (Glenberg, Witt, & Metcalfe, 2013). If this is true, then it seems prudent to design learning games that take advantage of how the body moves to reify concepts to be learned.

Embodied Educational Games

Creating educational games that are also embodied may be especially useful for topics that have traditionally been "tough to teach". This lab focuses on science for several reasons. First, it is a closed problem space, there is usually one answer, so it is a less ambiguous space to design for. Second, computer-aided instruction can be used to facilitate comprehension of content that is not readily apparent to human perceptual systems. This means making the macro (e.g., astronomy) and the micro (e.g., bacteria, or the genome) accessible or what some term, making the unseen seen. With the advent of affordable VR, others are pushing for VR in education to be used to take advantage of the fantastical (Slater & Sanchez-Vives, 2016). Third, an informed citizenry is crucial; there is concern that too many students are leaving the science pipeline around middle school. Games may be a way to engage and retain youth in the sciences. Games offer students an opportunity for stepping out of their usual identities and trying on new ones. When a learner is able to take on the "identity" of an expert (Shaffer et al., 2009), s/he can begin to feel and react like an expert. If the expert is a scientist then the learner might show outcomes like volunteering more answers in class, mentoring others, or spontaneously writing a letter to the a city's mayor about zoning laws learned in the game (Squire & Klopfer, 2007).

Gestures. Gestures may facilitate novices on their journey to becoming experts. By definition a novice is someone whose knowledge is fragmented. The "knowledge in pieces" paradigm (DiSessa, 1988), posits that learners as novices do not yet hold a coherent whole model, they perhaps have pieces that do not fit together. They understand that gears spin and can aid in "work", but do not understand how the input diameter of a gear train affects the work performed. By adding the extra modality of gesture in engaging embodied games, we may aid in the creation of coherent knowledge structures for these novices. The mental model might cohere better.

Other educational researchers have been supporting the use of movement, or body-based metaphors, in learning before motion capture and games were added to the mix (Nathan et al., 2014). Indeed, Cook and Goldin-Meadow (Cook & Goldin-Meadow, 2006) manipulated children's gesture during instruction on new mathematical concepts. The children who were prompted to gesture while learning retained the knowledge they had gained better than the children who were not prompted. Cook et al. postulate that gesturing serves a causal role in learning, perhaps by giving learners an alternative, embodied way of representing new ideas. Goldin-Meadow states, "…perhaps it is the motor aspects of gesture that are responsible for the cognitive benefits" (Goldin-Meadow, 2011). She also posits that gestures may help to "off-load" cognition. Nathan and Alibali (Nathan et al., 2014) found a significant relationship between action and cognition and experimenter's language (i.e., prompts and hints) as participants learned geometry proofs. Education could benefit from having more body-based, gesture-oriented games. However, game designers need a set of guidelines to help them design such games. One set has been proposed by Lindgren and Johnson-Glenberg (2013), and this chapter ends with a reiteration of the set proposed in 2015.

How can embodiment affect education? The goal was to create a game that would add a meaningful motor trace to the act of learning, in this way the game might enhance encoding and retention. The game should not activate just any motor trace, the game should activate a trace that contains overlap with the content to be learned. This overlap has been called gestural congruency (Black, Segal, Vitale, & Fadjo, 2012; Segal, Black, & Tversky, 2010). The physical gesture should match the abstract content to be learned.

This lab has attempted to be systematic when designing games and follows the tenets mentioned in the Discussion section and further extrapolated in our other articles (Johnson-Glenberg, Birchfield, et al., 2014; Lindgren & Johnson-Glenberg, 2013). It should be noted that games can be either low or high on the embodiment spectrum and several taxonomies have emerged that attempt to "quantify" the amount of embodiment in educational content (Johnson-Glenberg, 2017; Johnson-Glenberg & Megowan-Romanowicz, 2017; Skulmowski & Rey, 2018).

As an example of a high embodied gesture that overlaps very physically with the concept to be learned, consider the *Alien Health* game (Johnson-Glenberg, Savio-Ramos, & Henry, 2014). In that game using the *Kinect* sensor, the virtual food item is grasped by the learner's hand and placed close to the avatar's mouth, as opposed to merely hitting an "eat" button. That is, the human player makes the motion of bringing the virtual item to his/her mouth as the *Kinect* maps and makes the virtual object move on screen toward the avatar mouth. As a more conceptual example, consider, moving the hand "up" to connote the concept of "more". In one of our new VR games with hand controls, the player raises the physical hand upwards; in real time as the hand moves the virtual graph begins filling upwards with either numbers or the amount of butterflies collected. This is a kinesthetic prediction task, players are showing a numerical amount not by writing down symbols or speaking language, but by using the body. As the player lowers the hand, that action simultaneously lowers the graph (Johnson-Glenberg, submitted).

Gesture also implies that the body is being active. Therefore, these are sometimes referred to as active games. The increased sensorimotor input that occurs during active, high embodied learning may also positively affect learning. Better learning outcomes are reported in an RCT study on the electric field (Johnson-Glenberg & Megowan-Romanowicz, 2017). The groups that had agency over the content (could move content on screen with either their hands or tracking of the knees) learned significantly more than the group that interacted in a low embodied manner or with only text and symbols.

The genesis. For over a decade, members of the lab have been designing learning games and simulations for mixed and augmented reality (MR and AR) platforms. The term 'mixed reality' was first used by Milgram and Kishino (Milgram & Kishino, 1994) to connote realities that have been projected or used virtual overlays, although aspects of the real world were still present. (This distinguishes it from immersive VR where a 360° headset insures there is no intrusion of the real world.) The first three authors have published extensively on the MR platform called *SMALLab* (Situated Multimedia Arts Learning Lab). The *SMALLab* motion-capture platform uses 12 ceiling-mounted infrared *Optitrack* cameras to track players while holding a rigid body trackable object. The experience feels immersive because the projected floor and tracked space is large (15 x 15 X 15 feet). The players can see the outside world and that also makes it collaborative. (Videos can be found at www.smallablearning.com.) Entire classrooms can sit around the projected perimeter and observe and interact with active students in the space. When learning in this MR platform was compared with traditional instruction (teacher and content held constant) significant gains, and several trends, were seen that favored the MR platform (Johnson-Glenberg, Birchfield, et al., 2014; Johnson-Glenberg, Birchfield, Megowan-Romanowicz, Tolentino, & Martinez, 2009; Johnson-Glenberg, Birchfield, Megowan-Romanowicz, & Uysal, 2009)

As Connolly et al. (Connolly, Boyle, MacArthur, Hainey, & Boyle, 2012) noted, newer platforms like mobile, virtual worlds, and augmented reality mobile kits will continue to come to market and should have profound effects on educational gaming. With the advent of more cost-effective sensors, several of us opted to focus on designing educational content for smaller sensors like the Microsoft *Kinect*'s joint tracking system. The original *Kinect* (*Kinect 360*) was used in this study. It captured up to 20 joints on the body at approximately 30 frames per second.

Game Design

This chapter reports findings on two science games. The first game was easier to play, it was called Tour de Force; the second game was more difficult, it was called the Winching Game. These were part of a series of six short games created to help middle school students understand how simple machines, gears and levers, worked. The topic of simple machines is attractive because several parts of the body can simulate the action of gears or levers (the arm is a natural lever). After the topic space was chosen we needed to reframe it through the epistemology of children's scientific thinking. The design was premised on the concept of naïve science learners from diSessa's theory (diSessa, 1988) that human knowledge consists of many, loosely organized, fragmented pieces of knowledge. These building blocks of understanding are called phenomenological primitives (p-prims) (diSessa, 1988). They are small knowledge elements whose origins stem from repeated abstractions of very familiar events. We hold that these familiar events are experienced in an embodied manner at the earliest age. For example, many students come to kinematics and other science topics with misconceptions, i.e., that force is not an action with an equal and opposite reaction.

In a *SMALLab* sponsored summer camp, 17 middle schoolers helped to pilot many of the study's test items (see test as Appendix of the original article). Approximately 95% of students incorrectly answered that the largest input gear in a gear train would always lift the largest and heaviest item. When queried why, they replied with a variant of, "bigger is always better" - unpublished data - (Johnson-Glenberg, 2012). With repeated exposure to appropriate games, leveled content, and scaffolded discovery from the teacher, the goal was to re-organize a student's network of fragmented knowledge elements into a coherent and correct (more expert-like) model. The students may need to "experience" how the construct is incorrect and why. They may need to use *physical* body actions to *virtually* manipulate smaller and larger objects to really understand why their current gear mental model is incorrect. With this experience, and a new motor memory trace, students' knowledge structures may over time begin to resemble experts' knowledge structures.

The Beauty of Gears

To understand gears, we wanted to encourage students to explore the relationships between a number of *embodiable* concepts including gear size, speed of rotation, and direction. One challenge we confronted was how to embody the idea of diameter (size) and mechanical advantage when two gears interact. The first few questions on the test were designed to measure students' conceptual coherence and were influenced by an early study by Metz (1985). Her participants worked with a set of physically manipulable gears fashioned with a wooden crank. Two of the gears were marked with the form of a man. When a marked gear was turned clockwise, the man pictured on it somersaulted feet-first. Participants were instructed to arrange articulating gears so that they could "make the two men somersault in the same direction." Via trial and error, participants learned the relationship of parity between gear elements. E.g., if there were an odd number of gear elements between the marked gears, then the two marked gears turned in the same direction. Eleven and 12 years-olds were able to understand this rule. The Metz study demonstrates that students are able to construct complex knowledge through the direct manipulation of physical systems. Our goal was to preserve the powerful learning that can occur via this type of physical embodied experience and integrate it into the affordances of digital media in a game-like manner.

Gears also afford the concept of mechanical advantage (MA). A robust energy concept is central to an understanding of all science and MA as well. Although energy is often treated as if it were a straightforward and easily defined quantity, energy is notoriously difficult for people to understand. The third author was a physics teacher for 25 years and often her high school and college students confounded energy with the concepts of force and power (and even speed). [1]

Gears are a good choice for study, besides being able to be embodied, they involve both mathematical and scientific concepts. Gears require the application of both descriptive and causal conceptual models. Their motion and action are familiar (bicycles, pulleys, etc.) and easy to visually perceive because there is no hidden mechanism at work, but gears also reveal stubborn misconceptions regarding both simple (e.g., size, speed, and direction) and complex (e.g., mechanical advantage) constructs. In the games for this series, students were only exposed to double gear systems. There was one input gear and one output gear; players controlled the input gear's diameter. The output gear size was always preset and constant throughout the game. The mechanical advantage construct is a ratio, and it is Output to Input, or O:I. That is, diameter of the output gear divided by the diameter of the input gear.

The lab created a series of six simple machines games, three of these were games on levers. The three lever games were of such short duration (less than one minute each and only resulted in two lengths of the arm being captured by the sensor) that a meaningful frequency of change in a lever game was difficult to extract. Thus, we focus on only the gears games for this paper which had three unique diameters. Figure 1 shows the standard stance for the gears games with the arm extended out in front. Turning the whole arm (that is revolving the wrist joint around the shoulder joint) would make the input gear spin in the same direction and would control the input gear's diameter size.

Figure 1.
Videos of the two games are at: Tour de Force at https://www.youtube.com/watch?v=kSsiJZOUKt4
The Winching game https://www.youtube.com/watch?time_continue=1&v=NHLwQ8kZQ5A
Or at https://www.embodied-games.com/games/ at the bottom of page, under video highlights.

Research Questions. The test covered a range of gear concepts. We wanted to know how in-game play would correlate with both pretest and posttest knowledge. In the case of manipulating the bikes up hills of varying slopes, a student who understands that a smaller gear will get the bike up a steeper hill is one who does not show uncertainty about gear size as the hills change slope. That student will not bounce around trying many different gear diameters. Our hypothesis was that the students who were confused about the optimal gear diameters for mechanical advantage (MA) would be the ones who switched gear size more often. In addition, those who switched gear size more often during play would be the ones who demonstrated the lowest scores on the traditional paper and pencil knowledge pretests. This means there should be a negative correlation between number of gear switches and scores on the pretest, demonstrating that those who started with lower prior knowledge would probably not perform as well during gameplay.

Regarding the correlations for a posttest, we considered this study to be exploratory. Poor in-game performance could translate to poor posttest performance if the game is sensitive to, and calibrated for, specific knowledge structures that might be altered by posttest. On the other hand, the game is played in pairs (dyads) and dyadic performance would affect play in ways we were uncertain about. This study represents our first explorations of how dyads perform in front of a class in an active and observed-over-time game. The issue of how to design games that gather meaningful knowledge information during play (sometimes called in-process) is a timely one, because if serious "construct sensitive" games that gather meaningful in-game data that predict the amount of content learned can be created, then educators will not be forced to waste learners' class time giving repetitive or summative paper/pencil posttests.

METHODS

Participants

Participants were 23 7th graders from a middle school with 160 students in urban CA. The study began with 25 participants, but two (one from each class) were absent the day of the posttest, or their in-process data were corrupted. Fifty percent at the school received financial aid and 52% of the students were described as "people of color" by the Principal. There were 11 females in the two classes. There were no significant knowledge test differences due to gender. Two science classrooms were used in the study and the same teacher covered the same content in both classes.

Procedure

The entire study was a seven day-long intervention on Simple Machines. The study began with the concept of gears and then moved onto levers. There were three class sessions during which instruction was focused on gears. On Day 1, the pretest was given and then students played the Ratio Match gears tutorial game to get used to the arm spinning mechanic. On Day 2, students played the easier Tour de Force game, and on day 3, they played the more difficult Winching game. On day 4, students took the gears posttest and then continued on with the levers content. Participants were quasi-randomly assigned to dyads (more on this in the Discussion section).

The classroom lessons were co-designed with two science teachers, the project's lead programmer, a cognitive psychologist, an experienced game designer, and a physics subject matter expert. The classroom teacher in this study was engaged and very innovative, e.g., he brought in his own manipulatives like planks and bricks for levers, and his own bicycle to demonstrate gears. Thus, the content for the week of lessons was not solely based on the supplied *Kinect* games, the teacher interspersed short lectures that he devised. The teacher was provided with a scripted guide for the *Kinect*-based games, which he followed closely.

Day 1- Gears Tutorial Game. Student dyads took turns learning the mechanics of the *Kinect* using the Gear Ratio Tutorial Game that Dr. Birchfield designed. Two players either volunteered or were asked to come to the front of the room. The regular classroom projector projected the image (approximately 80 inch diagonal) on the wall. The dyad would stand in front of the *Kinect* sensor with their backs to the class and practice matching gear diameters in this sandbox-style tutorial game. (Video available https://www.youtube.com/watch?v=kSsiJZOUKt4&feature=youtu.be.)

Figure 2 shows the screenshot of the tutorial *Ratio Match* game. The *Kinect* is tracking two key joints on each players' bodies, i.e., the wrist and shoulder. The shoulder is the pivot point. Revolving the wrist joint around the shoulder joint creates one of three preset diameters on the screen.

The input gear rotates in real time with the player, and in the same direction as the player's arm. This is a strong example of gestural congruency. The virtual input gear diameter snaps to three different sizes. If a player makes a very wide circle around the shoulder joint it will result in the largest gear diameter of 12- the outer, red area. In Figure 2, the players are being prompted to match to a ratio, in this case an input size of 12, and the output gear on the inside is locked at a diameter of 5. Thus, 12:5 is the target ratio. The player that first completes two revolutions with an input maintained at the largest size 12 revolution will win the point. The game ends when the 45 second timer runs out. The total number of

Figure 2.

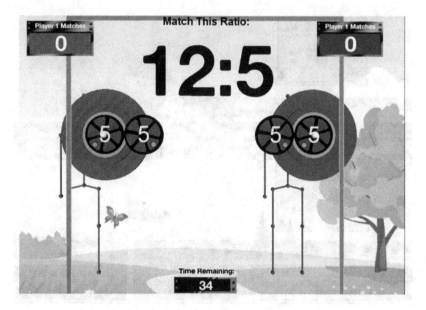

matches are presented in the boxes on top. (Note: we did not gather in-process data on this short tutorial.) Every student in the two classes was able to engage in this sand-box tutorial.

Day 2 - Tour de Force Game. On the second day, dyads played the *Tour de Force* biking game. The teacher first asked for volunteers and then the non-volunteering students were placed together in dyads. Thus, dyads were "quasi-randomly" assigned; they were not preset. Friends often chose each other in the early rounds. The game had a cut-off play time of 240 seconds. On average the last player usually crossed the finish line by two minutes (120 seconds). Figure 1 showed a player with her arm out in front as she turned the input gear on the pink bike on the top of the screen, the bike is going up a small hill. The second player is lagging behind on the green bike.

As players came to the front of the class, the experimenter entered their subject IDs into the computer from a prepopulated list of students. The size of the input gear, as measured via distance from the wrist to the shoulder pivot point, would vary (snap to) three sizes. The diameter changes were time stamped and mapped to subject ID. Figure 3 shows a close up of the opening screenshot.

Players are also able to see statistics on their performance such as input force, output force, kilometers per hour, and time played so far. At the beginning of the lesson the teacher guided student exploration of the equation: *Work = Force X Distance*. The lecture included the concept that there was a limited amount of input force, that is, they had only so much effort they could exert on the input gear. There were three input gear sizes to choose from in this game: 4, 5, and 16. The winner was the one who crossed the finish line first. To be the fastest, a player needed to show facility with critical constructs associated with the input gear (the pedal gear). They needed to quickly deduce that on the flat section of the race course the largest gear (size 16) should be used. Then, on the steep hill sections, the smallest gear (size 4) should be switched to for optimal performance. The gear switch needs to be well-timed and maintained as long as the player was on that specific terrain. If the player was not generating enough output force the bike would remain stationary. It did not slide backwards.

Figure 3.

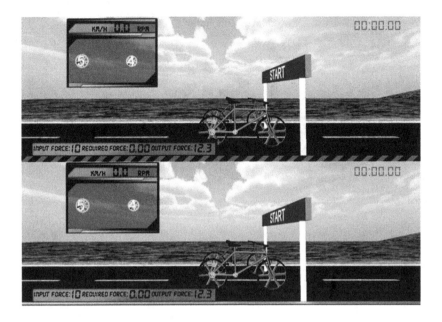

A learner who understood (intuited) mechanical advantage would exhibit both a very fast time *and* a minimal amount of gear switching. The biking course had 16 waypoints, that is, places where the hill slope could change. All participants played on the same default course with the same hills. On the far right in Figure 3, you can see the beginning of a small hill.

Configuration Panel - Tour de Force. Because we strive for players to also be creators, or generative in the games, a configuration panel, accessed with the key strokes "ctrl c" was included. The panel (see Figure 4) allowed for the slopes of the hills to be varied by altering the Y coordinates. In this way slopes that were impassable could be created and discussion could occur around math concepts like graphing, mechanical advantage, and game design, e.g., what makes for a "fun" and challenging game, versus a simply frustrating experience (not being able to ascend a hill of 80°). Pedal force (input force) and bike weight could also be altered in a different section of the configuration panel. (In the Discussion section we explore why this was never used.)

Profile of the Player. Players come to games with varying amounts of prior knowledge, both in terms of comfort with game play and knowledge of the content to be learned.[2] Regarding prior content knowledge, middle schoolers often approach gear trains with a knowledge structure that includes a misconception regarding diameter and which size input gear would be most efficacious given the circumstances. One way we measured whether they understood that they needed a smaller input gear to get up a steeper hill was via the number of diameter switches they made during play. Students often attempted many different gear diameters before they began to address their most common misconception - "bigger is always better". The students who either understood mechanical advantage on the bike gear train, or who could use the formula of the ratio of O:I (output to input) made the switch quickly to the smallest input gear size and stuck with it until they had reached the top of the hill. At the top, when the course would flatten, players who got it would switch adroitly back to the bigger gear and maintain that diameter for optimal speed until the next waypoint.

Figure 4.

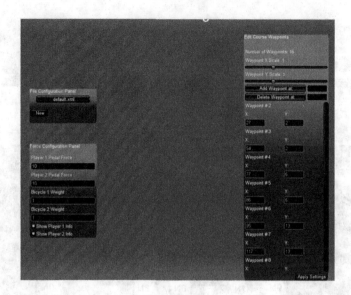

Students who did *not* understand the concept of smaller gears for steeper hills would bounce around trying the three different sizes of input gear until the bike finally moved. We labeled them the "Bouncers". The students who were more efficient, and consistently demonstrated they got it - were labeled the "Got its". It appeared that all students attacked the first couple of hills with the type of exploration technique commonly seen in mastering new games, but the Bouncers never really moved from exploration to "exploitation" during these games. We wanted to know if some of this behavior could be captured via in-process data and if overall number of switches would correlate with other subject variables like prior knowledge.

Day 3. The Winching Game - On the third day, dyads played the Winching Game. (See Figure 5.) The goal was to lift boulders of varying weight (force) from a pit onto a conveyor belt. The player with the most boulders lifted when the timer buzzed at 90 seconds won. In Figure 5, the input gear is the black circle on top. The output gear was locked at always be set at 5. Students needed to understand how to change the size of the input gear to efficiently winch up the larger boulders. The input gear sizes were set to 5, 7 or 9.

Winching is harder. This game was more difficult than the previous biking one because the input gear now moved in *two* directions. Spinning to the right would hoist the cable up, and spinning to the left would drop the cable back down to get the next boulder. The optimal diameter for the input gear changed with each boulder's mass (see the bottom of Figure 5). Players needed to deduce that a smaller diameter was needed for the heavier boulders. Because the game is timed, players need to rapidly lower the cable (with magnetic head) down and it was always best to do that with the largest diameter. Boulders were randomly seeded at the bottom of the screen and moved on a second conveyor belt, they ranged in weight from 2 Newtons (N) to 9 N for this game. A Newton is a measure of force and can be thought of as 0.22 lb. One of the constraints was that the largest input gear would *not* lift the largest boulder. The boulder could not be moved no matter how rapidly the player spun his or her arm, a new diameter had to be chosen. The player with the most boulders at the end of the timed cycle was the winner.

Figure 5.

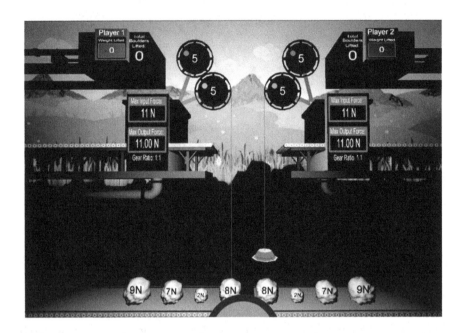

Configuration Panel - Winching Game - This game also included a configuration panel for user-created content. Users could alter start conditions varying in weight ranges and preset output gear diameters, etc.; however, that panel was not used during this study.

Measure

Gears Knowledge Measure. This measure was an experimenter-designed test created with several middle school teachers and a physics subject matter expert. (See test in original article.) It was pilot-tested to be age-appropriate. There were 13 items to be answered on the gears test, either multiple choice, open-ended, or fill in the blank items. The very last item queried students to choose the correct relatively-sized gear to winch up objects of varying mass. The maximum score achievable on this subtest was 54 points. Multiple choice questions were worth three points and open-ended questions ranged from zero to five points. It included both near and far transfer items. The invariant test is the same from pretest to posttest. There were not ceiling effects as the highest score achieved on the posttest was 37.

The Gears Lessons: Learning Goals

The instructional goals in the teacher's guide were:

1. Understand energy interactions in terms of transfer and storage
2. Develop a concept of work as a mechanism for energy transfer
3. Apply the concept of conservation of energy
4. Understand and demonstrate comprehension of calculations of the efficiency of a simple machine, specifically mechanical advantage via game play

5.   Define and show comprehension of mechanical advantage (*the factor by which the input force is multiplied by the use of a machine to transfer energy*)

Results

Knowledge test. All results were run with SPSS v22. All alphas levels were set to .05 and were two-tailed.

Pretest and Classroom Differences. The two classes differed significantly on gears knowledge pretest. The teacher was surprised by this result because he had been teaching the students for four months and stated the two class skill-levels were equally matched. He hypothesized the difference in pretest may have been due to a before and after lunch distinction. The AM class scored 20.08 (SD 6.56), and the PM class scored 12.08 (SD 9.89) on the pretest. An independent *t* test revealed a significant difference, $t_{(22)}$ = 2.32 p = .03. (Note, the classroom scores by posttest were no longer significantly different by class, $t_{(22)}$ = 1.57 p < .14, and a General Linear Model analysis using the interaction of time by class was not significant, $F_{(1,20)}$ = .08.) Thus, the decision was made to combine the classes into one dataset to increase overall power for the study since all students received the exact same instruction by the same teacher.

Combined classrooms - Posttest. As a combined group, the gears knowledge test results for the 23 participants were: pretest M = 16.81 (*SD* 8.89); posttest M = 21.19 (*SD* 7.90). This gain was significant on a paired *t* test: $t_{(22)}$ = 2.33, p =.03. The effect size was medium. Cohen's *d* is typically reported in the cognitive sciences, it is the mean difference between scores divided by the pooled average of the pretest and posttest standard deviations, d = .52.

In-Process Gameplay Analyses – Tour de Force – Entire Sample. Our hypothesis was that the students who were more efficient with their gear changes, that is, the "Got Its" with fewer switches during game play, would do better on the paper and pencil test. The metric used was gear diameter switches - the average frequency of change of gear size during play. The game cut off after four minutes of play. During the first round of play students interacted with the *Tour de Force* game for a mean of 78.41 seconds (Range = 32 to 190, *SD* = 36.37 seconds). Students averaged 72.27 gear switches (SD = 41.52 switches). The prediction was that the "Got Its" who understood mechanical advantage would use fewer switches and would cross the finish line faster. This was evident with the entire sample. Overall those with shorter times used fewer switches, $r(22)$ = .82 p < .001. But, were these faster players the winners within their dyads?

Tour de Force - Dyadic Analysis. Tour de Force lent itself to analyses using the pair of players (the dyad) as the unit of analysis because the game course did not alter between dyads. We saw that if the winner was faster, the loser was comparatively faster as well within the whole sample. Thus, partnerships affected play across the sample. However, we only had 11 dyads on the day Tour de Force was played. (We only used first time play data and one student went twice, with a first time player and so we did not include that dyad.) We note that statistical power is an issue in the following analyses, indeed, *G Power* (v 3.1) provides an estimate of only .26 to find significance at a .05 alpha level using a .50 effect size; if we wanted .80 power we would need 34 pairs.

With more pairs, we would be able to consider using other types of analyses like Hierarchical Linear Modeling (HLM). Although the case could be made that these data are not traditionally nested. HLM assumes the structure of the data are nested at a level we never considered in this small study, e.g., teacher, school, or district. It may be the case that position of play (first or last pair to play after observing) had an effect on scores and time, but we did not store those data. We do consider the paired to be linked, or yoked, within their game space. In this manner each dyad player is not independent (i.e., one wins – ergo the other *must* lose). An analysis of interest might be whether the number of gear switches separating the winner versus loser within dyad was significantly different, and that analysis was run.

Analyzing the set of first-time play dyads, the winner switched frequency of gear diameters on average 51.91 times (*SD*= 20.67), the loser switched 91.55 times (*SD*= 53.13). When students were analyzed as the winner (coded as 1) and loser (coded as 0) within dyads, the frequency of switch between players was correlated as well, $r = .68$, $p = .02$. Faster dyads had fewer switches overall and some of the losers in a faster dyad would have been the winners in a slower dyad. This supports the hypothesis that partners affected each other's' play.

We wanted to know if the difference between switches was statistically significant regardless of whether the yoked pair were in a relatively faster or slower dyad. Using a *paired* t-test within dyad we account for some variance between dyads. But because this may seem controversial, we also ran independent *t* tests. The paired *t* test revealed that the difference between the winners' and losers' switch frequency was significant, see Table 1, $p = .01$, with a large effect size (Cohen's *d*) of .95. Independent and bootstrap analyses are also reported and were also significant supporting the hypothesis that winners used significantly fewer switches within play, Bootstrap $t = 2.03$, bias $= -.02$, $p = .03$ (SE = 11.70).

In Gameplay and the Knowledge Test. The next question was whether the winners in the game showed greater gains on the knowledge posttest. The effect of change on test scores was moderate, $d = .56$. See Table 1. The inferential paired *t* test was not statistically significant because we only had 8 dyads in that analysis (several players missing data or posttest knowledge scores). We note again the power issue, but the direction of the *t* value would support the hypothesis that winners in the game dyad did better on the knowledge posttest than the losers within a dyad. There was a sort of "switchover" seen as well. That is, the dyad losers did better on the pretest (by two points on average) but *worse* on the posttest (again by two points on average). This may suggest that in-game processes were capturing knowledge as it changed. Winner and loser knowledge pretests were not significantly different within dyad (paired *t* value < .80), perhaps suggesting that friends who score similarly on tests often choose each other to play with. The amount of switching was not significantly correlated with pretest scores within dyads, $r < .25$.

Table 1. Paired and Independent t Tests Comparing Dyadic Winners and Losers

Dyad Comparison	df	M Difference (SD)	Cohen's d	t Test sig. Level
# of Gear Switches (Loser - Winner)	10	39.65 (41.91)	.95	Paired = 3.14** $p = .013$**
				Independent = 2.03 $p = .032$*
Knowledge Test Gains Score (Loser Gain – Winner Gain)	8	- 5.78 (10.40)	.56	Paired =- 1.67 $p = .13$

Tour de Force Gameplay and Knowledge Test - Whole sample. Using the sample as a whole group, we had predicted a negative correlation such that the students who made fewer gear switches would have higher test scores. There was significant evidence of this on the pretest, $r = -.41$, $p = .05$; however, at posttest this negative correlation did not hold, $r = .12$, $p = .29$, NS.

The Harder Game - In Process Analyses – Winching Game – Whole sample. In the Winching Game was reported to be somewhat more difficult than the first game. During the Winching Game the students lifted on average 17.7 rocks ($SD = 8.47$). All teams played for the same amount of time (90 seconds). The range of gear size switches was $43 - 140$; $M = 75.28$ ($SD = 27.61$). The number of gear switches was not predictive of number of rocks successfully lifted, $r = -.10$. Although, in this small sample we still see that the valence is negative.

Gameplay and Knowledge Test - Winching Game - Whole Sample. We predicted a negative correlation between number of switches and test scores, such that the students who made fewer switches, would have higher test scores. We saw some evidence of this on the pretest, $r = -.26$ (NS) and stronger evidence on the posttest, $r = -.37$, $p = .07$, which represents a statistical trend.

We did not run the same of sort of comparative dyadic analysis on this game because each player within each dyad was confronted with a different game course. That is, rock sizes were randomly seeded for each game and for each player on the bottom conveyor belt. It was possible for three rocks of the same size to come out in a row making one player's task much easier than the other player's task. This is different than the Tour de Force Game where the hill series never varied within or between dyads.

DISCUSSION

Both the gears Winching Game and Tour de Force Game were designed as playful environments for students to practice and demonstrate their understanding of gear trains and mechanical advantage. On average the two classes demonstrated statistically significant gains in learning on the knowledge post-test after the intervention. The games were embodied and innovative; they used the *Kinect* sensor as the input device so the body could mimic the tool of instruction (a spinning gear or a pumping lever). Our goal was to make the learners' movements map to the content to be learned with gestural congruency. We mined student performance during gameplay to explore how "physical" arm rotations and "virtual" gear diameter shifts related to dyadic performance and on more traditional paper and pencil tests.

In the game Tour de Force, the faster students were always the winners in the dyad and the faster students also used significantly fewer gear switches (at least in nine of the 11 Tour de Force dyads). A key research question is whether in-process gameplay correlates with performance on more traditional tests. The results here also suggest that outcomes may depend on the difficulty of the game. In the easier Tour de Force game where arm spin rotation was only in one direction, the "Got Its" did significantly better on the pretest (as would be predicted). However, the players' in-game performance was not predictive of posttest, that is, students' knowledge post-intervention was not correlated with diameter gesture-choices during learning. Perhaps because Tour de Force was rather easy to master and all students got the basics by the end of the race course, so it lacked precision as a predictive tool.

For the more difficult Winching Game, the valences of the pretest and posttest correlations remained negative, as we had predicted. By posttest the better learners were generally using fewer switches representing a trend for more learning ($p < .07$). Thus, there is some evidence that in-game performance on appropriately calibrated (i.e., harder, more effortful) games can reveal a learner's profile. These findings suggest that when students are in a more challenging game, one that might match their Zone of Proximal Development (Vygotsky, 1978), they might exhibit patterns of movement that suggest ongoing comprehension. The negative correlations support the hypothesis that the "Got It" players, the ones who rapidly understood how mechanical advantage worked during the game, also showed greater gains on the posttest. These were the ones who could see a larger boulder coming down the belt, switch expeditiously to a smaller input gear to grab it, and then switch back to a larger gear (and use a different direction) to spin the cable back down to grab another boulder.

In Tour de Force, within a dyad, the winners in the dyads did not start with statistically higher pretest scores (as a simplistic prior knowledge-based hypothesis might predict). However, when the winners took the posttest they did on average have higher *posttest scores* than the dyadic losers. This suggests that the game may have been capturing some moments where knowledge may have "switched over", that is, a time when pretest was no longer the sole predictor of performance – at some point during the three day intervention a *different sort of learning* may have been occurring that was not contingent on the previous knowledge the student arrived to the task with. Or, it may be that the quasi-random nature of the dyadic pairings added too much noise, e.g., "smarter kids hang together" so there was self-selection bias. In addition, the smarter, more confident, friend pairs were usually the first to volunteer, so that when whole group correlations are run many nuances are lost. The later-playing students could have benefitted from observing earlier rounds, although we did note some boredom in the class by the very end. A final, equally speculative, assumption might be that the paper and pencil static test may be capturing a different sort of declarative, or crystalized, knowledge that is very different from what gestures can show. Gestures can reveal knowledge that is internalized, but not captured on other types of tests or present in speech acts (Goldin-Meadow, 2014). We have recently begun to gather movement data using a touch-sensitive assessment tool, a large *WACOM Pro* tablet (Johnson-Glenberg & Megowan-Romanowicz, 2017), these sorts of gesture-based assessments show promise for more sensitive analyses of gains on embodied educational applications.

Larger studies are needed, as well as low-embodied control groups. Nonetheless, this study represents a start in gathering the sorts of effect sizes and results that can be expected in embodied multi-media science games. Learning scientists have speculated for years regarding the constraints associated with gathering validity and reliability on gameplay data. One timely question, given a test-besotted school environment, would be: "Is it possible to gather valid knowledge information about comprehension in-vivo during gesture-based gameplay?" Our results suggest *"yes"*, in-process data can be predictive of knowledge – if the games are in a cognitively appropriate zone of playability. If this is the case, then why should we force students to work through lengthy paper and pencil tests post-gameplay? If a student demonstrates in real time that s/he has mastered the concept, then a traditional multiple-choice type test need not be administered (Gee & Shaffer, 2010).

Game design principles. With this revision, the guidelines which had first been listed in the introduction have now been moved to the discussion section. The first author has just submitted an article for design practices using hand controls in VR for education (Johnson-Glenberg, submitted), as well as a chapter (Johnson-Glenberg, 2017). The six principles listed below are core and appear in all newer sets. Although this first set (from 2015) for mixed reality does have a have a special emphasis on "social". The socio-collaborative component is very important in education, but we note it is still expensive to make synchronous, social VR environments.

The tenets remain. Designers should strive to make games:

1. **Embodied**: Include as much "gestural congruency" as possible
2. **Socio-Collaborative:** Build games that encourage discourse with others. This series of games used dyads (pairs of students), but it also gave the observing students tasks to keep the whole class engaged

3. **Generative**: Also called Active. Learning games should encourage learners to be physically active. When learners manipulate content on screen in realtime that also gives them ownership and agency over the lesson
4. **Immediate Performance Feedback:** Feedback should not be intrusive, constant, or too negative. Low stakes failure should be built into the beginning to encourage exploration
5. **Cycle of Expertise:** Level up in difficulty as the player shows competence. If the funds are available, make your game adaptive with branches of difficulty
6. **Include User-Created Content:** This is last because it is difficult to do. Ideally students should be contributors and not just passive consumers of media. E.g., these games included in-game editors that allowed students to create personalized virtual race courses for their peers. This is highly generative and we have seen that it encourages students to take 'ownership' of the content (Johnson-Glenberg, Birchfield, et al., 2014). (The teacher did not use them in this study.)

LIMITATIONS AND FUTURE DIRECTIONS

The *Kinect* sensor was used as the input device; however, these sorts of movement and data-driven decision analyses can be accomplished with other technologies (e.g., the *Leap Motion*, embedded blob detection cameras, tracking on latest generations of immersive VR headsets with hand controls). This lab focuses on games that use as much sensori-motor activity as possible, so the whole arm is used to spin a gear, but perhaps circling the finger to spin a gear on a tablet may be just as effective? The amount of sensorimotor activation is a question for future studies. We agree with Nathan et al.'s (2014) observation in a paper that also assessed gear knowledge. The authors state that "...grounding actions may be most effective when the underlying mathematical ideas...align with the physical and spatial relation..." (p.192). Nonetheless, the gesture they used of "tapping on" virtual gears to learn the parity rule, may not have been as powerful as using a full-arm gesture to simulate turning the virtual gears in real time, as we did in our study.

New assessment metrics. This emerging field of game analyses is in need of more adroit, more sophisticated inferential tools. We were uncertain how to deal with the dynamic fluxes occurring over the class-long hour of play. For example, many of the beginning-of-play dyads were not truly randomly assigned (e.g., friends), but the end-of-play dyads were randomly assigned by the teacher from a pool without replacement. Perhaps we could add a decay function to an analysis to account for increasing randomness or independence of the pairs? Additionally, the end-of-play dyads, who may have been more introverted, observed more bouts of play before their turns. In this manner, one might expect the end-of-play dyads to pick up faster on the optimal mechanical advantage gear switch. Anecdotally, this was not seen in either the gears or levers games. The end-of-play dyads were generally composed of the slower and poorer performing players. One hypothesis is that they are the more uncertain students, and observation can only take you so far in an active game. For future studies, teachers might use random number generated pairs for play. We could also include a metric to assess students' self-efficacy, self-regulation (likelihood to persist) or goal structure (performance vs. mastery) with respect to learning games.

Clearly this exploratory study needs more dyads for power considerations. In addition, with a longer time series Hurst exponents and other persistence measures could have been reliably gathered. Hurst exponents are interesting measures for predictivity in a time series. As an example, in a social experiment with children, DiDonato (DiDonato et al., 2012) showed that when young children demonstrated flexibility and nonpersistence (as in, a Hurst exponent closer to .5 which connotes more randomness and less pink noise), the exponent was a positive indicator for later behaviors. They found that preschool children who were more gender flexible with play partners during earlier play showed better positive adjustment on several sociability scales six months later. In the learning and computer aided instruction literature, Snow et al. (Snow, Allen, Jacovina, & McNamara, 2015) investigated how log data can be used as a proxy for self-regulated learning and agentic behavior. Specifically, they identified patterns of behaviors that indicated controlled and ordered processes as students made choices through two computer-based tutors using various dynamic time series methodologies (i.e., Hurst, Entropy, Random Walks).

The Hurst exponent from a time series is certainly a more nuanced metric than the measures of central tendency used in this paper. With a longer series than the few minutes of play, perhaps a delta of variance may have emerged as a meaningful change over time metric. We will borrow terminology from Stafford and Dewar (Stafford & Dewar, 2013) who categorized players as either *Explorers* (what we might call Bouncers) or *Exploiters* (what we call the Got Its). Stafford and Dewar gathered statistics on hundreds of thousands of on-line players on a simple perceptual/motor game called *Axon*. They first binned players into percentile groups based on variance during first five times of play (higher variance = *explorers*) and then correlated that with subsequent performance data (plays six through 10: $r = .59$, $p < .0001$). The Explorers were not overly concerned with getting it right the first few times they played. Explorers moved all over the screen and spaced their practice sessions out. The Exploiters massed their practice sessions and were primarily goal-driven. *Explorers did better* at later gameplay even though all players practiced the same amount of time. This is an in-game metric that tells us something about the player profile over time. In the Tour de Force game, performance through gameplay like latency-to-switch-for-hill could reveal intriguing dynamic player profiles over time of play.

Prior Knowledge. We are interested in the construct of prior knowledge and how it interacts with intervention. Low and moderate pre-intervention knowledge students may be able to learn more in an embodied game because the learning is not driven primarily by language or memorizing symbols. These students may demonstrate higher gains when in an embodied condition. On the other hand, it may be the case that using the body is overwhelming at first, sensory overload may occur. Low prior knowledge learners might actually benefit from a symbolic tutorial before attempting an embodied session. We should also gather spatial abilities. The new 3D tools will be interesting to work with and prior spatial skills may interact with learning. Jang, Vitale, Jyung, and Black (2016) found that low spatial ability participants learned more from a direct 3D manipulation condition compared to the low spatial, yoked group in the observe condition (topic: functioning of the inner ear). Our study, unfortunately, did not have the power to run aptitude by treatment interactions (Cronbach & Snow, 1977).

Transfer. Transfer remains a thorny issue. In a relevant gears example, Dixon and Dohn (Dixon & Dohn, 2003) directly instructed participants to use the alternation (parity) strategy on a structurally analogous task in which balance beams were connected end-to-end in a series. Participants were asked to predict whether the last balance beam in the series would go up or down, given the movement of first beam. After being instructed on alternation and solving 10 problems using alternation, participants were given gear-train system problems. Despite immediate prior mastering of the alternation strategy, participants showed no evidence of transfer. Their median discovery trial did not differ from that of uninstructed participants. In our study, the final test question (item 10) asked about relative input gear size when winching up objects of varying masses. On the pretest only three participants chose the correct answer for the heaviest object (the mattress, 13%), on the posttest only six chose the correct answer (25%, paired $t < .80$, NS). This was not the sort of robust transfer gain we had hoped to see. It reminds us that teachers may still need to be very explicit with students about what was learned, and perhaps remind students to transfer and apply the MA knowledge to other similar content.

Adaptivity. For future design, we will work towards tracking behavior and integrating what we know about in ludo performance and placing learners in appropriate levels. If the student is a Bouncer and remains a Bouncer throughout several games, then the system should be able to place the student into a tutorial that goes over the concept of MA again, or flag the teacher to come and make sure the student fully understands the mechanics of the physical gameplay and/or the concepts.

Observation as an IV. Many of our games are designed with a performative aspect. The student(s) go to the front of the class to play and demonstrate their knowledge. There may be effects related to position or time of play. As in, the final students have observed more play and seen the mistakes of the earlier players so they should be at some advantage. Previous ranked player analyses have not shown a significant difference due to time of play (Johnson-Glenberg & Hekler, 2013), although that was also a small n study. We do know that after 20 minutes of observation the students who have already played these short games begin to get restless. We now recommend that teachers use these short games as "stations", and not make the entire class watch for more than six or so sessions.

Students as Creators. Finally, we are excited about building in-game editors and allowing students to alter gameplay for peers. We would like to understand why the configuration panels were not fully used. For the final few instructional minutes of the Tour de Force game, the teacher demonstrated to the students the panel. He changed the Y axis on one hill so that the extremely steep hill would be impossible to ascend. However, the teacher did not let the students explore this on their own; he did not encourage them to build or sketch out separate race courses for different teams to play. One idea for the next classroom instantiation is for us to include some locking code in the game that will not advance after five play sessions unless some of the hill parameters are altered and played through. Teachers often report feeling a press to get through topics and so changing around the game and going deeper to explore different start states may feel like a luxury to them. A hypothesis worth testing is whether students in the "creator condition" retain more information than those who never alter the game.

CONCLUSION

Two games called Tour de Force and the Winching Game were designed to instruct middle schoolers in the concepts associated with gear trains. Learners used the body to map the relatively abstract concept of mechanical advantage to physical, kinesthetic sensations. The games used the *Kinect* sensor as the input device to track the changing diameter of the player-created input gear. Paper and pencil tests were administered before and after the game intervention and significant gains in learning were made. In addition, dyadic data were gathered during play regarding amount of gear switches made during play on the easier game. Data were examined to understand student movement performance and explore how the arm rotations and gear diameter shifts related to scores on more traditional tests. Negative correlations were predicted, such that, players with fewer gear changes would score higher on the tests. The valence and magnitude of the correlations between gear switches varied between the two games. For the easier first game, movement data significantly negatively predicted pretest score, but not posttest score. For the more difficult second game, The Winching Game, gear switches were negatively associated with both pre- and posttests.

These exploratory data provide a window onto how students might perform on traditional tests. One take-away for our lab was that not all embodied games are created equal, even though the same team created the games and play-tested them with several students. We at first thought the games were of equal difficultly. However, the "in the wild" classroom students reported that the Winching Game was more difficult to master. It may be that the predictive effects of games emerge only from a game that is sufficiently challenging, or in the learner's appropriate Zone of Proximal Development (ZPD) (Vygotsky, 1978). If a game is too easy, it has low sensitivity, then being a winner or loser in a dyad will not reveal much about differences in comprehension. We also make note that the game might be capturing a different sort of knowledge than the crystalized paper and pencil test. Goldin-Meadow contends learners' gestures "precede, and predict" the acquisition of structures in speech (Goldin-Meadow, 2014). Thus, the learner may be understanding the concept and gesturing adroitly in the game, but still not be able to demonstrate that comprehension on a symbolically-oriented assessment measure.

Although the study sample size was small for inferential statistics, effect sizes that might be associated with short in-class, embodied games are reported. One primary goal is to use immediate game-style feedback to attenuate the need to give repetitive, time-wasting paper and pencil tests. We find this to be a promising intersection of gesture-based STEM instruction and in ludo assessments.

REFERENCES

Black, J. B., Segal, A., Vitale, J., & Fadjo, C. L. (2012). Embodied cognition and enhancing learning and motivation. In D. Jonassen & S. Land (Eds.), *Theoretical foundations of learning environments*. New York: Routledge.

Coller, B., & Scott, A. A. (2009). Effectiveness of using a video game to teach a course in mechanical engineering. *Computers & Education*, 53(3), 900–912. doi:10.1016/j.compedu.2009.05.012

Connolly, T. M., Boyle, E. A., MacArthur, E., Hainey, T., & Boyle, J. M. (2012). A systematic literature review of empirical evidence on computer games and serious games. *Computers & Education*, 59(2), 661–686. doi:10.1016/j.compedu.2012.03.004

Cook, S., & Goldin-Meadow, S. (2006). The Role of Gesture in Learning: Do Children Use Their Hands to Change Their Minds. *Journal of Cognition and Development*, 7(2), 211–232. doi:10.120715327647jcd0702_4

Cronbach, L., & Snow, R. (1977). *Aptitudes and Instructional Methods: A Handbook for Research on Interactions*. New York: Irvington.

DiDonato, M. D., Martin, C. L., Hessler, E. E., Amazeen, P. E., Hanish, L. D., & Fabes, R. A. (2012). Gender consistency and flexibility: Using dynamics to understand the relation between gender and adjustment. *Nonlinear Dynamics Psychology and Life Sciences*, 16(2), 159–184. PMID:22452931

diSessa, A. (1988). Knowledge in pieces. In G. Forman & P. B. Pufall (Eds.), *Constructivism in the Computer Age*. Hillsdale, NJ: Lawrence Erlbaum Associates.

Dixon, J. A., & Dohn, M. C. (2003). Redescription disembeds relations: Evidence from relational transfer and use in problem solving. *Memory & Cognition, 31*(7), 1082–1093. doi:10.3758/BF03196129 PMID:14704023

Gee, J. P., & Shaffer, D. W. (2010). Looking where the light is bad: Video games and the future of assessment. *EDge, 6*(1), 2–19.

Glenberg, A. M., Witt, J. K., & Metcalfe, J. (2013). From the revolution to embodiment: 25 years of cognitive psychology. *Perspectives on Psychological Science, 8*(5), 573–585. doi:10.1177/1745691613498098 PMID:26173215

Goldin-Meadow, S. (2011). Learning through gesture. *Wiley Interdisciplinary Reviews: Cognitive Science, 2*(6), 595–607. doi:10.1002/wcs.132 PMID:24187604

Goldin-Meadow, S. (2014). Widening the lens: What the manual modality reveals about learning, language and cognition. *Philosophical Transactions of the Royal Society, Biological Sciences., 369*(20130295).

Hanus, M., & Fox, J. (2015). Assessing the effects of gamification in the classroom: A longitudinal study on intrinsic motivation, social comparison, satisfaction, effort, and academic performance. *Computers & Education, 80*, 152–161. doi:10.1016/j.compedu.2014.08.019

Hauk, O., Johnsrude, I., & Pulvermüller, F. (2004). Somatotopic representation of action words in human motor and premotor cortex. *Neuron, 41*(2), 301–307. doi:10.1016/S0896-6273(03)00838-9 PMID:14741110

Jang, S., Vitale, J., Jyung, R., & Black, J. (2016). *Direct manipulation is better than passive viewing for learning anatomy in a three-dimensional virtual reality environment* (Vol. 106). Academic Press.

Johnson-Glenberg, M. C. (2012). *Pilot study with SMALLab summer camp attendees.* Unpublished.

Johnson-Glenberg, M. C. (2017). Embodied education in mixed and mediated realities: Principles for content design. In D. Liu, C. Dede, & J. Richards (Eds.), *Virtual, Augmented, and Mixed Realities in Education* (pp. 193–218). Springer Verlag. doi:10.1007/978-981-10-5490-7_11

Johnson-Glenberg, M. C. (submitted). *Immersive VR and education: Embodied design principles that include gesture and hand controls.* Academic Press.

Johnson-Glenberg, M. C., Birchfield, D., Koziupa, T., & Tolentino, L. (2014). Collaborative embodied learning in mixed reality motion-capture environments: Two science studies. *Journal of Educational Psychology, 106*(1), 86–104. doi:10.1037/a0034008

Johnson-Glenberg, M. C., Birchfield, D., Megowan-Romanowicz, M. C., Tolentino, L., & Martinez, C. (2009). Embodied Games, Next Gen Interfaces, and Assessment of High School Physics. *International Journal of Learning and Media, 1*(2). doi:10.1162/ijlm.2009.0017

Johnson-Glenberg, M. C., Birchfield, D., Megowan-Romanowicz, M. C., & Uysal, S. (2009). SMALLab: Virtual geology studies using embodied learning with motion, sound, and graphics. *Educational Media International, 46*(4), 267–280. doi:10.1080/09523980903387555

Johnson-Glenberg, M. C., & Hekler, E. B. (2013). Alien Health game: An embodied, motion-capture exer-game teaching nutrition and *MyPlate. Games for Health Journal, 6*(2). doi:10.1089/g4h.2013.0057

Johnson-Glenberg, M. C., & Megowan-Romanowicz, M. C. (2017). Embodied science and mixed reality: How gesture and motion capture affect physics education. *Cognitive Research: Principles and Implications, 2*(24). doi:10.118641235-017-0060-9 PMID:28603770

Johnson-Glenberg, M. C., Savio-Ramos, C., & Henry, H. (2014). "Alien Health": A nutrition instruction exergame using the *Kinect* sensor. *Games for Health Journal: Research, Development, and Clinical Applications, 3*(4), 241–251. doi:10.1089/g4h.2013.0094 PMID:25083315

Lindgren, R., & Johnson-Glenberg, M. C. (2013). Emboldened by embodiment: Six precepts regarding the future of embodied learning and mixed reality technologies. *Educational Researcher, 42*(8), 445–452. doi:10.3102/0013189X13511661

Lui, M., Kuhn, A., Acosta, A., Niño-Soto, M. I., Quintana, C., & Slotta, J. D. (2014). Using mobile tools in immersive environments to support science inquiry. *CHI '14 Extended Abstracts on Human Factors in Computing Systems, 978*, 403-406. doi:10.1145/2559206.2574796

Merchant, Z., Goetz, E. T., Cifuentes, L., Keeney-Kennicutt, W., & Davis, T. J. (2014). Effectiveness of virtual reality-based instruction on students' learning outcomes in K-12 and higher education: A meta-analysis. *Computers & Education, 70*, 29–40. doi:10.1016/j.compedu.2013.07.033

Metz, K. (1985). The development of children's problem solving in a gears task: A problem space perspective. *Cognitive Science, 9*(4), 431–471. doi:10.120715516709cog0904_4

Milgram, P., & Kishino, A. F. (1994). Taxonomy of mixed reality visual displays. *IEICE Transactions on Information and Systems, E77-D*(12), 1321–1329.

Mishra, J., Anguera, J. A., & Gazzaley, A. (2016). Video Games for Neuro-Cognitive Optimization. *Neuron, 90*(2), 214–218. doi:10.1016/j.neuron.2016.04.010 PMID:27100194

Mislevy, R. J., Behrens, J. T., DiCerbo, K. E., & Levy, R. (2012). Design and discovery in educational assessment: Evidence-centered design, psychometrics, and educational data mining. *JEDM-Journal of Educational Data Mining, 4*(1), 11–48.

Nathan, M. J., Walkington, C., Boncoddo, R., Pier, E. L., Williams, C. C., & Alibali, M. W. (2014). Actions speak louder with words: The roles of action and pedagogical language for grounding mathematical reasoning. *Learning and Instruction, 33*, 182-193.

Papastergiou, M. (2009). Digital Game-Based Learning in high school Computer Science education: Impact on educational effectiveness and student motivation. *Computers & Education, 52*(1), 1–12. doi:10.1016/j.compedu.2008.06.004

Segal, A., Black, J., & Tversky, B. (2010). *Do Gestural Interfaces Promotoe Learning? Congruent Gestures Promote Performance in Math.* Paper presented at the 51st Meeting of the Psychonomic Society Conference, St. Louis, MO.

Shaffer, D., Hatfield, D., Svarovsky, G., Nach, P., Nulty, A., Bagley, E., ... Mislevy, R. (2009). Epistemic Network Analysis: A Prototype for 21st Century Assessment of Learning. *International Journal of Learning and Media*, *1*(1).

Skulmowski, A., & Rey, G. D. (2018). Embodied learning: Introducing a taxonomy based on bodily engagement and task integration. *Cognitive Research*, *3*(1), 6. doi:10.118641235-018-0092-9 PMID:29541685

Slater, M., & Sanchez-Vives, M. V. (2016). Enhancing our lives with immersive virtual reality. *Frontiers in Robotics and AI*, *3*(74). doi:10.3389/frobt.2016.00074

Snow, E. L., Allen, L. K., Jacovina, M. E., & McNamara, D. S. (2015). Does agency matter?: Exploring the impact of controlled behaviors within a game-based environment. *Computers & Education*, *26*, 378–392. doi:10.1016/j.compedu.2014.12.011

Squire, K., & Klopfer, E. (2007). Augmented Reality Simulations on Handheld Computers. *Journal of the Learning Sciences*, *16*(3), 371–413. doi:10.1080/10508400701413435

Stafford, T., & Dewar, M. (2013). Tracing the trajectory of skill learning with a very large sample of online game players. *Psychological Science*. doi:10.1177/095679761351146

Vygotsky, L. S. (1978). *Mind in Society: The Development of Higher Psychological Processes*. Cambridge, MA: The Harvard University Press.

Wilson, M. (2002). Six views of embodied cognition. *Psychonomic Bulletin & Review*, *9*(4), 625–636. doi:10.3758/BF03196322 PMID:12613670

Wouters, P., Nimwegen, C., Oostendorp, H., & van der Spek, E. (2013). A meta-analysis of the cognitive and motivational effects of serious games. *Journal of Educational Psychology*, *105*(2), 249–265. doi:10.1037/a0031311

Young, M. F., Slota, S., Cutter, A. B., Jalette, G., Mullin, G., Lai, B., ... Yukhymenko, M. (2012). Our Princess Is in Another Castle: A Review of Trends in Serious Gaming for Education. *Review of Educational Research*, *82*(1), 61–89. doi:10.3102/0034654312436980

ENDNOTES

[1]   Energy is usually defined simply as "the ability to do work", a more general and useful definition is "the ability to cause a change". One reason to use the more general definition is that the term work is one that is often misunderstood as well. There are two things that can be done with energy: it can be stored and/or it can be transferred. The transfer of energy by means of work happens by exerting a force on something across some distance. The product of the input force and the distance travelled is the work done on the object. Working is the mechanism for energy transfer. Simple machines (e.g., levers and gears) are devices that make work easier by changing the magnitude and/or direction of a force and the displacement of the object to which the force is applied. This allows for useful work to be done on some object that would be difficult, or impossible, to accomplish otherwise. Examples of tasks that are hard for humans to do alone are lifting heavy boulders, moving pianos up stairs without pulleys or planes, and cycling up very steep hills.

[2]   Mislevy, et al. (2012) make intriguing points about how game designers and statisticians can work together in designing games to mitigate some of the prior gameplay knowledge that surely adds noise to all knowledge gain scores. They stress how the assessment design framework called Evidence Centered Design (ECD) can complement game design principles, so that designers can address assessment criteria such as reliability and validity jointly with game criteria like engagement and interactivity in mind (Mislevy, Behrens, DiCerbo, & Levy, 2012).

Regarding prior gameplay knowledge, we posit that the gameplay mechanism in this study was novel for all participants since the *Microsoft* Kinect for *XBOX* suite at the time did not have any products similar to our gears games when eth study ran. It was novel, yet intuitive; players did not need to use cognitive resources to recall the affordances of buttons A and B on a remote.

Chapter 53
Creativity and Digital Games:
A Study of Developing Creativity Through Digital Games

Werner Walder Marin
Mackenzie Presbyterian University, Brazil

Pollyana Notargiacomo
Mackenzie Presbyterian University, Brazil

ABSTRACT

In the last decades the interest in creativity has grown. One of the questions that has risen from this interest is whether it is possible to aid the development of creativity. This chapter reviews a study on the possibility of developing a digital game with this. The game Luovus was created, utilizing previous research on the subject of creativity and digital games as learning aids. The game has been tested with a group of users and seems to be an effect on the player's self-perceived creative capabilities and society's impact on their creativity. This chapter will also cover studies and past experiments on the subject and how they can be of interest to future experiments.

INTRODUCTION

Although creativity began to be studied in the early 40s by Maslow (1943), among others, increasing importance is being given to this topic, not only to its consequences to individual life but also to the possible benefits that creativity might bring to society as a whole (Alencar, Fleith, & Bruno-Faria, 2010). As interest in this topic grew, one of the questions studied throughout the years is how to exercise and/ or develop the creative thought.

It seems, therefore, that the interest of psychology in creativity is relatively recent (Alencar, Fleith, & Bruno-Faria, 2010). This interest occurs more intensely from 1950, thanks to various factors such as the influence of the humanist movement. Rogers (1959) and Maslow (1959) both draw attention to mental health as a source of creative impulses. They also point out the human potential for self-realization and

DOI: 10.4018/978-1-6684-7589-8.ch053

explain conditions that ease the expression of creativity. Rogers and Maslow conclude that creativity is the result of a mutually beneficial interaction between an individual and the environment in which this individual is inserted. Rogers also defends that autonomy and protection from excessive social control are fundamental for a creative activity.

According to Alencar et al. (2010) the idea of developing creative competencies is not yet a topic in which consensus has been reached. That said, it is already legitimized by studies that have shown positive results with programs that attempt to develop said creative competencies. Therefore, it is possible to theorize that any and every person has a creative potential that can be systematically explored and developed (Runco, 2014). There are currently multiple strategies that aim at training the creative thought, from programs, to software to digital games (Runco & Jaeger, 2012).

Azevedo et al. (2017) conducted a study on the Future Problem Solving Program International. Developed with the objective of training the creative thoughts of children and teenagers, the FPSPI is a program that has been applied for decades and in various countries. This program came to be in the United States and has spread to other countries including, but not limited to, Australia, England, Singapore, etc. Every year an international competition takes place, in which children and teenagers from all around the world present projects developed with the aid of the program's methodology. In the experiment conducted by Azevedo et al. (2017) a group of teenagers showed significant positive results to being submitted to this program.

Based on this scenario, it seems that the interest in understanding creativity has consistently grown in the last decades. This brings forth the question of the possibility of aiding the development of creative thought. This study is concerned with investigating the possibility of developing a digital game capable of such. For this the game *Luovus* was created, based on past research on creativity and digital games as learning tools. The game was tested on a group of users and although the results are not enough to come to a conclusive answer to the main question proposed by this study, there seems to be an effect on the player's self-evaluation of their own creative capabilities and society's impact on their creativity.

Other studies and experiments that are similar or relevant to this topic will also be analyzed. Many of them are important to comprehend the relationship of the various factors involved in the exercise of creative thought, such as positive psychology and mental state of flow.

BACKGROUND

Creativity: Definition and Involved Variables

Creativity can be defined as an interaction between a person and the environment this person is inserted in, this being a beneficial interaction. This interaction needs autonomy, and also needs to be shielded from excessive social control to be effective. Some aspects commonly associated with creativity are strategies, decision making, thought managing, learning style, personality traits, motivation, aspects of cognitive abilities, etc. Creativity is a psychosocial phenomenon, which is born both from an individual's characteristics and the social environment in which this individual exists (Alencar, Fleith, & Bruno-Faria, 2010). In other words, creativity is a result both from the individual as well as the environment.

Creativity can be divided in two types. These two types are individual creativity and team creativity. These two types of creativity function in different ways, as are the variables that influence their manifestation. Each type has its advantages, but also its disadvantages. Individual creativity flourishes more easily in isolated tasks, while team creativity is believed to flourish more easily in tasks where there is a stronger interdependency between the tasks of each member of the team. Therefore, in the model proposed by Wang (2013), individual autonomy promotes the feeling of propriety of the task at hand, which in turn promotes motivation. Motivation mediates the positive relationship between individual autonomy and individual creativity. The autonomy of an individual or of a team is one of the variables that may affect the capacity to find creative solutions studied by Wang. The other variable is the interdependence of the tasks a team is responsible for.

One factor that influences the creative thought is psychological well-being. De Rooij et al. (2015) found a connection between satisfaction and the capacity to produce creative ideas. Another factor that influences the creative thought is the way in which a person receives feedback on their work. Qiong, Wee, and Li remark that past studies focused on the negative aspects of psychological stress caused by work, but that a reduced number of studies were conducted on the positive aspects of psychological stress, one of which, they say, is the likelihood to come to a creative solution thanks to continuing to visualize the problem outside of work (Li, Qiong, & Wee, 2014).

If on the one hand an individual may come to more creative ideas for focusing on the task for longer periods of time, on the other hand there is the possibility that a longer session of creative thought may lead to cognitive exhaustion and, thus, subpar results (Coppi, 2015).

Coppi (2015) noted that there was a problem in the initially proposed duration of her experiment. Having a duration superior to two hours, the attention span of the children participating in the experiment may have been negatively affected, which consequently affected the post test. No signs were found that the children's capacity to produce creative ideas was affected, only their capacity to focus on a single task.

In regards to group creativity, it manifests more frequently in tasks where there is a stronger interdependence between the tasks of each member of the team. In the model proposed by Wang (2013), when a task is approached by a team, in the case the interdependence of the responsibilities of each member of the team is high, the team's total creativity is approximately the sum of the individual creativity of each member of the team. On the other hand, if the interdependence between the responsibilities of each member is low or the individual autonomy of each member is high, it may lead to conflicts between the members of the team, which has a negative impact on the team's creativity.

High interdependence and high team autonomy promote the exchange of ideas, discussions of strategies and viewpoints, feedback exchange, integration among tasks, as well as interpersonal interactions, communication and cooperation (Wang, 2013). Alternatively, when interdependence is low, the lack of internal communication in the team and the low coordination may lead to a decrease of motivation, which has a negative impact on the team's creativity.

Wang also says that when individual autonomy is high, each member of the team may choose how to accomplish their own tasks without having to consider the others. This may lead to an increase in intrinsic motivation, through an increased feeling of propriety and authorship over the task and responsibility over the outcome. This feeling is considered key to leading to creative thinking. In a scenario in which task interdependence is low, this arrangement will not lead to conflicts in the team and the total creativity may be calculated as the sum of each member's individual creativity. But if it is not the case, and task interdependence is high, the high individual autonomy may cause each member to act in a way that, although beneficial to themselves, is not beneficial to the rest of the team. I addition to that, it may be the case that each member's intrinsic motivation is incompatible with each other. The necessary coordination for a team to be productive is compromised, which also affects the team's capacity to act and implement creative solutions.

Relationship Between Positive Psychology and Creativity

A psychologically healthy person is in a position where they may find it easier to express their creativity and originality. An important step to prepare oneself to a task that requires creative thinking is to care for one's well-being.

In their study, De Rooij, Corr, and Jones (2015), conducted a study in which they developed a system that would evaluate the originality of ideas. Then participants were asked to present ideas and the system would evaluate those ideas. The evaluations were manipulated, though, so that while some evaluations would be legitimate, some would be either more favorable or less favorable than they should be. This was done to measure the impact that feedback can have on the ability of the participants to conceive creative ideas.

De Rooij et al. (2015) analyzed the influence that the positive or negative emotions caused by the feedback had on the participants and found a significant positive correlation between satisfaction and originality. In other words, when the participants received a positive evaluation, they had a higher probability of conceiving creative ideas in subsequent stages of the experiment. Participants that received neutral evaluations had a smaller probability of conceiving creative ideas in subsequent stages of the experiment. Participants that received negative evaluations had the smallest probability of conceiving creative ideas in subsequent stages of the experiment.

De Rooij et al. defend that this correlation can only be explained by the feelings of satisfaction and frustration caused in the participants by the feedback, since there was no observed difference in the performance of participants that had their evaluations manipulated and the participants that did not have their evaluations manipulated.

It is important to note that the system was developed taking into consideration that an exaggeratedly positive feedback could be detected as insincere or irrelevant by being disconnected from reality by the participants, and would therefore be counterproductive to their study. It is also important to note that De Rooij et al. (2015) admit the possibility that is not the positive feelings of satisfaction that promote originality, but negative feelings of frustration that inhibit creative thought, although the fact that participants who received positive evaluations were more productive than participants who received neutral evaluations might indicate this is not the case.

Creativity Under Stress

One of the positive effects of stress, say Qiong, Wee, and Li (2014), is to increase the duration of the creative thinking process a worker dedicates to a task. They propose that when a worker becomes stressed by a task, they think about it even out of the workplace. Therefore, the solution this worker finds for this task has the potential to be even more creative than it would be if this worker thought about this task only during work hours. This effect becomes even more intense proportionally to the control the worker has over this task (Li, Qiong, & Wee, 2014).

Qiong et al. (2014) call this stress a cognitive irritation. They analyzed the relationship between the control a worker has over a task and their creativity, mediated by this cognitive irritation. While they observe there are negative aspects to this cognitive irritation, such as potential health problems, depression and conflicts in the family environment, the authors argue that the positive aspects are mostly ignored. When workers possess high autonomy and control over their tasks, they also suffer with the stress of the responsibility over these tasks. In the scenario that the worker feels as if they are not progressing in finding a solution for this task, they may continue to simulate the process of solving this task in their mind. For instance, a factory worker tasked with increasing productivity in their production line that is struggling to complete such task may continue to visualize their daily tasks at work and try to find a way to increase productivity. When the worker enters this state of cognitive irritation, they continue to think about their task even outside the workplace. Since they spend longer thinking about the task, they have a higher probability of developing and elaborating creative ideas and strategies, and therefore has a higher probability of generating creative ideas. On the other hand, with no cognitive irritation the worker may still think creatively about their task, but will limit these creative thinking sessions to the workplace.

Also, positive stress can contribute even in areas such as entrepreneurship, as there is enthusiasm and positive experiences associated with situations that cause reflective practices, work organization, mental preparation and recovery, as well as joy appreciation and positive pressure encouragement (Berg, Dutton, & Wrzesniewski, 2013); elements that can also integrate creative processes.

Types and Effects of Feedback on Creative Work

In the office environment, workers that receive feedback on their work from a superior show a positive growth of their creative thinking capabilities (Amabile & Gryskiewicz, 1987).

Zhou et al. (2013) theorize that this growth depends a great deal in the worker's habit to self-monitor. A worker that self-monitors themselves is more likely to adapt to their context. Therefore, this worker will react to their social environment in an active manner. According to Zhou et al., this may lead the worker to having a more constructive reaction to their superior's feedback.

Even if a superior supply their subordinates with feedback, the relationship between those subordinate's feedback and their creativity is mediated by the self-monitoring habit of each one of these subordinates, in such a way that different workers will be affected differently by the feedback given by the same superior. Zhou et al. note that the feedback also has an effect on the worker's creativity by means of aiding these workers at becoming better at their tasks. In other words, the feedback will make the workers better at performing their tasks, which will increase their interest in the task. This interest, in turn, will incentivize the worker's to take risks and experiment with new approaches, which are key behaviours in finding creative solutions.

In their study, Zhou et al. observed that people who possess the habit of self-monitoring are more sensitive to social and environmental signs, which in turn gives them better chances at adapting their behaviour to the context they are currently inserted into. This way, these people react in a much more active and agile way, which leads them to having a more positive response to feedback. People who do not have the habit of self-monitoring, however, tend to not catch these social and environmental signs, therefore they are not capable to react as well to them and can only have a passive reaction to feedback. They are not capable to alter their behaviour in an active way (Gangestad & Snyder, 2000).

The Effects of Too Many or Too Few Restrictions

The restrictions imposed on a person when attempting to find a solution to a given task may impact that person's capacity to find a creative solution for said task. Moffat and Shabalina (2016) conducted an experiment and arrived at the conclusion that none, too many or too strong restrictions may impact negatively a person's capacity to reach a creative solution, but a moderate amount of restrictions may in turn have a positive effect. On the one hand, restrictions suppress creativity. On the other hand, they force the person to focus their creativity. In other words, a balance in restrictions forces a non-conventional solution without also restricting too much the possibilities of how to solve the task.

In an experiment conducted by Yokochi and Okada (2015), an artist was asked to complete a painting incorporating line that were previously painted on the canvas by the researchers. After the experiment, the artist stated that the resulting paintings were more creative than his usual paintings, which were painted without any form of restriction.

Too much freedom of choice, it seems, makes the creative process harder, as with the lack of any restriction or condition there are possibilities and options that must be considered. While this factor becomes less impactful as experience is acquired, as it permits more familiarity and comfort with the number of choices, less experienced people may find it easier to arrive at creative solutions if they must act under some restrictions (Chua, & Iyengar, 2008).

In their study, Moffat et al. (2016) asked a group of students to participate in some creative exercises. These exercises consisted of ideating short digital games. These games were then evaluated by their colleagues participating in the experiment. Many games were designed in different stages of the experiment. In the first stage the games were designed with no restrictions. In the second stage some restrictions were imposed on the students. In the third stage were imposed even harsher restrictions than in the previous stage.

When the students were interviewed after the experiment, it was put forward the opinion that the restrictions limited the students' creativity, but that it also forced their focus to be trained on specific areas. That means some restrictions may have a positive impact, while other restrictions may have a negative impact. Indeed, the results of the evaluations of the games designed in the experiment indicate that the evaluations for games designed with no restrictions were consistent, while the evaluations for games with some or many restrictions showed higher variation, with some ideas receiving positive and negative evaluations simultaneously.

Relevant Works

The first step in this research was to find tools and strategies to develop a person's creativity. Some experiments of interest to this research were found, including workplace activities (Wang, 2013) and pedagogical exercises with children (Coppi, 2015).

Buzady (2017) studied the serious game FLIGBY as a tool to develop leadership skills using the mental state of flow. Buzady describe the benefits of the flow state in a serious game, such as strong engagement and a feeling of satisfaction. The usefulness of the feeling of satisfaction has been previously discussed by De Rooij et al. (2015). In Buzady's study it is possible to see potential in serious games as tools to train soft skills.

The experiment conducted by Azevedo et al. (2017) with the *Future Problem Solving Program International* had positive results. All the competencies showed a significant increase in the experimental group. The prospect of developing a game that can aid the development of creativity applying the principles of the FPSPI is promising.

While there is no conclusive evidence that it is possible to develop a game that develops a player's creativity, it is possible to develop a game that aims to do so, with past experiments showing promising results, such as Coppi (2015) and Buzady (2017).

There is reason to believe that the player's age has an impact on the final experience. The study conducted by Vella et al. (2013) with people ranging from 12 to 52 years of age found a positive relationship between age and the player's well-being. The higher their age, the stronger their feelings of well-being. In other words, the same game will have different effects on two players of different ages (Vella, Johnson, & Hides, 2013). Therefore, it is unlikely to develop a game that has equally satisfying results across all ages. It might be more effective to develop a game with a specific demographic in mind.

The study conducted by Vella et al. (2013) had three primary objectives: investigate whether there was any difference in the creativity levels of students in distinct stages of high school, the generalization or specification of creativity in relationship to different school subjects and to what extent creativity is related to performance. For the purpose of this research, the most relevant is the first objective.

Analyzing the results of their study, Vella et al. (2013) concluded that students at the end of high school exhibited the highest capacity to express creative thoughts. Vella et al. call attention to the competencies of producing ideas, producing original ideas and producing abstract ideas that give new meaning to known ideas. In other words, the further a student's education, the higher their creative capacities.

It is not clear, however, if this positive relationship between formal education and creative capability happens thanks to psychological and intellectual maturation reached naturally through the aging process of a child. It is possible this ease at expressing creative thought is a consequence either of intellectual maturity or of formal education, potentially both. It is also not clear if, in case this is caused by formal education, this formal education must also attempt to intentionally exercise the child's creativity. It is possible that merely by acquiring general knowledge the child also acquires better tools with which to express their creativity.

Vella et al. (2013) argue that the found data does not allow to confidently say the causal influence of these variables, but that studies of children with no formal education of the same age range may come to shed light on the relationship between education, age and creativity. That said, Vella et al. (2013) state that the data is in accord with most studies on the subject, which also point to a positive relationship between the capacity to think creatively and the end of adolescence (Lau & Cheung, 2010; Torrance, 1979).

Measuring Creativity

In the search for a reliable method to measure creativity, some tests were developed. The most famous among them are probably the *Torrance Tests of Creative Thinking*, in which was later based the *Abbreviated Torrance Test for Adults*, a reduced version focused on adults. The TTCT scores individuals on the attributes of Fluency, Originality, Elaboration and, at later versions of the test, Abstractness of Titles and Resistance to Premature Closure. Earlier versions of the test also evaluated Flexibility, but Torrance removed it from later versions as he believed it overlapped with Fluency. Also evaluated are the criterions of emotional expressiveness, storytelling articulateness, movement or action, expressiveness of titles, synthesis of incomplete figures, synthesis of lines or circles, unusual visualization, internal visualization, extending or breaking boundaries, humor, richness of imagery, colorfulness of imagery and fantasy. The TTCT are widely trusted and frequently referred to in studies about the measurement of creativity (Cramond, Matthews-Morgan, & Bandalos, 2005).

Torrance concluded that the *Torrance Tests of Creative Thinking* do not cover all dimensions of creativity and suggested that a second form of measurement should also be used to reach more reliable results (Treffinger, 1985). However, The TTCT are a good measuring tool, not only to detect particularly creative individuals, but also to discover and encourage creative thinking in the populace in general (Kim, 2006). In addition to this, the TTCT are still some of the most used tests in the field of creativity. The reasons for using it are as relevant today as they were in 1966: promoting the comprehension of the human mind, aiding the development of individual instruction, provide information for psychotherapeutic programs, understand the efficacy of different educational materials and reveal potentials that might otherwise go unnoticed (Cramond, Matthews-morgan, & Bandalos, 2005).

Another creativity test to be considered is the *Abedi Test for Creativity*. Developed by Ahmadi (2011). In contrast to the previously mentioned TTCT and ATTA, the ATC is a self-evaluative test. In this case it is possible to gain some understanding of how a person perceives their own creative capabilities, in such a way that the TTCT and the ATC may be used for distinct reasons. The questionnaire consists of 60 questions divided between expansiveness, originality, fluency and flexibility.

Last to be covered in this research is the test for creativity developed by Alencar et al. (2010). Just as the ATC, this test is self-evaluative. The relevance for this research is primarily the language in which it was developed. The game developed in this research will be played by native portuguese speakers, the language in which the test developed by Alencar et al. was originally conceived.

Experiments on the Development of Creativity

Azevedo et al. (2017) conducted a study to test the possibility of developing creative thought in adolescents, applying the *Future Problem Solving Program International* methodology, which was in turn developed based in the *Creative Problem Solving* methodology, the latter being developed by the likes of Isaksen, Dorval and Treffinger (2011). The FPSPI methodology proposes six stages of problem resolution, starting with the definition of the problem to be approached to the communication of the solution in such a way that it is accepted. This methodology assumes that for any problem there is always at least one solution, the question being finding and applying this solution.

The six stages of the FPSPI are, in order, defining a generic problem, selecting the problem to be tackled, producing decision criteria, evaluating the proposed solutions and finally implementing the selected solution.

At the end of the program, which lasts one school year, Azevedo et al. noted that the results indicate that the program had a positive effect on its participants. All the competencies practiced and evaluated in the FPSPI program showed significant growth in the experimental group, even in competencies in which this group already had above average scores.

An experiment conducted by Buzady (2017) concerned itself with studying the relevance of the mental state of flow, a concept of the field of Positive Psychology. For such, the serious game FLIGBY was used, a simulation game aimed towards teaching and training on how to manage and lead people based on the principles of "flow-based leadership". Buzady did not focus on evaluating the efficiency of a framework in particular, neither did the research had the objective of arriving at new numerical findings. Instead, Buzady was mainly concerned in presenting a case study as inspiration for possible future works in this field of psychology.

The state of flow is reached when there is a balance between two states extreme to each other: the state of anxiety and the state of boredom. The state of anxiety is reached when the level of skill required to perform a task is significantly higher than the level of skill a person possesses. The state of boredom, on the other hand, is reached when the level of skill a person possesses is significantly higher than the level of skill required to perform a task. The state of flow can be reached from either extreme. When in a state of anxiety, a person begins to develop their skills and acquire the knowledge necessary to perform the task, eventually migrating to the state of flow. Alternatively, a person in a state of boredom will feel compelled to seek tasks that challenge them and that demand new skills and knowledge, which will lead them to a situation in which they can reach the state of flow.

This mental state has received the name of "flow" because individuals that experience this state commonly describe it as a state in which their energy flows freely and in which their consciousness is carried by the task at hand (Csikszentmihalyi, 1975).

Another proposal, by Coppi (2015), resulted in the development of the game "Over the Gate". This game had as a premise to train the creativity of children by means of games and storytelling through digital media. In her article, Coppi not only describes the development of the game but also explains the pilot study conducted on top of this game.

"Over the Gate" is presented in the format of an electronic book, with story accompanied by illustrations and composed of verbal and visual games based on different aspects of creativity, such as originality, flexibility, fluency, etc. Some of the challenges presented to the players are riddles in which the player must find more than one answer, complete unfinished drawings, manipulate geometric shapes so as to form figures, choose different titles for stories, complete unfinished poems and solve logical challenges with rules similar to chess. Afterwards the player is told a story that illustrates the importance of creativity.

Based on this study it is possible to see potential in the use of digital games as a tool to develop creativity. Coppi concludes that some changes should be implemented in the game to reach better results, suggesting a deeper reading of the literature to better understand the required changes. These alterations show themselves to be necessary thanks to a possible problem that may be identified with the duration of the game, which is longer than two hours, negatively affecting the player's attention span as they are children. This negative impact may have affected the post test results. Coppi also proposes changes to the user interface, a reduction of the duration of the story told to the player and the introduction of a scoring system.

METHODOLOGY

To test the hypothesis proposed in this research, a game called *Luovus* was developed. This name was chosen for the similarity with the words *luovuus*, which means "creativity", and the word "love" in English, as a reminder of a positive feeling. While the literature indicates the potentially positive effect of positive feelings on creativity (De Rooij, Corr, & Jones, 2015), this benefit was not considered when choosing the title for the game. It is merely an artistic choice.

The game *Luovus* was developed in the JavaScript programming language, using the PixiJS graphical engine. This combination was chosen for its ease of universal access, seeing as a web-based page is easier to access than an application programmed for a specific operating system. Modules are attached to the main .html page that may be activated or deactivated as needed. Each module corresponds to a questionnaire, a game scene or a game screen. The modules are managed by an engine programmed specifically for *Luovus*, also in JavaScript, called *Vorhees* (Figure 1). This engine is tasked with initializing PixiJS and deciding which modules to activate and deactivate based on a state diagram.

When a scene module is loaded, Vorhees loads a .json file corresponding to the correct scene, containing information such as character art, dialogue and background graphics. Vorhees interprets this information and, in tandem with PixiJS, draws the scene on screen. Vorhees then receives and interprets the player's input and reacts accordingly.

Figure 1. Vorhees' state diagram
Source: (Marin & Notargiacomo, 2019)

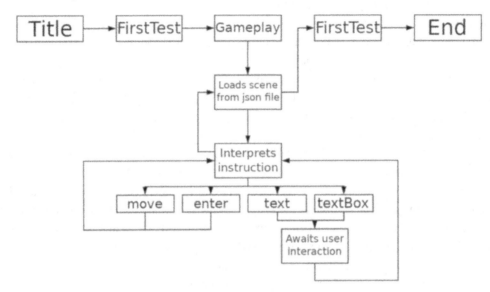

The results of the questionnaires answered by the players are each saved in a different *.json* file. These files do not contain any information that may compromise the privacy and anonymity of the players. Each file is identified by a randomly generated identification number.

Upon accessing the game by means of a chosen we browser, the user is presented the title screen, which contains the options "start" and "about." When the player selects the "start" option they are asked to complete the self-evaluative questionnaire for creativity created by Alencar et al. (2010) (Figure 2).

This specific creativity test was chosen for having been originally conceived in the portuguese language. This experiment was conducted with native portuguese speaking participants and keeping the test in its original language guarantees its integrity. The questionnaire consists of 66 questions in the format "I would be more creative if..." followed by a statement. For example, "I would be more creative if I were less shy to expose my ideas". For each statement the player must choose if they "completely disagree", "somewhat disagree ", is "uncertain", "somewhat agree" or "completely agree." The results are analyzed in a Likert scale. This initial questionnaire is used to evaluate the player's perception of their own creativity before their interaction with the game. The results of this questionnaire will posteriorly be compared to the results of the questionnaire completed by the player at the end of the game. This way, it is possible to examine the impact that the game had on the player and how their perception of their own creativity was affected after playing the game.

After completing the questionnaire, the player is presented to the game through a story.

This experiment counted on 15 participants. Of these 15 participants, 8 were female and 7 were male. The youngest participant was 20 years old and the oldest participant was 25 years old. The average of the ages of all participants is 22 years of age. Each player undertook the questionnaire twice. The questionnaire was identical to all players, consisting of the same 66 questions in the "I would be more creative if..." format with 5 replies on the Likert scale that were consisted throughout the questionnaire.

Figure 2. Translated questionnaire used in the game
Source: (Marin & Notargiacomo, 2019)

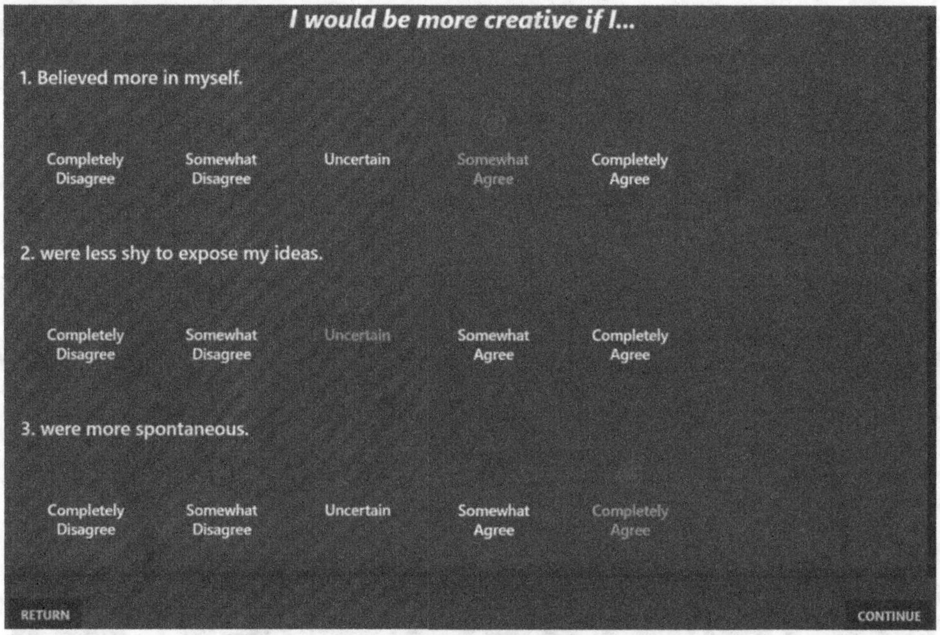

RESULTS AND ANALYSIS

Based on the developed computational application described in the methodology, the game *Luovus*, tests were conducted with real users. The players were asked to play the game, which included answering the two questionnaires, and then answer a few informal questions. Upon starting the game, the player is introduced to the *Artist*, a character that will serve as a guide and companion to the player throughout the game. The artist also serves as an interpreter to the player, as the player takes control of a silent character. Throughout the game the player will also meet other characters. In each interaction with one of these characters the player will be presented with challenges, that they must find a solution to in order to progress (Figure 3). The solutions presented by the player will be integrated into the game and commented on by other characters so that the player will have the opportunity to see that the solutions they present are being acknowledged by the game.

Throughout the game the player will meet new characters with whom they must interact. Each interaction affects the events of the story in a perceptible way. At the end, the artist will show the player the story they wrote. This story incorporates elements of the interactions between the player and the world. This approach is based on the structure of the game in which the player will meet characters that need assistance with a problem. Therefore, it is asked of the player that they propose a solution to this problem. The player receives a suggestion of what kind of solution they should propose, but the player has complete freedom to propose any solution they like. An example of a problem the player will be faced with is assisting a local bar owner with attracting clients to their establishment. This approach was chosen based on the study by Moffat and Shabalina (2016), and takes into consideration their findings and that and that a balance of some restrictions should be aimed for, as too many restrictions would suppress the players creativity, but too few restrictions may leave the player feeling confused and unsure of how to proceed. The character's reactions to the solutions presented by the player seek to be fun and gratifying, without being exaggeratedly congratulatory. While generating positive feelings of satisfaction on the player has a positive impact on their capacity to express their creativity, this effect would be loss if the player felt a disconnection between their performance and the feedback given by the game (De Rooij, Corr, & Jones, 2015).

Figure 3. Translated scene from the game in which the player is presented with a challenge
Source: (Marin & Notargiacomo, 2019)

> Patovsky
>
> I want something that stands out. Something no one ever thought of doing! What do you think would catch the the attention of anyone walking by?

Since the solutions presented by the player, by means of their interactions with other characters, have an impact on the story and are discussed by other characters, at the end of the game the *Artist* character uses the player's suggestions as inspiration to write his story. This story is shown to the player and is altered to include the player interactions. For instance, at some point in the game the player is asked for a suggestion of which material to use to build a certain object. In the artist's story some object will be a reference to the material chosen by the player. The art style and direction of the game were chosen to be unobtrusive and simple, while also being fantastic, as to invite the player to think beyond the realm of the obvious.

It should also be noted that the challenges in the game were designed in such a way as not to limit the options of what the player can do, but also suggest a guide as to how to come to a solution. Based on the study by Moffat et al. (2016), an effort was made towards neither restricting too much the player's creative freedom, nor leave the solution so open that the player may feel lost or confused about how to progress (Figure 4). A high number of restrictions or restrictions that are too strict might impede the player from feeling they have autonomy to find their own solution, which according to Wang (2013) would have a negative impact on the player's motivation, which would, in turn, impact negatively the player's ability to find creative solutions to the challenges presented by the game. On the other hand, none or few restrictions could leave the player confused and without an idea of how deeply they can explore the game mechanics.

The game was limited to three scenarios to avoid eroding the player's motivation. As this study depends on the post test results, it was deemed important to avoid having the player reach the end of the game feeling uninterested or cognitively exhausted, as this could affect the post test (Coppi, 2015).

Finally, the story presented by the artist at the end of the game is a way to show the player a different way that their solutions could be interpreted, and possibly incentivize reflection about how their input could have been interpreted had they come up with different solutions to the challenges presented by the game, as self evaluation is a catalyst for self development (Zhou & Li, 2013). A non intentional benefit was observed in the story presented to the player by the artist at the end of the game: it promoted discussion among the participants, as they compared their resulting stories and discussed the effects of each one's solutions.

Figure 4. Translated scene from the game in which the player is asked for input
Source: (Marin & Notargiacomo, 2019)

At the end of the game the player is once again taken to the questionnaire taken at the start of the game. The purpose of this post test is to examine how the game influenced the player, specifically how their perception of their capacity to think creatively was altered. This second test allowed an analysis of a player's total variation, as well as the variation in the score for each question among all players.

The test for creativity implemented in the game Luovus was the one developed by Alencar et al. (2010). As the experiment was conducted with people whose primary and possibly only language is Portuguese, this test was chosen over the ATC. A self-evaluative test was chosen for the opportunity it grants to incentivize the player to reflect on their own creativity and to understand how each participant sees their own capacity to find creative solutions for a given task. A self-evaluative test was chosen to promote the practice of self-monitoring during the game on the player. As noted by Zhou et al. (2013), self-monitoring is a useful practice when attempting to train creative thought.

When analysing the results of the experiment, it is possible to observe that not significant variation was found on the player's perception of their own creativity on the post-test in comparison to the pre test. The average variation on player score is -6 on a scale of -132 to 132 (Figure 5). This slight negative variation may have been caused by cognitive exhaustion on the players' side.

Figure 5. Creativity score variation for users between pretest and post-test
Source: (Marin & Notargiacomo, 2019)

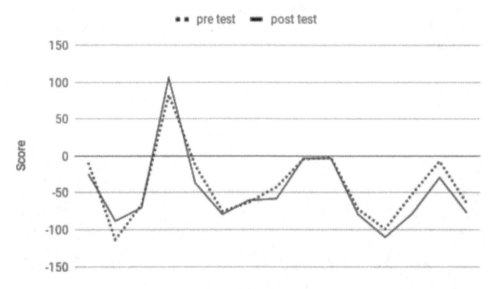

The individual variation on the answers for each specific question was also analyzed (Figure 6). In other words, an analysis of the variation for the score of each question for all players. In this analysis it is possible to see which questions had the greatest variation between the pretest and post-test.

Figure 6. Average score variation for each question between pretest and post-test
Source: (Marin & Notargiacomo, 2019)

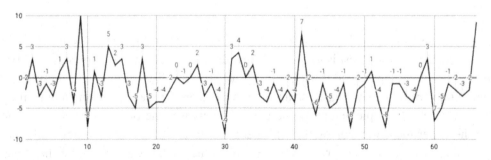

The variation for most questions was of 5 points or less, not presenting a significant variation. That said, some questions did present a more significant variation. The highest variation for a specific question found was of 10 points. The questions with variations considered significant were questions 9, 10, 30, 41, 43, 48, 53, 60 and 66 (Table 1).

Table 1. Questions with most significative score variation

Question	"I would be more creative if..."	Variation
9	"I had more initiative"	10
10	"I weren't afraid to contradict people"	-8
30	"I weren't afraid to be misunderstood"	-9
41	"I had more resources to put my ideas into practice"	7
43	"I hadn't been suppressed by my teachers"	-6
48	"there was more cooperation between people"	-8
53	"people valued new ideas more"	-8
60	"I had a stronger sense of humor"	-7
66	"I had more knowledge"	9

Source: (Marin & Notargiacomo, 2019)

CONCLUSION AND FUTURE WORKS

This experiment was proposed with the idea of testing the possibility of developing a game that could aid the player in training their creativity, based on past experiments. While the results were not conclusive, they indicate a promising possibility that it is possible to have at least some impact on a person's creativity by means of a digital game, be it in the form of exercising their creative capabilities or promoting self-monitoring and reflection on their own creativity.

Analysing the results of the experiment it is not possible to state that the game did actually impact the player's self-perceived creativity. The slight negative variation found on the average score of all players might be explained by the self-evaluative nature of the test chosen for this experiment. It is possible that the players evaluated themselves more strictly after playing the game.

After the game the players were asked about their experience with Luovus. 11 of the participants said they found the game "fun", "interesting" or "cool". This means that over two thirds of the 15 participants reported having a positive experience with the game. On the other hand, 5 of the participants also said they found the game too short or expressed a desire that the game be longer. This means their experience may have been cut short while they were in the *flow* state of mind. A longer game might have been more successful in giving players ampler opportunities to exercise their creativity without becoming exhausting.

Also worth noting is that 7 of the participants complained about the extension of the creativity test chosen for this experiment, arguing that the high number of questions (66 questions to be exact) and taking the test twice was tiring. This number represents almost half of participants, so this factor should not be ignored. This problem points back to the problem found by Coppi (2015) in her experiment, in which the duration of the experiment may have negatively affected the post test results because of the cognitive exhaustion it may have caused on the players. This is another possible explanation for the negative average score variation found in this experiment. This effect might be mitigated by employing a shorter questionnaire or by integrating the test in the game in a way that is nearly or completely imperceptible to the player.

Roughly speaking the score variation for each player did not present a significant variation. That said, some questions presented higher average variations and are therefore worthy of deeper analysis. These questions had variations higher than 5 points, whether negative or positive. Analysing the questions with positive variations it is possible to theorize that the game made the players more confident in their capacity to express creative thoughts without the need of external material or intellectual resources. Questions such as "I would be more creative if I had more initiative" and "I would be more creative if I had more knowledge" had a notably positive variation, which may indicate that the experience of practicing their creativity led the players to feel more secure in their capacity to be creative without the need of external aid. On the other hand, analysing the questions that presented a negative variation it seems the players may have become less secure in their ideas being socially accepted. The analysis of questions such as "I would be more creative if I weren't afraid of being misunderstood" and "I would be more creative if there were higher cooperation between people" had a notably negative variation. This may be a sign that that, after playing the game, players became more critical of the impact that society and their environment had in the development of their creativity.

This hypothesis may be further explored in future experiments. Future studies may also reach more enlightening results by employing other tests for creativity, especially if tests that are not self-evaluative are also employed. The *Torrance Tests of Creative Thinking are suggested*, in conjunction with another test, as suggested by Torrance (Treffinger, 1985). Future investigations may benefit from a larger number of participants in future experiments, as this may function as a proof of concept of the game developed. Another technology that may be used in future experiments is telemetry, as a way to use data mining and neural networks to verify the formation of clumps that might allow a better understanding of how different player profiles interact with the game

REFERENCES

Ahmadi, G. A., Abdolmaleki, S., & Khoshbakht, M. (2011). Effect of computer-based training to increase creativity and achievement science, students in fourth grade of elementary. *Procedia Computer Science*, *3*, 1551–1554. doi:10.1016/j.procs.2011.01.047

Alencar, E. M. L. S., Fleith, D. S., & Bruno-Faria, M. F. (2010). A medida da criatividade: Teoria e prática. *The Art of Medication.*

Amabile, T. M., & Gryskiewicz, S. S. (1987). *Creativity in the R&D laboratory.* Center for Creative Leadership.

Azevedo, I., Morais, M. D. F., & Martins, F. (2017). Educação para a criatividade em adolescentes: Uma experiência com future problem solving program international. *Revista Electrónica Iberoamericana sobre Calidad, Eficacia y Cambio en Educación*, 75–87.

Berg, J. M., Dutton, J. E., & Wrzesniewski, A. (2013). Job crafting and meaningful work. In B. J. Dik, Z. S. Byrne, & M. F. Steger (Eds.), *Purpose and meaning in the workplace* (pp. 81–104). Washington, DC: American Psychological Association. doi:10.1037/14183-005

Buzady, Z. (2017). Flow, leadership and serious games – a pedagogical perspective. *World Journal of Science, Technology and Sustainable Development*, 14(2-3), 204-217.

Chua, R. Y.-J., & Iyengar, S. S. (2008). Creativity as a matter of choice: Prior experience and task instruction as boundary conditions for the positive effect of choice on creativity. *The Journal of Creative Behavior*, 42(3), 164–180. doi:10.1002/j.2162-6057.2008.tb01293.x

Coppi, A. E. (2015). Fostering creativity through games and digital storytelling. In *Proceedings of the International Conference on Interactive Technologies and Games* (pp. 17-21). Academic Press. 10.1109/iTAG.2015.12

Cramond, B., Matthews-Morgan, J., Bandalos, D., & Zuo, L. (2005). A report on the 40-year follow-up of the torrance tests of creative chinking: Alive and well in the new millennium. *Gifted Child Quarterly*, 49(4), 283–291. doi:10.1177/001698620504900402

Csikszentmihalyi, M. (1975). *Beyond boredom and anxiety: Experiencing flow in work and play*. Jossey-Bass.

De Rooij, A., Corr, P. J., & Jones, S. (2015). Emotion and creativity: Hacking into cognitive appraisal processes to augment creative ideation. In *Proceedings of the 2015 ACM SIGCHI Conference on Creativity and Cognition* (pp. 265-274). ACM. 10.1145/2757226.2757227

Gangestad, S. W., & Snyder, M. (2000). Self-monitoring: Appraisal and reappraisal. *Psychological Bulletin*, 126(4), 530–555. doi:10.1037/0033-2909.126.4.530 PMID:10900995

Isaksen, S. G., Dorval, K. B., & Treffinger, D. J. (2011). *Creative approaches to problem solving: A framework for change. Sage.*

Kim, K. H. (2006). Can we trust creativity tests? A review of the Torrance tests of creative thinking (TTCT). *Creativity Research Journal*, 18(1), 3–14. doi:10.120715326934crj1801_2

Lau, S., & Cheung, P. C. (2010). Developmental trends of creativity: What twists of turn do boys and girls take at different grades? *Creativity Research Journal*, 22(3), 329–336. doi:10.1080/10400419.2010.503543

Li, Z., Qiong, B., & Wee, S. (2014). Impact of job control on employee creativity: The moderating effect of cognitive irritation. In *Proceedings of the 21th International Conference on Management Science & Engineering* (pp. 873-878). Academic Press.

Marin, W. W., & Notargiacomo, P. (2019). Study of development of creativity through digital games. In *Proceedings of the IADIS International Conference Game and Entertainment Technologies 2019* (pp. 391-395). Academic Press. 10.33965/g2019_201906C055

Maslow, A. H. (1943). A theory of human motivation. *Psychological Review*, 50(4), 370–396. doi:10.1037/h0054346

Maslow, A. H. (1959). Creativity in self-actualizing people. In H. H. Anderson (Ed.), *Creativity and its cultivation* (pp. 83–95). New York: Harper & Row.

Moffat, D. C., & Shabalina, O. (2016). Student creativity exercises in designing serious games. In *Proceedings of the European Conference on Games Based Learning* (pp. 470-478). Academic Press.

Rogers, C. R. (1959). Toward a theory of creativity. In H. H. Anderson (Ed.), *Creativity and its cultivation* (pp. 69–82). New York: Harper & Row.

Runco, M., & Jager, G. (2012). The standard definition of creativity. *Creativity Research Journal*, *24*(1), 92–96. doi:10.1080/10400419.2012.650092

Runco, M. A. (2004). Creativity. *Annual Review of Psychology*, *55*(1), 657–687. doi:10.1146/annurev. psych.55.090902.141502 PMID:14744230

Torrance, E. (1979). Unique needs of the creative child and adult. In A. Passow (Ed.), The gifted and the talented: Their education and development (pp. 352-371). National Society for the Study of Education.

Treffinger, D. J. (1985). Review of the torrance tests of creative thinking. In J. V. Mitchell Jr., (Ed.), *The ninth mental measurements yearbook* (pp. 1632–1634). Lincoln: University of Nebraska, Buros Institute of Mental Measurements.

Vella, K., Johnson, D., & Hides, L. (2013). Positively playful: When videogames lead to player wellbeing. *Proceedings of the Gamification*, 99–102.

Wang, K. (2013). The effect of autonomy on team creativity and the moderating variables. In *Proceedings of PICMET '13: Technology Management for Emerging Technologies* (pp. 1156-1160). Academic Press.

Yokochi, S., & Okada, T. (2005). Creative cognitive process of art making: A field study of a traditional Chinese ink painter. *Creativity Research Journal*, *17*(2-3), 241–255. doi:10.1080/10400419.2005.9651482

Zhou, M.-J., & Li, S.-K. (2013). Can supervisor feedback always promote creativity? The moderating role of employee self-monitoring. In *Proceedings of the 6th International Conference on Information Management, Innovation Management and Industrial Engineering* (pp. 510-512). Academic Press. 10.1109/ICIII.2013.6703200

KEY TERMS AND DEFINITIONS

Autonomy: The social freedom to act as desired, without the need to follow orders or be watched.

Feedback: Constructive criticism received on a performed task or solution

Flow: The mental state achieved with the balance of the mental states of anxiety and boredom in which a person may be best suited to perform a task.

JavaScript: A programming language often employed in the development of web based applications.

Motivation: The intrinsic desire to perform a task or find a solution.

Restriction: A condition or limit imposed on the performance of a task or on possible solutions to a problem.

Solution: One of possibly many answers to a problem proposed to a person or group, be it in the form of an idea or a process.

Task: An activity or process to be executed by a person or group.

Well-Being: A positive emotion, achieved when a person has or is feeling satisfied.

This research was previously published in Interactivity and the Future of the Human-Computer Interface; pages 96-113, copyright year 2020 by Engineering Science Reference (an imprint of IGI Global).

Chapter 54
Development of Habitual Behaviour in Online Social Gaming:
Understanding the Moderating Role of Network Externality

Nan Jiang
Taylor's University, Malaysia

Manmeet Kaur
Taylor's University, Malaysia

Mohd Muttaqin Bin Mohd Adnan
Taylor's University, Malaysia

Jason James Turner
Asia Pacific University of Technology and Innovation, Malaysia

See Kwong Goh
Taylor's University, Malaysia

ABSTRACT

Game habit and game addiction are distinguished in terms of psychological motivation, meaning, and a player's experience of gaming. The majority of contemporary studies address either the challenges or difficulties of particular habit formation often in the context of disciplined force or negative consequences of game addiction. Game habit does not necessarily imply game addiction. The objective of this study is to investigate the key antecedents of game habit formation using a quantitative study with 341 respondents collected in West Malaysia and analysed via structural equation modeling. The results demonstrate that game habit formation is formed more naturally with automatic control mechanisms, influenced by play intensity, flow experience, and self-efficacy, and the effect of play intensity towards game habit is interacted by network externality.

DOI: 10.4018/978-1-6684-7589-8.ch054

INTRODUCTION

The gaming industry is one of those sectors which seems impervious to recession, with annual growth around 9 percent and revenue expected to surpass $200 billion by 2023 (Peckham, 2020). Unlike most industries which have been negatively impacted by Covid-19, gaming has seen an increase in the number of players, the frequency of use and as a consequence, the amount of revenue generated by in-game advertising (Bashir, 2020; Elliott, 2020). Game play has come to impact all aspects of our lives and influence daily routines as well as personal and social behaviour, with its merits, often viewed in rather polarized context. Gaming can be perceived as either a medium which encourages an unproductive use of time, a behavioral script which can be stored in the memory (Verplanken & Aarts, 1999), considered in the context of a less cognitively demanding task (Wohn et al; 2012), or as a medium which develops employability skills such as critical thinking and determination (Sani, 2017). A further dimension to this debate is that of dependancy or addiction to gaming and whether an increased engagement with gaming is not only unproductive but unhealthy. Previous research has examined the role of technological features and social dimensions associated to online gaming (Gan et al; 2017), and the negative impacts of online gaming, such as game addiction (CC. Wang & CH. Wang, 2008; Huang et al; 2019) or internet dependence (Kim et al; 2017) but arguably overlooked the difference between game habit and game addiction. Game habit primarily refers to automated cognitive heuristic behavour or non-conscious social behaviour formation, in contrast, game addiction is more related to a psychological and pathological investigation (Griffiths, 2018). Game habit, even one which can be perceived as excessive is a personal routine which is not necessarily addictive behaviour. The aim of this study is to address this gap in the literature and provide emerging insight into game habit formation. This quantitative study will investigate the perceptions of Malaysia gamers which will assist academics and practitioners develop better understanding of how players engage with online games and the antecedents which are intrinsically linked to game habit formation.

LITERATURE REVIEW

Habit is a goal-directed behaviour formed when conducting the same behaviour frequently and consistently in a similar context for the same purposes (Ouellette & Wood, 1998; Carden & Wood, 2018). Consequently, the conscious efforts to plan and initiate goal-directed behavior become redundant (Danner et al; 2008). A significant contribution in the field of habits and attitude-behavior models was made by Bentley & Speckart (1979) who investigated the students' consumption of alcohol and marijuana and concluded that habitual behavior can be instigated without the mediation of intentions, such as deliberation or thought. This work has been replicated across a range of areas, including mass communication (Chiu & Huang, 2015), psychology (Gardner & Rebar, 2019), online gambling (Salonen et al; 2018), physical fitness (Kaushal et al; 2017), media consumption (LaRose, 2017), impulsive buying (Iram & Chacharkar, 2017), and junk food consumption (Hemmingsson, 2018). Similarly, this concept could be applied to social gaming where gamer's continuous interest and enjoyable interaction may encourage excessive playing, then could develop habitual behaviour or even become addictive (Lee et al; 2019). Although game habit and addiction are used interchangeably, there is a difference between the two concepts: '…*healthy excessive enthusiasms add to a person's life whereas addiction takes away from it…*' (Griffiths 2018, p.19). The majority of previous studies on game addiction adopt existing measurement scales from other fields: gambling addiction or exercise addiction (Ng & Wiemer-Hastings, 2005; Smahel et al; 2008; Hussain & Griffiths, 2009) and claim the addictive behaviour based on self-report accounts of excessive use of the internet, such as up to 80 hours per week (Chappell et al; 2006). Although most addictive behaviour shares certain similar characteristics, such as salience, mood modification, tolerance, withdrawal symptoms, conflict and relapse, the way of determining a non-chemical addiction (i.e. social game addiction) is debated in much of the literature. Arguably, the only way to confirm or to disconfirm addictive behaviour is to compare the observed or scaled behaviour against clinical criteria. However, most previous research has failed to do so, perpetuating the skepticism around whether a gamer is really addicted or just an excessive player (Griffiths, 2018). The reality of game addition remains ambiguous in most studies.

Certain research on habit emphasizes its moderating impact on certain associations. Triandis (1980) investigated the association between habit and intention, assuming that when the same behaviour is more frequently executed in the past and increases in habit strength; it is less guided by the intention to perform such behaviour. Habit moderates the relationship between intentional and actual behaviour. Gan et al (2017) investigated the moderating impact of habit on the strength between gratification and continuance intention, concluding that the associated strength will be reduced by habit due to the unconscious mind. Although the moderating role of habits in intention and behaviour relationship offers a promising perspective on assessing the habitual nature of goal-directed behaviour, in fact, the interactive effect of habit was found to be small to moderate or had no impact in most marketing, psychological and media usage studies. The formation of game habit is arguably more natural and effortless as cognitive processing, and the deliberate control of individual players are minimal. Rather than a negative consequence, the game habit may also lead to certain positive effects, such as reduce anxiety and stress, improve interpersonal relationships (Chou & Hsiao, 2000; Liao et al; 2020), develop critical thinking and determination (Sani, 2017) or even just passing the spare time (Wattanapisit et al; 2018). The associated antecedents of game habit formation could vary depending on the context.

Play Intensity

Previous work on habits emphasises a significant role of repetitive nature of goal-directed behavior (Aarts & Dijksterhuis, 2000; Carden & Wood, 2018) and states that '...*habits are directly mentally accessed in the context at hand as a result of frequently and consistently having performed that behavior in the past...*' (Danner et al; 2008, p.246). Similarly, game players constantly engage with intensive social games, such as the Massively Multiplayer Online Role-Playing Games (MMORPGs) for many hours a day over the courses of years. Excessive time spent in this manner could lead to game habit or even problematic behaviour known as internet dependency (Kim et al; 2017) or technological addiction (Griffiths, 2018). Current research has highlighted the significant role of repetition or frequency in relation to habit, but in the context of online social games, play intensity is more appropriate. Because the formation of game habit is driven by perceived enjoyment and gratification, habit is formed more naturally, rather than through a frequent and repetitive disciplined force. In certain circumstances, frequent or repetitive behavior may not have any impact on habit formation. For instance, frequently paying highway tolls or travel pass (i.e. bus or train ticket) in the daily commuter routine does not necessarily lead to any spending habit or loyalty.

A number of studies into the effect of play intensity in relation to social game addiction and concluded that intensive playing has negative effects on the gamer's life (Shen & Williams, 2011), measuring play intensity in the context of number of hours spent per week (or per day) of game playing. According to Ng & Wiemer-Hastings (2005), only 6 percent of gamers spend 20 hours weekly playing online games and this can be considered as high intensity, whereas 84 percent of other players spend less than 6 hours weekly in gaming. Marchetti et al (2016) also found that gamers play intensively and spend more than 20 hours per week playing the MMORPGs. But there are no clear criteria to confirm such behaviour is as a result of game addiction or game habit. Gamers might fully engage in games and occupy their time while detaching themselves from the real world, so reflecting as addictive behavior. However, the defined criteria of game addiction in most previous studies are ambiguous and the clinical benchmark of game addiction is not fully adopted. Games with low play intensity are normally considered as a way of relaxation for the players, thus requiring them to spend fewer hours; whereas games with high play intensity are normally goal-motivated, which may request more hours spent in playing. The strength of play intensity may not directly lead to game addiction, but there is a possibility to develop a habitual gaming behaviour at an early stage which gives rise to:

H1: Play intensity is positively associated with game habit formation.

Flow Experience

Flow experience refers to optimal and pleasing activities experienced by individuals with full involvement, concentration, and a sense of time distortion (Lee, 2009), defined as "...*the holistic experience that people feel when they act with total involvement...*" (Nakamura & Csikszentmihalyi, 2009, p.197). Current literature treats flow as a multi-dimensional construct (Figure 1) that also syncs with Bandura's (1989) social cognitive theory, postulating that behaviour, environmental influences, physiological and cognitive factors could operate as interesting determinants of each other. When players become absorbed in gaming: their awareness is narrowed to the game itself; they may lose self-consciousness and feel in control of their environment. The mental state in which gamers are fully immersed in what they are doing is, characterized by gratification, concentration, control, curiosity, intrinsic interest or even frustration (Shin, 2010; Procci et al; 2012).

This flow experience can only occur when both challenges and skills exceed a certain level of difficulty that is typical for the individual's day-to-day experiences. It is also applied to various aspects of leisure activities, such as sports, shopping, rock climbing, and dancing (Csikszentimihalyi, 2014). In the context of online gaming, players are willing to be continually challenged with more difficult tasks (i.e. to gain advanced privilege, possess more powerful arms, gain specific properties), aiming that the level of complexity is consistent with individual level of game skill. In a virtual game environment, members can interact with others anonymously and instantaneously, assume various roles, exchange virtual assets, develop strong relationships, as well as strengthen social ties (Williams, 2006). Research indicates that flow experience appears to prolong game addiction or excessive internet and media usage (Hsu & Lu, 2004). However, many of these studies have addressed the concept of flow in relation to computer-human interaction, IT/IS or website operation, such as TAM or Telepresence; and on psychological or physical activities or medical behaviour. Only a handful of studies examine the role of flow associated with the habitual formation of social gaming and gives rise to:

H2: Flow experience is positively associated with game habit formation.

Figure 1. Characteristics of Flow. Source: Hsu, C. L., & Lu, H. P. (2004). Why do people play on-line games? An extended TAM with social influences and flow experience. Information & Management, 41, p.856.

Authors	Applications	Construct	Characteristics
Ghani et al	Human-Computer Interaction	Flow	Concentration, enjoyment
Trevino and Webster	Human-Computer Interaction	Flow	Control, attention focus, curiosity, intrinsic interest
Webster et al	Human-Computer Interaction	Flow	Control, attention focus, curiosity, intrinsic interest
Ghani and Deshpande	Human-Computer Interaction	Flow	Concentration, enjoyment
Hoffman and Novak	Website	Flow	Skill/control, challenge/arousal, focused attention, interactivity, telepresence
Hoffman and Novak	Website	Flow	The seamless sequence of responses, intrinsically enjoyable, loss of self-consciousness, self-reinforcing
Novak et al	Website	Flow	Skill/control, challenge/arousal, focused attention, interactivity, telepresence
Agarwal and Karahanna	Website	Cognitive Absorption	Control, attention focus, curiosity, intrinsic interest
Moon and Kim	Website	Playfulness	Enjoyment, concentration, curiosity
Koufaris	Website	Flow	Perceived control, shopping enjoyment, concentration

Flexibility

Mobile social games are perceived as leisure activities rather than hardcore competition. It has easy learning curves and accommodates a greater variety of games (Wei & Lu, 2014). Flexibility in terms of time-saving, convenience, free-downloads, and various locations has been well facilitated by portable mobile devices, such as smartphones or tablets in recent times. Compared to PCs or game consoles, mobile devices seem to be ideal gaming platforms because of their small size and visual effects (Chou & Hsiao, 2000). Furthermore, flexible portability also has the potential to remove the spatial constraints of larger platforms and allow for short entertainment time periods (Bose & Yang, 2011). The terms 'flexibility' and 'mobility' have been used interchangeably in previous studies to emphasize the feature of playing anywhere, anytime and while on-the-go (Korhonen & Koivisto, 2006).

Flexibility does not only pair with portable devices or wireless internet connection; it also can be perceived as psychological or process-based freedom, such as passing spare time or relaxation. Most players described mobile gaming as a flexible way to fill their time between daily activities, valued especially for ubiquitous availability and instant entertainment, such as waiting for grab or public transportation, relaxing on the couch while watching TV, or laying before bedtime (Wei & Lu, 2014). Although such perceived entertainment is primarily experienced in a short period of time, it does not necessarily obstruct the emergence of game habit or its development. In contrast, just because of these frequent and short-time gratifications, it could further enhance the formation of game habit. Most players may psychologically feel that they are flexible and described mobile social gaming as casual daily activities that can be conducted anytime and anywhere. Therefore, gamers with higher flexibility have high possibilities to develop a game habit; while those individuals who are less flexible may experience less fun interaction, thus are more independent from social games:

H3: Flexibility is positively associated with game habit formation.

Self-Efficacy

Self-efficacy refers to "...*people's believes about their capacities to exercise control over their own level of function and events that affect their lives*" (Bandura, 2010, p.257). As one of the key determinants of behaviouor under social-cognitive theory (LaRose et al; 2010), self-efficacy addresses personal belief on the individual capability to organize and execute a particular course of action. It plays a central role within the self-regulation mechanism in the exercise of personal agency by its strong impact on thought, affects, motivation and action. Self-efficacy lies at the core of causal processes, including internet usage (Kim et al; 2017), excessive media consumption (LaRose, 2009), impulsive buying (Iram & Chacharkar, 2017), and binge eating disorder (Linardon, 2018). The phrase is often interchangeably used with self-control or self-regulation in which "...*individual's capacity to override or change their inner response, as well as to interrupt undesired behavioral tendencies, then refrain from action on themselves...*" (Tangney et al; 2004, p.275). Previous studies have investigated the effect of self-efficacy in relation to media dependency or social game addiction but largely overlooked the fact that many individuals actually can overcome such 'dependence' or 'addiction' by themselves without going through professional intervention or clinical treatment (Peele, 2000; Hall & Parsons, 2001). But why and how could people succeed in recovering from these 'addictive diseases'? In fact, they may not be addictive at all; it may just be a subjective habitual pattern, which could be manipulated by self-efficacy. If players are indeed addicted or diseased, it may only be curable through clinical intervention or professional treatment. Neither learning theory nor addictive personality formulation can explain the above circumstance.

Habit is initially defined as "*situation-behaviour sequence that becomes automatic, so that it occurs without self-instruction*" (Triandis, 1980, p.204). The game habit could be formed through diminishing self-efficacy or deficient self-regulation, where self-efficacy is not an all or-nothing condition. The size of the effect could be controllable (normal status) or uncontrollable (addictive status) or some phenomenon in between. Habitual gamers may experience lapses in their self-efficacy just the same as the addictive players do. However, even heavily addicted media users also can restore their self-efficacy, at least temporarily (LaRose et al; 2010). Previous studies indicated that self-efficacy was a significant moderated force for a broad range of addictive behaviors or interpersonal relationships (Kim et al; 2008) but the assumed moderation effect could also prove potentially limited (Du et al; 2019; Muraven & Slessareva, 2003) and therefore it is necessary to investigate whether self-efficacy could directly influence the development of game habit through a negative way:

H4: Self-efficacy is negatively associated with game habit formation.

Network Externalities

The network externalities refer to the phenomenon that an individual's evaluation of a product increases as the corresponding product's network expands (Zhang et al; 2017). Network externality is also called network effect or demand-side economies of scale and are widely adopted in various studies, typically in the fields of economics, social media (Sledgianowski & Kulviwat, 2009) and IS/IT (Yang & Mai, 2010). It implies that individual consumer adopts or possesses a particular product or service according to the total number of other users of that product or service (Tirole, 1988). For instance, people are more likely to click certain YouTube videos or subscribe to particular YouTube channels with a significant visit record or a large number of total 'viewed' or 'thumbed up' notifications. Similarly, new drivers always download 'Waves' or 'Google Map' apps as most existing drivers are using them now. Because when more users install these apps and join the traffic network, more accurate real-time location and traffic information could be provided to all users simultaneously. Chun & Hahn (2007) investigated a total of three dimensions of network externalities on people's intention to use network services: i) total network size, ii) local network size, iii) network strength, and concluded that the first two dimensions have more significant impact compared to the third dimension. The network effect only occurs when the size (total and local) of the network reaches a critical mass (the minimum size or effectiveness), especially when more peers join (Sledgianowski & Kulviwat, 2009). Within the online social gaming context, network externality refers to the context stability (Ouellette & Wood, 1998; Aarts & Dijksterhuis, 2000), the consistency aspect of the gaming environment, in which the similar activities have been executed in the past. Stability of context plays an interactive role in the establishment of any habit as it is based on the assumption that people are sensitive to the changes of such context (Verplanken & Asrts, 1999; Wood et al; 2005), i.e. perceived network externality where gamers play if more players join. A famous game could become even more popular through an overwhelming awareness created by the network effect.

Consistently, network effect sounds similar to the Bandwagon impact embedded in the theory of consumers' demand (Leibenstein, 1950; Shaikh et al; 2017). However, previous studies emphasize the direct network effect on user's perceptions of IT/IS application, impulsive purchasing or online game loyalty, but overlook the interaction effect of network externality in the relationship between play intensity and habit emerge. The current investigation of context stability emphasizes its moderated effect between intentional behaviour and habitual formation or internet and media usage (Verplanken & Asrts, 1999; Danner et al; 2008; Kim et al; 2017). Logically, an intensive network could offer higher utility or greater gratification for gamers. The large-sized network is crucial for game habit, especially if new players trust online searched-attributes evaluations more than experienced attributes estimation. When the stability aspect is taken into account, the examination of habit formation assumes that such behaviour is performed in a stable network context (Ouellette & Wood, 1998; Wood et al; 2005 as cited in Danner et al; 2008). The significant number of game peers and the size of the game network could enhance play intensity and impact habitual game behaviour. A larger network could enhance the high intensity of the virtual games, leading to a more emotive form of game habit; while low play intensity interacted with a weak network externality could result in a lesser form of habit, or no habit formation at all. The strength of the association between play intensity and habitual game behaviour varies with interacted network externality (Figure 2):

H5: Network externality moderates the relationship between play intensity and habit formation.

Figure 2. Conceptual framework

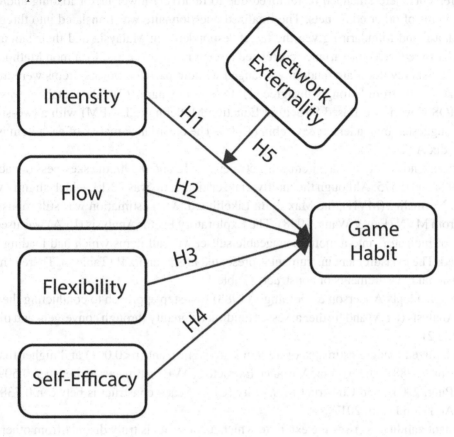

METHODOLOGY

Measurement and Data Collection

This study gathered empirical data using a partial self-reported questionnaire among adult gamers from the Klang Valley, Malaysia, over a period of four weeks. To encourage awareness and completion, the questionnaire link was posted on to Malaysia's game-related bulletin boards with the provision of an incentive (the opportunity to win one of three RM100 -- US$25 petrol gift vouchers). The research adhered to appropriate ethical practice in research, ensuring respondents provided informed consent, had the right to withdraw from the study at any time, and had their privacy protected with data kept confidential and aligned with the Personal Data Protection Act (2010). Ethical approval was granted for the research by the Human Ethics Committee from the authors' university.

This study adopts non-probability sampling with convenience technique, which coincides with previous research. The overall population of online gamers in Malaysia could be large to examine. Therefore, this study opts convenience sampling to target a sample that could represent the entire population. In addition, speed, cost-effectiveness, and ease of sample availability are also considered in sampling procedure and data collection. A total of 562 questionnaires were returned with 341 considered valid. A pilot study was conducted with 62 respondents to ensure respondents understand all the item questions and to validate the reliability of measurement instruments. Based on the respondent's feedback, certain item measurements were amended or removed due to relatively lower factor loading and/or crossed-loaded with items of other constructs. The finalized questionnaire was translated into three languages (English, Bahasa and Mandarin) given the target respondents in Malaysia and their language preferences. In order to reduce error variance correlated among items and avoid Common Methods Variance (CMV) bias, all survey items are randomly arranged without particular order. Items were measured on a 7-point Likert scale from 'strongly disagree (1)' to 'strongly agree (7)'. Data analysis was conducted through AMOS Covariance-Based Structural Equation Modeling (CB-SEM) with a two-step analysis approach as suggested by Anderson & Grebin (1988). The covariance matrix of each item is presented in the Appendix A (Table 7).

The univariate normality of each item was between -1.212 and 0.290; the skewness of each item was between -0.904 and 0.575. Although the multivariate critical ratio was 22.13, which slightly violates the Multivariate Normality (MVN), the Maximum Likelihood (ML) estimation was still robust with mild departures from MVN (Fan & Wang, 1998). The Exploratory Factor Analysis (EFA) was used to reduce the large set of indicators into a more manageable subset with all items which had loading lower than 0.6 eliminated. The measurement instrument is presented in Appendix B (Table 8). There is no violation of unidimensional measurements of constructs (Table 1).

This research adopts Anderson & Gerbing's (1988) two-step approach to conducting the Confirmatory Factor Analysis (CFA) and further assesses unidimensionality through convergent and discriminant validity (Table 2).

The standardized loading estimates of all items are significant (p<0.001) and higher than 0.6 (Anderson & Gerbin, 1988). The Average Variance Extracted (AVE) estimates are between 0.509 and 0.675 (above 0.5, Ping, 2004), and Construct Reliability (CR) of each construct is between 0.738 and 0.892 (above 0.7, Ab Hamid et al; 2017).

Discriminant validity assesses the extent to which a construct is truly distinct from other constructs (Hair et al; 2017). The correlations among all latent variables are between 0.146 and 0.670 (Table 3). The AVE square root of each variable is larger than any correlation between a particular variable and any other variables, which indicates that the Type II error rate is low.

Analysis of Result and Discussion

Structural equation modeling is used to examine the research hypotheses contained within the constructed model. The goodness-of-fit indices are within an acceptable range (chi-square =142.316, df=67, p<0.001, chi-square/df=2.124, GFI=0.946, AGFI=0.915, RMSEA=0.057, TLI=0.951, RFI=0.911, IFI=0.964, CFI=0.964, NFI=0.934). The standard errors of variance are relatively small between 0.062 and 0.115. Most hypotheses are supported, except H3 (p=0.097) indicating that flexibility had no impact on game habit formation (Table 4). The parameter estimates for the relationships of game habit with play intensity (0.585, p<0.001, H1), self-efficacy (-0.404, p<0.001, H4), and flow experience (0.428, p<0.001, H2) are statistically significant and coincide with the research hypotheses. The exogenous constructs can explain 51.30% of the variation in the game habit formation, indicating a relatively moderate to high predictive relevance. The calculated effect size f^2 (0.170) was used to compute achieved predictive power of the constructed model (f^2=0.170, σ=0.05, n=341), indicating a reliable predictive power (1-β error prob) = 0.807 (above 0.8, MacCallum & Austin, 2000).

Table 1. EFA and unidimensionality

	Rotated Component Matrix				
			Component		
	1	2	3	4	5
Flow3	.851				
Flow2	.837				
Flow1	.785				
Flow4	.748				
Intensity2		.812			
Intensity1		.762			
Intensity3		.759			
Flexibility2			.812		
Flexibility1			.739		
Flexibility4			.660		
Self_E4				.862	
Self_E3				.777	
Habit2					.855
Habit1					.775

Extraction Method: Principal Component Analysis.
Rotation Method: Varimax with Kaiser Normalization.
a. Rotation converged in 6 iterations.

Cross-Validation examined the stability and generalizability of the proposed model and enhances research validity and generalizability of findings. With good model stability (ΔTLI <0.01, ΔCFI<0.05, p>0.05, Table 5), the predictive validity of this model can be generalized to other distribution samples as well.

Network externality interacted with play intensity in such a way to impact on a player's game habit (H5). The association could be stronger with a greater influence of external network, and weaker with a lower level of context stability. The initially published implementation of indicant product analysis was proposed by Kenny & Judd (1984). However, their approach cannot be specified in a straightforward manner in SEM, especially with nonlinear loadings and error terms (Hayduk, 1987). Their approach lacked significant testing statistics (Bollen, 1989) or/and loss of statistical power in product term regression analysis as the reliability declines (Aiken & West, 1991). Cohen, J & Cohen, P (1983) suggest the use of the product of summed indicants to estimate an interaction or quadratic variable (cited in Ping, 1995, p.338). This study applies Ping's sophisticated technique (1995) and converts the related variables into a single indicant and specifies the loading and error terms for the single indicants in the structural model. The moderation effect of network externality in the relationship between play intensity and game habit formation is supported with acceptable goodness-of-fit indices (chi-square = 31.929, df=17, p=0.015, chi-square/df=1.878, GFI=0.977, AGFI=0.952, RMSEA=0.051, CFI=0.964, Table 6). A stronger association occurs when players are highly influenced by the external network; a relatively weaker relationship emerges with lower-influenced network externality (0.101, t=2.589, p=0.009, H5). The Moderator plot presents the interacting effect of network externality (Figure 3).

Table 2. CFA and convergent validity (n=341)

CR & AVE	UNSTD	S.E.	T-Value	P	Estimate	SMC	1-SMC	C.R	AVE
Flow1 <--- Flow	1				0.773	0.598	0.402	0.892	0.675
Flow4 <--- Flow	0.954	0.065	14.585	***	0.753	0.567	0.433		
Flow3 <--- Flow	1.147	0.063	18.302	***	0.924	0.854	0.146		
Flow2 <--- Flow	1.001	0.062	16.256	***	0.824	0.679	0.321		
Intensity1 <--- Intensity	1				0.783	0.613	0.387	0.806	0.581
Intensity3 <--- Intensity	1.016	0.082	12.315	***	0.741	0.549	0.451		
Intensity2 <--- Intensity	1.146	0.091	12.535	***	0.762	0.581	0.419		
Flexibility1 <--- Flexibility	1				0.873	0.762	0.238	0.752	0.509
Flexibility2 <--- Flexibility	0.667	0.084	7.969	***	0.614	0.377	0.623		
Flexibility4 <--- Flexibility	0.724	0.073	9.878	***	0.624	0.389	0.611		
Self_E3 <--- Self_E	1				0.872	0.760	0.240	0.739	0.591
Self_E4 <--- Self_E	0.705	0.103	6.856	***	0.650	0.423	0.578		
Habit1 <--- Habit	1				0.836	0.699	0.301	0.738	0.587
Habit2 <--- Habit	0.843	0.087	9.630	***	0.690	0.476	0.524		

Table 3. Discriminant validity

	Habit	Self_E	Flexibility	Intensity	Flow
Habit	**0.766**				
Self_E	0.146	**0.769**			
Flexibility	0.501	0.367	**0.713**		
Intensity	0.528	0.628	0.448	**0.762**	
Flow	0.575	0.405	0.670	0.484	**0.822**

Notes: Square root values of average variance extracted on the diagonal.

Table 4. Structural Regression Weight (n=341)

CR & AVE	Estimate	S.E.	T-Value	P	STD	SMC	Hypothesis
Habit <--- Intensity	0.585	0.115	5.069	***	0.520	0.513	H1: Supported
Habit <--- Flow	0.428	0.106	4.032	***	0.373		H2: Supported
Habit <--- Flexibility	0.149	0.090	1.660	0.097	0.161		H3: Rejected
Habit <--- Self_E	-0.404	0.105	-3.846	***	-0.391		H4: Supported

Table 5. Cross-Validation

Model	NPAR	CMIN	DF	ΔDF	ΔCMIN	P	ΔTLI	ΔCFI
Unconstrained	76	236.982	134					0.951
Measurement weights	67	243.07	143	9	6.087	0.731	-0.006	0.002
Structural weights	63	246.907	147	4	3.838	0.428	-0.002	0.000
Structural covariances	53	254.012	157	10	7.104	0.716	-0.005	0.001
Structural residuals	52	255.156	158	1	1.144	0.285	0.000	0.000
Measurement residuals	38	291.906	172	14	36.750	0.001	0.007	-0.011

Table 6. Moderation model

Model	DF	CMIN	P	NFI Delta-1	IFI Delta-2	RFI rho-1	TLI rho2
Moderator Model	17	31.929	0.015	0.958	0.980	0.931	0.967
			UNSTD	S.E.	T-Value	P	Label
Habit	<---	Moderator	0.101	0.039	2.589	0.009	Network Externality

Figure 3. Moderation plot

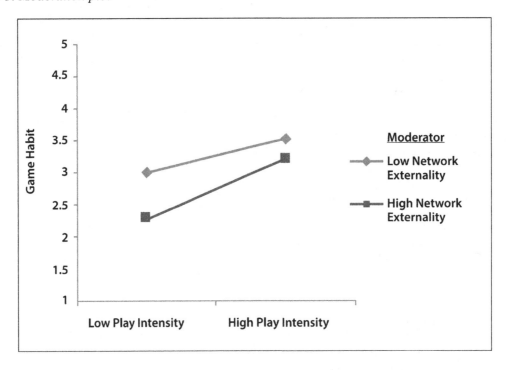

CONCLUSION AND IMPLICATIONS

Game habit is not a goal-directed behaviour, and excessive gaming does not necessarily mean addiction. The intensity of play is considered the most effective antecedent towards game habit, which is partially consistent with previous studies of frequency or repetitive impact on habit formation across a variety of behavioural investigations. However, frequency and intensity are two distinguished concepts with the former referring to the occurrence rate of gaming behaviour and the latter addressing the strength and concentration of such behaviour. Consecutive repetition of past behaviour may not significantly initiate players' cognitive involvement in gaming, while play intensity immersed such experience. The game habit is expected to emerge when more peers play popular games even with the same degree of intensity, and could be scaled from low to high with intensity impact in a comparatively weak to strong context stability. For game vendors, popular games could become even more famous or overwhelmed, while less popular ones may struggle to survive with unachieved critical mass.

With flow experience, continual challenges embedded around more difficult tasks are more attractive and fun for gamers. Their emotional state embracing perceptional gratification and enjoyment reflects a stronger impact on game habit formation (0.428, t=4.032). Unique game features and playful experiences could shift a common mode of experience into an absorbed status, which could further strengthen their gaming habits. The reported effect of self-efficacy is moderate (-0.404, t=-3.846), implying the reality of most habit strength, especially with diminishing self-regulation. Since the associated absolute effect values of self-efficacy (-0.404) and flow experience (0.428) are similar, these two opposite impacts may outweigh each other in predicting game habit.

Flexibility in terms of time, perceived convenience (i.e. portable devices), and flexible locations had no effect on game habit (H3, p=0.097). This implies that the formation of a particular habit is not necessarily determined by flexible capability. A gamer's initial rationale for gaming engagement could be as simple as the experience of fun. The flexible capability may facilitate that fun but is arguably not efficient enough to develop habitual game behaviour.

Regarding the research limitations, it is acknowledged that this study could have benefitted from including a qualitative dimension to better understand a player's feelings and attitude towards gaming habit formation. Another limitation is the fact that this study focused on Malaysia, which although consolidated existing research and provides insight into a country relatively unresearched in the context of online gaming, does carry the limitation of generalisability. Data collected in one country may not be robust enough to explain more complex phenomenon in other countries.

Further study intends to explore potential themes from a particular context and takes literature forward the area of game habit strength. It would be interesting to examine a broader range of gamers from different regions to gain a more holistic understanding of their game habit formation and strength. A further research area would be to investigate the characteristics of age and gender, comparing different popular online games which would enable more insights into the relationship between players and levels of habit, gaming intensity, and addiction, further exploring the research finding that a simple repetition of past behaviour may not significantly reflect a player's cognitive involvement in gaming.

REFERENCES

Aarts, H., & Dijksterhuis, A. (2000). Habits as knowledge structures: Automaticity in goal-directed behavior. *Journal of Personality and Social Psychology*, 78(1), 53–71. doi:10.1037/0022-3514.78.1.53 PMID:10653505

Ab Hamid, M. R., Sami, W., & Sidek, M. M. (2017, September). Discriminant validity assessment: Use of Fornell & Larcker criterion versus HTMT criterion. *Journal of Physics: Conference Series*, 890(1), 012163. doi:10.1088/1742-6596/890/1/012163

Aiken, L. S., West, S. G., & Reno, R. R. (1991). Multiple Regression: Testing and Interpreting Interactions. *Sage (Atlanta, Ga.)*.

Anderson, J. C., & Gerbing, D. W. (1988). Structural equation modeling in practice: A review and recommended two-step approach. *Psychological Bulletin*, 103(3), 411–423. doi:10.1037/0033-2909.103.3.411

Bandura, A. (1989). Human agency in social cognitive theory. *The American Psychologist, 44*(9), 1175–1186. doi:10.1037/0003-066X.44.9.1175 PMID:2782727

Bandura, A. (2010). Self-efficacy. The Corsini Encyclopedia of Psychology, 1-3.

Bashir, D. (2020). *Malaysian gamers spent $673 million on video games along in 2019*. Retrieved from https://sea.ign.com/mobile-legendsbang-bang/157398/news/mala ysian-gamers-spent-673-million-on-video-games-alone-in-2019

Bentler, P. M., & Speckart, G. (1979). Models of attitude-behaviour relations. *Psychological Review, 86*(5), 452–464. doi:10.1037/0033-295X.86.5.452

Bollen, K. A. (1989). A new incremental fit index for general structural equation models. *Sociological Methods & Research, 17*(2), 303–316. doi:10.1177/0049124189017003004

Bose, I., & Yang, X. (2011). Enter the Dragon: Khillwar's foray into the mobile gaming market of China. *Communications of the Association for Information Systems, 29*(1), 29–41. doi:10.17705/1CAIS.02929

Brockmyer, J. H., Fox, C. M., Curtiss, K. A., McBroom, E., Burkhart, K. M., & Pidruzny, J. N. (2009). The development of the game engagement questionnaire: A measure of engagement in video game-playing. *Journal of Experimental Social Psychology, 45*(4), 624–634. doi:10.1016/j.jesp.2009.02.016

Carden, L., & Wood, W. (2018). Habit formation and change. *Current Opinion in Behavioral Sciences, 20*, 117–122. doi:10.1016/j.cobeha.2017.12.009

Chappell, D., Eatough, V., Davies, M. N., & Griffiths, M. (2006). EverQuest - It's just a computer game right? An interpretative phenomenological analysis of online gaming addiction. *International Journal of Mental Health and Addiction, 4*(3), 205–216. doi:10.100711469-006-9028-6

Chiu, C. M., & Huang, H. Y. (2015). Examining the antecedents of user gratification and its effects on individuals' social network services usage: The moderating role of habit. *European Journal of Information Systems, 24*(4), 411–430. doi:10.1057/ejis.2014.9

Chou, C., & Hsiao, M. C. (2000). Internet addiction, usage, gratification, and pleasure experience: The Taiwan college students' case. *Computers & Education, 35*(1), 65–80. doi:10.1016/S0360-1315(00)00019-1

Chun, S. Y., & Hahn, M. (2007). Network externality and future usage of Internet services. *Internet Research*, (April), 10.

Cohen, J., & Cohen, P. (1983). *Applied Multiple Regression/Correlation Analyses, for the Behavioral Sciences*. Lawrence Erlbaum.

Csikszentmihalyi, M. (2014), The concept of flow. In Flow and the Foundations of Positive Psychology. Springer.

Danner, U. N., Aarts, H., & de Vries, N. K. (2008). Habit vs. intention in the prediction of future behaviour: The role of frequency, context stability and mental accessibility of past behaviour. *British Journal of Social Psychology, 47*(2), 245–265. doi:10.1348/014466607X230876 PMID:17678574

Du, J., Kerkhof, P., & Van Koningsbruggen, G. M. (2019). Predictors of social media self-control failure: Immediate gratifications, habitual checking, ubiquity, and notifications. *Cyberpsychology, Behavior, and Social Networking, 22*(7), 477–485. doi:10.1089/cyber.2018.0730 PMID:31295024

Elliott, R. (2020). *Insights into Malaysia's games market and its gamers*. Retrieved from https://newzoo.com/insights/articles/insights-into-malaysias-games-market-and-its-gamers/

Fan, X., & Wang, L. (1998). Effects of potential confounding factors on fit indices and parameter estimates for true and mis specified SEM models. *Educational and Psychological Measurement, 58*(5), 701–735. doi:10.1177/0013164498058005001

Gan, C., Liang, X., & Yu, X. (2017). Continuance intention on mobile social networking service: examine the effects of habit and gratifications. *Wuhan International Conference on e-Business. Association for Information Systems, Summer*, 222-231.

Gardner, B., & Rebar, A. L. (2019). Habit Formation and behavior change. *Oxford Research Encyclopedia of Psychology*.

Griffiths, M. D. (2018). Psychometric tools in the study of behavioural addiction: A personal overview. *Assessment & Development Matters, 10*, 18–21.

Hair, J. F. Jr, Matthews, L. M., Matthews, R. L., & Sarstedt, M. (2017). PLS-SEM or CB-SEM: Updated guidelines on which method to use. *International Journal of Multivariate Data Analysis, 1*(2), 107–123. doi:10.1504/IJMDA.2017.10008574

Hall, A. S., & Parsons, J. (2001). Internet addiction: College student case study using best practices in cognitive behavior therapy. *Journal of Mental Health Counseling, 23*(4), 312–331.

Hayduk, L. A. (1987). *Structural Equation Modeling with LISREL: Essentials and Advances*. Jhu Press.

Hemmingsson, E. (2018). Early childhood obesity risk factors: Socioeconomic adversity, family dysfunction, offspring distress, and junk food self-medication. *Current Obesity Reports, 7*(2), 204–209. doi:10.100713679-018-0310-2 PMID:29704182

Hsu, C. L., & Lu, H. P. (2004). Why do people play on-line games? An extended TAM with social influences and flow experience. *Information & Management, 41*(7), 853–868. doi:10.1016/j.im.2003.08.014

Huang, C. L., Yang, S. C., & Hsieh, L. S. (2019). The cyberbullying behavior of Taiwanese adolescents in an online gaming environment. *Children and Youth Services Review, 106*, 104461. doi:10.1016/j.childyouth.2019.104461

Huang, J., Yan, E., Cheung, G., Nagappan, N., & Zimmermann, T. (2017). Master maker: Understanding gaming skill through practice and habit from gameplay behavior. *Topics in Cognitive Science, 9*(2), 437–466. doi:10.1111/tops.12251 PMID:28198102

Hussain, Z., & Griffiths, M. D. (2009). Excessive use of massively multi-player online role-playing games: A pilot study. *International Journal of Mental Health and Addiction, 7*(4), 563–571. doi:10.100711469-009-9202-8

Iram, M., & Chacharkar, D. Y. (2017). Model of impulse buying behavior. *BVIMSR's. Journal of Management Research*, *9*(1), 45.

Jackson, S. A., & Eklund, R. C. (2002). Assessing flow in physical activity: The flow state scale-2 and dispositional flow scale-2. *Journal of Sport & Exercise Psychology*, *24*(2), 133–150..doi:10.1123/jsep.24.2.133

Kaushal, N., Rhodes, R. E., Spence, J. C., & Meldrum, J. T. (2017). Increasing physical activity through principles of habit formation in new gym members: A randomized controlled trial. *Annals of Behavioral Medicine*, *51*(4), 578–586. doi:10.100712160-017-9881-5 PMID:28188586

Kenny, D. A., & Judd, C. M. (1984). Estimating the nonlinear and interactive effects of latent variables. *Psychological Bulletin*, *96*(1), 201–218. doi:10.1037/0033-2909.96.1.201

Kim, D. J., Kim, K., Lee, H. W., Hong, J. P., Cho, M. J., Fava, M., Mischoulon, D., Heo, J.-Y., & Jeon, H. J. (2017). Internet game addiction, depression, and escape from negative emotions in adulthood: A nationwide community sample of Korea. *The Journal of Nervous and Mental Disease*, *205*(7), 568–573. doi:10.1097/NMD.0000000000000698 PMID:28598958

Kim, E. J., Namkoong, K., Ku, T., & Kim, S. J. (2008). The relationship between online game addiction and aggression, self-control and narcissistic personality traits. *European Psychiatry*, *23*(3), 212–218. doi:10.1016/j.eurpsy.2007.10.010 PMID:18166402

Korhonen, H., & Koivisto, E. M. (2006, September). Playability Heuristics for Mobile Games. In *Proceedings of the 8th conference on Human-computer interaction with mobile devices and services*. ACM. 10.1145/1152215.1152218

LaRose, R. (2009). *Social Cognitive Theories of Media Selection. In Media Choice*. Routledge.

Larose, R. (2017). Media habits. The International Encyclopedia of Media Effects, 29, 1-9.

LaRose, R., Kim, J., & Peng, W. (2010). *Social networking: addictive, compulsive, problematic, or just another media habit? In A Networked-self*. Routledge.

Lee, J. Y., Ko, D. W., & Lee, H. (2019). Loneliness, regulatory focus, inter-personal competence, and online game addiction: A moderated mediation model. *Internet Research*, *29*(2), 381–394. doi:10.1108/IntR-01-2018-0020

Lee, M. C. (2009). Understanding the behavioural intention to play online games: An extension of the theory of planned behavior. *Online Information Review*, *33*(5), 849–872. doi:10.1108/14684520911001873

Leibenstein, II. (1950). Bandwagon, snob, and Veblen effects in the theory of consumers' demand. *The Quarterly Journal of Economics*, *64*(2), 183–207. doi:10.2307/1882692

Liao, G. Y., Tseng, F. C., Cheng, T. C. E., & Teng, C. I. (2020). Impact of gaming habits on motivation to attain gaming goals, perceived price fairness, and online gamer loyalty: Perspective of consistency principle. *Telematics and Informatics*, *49*, 101367. doi:10.1016/j.tele.2020.101367

Linardon J. (2018). *The relationship between dietary restraint and binge eating: Examining eating-related self-efficacy as a moderator*. Academic Press.

MacCallum, R. C., & Austin, J. T. (2000). Applications of structural equation modeling in psychological research. *Annual Review of Psychology*, *51*(1), 201–226. doi:10.1146/annurev.psych.51.1.201 PMID:10751970

Marchetti, J., Sankey, C., & Varescon, I. (2016). Psychological Predictors of Intensive Practice of Massively Multiplayer Online Role-Playing Games. *Psychology (Irvine, Calif.)*, *6*(11), 676–683.

Muraven, M., & Slessareva, E. (2003). Mechanisms of self-control failure: Motivation and limited resources. *Personality and Social Psychology Bulletin*, *29*(7), 894–906. doi:10.1177/0146167203029007008 PMID:15018677

Nakamura, J., & Csikszentmihalyi, M. (2009). Flow theory and research. Handbook of Positive Psychology, 195-206.

Ng, B. D., & Wiemer-Hastings, P. (2005). Addiction to the internet and online gaming. *Cyberpsychology & Behavior*, *8*(2), 110–113. doi:10.1089/cpb.2005.8.110 PMID:15938649

Ouellette, J. A., & Wood, W. (1998). Habit and intention in everyday life: The multiple processes by which past behavior predicts future behavior. *Psychological Bulletin*, *124*(1), 54–74. doi:10.1037/0033-2909.124.1.54

Peckham, E. (2020). *Newzoo forecasts 2020 global games industry will reach $159 billion*. Retrieved from https://techcrunch.com/2020/06/26/newzoo-forecasts-2020-global-games-industry-will-reach-159-billion/

Peele, S. (2000). What addiction is and is not: The impact of mistaken notions of addiction. *Addiction Research*, *8*(6), 599–607. doi:10.3109/16066350008998991

Personal Data Protection Act. (2010). *Law of Malaysia Act (709)*. Retrieved from http://www.agc.gov.my/agcportal/uploads/files/Publications/LOM/EN/Act%20709%2014%206%202016.pdf

Ping, R. A. Jr. (1995). A parsimonious estimating technique for interaction and quadratic latent variables. *JMR, Journal of Marketing Research*, *32*(3), 336–347. doi:10.1177/002224379503200308

Ping, R. A. Jr. (2004). On assuring valid measures for theoretical models using survey data. *Journal of Business Research*, *57*(2), 125–141. doi:10.1016/S0148-2963(01)00297-1

Procci, K., Singer, A. R., Levy, K. R., & Bowers, C. (2012). Measuring the flow experience of gamers: An evaluation of the DFS-2. *Computers in Human Behavior*, *28*(6), 2306–2312. doi:10.1016/j.chb.2012.06.039

Puerta-Cortés, D. X., Panova, T., Carbonell, X., & Chamarro, A. (2017). How passion and impulsivity influence a player's choice of videogame, intensity of playing and time spent playing. *Computers in Human Behavior*, *66*, 122–128. doi:10.1016/j.chb.2016.09.029

Salonen, A. H., Hellman, M., Latvala, T., & Castrén, S. (2018). Gambling participation, gambling habits, gambling-related harm, and opinions on gambling advertising in Finland in 2016. *Nordisk Alkohol- & Narkotikatidskrift*, *35*(3), 215–234. doi:10.1177/1455072518765875 PMID:32934528

Sani, R. (2017). *Not just play, gaming a booming industry for careers*. Retrieved from https://www.nst.com.my/education/2017/06/248816/not-just-play-gaming-booming-industry-careers

Shaikh, S., Malik, A., Akram, M. S., & Chakrabarti, R. (2017). Do luxury brands successfully entice consumers? The role of bandwagon effect. *International Marketing Review*, *34*(4), 498–513. doi:10.1108/IMR-09-2014-0302

Shen, C., & Williams, D. (2011). Unpacking time online: Connecting internet and massively multiplayer online game use with psychosocial well-being. *Communication Research*, *38*(1), 123–149. doi:10.1177/0093650210377196

Shin, D. H. (2010). Analysis of online social networks: A cross-national study. *Online Information Review*, *34*(3), 473–495. doi:10.1108/14684521011054080

Sledgianowski, D., & Kulviwat, S. (2009). Using social network sites: The effects of playfulness, critical mass and trust in a hedonic context. *Journal of Computer Information Systems*, *49*(4), 74–83.

Smahel, D., Blinka, L., & Ledabyl, O. (2008). Playing MMORPGs: Connections between addiction and identifying with a character. *Cyberpsychology & Behavior*, *11*(6), 715–718. doi:10.1089/cpb.2007.0210 PMID:18954271

Tangney, J. P., Baumeister, R. F., & Boone, A. L. (2004). High self-control predicts good adjustment, less pathology, better grades, and interpersonal success. *Journal of Personality*, *72*(2), 271–324. doi:10.1111/j.0022-3506.2004.00263.x PMID:15016066

Tirole, J. (1988). *The Theory of Industrial Organization*. MIT Press.

Triandis, H. C. (1980). Values, Attitudes, An Interpersonal Behaviour. In *Nebraska Symposium on Motivation*. University of Nebraska Press.

Verplanken, B., & Aarts, H. (1999). Habit, attitude, and planned behaviour: Is habit an empty construct or an interesting case of goal-directed automaticity? *European Review of Social Psychology*, *10*(1), 101–134. doi:10.1080/14792779943000035

Wang, C. C., & Wang, C. H. (2008). Helping others in online games: Prosocial behavior in cyberspace. *Cyberpsychology & Behavior*, *11*(3), 344–346. doi:10.1089/cpb.2007.0045 PMID:18537505

Wattanapisit, A., Saengow, U., Ng, C. J., Thanamee, S., & Kaewruang, N. (2018). Gaming behaviour with Pokémon GO and physical activity: A preliminary study with medical students in Thailand. *PLoS One*, *13*(6), e0199813. doi:10.1371/journal.pone.0199813 PMID:29958272

Wei, P. S., & Lu, H. P. (2014). Why do people play mobile social games? An examination of network externalities and of uses and gratifications. *Internet Research*, *24*(3), 313–331. doi:10.1108/IntR-04-2013-0082

Williams, D. (2006). Groups and goblins: The social and civic impact of an online game. *Journal of Broadcasting & Electronic Media*, *50*(4), 651–670. doi:10.120715506878jobem5004_5

Wohn, D., Velasquez, A., Bjornrud, T., & Lampe, C. (2012, May). Habit as an explanation of participation in an online peer-production community. In *Proceedings of the SIGCHI Conference on Human Factors in Computing Systems*. ACM. 10.1145/2207676.2208697

Wood, W., Tam, L., & Witt, M. G. (2005). Changing circumstances, disrupting habits. *Journal of Personality and Social Psychology*, *88*(6), 918–933. doi:10.1037/0022-3514.88.6.918 PMID:15982113

Yang, J., & Mai, E. S. (2010). Experiential goods with network externalities effects: An empirical study of online rating system. *Journal of Business Research*, *63*(9), 1050–1057. doi:10.1016/j.jbusres.2009.04.029

Zhang, C. B., Li, Y. N., Wu, B., & Li, D. J. (2017). How WeChat can retain users: Roles of network externalities, social interaction ties, and perceived values in building continuance intention. *Computers in Human Behavior*, *69*, 284–293. doi:10.1016/j.chb.2016.11.069

This research was previously published in the International Journal of Cyber Behavior, Psychology and Learning (IJCBPL), 11(1); pages 20-37, copyright year 2021 by IGI Publishing (an imprint of IGI Global).

APPENDIX A: COVARIANCE MATRIX

Table 7. Covariance Matrix

Rowtype_	Varname_	Flexibilty4	Self_E3	Self_E4	Flexibility1	Flexibility2	Habit1	Habit2	Intensity1	Intensity2	Intensity3	Flow_E1	F
COV	Flexibility4	3.425											
COV	Self_E3	-0.496	3.701										
COV	Self_E4	-0.349	1.984	3.31									
COV	Flexibility1	1.744	-0.731	-0.64	4.026								
COV	Flexibility2	1.351	-0.795	-0.44	2.046	3.616							
COV	Habit2	1.018	-1.244	-0.794	1.18	0.912	3.358						
COV	Habit2	0.717	-1.045	-0.623	0.89	0.925	1.978	3.504					
COV	Intensity1	0.773	-0.923	-0.689	0.783	0.945	0.972	0.845	2.872				
COV	Intensity2	1.275	-0.777	-0.571	1.138	0.86	1.351	1.177	1.972	3.984			
COV	Intenity3	0.828	-0.988	-0.853	0.641	0.709	1.012	0.913	1.816	2.07	3.309		
COV	Flow_E1	1.042	-0.751	-0.506	1.331	0.769	1.12	0.927	1.182	1.257	0.855	2.757	
COV	Flow_E2	1.031	-0.949	-0.663	1.384	0.804	1.07	1.002	0.77	0.959	0.604	1.628	2.

APPENDIX B: MEASUREMENT INSTRUMENT

Table 8. Measurement Instrument

Appendix 2: Measurement Instrument & EFA Loading	Items	EFA Factor Loading
Flow Experience	**Flow**	
I forget about time passing and find it difficult to pause while playing the game.	Flow4	0.748
I really attach onto my desired avatar (online game character) and develops a strong affection for it.	Flow3	0.851
I like to be challenged by new levels/items/units.	Flow2	0.837
I feel immersed into the game and almost forget other things.	Flow1	0.785
*Source: Jackson & Eklund (2002), Brockmyer et al (2009), Procci et al (2012)		
Play Intensity	**Intensity**	
I feel out of touch when I don't access online games after a while.	Intensity3	0.759
I consistently spend more time playing games.	Intensity2	0.812
I often indulge in same gaming and occupy plenty of my spare times.	Intensity1	0.762
*Source: Huang et al (2017), Puerta-Cortes et al (2017)		
Flexibility	**Flexibility**	
My device enables me to play online games anytime and anywhere.	Flexibilty4	0.660
There are many small and short time slots available for game playing.	Flexibility2	0.812
My game device is convenient, handy and portable.	Flexibility1	0.739
*Source: Korhonen & Koivisto (2006), Wei & Lu (2014)		
Self_Efficacy	**Self_E**	
Gaming should give a way to other things that is more important or urgent.	Self E4	0.862
I have the capability to exercise control over my time of game playing.	Self E3	0.777
*Source: Tangney et al (2004), LaRose et al (2010)		
Game Habit	**Habit**	
I normally play game at the similar time slots, e.g. after dinner / before bed.	Habit2	0.855
Gaming has become part of my life routine that i always find myself playing.	Habit1	0.775
*Source: Griffiths (2018), Lee et al (2019)		

Chapter 55

Using Sentiment Analytics to Understand Learner Experiences in Serious Games

Linda William
Temasek Polytechnic, Singapore

Ruan Yang
Temasek Polytechnic, Singapore

ABSTRACT

A serious game has been introduced as an alternative tool to support teaching and learning. It integrates entertainment and non-entertainment elements to encourage the voluntary learning of knowledge and skills. One of the essential entertainment elements in the serious game to motivate learning is the enjoyment element. However, studies on models to analyze this enjoyment element are still limited. Most models present isolated and specific approaches for specific games that cannot scale to other games. In this chapter, a generic enjoyment analytics framework is proposed. The framework aims to capture learners' enjoyment experience using open-ended feedback, analyze the feedback using sentiment analytics models, and visualize the results in an interactive dashboard. Using this framework, the lecturers would interpret the learners' experience towards the topic and the game and capture difficulties the learners may encounter during the game. It would help the lecturers to decide follow-up actions required for the learners to improve the learning.

1. INTRODUCTION

The serious game is defined as a (digital) game designed and created not with the primary purpose of pure entertainment but with the serious intention of using it in training, education and healthcare (Loh, Sheng, & Ifenthaler, 2015). It can be used as an alternative or interactive tool to improve skills/performance as well as to broadcast messages to the learners (Liu, Alexandrova, & Nakajima, 2011; Ma, Oikonomou, & Jain, 2011; De Freitas & Liarokapis, 2011; Loh, Sheng, & Ifenthaler, 2015). Serious game infuses

DOI: 10.4018/978-1-6684-7589-8.ch055

knowledge and skills into the game environment while maintaining the entertainment elements that keeping the learners engaged and interacted with the game. Learners who train and learn with a serious game will "play as they learn and learn as they play". Through the engagement and interaction with information, tools, materials and other learners in the serious game, learners would voluntarily learn and master their knowledge and skills (Kim, Park, & Baek, 2009).

Serious game has been implemented in various areas, including computer programming (Coelho, Kato, Xavier, & Gonçalves, 2011; Muratet, Torguet, Jessel, & Viallet, 2009), healthcare (Garcia-Ruiz, Tashiro, Kapralos, & Martin, 2011; de Freitas & Jarvis, 2008; Graafland, Schraagen, & Schijven, 2012), military applications (Lim & Jung, 2013), city planning (Gómez-Rodríguez, González-Moreno, Ramos-Valcárcel, & Vázquez-López, 2011) and supply chain management (William, Rahim, Souza, Nugroho, & Fredericco, 2018). According to a recent report, about 25% of the Global Fortune 500 companies, particularly from the United States, Britain and Germany, have already adopted serious games for their training and education (Loh, Sheng, & Ifenthaler, 2015). Main objectives for the implementation include broadcasting information related to a specific topic (i.e. refugees (United Nations High Commissioner for Refugees, 2021; United Nations High Commissioner for Refugees, 2005; Canadian Red Cross, 2021)), improving the skills and performance of the learners (i.e. python programming language (CodeCombat, 2021)), and testing and evaluating learner's skills as an assessment tool (William, Abdul Rahim, Wu, & de Souza, 2019).

Numerous studies have revealed the benefits of using serious game (Ma, Oikonomou, & Jain, 2011). The benefits include enhancing and encouraging engagement, curiosity, motivation, self-monitoring and problem solving (Ma, Oikonomou, & Jain, 2011; Rieber, 1996; Knight, et al., 2010; Kumar, 2000) to improving the learner's knowledge and skills for specific topics or subjects. The serious game would encourage active participation and interaction from the learners to eventually increase their understanding of particular knowledge and skills (Hou, 2015). The learners would gain experience implementing the new knowledge and skills by completing tasks and challenges in the game.

One of the serious game's essential entertainment elements is learners' enjoyment (Sweetser & Wyeth, 2005). Enjoyment comes from positive experience while playing the game. This enjoyment element helps to decide whether learners would or would not continue playing the game. In the serious game, the enjoyment element is also believed to intrinsically motivate learners to learn new knowledge and skills (IJsselsteijn, De Kort, Poels, Jurgelionis, & Bellotti, 2007; Sweetser & Wyeth, 2005). Enjoyment allows learners to encounter flow experience for a total absorption or engagement in the game (immersive). During the optimal flow experience, the learners are in a state where they are so involved in the game that nothing else seems to matter (Kiili, 2006). It encourages the learners to complete and win the game by achieving new skills and understanding new concepts voluntarily (Kiili, 2006).

However, studies on models for assessing learners' enjoyment and its impacts to improve the learners' knowledge and skills are still limited (Sweetser & Wyeth, 2005; Giannakos, Chorianopoulos, Jaccheri, & Chrisochoides, 2012). Most of the models present isolated and non-repeatable heuristics approaches for evaluating the enjoyment element. It may only focus on only one specific aspect or concept, such as the interface (game control and display), the mechanism (interaction and feedback in the game world), and the gameplay (game problems and challenges). The main challenges in developing the model are 1) collecting the inputs and feedback from the learners, 2) analyzing the inputs and feedback, and 3) interpreting the enjoyment based on these inputs or feedback. The results of the game alone may be minimal and may not be able to represent the learners' enjoyment in the game. Additionally, for existing games (or serious games) in the industry, learners' inputs are mainly used to improve gameplay quality instead of understanding the learning process.

This chapter aims to design a generic enjoyment analytics framework to tackle these three challenges using machine learning models. The proposed framework focuses on open-ended feedback from learners while they are playing the game. This framework has three main components: 1) feedback gathering component, 2) feedback analytics component, and 3) feedback visualization component. The first component, the feedback gathering component, is embedded in the game itself. It allows the learners to provide open-ended feedback regarding the serious game frequently. The second component, the feedback analytics component, analyzes the feedback using machine learning models to detect favorable (positive) or unfavorable (negative) sentiments. These sentiments would be used to indicate the learners' enjoyment experience toward the topics and game itself. Nine machine learning models were developed to perform sentiment analytics. After comparing the models, the best model with the highest accuracy will be implemented in the enjoyment analytics framework. The third component, the feedback visualization component, provides an interactive dashboard to present the sentiment analytics results. It can be used to interpret the learners' experience. Detailed information about the sentiment analytics results and the learners' information is also provided in an interactive dashboard. The framework was evaluated using semi-structured interviews with several lecturers in Singapore. These interviews captured the usefulness of the framework to understand the learners' learning and experience better. The proposed framework is designed to implement it to different games and different topics with no or limited changes required.

The remaining of the chapter will be organized as follows: Section 2 presents the literature review on serious game design, enjoyment in serious game, and sentiment analytics. Section 3 discusses the overview of the proposed enjoyment analytics framework and its three components. Section 4 captures the evaluation of the framework. Section 5 and section 6 present the future research direction and conclusion.

2. LITERATURE REVIEW

This literature review includes: how a serious game can be designed, the impact of enjoyment in a serious game, how emotion can influence learning, the definition of sentiment analytics, and how sentiment analytics can be applied in text feedback.

2.1. Serious Game Design

The serious game has been defined as games with a purpose to educate (Yu, 2019). There is a consensus that serious game has a significant potential as a tool for instruction (Bellotti, Kapralos, Lee, Moreno-Ger, & Berta, 2013). In recent years, there is a sudden increase in serious game usage in education and training (Cowan & Kapralos, 2014). It is found that learners who had serious games integrated into their curriculum had a remarkable performance compared to those who had only a typical curriculum (Blunt, 2009). Additionally, it is also identified that serious game's learners had a drastic improvement in the topics compared to the non-serious game's learners (Guillén-Nieto & Aleson-Carbonell, 2012).

Serious game needs to balance the entertainment and non-entertainment (i.e. teaching pedagogy) to let the learners enjoy the game and learn from the game. Techniques to balance these two elements have been discussed as practices and frameworks in serious game design (Van Staalduinen & de Freitas, 2011). These best practices and frameworks combine game design and instructional design components to balance the entertainment and non-entertainment components in serious game. A few of these frameworks are the Game Object Model (Amory & Seagram, 2003; Amory, 2007), the Experiential Gaming Model (Kiili, 2005a; Kiili, 2005b; Kiili, 2005c), the Four-Dimensional Framework (De Freitas & Oliver, 2006; De Freitas & Jarvis, 2009), and the Game-based Learning Framework (Van Staalduinen & de Freitas, 2011).

The game object model is based on the object-oriented programming concept (Amory & Seagram, 2003; Amory, 2007). Pedagogy elements are combined with game elements that can implement the pedagogy elements in a game, such as a story, plot, and interaction. In contrast, the experiential gaming model describes the relationship between the gameplay and experiential learning to facilitate flow experience (Kiili, 2005a; Kiili, 2005b; Kiili, 2005c). It uses flow theory, which is defined as a total engagement in the game that motivates players to win the game by acquiring new skills and understanding new concepts voluntarily (Kiili, 2006). The four-dimensional framework introduces four dimensions in game design: learning specification, pedagogy, representation and context (De Freitas & Oliver, 2006; De Freitas & Jarvis, 2009). Lastly, the game-based learning framework explores the relationship between game elements and expected learning outcome (Van Staalduinen & de Freitas, 2011). It includes three components, namely: learning, instruction and assessment.

2.2. Enjoyment in Serious Game

In serious game design, enjoyment is one of the essential entertainment elements to be included. It plays a significant role in the learners' decision to continue playing the game and motivate them to achieve certain tasks, such as learning a specific concept (IJsselsteijn, De Kort, Poels, Jurgelionis, & Bellotti, 2007; Sweetser & Wyeth, 2005). Enjoyment would make the learners immerse and engage with the game entirely. This experience is referred to as a "flow" experience. "Flow" experience is denoted as a state during the game where the learners are so involved in the game that nothing else seems to matter (Kiili, 2006). They are fully concentrating on the tasks in the game and less conscious of the passage of time. The "flow" experience would encourages the learners to complete and win the game and help learners to unknowingly learn new skills and knowledge (Kiili, 2006), which result in a better learning process (Nagle, Wolf, Riener, & Novak, 2014).

The most significant factor in game enjoyment is emotion (Lazzaro, 2009). Emotion is a complex behavioural phenomenon involving many neural and chemical integration levels in the body (Lindsley, 1951) that can be classified into two superset terms, namely: positive and negative (Bower, 1992). Emotions can control conscious thought, such as attention focus (Lazzaro, 2004). It is crucial and drives focus, which drives learning and memory (Sylwester, 1994). Learners' emotions would affect their self-regulated learning and determination, which subsequently affect their accomplishment (Mega, Ronconi, & Beni, 2014).

Emotion can be perceived from facial expressions and communication language (Barrett, Lindquist, & Gendron, 2007). Language, including written language (i.e. text), can express emotions, and it helps with categorizing sensations into emotion categories such as anger, disgust, and fear (Lindquist, Satpute, & Gendron, 2015). Emotions in written language can be identified from different writing style (Hancock, Landrigan, & Silver, 2007).

2.3. Sentiment Analytics

Sentiment analytics has been widely used to study opinions, sentiments, and emotions expressed in the text (Miner, Elder IV, & Hill, 2012). It is generally known as computational identification of opinions, sentiments, emotions, and subjectivity from a given text (Medhat, Hassan, & Korashy, 2014). Sentiment analytics can be used to find out about the point of view of the public regarding a topic or individual (Medhat, Hassan, & Korashy, 2014), context to social conversations (Godsay, 2015), and different emotions (Altrabsheh, Gaber, & Cocea, 2013). The objectives of sentiment analytics are to identify the sentiments expressed in a text and classify their polarity. The sentiments can be categorized into two categories: positive and negative, or into an n-point scale, such as very good, good, neutral, bad, and very bad.

Based on its coverage, sentiment analytics can be divided into three levels, namely: document-level, sentence-level, and aspect-level (Medhat, Hassan, & Korashy, 2014). Document-level sentiment analytics focuses on analyzing the whole document and classifying the sentiments for that document. Sentence-level sentiment analytics only focuses on sentiments for each statement. Aspect-level sentiment analytics aims to identify sentiments for specific aspects of the text.

There are two main approaches to solving sentiment analytics: the lexicon-based approach and the machine learning approach (Sommar & Wielondek, 2015). Lexicon-based approaches use a list of predefined words, where each expression is associated with a specific sentiment (Gonçalves, Araújo, Benevenuto, & Cha, 2013). For example, the term "good" is associated with positive sentiment, while the word "bad" is associated with negative sentiment. In the lexicon-based approach, it is essential to have a complete lexical-based dictionary. Different languages and topics would require a different dictionary. This dictionary will determine the accuracy of the sentiment analytics results. Preparing a suitable dictionary is one of the main challenges in a lexical-based approach.

Machine learning approaches for sentiment analytics generally use a supervised classification approach. In this classification, each sentiment is considered as one label. Machine learning-based sentiment analytics approaches have been commonly used and gained popularity in recent years (Agarwal & Mittal, 2015). These approaches require labelled data as a training dataset (Pang, Lee, & Vaithyanathan, 2002). Machine learning approaches for sentiment analytics would generally train the model using the pre-labelled dataset to find patterns in the data and classify the text into specific sentiments (Sommar & Wielondek, 2015). The model will then be used to predict sentiments in new or "real" text. One main benefit of using machine learning approaches is adapting and creating trained models based on the specific context. It can also adjust to the changes in the "real" dataset in the implementation phase. Machine learning approaches are believed to have better performance than the lexicon-based approach (Pang, Lee, & Vaithyanathan, 2002). One main challenge in these machine learning approaches is preparing the pre-labelled dataset, which can be costly or even prohibited for a particular context.

3. PROPOSED ENJOYMENT ANALYTICS FRAMEWORK

To tackle the above challenges, an enjoyment analytics framework is proposed. This proposed framework aims to collect, analyze, and interpret learners' open-ended feedback while using a serious game. It is used to understand their learning experience through a serious game. It has three main components, namely: 1) feedback gathering during game session, 2) data analytics for the analyzing the feedback using sentiment analytics, and 3) visualization of the feedback and sentiments result for interpreting the learners' experience. The three components are summarized in Figure 1.

Figure 1. Components of the proposed enjoyment analytics framework

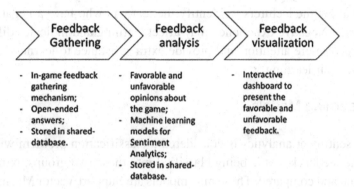

3.1. Feedback Gathering Component

The feedback gathering process is conducted through the serious game itself using open-ended question. The answers will then be stored in a shared database for further processes. This mechanism enables frequent feedback while playing a serious game rather than single feedback at the end of a game. It would help the current learners and act as checkpoints to early identification of learning challenges.

The feedback is collected after each topic for a particular subject. For example, the subject "Introduction to Programming" has two topics, namely: "Condition" and "Loop". The subject would collect two pieces of feedback, one for each topic. The steps for gathering the feedback are as follows:

1. After completing a particular topic, the game will prompt the learners for their feedback. The interface for feedback collection is shown in Figure 2.
2. After they pressed the 'Submit' button, their feedback will be stored in a table of the database for further processes.

Figure 2. Example of one feedback gathering UI interface

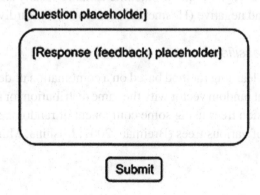

3.2. Feedback Analytics Component

Feedback analytics is conducted for learners' feedback stored in a shared database. It uses a sentiment analytics model to identify learners' enjoyment experience towards the topic and the game itself. The model needs to identify two enjoyment experience categories, namely: positive and negative. The sentiment analytics will allow the lecturers to identify the learners who have a negative experience with the topics and the game. Negative experience may affect learning and indicates difficulties during the game. Lecturers can give more attention and provide extra assistance to learners who have a negative experience to improve their learning.

3.2.1. Machine Learning Models

For this component, sentiment analytics is considered a classification problem with two labels: positive and negative. The feedback text is being classified into these two groups. Nine machine learning models were developed and compared. These nine models are Support Vector Machine (SVM), Logistic Regression, Random Forest Classifier, K-Nearest Neighbour (KNN), Naïve Bayes, Simple Neural Network (SNN), Convolutional Neural Network (CNN), Recurrent Neural Network with Long-Sort Term Memory (RNN-LSTM), and Bi-directional Recurrent Neural Network with Long-Sort Term Memory (Bi-RNN-LSTM). SVM, Logistic Regression, Random Forest Classifier, KNN, and Naïve Bayes are supervised models, while SNN, CNN, RNN-LSTM, and Bi-RNN-LSTM are neural network models. A brief description of these models is as follows.

3.2.1.1. Support Vector Machine (SVM)

SVM is a supervised learning method that generates input-output mapping functions from a training dataset (Vapnik, 1995). An SVM model maps the training dataset to a point in high-dimensional feature space to maximize the gap between categories (i.e. positive and negative sentiment). There are four fundamental concepts of SVM, namely: (1) the separating hyperplane, (2) the maximum-margin hyperplane, (3) the soft margin, and (4) the kernel function (Noble, 2006).

3.2.1.2. Logistic Regression

Logistics regression is a supervised learning method that uses a logistics function to find the best fitting model to explain the relationship between an outcome (dependent) variable and a set of independent (predictor) variables. In logistics regression, the outcome variable usually is binary or dichotomous, such as true and false or positive and negative (Hosmer Jr, Lemeshow, & Sturdivant, 2013).

3.2.1.3. Random Forest Classifier

Random forest is a supervised learning method based on a combination of decision tree predictors. Each tree depends on an independent random vector with the same distribution for all the forest trees (Breiman, 2001). It builds multiple decision trees using some component of randomness and determines the classification using the majority of various trees (Breiman, 2001; Mishina, Murata, Yamauchi, Yamashita, & Fujiyoshi, 2015).

3.2.1.4. K-Nearest Neighbour (KNN)

KKN is a supervised learning method that classifies the input data based on their nearest neighbour's group (Kataria & Singh, 2013). The nearest neighbour's distance can be calculated using any distance measurement such as Euclidian distance and Manhattan distance.

3.2.1.5. Naïve Bayes

Naïve Bayes is a supervised learning method that assigns the most likely group to the data based on its probability (Rish, 2001). Naïve Bayes classifier assumes that the effect of an attribute value on a given group is independent of the other attributes' values.

3.2.1.6. Simple Neural Network (SNN)

SNN is a basic neural network model with interconnected nodes (referred to as neurons) that collectively learn from the input dataset to produce the optimized final output (O'Shea & Nash, 2013). It usually has an input layer, hidden layer and output layer. Each layer would have one or more nodes.

3.2.1.7. Convolutional Neural Network (CNN)

CNN is an extension of SNN that is primarily used in pattern recognition within images (O'Shea & Nash, 2013). It encodes image-specific features into the network.

3.2.1.8. Recurrent Neural Network With Long-Sort Term Memory (RNN-LSTM)

RNN is a neural network with a feedback (closed-loop) connection (Medsker & Jain, 2001). The architecture can be a fully interconnected net to a partially connected net. LSTM is a storing mechanism to save representation of recent input event in the form of activation (Hochreiter & Schmidhuber, 1997). LSTM is implemented in RNN to solve the vanishing gradient problem that significantly increased computational costs by exponentially grows the network.

3.2.1.9. Bi-directional Recurrent Neural Network With Long-Sort Term Memory (Bi-RNN-LSTM)

Bi-RNN LSTM is similar to RNN LSTM. But in Bi-RNN LSTM, the feedback connection can work in both directions (forward and backwards).

3.2.2. Data Preprocessing

Before applying the models, the dataset undergoes data pre-processing to remove any data quality problems and transform the dataset to fit the models. The steps in the data pre-processing are as follows:

1.   Change to lower case

The models might not recognize the same word with different capitalizations, thus changing all words to the lower case can help mitigate the issue.

2.   Remove characters

Several characters, such as special characters, extra white spaces, numbers, single-character word, and punctuations, may not provide much meaning to the sentiment analytics. Hence, these characters are removed. Few research in the literature stated punctuations could provide meaningful sentiment in VADER (Valence Aware Dictionary and sEntiment Reasoner) using specific models (Hutto & Gilbert, 2014). The models in this work are built from scratch and do not have such advanced technology to recognize punctuations' meaning. Thus, punctuations were removed.

3.   Split the dataset

The dataset is split into train and test dataset to evaluate the quality of the models' performance.

4.   Change the feedback text to vectors.

As the models cannot process feedback text in its raw form, changing the feedback text into vectors helps the models process the text.

For supervised models, Term Frequency–Inverse Document Frequency (TF-IDF) was used to transform the feedback text to vector (Roelleke, 2013). TF-IDF put more weight on rare occurring terms and was more suitable for simple machine learning.

The following methods were implemented for neural network models: a tokenizer, padding sequence, and GloVe. Tokenizer changes each text into a sequence of vectors where each token's coefficient could be binary based on TF-IDF (Manning, Raghavan, & Schütze, 2008). It fits its internal vocabulary based on the train data and transforms the text to a sequence of integers based on that internal vocabulary. The padding ensures that the sequences of integers generated have the same length as the longest sequences for training (Manning, Raghavan, & Schütze, 2008). The gloVe is an unsupervised learning model for obtaining vector representation of words (Pennington, Socher, & Manning, 2014). It is a count-based model as it learns the vectors by reducing the occurrence counts matrix. It aims to find the lower dimensional that is the best representation of the high dimension data. Examples of these changes are in Table 1.

Table 1. Examples of changes from feedback text to vector

Method	Text				Vector			
TF-IDF	Term	First document (Term Frequency)	Second Document (Term Frequency)		First document (TF-IDF)	Second Document (TF-IDF)		
	The	1	1		0	0		
	Quick	1	0		0.043	0		
	Brown	0	2		0	0.086		
	Fox	1	1		0	0		
	Jumps	1	1		0	0		
	Over	1	1		0	0		
	Dry	1	0		0.043	0		
	Log	1	1		0	0		
Tokenizer	['Well done!', 'Good work', 'Great effort', 'nice work', 'Excellent!']				[[0. 0. 1. 1. 0. 0. 0. 0. 0.] [0. 1. 0. 0. 1. 0. 0. 0. 0.] [0. 0. 0. 0. 0. 1. 1. 0. 0.] [0. 1. 0. 0. 0. 0. 0. 1. 0.] [0. 0. 0. 0. 0. 0. 0. 0. 1.]]			
Padding sequence	[[1], [2, 3], [4, 5, 6]]				[[0, 0, 1], [0, 2, 3], [4, 5, 6]]			
GloVe	The pre-trained version was implemented. There is no additional change using the dataset.							

3.2.3. Comparison Method

3.2.3.1. Dataset

Two different datasets were employed for comparing these models. The first dataset is a movie review dataset from IMDB (Maas, et al., 2011), consisting of current game reviews with pre-labelled sentiments. It has more than 50,000 reviews with a wide variety of vocabulary. Examples of the data are shown in Figure 3. The text column refers to the text review, and the label column is the sentiment label. 0 means negative sentiment, and 1 means positive sentiment. The number of reviews with positive sentiments and the number of reviews with negative sentiments in this dataset are similar.

Figure 3. Part of the data from the movie review dataset

text	label
I grew up (b. 1965) watching and loving the Thunderbirds. All my mates at school watched. We played "Thunderbir	0
When I put this movie in my DVD player, and sat down with a coke and some chips, I had some expectations. I was	0
Why do people who do not know what a particular time in the past was like feel the need to try to define that time	0
Even though I have great interest in Biblical movies, I was bored to death every minute of the movie. Everything is l	0
Im a die hard Dads Army fan and nothing will ever change that. I got all the tapes, DVD's and audiobooks and every	1
A terrible movie as everyone has said. What made me laugh was the cameo appearance by Scott McNealy, giving a	0
Finally watched this shocking movie last night, and what a disturbing mindf**ker it is, and unbelievably bloody and	1
I caught this film on AZN on cable. It sounded like it would be a good film, a Japanese "Green Card". I can't say I've	0
It may be the remake of 1987 Autumn's Tale after eleven years, as the director Mabel Cheung claimed. Mabel emp	1
My Super Ex Girlfriend turned out to be a pleasant surprise for me, I was really expecting a horrible movie that wo	1
I can't believe people are looking for a plot in this film. This is Laural and Hardy. Lighten up already. These two wer	1
If you haven't seen the gong show TV series then you won't like this movie much at all, not that knowing the series	0
I have always been a huge fan of "Homicide: Life On The Street" so when I heard there was a reunion movie comin	1
Greg Davis and Bryan Daly take some crazed statements by a terrorists, add some commentary by a bunch of uber	0
A half-hearted attempt to bring Elvis Presley into the modern day, but despite a sexy little shower scene and a pseu	0

The second dataset is an actual serious game review from learners (William, 2021). The serious game review dataset is a small dataset with an imbalance number of positive and negative reviews. Examples of the dataset are shown in Figure 4. The feedback column is the text feedback from learners, while the label column is the sentiment labels.

Figure 4. Part of the data from a serious game review dataset

feedback	label
it's fine	0
Too easy	1
It is a good game that we are able to learn and play at the same time.	1
A refreshing way to learn and understand python	1
It is an interesting educational coding game, good for beginners.	1
It was a great beginner course	1
It was stimulating	1
I felt that this was the best method to learn coding.	1
I think we need more assignments with the game	1
I felt that the levels did not cover much content in Python in the sense that m	0
Bad Game	0
Great	1
It is a intresting way to learn coding	1
Fun	1
It was fun as it makes me practise with my coding with playing a game	1
It was fun and im able to learn within the game	1

3.2.3.2. Preliminary Test

A preliminary test was conducted to eliminate the machine learning models that are not performing well with the given dataset. In this preliminary test, those nine machine learning models were trained and tested using the first dataset (IMDB movie revise dataset) in their default parameter values. No optimization was performed in this preliminary test. The performance of the models was evaluated using accuracy measurement. Accuracy is the ratio of the correct number of observations to the total number of observations. It can be a good indicator for the model's performance when the data is balanced, as in the first dataset. The test results are shown in Table 2.

Table 2. Preliminary test for sentiment analytics models

Method	Accuracy	Prediction Time*
Support Vector Machine (SVM)	89%	75 s
Logistic Regression	89%	61.2 µs
Random Forest Classifier	85%	575 µs
K-Nearest Neighbour	83%	562 µs
Naïve Bayes	79%	7.81 s
Simple Neural Network	72%	1.21 s
Convolutional Neural Network	83%	1.84 s
Recurrent Neural Network with LSTM	83%	1.59 s
Bi-directional Recurrent Neural Network with LSTM	85%	5.83 s

*Timings may differ due to computer specifications.

Table 2 shows that the best-supervised models are Support Vector Machine (SVM) and Logistic Regression, with an accuracy of 89%. The best neural network model is Bidirectional Recurrent Neural Network with Long Short Term Memory (LSTM), with an accuracy of 85%. However, SVM cannot handle large dataset and took a longer time than Logistics Regression. Hence, only Logistics Regression and Bidirectional Recurrent Neural Network with Long Short Term Memory (LSTM) are considered further.

3.2.3.3. Hyper Parameter Tuning

Logistics Regression and Bidirectional Recurrent Neural Network with Long Short Term Memory (LSTM) models are further tuned to improve their accuracy. The model tuning was performed using Grid Search Cross-Validation (GridSearchCV) to find the best hyperparameters, known as hyper-parameter tuning (Krstajic, Buturovic, Leahy, & Thomas, 2014). This model is to ensure the model will be able to perform at its best with suitable hyper-parameters. GridSearchCV runs through the possible combinations of the parameters and determines the parameters with the best performances. Due to time constraint, only several parameters were optimized. The results of GridSearchCV for both models are in Figure 5 and 6.

After the hyper-parameter tuning, the new parameters were used to perform training and testing using the IMDB movie review dataset. The performance results of these two models are shown in Table 3. The performance for both models did not significantly increase. It was still around 89% for Logistics Regression and 85% for Bi-directional Recurrent Neural Network with LSTM.

Figure 5. The results of GridSearchCV for Logistic Regression

Logistic Regression:

```
Best params: {'clf__C': 1.0, 'clf__penalty': 'l2', 'clf__solver': 'liblinear'}
```

Figure 6. The results of GridSearchCV for Bidirectional Recurrent Neural Network with Long-Sort Time Memory

Bidirectional Recurrent Neural Network with LSTM:

```
Best: 0.859594 using {'batch_size': 50, 'epochs': 6}
Best: 0.838281 using {'optimizer': 'Adam'}
```

Table 3. Performance of sentiment analytics models after parameter tuning

Method	Accuracy	Prediction Time*
Logistic Regression	89%	43.9 µs
Bi-directional Recurrent Neural Network with LSTM	85%	778 µs

*Timings may differ due to computer specifications.

To further test these models, the second dataset (serious game review from learners) was used for testing. The new parameter values from the hyper-parameter tuning were used. F1 was used to measure the performance instead of accuracy because the second dataset has data imbalance (Raschka, 2021). The number of positive sentiments and the number of negative sentiments significantly differ for the serious game review dataset. F1 score is a better indicator than accuracy when the data is imbalanced. The results are shown in Table 4. Bidirectional Recurrent Neural Network with LSTM is performing better than Logistic Regression by 1%.

Table 4. Performance of sentiment analytics models for serious game review dataset

Method	F1	Prediction Time*
Logistic Regression	85%	29.5 µs
Bi-directional Recurrent Neural Network with LSTM	86%	69.8 µs

*Timings may differ due to computer specifications.

Bi-directional Recurrent Neural Network with LSTM model performs better for the second dataset (serious game review dataset) compared to the first dataset (IMDB movie review dataset). It is common as the Bi-directional Recurrent Neural Network with the LSTM model has dropout layers that ignore some of the neurons during training (Brownlee, 2018). The dropout layer is used to reduce overfitting. During training, the model faces more difficulty to predict the correct answer because of the dropout layer and not all neurons are utilized. During testing, the model has all neurons utilized, thus it has the full computational power and might perform better.

The results indicate that the Bi-directional Recurrent Neural Network with the LSTM model performed better than Logistic Regression. Thus, Bi-directional Recurrent Neural Network with LSTM is used for the feedback analytics component.

3.3. Feedback Visualization Component

Sentiment analytics results from the second component are visualized in an interactive dashboard. It is displayed as a column chart with a red bar representing negative feedback while a green bar represents positive feedback, as illustrated in Figure 7. The X-axis of the column chart is the different categories of learners' sentiments, while the Y-axis is the count of learners having the sentiment for that question. Detailed information about the learners with positive and negative sentiments can be shown by clicking the respective bar.

This information can be used by lecturers to interpret the learners' enjoyment experience towards the topic and the game itself. Lecturers would be able to identify learners that have negative sentiments and find out the difficulties that they are encountered. A lecturer can guide them to solve their challenges and improve their learning.

Figure 7. Sentiment analytics results represented in a column chart

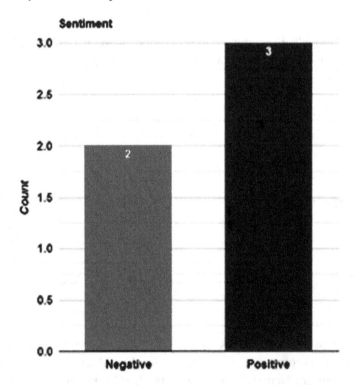

4. EVALUATION OF THE ENJOYMENT ANALYTICS FRAMEWORK

To evaluate the proposed enjoyment analytics framework, seven semi-structured interviews with lecturers in Temasek Polytechnic, Singapore, were conducted. The sessions were held in December 2020 with the different lecturer for each session. During the interview sessions, the framework design was briefly described, and the lecturer's opinions regarding the framework and their suggestions were captured. The questions asked during the semi-structured interviews are listed in Table 5.

Table 5. Evaluation Questions

#	Question
1	Based on the current features in the enjoyment analytics framework, would the framework help you to monitor the student's learning?
2	Based on the current features in the enjoyment analytics framework, would the framework help you to evaluate the student's learning?
3	Does the current enjoyment analytics framework provide sufficient insights to understand the student's learning?
4	Does the positive and negative sentiments help you to understand the student's learning?
5	What are other features that you would like to be included in the enjoyment analytics framework?

From these sessions, the lecturers think that the framework would help to monitor and evaluate the student's learning. The insights that were captured in the framework are useful for the lecturers to understand the learners' experience and learning better. Learners with positive feedback would be able to enjoy the game and, at the same time, learn new knowledge and skills. The lecturers would be able to monitor this learning through the feedback visualization. Learners with unfavorable (negative) sentiments can also be identified. Negative sentiments may indicate difficulties in learning. The lecturers would be able to approach the learners and conduct follow-up discussions to improve their learning.

The lecturers also proposed additional features to improve the enjoyment analytics framework. These features include exporting the data to Ms Excel, filtering the sentiments based on the topics and filtering the sentiments based on the classes. These additional features are currently being evaluated to be added in the framework.

5. FUTURE RESEARCH DIRECTIONS

A serious game for learning has received a lot of attention from educators as well as game designers. It provides a more interactive approach to engage the learners to learn new skills and knowledge. However, there are very limited works on the effectiveness of serious games as a learning tool in a different learning environment (such as problem-based learning). Most of the works focused on specific aspects of serious games or a specific serious game. More works to evaluate serious games effectiveness and to develop a generic framework to assess it are needed.

One of the approach to evaluate the effectiveness of learning is through understanding the learners' enjoyment experience. It may provide insights into the effectiveness of the serious game. These insights are proposed in the enjoyment analytics framework. There are at least two possible research opportunities to extend the enjoyment analytics framework. First, in addition, to understand the sentiments, identifying specific difficulties in a topic can also be included in the framework. Machine learning models for keyword discovery can be implemented for this purpose to the feedback text. It would be able to help the lecturers to focus their scaffolding on removing these difficulties. Second, finding and analyzing learners' learning patterns can be developed. Learners with the same enjoyable experience and learning patterns may act and perform similarly in the game. It would help the lecturers to identify a group of learners that would need more help.

6. CONCLUSION

This chapter reviews the proposed enjoyment analytics framework for a serious game using sentiment analytics. The framework aims to identify learners' sentiments to understand their enjoyable experience while learning a particular subject using a serious game. In addition to that, the framework would also help to provide insight for the lecturers to identify learners with a negative experience. It is assumed that learners with negative experience may have difficulties with the topic and the game. Lecturers would be able to pay more attention to these learners and provide more scaffolding for them.

The proposed framework consists of three main components: feedback gathering, feedback analytics and feedback visualization. The first component, feedback gathering, is embedded in the serious game itself. It allows the learners to submit text feedback regarding the topics and serious game. The second component, feedback analytics, uses machine learning models to identify learner's sentiments based on their feedback. It classifies the sentiments into two categories, positive and negative sentiments. And the third component, feedback visualization, shows the sentiment to the lecturers using an interactive dashboard where the lecturers can drill down the information to understand the sentiments and the learners better. This framework can be implemented for any serious game with different subjects with no (or limited) changes required.

ACKNOWLEDGMENT

This research is supported by the Ministry of Education, Singapore, under its Translational R&D and Innovation Fund (TIF) Grant (12th Award, MOE2019-TIF-0009). Any opinions, findings and conclusions or recommendations expressed in this material are those of the author(s) and do not reflect the views of the Ministry of Education, Singapore.

REFERENCES

Agarwal, B., & Mittal, N. (2015). Machine Learning Approach for Sentiment Analysis. In B. Agarwal & N. Mittal (Eds.), *Prominent Feature Extraction for Sentiment Analysis*. Springer.

Altrabsheh, N., Gaber, M. M., & Cocea, M. (2013). Sentiment analytics for education. In *5th KES International Conference on Intelligent Decision Technologies (KES-IDT 2013)*. Sesimbra, Portugal: IOS Press.

Amory, A. (2007). Game object model version II: A theoretical framework for educational game development. *Educational Technology Research and Development, 55*(1), 51–77. doi:10.100711423-006-9001-x

Amory, A., & Seagram, R. (2003). Educational game models: conceptualization and evaluation: the practice of higher education. *South African Journal of Higher Education, 17*(2), 206–217.

Barrett, L. F., Lindquist, K. A., & Gendron, M. (2007). Language as context for the perception of emotion. *Trends in Cognitive Sciences, 11*(8), 327–332. doi:10.1016/j.tics.2007.06.003 PMID:17625952

Bellotti, F., Kapralos, B., Lee, K., Moreno-Ger, P., & Berta, R. (2013). Assessment in and of Serious Games: An Overview. *Advances in Human-Computer Interaction, 2013*, 11. doi:10.1155/2013/136864

Blunt, R. (2009, December). *Do Serious Games Work? Results from Three Studies*. Retrieved from eLearn Magazine: https://elearnmag.acm.org/archive.cfm?aid=1661378&doi=10.1145%2F1661377.1661378

Bower, G. H. (1992). How Might Emotions Affect Learning? In S. Å. Christianson (Ed.), *The Handbook Of Emotion And Memory*. Lawrence Erlbaum Associates.

Breiman, L. (2001). Random forests. *Machine Learning, 45*(1), 5–32. doi:10.1023/A:1010933404324

Brownlee, J. (2018, December 3). *A Gentle Introduction to Dropout for Regularizing Deep Neural Networks*. Retrieved from Machine Learning Mastery: https://machinelearningmastery.com/dropout-for-regularizing-deep-neural-networks/

Canadian Red Cross. (2021). *In Exile For A While*. Retrieved April 30, 2018, from https://www.redcross.ca/cmslib/general/inexileforawhilekit.pdf

CodeCombat. (2021). *Code Combat*. Retrieved from https://codecombat.com/

Coelho, A., Kato, E., Xavier, J., & Gonçalves, R. (2011). Serious game for introductory programming. In *International Conference on Serious Games Development and Applications* (pp. 61-71). Lisbon, Portugal: Springer. 10.1007/978-3-642-23834-5_6

Cowan, B., & Kapralos, B. (2014). A Survey of Frameworks and Game Engines for Serious Game Development. In *2014 IEEE 14th International Conference on Advanced Learning Technologies*. Athens: IEEE.

de Freitas, S., & Jarvis, S. (2008). Towards a development approach for serious games. In T. Connolly, M. Stansfield, & E. Boyle (Eds.), *Games-based learning advancements for multi-sensory human-computer interfaces: Techniques and effective practices* (pp. 215–231). IGI Global.

De Freitas, S., & Jarvis, S. (2009). Towards a development approach to serious games. In T. Connolly, M. Stansfield, & L. Boyle (Eds.), Games-based learning advancements for multi-sensory human computer interfaces: Techniques and effective practices (pp. 215-231). IGI Global. doi:10.4018/978-1-60566-360-9.ch013

De Freitas, S., & Liarokapis, F. (2011). Serious games: a new paradigm for education? In M. Ma, A. Oikonomou, & L. Jain (Eds.), *Serious Games and Edutainment Applications* (pp. 9–23). Springer. doi:10.1007/978-1-4471-2161-9_2

De Freitas, S., & Oliver, M. (2006). How can exploratory learning with games and simulations within the curriculum be most effectively evaluated? *Computers & Education*, *46*(3), 249–264. doi:10.1016/j.compedu.2005.11.007

Garcia-Ruiz, M., Tashiro, J., Kapralos, B., & Martin, M. (2011). Crouching Tangents, Hidden Danger: Assessing Development of Dangerous Misconceptions within Serious Games for Healthcare Education. In *Gaming and Simulations: Concepts, Methodologies, Tools and Applications* (pp. 1712–1749). Information Resources Management Association. doi:10.4018/978-1-60960-195-9.ch704

Giannakos, M. N., Chorianopoulos, K., Jaccheri, L., & Chrisochoides, N. (2012). *This game is girly!" Perceived enjoyment and learner acceptance of edutainment. In Edutainment 2012/GameDays 2012.* Springer.

Godsay, M. (2015). The Process of Sentiment Analysis: A Study. *International Journal of Computer Applications*.

Gómez-Rodríguez, A., González-Moreno, J., Ramos-Valcárcel, D., & Vázquez-López, L. (2011). Modeling serious games using AOSE methodologies. *11th International Conference on Intelligent Systems Design and Applications (ISDA)*, 53-58.

Gonçalves, P., Araújo, M., Benevenuto, F., & Cha, M. (2013). Comparing and combining Sentiment analytics methods. ACM conference on Online Social Networks, 27-38.

Graafland, M., Schraagen, J., & Schijven, M. (2012). Systematic review of serious games for medical education and surgical skills training. *British Journal of Surgery*, *99*(10), 1322–1330. doi:10.1002/bjs.8819 PMID:22961509

Guillén-Nieto, V., & Aleson-Carbonell, M. (2012). Serious games and learning effectiveness: The case of It's a Deal! *Computers & Education*, *58*(1), 435–448. doi:10.1016/j.compedu.2011.07.015

Hancock, J. T., Landrigan, C., & Silver, C. (2007). Expressing emotion in text-based communication. *2007 Conference on Human Factors in Computing Systems*.

Hochreiter, S., & Schmidhuber, J. (1997). Long Short-Term Memory. *Neural Computation*, *9*(8), 1735–1780. doi:10.1162/neco.1997.9.8.1735 PMID:9377276

Hosmer, D. Jr, Lemeshow, S., & Sturdivant, R. (2013). *Applied Logistic Regression* (Vol. 398). John Wiley & Sons. doi:10.1002/9781118548387

Hou, H. (2015). Integrating cluster and sequential analysis to explore learners' flow and behavioral patterns in a simulation game with situated-learning context for science courses: A video-based process exploration. *Computers in Human Behavior*, *48*, 424–435. doi:10.1016/j.chb.2015.02.010

Hutto, C., & Gilbert, E. (2014). Vader: A parsimonious rule-based model for Sentiment analytics of social media text. *International AAAI Conference on Web and Social Media*, 2-10.

IJsselsteijn, W., De Kort, Y., Poels, K., Jurgelionis, A., & Bellotti, F. (2007). Characterizing and measuring user experiences in digital games. *International conference on advances in computer entertainment technology, 2*, 27.

Kataria, A., & Singh, M. (2013). A review of data classification using k-nearest neighbour algorithm. *International Journal of Emerging Technology and Advanced Engineering, 3*(6), 354–360.

Kiili, K. (2006). Evaluations of an experiential gaming model. *Human Technology: An Interdisciplinary Journal on Humans in ICT Environments, 2*(2), 187–201. doi:10.17011/ht/urn.2006518

Kiili, K. (2006). Evaluations of an Experiential Gaming Model. *An Interdisciplinary Journal on Humans in ICT Enviroments, 2*(2), 187–201.

Kim, B., Park, H., & Baek, Y. (2009). Not just fun, but serious strategies: Using meta-cognitive strategies in game-based learning. *Computers & Education, 52*(4), 800–810. doi:10.1016/j.compedu.2008.12.004

Knight, J., Carly, S., Tregunna, B., Jarvis, S., Smithies, R., de Freitas, S., ... Dunwell, I. (2010). Serious gaming technology in major incident triage training: A pragmatic controlled trial. *Resuscitation Journal, 81*(9), 1174–1179. doi:10.1016/j.resuscitation.2010.03.042 PMID:20732609

Krstajic, D., Buturovic, L., Leahy, D., & Thomas, S. (2014). Cross-validation pitfalls when selecting and assessing regression and classification models. *Journal of Cheminformatics, 6*(1), 1–15. doi:10.1186/1758-2946-6-10 PMID:24678909

Kumar, D. (2000). Pedagogical Dimensions of Game Playing. *ACM Intelligence Magazine, 10*(10), 9–10.

Lazzaro, N. (2004). Why We Play Games: Four Keys to More Emotion in Player Experiences. *Game Developer Conference 2004.*

Lazzaro, N. (2009). Why we play: affect and the fun of games. *Human-Computer Interaction: Designing for Diverse Users and Domains,* 155.

Lim, C., & Jung, H. (2013). A study on the military Serious Game. *Advanced Science and Technology Letters, 39,* 73–77. doi:10.14257/astl.2013.39.14

Lindquist, K. A., Satpute, A. B., & Gendron, M. (2015). Does Language Do More Than Communicate Emotion? *Current Directions in Psychological Science, 24*(2), 99–108. doi:10.1177/0963721414553440 PMID:25983400

Lindsley, D. B. (1951). Emotion. Handbook of experimental psychology, 473–516.

Liu, Y., Alexandrova, T., & Nakajima, T. (2011). Gamifying intelligent environments. *Proceedings of the 2011 international ACM workshop on Ubiquitous meta user interfaces.* 10.1145/2072652.2072655

Loh, C., Sheng, Y., & Ifenthaler, D. (2015). Serious Game Analytics: Theoretical Framework. In C. Loh, Y. Sheng, & D. Ifenthaler (Eds.), *Serious Game Analytics: Methodologies for Performance Measurement, Assessment and Improvement* (pp. 3–30). Springer. doi:10.1007/978-3-319-05834-4_1

Ma, M., Oikonomou, A., & Jain, L. (2011). Innovations in Serious Games for Future Learning. In *Serious Games and Edutainment Applications* (pp. 3–7). Springer. doi:10.1007/978-1-4471-2161-9_1

Maas, A., Daly, R., Pham, P., Huang, D., Ng, A., & Potts, C. (2011). Learning Word Vectors for Sentiment Analysis. *The 49th Annual Meeting of the Association for Computational Linguistics: Human Language Technologies,* 142-150.

Manning, C., Raghavan, P., & Schütze, H. (2008). *Introduction to Information Retrieval*. Cambridge University Press. doi:10.1017/CBO9780511809071

Medhat, W., Hassan, A., & Korashy, H. (2014). Sentiment analytics algorithms and applications: A survey. *Ain Shams Engineering Journal*, *5*(4), 1093–1113. doi:10.1016/j.asej.2014.04.011

Medsker, L., & Jain, L. (2001). *Recurrent Neural Networks*. CRC Press.

Mega, C., Ronconi, L., & Beni, R. D. (2014). What Makes a Good Learner? How Emotions, Self-Regulated Learning, and Motivation Contribute to Academic Achievement. *Journal of Educational Psychology*, *106*(1), 121–131. doi:10.1037/a0033546

Miner, G., Elder, I. V. J., & Hill, T. (2012). *Practical text mining and statistical analysis for non-structured text data applications*. Academic Press.

Mishina, Y., Murata, R., Yamauchi, Y., Yamashita, T., & Fujiyoshi, H. (2015). Boosted Random Forest. *IEICE Transactions on Information and Systems*, *98*(9), 1630–1636. doi:10.1587/transinf.2014OPP0004

Muratet, M., Torguet, P., Jessel, J., & Viallet, F. (2009). Towards a serious game to help learners learn computer programming. *International Journal of Computer Games Technology*, *2009*, 1–12. doi:10.1155/2009/470590

Nagle, A., Wolf, P., Riener, R., & Novak, D. (2014). The use of player-centered positive reinforcement to schedule in-game rewards inreases enjoyment and performance in a serious game. *International Journal of Serious Games*, *1*(4), 35–47. doi:10.17083/ijsg.v1i4.47

Nasim, Z., Rajput, Q., & Haider, S. (2017). Sentiment analytics of learner feedback using machine learning and lexicon based approaches. In *2017 International Conference on Research and Innovation in Information Systems (ICRIIS)* (pp. 1-6). Langkawi: IEEE.

Noble, W. S. (2006). What is a support vector machine? *Nature Biotechnology*, *24*(12), 1565–1567. doi:10.1038/nbt1206-1565 PMID:17160063

O'Shea, K., & Nash, R. (2013). *An Introduction to Convolutional Neural Networks*. Retrieved from https://white.stanford.edu/teach/index.php/An_Introduction_to_Convolutional_Neural_Networks

Pang, B., Lee, L., & Vaithyanathan, S. (2002). *Thumbs up? Sentiment Classification using Machine Learning. In Conf. on Empirical Methods in Natural Language Processing*. EMNLP.

Pennington, J., Socher, R., & Manning, C. (2014). Glove: global vectors for word representation. *The 2014 Conference on Empirical Methods in Natural Language Processing (EMNLP)*, 1532-1543.

Raschka, S. (n.d.). *How can the F1-score help with dealing with class imbalance?* Retrieved from Sebastian Raschka: https://sebastianraschka.com/faq/docs/computing-the-f1-score.html

Rieber, L. (1996). Seriously considering play: Designing interactive learning environments based on the blending of microworlds, simulations, and games. *Educational Technology Research and Development*, *44*(2), 43–58. doi:10.1007/BF02300540

Rish, I. (2001). An empirical study of the naive Bayes classifier. *IJCAI 2001 workshop on empirical methods in artificial intelligence, 3*, 41-46.

Roelleke, T. (2013). *Information Retrieval Models: Foundations and Relationships.* Morgan & Claypool.

Sommar, F., & Wielondek, M. (2015). *Combining Lexicon- and Learning-based Approaches for Improved Performance and Convenience in Sentiment Classification* (Dissertation). Retrieved from DiVA: http://urn.kb.se/resolve?urn=urn:nbn:se:kth:diva-166430

Sweetser, P., & Wyeth, P. (2005). GameFlow: a model for evaluating player enjoyment in games. *Computers in Entertainment (CIE), 3*(3), Article 3A.

Sylwester, R. (1994). How Emotions Affect Learning. *Reporting What Learners Are Learning*, 60-65.

United Nations High Commissioner for Refugees. (2005, December 7). *Surviving against the odds: a taste of life as a refugee.* Retrieved April 30, 2018, from https://www.unhcr.org/4397174b4.html

United Nations High Commissioner for Refugees. (2021). *Passages: An Awareness Game Confronting The Plight of Refugees.* Retrieved April 30, 2018, from https://www.unhcr.org/473dc1772.html

Van Staalduinen, J., & de Freitas, S. (2011). A game-based learning framework: Linking game design and learning. In M. Khine (Ed.), *Learning to play: exploring the future of education with video games* (pp. 29–54). Peter Lang.

Vapnik, V. (1995). *The Nature of Statistical Learning.* Springer. doi:10.1007/978-1-4757-2440-0

William, L. (2021). Improving Learners Programming Skills using Serious Games. *14th International Symposium on Advances in Technology Education.*

William, L., Abdul Rahim, Z., Wu, L., & de Souza, R. (2019). Effectiveness of Supply Chain Games in Problem Based Learning Environment. In D. K. Ifenthaler (Ed.), *Game-Based Assessment Revisited* (pp. 257–280). Springer. doi:10.1007/978-3-030-15569-8_13

William, L., Rahim, Z., Souza, R., Nugroho, E., & Fredericco, R. (2018). Extendable Board Game to Facilitate Learning in Supply Chain Management. *Advances in Science, Technology and Engineering Systems Journal, 3*(4), 99–111. doi:10.25046/aj030411

Yu, Z. (2019). A Meta-Analysis of Use of Serious Games in Education over a Decade. *International Journal of Computer Games Technology*, 8.

ADDITIONAL READING

Bing, L. (2015). *Opinions, sentiment, and emotion in text.* Cambridge University Press.

Dörner, R., Göbel, S., Effelsberg, W., & Wiemeyer, J. (Eds.). (2016). *Serious Games.* Springer International Publishing. doi:10.1007/978-3-319-40612-1

Ifenthaler, D., & Kim, Y. J. (Eds.). (2019). *Game-Based Assessment Revisited.* Springer International Publishing. doi:10.1007/978-3-030-15569-8

Kiili, K. (2005). *On educational game design: Building blocks of flow experience*. Tampere University of Technology.

Kiili, K., De Freitas, S., Arnab, S., & Lainema, T. (2012). The design principles for flow experience in educational games. *Procedia Computer Science*, *15*, 78–91. doi:10.1016/j.procs.2012.10.060

Kubat, M. (2017). *An Introduction to Machine Learning*. Springer International Publishing. doi:10.1007/978-3-319-63913-0

Loh, C. S., Sheng, Y., & Ifenthaler, D. (Eds.). (2015). *Serious games analytics*. Springer International Publishing. doi:10.1007/978-3-319-05834-4

KEY TERMS AND DEFINITIONS

Classification: A process of categorized the item in a dataset into predefined labels (such as positive and negative).

Flow Experience: A state during a game session where the players are fully engaged and concentrated with the game that nothing else seems to matter.

Interactive Dashboard: A visualization tool that analyzes, monitors, and visualizes key insights while allowing the users to drill down and filter the information directly.

Machine Learning: A computer algorithm that can learn and adapt without following explicit instructions by identifying and analyzing data patterns.

Neural Network: A machine learning model that mimics the human brain's neural network. It contains layers of interconnected nodes (referred to as neurons) to understand and learn from the data.

Sentiment Analytics: A method used to identify opinions, sentiments, and subjectivity from a given dataset.

Serious Game: A (digital) game designed and created not with the primary purpose of pure entertainment. It includes non-entertainment components such as learning specific skills and knowledge or building awareness on particular topics.

Supervised Learning: A machine learning model that maps an input to an output based on predefined input-output pairs (training examples). It requires a pre-labelled (with input and output) training dataset.

This research was previously published in Next-Generation Applications and Implementations of Gamification Systems; pages 145-165, copyright year 2022 by Engineering Science Reference (an imprint of IGI Global).

Chapter 56
The Social Facilitation of Performance, Emotions, and Motivation in a High Challenge Video Game:
Playing People and Playing Game Characters

Russell Blair Williams
Zayed University, Dubai, UAE

ABSTRACT

The objective of this study is to analyze motivation, performance, state hostility, and targeted affect in a computer-based car racing game when social actors are opponents, and when game characters are opponents. This is a between-subjects, experimental, study of social facilitation with 97 Gulf Arab women. The social facilitation of performance and finishing time does not take place. There is no difference in state hostility based on social facilitation, but there is in emotions targeted at opponents. People are viewed more positively than NPCs after play. Intrinsic engagement and extrinsic motivation are both facilitated by the presence of human opponents. There is evidence that the experience of playing a game character and playing a person is substantially different even though the outcomes of performance and state hostility are not.

INTRODUCTION

Playing video games is a very social leisure activity (Cairns, Cox, Day, Martin & Perryman., 2013). The presence of other people, co-located or network-connected, may be the heart of the video game play experience (Bowman, et al., 2013). Yet, video games can also be a part of a very solitary pursuit where the player is alone and opponents are Non-Player Characters (NPCs), the product of programming within

DOI: 10.4018/978-1-6684-7589-8.ch056

the game. The experience and outcome of play can be very different when playing alone and playing with others (e.g. Williams & Clippinger, 2002; Schmierbach, 2010; Shafer, 2012).

It has been theorized that the presence of other people can facilitate improved performance in a wide array of activities (Triplett, 1898; Zajonc, 1965) and that this social facilitation of performance also occurs in video game play (Bowman et al., 2013). The presence of an audience has been found to improve performance when the game being played does not offer a great deal of challenge (Bowman et al., 2013). Co-located human opponents are not the same as having a live audience, but the physical presence of a human opponent has been shown to facilitate differences in the game play experience and post-play affect (Williams & Clippinger, 2002; Schafer, 2013). This physical presence of a human as an opponent could also impact performance and by extension experience and post-play affect.

The key question in this study is whether there is social facilitation of performance, experience and affect with the play of a complex video game. This study will look at the social facilitation of intrinsic engagement, extrinsic motivation, performance and post-play affect. It is an exploration of the social facilitation of engagement, motivation and affect alongside performance in a video game. It examines targeted affect alongside the state hostility scale (SHS). The play experience, motivation and performance, are then be examined for their role in particular affective outcomes when playing a human and an NPC opponent. The affective impact of video games has been largely studied on the basis of single variables, increasing attention is being given to the role of experience (e.g. Abbassi et al., 2019; Johnson et al., 2018), and the role of performance in the process is also becoming more important to understand (e.g. Röhlcke et al., 2018; Bowman, Kowert, & Cohen, 2015; Bowman et al., 2013).

BACKGROUND

Social Facilitation

Social Facilitation Theory (SFT) comes out of Triplett's (1898) work which was the first experimental study of social psychology (Zajonc, 1965). Triplett (1898) concluded that the physical presence of another person in a competition would increase the amount of energy available to perform in a competition. Zajonc (1965) reported that social facilitation research looks at behavior in front of an audience of non-participants or in the presence of another person or persons engaged in the same activity. Either one can have an impact on performance in an activity. Bowman et al. (2013) looked at performance in front of an audience and found facilitation effects with simple games. VanTuinen and McNeel (1975) looked at competitive pairs and found facilitation effects, but did not find effects with non-competitive pairs and playing alone in non-competitive situations. The study of Social Facilitation has had mixed results on the basis of task, social context, respondents and theoretical perspective (Strauss, 2002).

The first applications of SFT to video game play (Brown, Hall, & Holtzer, 1997; Kimble & Rezabek, 1992) demonstrated that the presence of an audience decreased performance in what is considered a complex task. Based on a flight simulator, Worchel, Shebilske, Jordan, and Prislin (1997) concluded that increases in performance were a function of challenge and not the presence of an audience. Zajonc (1965) argued that competition and challenge could push performance in the same way as an audience and this could confound findings. Bowman et al. (2013) argued that either challenge or audience will push a player to their limit so that when the game is more complex it will consume all of the potential of drive and ability and reduce the effect of an audience. When a game is simple there is enough cognitive capacity for improvement and the audience can have an effect on an individual's performance. When a game is complex there is not enough cognitive capacity for an audience to have an effect on performance. Bowman et al. (2013) concluded that the presence of audience members during play in low-challenge, simple, video games increased performance.

In this study the social facilitation of performance has been examined with an off-the-shelf driving simulation game that is neither low-challenge or simple. Cognitive load in the game will be high regardless of the situation of play and based on previous findings this is likely to negate the impact of a human opponent on performance. The measure of performance in this study is based on time, an absolute metric. Based on previous research the hypothesis here will be:

Hypothesis 1: Performance will not be significantly different for respondents playing co-located humans and playing game-generated characters.

Video Games and Opponent Identity

Social interaction can facilitate or inhibit more than performance. It can also have an impact on post-activity affect and engagement. Williams and Clippinger (2002) found that scores on the State Hostility Scale were significantly higher when respondents were playing against the character than when they played against a person. Mandryk, Inkpen, and Calvert (2006) concluded that participants preferred playing against a friend rather than playing against a game character. Respondents found human competition to be less boring, more fun and more competitive. Ravaja et al. (2006) reported that playing against people rather than a character resulted in more engagement, higher post-game challenge appraisals and greater arousal. There is clearly the possibility that different play experiences are socially facilitated.

Weibel, Wissmath, Habegger, Steiner, and Groner (2008) found that people like to compete against people and that there seems to be more challenge if the opponent is at least thought to be controlled by a person. Respondents enjoyed playing a person more even when they lost the contest and reported higher levels of presence and intrinsic engagement. Ravaja (2009) found that even without co-location respondents experienced more pleasure playing against a human. Schmierbach (2010) concluded that playing against a game-generated character can make people frustrated and angry. Mihan, Anisimowicz, and Nicki (2015) concluded that playing alone was more aggravating than playing either competitively or cooperatively with a co-located individual.

Shafer (2012) conducted the only study where playing people resulted in greater post-play hostility than playing game characters. This increase in hostility also reduced reported enjoyment of the game. Shafer (2012) employed a pre-test/post-test of state hostility and looked specifically at the difference of pre/post SHS scores. In spite of this one study it appears that human social interaction facilitates less hostility and frustration on the part of game players.

Hypothesis 2: State hostility will be lower for respondents after playing co-located humans than after playing game-generated characters.

Targeted Affect

Affect can be understood as a general state or it can be directed at something specific. The target can be self, other people, an object or something less tangible. Targeted affect has been studied in relation to stereotyping and racism where often respondents have negative self-directed emotions when they behave contrary to their stated belief systems and core values (e.g Monteith, Devine & Zuwerink, 1993; Costarelli & Colloca, 2004; Fehr & Sassenberg, 2010). Targeted affect has also been considered in terms of newcomers to an organization and the feelings they generate toward their supervisors on the basis of experience (Nifadkar, Tsui, & Ashforth, 2012). There have been two media-centered studies discussing targeted affect. Holbert et al. (2007) looked at priming targeted emotions toward presidential candidates in a debate after viewing a politically-charged documentary. King and Behnke (2000) considered the intervention of directed-task affect in dealing with various levels of communication load in listening. They found significant correlations between directed task affect and listening performance.

Because this construct is not found in video game research, the conclusions using general measures of hostility create an expectation for the direction of targeted emotions after play. The dominant finding of lower levels of state hostility associated with human opponents provides a starting point for understanding the emotions targeted to opponents and self.

Hypothesis 3: Emotion directed towards opponents will be more positive after playing co-located humans than after playing game-generated characters.

Hypothesis 4: Emotion directed toward self will be more positive after playing co-located humans than after playing game-generated characters.

Experience of Play

Mandryk et al. (2006) concluded that human competition is less boring, more fun and more competitive than playing against a game character. Differential play experiences on the basis of opponents were also identified by Ravaja et al. (2006). They reported that playing against people rather than a character resulted in more engagement and greater arousal. Ravaja (2009) found respondents experienced more pleasure playing against a human.

The experience of video game play can also be examined through the report of intrinsic engagement and extrinsic motivation. Intrinsic engagement is playing the game for the experience and extrinsic motivation works against this state of optimal experience (Csiksentmihalyi, 1990). Here there is no imposition of extrinsic motivators by the researcher (e.g. Pittman, Emery & Boggiano, 1982; Newby & Alter, 1989; Abeyta, Routledge & Sedikides, 2017). This is a query of intrinsic and extrinsic factors that were experienced during play and identified by respondents. Intrinsic and Extrinsic factors are understood here as endogenous to the individual and not the products of outside forces (Malhotra, Galletta, & Kirsch, 2008). Abuhamdeh and Csikszentmihalyi (2009) define intrinsic engagement as doing an activity for its own sake. The activity brings the pleasurable experience of immersion and control (Ryan, Rigby & Przybylski, 2006) and often leads to higher performance levels (Abuhamdeh & Csikszentmihalyi, 2009). Extrinsic motivation drives a person to participate for the outcome or reward, rather than the experience itself (Pittman et al., 1982; Abuhamdeh & Csikszentmihalyi, 2009). It is often thought that extrinsic and intrinsic motivations work against each other. Gong, Wu, Song, and Zhang (2017), however, hypothesized that the two could be working together.

On the basis of this literature to following hypotheses are proposed:

Hypothesis 5: Intrinsic engagement will be higher for respondents playing co-located humans than playing game-generated characters.

Hypothesis 6: Extrinsic motivation will be higher for respondents playing co-located humans than playing game-generated characters.

Hypothesis 7: Intrinsic engagement will be negatively related to extrinsic motivation.

METHOD

The method employed in this study is an experiment and involves within-subjects tests which Barlett, Harris and Baldassaro (2007) found to be useful for video game research. This study seeks to address the important issue of ecological validity emphasized by Weibel et al. (2008) and Brasel (2011) by using a commercial game as the stimulus. There is a loss of experimental control using a game off of a store shelf but there is a more complex experience in terms of game aesthetics and mechanics for study respondents. It is more realistic as game play and involves that a game respondent might play by choice. Two weeks previous to research play respondents filled out a questionnaire on demographics, game play experience and game interest.

Each participant drove in two identical driving sessions separated by a week. This separation was intended to eliminate the overlap of emotion from one condition to the other. Controlling for ordering effects players were randomly assigned to two groups, half playing people first. Each play session lasted 20 minutes. Three study participants were scheduled for each session and all three would drive against the game-generated characters or against one another. Respondents spent the first five minutes of each session learning the controls, exploring the game world and learning context-specific attributes. Respondents then drove three races on the same course through Hollywood in the fifteen minutes available. After racing they immediately completed an experiential and affective state questionnaire using Survey Monkey on an iPad. Across both sessions respondents were exposed to the game for a total of 40 minutes of play. While this is not representative of the time one would spend playing a video game in the real world it is substantially longer than subjects have spent playing video games in other studies. In order to adjust for this less than realistic time subjects only competed in one race in both sessions. This represents a very small portion of the game world but gave focus to the play so that there would be less confusion about the demands during play.

Stimulus

Midnight Club: Los Angeles, (MC:LA) is a commercially produced street racing simulation from Rockstar Games. It is the last installment of their second highest selling franchise with more than 4.7 million units sold worldwide, across platforms (VGChartz, 2017) (While VGChartz may not be completely reliable it is the only source of this sales information). The game was first released in 2008. MC:LA is an open world game which offers almost unlimited navigational choice for players. They must hit checkpoints in a race but the path to those checkpoints is not fixed. The game is based on Los Angeles, including significant local landmarks. While there are aggressive elements, MC:LA is not violent (Smith et al., 1998). There is no 'credible threat of physical force or the actual use of such force intended to physically harm an animate being or group of beings' (p. 30).

Participants played MC:LA on the Xbox 360. For this research Xbox game platforms were connected to 50-inch HDTV monitors. When playing against game characters participants used headphones while sitting in comfortable chairs set approximately two meters away from the monitors. Machines were separated by dividing screens. When playing head-to-head room dividers were removed, participants took off their headphones and turned up the sound on the monitors to enable player interaction during races. Each participant played on individual machines that were connected by a wired LAN. Sound effects were a part of the experience, but the music portion of the sound environment was muted (Halko, Mäkelä, Nummenmaa, Hlushchuk, & Schürmann, 2013). All races were configured at midnight with skies clear and no other traffic on the streets. In races against game characters the difficulty level was medium to provide a challenging and equivalent level of computer-generated competition for all players.

Participants

The participants in this study were 97 young women from the Arabian Gulf. The sample started at 115 but 18 respondents were eliminated from the pool because they did not complete all elements of study on time or in the right sequence. All were students in a federal university of more than 6,000 students in the United Arab Emirates where women and men are taught separately. All respondents received extra credit for their participation. Vermeulen and Looy (2016), in line with Durkin and Barber (2002) and Schmierbach, Boyle, Xu, and McLeod (2011), defined high frequency gamers as those who play at least once a week. Based on this criterion 38% of Emirati women in the UAE are high frequency gamers while only 20% do not play video games at all. The remaining 42% can be identified as casual gamers (PARC, 2014).

Women in the gulf region are underrepresented in all forms of media and video game research so this is an opportunity to learn more about them as people and players (Jerabeck & Ferguson, 2013). There is also the question of gender in face-to-face gaming situations. Vermeulen, Castellar, and Looy (2014) found that gender played a role in how players perceived themselves and their opponents in terms of gaming ability. This could have an impact on the affective state and experience of a player as well as performance. It is controlled here through the exclusion of male players.

The average age of the participants was 22.20 (sd=2.30). Fifteen (15.4%) were married and 13 had children. Participants came from families with an average of more than six children (sd=2.33). They reported spending an average of 2.69 hours per week playing console games (sd=4.87). On a six point scale where zero is no interest and five is great interest participants averaged a 3.13 (sd=1.70) level of interest in driving simulation games with role-playing games coming in second and fighting games in third.

Analysis

There were a number of tools of measurement used in this study. Performance was measured by race times. Times were then averaged across the three races in a session. Race times were recorded for respondents at the conclusion of each race. Race times are an absolute measure of performance. It is the individual player against the clock (Figure 1).

Frustration was measured using the State Hostility Scale (SHS) devised by Anderson, Deuser, and DeNeve (1995). This is a 35-item scale used to determine the level of hostile feelings a person possesses at a given moment in time. Williams and Clippinger (2002) used an edited scale with only 20 items for their study and that was the starting point in this research. Other video game researchers have used this scale and edited versions (Velez, Mahood, Ewoldsen, & Moyer-Gusé, 2014; Przybylski, 2014; Crouse-Waddell & Wei, 2014). Because of item confusion among respondents two items were dropped from the edited list of 20 to make the SHS used in this study an 18-item scale ($\alpha = .91$).

Figure 1. Race times

Intrinsic engagement and extrinsic motivation were measured using Engeser and Rheinberg's (2008) 11 item Flow Short Scale. Eight items reported the experience of play and this is the intrinsic engagement scale including "I don't notice time passing," "I have no difficulty concentrating" and "I am totally absorbed in what I am doing." Three items measured extrinsic motivation. These are questions about fear of failure, desire to make no mistakes and sense that there is something important at stake. All item responses were on a 7-point scale from strongly agree to strongly disagree and scored from 6 to 0. The instrument has been validated and successfully used previously in experimental and correlational studies (see Rheinberg, Vollmeyer, & Engeser, 2003; Schuler, 2007) (Figure 2).

Figure 2. A series of 7 faces to gauge emotions

The Targeted Affect Manikin (TAM) has been devised for measuring targeted emotions in this study. This is a series of seven faces that respondents used to express their emotions about themselves and their opponents. The seven faces gave respondents a visual clue to the meaning of the associated words and enabled them to respond at a visual as well as verbal level. Inspired by the Self-Assessment Manikin (Bradley & Lang, 1994) this simplifies item responses.

RESULTS

Hypothesis One: Performance

Hypothesis 1 states that absolute performance will not be significantly different for respondents playing against a co-located person and playing against a game character. Using t-tests (Table 1) there is no statistically significant difference between playing a co-located human and playing the game-generated character on the measure of time. Hypothesis 1 is supported in terms of absolute performance. There is not a statistically significant difference even though the average time to finish the race was 5 seconds faster when facing human opponents.

Table 1. Results of t-test and Descriptive Statistics for Average Time (seconds): Hypothesis One A

Outcome	H-Ave Time		G-Ave Time		n	95% CI for Mean Difference	t	df
	M	SD	M	SD				
	217.8	78.7	222.6	59.6	97	-21.45, 11.88	-.571	96

Hypothesis Two: State Hostility

Hypothesis Two indicates that scores on the state hostility scale will be lower for respondents playing against a person than playing against a machine. A t-test demonstrates that the differences in the two scores on the SHS are not statistically significant for these respondents (Table 2). The hypothesis is not supported.

Table 2. Results of t-test and Descriptive Statistics for State Hostility Scale (SHS): Hypothesis Two

Outcome	H-SHS		G-SHS		n	95% CI for Mean Difference	t	df
	M	SD	M	SD				
	47.7	10.42	47.6	10.33	97	-2.04, 2.15	.053	96

This finding is not consistent with previous studies of state hostility after game play with different opponents. This could be a cultural artifact of the study participants as this general measure of negative affect may not effectively capture their emotional state.

Hypothesis Three: Affect Targeted to Opponents

The third hypothesis is that emotion targeted towards opponents will be more positive after respondents play co-located humans than after playing game-generated characters. This is true for this sample. The opponent targeted affect averaged 3.23 (sd = 1.50) after playing with people. This is significantly higher than the opponent targeted affect average of 2.81 (sd=1.47) after playing against a character (t

= 2.21, df = 96, p < .05). The hypothesis is supported. More positive affect targeted toward opponents is socially facilitated. This is consistent with the majority of studies on state hostility. Breaking down affect according to targets can be a useful way to consider the emotional outcomes of video game play.

Hypothesis Four: Affect Targeted to Self

The fourth hypothesis is that emotion targeted towards self will be more positive after respondents play co-located humans than after playing game-generated characters. This is not true for this sample. The self-targeted affect averaged 3.58 (sd = 1.58) after playing with people. The self-targeted affect averaged of 3.63 (sd=1.30) after playing against a character (t = 2.21, df = 96, p > .50). The difference is not statistically significant. The hypothesis is rejected.

Hypothesis Five: Intrinsic Engagement

The fifth hypothesis states that intrinsic engagement will be higher for respondents playing against a person than playing against a machine. The results of a t-test show that intrinsic engagement scores are higher, and the difference is statistically significant, when playing people than when playing characters. The hypothesis is supported (Table 3).

Table 3. Results of t-test and Descriptive Statistics for Intrinsic Engagement: Hypothesis Five

Outcome	H-Intrinsic		G-Intrinsic			95% CI for Mean Difference	t	df
	M	SD	M	SD	n			
	31.5	4.74	30.3	5.09	97	.177, 2.10	2.35*	96

* p < .05.

There is social facilitation of intrinsic engagement. This is consistent with the findings of previous research (Mandryk et al., 2006; Ravaja et al., 2006; Ravaja, 2009; Weibel et al., 2008).

Hypothesis Six: Extrinsic Motivation

The sixth hypothesis indicates that extrinsic motivation will higher for respondents playing against a person than playing against a machine. The hypothesis is supported because a t-test show that extrinsic motivation scores are higher at a statistically significant level when playing a person rather than when playing a game-generated character (Table 4).

Table 4. Results of t-test and Descriptive Statistics for Extrinsic Motivation: Hypothesis Six

Outcome	H-Extrinsic		G-Extrinsic		n	95% CI for Mean Difference	t	df
	M	SD	M	SD				
	11.59	2.64	11.02	2.64	97	.133, 1.00	2.59*	96

* p < .05.

Though it was not found in previous research, here there is social facilitation of extrinsic motivation. The presence of other people appears to increase the external pressure to perform. When playing alone against game characters there is no social pressure in any aspect of the game. When playing against people the exogenous pressures increase. In this study both intrinsic engagement and extrinsic motivation were socially facilitated (Tables 5 and 6).

Table 5. Pearson correlations

Co-Located Human Opponents	
n=97	1
Intrinsic Engagement – 1	
Extrinsic Motivation – 2	.158

Table 6. Pearson correlations

Game-Generated Character Opponents	
n=97	1
Intrinsic Engagement - 1	
Extrinsic Motivation - 2	.326**

$**p < .01$

Hypothesis Seven: Intrinsic Engagement and Extrinsic Motivation

The seventh hypothesis indicates that intrinsic engagement will have a negative relationship with extrinsic motivation. This is considered within each context of play. There is a positive correlation between the two variables in both contexts of play, which is in conflict with the hypothesis. The hypothesis is rejected in both situations. When playing a game-character the two operate in concert at a statistically significant level while this is not true with a human opponent.

DISCUSSION

The objective of this study was to analyze the social facilitation of performance, intrinsic engagement and extrinsic motivation, state hostility and affect targeted to opponents and self in a video driving game when the social actors are competitors and not simply observers. Agreeing with previous research it appears that social facilitation of performance does not take place when the task is complex, specifically car racing. Opposing most previous research there is no social facilitation of state hostility in either direction in this study. This could be a factor of the game details and its genre. This needs to be examined with other genre of games as well. Targeted affect to opponents and self does show significant differences between the two contexts of play. There is significant social facilitation of positive affect toward opponents. This points to the value of measuring targeted affect beyond state hostility or any other generalized measure of affective state.

Intrinsic engagement and extrinsic motivation are both facilitated by human interaction in the course of play. Intrinsic engagement is higher when playing a human opponent in this racing game. Extrinsic motivation is also higher when playing a human opponent in this game. Engagement and motivation are socially facilitated regardless if there is an impact on performance or post-play affect.

Social facilitation is relevant to every aspect of play with this particular car racing video game and this population of players. When driving absolute performance is not likely to change between opponent identity conditions. Intrinsic engagement and extrinsic motivation play a role in the outcomes of play, but they are not always in opposition. There is value in examining targeted affect in addition to general states of affect. Targeted affect may be more indicative of emotions that can lead to directed behaviors.

LIMITATIONS

The most obvious limitation in this study may be its strength. Engaging a culturally homogenous group of women makes it difficult to generalize the finding to broader populations. But that is a problem with all experimental and quasi-experimental designs, regardless of the specific demographic profile and national culture of respondents. By engaging a specific group of respondents with a single genre game, the isolation of variables is enhanced and empowered. There are only limited explanations for the changes that occur when the key differences between respondents are their performance and responses. It also enables the recognition and consideration of the impact of culture on the findings. No research can have a globally representative sample but by isolating and identifying variables and relationships in an experimental setting with a very specific group of players it becomes possible to re-examine those relationships and variables across cultural and national contexts from one study to another. Video game studies should not be exclusively conducted in a single region of the world. Video games are international phenomena with international impact. These findings come from a very different population than is normally seen in video game research, yet the findings connect with previous research and expand the understanding of social facilitation, the experience, and the outcomes of game play.

At the structural level this research has been limited by the number of available gaming stations in the lab. Because there were only three game systems, the finishing positions for both racing conditions was limited to those three. With more systems available in the local network it will be possible to have more players and more finishing positions which will create a greater opportunity for variations in experience, performance and the associated emotional responses. This can be adjusted at any time for game characters, but it can only be matched in the physical world with the presence of more connected game systems.

FUTURE RESEARCH

In spite of the fact that social facilitation was first studied in relation to competitive cycling (Triplett, 1898), social facilitation in video game studies are focused on audiences for play rather than human competitors. The complexities of the competitor relationship are being overlooked (Zajonc, 1965). Future research needs to take a more theory-based approach to the exploration of play experiences and outcomes and include variations in the identity and location of opponents. Social Facilitation can be very useful for informing these studies.

A more broadly accepted vision of intrinsic engagement and extrinsic motivation will also be useful across dependent variables and gaming situations. Looking at the two as endogenous (Malhotra et al., 2008) aspects of experience will expand an understanding of the intrinsic engagement and extrinsic motivation as well as the experiential nature and outcomes of video game play. There also exists the possibility of examining performance and outcomes in networked social play as well as in larger groups of co-located opponents. Finally, future research needs to take account of participant interest in playing video games, and particular genre of video games, as well as the time they spend each week playing video games. These variables can clearly influence the experience and outcomes of play.

REFERENCES

Abeyta, A. A., Routledge, C., & Sedikides, C. (2017). Material meaning: Narcissists gain existential benefits from extrinsic goals. *Social Psychological & Personality Science*, *8*(2), 219–228. doi:10.1177/1948550616667618

Abuhamdeh, S., & Csikszentmihalyi, M. (2009). Intrinsic and extrinsic motivational orientations in the competitive context: An examination of person–situation interactions. *Journal of Personality*, *77*(5), 1615–1635. doi:10.1111/j.1467-6494.2009.00594.x PMID:19678872

Anderson, C. A., Deuser, W. E., & DeNeve, K. M. (1995). Hot temperatures, hostile affect, hostile cognition, and arousal: Tests of a general model of affective aggression. *Personality and Social Psychology Bulletin*, *21*(5), 434–448. doi:10.1177/0146167295215002

Barlett, C. P., Harris, R. J., & Baldassaro, R. (2007). Longer you play, the more hostile you feel: Examination of first person shooter video games and aggression during video game play. *Aggressive Behavior*, *33*(6), 486–497. doi:10.1002/ab.20227 PMID:17694539

Bowman, N. D., Weber, R., Tamborini, R., & Sherry, J. (2013). Facilitating Game Play: How Others Affect Performance at and Enjoyment of Video Games. *Media Psychology*, *16*(1), 39–64. doi:10.1080/15213269.2012.742360

Bradley, M. M., & Lang, P. J. (1994). Measuring emotion: The self-assessment manikin and the semantic differential. *Journal of Behavior Therapy and Experimental Psychiatry*, *25*(1), 49–59. doi:10.1016/0005-7916(94)90063-9 PMID:7962581

Brasel, S. A. (2011). Nonconscious drivers of visual attention in interactive media environments. *Journal of Brand Management*, *18*(7), 473–482. doi:10.1057/bm.2011.11

Brown, R. M., Hall, L. R., Holtzer, R., Brown, S. L., & Brown, N. L. (1997). Gender and video game performance. *Sex Roles*, *36*(11/12), 793–812. doi:10.1023/A:1025631307585

Cairns, P., Cox, A. L., Day, M., Martin, H., & Perryman, T. (2013). Who but not where: The effect of social play on immersion in digital games. *International Journal of Human-Computer Studies*, *71*(11), 1069–1077. doi:10.1016/j.ijhcs.2013.08.015

Crouse Waddell, J., & Wei, P. (2014). Does it matter with whom you slay? The effects of competition, cooperation and relationship type among video game players. *Computers in Human Behavior*, *38*, 331–338. doi:10.1016/j.chb.2014.06.017

Csiksentmihalyi, M. (1990). *Flow: The psychology of optimal experience*. New York: Harper & Row.

Durkin, K., & Barber, B. (2002). Not so doomed: Computer game play and positive adolescent development. *Journal of Applied Developmental Psychology*, *23*(4), 373–392. doi:10.1016/S0193-3973(02)00124-7

Engeser, S., & Rheinberg, F. (2008). Flow, performance and moderators of challenge-skill balance. *Motivation and Emotion*, *32*(3), 158–172. doi:10.100711031-008-9102-4

Gong, Y., Wu, J., Song, L. J., & Zhang, Z. (2017). Dual tuning in creative processes: Joint contributions of intrinsic and extrinsic motivational orientations. *The Journal of Applied Psychology, 102*(5), 829–844. doi:10.1037/apl0000185 PMID:28150986

Halko, M.-L., Mäkelä, T., Nummenmaa, L., Hlushchuk, Y., & Schürmann, M. (2013). Music influences risk taking: how emotion and decision making circuits interact when making risky choices. *NeuroPsychoEconomics Conference Proceedings, 28.*

Jerabeck, J. M., & Ferguson, C. J. (2013). The influence of solitary and cooperative violent video game play on aggressive and prosocial behavior. *Computers in Human Behavior, 29*(6), 2573–2578. doi:10.1016/j.chb.2013.06.034

Malhotra, Y., Galletta, D. F., & Kirsch, L. J. (2008). How endogenous motivations influence user intentions: Beyond the dichotomy of extrinsic and intrinsic user motivations. *Journal of Management Information Systems, 25*(1), 267–299. doi:10.2753/MIS0742-1222250110

Mandryk, R. L., Inkpen, K. M., & Calvert, T. W. (2006). Using psychophysiological techniques to measure user experience with entertainment technologies. *Behaviour & Information Technology, 25*(2), 141–158. doi:10.1080/01449290500331156

Mihan, R., Anisimowicz, Y., & Nicki, R. (2015). Safer with a partner: Exploring the emotional consequences of multiplayer video gaming. *Computers in Human Behavior, 44*, 299–304. doi:10.1016/j.chb.2014.11.053

Newby, T. J., & Alter, P. A. (1989). Task motivation: Learner selection of intrinsic versus extrinsic orientations. *Educational Technology Research and Development, 37*(2), 77–89. doi:10.1007/BF02298292

PARC. (2014). TGI UAE 2014. Pan Arab Research Center.

Pittman, T., Emery, J., & Boggiano, A. (1982). Intrinsic and extrinsic motivational orientations: Reward-induced changes in preference for complexity. *Journal of Personality and Social Psychology, 42*(5), 789–797. doi:10.1037/0022-3514.42.5.789

Ravaja, N. (2009). The Psychophysiology of Digital Gaming: The Effect of a Non Co-Located Opponent. *Media Psychology, 12*(3), 268–294. doi:10.1080/15213260903052240

Ravaja, N., Saari, T., Turpeinen, M., Laarni, J., Salminen, M., & Kivikangas, M. (2006). Spatial Presence and Emotions during Video Game Playing: Does It Matter with Whom You Play? *Presence (Cambridge, Mass.), 15*(4), 381–392. doi:10.1162/pres.15.4.381

Rheinberg, F., Vollmeyer, R., & Engeser, S. (2003). Die Erfassung des Flow-Erlebens [The assessment of flow experience]. In J. Stiensmeier-Pelster & F. Rheinberg (Eds.), *Diagnostik von Selbstkonzept, Lernmotivation und Selbstregulation* [*Diagnosis of motivation and self-concept*] (pp. 261–279). Gottingen: Hogrefe.

Ro"hlcke S, Ba"cklund C, So"rman DE, Jonsson B (2018) Time on task matters most in video game expertise. *PLoS ONE, 13*(10): e0206555. . pone.0206555 doi:10.1371/journal

Ryan, R. M., Rigby, C. S., & Przybylski, A. (2006). The motivational pull of video games: A Self-Determination Theory approach. *Motivation and Emotion*, *30*(4), 344–360. doi:10.100711031-006-9051-8

Schmierbach, M. (2010). "Killing spree": Exploring the connection between competitive game play and aggressive cognition. *Communication Research*, *37*(2), 256–274. doi:10.1177/0093650209356394

Schmierbach, M., Boyle, M. P., Xu, Q., & McLeod, D. M. (2011). Exploring third-person differences between gamers and nongamers. *Journal of Communication*, *61*(2), 307–327. doi:10.1111/j.1460-2466.2011.01541.x

Schuler, J. (2007). Arousal of flow-experience in a learning setting and its effects on exam-performance and affect. *Zeitschrift fur Padagogische Psychologie*, *21*(3/4), 217–227. doi:10.1024/1010-0652.21.3.217

Shafer, D. M. (2012). Causes of state hostility and enjoyment in player versus player and player versus environment video games. *Journal of Communication*, *62*(4), 719–737. doi:10.1111/j.1460-2466.2012.01654.x

Strauss, B. (2002). Social facilitation in motor tasks: A review of research and theory. *Psychology of Sport and Exercise*, *3*(3), 237–256. doi:10.1016/S1469-0292(01)00019-X

Triplett, N. (1898). The dynamogenic factors in pacemaking and competition. *The American Journal of Psychology*, *9*(4), 507–533. doi:10.2307/1412188

VanTuinen, M., & McNeel, S. P. (1975). A test of the social facilitation theories of Cottrell and Zajonc in a coaction situation. *Personality and Social Psychology Bulletin*, *1*(4), 604–607. doi:10.1177/014616727500100412

Velez, J. A., Mahood, C., Ewoldsen, D. R., & Moyer-Gusé, E. (2014). Ingroup Versus Outgroup Conflict in the Context of Violent Video Game Play: The Effect of Cooperation on Increased Helping and Decreased Aggression. *Communication Research*, *41*(5), 607–626. doi:10.1177/0093650212456202

Vermeulen, L., Castellar, E. N., & Looy, J. V. (2014). Challenging the Other: Exploring the Role of Opponent Gender in Digital Game Competition for Female Players. *Cyberpsychology, Behavior, and Social Networking*, *17*(5), 303–309. doi:10.1089/cyber.2013.0331 PMID:24724802

Vermeulen, L., & Looy, J. V. (2016). "I Play So I Am?" A Gender Study into Stereotype Perception and Genre Choice of Digital Game Players. *Journal of Broadcasting & Electronic Media*, *60*(2), 286–304. doi:10.1080/08838151.2016.1164169

VGChartz.com. (n.d.). Game Database. Retrieved from http://www.vgchartz.com/gamedb/

Smith, S. L., Wilson, B. J., Kunkel, D., Linz, D., Potter, W. J., Colvin, C. M., & Donnerstein, E. (1998). Violence in television programming: University of California, Santa Barbara study. In National Television Violence Study (Vol. 3, pp. 5–220). Newbury Park, CA: Sage.

Weibel, D., Wissmath, B., Habegger, S., Steiner, Y., & Groner, R. (2008). Playing online games against computer- vs. human-controlled opponents: Effects on presence, flow, and enjoyment. *Computers in Human Behavior*, *24*(5), 2274–2291. doi:10.1016/j.chb.2007.11.002

Williams, R. B., & Clippinger, C. A. (2002). Aggression, competition, and computer games: Computer and human opponents. *Computers in Human Behavior*, *18*(5), 495–506. doi:10.1016/S0747-5632(02)00009-2

Worchel, S., Shebilske, W. L., Jordan, J. A., & Prislin, R. (1997). Competition and Performance on a Computer-Based Complex Perceptual-Motor Task. *Human Factors*, *39*(3), 410–416. doi:10.1518/001872097778827025 PMID:9394634

Zajonc, R. B. (1965). Social Facilitation. *Science. New Series*, *149*(3681), 269–274. PMID:14300526

This research was previously published in the International Journal of Gaming and Computer-Mediated Simulations (IJGCMS), 11(3); pages 38-54, copyright year 2019 by IGI Publishing (an imprint of IGI Global).

Chapter 57
Experiencing Presence in a Gaming Activity Improves Mood After a Negative Mood Induction

Stefan Weber
University of Bern, Switzerland

Fred W. Mast
University of Bern, Switzerland

David Weibel
University of Bern, Switzerland

ABSTRACT

Research suggests that immersion in computer games is beneficial for recovering from stress and improving mood. However, no study linked explicit measures of presence—individually experienced immersion—to mood enhancement. In the present experiment, immersion of a gaming activity was varied, and levels of presence and enjoyment were measured and connected to mood repair after a stress-induction. The participants (N = 77) played a game in virtual reality (VR; high immersion), on the desktop (medium immersion), or watched a recording of the game (low immersion). Positive emotions were enhanced in the high and medium, but not the low immersion condition. Presence was a significant predictor in the VR condition. Furthermore, an explanatory mediation analysis showed that enjoyment mediated the effect of presence on mood repair. These findings demonstrate positive effects of presence experiences in gaming. Strong presence in VR seems especially helpful for enhancing mood and building up positive emotional resources.

DOI: 10.4018/978-1-6684-7589-8.ch057

INTRODUCTION

In recent years, research about media use – especially *gaming* – has shifted its focus towards the investigation of positive effects (cf. Reinecke & Eden, 2016). A case in point is mood improvement. A number of authors suggest that interactive elements and high immersiveness of a computer game positively affect mood and may help to recover from work-related stress and strain (Bowman & Tamborini, 2012; 2015; Reinecke, Klatt, & Krämer, 2011; Rieger, Frischlich, Wulf, Bente, & Kneer, 2015). Interactivity and immersion are closely linked to *presence* – the feeling of *being there* in a mediated environment (Steuer, 1992; Witmer & Singer, 1998; Wissmath, Weibel, Schmutz, & Mast, 2011). Presence is often used synonymously with immersion (cf. McMahan, 2003). However, unlike interactivity and immersion, presence is a clearly defined term and is widely used in virtual reality (VR) and gaming research (cf. McMahan, 2003). As mentioned, it is believed that immersing oneself in the world of a computer game can have a positive effect on one's mood. Surprisingly, however, the role of presence has not yet been investigated in the context of mood repair and gaming. The present study aims to close this gap.

BACKGROUND

Presence has been described as mediated contents being experienced as real and one's self-awareness being immersed into another world (Draper, Kaber, & Usher, 1998). According to Lombard and Ditton (1997), presence is a perceptual illusion of non-mediation. Following a proposition by Slater and Wilbur (1997), the term presence is separated from immersion in more recent literature (Cummings & Bailenson, 2015; Hein, Mai, & Hußmann, 2018; Wu, Gomes, Fernandes, & Wang, 2018). Immersion is based on technical properties of the system and is objectively quantifiable. Presence, however, is the individual psychological response to the properties of the system (Norman, 2010; Wirth et al., 2007; Witmer & Singer, 1998). Empirical findings show that presence is indeed modulated by individual expectations and personality traits (Bucolo, 2004; Weibel, Wissmath, & Mast, 2010; 2011a; 2011b). This distinction will be used henceforth in this article by examining the influence of immersion (the characteristic of a computer game) as well as presence (the individual experience of immersion).

According to Reinecke (2009a; 2009b), the immersive experience (i.e. presence) is a key factor that accounts for the recovery experience of computer games. *Recovery* is a concept from organizational psychology and describes the renewal of depleted physical and psychological resources after phases of stress and strain (Sonnentag & Fritz, 2007; Sonnentag & Zijlstra, 2006). Sonnentag and Fritz (2007) proposed four central aspects of successful recovery: *Psychological detachment* (mental disengagement from work-related stress), *relaxation* (deactivation of arousal and increased positive affect), *mastery* (building up new internal resources through challenging experiences and learning opportunities), and *control* (increased self-efficacy and feelings of competence through experiencing personal control). The results of Reinecke (2009a; 2009b) suggest that presence goes along with psychological detachment, which contributes to the recovery experience of gaming activity. Additionally, entertaining media are an ideal way to stop negative cognitions and preventing episodes of rumination by letting their users immerse in the mediated environment. This is in line with Tamborini and Skalski (2006) who suggest that playing computer games requires the full attention of the player and strongly binds cognitive capacities to the screen, what in turn leads to a highly immersive experience. Games also often require taking over new roles (Bessière, Seay, & Kiesler, 2007) and experiencing fictional worlds (Yee, 2006). They provide opportunities to control the progress of events or characters (Klimmt & Hartmann, 2006) and to experience feelings of autonomy, challenge, and competition (Klimmt & Hartmann, 2006; Ryan, Rigby, & Przybylski, 2006). Thus, computer games contribute to all four aspects of successful recovery and are likely to enhance mood and support recovery form stress and strain (Collins & Cox, 2014; Reinecke, 2009a; 2009b; Reinecke et al., 2011).

Empirical investigations into the role of computer games in recovery are provided by three correlational online studies. In two studies by Reinecke (2009a; 2009b), levels of work-related fatigue and exposure to daily hassles were positively related to the use of games for recovery. Thus, participants who associated playing games with recovery played more extensively after stressful events. In addition, Collins and Cox (2014) found a relation between the amount of gaming activity and recovery from work-related stress.

In experimental studies, *interactivity* was manipulated by comparing active gaming with watching gameplay recordings and videos. There is no consensus about the definition of interactivity (cf. Smuts, 2009), but the respective authors focused on "active participation of the player" and having "control over the progress" of the game (Collins, Cox, Wilcock, & Sethu-Jones, 2019; Reinecke et al., 2011). As such, interactivity shares strong similarities with the immersion of games. In these experiments, interactivity has been shown to play a crucial role in recovery. Recovery in turn was shown to affect other measures such as cognitive performance (Reinecke et al., 2011) and enjoyment (Reinecke et al., 2011; Tamborini, Bowman, Eden, Grizzard, & Organ, 2010; Tamborini et al., 2011). In the study by Reinecke and colleagues (2011), a repetitive and tedious working task was used to induce a need for recovery. Participants were then assigned to one of four conditions that varied in interactivity (video game, recording of a video game, an animated video clip, and a control condition). The degree of interactivity of the condition positively affected the *involvement* in the game. Involvement was measured with the involvement subscale of the presence-questionnaire by Witmer and Singer (1998). Therefore, involvement is part of the presence experience as defined by Witmer and Singer. Involvement was positively associated with recovery, which in turn was positively associated with enjoyment. In a recent study, Collins et al. (2019) found that only a digital game condition could improve recovery as opposed to a mindfulness app and a non-media condition. Tamborini et al. (2010; 2011) showed that recovery through gaming was positively associated with enjoyment. Recovery in these studies was operationalized with need satisfaction (cf. Reinecke et al., 2011). Taken together, previous research on recovery from work-related stress has demonstrated that interactivity, and thus also likely immersion, supports recovery and that feelings of presence and enjoyment could serve as important individual enhancing factors for successful recovery. However, the different contributions of a game's immersion and the individual presence experience have not been worked out so far.

Instead of recovery from work-related stress, yet other studies used *mood repair* as a measure of the immediate effect of gaming on current mood. This approach is mainly inspired by mood management theory (Zillmann, 2000). Mood management assumes that individuals seek to avert negative mood and maximize positive mood by selecting appropriate media (Bryant & Zillmann, 1984; Knobloch & Zillmann, 2002; Mastro, Eastin, & Tamborini, 2002). Thus, mood repair is defined as the change in positive and negative mood after an intervention to regain an "optimal" state of mood (Bowman & Tamborini, 2012, p. 1339). In two studies by Bowman and Tamborini (2012; 2015), the task demand of a computer game was manipulated in order to influence mood repair (task demand is similar to the concept of interactivity, according to the authors). The results of both studies showed a curvilinear effect of task demand on mood repair, meaning that a medium level of task demand was evoking the strongest mood repair (Bowman & Tamborini, 2012; 2015). In a study by Rieger et al. (2015), high interactivity (i.e. gaming compared to watching a recording of the game and a control condition) was positively associated with mood repair. Positive emotions generally increased across conditions, whereas negative emotions only decreased in the highly interactive condition. The same result was previously obtained in a study by Chen and Raney (2009).

Even though immersive experiences were postulated to affect mood and recovery and related concepts such as involvement, interactivity, or task demand were empirically investigated, there is a lack of studies that differentiate between immersion and presence. Particularly, there is a lack of studies that specifically link subjective immersion in the sense of *presence* (being there in a mediated environment; Steuer, 1992) with mood repair or recovery after playing video games. Presence is of great importance in VR research as a VR display completely surrounds the user with another world as opposed to a desktop display that provides a discontinuity between the screen and the user in front of the screen (Slater & Wilbur, 1997) According to Steuer (1992), presence is the underlying concept of VR. Thus, it is important to include VR conditions in the study of stress recovery and mood repair in order to understand the impact of presence. However, surprisingly, no study so far has manipulated presence with a VR gaming condition.

A few studies have assessed presence in the context of relaxation tasks in a nature setting specifically designed to induce stress recovery or *restoration* (e.g. de Kort, Meijnders, Sponselee, & IJsselsteijn, 2006; Sponselee, de Kort, & Meijnders, 2004). Restoration was defined as renewing resources, enhancing the ability to focus one's attention, reducing stress, and promoting positive affect (cf. de Kort et al., 2006). These studies show a beneficial effect of presence on reducing stress and enhancing mood. It would be of high interest to study presence also in the context of computer games as it is an important concept in the gaming community and has been shown to be one of the driving factors for playing computer games (Yee, Ducheneaut, & Nelson, 2012). Jennett et al. (2008, p. 644) even describe it as being "key to a good gaming experience". As Reinecke (2009a; 2009b) pointed out, immersive experiences in games (i.e. presence) are also crucial for the recovery experience. However, empirical findings for this claim are sparse and none of the reported studies explicitly measured presence. Thus, in the present experiment, an explicit measure of presence was used and it was linked to mood repair following a phase of computer gaming. To induce increased variability in presence and to look at differences between the immersion of conditions, the mode of presentation of the gaming activity was manipulated, including a VR condition. This study is the first to include a VR condition in the context of gaming and mood improvement. Again, the available literature is mainly based on research on VR therapy and stress reduction in relaxing virtual environments (VEs). Although, results of these studies show a clear effect of presence in VEs on stress reduction and mood enhancement, it is not clear whether computer games would elicit the same effect (e.g. Annerstedt et al., 2013; Freeman, Lessiter, Keogh, Bond, & Chapman, 2004; Liszio, Graf, & Masuch, 2018; Valtchanov & Ellard, 2010; Villani & Riva, 2012; Villani, Riva, & Riva, 2007; Villani, Luchetta, Preziosa, & Riva, 2009; for an overview see Villani, Cipresso, Gaggioli, & Riva, 2016).

Thus, the aims of the present study were 1) to link presence with mood repair following a gaming experience, 2) to differentiate between the effect of individual experienced presence and the effect of immersion as a property of the system, and 3) to add a VR gaming condition. For this purpose, 77 participants underwent a stress-induction to create a need for mood repair. Afterwards, they were assigned to one of three immersion conditions in which they either played a computer game in VR using a Head-mounted display (HMD), played the same game on a desktop computer, or – in a control condition – watched a recording of the same game. To assess mood repair after the respective experience, mood ratings before gaming (after the stress-induction, respectively) and after gaming were assessed and both measures were compared. The individual level of presence was assessed with a questionnaire.

A measure of enjoyment was also included since enjoyment was shown to be related to recovery or need satisfaction and involvement (Reinecke et al., 2011; Tamborini et al., 2010; 2011). Additionally, Wirth et al. (2007) proposed that presence acts as a booster of media effects such as enjoyment. Thus, relationships between enjoyment, individual presence and mood repair were explored.

In accordance with the literature review above, the authors stated the following hypotheses:

Hypothesis One: The higher the immersion of the gaming activity, the stronger the effect of mood repair.
Hypothesis Two: The higher the level of individual presence, the stronger the effect of mood repair.
Hypothesis Three: Enjoyment is positively related to (a) mood repair and (b) presence.

Insights into these issues could help us to better understand the potential of computer games as a means for mood repair and the role of presence.

METHOD

Participants

77 participants (24 male and 53 female) took part in the experiment. Five participants were excluded because they guessed the hypotheses (see Procedure for details). The average age was 23.1 years ($SD = 5.7$ years). Participants received either course credit or a little token of appreciation (chocolate bar) for their participation and were debriefed after the experiment. The study was approved by the ethics committee of the Human Sciences Faculty of the University of Bern and participants were treated according to the declaration of Helsinki (World Medical Association, 1991).

Design

A mix of group comparisons and correlational analyses was used. On the one hand, groups were used to investigate influences on mood ratings in terms of immersion. On the other hand, the relationship between mood ratings and individual presence scores of participants across conditions was explored. Participants were randomly assigned to one of three groups: *VR*, *desktop*, and *video* condition. The conditions varied in the level of immersion, with the *VR* condition having the highest immersion and the *video* condition having the lowest immersion. Using a meta-analysis, Cummings and Bailenson (2015) demonstrated that the level of immersive quality of a system leads to higher experienced presence, which especially applies to the level of user tracking and the use of stereoscopic visuals. Thus, the *VR* condition should evoke the highest presence levels. Additionally, two studies have shown that actively playing a game evoked more presence than watching a pre-recorded playing session (Kätsyri, Hari, Ravaja, & Nummenmaa, 2013; Wong, Rigby, & Brumby, 2017). Nevertheless, watching pre-recorded video games can still lead to feelings of presence (Collins et al., 2019; Wong et al., 2017), which means that all conditions should lead to at least some degree of presence and that the average level of presence should vary between conditions.

The *VR* and *desktop* conditions involved playing the game *Star Conflict*, with ($n = 31$) and without the addition of an HMD ($n = 29$). The *video* condition required participants to watch a recording of the same game ($n = 17$). See Material below for more information. Different subsample sizes were obtained because the *video* condition was later added as a control condition. However, unequal group size is not a requirement for simple group comparisons (i.e. non-factorial designs; cf. Miliken & Johnson, 1984). The possible loss of statistical power implies a conservative testing of the hypotheses. For correlational analyses, data points were weighted according to the size of the group (cf. Meinck & Rodriguez, 2013) or included the condition as a factorial variable.

The measured variables were feelings of *presence* while playing, ratings of momentary mood (*positive* and *negative*), and *enjoyment*. Before being randomly assigned to a condition, participants had to undergo a stress-induction procedure. Differences between mood ratings before and after the procedure served as a check whether the stress-induction worked as expected. In order to assess *mood repair*, differences in positive and negative mood ratings between after the gaming activity and after the stress-induction were computed. Mood repair was defined as a change of mood ratings in the desired direction (positive values indicating an increase in positive mood and a decrease in negative mood). A summary of the experimental design is shown in Figure 1.

Figure 1. Graphical representation of the procedure

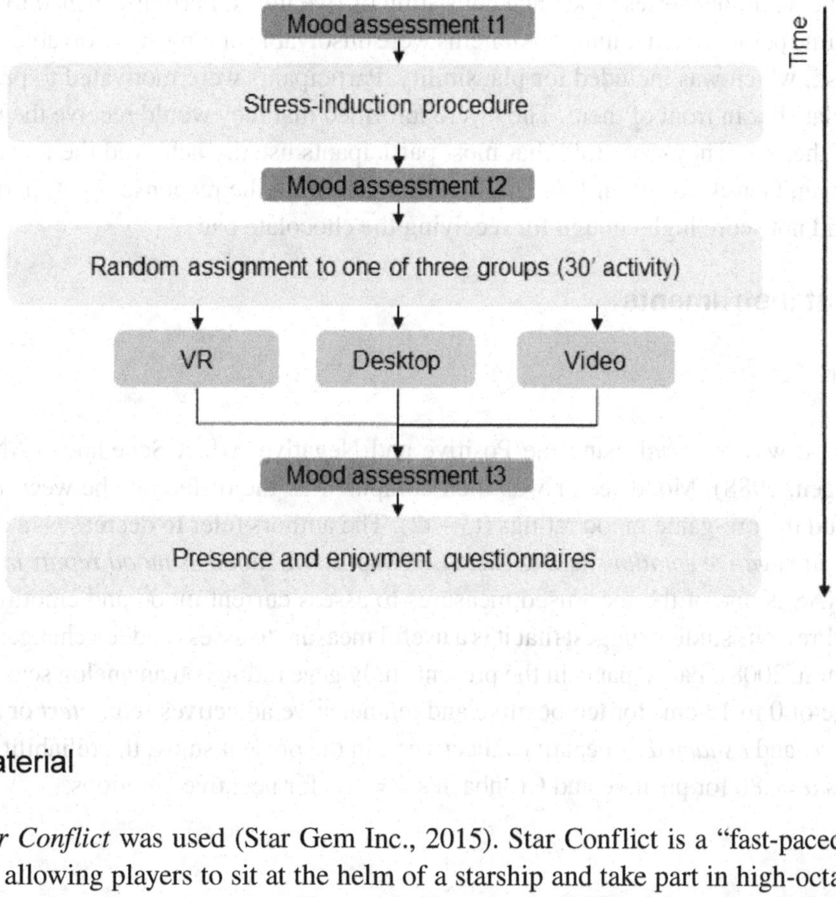

Material

Stimulus Material

The game *Star Conflict* was used (Star Gem Inc., 2015). Star Conflict is a "fast-paced, third person space shooter, allowing players to sit at the helm of a starship and take part in high-octane skirmishes for control of ancient alien artefacts" (Star Conflict Wiki, 2015). The game involves elements of strategy and action. Five subjects that were tested in a pilot test prior to the actual experiment described the game as non-violent and fun to play. Whereas the original game is a multiplayer online game, in this study only the initial tutorials of the game were used, where participants learned to control the ship and how to take over an enemy base. The authors chose the game because full technical support for playing in VR was given and it was freely available. Furthermore, the game is described as highly immersive by players in online forums (Oculus VR, 2015). Additionally, the genre of the game is suitable for detecting effects on mood enhancement: Collins and Cox (2014) showed that first person shooters and action games were most highly correlated with recovery experiences, whereas the recovery potential of sports games turned out to be lower.

For the desktop and the video condition, a commonly available gaming notebook with a 15.6-inch LED screen was used (resolution: 1920 x 1080 pixels). In the VR condition, participants played with the Oculus Rift DK 2 (Oculus VR, 2014). Both active playing groups used an Xbox 360 controller (Microsoft Corporation, 2005) as input device.

Stress-Induction

Two stress-induction procedures suggested by Bauer, Pripfl, Lamm, Prainsack and Taylor (2003) and McLaughlin, Lefaivre and Cummings (2009) were combined. The resulting procedure comprised an anagram task and a number series task, each consisting of five items. Participants had to find solutions within a given time period of ten minutes. All items were unsolvable or almost unsolvable, except for one item in each task, which was included for plausibility. Participants were motivated to perform well by putting a chocolate bar in front of them. They were informed that they would receive the bar depending on the score in the test. They were told that most participants usually achieved the required score (cf. Henna, Zilberman, Gentil, & Gorenstein, 2008). After returning the response sheet, participants were told that they did not score high enough for receiving the chocolate bar.

Measurement Instruments

Mood Repair

Momentary mood was assessed using the Positive and Negative Affect Schedule (PANAS; Watson, Clark, & Tellegen, 1988). Mood repair was then computed as the difference between the post-game mood ratings and the pre-game mood ratings (t3 – t2). The authors refer to decreases in negative mood as *mood repair in negative emotions* and to increases in positive mood as *mood repair in positive emotions*. The PANAS is one of the most used measures to assess current mood and emotions (Watson & Vaidya, 2003). Previous studies suggest that it is a useful measure to assess sudden changes in mood (e.g. Russell & Newton, 2008). Participants in the present study gave ratings on an analog scale (measured in cm with a range of 0 to 13 cm) for ten positive and ten negative adjectives (e.g. *alert* or *determined* as positive and *upset* and *ashamed* as negative adjectives). In the present study, the reliability of the scales was Cronbach's $\alpha = .86$ for positive and Cronbach's $\alpha = .84$ for negative emotions.

Presence

Feelings of presence were obtained by the Pictorial Presence SAM questionnaire (Weibel, Schmutz, Pahud, & Wissmath, 2015). The SAM questionnaire – which was inspired by the widely used Self-Assessment Manikin to measure emotion (Lang, 1980) – was recently developed to assess presence intuitively and unambiguously. It has been shown to be a valid and sensitive measure for assessing spatial presence

(Weibel et al., 2015). For six items representing the sensation of presence, participants choose one of five graphical representations that best matches their sensations. In the present study, the SAM questionnaire showed a sufficient reliability with Cronbach's $\alpha = .67$.

Enjoyment

In line with various other studies (Green, Brock, & Kaufman, 2004; Knobloch & Zillmann, 2002; Weibel et al., 2011; Weibel, Wissmath, & Stricker, 2011c) enjoyment was measured with one single item: "On a scale from one to ten, how much fun have you had?" (1 = *no fun at all*; 10 = *a lot of fun*).

Procedure

In order to assure the feasibility of the procedure, participants were told that the study served the purpose to relate their ability to solve a rule-based cognitive task with their ratings of presence in a gaming task. Furthermore, they were told that the ratings of current emotions would serve as a control variable.

The procedure of the experiment is summarized in Figure 1. First, participants filled out the PANAS. Then they were introduced to the anagram and the number series task. They had ten minutes to complete the tasks. After explaining the results of the test, participants filled out the PANAS again in order to test whether the stress-induction was successful. Next, participants were randomly assigned to one of the three experimental conditions. First, the handling of the controller was explained. Furthermore, in the *VR* condition, they were instructed on how to use the HMD and were told to immediately report any feelings of nausea. Participants were asked to freely play the game or watch the recording. The duration of this phase was 30 minutes in each condition. Afterwards, participants filled out the PANAS a third time in order to test whether playing the computer game led to mood repair. Finally, participants filled out the presence scale and answered the enjoyment question, followed by a demographic questionnaire. The authors carefully interviewed each participant after the experiment to make sure not to include participants who guessed the hypotheses. Only five participants reported that they drew a link between the gaming task and the mood questionnaires and were therefore excluded. Upon completion of the experiment, the participants were debriefed.

RESULTS

Strategy of Analyses

Two different approaches were used to test the hypotheses: In an experimental approach, the three experimental conditions were compared in terms of positive and negative mood repair, presence, and enjoyment, using one-way analyses of variance (ANOVAs) or Kruskal-Wallis tests. In a correlational approach, measures of association between individual levels of presence, enjoyment, and mood repair were calculated. Group-size-weighted bivariate correlations with Pearson coefficients were used. Additionally, a moderated regression model was calculated to differentiate the effect of individual presence on mood repair from the group-level effect of presence. This is important because of the hierarchical structure of the data: Individual presence and mood repair are nested in the three conditions and, thus, the overall level of presence and mood repair could vary between groups (contextual effect). Therefore, analyzing the effect of presence only on the individual level would potentially result in a *Simpson's paradox* (cf. Ameringer, Serlin, & Ward, 2009). An exploratory mediated regression model to test whether enjoyment serves as a mediator variable between presence and mood repair is also reported. Since mood repair in positive and negative emotions were both left skewed, a log-transformation with an added constant on both variables was performed. This way normally distributed residuals for the correlational analyses were obtained.

Descriptive Statistics

A summary of descriptive statistics for the whole sample is presented in Table 1. All but six participants had never used an HMD before. Additionally, the average time participants spend playing computer games in a week was 66 minutes ($SD = 164$ minutes).

Table 1. Descriptive statistics for variables across all conditions

Variable	*min*	*max*	*M*	*SD*
Enjoyment	1	10	5.70	2.75
Pictorial Presence SAM	1.00	5.00	3.40	0.85
Mood repair in positive emotions	-2.21	7.46	0.80	1.84
Mood repair in negative emotions	-1.18	9.10	1.27	1.61
Enjoyment	1	10	5.70	2.75
Pictorial Presence SAM	1.00	5.00	3.40	0.85

Notes: N = 76 for Pictorial Presence SAM and 77 for all other variables

Manipulation Checks

To examine the stress-induction procedure, differences in the PANAS ratings before and after the stress-induction (t2 – t1) were analyzed. As expected, the mean value for positive emotions after the stress-induction ($M = 6.41$, $SD = 2.37$) was lower than the baseline mean value assessed before the stress-induction ($M = 7.42$, $SD = 1.85$). This indicates that the stress-induction for positive emotions was successful, $t(76) = -6.81$, $p < .001$, $d = -0.78$. Similarly, ratings for negative emotions were higher after the stress-induction ($M = 2.70$, $SD = 2.08$) than before the stress-induction ($M = 1.57$, $SD = 1.33$), $z = 2652$, $p < .001$, $d = 0.67$ (a Wilcoxon signed-rank test was used because residuals were not normally distributed).

A one-way Kruskal-Wallis test was used to assess differences in presence scores between conditions for the SAM questionnaire because residuals were not normally distributed. This served as a check whether the manipulation of designated immersion worked as intended. The test revealed a significant effect, $\chi^2(2) = 19.0$, $p < .001$, $\varepsilon^2 = 0.25$. Post hoc comparisons (Dwass-Steel-Critchlow-Fligner) showed that presence scores were lower in the *video* condition compared to the *desktop* and *VR* conditions (both $p < .01$). Descriptively, there was a linear trend, which suggests that the higher the intended immersion of the condition, the more presence was reported by participants. This is in accordance with expectations. Presence scores for each condition are shown in Figure 2.

A one-way ANOVA revealed also a significant difference between conditions in enjoyment, $F(2, 74)$ = 12.2, $p < .001$, $\eta_p^2 = 0.25$. Post-hoc comparisons (Tukey) indicated that the *video* condition involved lower enjoyment compared to the other conditions (both $p < .001$). Enjoyment scores for each condition are shown in Figure 3.

*Figure 2. Mean presence SAM scores for each condition. Error bars represent standard errors. Significance codes: ** p < .01, *** p < .001.*

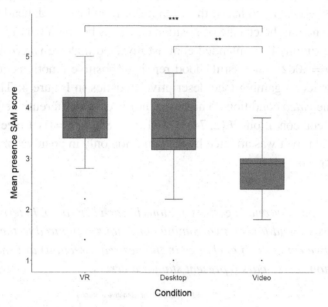

*Figure 3. Mean enjoyment scores for each condition. Error bars represent standard errors. Significance codes: ** p < .01, *** p < .001.*

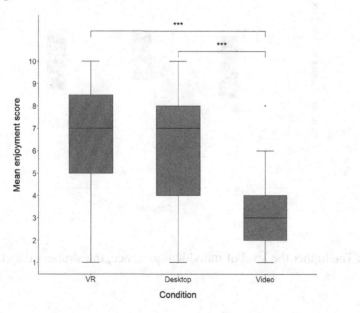

Testing the Hypotheses

Hypothesis One: The higher the immersion of the gaming activity, the stronger the effect of mood repair.

Mood ratings were investigated to test the first hypothesis. Overall, there was a change in emotional ratings from before gaming to afterwards across conditions for positive, $t(76) = 3.82$, $p < .001$, $d = 0.44$, and negative emotions, $t(76) = -6.90$, $p < .001$, $d = -0.79$ (see Table 1 for descriptive statistics). This means that overall, a significant effect of mood repair in positive and negative emotions could be observed. In line with the first hypothesis, the strength of mood repair depends on immersion: There was a significant difference in the change of positive emotions between conditions, $F(2, 74) = 5.18$, $p = .008$, $\eta_p^2 = 0.12$ (see Figure 4). A planned contrast revealed that the *video* condition differed from the other conditions, $p = .002$. Successful mood repair in positive emotions could only be observed in conditions involving active gaming (see descriptive statistics in Figure 4: There was a decrease in positive emotions for the *video* condition). There was, however, no differential effect for mood repair in negative emotions between conditions, $F(2, 74) = 0.21$, $p = .811$, $\eta_p^2 = 0.01$ (see Figure 4). This means that the strength of mood repair was affected by the condition only in positive emotions, which partially supports the first hypothesis.

Figure 4. Mood repair in positive and negative emotions in each condition. In terms of positive emotions, stronger mood repair was found for the two gaming conditions compared to the video condition. Note that decreases in negative emotions (i.e. change in the desired direction) are shown as positive values to facilitate interpretation. Error bars represent standard errors.

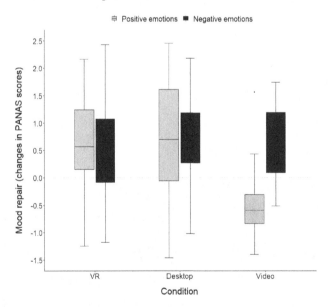

Hypothesis Two: The higher the level of individual presence, the stronger the effect of mood repair.

Weighted bivariate correlations were computed using the *weights* package in *R* (Pasek, 2018; R Core Team, 2019). The results show that individual presence is related to mood repair in positive emotions but not in negative emotions (see Table 2 for an overview). This means that a higher individual presence rating was associated with stronger mood repair in positive emotions. This partially supports the second hypothesis stating that individual presence levels enhance mood repair.

Table 2. Bivariate weighted correlations between variables (across conditions)

	1	2	3	4
1. Mood repair in positive emotions	-			
2. Mood repair in negative emotions	.20	-		
3. Pictorial Presence SAM	.34**	.14	-	
4. Enjoyment	.52***	.12	.51***	-

Notes: * p < .05, ** p < .01, *** p < .001 (one-tailed). All p-values were adjusted using the Bonferroni method. Mood repair in positive and negative emotions was log-transformed to obtain normally distributed residuals. N = 76 for Pictorial Presence SAM and 77 for all other variables

To control for a potential Simpson's paradox, moderated regression models with presence as a linear predictor and immersion as a factorial predictor were calculated. The dependent variables were mood repair in positive and negative emotions. The results for positive emotions are shown in Table 3. The model for negative emotions yielded no significant prediction of mood repair ($R^2 = .08$, $F(5, 70) = 1.14$, $p = 0.346$). A simple slope analysis revealed that presence predicted mood repair in positive emotions only in the VR condition ($b_{VR} = 0.15$, $p = 0.002$; other slopes both $p > 0.05$; see Figure 5). Therefore, the positive effect of individual presence on mood repair in positive emotions was limited to the VR condition.

Table 3. Mood repair in positive emotions predicted by presence (focal predictor) and immersion (moderator)

Predictor	b	SE	95% CI	Predictor
Intercept	0.33	0.07	0.19	0.46
Presence	-0.06	0.07	-0.20	0.08
Desktop condition	0.25	0.08	0.10	0.40
VR condition	0.18	0.08	0.03	0.34
Presence x desktop condition	0.11	0.08	-0.06	0.27
Presence x VR condition	0.21	0.08	0.04	0.38

Notes: $R^2 = 0.27$, F(5, 70) = 5.18, p < .001. The video condition was used as the reference group (dummy coding). Presence was centered. Mood repair in positive emotions was log-transformed in order to obtain normally distributed residuals

Hypothesis Three: Enjoyment is positively related to (a) mood repair and (b) presence.

Figure 5. Simple slope analysis for the effect of presence on mood repair in positive emotions. Only the simple slope in the VR condition was significant (p = .002).

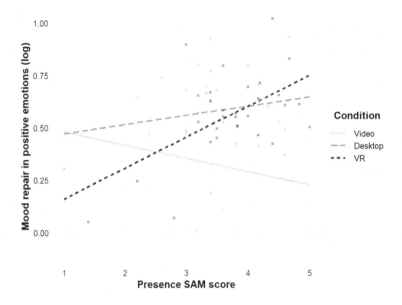

Enjoyment was positively associated with mood repair in positive emotions but not negative emotions (see Table 2). Enjoyment was also positively associated with presence. Thus, hypothesis 3a was partially and hypothesis 3b fully supported.

To further investigate the relationship between the variables presence, enjoyment and mood repair in positive emotions, an explorative mediation model using the *jAMM* module in *jamovi* (Gallucci, 2019; The jamovi project, 2019) was performed. This tested whether enjoyment mediates the relationship between individual presence and mood repair in positive emotions. To again control for possible contextual effects, the immersion of the condition was entered as an additional explanatory variable (all possible moderation effects of immersion were non-significant and were therefore not included in the final model). An overview is provided in Figure 6. The results show that the relationship between presence and mood repair in positive emotions is mediated by enjoyment. The unstandardized regression coefficients between presence and enjoyment and between enjoyment and mood repair in positive emotions were statistically significant. The indirect effect was tested using bootstrapping procedures (1000 samples) as proposed by Hayes (2017). The unstandardized indirect effect of presence on mood repair in positive emotions was significant, $B = .29$, $SE = .14$, 95% $CI = .07, .62$. There was, however, no total and no direct effect of presence on mood repair in positive emotions (both $p > .05$). These results are consistent with indirect-only mediation (Zhao, Lynch, & Chen, 2010). The indirect effects of the immersion conditions on mood repair in positive emotions were not significant (both $p > .05$).

Figure 6. Unstandardized regression coefficients for the relationship between presence and mood repair in positive emotions as mediated by enjoyment. Immersion was entered as an explanatory variable to control for contextual effects. This categorical independent variable is shown with only one rectangle, but its effects are estimated using contrast variables (dummy coding with the video condition as reference category). Presence was centered. Covariances among independent variables are estimated but not shown. The total effect between presence and mood repair is in parentheses. Bias-corrected bootstrapping (1000 samples) was used to obtain p-values. *p < .05, **p < 0.01, ***p < 0.001.

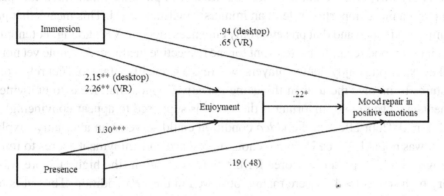

CONCLUSION

The present study investigated whether immersive gaming conditions led to improved mood repair after a stress-induction and whether the individual level of presence was associated with better mood repair. High immersion was operationalized with a VR gaming condition, medium immersion with a desktop gaming condition, and low immersion with a passive video condition. Supporting the authors' expectation, the level of presence varied between the conditions, with the *VR* condition evoking the highest levels and the *video* condition evoking significantly lower levels than the two active gaming conditions. The active gaming conditions were also evoking higher levels of enjoyment and stronger mood repair in positive emotions. This supports the idea that immersion in video games improves the overall state of mood after episodes of stress. However, whereas negative emotions generally decreased after the gaming activity, the immersion of the condition and the individual level of presence did not affect mood repair in negative emotions. Furthermore, using a moderation analysis, the present study could show that the individual level of presence was a significant predictor for mood repair in positive emotions, after controlling for immersion. However, presence only led to significantly improved mood repair in the VR condition. Finally, using an exploratory mediation analysis, the present study showed that only the individual level of presence led to improved mood repair in positive emotions by evoking higher levels of enjoyment (indirect-only mediation). Immersion was also associated with higher enjoyment but showed no indirect effect on mood repair.

The main result of the present study is that individual presence levels are favorable for attaining an overall improved mood state. This provides empirical support for the claim that presence experiences in gaming enhance well-being and mood (Collins & Cox, 2014; Reinecke, 2009a; 2009b; Reinecke et al., 2011). Previous research has linked effects of mood enhancement to the extent of experienced presence in relaxing VR environments (e.g. Freeman et al., 2004; Villani et al., 2007; Villani et al., 2009). The results from the present study suggest that presence contributes to mood repair not only in immersive environments designed to be relaxing, but also in games. The present study could show that presence was associated with mood repair in positive emotions. There seemed to be a weak association with mood repair in negative emotions, but this finding did not reach statistical significance. After controlling for immersion, the present study could demonstrate that individual presence affects mood repair in positive emotions independent of the differences between the conditions. However, this effect was limited to the *VR* condition. In the *desktop* condition, there was a small but non-significant effect, and in the *video* condition, the effect was negative but also non-significant. A possible explanation for these results is that presence plays a more important role in an immersive virtual world. This means that gaming itself is crucial for improved mood and that presence only enhances mood in VR gaming. Potentially, presence is only beneficial for mood repair if it is relevant for the respective medium: A simple yet non-immersive game can still evoke strong enjoyment in players, whereas a game like Star Conflict relies on immersive gameplay features to involve the user in the game narrative, which then leads to enjoyment. The immersive elements are even more important if the world is supposed to appear convincingly realistic as in a VR condition. A floor effect in the *video* condition could serve as an alternative explanation: the *video* condition was not able to lead to large enough presence and enjoyment scores to improve mood. Indeed, there were no high presence scores for the *video* condition (the highest score was 3.80). Additionally, very high scores (> 4.5) were mainly observed in the *VR* condition. Thus, it is possible that presence scores were not high enough in the *desktop* condition to evoke an individually increasing effect on mood repair, whereas the *VR* condition provided participants with the opportunity to experience large increased presence scores, leading to highly improved mood. There are also other possible explanations and additional studies using VR gaming are needed to confirm the results.

Apart from the effect of presence on mood repair, the results from the present study also confirm previous findings: A gaming activity led to an overall improved mood state after a stress-induction (cf. Collins & Cox, 2014; Reinecke 2009a; 2009b). The size for this effect was small to medium in positive emotions (0.44) and large in negative emotions (-0.79; Cohen, 1988). As in previous studies, active gaming led to an overall improved mood state compared to watching a video (Chen & Raney, 2009; Collins et al., 2019; Reinecke et al., 2011; Rieger et al., 2015). Thus, positive mood only increased in the gaming conditions. There was no difference between the VR and the desktop condition, which means that VR as a medium might not be overall better at improving mood than desktop gaming, despite offering a higher potential for strong presence experiences. It is possible that the interactivity of active playing led to already strong mood repair in the gaming conditions and that the VR condition was simply not offering an additional benefit in the present study. After all, Star Conflict is described as fun to play in online forums (Oculus VR, 2015). This assumption could be tested in future studies by comparing VR and desktop conditions using games with different potentials for mood improvement.

In contrast to the active gaming conditions, positive mood showed a small decrease in the video condition. Generally, this is in line with the authors' expectations but could indicate that watching a pre-recorded gaming session does not provide a boost in positive emotions. This is an important finding because watching others playing games on YouTube, Twitch.tv, or at e-sports tournaments is increasingly popular among gamers (Gandolfi, 2016; Smith, Obrist, & Wright, 2013). Studies suggested that watching such videos involves experiences of presence (Collins et al., 2019; Wong et al., 2017). In a previous study by Chen and Raney (2009), the increase in positive mood was higher in an interactive condition but was also positive in a non-interactive condition and a control condition. Rieger et al. (2015) found a similar increase of positive emotions in all interactivity conditions. In contrast to positive emotions, negative emotions in the experiment decreased in each condition to about the same amount, indicating no advantage of active gaming and VR technology. Interestingly, previous studies (Chen & Raney, 2009; Rieger et al., 2015) found that negative emotions did not decrease in a non-interactive condition but only in an interactive condition. Thus, the *video* condition in the experiment showed a surprising decrease in negative emotions but also a decrease in positive emotions. A reason for this could be the different choice of games. Star Conflict probably involves more action and strategy than games used in previous studies, which could enhance the potential for increasing positive emotions. Another reason could lie in different measurements of mood repair: Rieger et al. (2015), for example, operationalized positive and negative mood with measures for happy and depressed mood. In contrast, the PANAS questionnaire, which was used in the present study, is targeted at more general mood states, including items such as *attentive* and *nervous*. However, the *video* condition in the present experiment evoked also less presence and enjoyment scores than the active gaming conditions. This is in line with anecdotal reports of participants. It is plausible, therefore, that the low overall enjoyment of the video led to the unimproved positive mood. Additionally, there was arguably a lack of competition in the *video* condition. According to Reinecke (2009a; 2009b), successful recovery demands for a task structure that enables competence and mastery experiences. The same could be true for mood repair. As for negative mood, it is possible that negative emotions decreased naturally over time. It is not possible to separate the effect of time from the overall effect of the gaming activity since there was no non-medium control condition. Thus, further studies should investigate the specific advantage of watching others play by contrasting it with a non-medium control condition.

Another important point is that no meaningful associations involving mood repair in negative emotions were found. Interestingly, the two measures of mood repair showed no substantial correlation. Negative emotions could, therefore, activate other processes than positive emotions. It is possible that gaming is especially helpful for restoring positive affect but not as effective as previously thought in reducing negative affect. Interestingly, recent findings from organizational psychology provide evidence that recovery from work-related stress goes beyond the replenishing of depleted resources and involves preemptively building up resources to increase coping capabilities and to avoid future loss of resources (Conservation of Resources Theory; Hobfoll, 1989; cf. Reinecke & Eden, 2016). Thus, preemptively building up a positive mood state by increasing positive emotions could be more functionally relevant for gamers and more easily achievable than eliminating negative emotions. It is worth noting, however, that previous studies did find a beneficial effect of gaming for negative emotions. Context (i.e. the type of game and the method for inducing a negative mood state) could play an important role. This discrepancy should be addressed in further research by specifically comparing the effects of positive and negative mood repair and by varying the type of computer game and other variables such as the length of media exposure.

Lastly, the present study showed that enjoyment mediated the effect of presence on mood repair in positive emotions. This supports the expectation that presence is beneficial for mood repair because it leads to a higher enjoyment of a game. Wirth et al. (2007) suppose that increased presence in entertaining media leads to increased enjoyment of the media's content. Accordingly, Teng (2010) proposes that immersion in games is pleasurable and satisfies the user's need. In accordance with this assumption, Weibel and Wissmath (2011) were able to show for various computer games that presence has a positive influence on enjoyment. Reinecke and coworkers (2011) noted that enjoyment could be an important amplifier for the recovery effect. Enjoyment was also related to involvement in their study. The results from the present study support these conclusions. Presence was highly correlated with enjoyment and higher enjoyment led to increased mood repair in positive emotions. However, these results should be considered exploratory and further studies are needed to confirm this relationship.

The results from the present study clearly demonstrate positive effects of gaming. However, it is important to note that this might not always be the case and that there could also be negative effects. Bowman and Tamborini (2012; 2015), for example, showed that high task demand – as opposed to medium demand – led to less mood repair. Task demand was not measured, but it is likely that task demand was medium and not high in the present study: the control of the ship in Star Conflict is comparatively complex, but participants only played a beginner's tutorial. Consequentially, all participants managed to complete the tutorial successfully. However, if the demand of a game is too high, effects of mood repair could be severely impaired (Bowman & Tamborini, 2012; 2015). Furthermore, a recent experience sampling study found that more than half of the studied media occurrences (including gaming) showed at least some degree of conflict with other goals and responsibilities (Reinecke & Hofmann, 2016). This goal conflict as well as the evaluation of one's own media use as a form of procrastination can result in feelings of guilt that reduce enjoyment and impair situational well-being (Reinecke, Hartmann, & Eden, 2014; Reinecke & Hofmann, 2016). Reinecke and Eden (2016) propose that prolonged media exposure may turn media use from a resource-providing into a resource-consuming activity. Thus, prolonged gaming could lead to impaired mood, even when short-term effects are positive. Successful media-induced recovery and mood repair seem to depend on the right dosage.

In conclusion, the results from the present study show that gaming improves mood. Furthermore, the individual level of presence enhances the effect of mood repair in VR and presence is also strongly related to media enjoyment. The results show that the presence experience in a game affects mood repair beyond the effect of the game's immersion and that only presence might influence positive emotions by evoking higher enjoyment. The individual level of presence is especially important for VR games as they may potentially offer greater opportunities for experiencing high levels of presence. Presence experiences effectively enhance mood states and build up resources. This has implications for the VR gaming industry as well as health research. The positive effect of presence in VR could be used for the treatment of stress and negative affect. In addition to relaxing environments, games offer challenges and competition and are a form of treatment that can draw from thousands of readily available experiences. Additionally, immersive experiences in games are beneficial for mood repair and show that the immersion of a game combines with the individual's reaction towards the game to promote psychological well-being and recovery from stress and negative mood states.

REFERENCES

Ameringer, S., Serlin, R. C., & Ward, S. (2009). Simpson's paradox and experimental research. *Nursing Research*, *58*(2), 123–127. doi:10.1097/NNR.0b013e318199b517 PMID:19289933

Annerstedt, M., Jönsson, P., Wallergård, M., Johansson, G., Karlson, B., Grahn, P., Hansen, Å. M., & Währborg, P. (2013). Inducing physiological stress recovery with sounds of nature in a virtual reality forest—Results from a pilot study. *Physiology & Behavior*, *118*, 240–250. doi:10.1016/j.physbeh.2013.05.023 PMID:23688947

Bauer, H., Pripfl, J., Lamm, C., Prainsack, C., & Taylor, N. (2003). Functional neuroanatomy of learned helplessness. *NeuroImage*, *20*(2), 927–939. doi:10.1016/S1053-8119(03)00363-X PMID:14568463

Bessière, K., Seay, A. F., & Kiesler, S. (2007). The ideal elf: Identity exploration in World of Warcraft. *Cyberpsychology & Behavior*, *10*(4), 530–535. doi:10.1089/cpb.2007.9994 PMID:17711361

Bowman, N. D., & Tamborini, R. (2012). Task demand and mood repair: The intervention potential of computer games. *New Media & Society*, *14*(8), 1339–1357. doi:10.1177/1461444812450426

Bowman, N. D., & Tamborini, R. (2015). "In the Mood to Game": Selective exposure and mood management processes in computer game play. *New Media & Society*, *17*(3), 375–393. doi:10.1177/1461444813504274

Bryant, J., & Davies, J. (2006). Selective exposure to video games. In P. Vorderer & J. Bryant (Eds.), *Playing video games: Motives, responses, and consequences* (pp. 181–194). Lawrence Erlbaum.

Bryant, J., & Zillmann, D. (1984). Using television to alleviate boredom and stress: Selective exposure as a function of induced excitational states. *Journal of Broadcasting*, *28*(1), 1–20. doi:10.1080/08838158409386511

Bucolo, S. (2004, June). Understanding cross cultural differences during interaction within immersive virtual environments. In *Proceedings of the 2004 ACM SIGGRAPH International Conference on Virtual Reality Continuum and its Applications in Industry* (pp. 221-224). ACM. 10.1145/1044588.1044634

Chen, Y., & Raney, A. A. (2009, May). *Mood management and highly interactive video games: An experimental examination of Wii playing on mood change and enjoyment.* Paper presented at the Annual Meeting of the International Communication Association (ICA), Chicago, IL.

Cohen, J. (1988). *Statistical Power Analysis for the Behavioral Sciences* (2nd ed.). Erlbaum.

Collins, E., & Cox, A. L. (2014). Switch on to games: Can digital games aid post-work recovery? *International Journal of Human-Computer Studies*, *72*(8-9), 654–662. doi:10.1016/j.ijhcs.2013.12.006

Collins, E., Cox, A., Wilcock, C., & Sethu-Jones, G. (2019). Digital Games and Mindfulness Apps: Comparison of Effects on Post Work Recovery. *JMIR Mental Health*, *6*(7), e12853. doi:10.2196/12853 PMID:31322125

Cummings, J., & Bailenson, J. (2015). How immersive is enough? A meta–analysis of the effect of immersive technology on user presence. *Media Psychology*, *19*(2), 272–309. doi:10.1080/15213269.2015.1015740

Davis, J. P., Steury, K., & Pagulayan, R. (2005). A survey method for assessing perceptions of a game: The consumer playtest in game design. *Game Studies, 5*(1).

de Kort, Y. A. W., Meijnders, A. L., Sponselee, A. A. G., & IJsselsteijn, W. A. (2006). What's wrong with virtual trees? Restoring from stress in a mediated environment. *Journal of Environmental Psychology*, *26*(4), 309–320. doi:10.1016/j.jenvp.2006.09.001

Draper, J. V., Kaber, D. B., & Usher, J. M. (1998). Telepresence. *Human Factors*, *40*(3), 354–375. doi:10.1518/001872098779591386 PMID:9849099

Freeman, J., Lessiter, J., Keogh, E., Bond, F. W., & Chapman, K. (2004). Relaxation Island: virtual, and really relaxing. In *Proceedings of 7th International Workshop on Presence* (pp. 67-72). Academic Press.

Gallucci, M. (2019). *jAMM: jamovi Advanced Mediation Models* (Version 1.0.2) [Computer Software]. Retrieved from https://jamovi-amm.github.io/index.html

Gandolfi, E. (2016). To watch or to play, it is in the game: The game culture on Twitch.tv among performers, plays and audiences. *Journal of Gaming & Virtual Worlds*, *8*(1), 63–82. doi:10.1386/jgvw.8.1.63_1

Green, M. C., Brock, T. C., & Kaufman, G. F. (2004). Understanding media enjoyment: The role of transportation into narrative worlds. *Communication Theory*, *14*(4), 311–327. doi:10.1111/j.1468-2885.2004.tb00317.x

Hayes, A. F. (2017). *Introduction to mediation, moderation, and conditional process analysis: A regression-based approach*. Guilford Publications.

Hein, D., Mai, C., & Hußmann, H. (2018). The Usage of Presence Measurements in Research: A Review. In *Proceedings of the International Society for Presence Research Annual Conference (Presence)*. The International Society for Presence Research.

Henna, E., Zilberman, M. L., Gentil, V., & Gorenstein, C. (2008). Validity of a frustration-induction procedure. *Revista Brasileira de Psiquiatria (Sao Paulo, Brazil)*, *30*(1), 47–49. doi:10.1590/S1516-44462006005000057 PMID:17713692

Hobfoll, S. E. (1989). Conservation of resources: A new attempt at conceptualizing stress. *The American Psychologist*, *44*(3), 513–524. doi:10.1037/0003-066X.44.3.513 PMID:2648906

Jennett, C., Cox, A. L., Cairns, P., Dhoparee, S., Epps, A., Tijs, T., & Walton, A. (2008). Measuring and defining the experience of immersion in games. *International Journal of Human-Computer Studies*, *66*(9), 641–661. doi:10.1016/j.ijhcs.2008.04.004

Klimmt, C., & Hartmann, T. (2006). Effectance, self-efficacy, and the motivation to play video games. In P. Vorderer & J. Bryant (Eds.), *Playing video games: Motives, responses and consequences* (pp. 133–146). Erlbaum.

Kätsyri, J., Hari, R., Ravaja, N., & Nummenmaa, L. (2013). Just watching the game ain't enough: Striatal fMRI reward responses to successes and failures in a video game during active and vicarious playing. *Frontiers in Human Neuroscience*, *7*, 278. doi:10.3389/fnhum.2013.00278 PMID:23781195

Knobloch, S., & Zillmann, D. (2002). Mood management via the digital jukebox. *Journal of Communication*, *52*(2), 351–366. doi:10.1111/j.1460-2466.2002.tb02549.x

Lang, P. J. (1980). Behavioral treatment and bio-behavioral assessment: Computer applications. In J. B. Sidowski, J. H. Johnson, & T. A. Williams (Eds.), *Technology in mental health care delivery systems* (pp. 119–137). Ablex.

Liszio, S., Graf, L., & Masuch, M. (2018). The Relaxing Effect of Virtual Nature: Immersive Technology Provides Relief in Acute Stress Situations. *Annual Review of Cybertherapy and Telemedicine*, *2018*, 87.

Lombard, M., & Ditton, T. (1997). At the heart of it all: The concept of presence. *Journal of Computer-Mediated Communication*, *3*(2), 0. doi:10.1111/j.1083-6101.1997.tb00072.x

Mastro, D. E., Eastin, M. S., & Tamborini, R. (2002). Internet search behaviors and mood alterations: A selective exposure approach. *Media Psychology*, *4*(2), 157–172. doi:10.1207/S1532785XMEP0402_03

McLaughlin, E., Lefaivre, M. J., & Cummings, E. (2009). Experimentally-induced learned helplessness in adolescents with type 1 diabetes. *Journal of Pediatric Psychology*, *35*(4), 405–414. doi:10.1093/jpepsy/jsp061 PMID:19700419

McMahan, A. (2003). Immersion, engagement, and presence: A method for analyzing 3-D video games. In M. J. P. Wolf & B. Perron (Eds.), *The video game theory reader* (pp. 67–86). Routledge.

Meinck, S., & Rodriguez, M. C. (2013). Considerations for correlation analysis using clustered data: Working with the teacher education and development study in mathematics (TEDS-M) and other international studies. *Large-Scale Assessments in Education*, *1*(1), 7. doi:10.1186/2196-0739-1-7

Microsoft Corporation. (2005). *Xbox 360 Controller* [apparatus]. Microsoft Corporation.

Miliken, G. A., & Johnson, D. E. (1984). Analysis of Messy Data: Vol. I. *Designed Experiments*. Van Nostrand Reinhold.

Nixon, A. E., Mazzola, J. J., Bauer, J., Krueger, J. R., & Spector, P. E. (2011). Can work make you sick? A meta-analysis of the relationships between job stressors and physical symptoms. *Work and Stress*, *25*(1), 1–22. doi:10.1080/02678373.2011.569175

Norman, K. (2010). *Development of instruments to measure immerse ability of individuals and immersiveness of video games*. Technical Report LAPDP-2010-03, HCIL Technical Report 12-5-10, University of Maryland.

Oculus, V. R. (2014). *Oculus Rift Development Kit 2* [apparatus]. Oculus VR, LLC.

Oculus, V. R. (2015). *Forum* [online]. Oculus VR, LLC. Retrieved from https://forums.oculus.com

Pajitnov, A. (1985). *Tetris* [Computer game]. Tetris Holding LLC. Retrieved from http://www.freetetris.org

Pasek, J. (2018). *Weights: weighting and weighted statistics* (Version 1.0) [Computer Software]. Retrieved from https://cran.r-project.org/package=weights

R Core Team. (2019). *R: A language and environment for statistical computing*. R Foundation for Statistical Computing. Retrieved from https://www.R-project.org/

Reinecke, L. (2009a). Games and recovery: The use of video and computer games to recuperate from stress and strain. *Journal of Media Psychology*, *21*(3), 126–142. doi:10.1027/1864-1105.21.3.126

Reinecke, L. (2009b). Games at work: The recreational use of computer games during working hours. *Cyberpsychology & Behavior*, *12*(4), 461–465. doi:10.1089/cpb.2009.0010 PMID:19619038

Reinecke, L., & Eden, A. (2016). Media-induced recovery as a link between media exposure and well-being. The Routledge Handbook of Media Use and Well-Being: International Perspectives on Theory and Research on Positive Media Effects, 106.

Reinecke, L., Hartmann, T., & Eden, A. (2014). The guilty couch potato: The role of ego depletion in reducing recovery through media use. *Journal of Communication*, *64*(4), 569–589. doi:10.1111/jcom.12107

Reinecke, L., & Hofmann, W. (2016). Slacking off or winding down? An experience sampling study on the drivers and consequences of media use for recovery versus procrastination. *Human Communication Research*, *42*(3), 441–461. doi:10.1111/hcre.12082

Reinecke, L., Klatt, J., & Krämer, N. C. (2011). Entertaining media use and the satisfaction of recovery needs: Recovery outcomes associated with the use of interactive and noninteractive entertaining media. *Media Psychology*, *14*(2), 192–215. doi:10.1080/15213269.2011.573466

Rieger, D., Frischlich, L., Wulf, T., Bente, G., & Kneer, J. (2015). Eating ghosts: The underlying mechanisms of mood repair via interactive and noninteractive media. *Psychology of Popular Media Culture*, *4*(2), 138–154. doi:10.1037/ppm0000018

Russell, W. D., & Newton, M. (2008). Short-term psychological effects of interactive video game technology exercise on mood and attention. *Journal of Educational Technology & Society*, *11*(2).

Ryan, R. M., & Deci, E. L. (2000). Self-determination theory and the facilitation of intrinsic motivation, social development, and well-being. *The American Psychologist*, *55*(1), 68–78. doi:10.1037/0003-066X.55.1.68 PMID:11392867

Ryan, R. M., Rigby, C. S., & Przybylski, A. (2006). The motivational pull of video games: A self-determination theory approach. *Motivation and Emotion*, *30*(4), 344–360. doi:10.100711031-006-9051-8

Slater, M., & Wilbur, S. (1997). A framework for immersive virtual environments (FIVE): Speculations on the role of presence in virtual environments. *Presence (Cambridge, Mass.)*, *6*(6), 603–616. doi:10.1162/pres.1997.6.6.603

Smith, T., Obrist, M., & Wright, P. (2013, June). Live-streaming changes the (video) game. In *Proceedings of the 11th European Conference on Interactive TV and Video* (pp. 131-138). ACM. 10.1145/2465958.2465971

Smuts, A. (2009). What is interactivity? *Journal of Aesthetic Education*, *43*(4), 53–73. doi:10.1353/jae.0.0062

Sonnentag, S., & Fritz, C. (2007). The recovery experience questionnaire: Development and validation of a measure for assessing recuperation and unwinding from work. *Journal of Occupational Health Psychology*, *12*(3), 204–221. doi:10.1037/1076-8998.12.3.204 PMID:17638488

Sonnentag, S., & Zijlstra, F. R. H. (2006). Job Characteristics and Off-Job Activities as Predictors of Need for Recovery, Well-Being, and Fatigue. *The Journal of Applied Psychology*, *91*(2), 330–350. doi:10.1037/0021-9010.91.2.330 PMID:16551187

Sponselee, A.-M., de Kort, Y. A. W., & Meijnders, A. L. (2004). Healing media: The moderating role of presence in restoring from stress in a mediated environment. *Proceedings of Presence*, *2004*, 197–203.

Stansfeld, S., & Candy, B. (2006). Psychosocial work environment and mental health—A meta-analytic review. *Scandinavian Journal of Work, Environment & Health*, *32*(6), 443–462. doi:10.5271jweh.1050 PMID:17173201

Star Conflict Wiki. (2015). *About the game.* Retrieved from http://wiki.star-conflict.com

Star Gem Inc. (2015). *Star Conflict* [Computer game]. Available from http://star-conflict.com

Steuer, J. (1992). Defining virtual reality: Dimensions determining telepresence. *Journal of Communication*, *42*(4), 72–92. doi:10.1111/j.1460-2466.1992.tb00812.x

Tamborini, R., Bowman, N. D., Eden, A., Grizzard, M., & Organ, A. (2010). Defining media enjoyment as the satisfaction of intrinsic needs. *Journal of Communication*, *60*(4), 758–777. doi:10.1111/j.1460-2466.2010.01513.x

Tamborini, R., Grizzard, M., Bowman, N. D., Reinecke, L., Lewis, R. J., & Eden, A. (2011). Media enjoyment as need satisfaction: The contribution of hedonic and nonhedonic needs. *Journal of Communication*, *61*(6), 1025–1042. doi:10.1111/j.1460-2466.2011.01593.x

Tamborini, R., & Skalski, P. (2006). The role of presence in the experience of electronic games. In P. Vorderer & J. Bryant (Eds.), *Playing video games: Motives, responses, and consequences* (pp. 225–240). Erlbaum.

Teng, C. I. (2010). Customization, immersion satisfaction, and online gamer loyalty. *Computers in Human Behavior*, *26*(6), 1547–1554. doi:10.1016/j.chb.2010.05.029

The Jamovi Project. (2019). *Jamovi* (Version 1.1.7.0) [Computer Software]. Retrieved from https://www.jamovi.org

Valtchanov, D., & Ellard, C. (2010). Physiological and affective responses to immersion in virtual reality: Effects of nature and urban settings. *Cybertherapy & Rehabilitation*, *3*(4), 359–373.

Villani, D., Cipresso, P., Gaggioli, A., & Riva, G. (2016). Positive technology for helping people cope with stress. In *Integrating Technology in Positive Psychology Practice* (pp. 316–343). IGI Global. doi:10.4018/978-1-4666-9986-1.ch014

Villani, D., Luchetta, M., Preziosa, A., & Riva, G. (2009). The role of interactive media features on the affective response: A virtual reality study. *International Journal of Human-Computer Interaction*, *1*(5), 1–21.

Villani, D., & Riva, G. (2012). Does interactive media enhance the management of stress? Suggestions from a controlled study. *Cyberpsychology, Behavior, and Social Networking*, *15*(1), 24–30. doi:10.1089/cyber.2011.0141 PMID:22032797

Villani, D., Riva, F., & Riva, G. (2007). New technologies for relaxation: The role of presence. *International Journal of Stress Management*, *14*(3), 260–274. doi:10.1037/1072-5245.14.3.260

Watson, D., Clark, L. A., & Tellegen, A. (1988). Development and validation of brief measures of positive and negative affect: The PANAS scales. *Journal of Personality and Social Psychology*, *54*(6), 1063–1070. doi:10.1037/0022-3514.54.6.1063 PMID:3397865

Watson, D., & Vaidya, J. (2003). Mood measurement: Current status and future directions. In J. A. Schinka, W. F. Velicer, & I. B. Weiner (Eds.), Handbook of psychology: Vol. 2. *Research methods in psychology* (pp. 351–375). John Wiley & Sons, Inc.

Weibel, D., Schmutz, J., Pahud, O., & Wissmath, B. (2015). Measuring spatial presence: Introducing and validating the pictorial presence SAM. *Presence (Cambridge, Mass.), 24*(1), 44–61. doi:10.1162/PRES_a_00214

Weibel, D., & Wissmath, B. (2011). Immersion in computer games – the role of spatial presence and flow. *International Journal of Computer Games Technology*, 1–14.

Weibel, D., Wissmath, B., & Mast, F. W. (2010). Immersion in mediated environments: The role of personality traits. *Cyberpsychology, Behavior, and Social Networking, 13*(3), 251–256. doi:10.1089/cyber.2009.0171 PMID:20557243

Weibel, D., Wissmath, B., & Mast, F. W. (2011a). Influence of mental imagery on spatial presence and enjoyment assessed in different types of media. *Cyberpsychology, Behavior, and Social Networking, 14*(10), 607–612. doi:10.1089/cyber.2010.0287 PMID:21352082

Weibel, D., Wissmath, B., & Mast, F. W. (2011b). The Role of Cognitive Appraisal in Media-Induced Presence and Emotions. *Cognition and Emotion, 25*(7), 1291–1298. doi:10.1080/02699931.2010.5430 16 PMID:21432638

Weibel, D., Wissmath, B., & Stricker, D. (2011c). The influence of neuroticism on spatial presence and enjoyment in films. *Personality and Individual Differences, 51*(7), 866–869. doi:10.1016/j.paid.2011.07.011

Wirth, W., Hartmann, T., Böcking, S., Vorderer, P., Klimmt, C., Schramm, H., ... Biocca, F. (2007). A process model of the formation of spatial presence experiences. *Media Psychology, 9*(3), 493–525. doi:10.1080/15213260701283079

Wissmath, B., Weibel, D., & Mast, F. W. (2010). The effects of virtual weather on presence. In F. Lehmann-Grube & J. Sablatnig (Eds.), *Facets of virtual environments* (pp. 68–78). Springer Berlin Heidelberg. doi:10.1007/978-3-642-11743-5_6

Wissmath, B., Weibel, D., Schmutz, J., & Mast, F. W. (2011). Being Present in More than One Place at a Time? Patterns of Mental Self-Localization. *Consciousness and Cognition, 20*(4), 1808–1815. doi:10.1016/j.concog.2011.05.008 PMID:21641823

Witmer, B. G., & Singer, M. J. (1998). Measuring presence in virtual environments: A presence questionnaire. *Presence (Cambridge, Mass.), 7*(3), 225–240. doi:10.1162/105474698565686

Wong, P. N., Rigby, J. M., & Brumby, D. P. (2017, October). Game & watch: are let's play gaming videos as immersive as playing games? In *Proceedings of the Annual Symposium on Computer-Human Interaction in Play* (pp. 401-409). ACM. 10.1145/3116595.3116613

World Medical Association. (1991). Declaration of Helsinki. *Law, Medicine & Health Care, 19*(3-4), 264–265. doi:10.1111/j.1748-720X.1991.tb01824.x PMID:11642954

Wu, T. L., Gomes, A., Fernandes, K., & Wang, D. (2019). The Effect of Head Tracking on the Degree of Presence in Virtual Reality. *International Journal of Human-Computer Interaction, 35*(17), 1569–1577. doi:10.1080/10447318.2018.1555736

Yee, N. (2006). Motivations for play in online games. *Cyberpsychology & Behavior*, *9*(6), 772–775. doi:10.1089/cpb.2006.9.772 PMID:17201605

Yee, N., Ducheneaut, N., & Nelson, L. (2012, May). Online gaming motivations scale: development and validation. In *Proceedings of the SIGCHI Conference on Human Factors in Computing Systems* (pp. 2803-2806). ACM. 10.1145/2207676.2208681

Zhao, X., Lynch, J. G. Jr, & Chen, Q. (2010). Reconsidering Baron and Kenny: Myths and truths about mediation analysis. *The Journal of Consumer Research*, *37*(2), 197–206. doi:10.1086/651257

Zillmann, D. (2000). The coming of media entertainment. In P. Vorderer & D. Zillmann (Eds.), *Media entertainment: The psychology of its appeal* (pp. 1–20). Erlbaum. doi:10.4324/9781410604811

This research was previously published in the International Journal of Gaming and Computer-Mediated Simulations (IJGCMS), 12(4); pages 1-22, copyright year 2020 by IGI Publishing (an imprint of IGI Global).

Chapter 58
The Fallacies of MDA for Novice Designers:
Overusing Mechanics and Underusing Aesthetics

Kenneth Chen
Drexel University, USA

ABSTRACT

Ever since MDA was publicized by Hunicke, Leblanc, and Zubek in 2004, it has become a building block for game developers and scholars. However, it has also incited several misconceptions that have spread among students and the gaming community. For example, players have overused the term "mechanics," to the point that it is virtually meaningless. On the other side, the terms "dynamics" and "aesthetics" have been comparatively neglected, despite their value. Building upon our experiences of teaching an undergraduate game design course, we argue that these misconceptions stem from the ways that consumers have misinterpreted the MDA framework. Game educators are not necessarily working with experienced designers: they are working with students who are often more passionate about playing games than making them. Thus, game educators need to target this misconception in order to shed light on preconceived biases.

INTRODUCTION

With the rise of game development as a viable career choice, more and more students are entering game design programs for higher education. Decades ago, potential designers were seen as solitary tinkerers, but now, they are players who feel inspired by games and have paths to turn that inspiration into production. However, this introduces a new problem: these players often develop misconceptions about game design based on their experiences from consuming games rather than creating them. On the academic level, instructors need to be aware of these misconceptions and specifically target them.

DOI: 10.4018/978-1-6684-7589-8.ch058

The misconception I want to discuss is the concept of mechanics. This word was popularized by Hunicke et al. in a 2004 workshop paper at GDC, along with dynamics and aesthetics in their foundational MDA model (Hunicke, Leblanc, Zubek, 2004). MDA argues that game design can be understood as the connections among mechanics (data, formulas, rules), dynamics (behaviors, interactions, decisions), and aesthetics (emotions, reactions, feelings). Since its inception, MDA has been appropriated by players and morphed into an amalgamation of different definitions. In its current state, the word "mechanics" is nearly meaningless, and has lost all of its insight into the MDA framework. Despite this, the word is still extremely common not only among players, but also among students who are relying on their previous experience as players.

For instructors in game development, it is not sufficient to teach students how to make games. They also need to unteach students how they thought games were supposed to be made. Many of the students who are entering university-level game design programs are primarily inspired by playing games rather than making games. Even though MDA was originally developed as a means to bridge this divide, I argue that it has unintentionally yet ironically widened it. However, if we become more aware of the problem, we can take steps to fix the situation.

Game Design and MDA

The field of game design, as a specific area of discipline within the larger context of game development, has faced misunderstandings and misinterpretations throughout its history. In the formative days of video games as an industry, there was no distinct role for a "designer." Often, there was only one programmer building everything, from graphics to rulesets. As productions grew larger, those programmers began to work with dedicated artists. Design became an explicit role with the rise of adventure games, where design overlapped with narrative in puzzles and dialogue (Williams, 2017).

Even today, "game design" is often used as a nebulous concept. For example, Drexel University's undergraduate game curriculum is called "Game Design and Production." However, this name is inaccurate, because the curriculum has historically not taught game design. It has focused on art production such as 3D modeling and animations which are then imported into games. In the past, the curriculum was accurately called "Game Art and Production," but it was renamed to "Game Design and Production" with very little change in the actual curriculum. There is still so much confusion among the terms "game design," "game development," and "game programming." In classes, students still struggle to even define a "game" in the first place, unaware that such arguments have already been explored (Juul, 2003) (Aarseth, 2015). Students are often surprised at how difficult game design can be when they first start plumbing its depths, which is why Jesse Schell quickly reassures readers to have the confidence to say "I am a game designer" in his textbook "The Art of Game Design" (Schell, 2008).

Game designers themselves seem to find difficulty in defining their role. Loosely, a game designer creates an experience for the player, but the precise manner in which this is achieved seems to be a black box. Daniel Cook likened this to the process of alchemy: experimenting wildly with different potions and brews, relying on mysticism and voodoo rather than logical scientific rigor (Cook, 2007).

The game design community has informally rallied around the "door problem" as an example of how game design differs from and interacts with other aspects of development (England, 2014). A game designer decides what a door does: how it opens, what the player does, when certain events associated with the door are triggered, and so on. This gives a concrete example of game design in practice, which the field sorely lacks.

Game design is naturally difficult to perceive. In various design-oriented communities, there is an informal mantra that "good design is invisible." Don Norman's seminal book, "The Design of Everyday Things," opens with this concept on its very first page (Norman, 2013):

"Good design is actually a lot harder to notice than poor design, in part because good designs fit our needs so well that the design is invisible, serving us without drawing attention to itself. Bad design, on the other hand, screams out its inadequacies, making itself very noticeable."

People who want to learn game design often end up fixating on bad design, simply because that is what they can actually observe. This has led to the mythos of the "idea guy," a person whose job is to think of ideas for games. For students and prospective designers, games seem filled with problems that could be solved if only there was someone who could think of an idea to fix those problems. "Idea guys" have become so prevalent that the game design industry treats the term as a pejorative descriptor, since the stereotype underplays the amount of effort that game design requires (Mullich, 2015).

The MDA model was created in order to relieve these tensions. Robin Hunicke, Mark LeBlanc, and Robert Zubek wrote the original whitepaper to clarify the process of game design for a whole range of audiences: not only other designers but also academics, researchers, and consumers. In particular, the paper focuses on the ways in which programming intersects with game design, especially with AI programming. An AI is driven by mechanics (code) in order to achieve certain dynamics (actions) which in turn are decided by the target aesthetics (experiences). When one part of the chain is changed, a ripple distorts everything else around it.

Since then, MDA has been widely integrated into the communities surrounding game design, to the point where it is almost regarded as an undisputed fact. It is used in textbooks (Kim, 2015), research foundations (Suh, Wagner, Liu, 2015), and exercises for workshops and game jams (Buttfield-Addison, Manning, Nugent, 2016). Although this paper's goal is to refute MDA, the framework is also an important milestone. MDA's history, popularity, and transformation can give us a greater understanding of not only game design itself, but also the way in which game design is understood outside of its field.

The Gap Between Definitions

The primary word to be discussed is "mechanics." Although the word "mechanics" is only one out of three words in the MDA framework, it has been disproportionately misused. Hunicke et al. defined mechanics as "the particular components of the game, at the level of data representation and algorithms." Modern discourse seems to have left this definition in the past, replacing it with personal interpretations, or worse, nothing.

Player/Consumer Definitions

Some of the more experienced and established members of the industry and academic communities might not be familiar with the ways in which the gaming community has twisted the word "mechanics." Although there isn't exactly a true dictionary definition, players have generally taken the term to mean something along the lines of the expression of skillful play through controlled intentional inputs. This is often paired with a positive connotation.

In some online gaming communities, mechanics are considered as an element of skill, separated from tactics or communication or foresight. Thus, mechanics in this sense become more closely related to reflexes or precision in timing and aiming. This approach to mechanics becomes especially prevalent in eSports communities which toe the line between consumers and creators. For example, in the game *League of Legends*, official casters and commentators discuss the teams and players in the eSports scene, and they will often invoke the term "mechanics" as a positively connoted quality. The following quote refers to a professional player nicknamed Goldenglue, written by an eSports journalist (Lam, 2018).

Goldenglue isn't some kind of prodigy. Neither are you or me. He doesn't have godly mechanics, and he's not likely to ever be a superstar. But what he did do was go to Korea on his own and play 400 games of Solo Queue. What he did do was keep his head down and grind out all of his opportunities even as the community wrote him off as deadweight. - Kien Lam

In this usage, we see that the word "mechanics" is no longer being used as a tool to analyze game design, but rather as a tool to analyze player performance in games. This is not intrinsically problematic: words and meanings naturally change over time. The problem occurs when people take their new definitions and try to use them in their previous contexts. For example, the following quote refers to a player's reaction to the boss monster Kushala Daora in *Monster Hunter World*, from the wiki page:

Technically among the worst designed enemies in the history of video games. Design and execution-wise obviously. Really*****ty and meaningless enemy design; sloppy hitboxes and stagger. This is how you literally ruin a mechanical game and turn it into a cheese/equipment fest. - Anonymous

This quote from a gaming wiki forum illustrates a different, but related use of "mechanics" than the one seen before in the player analysis. Here, the word is used to attempt to describe a fault in the game's design. The concepts of hitbox and stagger call back to the idea of mechanical skill where the player must accurately aim their attacks and time their dodges. We can reinterpret this passage to mean that the stifling of player skill is an indication of poor design. And yet, that is false, because the stifling of player skill is an important part of a game designer's toolbox. Perhaps the designer has decided that this is the point at which players should stop trying to muscle their way through a fight with quick reflexes, but rather take a more deliberate and methodical approach.

Clearly, the player is just frustrated and most likely not actually trying to conduct an insightful design analysis. This is just an exaggerated example of the overreaching mentality that I want to expose. When students emphasize the importance of mechanics as a skill, they fail to recognize the larger design implications behind these decisions. Even though both players and designers are saying "mechanics," they are not communicating the same meaning. If this anonymous player were a college-bound game design major, we as educators cannot teach them the formal definition of a mechanic until we first address their misconception of that definition.

Industry/Academic Definitions

Unfortunately, that may be slightly difficult because the industry has also wavered on the definition of mechanics for quite some time. This reflects a similar struggle across the gaming industry to create standardized terms for discussing design. Greg Costikyan wrote "I Have No Words & I Must Design" in 1999 (Costikyan, 1999), and in some respects we haven't evolved far since then.

"Mechanics" is just another term which has been caught in this crossfire. Some designers have circled around the concept of mechanics, such as the term "ludemes" which also refers to elements of gameplay (Parlett, 2007). Others have simply taken the word itself and ascribed their own meaning to it. Daniel Cook, whose article "The Chemistry of Game Design" was briefly discussed above, used the term mechanics to denote chunks of learned knowledge over the course of a game experience (Cook, 2007).

Mike Stout, formerly from Insomniac Games, wrote "Evaluating Game Mechanics For Depth" which formalizes the player/consumer definitions seen above, with a focus on player skill (Stout, 2010).

When I say 'game mechanic' I'm referring to any major chunk of gameplay in a video game. Using the classic The Legend of Zelda: A Link to the Past as an example, here are a batch of game mechanics: sword combat, block pushing, boomerang throwing, swimming, button-based puzzles, hazard-avoidance, use of specific weapons, etc... - Mike Stout

These are not truly mechanics in Hunicke et al.'s original sense of the term, but are instead extensions of the player's interpretation of mechanics as expressions of skill. This might be the definition that a designer would use if they wanted to answer the question, "How do we improve the Kushala Daora boss fight in *Monster Hunter World*?" However, Hunicke et al.'s use of the word would ask the question, "Should we improve the Kushala Daora boss fight in the first place? Certainly, it may be frustrating, but could that lead to the final experience that we want to create?"

We can see an especially odd use of this term in Martin Sahlin's GDC 2017 talk *"Unravel - Using Empathy as a Game Mechanic"* (Sahlin, 2017):

Unravel turned empathy into a game mechanic. I wanted players to fall in love... Then break their hearts! Then we make it all worth it. - Martin Sahlin

While these are certainly interesting and valuable goals for a game designer, the use of the word "mechanic" just invites even more confusion. Moreover, this is a point at which the term "aesthetics" from the original framework would have been perfectly appropriate. It is doubtful that Sahlin was unaware of the MDA framework. The word "mechanic" just communicated the point better, because the word has expanded to mean practically any part of a game.

When Sahlin uses the term "mechanics" instead of the more appropriate term "aesthetics," he reflects a similar shift in public perception. People are putting less emphasis on dynamics/aesthetics and more emphasis on mechanics, and then expanding the definition of mechanics to include dynamics/aesthetics. The whole purpose of MDA was to separate these three concepts so that designers could intelligently discuss how they interacted with each other. But the direction of modern discourse seems to indicate the opposite effect. If Greg Costikyan had no words to design with, we may end up with only one, which isn't a much better situation.

MISCONCEPTIONS AND MISTAKES

Although MDA is a victim of misinterpretation, I argue that it is also a perpetrator. I do not attack developers/academics/players for misinterpreting MDA out of faith in the framework. Rather, I believe that MDA cannot be treated as a truth of game design, and that we need to consider it along with other approaches. However, we cannot teach students how to deconstruct MDA if they did not understand MDA in the first place.

One of MDA's arguments is that designers experience games from mechanics to dynamics to aesthetics, whereas players experience games from aesthetics to dynamics to mechanics. The terms of mechanics, dynamics, and aesthetics are insightful and valuable. However, I believe that the illustrated progression from one to the next is not only false, but also a reason why the words have become so severely misinterpreted.

Players who want to talk about games in a more intelligent manner will try to use more advanced language, which from this perspective, is the word "mechanics." Anonymous could have written "Kushala

Daora beat me and I felt weak and helpless" and that would be an illustration of game aesthetics, but that's not how humans express frustration. Likewise, designers who want to appeal to players will use the same language that they use, as seen in Sahlin's GDC talk about empathy as a game mechanic.

We have ended up in a situation where we use the word "mechanics" far too often, and the word "aesthetics" far too rarely. It doesn't help that the word "aesthetic" is already commonly used to refer to artistic quality, which causes people to think that "game aesthetics" means "game art." In game design, aesthetics are one of the most important parts, and that we must not neglect the value of this term.

Players: From Mechanics to Aesthetics

Hunicke et al. state that "From the player's perspective, aesthetics set the tone, which is born out in observable dynamics and eventually, operable mechanics."

On the contrary, players need to first learn the mechanics and then the dynamics in order to properly appreciate the aesthetics. For example, let us examine chess. The mechanics of chess cover the core rules and the movement for each piece. The dynamics of chess illustrate different strategies, openings, counterattacks, sieges, and all the other types of events that can happen during play. The aesthetics represent the final experience: not only the joy of winning or the sadness of defeat, but also the cleverness of a tricky move, or the bravery of a reckless assault, or the desperation of an unlikely plan.

But when a player first sits down at the chess board, they cannot experience these emotions directly. They cannot be told to feel clever, or brave, or desperate, or joyful or sad. Those emotions need to be earned through gameplay. If the player does not know the rules, then they are not responsible for their actions. And if they are not responsible for their actions, they will not have an emotional attachment. Imagine a player who loses because they do not know the rules. Such a player will not feel disappointed: they will only feel bored. Thus, it makes more sense to say that players experience games from mechanics to dynamics to aesthetics: the complete opposite of what Hunicke et al. described.

The original players-from-aesthetics-to-mechanics position can be understood as a product of its time. MDA was first publicized in 2004, around the period of the ludology vs narratology debate (Aarseth, 2012). This was a period when mainstream AAA games operated primarily through cutscenes, and the indie market with more experimental narrative formats was still growing. Cutscenes can be interpreted as a shortcut to aesthetics which bypasses mechanics and dynamics (Klevjer, 2002). If the player watches enough cutscenes of their character being powerful, eventually they will feel powerful too despite never touching a button. In this context, it is understandable that Hunicke et al. said that aesthetics set the tone.

But today, long after ludology vs narratology, the field of game development has generally settled into the agreement that players are an important part of their own experience. We are seeing more and more games, AAA games even, which are breaking away from the strict cutscene-gameplay-cutscene-gameplay rhythm. Clint Hocking's work on ludonarrative dissonance (Hocking, 2007) has illustrated the importance of guiding players through mechanics to dynamics to aesthetics, rather than just forcing an aesthetic directly. The IMP framework (Elson, Breuer, Ivory, Quandt, 2014) is better suited to understand how cutscenes and other external forces influence the experience outside of the MDA loop.

Designers: From Aesthetics to Mechanics

Hunicke et al. state that "From the designer's perspective, the mechanics give rise to dynamic system behavior, which in turn leads to particular aesthetic experiences."

This progression from mechanics to dynamics to aesthetics can also be seen as a product of its time, although the argument is weaker. Modern approaches to game design have shown the importance of working backwards from a strong aesthetic goal. Matt Thorson, creator of *Towerfall* and *Celeste* described his process in a GDC talk in 2018 (Thorson, 2018). He starts with the experience that he wants players to have and then iterates his levels until they properly evoke the intended reaction. Each mechanic in *Celeste* such as dashing or climbing up walls is reverse derived from the final aesthetic experience.

However, this was a popular view even around the 2004 period. Tracy Fullerton's book "Game Design Workshop" quickly emphasizes that the first thing a designer should do is set "player experience goals": the type of experience that players will have during the game, or in other words, aesthetics (Fullerton, 2004). This is mirrored in Jesse Schell's "The Art of Game Design," where the very second chapter is titled "The Designer Creates An Experience" (Schell, 2008). Even outside of games, we can see the same kind of division between aesthetics/experiences and mechanics/handicraft in Scott McCloud's "Understanding Comics", where out of six steps, the idea is first and the form is second (McCloud, 1993). All of these established works of knowledge focus on the designer's ability to conceptualize a central vision and lay out the path carefully and deliberately.

Hunicke et al.'s argument, that designers start with mechanics which lead to dynamics which lead to aesthetics, seems haphazard in comparison. Is the designer supposed to throw together a bunch of mechanics with no plan or direction and just hope that it ends up being fun? There are several prominent modern designers who are exploring that exact question. Frank Lantz casts doubt on "the iconic image of the designer - smart, confident, sophisticated, stylish, informed" in his post "Against Design", and argues that perhaps we should say that games are discovered or composed rather than designed (Lantz, 2015).

This perspective exists because it is built on top of the previous one. There cannot be an "Against Design" if there is not a "Design" in the first place. Once we realize the limits of our ability to build aesthetics, we can come back to the mechanics-first approach. But starting with mechanics from the very beginning is hardly designing: it is only throwing a game together and hoping it sticks (Pulsipher, 2016).

Naturally, every game production has a different process: some start with aesthetics, some start with mechanics, some with a different approach altogether. However, when Hunicke et al. propose that designers start with mechanics, they don't acknowledge this full range of possibilities. They would not have been able to do so in a short workshop paper, but unfortunately that short workshop paper seems to have developed more traction than expected.

PEDAGOGICAL PROBLEMS

Through these twists and turns, this focus on mechanics has led to several subtle mindsets around game design which are harmful to the learning process. These are only a few mindsets that I have identified, and they are caused by a multitude of factors, not just MDA. However, we can see their effects propagating throughout the game design community, even into academia.

Lack of Resonance

From a philosophical perspective, artwork mirrors design in the way that it focuses on delivering a core experience. This is echoed in fields from poetry (Poe, 1846) to novels (Forster, 1985) to games, as discussed previously. When prospective designers focus on mechanics rather than aesthetics, they lose sight of this goal, causing their works to suffer from a lack of resonance.

We can see an explicit example of this effect in the *Super Mario Maker* games, which allow players to create 2D sidescrolling levels using characters, obstacles, and environments from the *Mario* series. These games are spaces for players to apply their knowledge of game design and create new, interesting levels using the same tools that Nintendo's designers use. However, *Super Mario Maker* games are infamous for being filled with low-quality levels (Thomson, 2015). In this case, quality does not refer to the overall level of production and polish, but rather the degree to which the design resonates with the player experience.

There are many forms of low-quality design. Some authors will create levels that are empty except for rows of coins that spell out their name. Others will create "automatic levels" which are elaborate Rube Goldberg machines that propel Mario to the finish through no player input whatsoever. Although these levels can become popular through spectacle and complexity, they are still a far cry from the types of experiences that made the mainline *Mario* games famous. These types of levels exist to make the designer feel clever about themselves, rather than the player.

Kaizo-style levels are a form of low-quality design that represents the problems of a lack of resonance, and the mechanics-first perspective. These levels are characterized by absurd difficulty, with hidden traps and unexpected deaths which are intended to frustrate the player (Newman, 2018). It is no wonder that Kaizo-style design doesn't exist in professional game design, and that it emerged from ROM hacking and pranks played on friends. Fullerton describes the role of a game designer as "an advocate for the player," (Fullerton, 2004) which is practically the complete opposite of a Kaizo-style level.

For this discussion, it is important to note that Kaizo-style levels are built using an extremely wide array of available mechanics. The solution typically involves some kind of unexpected interaction, including glitches, which involves multiple different mechanics. Since these interactions are so obscure, these levels are extremely difficult not only to beat, but to figure out how to beat.

This style of design is nearly the complete opposite of Nintendo's style, where each level revolves around the exploration of a small set of mechanics, gradually building up on top of each other to form a smooth difficulty curve. In an interview, the director Koichi Hayashida explained how he used four-panel comic structures as an inspiration for *Super Mario 3D Land* levels (Nutt, 2012). Each level introduces a new mechanic, ramps up the difficulty slightly, adds an unexpected twist, then finishes with a display of mastery. Even though Hayashida named this specific structure, other game designers have been using similar models of progression across all sorts of genres or styles.

There is a reasonable argument that a person who creates Kaizo-style levels is not practicing game design. While it is certainly better to create Kaizo-style levels than to create nothing at all, the mechanics-driven approach leads to a dead end because of a lack of resonance. Outside of *Super Mario Maker*, this same sentiment can be seen in the myth of the game design document, where aspiring designers believe that if they can fill out a form describing all of the aspects of their game, then they will be well on their way towards a finished product. Jesse Schell explicitly attacks this mentality (2008), arguing that design is a continuous process and must remain fluid. A list of mechanics neglects the aesthetic vision, and adhering to such a document can be dangerous.

Trophy Productions

I use the term "trophy productions" to temporarily discuss the production of games (or other forms of entertainment) where the process of creation is treated with greater regard than the actual result. This leads to a project which is seen much like a trophy: interesting to look at and discuss from a distance, but not necessarily usable as a tangible product.

This problem has plagued the field of interactive emergent narrative, which is an academic discipline which seeks to use games to create stories alongside the player rather than thrusting the player into a prewritten story. Interactive emergent narratives rely heavily on AI, not only for depicting individual characters but also for acting in a managerial/directorial role. These interactions closely follow the path which is charted in the MDA paper's treatment of AI: a designer cannot actually cause an AI to execute any specific behavior, but must work on the level of code and rules.

Ryan, Mateas, and Wardrip-Fruin feared that the field was judging its successes by the craftsmanship of successful simulations, rather than the interactive experience of a human player (Ryan et al, 2015). As a concrete example, we can see this situation in *Façade*, one of the earliest successes of interactive emergent narrative (Mateas & Stern, 2005). *Façade* is a game in which the player is a dinner guest at a dysfunctional couple's apartment, and may intervene as much or as little as they wish in order to defuse a routine argument. The simulation is built in order to dynamically follow dramatic narrative structures, pulling the player into new story beats.

Technically, *Façade* fulfills the fantasy of interactive emergent narrative, which is why we still consider it to be the foremost example of the field even despite its age. However, the original authors quickly realized that the actual experience of playing *Façade* was far different from what they intended. Players should have felt like a heartbroken friend, sad to see a couple breaking apart in front of them and desperate to repair their relationship. If the player places themselves in such a role, they can experience *Façade* in its fully realized glory.

But most players did not do this (El-Nasr, Milam, Maygoli, 2013). They struggled to figure out the system, or they treated the conversation like a puzzle game, or they pushed the boundaries of absurdist humor. In the end, *Façade* is more of a beneficial project for the field rather than an enjoyable playable product.

Although *Façade* does not map neatly into the MDA framework, it represents a high-level focus on systems over experiences. Coming back to game design education, we can see a similar focus. Students may build a game not for the sake of producing a good experience, but rather just to demonstrate that they are capable of working with the technology. While this is a good way to show skills in programming or art, design is naturally difficult to perceive, as discussed in a previous section.

Overemphasis on Skill

Game scholars have dedicated great amounts of research to identifying types of fun, and Lazzaro's eight kinds of fun are even a central part of the original MDA paper. However, the current consumer dialogue around game mechanics places a greater focus on fun through skillful play, even if it comes at the cost of fun through other means. While fun from skillful play is a useful tool in a designer's kit, it is only one aspect of games, and a designer must be able to wield many.

We can observe a prominent and recent example of this in the *Fortnite: Battle Royale* community. *Fortnite: BR* is a multiplayer shooter game where players collect resources such as ammunition or crafting components, which let them fight more effectively. Some time after the game's launch, the developers added "siphon," a mechanic which automatically transfers a player's materials to their killer if they are defeated. This can be said to have led to the dynamic of snowballing, where stronger players are able to maintain their lead by continuing to kill, rather than having to stop and lose time to collect resources after every skirmish. The aesthetic is that better players (those who are better at the "mechanics" of aiming, shooting, and building) can enjoy rapid sequences of action, whereas worse players spend comparatively long periods of time on resource gathering.

Siphon was removed from the game later, which caused a public opinion backlash in the *Fortnite: BR* community (spread across Twitter, Reddit, and other forums). Experienced players enjoyed siphon because it rewarded them for skillful play, whereas inexperienced players typically didn't self-select themselves into these communities in the first place. This is exemplified in a tweet by Daequan Loco, a professional *Fortnite: BR* player under the Team Solo Mid organization (Loco, 2019):

One day game developers will realize that you can't protect noobs from getting bopped. You add ranked, people will smurf. You separate casual and ranked, ppl will just go bot farm in casuals. You try to change game mechanics to save them, you ruin your game. History doesn't lie! - Daequan Loco

Daequan speaks with slang, which I will explain briefly. "Noobs" is a short way to say "newbies," which in turn is a short way to say "new player." This comes with a connotation of low skill, so "noobs" has actually evolved to be an insult rather than an objective statement: even highly experienced players can be called noobs if they make a blunder. "Bopped" refers to being defeated, especially in a humiliating one-sided manner. A player who is "smurfing" has manipulated the system in order to play against opponents at a lower skill level, which often results in a one-sided victory, or in other terms, a Smurf bopping noob. The terms "ranked," "casual," and "bot farm" are not as closely related to the topic at hand.

This example demonstrates a player/consumer attempting to make statements from a designer/creator perspective, but using the term "game mechanics" in the wrong context. On a pedantic level, the designers of *Fortnite: BR* were not necessarily trying to change game mechanics: they were trying to change the game aesthetics of the strong trampling the weak, which resulted in a need to change game dynamics, which resulted in a need to change game mechanics. Although this is only a minor misunderstanding, it indicates a misguided focus.

However, putting that aside, this tweet is still problematic because it is blatantly incorrect that "protecting noobs from getting bopped" will "ruin your game." Game designers devote great amounts of effort into ensuring that the path of mastery follows a smooth curve. This is the core concept of psychological flow (Chen, 2006) and the reason why learning is fun (Koster, 2003). Players are supposed to get better over time, the challenge is supposed to match their skill level, if it's too hard they experience anxiety, if it's too easy they experience boredom. The player has used the concept of mechanics in terms of skill in order to discuss the concept of mechanics in terms of design. Since these two concepts are different, the player fails to realize some of the most basic principles of game design.

There are plenty of historical examples of games that have found success by "protecting noobs from getting bopped." Virtually every game that has a reasonably-designed difficulty curve can be argued to have used such an approach. *Fortnite: BR* itself has not been ruined in the months since removing siphon. Many multiplayer games develop advanced matchmaking algorithms to keep new players separated from experienced ones (Menke, 2017). In player-vs-player modes for the *Gears of War* games, new players are given a damage boost to put them on the same level as more experienced ones, and combat is fast enough that people typically don't notice (Scheurle, 2018). By formal and informal standards, none of these games can be said to have been ruined by introducing an easing curve for new players.

A new player may be unskilled, but they still deserve to have fun and enjoy the game's experience. Professional players like Daequan are primarily concerned with winning, and winning is often conflated with entertainment. Skill and entertainment do not need to be linearly related, and entertainment is not a zero-sum resource. But if we swap the words around, skill and winning are linearly related, and winning is a zero-sum resource. The fallacy is that winning and entertainment should be treated as separate concepts, but the word "mechanics" is not sufficient by itself to reveal those differences.

PEDAGOGICAL SOLUTIONS

As teachers, being aware of the problem is the first step towards fixing it. MDA has spread various misconceptions about game design, whether through unfortunate misinterpretations or faulty logic in the paper itself. Instead of teaching MDA as an unquestioned part of a course syllabus, we can use it as a stepping stone to illustrate the divide between players and designers.

Reinforcing MDA Through Programming

Game design curriculums often neglect the importance of code, such as how Drexel renamed the Game Art major to Game Design. Full Sail University also keeps game art and game design closely related. However, MDA shows us a different perspective, because in the strictest sense, mechanics are code. When a designer is able to program, they are able to see the ramifications of decisions that they never would have considered. A single change in a mechanic can cause a butterfly effect to drastically change the player's experience.

For example, imagine that a student is designing some kind of card game, along the lines of *Hearthstone* or *Magic: The Gathering*. These types of games are filled with specific rules and orders to resolve certain interactions. One card may say "at the beginning of your next turn, gain five health" and the enemy may play a card that says, "at the beginning of your opponent's next turn, they lose five health." Which card resolves first, and why? If the player in question has less than five health at the time, this could be a win-or-lose situation.

Either way could completely change a player's tactics, which would in turn change that player's emotional experience. If the designer was not experienced in programming, they might not have realized that this was a decision between mechanics. They might have written these card effects in a document and handed it off to their programmer, who doesn't realize the ramifications of prioritizing one over the other. A designer with no programming knowledge does not recognize the choice, and a programmer with no design knowledge does not care about the choice. This is why MDA was originally written with a specific focus on AI developers coming from a programming background.

Other companies are already moving in directions that integrate game design and programming. Riot Games, creator of *League of Legends*, develops champions with teams called DNA (design, narrative, art) where the designer fulfills the roles of a programmer (Riot, 2017). Brian Schwab also argues for a greater degree of interaction between designers and programmers, and suggests the creation of a "technical designer" role to properly bridge the gap (Schwab, 2014). Colleges and universities can keep up by putting prospective game designers through a deeper programming background, with emphasis on interactivity through quick projects like game jams.

Emphasizing Emerging Gameplay/Design

An instructor could also explore the design-oriented questions from section 4.2 and present both perspectives: aesthetics-first, or mechanics-first. The mechanics-first approach could be discussed using the term "emergence," which has unique implications from a programming background. Emergence in programming refers to the ability for a system to create unintended behaviors based on a core set of rules. Conway's Game of Life is an iconic example of emergence (Gardner, 1970), but in video games specifically we can see the same patterns in *Middle Earth: Shadow of War*'s Nemesis System (Hoge, 2018).

Players often discuss emergent gameplay in titles like *Deus Ex* which allow them to make a wide variety of decisions. However, just like how emergent gameplay exists based on the rules of the game, we could also create emergent game design based on the rules of the class. Once students become familiar with programming, they can start to experiment with emergent game design. This could possibly be some kind of form of Exquisite Corpse, or perhaps some kind of platformer where every student is given a base template and an assignment to create some kind of obstacle. Then, the students experiment with various combinations of each other's obstacles to create levels in a collaborative manner. An exercise like this could highlight the importance of a guiding vision and its double-edged blade: on one hand it creates more cohesion, but on the other hand, sometimes some reckless experimentation will reveal a fun combination that no one would have thought to design intentionally.

Alternatives to MDA

Finally, MDA is not the only framework for understanding games. I briefly discussed Elson's IMP framework, but it is more about constructing social relationships rather than game design specifically. One exercise could ask students to develop their own synonyms for MDA to avoid the loaded definitions of "mechanics" and "aesthetics". A professor at SAE Institute renamed it to "elements, behaviors, experiences" in order to help their students understand the framework better.

One notable alternative to MDA is SSM, developed by Thomas Grip of Frictional Games (Grip, 2017). SSM stands for system, story, and mental model. The system encompasses mechanics and dynamics for gameplay, and the story encompasses the same for narrative (a mechanical in narrative is like a character, whereas a dynamic in narrative is a relationship between characters). However, the most important part is the mental model, which is a concept borrowed from psychology. Mental models represent the ways in which people make sense of the world around them and develop their own logic for why things happen. It is like the experience of an aesthetic, but it leans more heavily towards the player's perception rather than the game's actual rules. A mental model can be different from reality, and it is especially important for a game designer to recognize this and use it to their advantage.

The story is that Thomas Grip discovered this effect while working on *Amnesia: The Dark Descent*. When he was working on the sanity system, he tried various game mechanics in order to create specific dynamics, but the gameplay was either easily manipulated or unnoticeable. Eventually, he just removed all challenge from the sanity system and left it only as a visual effect. However, players did not realize this and played through the game believing that sanity would affect them, which pushed them towards interesting gameplay without having an actual mechanic driving this process. Mental models can describe behaviors that couldn't be described by the MDA framework.

CONCLUSION

MDA has been one of the most prominent game frameworks in not only industry and academia, but also player communities. We need to properly assess the impact of MDA in order to teach the next generation of game designers how to use it more effectively. In programming, we call this effect a "tech debt," when a whole system is built on top of a piece of outdated legacy code. Removing or refactoring that code could end up sending the whole system crashing down, but then you would be able to rebuild it stronger than before. The burden of handling this tech debt should fall to university teachers, who are in the best position to pinpoint this problem and turn it into a learning opportunity. MDA should be taught as one type of approach, rather than as an incontrovertible truth. Educators can use other models such as SSM (Grip, 2017) or DDE (Walk, 2017) as juxtapositions to better understand MDA and its relation to game design.

This research received no specific grant from any funding agency in the public, commercial, or not-for-profit sectors.

REFERENCES

Aarseth, E. (2012, May). A narrative theory of games. In *Proceedings of the International Conference on the Foundations of Digital Games* (pp. 129-133). ACM.

Aarseth, E., & Calleja, G. (2015, June). The Word Game: The ontology of an undefinable object. In FDG.

Buttfield-Addison, P., Manning, J., & Nugent, T. (2016, March). A better recipe for game jams: using the Mechanics Dynamics Aesthetics framework for planning. In *Proceedings of the International Conference on Game Jams, Hackathons, and Game Creation Events* (pp. 30-33). ACM. 10.1145/2897167.2897183

Chen, J. (2006). *Flow in games* (Doctoral dissertation, University of Southern California).

Cook, D. (2007). *The chemistry of game design*. Gamasutra. Retrieved from https://www.gamasutra.com/view/feature/129948/the_chemistry_of_game_design.php

Costikyan, G. (2005). I Have No Words & I Must Design. *The game design reader: A rules of play anthology*, 24.

El-Nasr, M. S., Milam, D., & Maygoli, T. (2013). Experiencing interactive narrative: A qualitative analysis of Façade. *Entertainment Computing*, 4(1), 39–52. doi:10.1016/j.entcom.2012.09.004

Elson, M., Breuer, J., Ivory, J. D., & Quandt, T. (2014). More than stories with buttons: Narrative, mechanics, and context as determinants of player experience in digital games. *Journal of Communication*, 64(3), 521–542. doi:10.1111/jcom.12096

England, L. (2014). *The door problem*. Retrieved from http://www.lizengland.com/blog/2014/04/the-door-problem/

Forster, E. M. (1985). *Aspects of the Novel* (Vol. 19). Houghton Mifflin Harcourt.

Fullerton, T. (2018). *Game design workshop: a playcentric approach to creating innovative games*. AK Peters/CRC Press.

Gardener, M. (1970). MATHEMATICAL GAMES: The fantastic combinations of John Conway's new solitaire game" life. *Scientific American, 223*, 120–123. doi:10.1038cientificamerican1070-120

Grip, T. (2017). *The SSM framework of game design*. Frictional Games. Retrieved from https://friction-algames.blogspot.com/2017/05/the-ssm-framework-of-game-design.html

Hocking, C. (2007). *Ludonarrative dissonance in Bioshock*. Typepad. Retrieved from https://clicknoth-ing.typepad.com/click_nothing/2007/10/ludonarrative-d.html

Hoge, C. (2018). *Helping players hate (or love) their nemesis* [YouTube Video]. Retrieved from https://www.youtube.com/watch?v=p3ShGfJkLcU

Hunicke, R., LeBlanc, M., & Zubek, R. (2004, July). MDA: A formal approach to game design and game research. In *Proceedings of the AAAI Workshop on Challenges in Game AI* (Vol. 4, No. 1, p. 1722).

Juul, J. (2018). The game, the player, the world: Looking for a heart of gameness. *PLURAIS-Revista Multidisciplinar, 1*(2).

Kim, B. (2015). *Understanding gamification*. ALA TechSource.

Klevjer, R. (2002, June). In Defense of Cutscenes. In *CGDC Conf*. Academic Press.

Koster, R. (2003). *Theory of fun for game design*. O'Reilly Media, Inc.

Lam, K. (2018). *Vault boy's emergence: Goldenblue's big break*. League of Legends. Retrieved from https://nexus.leagueoflegends.com/en-us/2018/09/vault-boys-emergence-goldenglues-big-break/

Lantz, F. (2015). *Against design*. Game Design Advance. Retrieved from http://gamedesignadvance.com/?p=2930cpage=1

Mateas, M., & Stern, A. (2005, June). *Structuring Content in the Façade Interactive Drama Architecture*. AIIDE.

McCloud, S. (1993). *Understanding comics: the invisible art*. Tundra Publishing.

Menke, J. (2017). *Skill, Matchmaking, and Ranking Systems Design* [YouTube video]. Retrieved from https://www.youtube.com/watch?v=-pglxege-gU

Mullich, D. (2015). *Sorry, there is no "idea guy" position in the game industry*. Retrieved from https://davidmullich.com/2015/11/23/sorry-there-is-no-idea-guy-position-in-the-game-industry/

Newman, J. (2018). Kaizo Mario Maker: ROM hacking, abusive game design and Nintendo's Super Mario Maker. *Convergence, 24*(4), 339–356. doi:10.1177/1354856516677540

Norman, D. (2013). *The design of everyday things: revised and expanded edition*. Basic Books.

Nutt, C., & Hayashida, K. (2012). The structure of fun: learning from Super Mario 3D Land's director. *Gamasutra*. Retrieved from Error! Hyperlink reference not valid.http://www.gamasutra.com/view/feature/168460/the_structure_of_fun_learning_.php

Parlett, D. (2017). What's a ludeme? Game & Puzzle Design, 2(2), 81.

Poe, E. A. (1846). The philosophy of composition.

Pulsipher, L. (2016). *Are you designing a game, or throwing one together? You can't design a game as though you were playing a video game*. Gamasutra. Retrieved from https://www.gamasutra.com/blogs/LewisPulsipher/20161214/287544/Are_you_designing_a_game_or_throwing_one_together_You_cant_design_a_game_as_though_you_were_playing_a_video_game.php

Riot Games. (2017). *Creative collaboration: making League of Legends champions* [YouTube video]. Retrieved from https://www.youtube.com/watch?v=j-k3TbFwMgI

Ryan, J. O., Mateas, M., & Wardrip-Fruin, N. (2015, November). Open design challenges for interactive emergent narrative. In *Proceedings of the International Conference on Interactive Digital Storytelling* (pp. 14-26). Springer. 10.1007/978-3-319-27036-4_2

Sahlin, M. (2017). *Unravel - using empathy as a game mechanic*. GDC Vault. Retrieved from https://www.gdcvault.com/play/1024661/-Unravel-Using-Empathy-as

Schell, J. (2008). *The art of game design: A book of lenses*. CRC Press. doi:10.1201/9780080919171

Scheurle, J. (2018). *Good game design is like a magic trick* [YouTube video]. Retrieved from https://www.youtube.com/watch?v=2YdJa7v99wM

Schwab, B. (2014). *Designers are from Saturn, programmers are from Uranus* [YouTube video]. Retrieved from https://www.youtube.com/watch?v=6b-o_-Xb50E

Suh, A., Wagner, C., & Liu, L. (2015, January). The effects of game dynamics on user engagement in gamified systems. In *Proceedings of the 2015 48th Hawaii International Conference on System Sciences* (pp. 672-681). IEEE. 10.1109/HICSS.2015.87

Thomsen, M. (2015). Super Mario Maker is an engine for circulating horrible new Mario levels. *The Washington Post*.

Thorson, M. (2018). *Level design workshop: Designing Celeste* [YouTube video]. Retrieved from https://www.youtube.com/watch?v=4RlpMhBKNr0

TSM_Daequan. (2019, March 29). One day game developers will realize that you can't protect noobs from getting bopped. You add ranked, people will smurf. You separate casual and ranked, ppl will just go bot farm in casuals. You try to change game mechanics to save them, you ruin your game.🎮♂️History doesn't lie! [Tweet]. Retrieved from https://twitter.com/tsm_daequan/status/1111744197294346240?lang=en

Walk, W., Görlich, D., & Barrett, M. (2017). Design, Dynamics, Experience (DDE): an advancement of the MDA framework for game design. In *Game Dynamics* (pp. 27–45). Cham: Springer. doi:10.1007/978-3-319-53088-8_3

Williams, A. (2017). *History of digital games: Developments in art, design and interaction*. Routledge. doi:10.1201/9781315715377

ADDITIONAL READING

De Koven, B. (2013). *The well-played game: A player's philosophy*. MIT Press. doi:10.7551/mitpress/9722.001.0001

Juul, J. (2011). *Half-real: Video games between real rules and fictional worlds*. MIT Press.

Sellers, M. (2017). *Advanced Game Design: A Systems Approach*. Addison-Wesley Professional.

Sylvester, T. (2013). *Designing games: A guide to engineering experiences*. O'Reilly Media, Inc.

KEY TERMS AND DEFINITIONS

AI: Artificial intelligence, a system which makes decisions independently based on its directed goals. Game AIs can focus on problem solving or user experience: in chess, a problem-solving AI will find the most optimal move, whereas a user experience AI will make moves that are fun and interesting to play against.

Aesthetics: The experiences and emotions which emerge out of dynamics.

Dynamics: The behaviors and tactics which emerge out of mechanics.

Emergence: The capacity for a system to produce outputs which were unexpected by the original designers.

Game Design: The process of ensuring that a game has a unified core theme, reinforces that theme throughout the act of playing, and delivers that theme intact to the player.

Game Development: The process of creating a game, including design, art, programming, and production, but typically not including marketing, PR, and manufacturing.

Fun: The subjective experience of enjoyment, often redefined by each individual designer. Notably, Raph Koster defines fun as learning, and the MDA paper introduces a taxonomy (including but not limited to sensation, fantasy, narrative, challenge, fellowship, discovery, expression, submission).

Mechanics: The rules and pieces of a game.

This research was previously published in Interactivity and the Future of the Human-Computer Interface; pages 190-205, copyright year 2020 by Engineering Science Reference (an imprint of IGI Global).

Chapter 59

The Role of Narrative Elements in Gamification Towards Value Co-Creation:
A Case of Mobile App Users in Malaysia

Cheah Wen Kit
Universiti Sains Malaysia, Malaysia

Izzal Asnira Zolkepli
Universiti Sains Malaysia, Malaysia

ABSTRACT

This article discusses the role of narrative element in gamification towards value co-creation in a crowdsourcing application system. The discourse addresses the gap of knowledge to understand the user motivation and experience to co-create value in a gamified system. Value co-creation is an interactive engagement process that refers to the act of collaborating with a group of intended consumers through a crowdsourcing approach. As the decentralisation of the web enables participation of people to shape the future based on their contributions, understanding Internet users' motivation and experience to co-create value is crucial in ensuring that the initiatives are reciprocated by the intended parties. As gamification has been widely utilised in numerous contexts in order to encourage users to contribute their resources of knowledge and skills, the effectiveness of its elements, namely narrative, remains questionable.

INTRODUCTION

The gaming industry is one of the fastest growing and emerging industries that connects Internet users from all over the world. Anyone with Internet connectivity is able to experience an immersive platform that offers fun and enjoyable moments. Understanding the penetration that the gaming industry has on the players, firms are leveraging on numerous gaming and gamification platforms to ensure the sustenance of their business through the customers value co-creation.

DOI: 10.4018/978-1-6684-7589-8.ch059

As the fourth industrial revolution (termed as Industry 4.0), is transforming communication from all areas, understanding online user engagement is crucially important to achieve effective collaboration between the firm and its target market for any intended purpose. Given its rapid growth, research efforts to extricate the complexity of digital communication between humans to humans, humans to machines, and machines and machines is intensified more than ever. For instance, the deployment of artificial intelligence (A.I.) is changing the immersive state of user during connectivity. Each smartphone user nowadays is carrying a personal A.I. in his or her pocket, which makes acquisition and dissemination of knowledge conveniently and swiftly. Advanced technology tools that rely on rich interactive media to connect with online users are gradually blurring the line between the virtual and real-world experience. The information that is found on numerous online platforms are based on the contribution of the users to other users. As users are more likely to engage with the information provided from other users, firms and content providers are heavily relying on the knowledge possessed by other users. One of the effective ways that firms use to motivate the initiative of other users to contribute their knowledge and skills in a collaborative platform is through the use of gamification, a process that draws the potential of games in non-game contexts.

Understanding the potential of gamification would be beneficial for firms in leveraging the game design elements to encourage engagement and induce immersion among its users to co-create value in marketing communication approach. In brief, a game refers to physical or mental contest that has goal or objective, whereby an individual or a group of individuals will play according to a pre-determined framework or rules in the game world (Huzinga, 1970). The use of game elements in practical context is called gamification. The fundamental understanding of how and why certain users behave in a gamified environment is only at the tip of the iceberg. Therefore, researchers are calling for more in-depth research into this context that was derived from the rapid progress of the world wide web technology.

The advancement of Semantic Web, which is also referred as Web 3.0, that witnesses more intelligent and intuitive application system is empowering users towards seamless user experience to reach more targeted communication goal. Such democratisation of the Internet enables all users to connect dynamically with each other, including in the context of business to consumers (B2C) and consumers to consumers (C2C), in which the connectivity between users happens in split seconds to reach the intended objectives. At one time, countless of information exchange processes takes place that help firms to understand its users or consumers better. For instance, a search engine understands the thinking patterns of the users better than the users would aware. It is able to predict the user's search patterns thereby offering possible findings of consumer behaviours at a rapid pace. From the firm's perspective, developers and marketers are able to understand users in greater detail with the assistance of big data, which is intensified by the decentralisation of the Internet.

As the decentralisation of the web enables participation of the people to shape the future based on their very own behaviours, understanding Internet users' psychological aspects, namely their motivation and experience in the dissemination of knowledge is crucial to spread the message on pressing global issues, such as on sustainable development in the age of urbanisation in emerging countries such as Malaysia.

Malaysia is holding the number one position in terms of its economic standing among the emerging markets due to her stable economic growth according to Bloomberg (2018).

The engagement and contribution of skills and knowledge from the people through value co-creation are vital to ensure the success of sustainability development initiatives. Since Sustainable Development Goals (SDG) was introduced by the United Nations in September 2015, firms from the developing nations have initiated numerous initiatives to tackle environmental issues such as on reducing carbon footprint from the use of transportation.

Since the penetration of Internet stands at close to 50 percent in Asia, which is the highest in the world (Miniwatts Marketing Group, 2018), a research from an emerging market in Asia such as Malaysia to investigate the effectiveness of marketing communication messages to encourage engagement pertaining to green issues is highly needed. As Malaysia is gearing towards developed nation that is bound to experience even more pressing green issues, namely sustainable consumption, pro-environmental effort from all parties, including government, firms and the people, the collaboration between all parties is highly needed, especially that collaborative green behaviour is integral in combating sustainable development issues on local and global front (Klöckner, 2013). While policymakers in Malaysia are intensifying the efforts to inculcate green behaviours by introducing numerous green initiatives such as through Environmental Protection Plan (The Star, 2018), it is argued that the initiatives would continue to face behavioral response setbacks if the people do not co-create value with the government or any organisations that attempt to tackle this issue, which greatly requires collaborative efforts. It was reported that green attitude has been found to be one of the key factors in determining environmental practices (Choe & Yap, 2018). Although it was surveyed that the majority of Malaysians are giving their moral support to the zero single use plastic campaign by the government (Malay Mail, 2019), it is unknown if the people are behaviorally contributing to the cause. Past studies have shown that environmental awareness among Malaysians are negatively correlated with their environmental behaviour, an indicator which has been a concern for policymakers in order to ensure the success of the green initiatives that will soon to implement in the future (Mei, Wai, & Ahamad, 2016).

One of the approaches that can be leveraged to encourage response in the context of green initiative is through the implementation of gamification. Since there are a number of gamification elements, namely through the use of points, badges, leaderboards, performance graphs, avatars, teammates, and meaningful stories (also referred to as narrative), practitioners are able to design the most appropriate strategies to execute an effective approach to motivate online users to co-create value in a given context. It has been reported that the commonly used gamification element, which are points and leaderboards (Morschheuser, Hamari, Koivisto, & Maedche, 2017), have demonstrated positive results to encourage value co-creation in gamified crowdsourcing system. However, for a gamification strategy to be well-designed that ensures continuous user engagement, other gamification elements needs to be investigated to ensure its effectiveness. While the gaming industry has been utilising the story element, the use of gamification is still at its infancy stage and warrants for further investigation. Although narrative element is often used in numerous gamification approach for value co-creation, it requires further understanding on its effectiveness. As to date, there is no empirical research that has been conducted in this context. In addition, the psychological outcomes from the integration of story element needs to be investigated for the validation of this approach. Therefore, the present article aims to shed light on the discourse gap by discussing the effectiveness of the story element in gamification towards value co-creation, which focuses on the user experiences in driving collaboration.

VALUE CO-CREATION

Value co-creation is a novel paradigm that is highly discussed by researchers from numerous disciplines, especially in marketing communication, management, and information system (Galvagno & Dalli, 2014).

Value creation is vital to ensure the sustainability of a firm through service offer, which is a fundamental basis of exchange (Vargo & Lusch, 2004). Generally, researchers agree that value co-creation is a process that refers to a collaborative process between an initiator and its actors, an umbrella term that refers to individual consumers, groups of consumers, brand communities, employees, and suppliers, among others (Storbacka, Brodie, Böhmann, Maglio, & Nenonen, 2016). Service marketing researchers highlighted that it is a process that serves as a way to increase value between the service provider and the intended consumer (Deng, Lu, Wei, & Zhang, 2010; Hollebeek & Andreassen, 2018). To further explain, Brodie, Hollebeek, Jurić, and Ilić (2011) mentioned that value co-creation is an interactive, creative and social process between stakeholders, which include consumers, suppliers and investors. Galvagno and Dalli (2014) have explored the definition by mentioning that it is a "joint, collaborative, concurrent, peer-like process of producing new value, both materially and symbolically". In brief, it is agreed that value co-creation is a way to increase value between the service provider and the intended consumer (Payne, Storbacka, & Frow, 2008; Vargo & Lusch, 2004). From the definitions gathered, it signifies that value co-creation is in reference of an interactive process that involves several parties in a multidimensional dissemnination of message that goes beyond dyadic communication (Li, Juric, & Brodie, 2017).

The success of value co-creation is highly dependent on the voluntary participation of the intended stakeholders. The emergence of new technologies such as Web 3.0, blockchain technology, big data, and social media are offering numerous new opportunities for value co-creation on various online platforms (Geri, Gafni, & Bengov, 2017; Xu, He, & Li, 2014).

Each of the constructs used in the value co-creation concept needs to be further discussed. Value can be referred to the utilitarian or hedonic aspect of the outcome, which is the creation, whereas "co-" refers to the actors, which is also the customers, who are collaborating with the initiator (Islam, Rahman, & Hollebeek, 2018). The process is aimed towards developing beneficial collaborative behaviour as intended by the initiator.

In line with the fundamental understanding described by Storbacka et al. (2016), value co-creation is an approach that creates offerings through ideation, design and development through customer engagement. Based on the mentioned descriptions of value co-creation in past literatures, the researchers tend to view consumers from a capitalistic point of view. Customers are perceived as 'partner employee' that is able to contribute to their supply chain of business. Hence, the psychological characteristics of the co-creators needs to be explored as these would ensure a continuously healthy and interactive process between the parties involved (Bendapudi & Leone, 2003; France, Grace, Merrilees, & Miller, 2018; Heinonen, 2018).

A definite conceptualisation of value co-creation is still incomplete as it fails to capture the psychological state of the co-creator, which is termed as actor disposition (Chandler & Lusch, 2015; Li, Juric, & Brodie, 2018; Storbacka et al., 2016).

Value Co-Creation and Crowdsourcing Explained

While the concept of both crowdsourcing and value co-creation are often discussed in overlapping manner, it needs to be clarified that the former refers to the approach performed by an initiator, which usually would be a firm or organisation, whereas the latter refers to the act of collaboration between two or more parties. Firms are leveraging on crowdsourcing system to co-create value with their consumers in order to build online brand community (Fuller, Hutter, & Faullant, 2011; Muniz & O'Guinn, Thomas, 2001; Schau, Muniz, & Arnould, 2009). Value co-creation is made possible especially as firms crowdsource resources from the intended consumers through an open call on the Internet. The purpose of carrying out a crowdsourcing approach is usually to innovate a product, service, or content by sourcing for ideas and solutions from the stakeholder's core competencies, such as expertise, knowledge and skills (Brabham, 2008; Duverger, 2015). Co-creation of value would be able to offer competitive advantage for the initiator as its collective outcome is catered to the consumers for a more personalised service.

Crowdsourcing was introduced by Jeff Howe in 2006 when he wrote an article on Wired magazine that caught the attention of many industry players (Howe, 2006). He sheds light on the rise of online platforms with the likes of iStockphoto, whereby publishers are able to source for user-submitted photos at a exceptionally low price rate instead of paying much higher to a photographer to capture the intended shots. The publisher ended up paying for only one dollar to the original owner of the photos instead of hundreds of dollars to a professional. These images are contributed by the Internet users on a dedicated website to showcase their talents and be discovered by industry players, aside from getting paid for their work. Another platform that rode on this dynamic approach was Innocentive, a website that allows industry players such as Procter and Gamble, DuPoint and Boeing to seek contributors' solution on the posted scientific, business and technical problems with a pre-determined prize money as incentive. Some of these problems seek to solve pressing global green issues. Hence, any Internet user who has solutions to the posted problems are able to contribute towards sustainable development while being rewarded for their resources, such as knowledge, skills, time and energy. Such phenomena have disrupted the market whereby a once confined industry becomes more permeable and receptive to anyone among the crowds. While not all the posted problems were solved, it was reported that about 30 percent of the problems were solved through the submitted ideas and solutions. However, 30 percent is still considered low compared to the high number of Internet users around the world who has untapped knowledge, skills and ideas. While offering prize money would be an easy solution to encourage value co-creation through user contribution, the downside would surface when the initiator does not possess sufficient financial resources for crowdsourcing. Incentivising the crowd with monetary value revolves around a carrot-and-stick method, whereby the crowd would be conditioned to only contribute ideas if there is financial reward, which many initiators, such as startups, nonprofit organisations and public-funded entities could not afford. Targeting the crowd's extrinsic motivation would be detrimental to the approach or campaign in the long run, whereby the consumers would only focus on the extrinsic reward. In order for an approach to provide the intended gameful experience, an experience that is unique to games, initiators would need to tap into the user's intrinsic motivation as well (Huotari & Hamari, 2012; Zhao & Zhu, 2014).

Realising the potential that the users possess, especially those who are enthusiastic towards contributing to a cause or brands, firms are beginning to engage their network of communities towards the company's initiatives through value co-creation that is made possible with the unique position that technology advancement offers.

With the proliferation of mobile applications (apps), websites, and social media due to the advancement of Web 3.0, the features and functionalities have been expanded with wide range of uses to encourage more users to co-create value. Understanding that the online users and consumers are demanding for more active role in an exchange of service (Labrecque, vor dem Esche, Mathwick, Novak, & Hofacker, 2013), individuals who engage with a particular Internet application are given the authority and autonomy to contribute their own ideas, skills and knowledge for a more personalised service experience (Füller & Bilgram, 2017). Such an approach takes steps forward to ensure that users are intrinsically motivated to co-create value. In addition, it leads to a win-win situation whereby the initiator is able to acquire the knowledge and skills from the users through their contributions and the users are able to enjoy a personalised service for a better experience. Without a doubt, value co-creation is growing at a rapid pace.

Researchers and marketers are beginning to understand the limitless harnessing potential that they are able to source from the online communities to ensure the success of their campaigns. For instance, a German-based skincare brand Nivea that is globally recognised for its extensive research and development efforts has been pushing boundaries with their technology-driven innovation capabilities. The firm has managed to hit the most successful sales from their 130-year history of product launch as they co-create a new deodorant with the consumers. Japanese consumer brand called Muji has also reported that the sales from its co-created products are higher than the internally developed ones.

Theoretical Underpinning of Value Co-Creation: Service-Dominant Logic

According to Vargo and Lusch (2004), value is no longer determined only when the delivery of goods or tangible products reaches the stakeholders. Goods are viewed as the transmitter of knowledge, but not as the end product, in a value creation process. That is, any form of products and services delivered to the stakeholders is categorised as service. The novel marketing theory builds on the fundamental understanding that service is uniquely derived from the delivery of goods (Hansen, 2017). This new understanding of logic is viewed as the Service-Dominant (S-D) Logic, which is stimulating discussions from marketing and management researchers (Baron, Patterson, Warnaby, & Harris, 2010; Cheah & Zolkepli, 2018; Grönroos, 2006; Payne et al., 2008).

Vargo and Lusch (2008) defined service as the application of competence, such as through knowledge and skills, in benefiting the service recipients. Hence, regardless if it is a goods-based (tangible) or service-based (intangible) product, the logic postulates that the firm is delivering value.

S-D Logic is viewed as a transcendence of goods-dominant (G-D) logic that conservatively focuses on the delivery of goods (Vargo & Lusch, 2008). The logic that has been viewed to tie the loose ends in the fragments of marketing theories appears to have broadened the understanding of values which benefit both the firms and stakeholders (Saarijärvi, Kannan, & Kuusela, 2013). In line with the paradigm shift, firms need to acknowledge the importance and potential of value in service as they communicate with their customers or prospective consumers.

Through this understanding, service is viewed as a unit of exchange, whereas goods and service products are the mediator of trade (Payne et al., 2008; Saarijärvi, Kannan, & Kuusela, 2013). In other words, consumers who are utilising, adapting, and maintaining the goods or products are determining the value created. It is no longer that the firms dictating the value of a goods or service delivery, but the customers. The basis of this customer-oriented communication gives rise to the understanding that value creation is a collaborative function between the service provider and the receiver. Hence, a service, being the common denominator, is always co-created and is never a one-way process when a trade is done.

There are five axioms or principles that form the understanding of S-D Logic which needs to be met, according to Vargo and Lusch (2008). The first one is that service is the integral unit of exchange. The second axiom states that customers or the prospective customers are always the co-creater of value. An update in the authors' foundational premise (FP) in almost a decade later suggested that value is co-created by multiple actors (Vargo & Lusch, 2016). This shows that the authors have taken into account the multidimensional communication that exists in the network, a view that is in-line with the systems perspective. The third axiom states that all actors, including industry players, service initiators, and even customers in the social and economic context are the resource integrators. In other words, they are the ones who do not merely provide the service, but consolidate and integrate the available resources through various means as well. Resources, specifically operant resources, primarily refers to knowledge and skills (Vargo & Lusch, 2016). The fourth axiom states that value is always determined by the beneficiary, who is also the co-creator, of the service in phenomenological sense. In other words, the customers of a service are always determining the value in a trade process, as mentioned earlier. While Vargo and Lusch (2008), have only mentioned four axioms in their original conceptualisation of S-D Logic, the scholars have revised the understanding of S-D Logic through the injection of the fifth axiom in the theory's foundational premise (FP), which states that "value co-creation is coordinated through actor-generated institutions and institutional arrangements" (Vargo & Lusch, 2016, p. 8). It needs to be noted that the term "institution" does not refer to an organisation but the rules, meanings, symbols, practice, and norms that are designed by humans, in enabling and constraining action in giving meaning to an individual's social life.

The central focus of the revised S-D Logic is to provide a holistic and meaning-ladden worldview of actor's experience that encourage co-creation of value (Vargo & Lusch, 2016). In line with the contemporary understanding in marketing, customer-centric firms are seeking ways to generate better engagement and experience for value co-creators (Vega-Vazquez, Revilla-Camacho, Cossío-Silva, & Cossı, 2013). The scenario is applied to the situation that involves any approach or initiative that is carried out by an organisation, including government bodies. Hence, the integrated study of experience and intrinsic motivation to co-create value with a crowdsourcing platform needs to be done to understand the antecedents of value co-creation from the actor's psychological perspective.

Motivations for Value Co-Creation

User engagement has been described to be a motivationally driven resource integration function through the interaction with a firm or organisation (Hollebeek & Andreassen, 2018). Therefore, the investigation on the motivations of an actor that influence his or her intention to co-create value with a firm shall provide more in-depth understanding on the antecedents of value co-creation. While extrinsic motivation such as obtaining the reward of money or other tangible prizes would enhance participation and involvement for users to co-create value, that is not always the case as there is no contract that abides users to integrate their resources (Zhao & Zhu, 2014). In other words, financial rewards may not always work if the actors are not intrinsically motivated to co-create value. Since users would consciously evaluate their contribution of service in the form of skills, knowledge, time and energy, practitioners would need to tap into the user's intrinsic motivation. Among the intrinsic motivations that could encourage participation in a co-creation approah include user's hedonic and utilitarian experience, the need for recognition and competition, and other forms of personal satisfaction (Zheng, Li, & Hou, 2011). A study based on the systems perspective has found that the experience of actors would be enhanced if the platform that actors engage on is able to provide usability and sociability (Zhao & Zhu, 2014). The study carried out by Zhao and Zhu (2014) showed that the two main dimensions that positively motivated the participants in a crowdsourcing contest are the attributes of hedonic and utilitarian. Concurrently, these values are able to be met through the elements of games, which is referred to as gamification (Deterding, 2011; Morschheuser et al., 2017). Immersive gamification is able to provide these functionalities towards the users. Users who are engaged on a crowdsourcing gamification platform are able to experience hedonism and utilitarianism, while being recognised in their contribution. Understanding that intrinsic motivation is able to influence participation efforts, the present article argues that actors who co-create value would be positively driven by the concept of gamification that is introduced on an interactive platform.

Gamification in Value Co-Creation

Gamification in value co-creation has been widely utilised in numerous contexts. For instance, a highly used community-based traffic and navigation mobile application called Waze is depending on the contribution of the motorist to report on the traffic conditions including congestions, road hazards, roadblocks and sharing place of interest, among others. It is reported that Waze has over 90 million global active users in 185 countries (Waze, 2018), whereas Malaysia is recorded for having the highest number of users in Asia and top 5 in the world (The Star, 2017). Realising the huge number of reach and engagement, brands are leveraging on the app for location-based marketing to advertise and target their marketing communication to the nearby users. In order to attract more users and ensure continuous usage, the app offers a variety of features and function, such as interactivity and gamification. Apart from being able to communicate with each other on the app, Waze users are granted points from every trip and contribution to the system that they make. These points would help them to level up, which makes more features available to the higher level users. The icon that represents each user would have their avatar changes as they climbs up the stage. The change in representation of the user is to signifiy that they have achieved a higher level and more features are unlocked. Users who are connected with each other on the app are also able to compare their rankings and marks on the system's leaderboard. The granting of points and the availability of leaderboards are part of the gamification affordances that are integrated in the app. Having said that, the app is not leveraging on other gamification affordance, namely story element, which is argued to be effective in sustaining usage rather than being used for pure navigation purpose. Such could be the reason as to why navigational app users in Malaysia seems to opt for Google Maps, as an online poll shows (Awani, 2019). Users do not seem to appreciate the gamification feature that the system offers, despite its high emphasis on points and leaderboard integration.

In addition, an e-hailing app in Malaysia called Grab is implementing the use of gamification features to reward loyal users. The feature is called GrabRewards membership. There are four levels in total, which are labelled as "member", "silver", "gold" and "platinum". The higher level that a user climbs enables him or her to unlock more rewards and benefits offered by the app. For instance, a "platinum" user is able to earn double the reward point through each booking, compared to a regular member. With more points earned, users are able to exchange it with a wide variety of offers such as discounts on their next Grab rides or with their partner merchants. While Grab has implemented such gamification features to ensure continuous usage among users, the use of extrinsic rewards such as financial benefit could exhaust user's motivation in the long run. Hence, firms and developers would need to tap into the use of intrinsic motivation in order for the users to continuously engaged in a long run, despite the presence of other competing players that would consume a larger market share.

In the context of green initiative, an app developer is collaborating with a non-profit environmental organisation to bring higher awareness to the public in preserving the environment through tree-planting. For instance, a Chinese-based gamification productivity app called "Forest" is in cooperation with Trees For The Future, a non-profit organisation based in Maryland of United States of America to plant trees in Africa. Apart from greening the earth, their mission is to elevate poverty. Based on the points in the form of virtual coins that users earned through their focus time during the app usage, they are able to co-create with the firm to exchange the value for tree-planting. The use of point-based system is an application of gamification that functions to encourage user's enjoyment and their focus time. The trees that they plant will wither if they happen to switch to other app when the app is in use, a phenomenon known as 'phubbing'. Such approach can be related to the use of story element whereby users are role-playing as the tree planters. It is also reported that the proceeds from the app sales has helped the organisation to purchase trees from their partners as well, apart from public donation on their green initiative. In the app and on the brand's social media profiles, Forest has integrated the narrative elements by actively describing about the trees that they offer the users to plant to ensure continuous use. However, it is not known if users are driven to use the app due to the story element, for its functional purpose, or both. It needs to be highlighted that the element of story is one of the affordances that form gamification.

Gamification Affordances Explained

Gamification affordances are the game design elements that motivates gameful experiences. These elements are the basic building blocks for games and gamified systems, in which each of them, or collectively, serves to propel the game towards its intended experience. Given its relatively novel area of study, game researchers have not come to conclusion the exact number of these elements that exists. For instance, Werbach and Hunter (2012) have suggested that there are 15 elements or components of a game, whereas Revees and Read (2009) suggested that there are 10 'ingredients' that make up an effective gamification approach. Having said that, many gamification systems do not utilize all of the available elements that exist. Based on Werbach and Hunter (2012), Sailer et al. (2017) proposed that there are seven common elements that are present in the previously discussed game literatures. The justification for the authors' selection are that these elements have direct visibility to the players, are easily activated and deactivated in experimental setting, and the ease of use in manipulating each variable to study the motivational aspect of players. For the benefit of the present context that revolves around user experience and motivation, the current study subscribes to the proposal by Sailer et al. (2017). The seven game elements are points, badges, leaderboards, performance graphs, avatars, and meaningful stories (Sailer et al., 2017).

Points is the most basic game element that is rewarded to player's based on his or her successful or accomplished task (Sailer et al., 2017; Werbach & Hunter, 2012). It serves to represent and track a player's progress numerically while providing feedback to the journey in the game. There are various types of points that have been used by game designers such as achievement or reputation points, experience points, redeemable points. There are apps that have integrated a combination of types of points as service. For instance, Grab, Southeast Asian e-hailing app that allows users to book a private ride, rewards reputation and redeemable points to its users. These points can be exchanged for ride discounts and other sales promotion discounts with their partners. Being the most basic form of game element, past research have revealed that the use of points has been shown to be effective in motivating users to participate in gamified crowdsourcing system (Morschheuser et al., 2017).

Badges are the visual representation, a sign, or symbol that indicates the achievements of the players, who would collect them throughout the game environment (Sailer et al., 2017; Werbach & Hunter, 2012). Badges visibly show player's achievement, which would give them a sense of pride and satisfaction. The use of badges would encourage continuous usage as players would be motivated to earn the available badges. However, once all the badges are earned, the motivation of players would perhaps deteriorate. Earning badges do not pose any narrative meaning. It is also not a compulsory task for players to journey forward in the gamified environment (Sailer et al., 2017). For instance, the use of badges is evident in the Forest app, a co-creative productivity app that encourages users to focus on a self-determined time.

Once users have achieved a targeted focus time, badges are awarded. However, these badges do not propel the gameplay journey forward as they are not necessary to be collected.

Leaderboards is a game element that quantifies players' success according to their achievements (Sailer et al., 2017). The quantification may be calculated through points or other forms or measurable outcomes. In other words, the utilisation of leaderboard is useful in ranking users against certain success criterion. It is able to create a competitive environment among the players while providing users a sense of pride and satisfaction in the gamified network. However, it might not be an effective gamification affordance as the usage motivation would deplete once a player reaches the highest level of the leaderboard. In the case of Waze the the gamified navigation app, a player or user would climb the leaderboard based on the distance that the person has travelled. The distance is converted into points for leaderboard quantification. There are five rankings that a user may reach. It is argued that once a user has reached the highest level in the leaderboard, the sense of excitement and hedonic experience of users who focus on this element would deplete as there will be no motivating factor in driving the gameplay journey.

Performance graphs contains information that is used to compare the player's current performance against their preceding performance (Sailer et al., 2017). It does not compare the said player's performance with other players but with his or her own previous performance so that the player is able to evaluate the achievement thus far. In a networked game environment that involves the participation of multi-players, it is argued that the sole use of performance graph might not be suitable as a main or focal game design element to encourage a strong motivation and optimal experience for continuous usage.

Avatar represents players visually in a gamification or gamified environment through the use of a virtual character (Sailer et al., 2017; Werbach & Hunter, 2012). Avatars are either assigned by the game designer or chosen by the player. Avatars can be depicted as a simple pictogram or complex three-dimensional animation (Werbach & Hunter, 2012). In certain games such as a popular simulation game *The Sims*, highly-rated strategy game *PlayerUnknown Battleground* or briefly known as *PUBG*, or even a networked simulation game called *Second Life*, players are allowed to customise their own avatars. The function of customisation is to set their avatar apart from other players in the network. The use of avatars would give users a sense of immersive experience in creating and adopting their own identity in becoming part of the game environment (Sailer et al., 2017). While the use of avatar is argued to be able to contribute towards user's optimal experience in the gameplay, it is not compulsory for game designers to introduce this element towards inducing a complete gameful experience.

Teammates refers to the use of other human or computer players to induce conflict, competition or cooperation (Kapp, 2012). The introduction of teams is able to foster collaboration among players towards a shared goal or objective (Werbach & Hunter, 2012). The use of teammates as game design element is apparent in most networked games. In fact, as most of the mobile games are connected over the Internet, it is easy for game designers to utilise this teammates to make a gameplay more interesting. While it is not the focus of the present study, it needs to be acknowledged that the use of teammates would influence a player's gameful experience.

Meaningful stories refers to the use of narrative element that gives and expresses the meaning of a game that goes beyond the quest for points and quantifiable achievements (Kapp, 2012; Sailer et al., 2017). While it does not relate to the player's performance, the use of meaningful stories as game element could enrich gameful experience and further motivate the players towards engagement (Sailer et al., 2017). Being an important element of gamification, the implementation of story is said to be more engaging if it was applied in a less stimulating non-game contexts. The overlay of narrative element is able to alter the real-world meaning while immersing the players towards value co-creation (Hansen, 2017; Sailer et al., 2017). The relationship between stories and human behaviour has been acknowledged, but not as cause and effect (Hansen, 2017). Stories is arguably to be able to influence behaviour as it organises perceptions and would symbolically restructure one's experience (Jackson, 2013). The understanding of how stories influence behaviour needs to be investigated.

Sailer et al. (2017) have conducted a study to investigate the effect of game elements on human motivation and performance using an online simulation. The authors have grouped the game design elements based on the focus of the study, which were psychological need satisfaction, which are the need for competence and autonomy in a gameplay. The need for competence revolves around the feedback that the players would be getting. On the other hand, the need for autonomy involves two aspects, which are experience of decision freedom and experience of task meaningfulness. It was found that badges, leaderboards, and performance graphs yield positive effect on competence need satisfaction and task meaningfulness. Whereas, avatars, teammates, and meaningful stories game elements have shown to affect experience and social relatedness. While the grouping of game design elements appeared to be relevant towards investigating both study variables, it is still unclear how individual game design element could afford specific outcomes, such as user motivation and optimal experiences as users participate in a gamified system. In the context value co-creation, it is proclaimed that value is deconstructed through stories (Hansen, 2017).

Story Immersion as Gamification Affordances

In order to win a game, players need to draw information presented to them as they navigate the gaming world. The information are often times given through a form of storyline. Hence, video game creators would need to employ interesting and immersive storyline in the dynamic, role-playing medium of gameplay (Baranowski, Buday, Thompson, & Baranowski, 2008). As a narrative series of events, a story functions to give meaning to a wide range of context, including gamification (Deterding, 2011; Green & Brock, 2000; Lu, Baranowski, Thompson, & Budday, 2012). A story takes place at a particular time (such as before World War II, during graduation, at year end), particular place (in a starship, on a mountain, in the prison), and usually has a character that lead the story forward, called the protagonist (Baranowski et al., 2008). Other character that opposes the protagonist is called antagonist. The struggle between both protagonist and antagonist refers to conflict, which is the motivating factor behind a story's plot.

A story is able to engage individuals by forming empathy with the protagonist. The engagement is even stronger and more effective when there is a change of value in the protagonist, such as being failure to a successful, betrayal to loyalty, cowardice to courage, so that the viewers or audiences is able to relate and exemplify the lessons to be learned from the story (Baranowski et al., 2008). The changes in value is usually presented as the protagonist's internal conflict. This conflict would be the common barriers towards individual's behaviour change (Baranowski et al., 2008). The change of behaviour as argued by Baranowski et al., (2008) implies that an individual would respond behaviorally upon presented persuasive message contained in the story. In this vein, the engaged individuals are immersed by the story element. The behavioral response as influenced by the story is argued to have the potential in engaging individuals towards value co-creation (Green & Brock, 2000; Lu et al., 2012).

In the context of game, the utilisation of narrative element in a gamification is able to transcend fantasy to the real-world scenario. It is said to be able to serve as analogies in the virtual world for user's understanding of the physical world (Sailer et al., 2017). While it is an emerging trend, there are not many studies to investigate that effectiveness of story element in gamified application systems which employ the use of story element to immerse players for continuous engagement. Although story element has been mentioned as one of the gamification affordances in numerous gamification literature (Morschheuser et al., 2017; Sailer et al., 2017), little to none empirical findings is found on the effectiveness this element. It remains questionable if users are driven to co-create value through a presented story element in gamification (Lu et al., 2012). Such gap of knowledge needs to be investigated especially that the common component of games is the story element (McKee, 1997). Now that everyone is able to create stories through user-generated content as mentioned earlier, an investigation on this gamification affordance is integral for co-creation of value approach. Hence, the present article encourages researchers to investigate the effectiveness of story immersion as an enabler in gamification towards value co-creation among online users. The studies would be beneficial to find out how users who are immersed in the narrative element during the process of gamification would respond to a call for collaboration towards pressing global issues.

WHAT'S IN A STORY?

Narrative, which is also known as story, derives from the Latin word *narrare*, which is "to recount". Narration is originated from the ancient oral culture that involves the sharing of life stories among people (Lu et al., 2012). It is the most basic form of human communication and is enjoyed by many. On societal level, a narrative element is seen as a pre-condition for community living to collaborate and unite with each other (Riessman, 2008). Present in every age and society, narrative is defined as the "quintessential form of customary knowledge" (Lyotard, 1984, p. 19) in postmodernism philosophy. As narrative or story is broadly defined, it may be fictional or non-fictional in any medium, from text to video (Green & Brock, 2000). In that sense, the story recipient or narratee could be termed as a viewer, reader or listener. A phenomenon worth noting is that a narratee would be immersed in the narration through story immersion, according to transportation theory, which will be discussed in the following section (Green & Brock, 2000; Lu et al., 2012).

As a person is immersed in a story, the individual would reach an optimal experience or flow (Csikszenmihalyi, 1990), which would then influence behaviour even in online environment (Hoffman & Novak, 2009). In line with the hypothesised argument that a narrative element would influence online behaviour, narrative might serve as a bridging element between gamification value co-creation. As a user is engaged on a gamified co-creation platform, there is a high chance that the individual will be exposed to a narrative element, especially as it sets the context for the game.

From managerial perspective, understanding the customers through their narrative worldview that is expressed through stories would allow the firms to strategise a more effective engagement approach, especially when value is always determined by the customers. According to the narrative theory is based on the assumption that human beings share stories to connect with the society, firms are able to harness the wisdom of the crowd through narration as medium. In this vein, narrative is seen to connect the dot of understanding in the context of gamification and value co-creation in investigating the motivation and experience of customers towards the intended engagement properties. Understanding the composition of a narrative element would further facilitate understanding for researchers and practitioners.

While it is generally known that a story is made up of a beginning, middle and end according to Aristotle, researchers agreed that it is made up of six elements, which include abstract, orientation, complication, evaluation resolution and coda (Labov, 1997; Rezadoost & Charvadeh, 2013). According to

Labov (1997), 'abstract' refers a short summary of the story; 'orientation' denotes the who, where and when of the story that requires the story recipient to understand who the characters are, and situation of the time and place. The element of 'complication' tells the exact happenings of the story. This element is the core or integrating factor of the story. As the name suggests, 'evaluation' refers to the analysing of story if it is worth to retelling. 'Resolution' refers to the last part of the story that concludes the narration. The last element in Labov's model, which is 'coda', which refers to the brief summary that explicitly states the retelling of the story by the story receiver.

From serious games perspective, an area that gamification borrows its understanding from, the element of story is widely found in most, if not all, of the game genres. The game genre that is heavily dependable on story element are games that are categorised in adventure, role-playing, strategy, action games, to name a few. For instance, the *Final Fantasy* series, *The Elder Scrolls*, *Assassin's Creed*, *Resident Evil*, *Tomb Raider*, are some of the highest-grossing games that are made available on numerous platforms, from computer, console to mobile. In fact, the successes of these games have spun off to big screen as films that garnered high number of viewers globally. Currently, the electronic game across platforms that appear to garner one of the highest number of players is *Player Unknown Battleground*, or *PUBG* for short. Released just a year, the shooter game has 32 million total players worldwide (Kain, 2018). Developed by Microsoft and Tencent, the game that has sold more than 20 million copies becomes one of the most talk-about online from players and practitioners (BBC News, 2018). It is a community-based connectivity game or termed as massive multiplayer online role-playing game (MMORPG) involves players from all over the world to connect and fight with each other to locate weapons and supplies in a remote island to survive and be the last person standing. A player is represented by each unique avatar or character of their choice. The game on mobile platform allows players to communicate with each other through voice as well. The success of the game suggests that players find enjoyment in the immersive gameplay experience through its story element as they collaborate with each other towards a common goal.

As for gamified systems, the elements of stories have been widely used as well. For instance, a highly-rated mobile exergame (integrating exercise and games) called 'Zombies, Run!' appears to leverage the element of story element as well. Developed in 2012, the app integrates science fiction storyline of zombie apocalypse that requires users to "survive" by running away from the "zombies". The gamified app introduces a series of missions as the players run, whereby they would need to collect items that help them to "survive" in the game. The users are playing as the characters called "Runner 5", which are also their representation in the game. The elements of points, avatars and storyline are created to influence users to be in the immersive state as they use the app while exercising or running. While most gamified apps contain story element, game designers and technology communication practitioners have yet to leverage on the potential that it brings. For instance, a top-rated productivity app called Forest, an example which was mentioned earlier, that serves as a timer while enabling users to collaborate with each other in trees planting in real life from the virtual coins that they earned, has hardly used the element of story. Although it features a hint of narrative element, such as the use of 'complication', it does not seem to have a fully utilise the concept of story that encourages users to be in an immersive state as they use the app. Having said that, the app appears to garner a high number of users. The question arises if being immersive in the story, or story immersion, is an essential element in a gamified app?

Story immersion as a construct has been proposed by Lu et al. (2012) in their conceptual framework. According to the authors who conducted a multidisciplinary literature reviews psychology, human computer interaction, communication to public health, it is proposed that story immersion would affect health behavioral change as mediated by intrapersonal psychological predictors such as attitude, observational learning, emotional arousal, self-efficacy, subjective norms and intrinsic motivation. However, the conceptual study did not show any empirical finding.

There are not many studies that reports the effectiveness of story element in the context of gamification. As to date, there are only seven studies that investigates storytelling as gamification affordances (Morschheuser et al., 2017). Therefore, such finding calls for more in-depth research on this dimension as it would facilitate gamified application designers, communication practitioners and researchers to understand the suitable elements that yields the strongest engagement towards co-creation of value.

However, the effectiveness of the story element approach in the context of gamification remains questionable. It is also unclear what motivates the users to integrate their resources of time, ideas and knowledge, since there is a lack of theoretical foundation to this novel phenomenon. Although it has found that stories have influenced beliefs (Green & Brock, 2000) and behaviours (Baranowski et al., 2008) through immersion, researchers have yet to conclude if individuals who are immersed in a story would co-create value with the initiator. It is not known if individuals in the virtual context or online users would carry out the behaviours as intended by the firm that initiates a crowdsourcing approach through the Internet. While previous findings have shown that gamification would serve as an effective strategy to motivate users to co-create value (Morschheuser et al., 2017; Piligrimiene, Dovaliene, & Virvilaite, 2015; Sailer et al., 2017), the effectiveness of the vital elements in gamification, which is its narrative element, remains unclear. In order to investigate the context of story that persuades and moves users towards an immersive state, its fundamental understanding is discussed further in the following section.

Theoretical Underpinnings of Story Immersion: Transportation Theory

Narrative has always been known to change beliefs. Its persuasive potential is leveraged by practitioners in social marketing to influence and induce certain behaviours among its intended target market (Davis, 2002; Kotler & Zaltman, 1971). For instane, public service announcements would use a form of narrative as a strategy to communicate its intended message for change in social marketing campaigns. Some of the examples of social marketing messages that utilise narrative element include anti-smoking campaigns, save the environment campaigns, road safety campaigns, to name a few. Similar approach is witnessed in green marketing as well, whereby brands would use narrative element to communicate its environmental concern while promoting their environmentally friendly products (Kalafatis, Pollard, East, & Tsogas, 1999). These messages could either be presented in the form print advertisement or video documentaries. Similar approach is seen in the context of video games as mentioned earlier. As more sophisticated technology systems, applications, and equipments are facilitating the widespread adoption towards virtual worlds such as Second Life virtual game, the use of story element to provide an immersive experience is witnessed as well. The utilisation of narrative element has been effective in engaging consumers through offline and online environment. However, the use of narrative element does not guarantee success in continuous engagement for value co-creation, which requires active customer collaboration, in the context of gamification. The transcendence of story element from a serious game to non-game contexts is questionable due to its adaptability potential. For instance, it is unclear if the use of story element would be effective in influencing participation and engagement, which are the basic component that ensures gamification success, in functional gamified platform such as Waze or Forest (Berkling & Thomas, 2013). As such, the current study proposes to investigate the effectiveness of story element in influencing user's optimal experience during engagement.

As a story raises questions, builds conflicts, presents a journey of activities that is related to the characters and storyline, it has the potential to encapsulate a user in an immersive experience, which is accounted as the construct of story immersion (Green & Brock, 2000; Lu et al., 2012; Rubio-Tamayo, Barrio, & García, 2017). The use of story element has the potential to shift a user's current real-world context to the environment portrayed in the game. Such is a phenomenon that can be explained through transportation theory as proposed by Green and Brock (2000). According to transportation theory, a person who is immersed in a story would be "transported" into the narrative world and become involved with the characters in the storyline. As an individual is transported into the narrative environment, he or she would undergo certain mental processes, such as a change of beliefs and attitudes, that has effect on their real-world context (Green & Brock, 2000). The psychological experiences are the effects that resulted from the integration of attention, imagery and feelings due to the exposure of the recipient.

The transportation theory is originated from the accounts described by Gerrig (1993) in describing one's narrative experience. As an individual travels upon performing certain actions, the traveller is on a journey that changes his or her original perspective. During the course of transportation, such experience makes some aspects of the original world becomes inaccessible, which is similar to the literal experience of traveling as conceptualised by Gerrig (1993). The action perform could be reading a text or watching a video that has communicates the narrative element. As a transported narratee would experience a loss of accessibility to the real-world environment, the individual may be unaware of his or her surroundings. For instance, on a physical level, if a person is transported into a story as he is watching a movie in the living room, he may not notice others entering the room. On psychological perspective, the person would have "subjective distancing from reality" (Green & Brock, 2000, p. 702). Transcending from the loss of access to real-world facts, the narratee would experience strong experience and motivation even when the individual knows that the world is unreal. Such engagement in the narrative context explains the occurrences whereby a viewer would cry when watching a tragic scene in a movie. It also explains a situation where viewers would actively think what could have happened next if an outcome was to be changed when an individual is presented with unhappy ending in a movie, a phenomenon that (Gerrig, 1993) termed as 'anomalous replotting'.

According to the transportation theory, there are three conditions that determine a transported individual who is immersed in a story, namely suspension of disbelief, personal experience and affection towards the character (Green & Brock, 2000; Lu et al., 2012). Methodologically, these are the variables that make up the construct of story immersion.

Suspension of disbelief refers to the situation where the narratee would be less likely to counter-argue a claim in the story. In other words, the person would be easily influenced in accordance to the story context. This argument is supported by Gilbert (1991) whereby people tend to believe anything that they read or hear. As disbelieving appears to be an effortful corrective mental process, it is found that transported individuals would be less motivated to exert such effort (Green & Brock, 2000). The individual is highly absorbed into the story that he or she is reluctant to critically analyse any reasonings presented in the narrative. Therefore, it is argued that the attitude and belief of the individual would be easily influenced through story immersion. To test this hypothesis, Green and Brock (2000) conducted an experiment that requires the participants to read a textual content and identify the statements that they believe to be false. The result shows that the highly immersed participants identified fewer false statements and showed greater acceptance towards the story content. This shows that the participants who are more immersed tend to suspend their disbelief towards false content and enjoy the story.

Personal experience refers to the situation when the events portrayed in the story feels more self-directed and real (Green & Brock, 2000; Lu et al., 2012). In other words, narrative events would become more of personal experience when a person is immersed in a story. As the event seems closer to reality, it is argued that the attitude of a transported individual would be changed according to the narrative since direct experience is a powerful measure of forming attitude (Slater & Rouner, 2002).

Affection for the character refers to the situation where the narratee develops strong feelings towards the character portrayed in the story (Green & Brock, 2000; Lu et al., 2012). As a viewer or reader develops a strong sense of attachment with the protagonist, the values of the characters would have influence on the immersion level of the narratee as he or she journeys through the story. It is likely for a person who is high on story immersion to have affection for the character as it drives a story forward. Similar to passive narration, a character can either be portrayed through an actual character or an avatar, which was discussed earlier. However, it is unclear if an avatar in a gamified context would yield similar result of transportation effect as compared to a situation where a person is exposed to textual or motion narrative, since an avatar is already a representation of the self or the player in the game context. One might question if the avatar that is controlled by the storyline would show similar effect of persuasiveness or would it be that the player imposes his or her value on the avatar, if given the freedom? The current study intends to investigate this uncertainty.

As transportation theory discusses about attitude change through one's cognitive exposure to narrative element, it needs to be clarified that it differs from an attitude change theory called elaboration likelihood model (ELM) (Petty & Cacioppo, 1981). The main distinguishing factor is that transportation is considered as a convergent process whereby ELM is a divergent process. In other words, a person who is engaged in elaboration process might be accessing his or her own mental schema such as previous knowledge, thoughts or opinions in evaluating a situation. On the contrary, an individual who is on high level of transportation would temporarily disregard or distance his or her previous schemas and experience (Green & Brock, 2000) While suspension of disbelief, personal experience and affection towards the character may be true for passive narratee as suggested by Green and Brock (2000) through the experiment conducted, individuals who are exposed to the story element in an active engagement context such as gamification is questionable. In addition, since there is no empirical evidence in the conceptual model proposed by Lu et al. (2012), the argument calls for further clarification. Therefore, the present study intends to extend the construct by Lu et al. (2012) by investigating the influence of story immersion as fundamentally supported by transportation theory.

Theoretical Underpinning of Story Immersion: Flow

In order to investigate the experience of users who are in story immersion, it is essential to discuss the flow theory as its fundamental understanding to facilitate value co-creation. As mentioned, it is argued that immersed users would undergo flow, a state that Csikszenmihalyi (1990) described as a process of optimal experience. Flow is used to account for an individual's experience of pleasure and immersion in numerous activities, from mundane tasks to learning a new skill (Jin, 2011). It is a state of mind in which a person is fully immersed in performing a particular activity that characterised by deep focus, complete involvement, intense attention, and achieves an equilibrium perception of skill and challenge (Csikszenmihalyi, 1990).

In total, there are nine elements or constructs that conceptualised flow, which are balance, control, feedback, goals, concentration, merging, loss of self-consciousness, timelessness, and enjoyment. Table 1 summarises nine flow characteristics as theorised by Csikszenmihalyi and how it applies to gamification.

Table 1. Characteristics of flow

No.	Construct	Description
1.	Balance	When a person achieves a match between the perception of skills and challenges at high level. Else, boredom or anxiety may occur. Challenges refers to demanding tasks whereas skills refer to the capacities that one has to reach the desired outcome.
2.	Control	When one feels that he or she is in control of the situation at any time, without a need to actively exert it.
3.	Feedback	When one continuously receives feedback over the achievements or activities that one makes immediately and unambiguously.
4.	Goals	When the objective of the activity is clearly defined distinctively. The person needs to be aware of requirements of the respective activity that he or she engages in.
5.	Concentration	When the person is completely focused on the task at hand. There will be no distracting thoughts and the attention is high.
6.	Merging	The element refers to the merging between awareness and action. When the individual has acts spontaneously without conscious effort, he or she experiences a unified consciousness of awareness and action.
7.	Loss of self-consciousness	When an individual's concern about the self is out of the way. Any disturbing thoughts that interferes with the activity fades away during engagement.
8.	Timelessness	When one feels that the perception of time is altered. Hours will be felt as though minutes has just passed by. The person finds that time moves slowly when he or she is experiencing timelessness.
9.	Enjoyment	When one believes that the situation is highly enjoyable. The person's state of mind gratifies. Therefore, he or she has the desire to repeat the activity for its own sake. In other words, the activity becomes autotelic.

The concept of flow has been applied in a wide variety of discipline, from social psychology, consumer research, human-computer interaction to user experience, including gamification (Choi, Kim, & Kim, 2007; Green & Brock, 2000; Hansen, 2017; Henke, 2013; Huang, Backman, & Backman, 2012; Jin, 2011; Lu et al., 2012; Topu, Reisoğlu, Yılmaz, & Göktaş, 2018). The nine characteristics of flow is able to explain the state of mind of an individual who engages on a gamification platform. As a user plays a game, the person is bound to be immersed in the world that the game creates (Jennett et al., 2008). In other words, the user or player would lose himself or herself in the game that nothing else seems to matter.

As noted, the flow theory was conceptualised by Csikszenmihalyi since 1975. Recently, there has been a development who proposes that the theory of flow to be revisited (Drengner, Jahn, & Furchheim, 2018). According to the authors, flow should be viewed as a parsimonious process. The author argued flow does not apply only to a person who engages in a active functioning but when he or she engages in passive activities such as watching television or meditating as these activities would require awareness and being in a state of mindfulness. In fact, academics are very much shifting their attention to researching the effect of mindfulness on well-being. To support the argument, they have found that there is a process that takes place whenever a person experiences flow.

Firstly, one would experience the constructs of flow antecedents, which is categorised as the task related conditions. These include the constructs of balance, control, feedback and goals. Then, a person would thereafter experience the flow process, which is engrossment that leads to enjoyment. According to the researchers who challenged the traditional understanding of flow theory (Drengner et al., 2018), four of the nine flow characteristics, which are Concentration, Loss of self-consciousness Merging and Timelessness, should be considered as the flow core characteristics in a revised conceptualisation of flow. These characteristics are conceptualised as flow.

Thereafter, an individual would experience the flow outcome, which refers to the intended consequence of the activity that the person hopes to experience or as influenced by the service provider. This suggests that when one experiences flow, it is likely for a person to co-create value with the system. For instance, a research has found that players who are in Second Life, the networked simulation game that builds on its players' contribution, are more likely to co-create value when they are in a flow state of mind (Kohler, Fueller, Matzler, & Stieger, 2011).

As like many other games, Second Life rides on the power of narrative to hook its players to collaborate in building the virtual world. Second Life is a true depiction of gamified value co-creation that sources for the wisdom of the crowd. The use of story element in games seems to be the deciding factor if players would continue to be engaged or disengage. The implementation of narrative element would encourage users to co-create value with the system.

The revisitation of flow theory on a recent finding sheds new light on the understanding of user experience from the perspective of flow. As gamification requires skills to overcome the challenge imposed, a user would need to achieve a balance between skill and challenge to navigate and stay engaged in the system. The elements of gamification, namely narrative element, encapsulates the user in a context so as to give an understanding of the worldview that he or she is in. As the user have a better understanding, he or she would know how to utilise the skills needed for the challenge. It is argued that once balance is achieved, it is likely for the user to be engrossed in the gamified environment.

As a user is engaged on a gamified platform, it is likely that the user takes the role of a character or an avatar, which is the virtual representation of the user in the gamified environment. It is common for the user to be in control over other gamification affordances as well, such as the story element presented in the gamified environment. As the user navigates in the gamified environment with the avatar, a user is said to have the control in creating the story. It was reported that users who are in control would be in engrossment and achieve optimal experience.

A game often provides feedback to the player if they have correctly navigated through the story. As a user experiences story immersion through the narrative presented in the gamified environment, he or she would have stronger engagement for a longer duration, resulting in the user receiving more feedback. The feedback that the user receives would translate to higher engrossment.

A user needs to have a clear goal as to why and how the game is played. The rules of the game is often stated at the start of the game so that the user have clear goal. The rules of a game is usually integrated in the story of a game. As a user navigates through a game, the user would need to know the finishing line. The motivation to reach the finishing line often influences the user to have high engrossment. When a user is highly engrossed, it is likely for the user to co-create value with the system, in which researchers refer to the flow outcome. The below framework shows a visual representation of the role of story immersion in gamification towards value co-creation, from the perspective of the revisitation of flow theory. Figure 1 shows the conceptual framework of the role of story immersion in gamification towards value co-creation.

Figure 1. The role of story immersion in gamification towards value co-creation

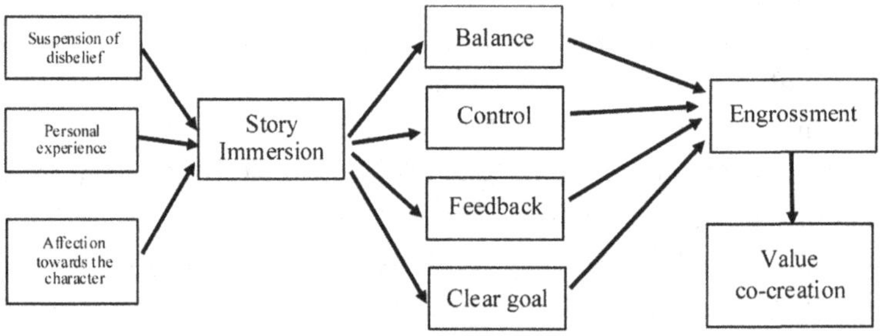

CONCLUSION

This article discussed the role of narrative element in gamification that motivates online users to co-create value. The derivation of gamification features in today's advanced technology ecosystem seems to be able to engage users for continued use. However, its effectiveness is still in question as discussed earlier. Despite the potential that gamification brings, the fact that Malaysia has the highest number of Waze users, but many seem to opt for Google Maps in a recent online poll brings questionable outcomes of gamification among Malaysian mobile app users.

To date, there has not been a study to validate the effectiveness of the gamification affordance, especially on narrative element. Hence the author encourages academics to conduct studies to fill the gap of knowledge so that practitioners are able to implement a more effective gamification approach. The study of user experience from a single gamification affordance as one engages on a gamified system would be a good start. As discussed, the potential that narrative element brings is worth considering, especially that it is able to transport its users into optimal experience of flow for continued usage and thereafter co-create value with the system. Its findings hold promising potential for businesses to engage with its prospects and customers for the sustenance of firm.

REFERENCES

Awani, A. (2019). Rakyat Malaysia lebih gemar Google Maps? Astroawani. Retrieved from http://www.astroawani.com/gaya-hidup/rakyat-malaysia-lebih-gemar-google-maps-217093

Baranowski, T., Buday, R., Thompson, D., & Baranowski, J. (2008). Playing for real: Video games and Stories for Health-Related Behavior Change. *American Journal of Preventive Medicine, 34*(1), 74–82. doi:10.1016/j.amepre.2007.09.027 PMID:18083454

Baron, S., Patterson, A., Warnaby, G., & Harris, K. (2010). Service-dominant logic: Marketing research implications and opportunities. *Journal of Customer Behaviour, 9*(3), 253–264. doi:10.1362/147539210X533179

Bendapudi, N., & Leone, P. R. (2003). Psychological implications of customer participation in co-production. *Journal of Marketing, 67*(1), 14–28. doi:10.1509/jmkg.67.1.14.18592

Berkling, K., & Thomas, C. (2013). Gamification of a software engineering course and a detailed analysis of the factors that lead to it's failure. *Proceedings of the 2013 International Conference on Interactive Collaborative Learning, ICL 2013* (pp. 525–530). Academic Press. 10.1109/ICL.2013.6644642

Bloomberg. (2018). Malaysia beats emerging market peers as Asia outshines. Retrieved from https://www.nst.com.my/business/2018/11/435823/malaysia-beats-emerging-market-peers-asia-outshines

Brabham, D. C. (2008). Crowdsourcing as a Model for Problem Solving: An Introduction and Cases. *Convergence (London)*, *14*(1), 75–90. doi:10.1177/1354856507084420

Brodie, R. J., Hollebeek, L. D., Jurić, B., & Ilić, A. (2011). Customer engagement: Conceptual domain, fundamental propositions, and implications for research. *Journal of Service Research*, *14*(3), 252–271. doi:10.1177/1094670511411703

Chandler, J. D., & Lusch, R. F. (2015). Service Systems: A Broadened Framework and Research Agenda on Value Propositions, Engagement, and Service Experience. *Journal of Service Research*, *18*(1), 6–22. doi:10.1177/1094670514537709

Cheah, W. K., & Zolkepli, I. A. (2018). Crowdsourcing and Service-Dominant Logic : The Interaction Effect of Brand Familiarity, Customer Experience an..... *Asia Pacific Journal of Advanced Business and Social Studies*, *4*(1), 154–162. doi:10.25275/apjabssv4i1bus16

Choe, K. H., & Yap, C. Y. (2018). Exploring Malaysian Attendee Attitude towards Green Practices in Exhibitions. *Proceedings of the 2017 Tokyo International Conference on Hospitality, Tourism, and Sports Management* (pp. 78–92). Academic Press.

Choi, D. H., Kim, J., & Kim, S. H. (2007). ERP training with a web-based electronic learning system: The flow theory perspective. *International Journal of Human-Computer Studies*, *65*(3), 223–243. doi:10.1016/j.ijhcs.2006.10.002

Csikszenmihalyi, M. (1990). *Flow: The Psychology of Optimal Experience*. New York: Harper & Row.

Da Xu, L., He, W., & Li, S. (2014). Internet of things in industries: A survey. *IEEE Transactions on Industrial Informatics*, *10*(4), 2233–2243. doi:10.1109/TII.2014.2300753

Davis, J. E. (2002). *Stories of change: Narrative and social movements*. New York: State University of New York Press.

Deng, Z., Lu, Y., Wei, K. K., & Zhang, J. (2010). Understanding customer satisfaction and loyalty: An empirical study of mobile instant messages in China. *International Journal of Information Management*, *30*(4), 289–300. doi:10.1016/j.ijinfomgt.2009.10.001

Deterding, S. (2011). Situated motivational affordances of game elements: A conceptual model. *Proceeding of ACM CHI Conference on Human Factors in Computing Systems*. ACM.

Drengner, J., Jahn, S., & Furchheim, P. (2018). *Flow revisited: process conceptualization and a novel application to service contexts. Journal of Service Management, 29*. doi:10.1108/JOSM-12-2016-0318

Duverger, P. (2015). Crowdsourcing innovative service ideas. *Journal of Hospitality and Tourism Technology*, *6*(3), 228–241. doi:10.1108/JHTT-10-2014-0063

France, C., Grace, D., Merrilees, B., & Miller, D. (2018). Customer brand co-creation behavior: Conceptualization and empirical validation. *Marketing Intelligence & Planning*, *36*(3), 334–348. doi:10.1108/MIP-10-2017-0266

Füller, J., & Bilgram, V. (2017). The moderating effect of personal features on the consequences of an enjoyable co-creation experience. *Journal of Product and Brand Management*, *26*(4), 386–401. doi:10.1108/JPBM-03-2016-1122

Fuller, J., Hutter, K., & Faullant, R. (2011). Why co-creation experience matters? Creative experience and its impact on the quantity and quality of creative contributions. *R & D Management*, *3*(41), 259–273. doi:10.1111/j.1467-9310.2011.00640.x

Galvagno, M., & Dalli, D. (2014). Theory of value co-creation: A systematic literature review. *Managing Service Quality*, *24*(6), 643–683. doi:10.1108/MSQ-09-2013-0187

Geri, N., Gafni, R., & Bengov, P. (2017). Crowdsourcing as a business model. *Journal of Global Operations and Strategic Sourcing*, *10*(1), 90–111. doi:10.1108/JGOSS-05-2016-0018

Gerrig, R. J. (1993). *Experiencing narrative worlds*. New Haven: Yale University Press.

Gilbert, D. T. (1991). How mental system believe. *The American Psychologist*, *46*(2), 107–199. doi:10.1037/0003-066X.46.2.107

Green, M. C., & Brock, T. C. (2000). The role of transportation in the persuasiveness of public narratives. *Journal of Personality and Social Psychology*, *79*(5), 701–721. doi:10.1037/0022-3514.79.5.701 PMID:11079236

Grönroos, C. (2006). Adopting a service logic for marketing. *Marketing Theory*, *6*(3), 317–333. doi:10.1177/1470593106066794

Hansen, A. V. (2017a). What stories unfold: Empirically grasping value co-creation. *European Business Review*, *29*(1), 2–14. doi:10.1108/EBR-08-2015-0080

Heinonen, K. (2018). Positive and negative valence influencing consumer engagement. *Journal of Service Theory and Practice*, *28*(2), 147–169. doi:10.1108/JSTP-02-2016-0020

Henke, L. L. (2013). Breaking through the clutter: The impact of emotions and flow on viral marketing. *Academy of Marketing Studies Journal*, *17*(2), 111–118.

Hoffman, D. L., & Novak, T. P. (2009). Flow Online: Lessons Learned and Future Prospects. *Journal of Interactive Marketing*, *23*(1), 23–34. doi:10.1016/j.intmar.2008.10.003

Hollebeek, L. D., & Andreassen, T. W. (2018). The S-D logic-informed "hamburger" model of service innovation and its implications for engagement and value. *Journal of Services Marketing*, *32*(1), 1–7. doi:10.1108/JSM-11-2017-0389

Howe, J. (2006). The Rise of Crowdsourcing. *Wired Magazine*, *14*(06), 1–5. doi:10.1086/599595

Huang, Y., Backman, S. J., & Backman, K. F. (2012). Exploring the impacts of involvement and flow experiences in Second Life on people's travel intentions. *Journal of Hospitality and Tourism Technology*, *3*(1), 4–23. doi:10.1108/17579881211206507

Huotari, K., & Hamari, J. (2012). Definining Gamification - A Service Marketing Perspective. *Proceeding of the 16th International Academic MindTrek Conference* (pp. 17–22). Tampere: Mindtrek. 10.1145/2393132.2393137

Huzinga, J. (1970). *Homo Ludens: A Study of the Play Element in Culture*. New York: J & J Harper.

Islam, J. U., Rahman, Z., & Hollebeek, L. D. (2018). Consumer engagement in online brand communities: A solicitation of congruity theory. *Internet Research*, *28*(1), 23–45. doi:10.1108/IntR-09-2016-0279

Jackson, M. (2013). *The politics of storytelling: Variations on a theme by Hannah Arendt*. Copenhagen: Museum Tusculanum Press.

Jennett, C., Cox, A. L., Cairns, P., Dhoparee, S., Epps, A., Tijs, T., & Walton, A. (2008). Measuring and defining the experience of immersion in games. *International Journal of Human-Computer Studies*, *66*(9), 641–661. doi:10.1016/j.ijhcs.2008.04.004

Jin, S. A. A. (2011). "I feel present. therefore, I experience flow:" A structural equation modeling approach to flow and presence in video games. *Journal of Broadcasting & Electronic Media*, *55*(1), 114–136. doi:10.1080/08838151.2011.546248

Kain, E. (2018). "PUBG" Tops 4 Million Players On Xbox One, Hands Out Free Stuff To Players. Forbes. Retrieved from https://www.forbes.com/sites/erikkain/2018/01/25/pubg-tops-4-million-players-on-xbox-one-hands-out-free-stuff-to-players/#5297c3d72621

Kalafatis, S. P., Pollard, M., East, R., & Tsogas, M. H. (1999). Green marketing and Ajzen's theory of planned behaviour: A cross-market examination. *Journal of Consumer Marketing*, *16*(5), 441–460. doi:10.1108/07363769910289550

Kapp, K. M. (2012). *The gamification of learning and instruction: Game-based methods and strategies for training and education*. San Francisco, CA: Pfeiffer.

Klöckner, C. A. (2013). A Comprehensive Model of the Psychology of Environmental Behaviour – a Meta-Analysis. *Global Environmental Change*, *23*(5), 1028–1038. doi:10.1016/j.gloenvcha.2013.05.014

Kohler, T., Fueller, J., Matzler, K., Stieger, D., & Füller. (2011). Co-Creation In Virtual Worlds: The Design Of The User Experience. *Management Information Systems Quarterly*, *35*(3), 773–788. doi:10.2307/23042808

Kotler, P., & Zaltman, G. (1971). Social Marketing: An Approach to Planned Social Change. *Journal of Marketing*, *35*(3), 3–12. doi:10.1177/002224297103500302 PMID:12276120

Labov, W. (1997). Some further steps in narrative analysis. *Journal of Narrative and Life History*, *7*(1/4), 395–415. doi:10.1075/jnlh.7.49som

Labrecque, L. I., vor dem Esche, J., Mathwick, C., Novak, T. P., & Hofacker, C. F. (2013). Consumer power: Evolution in the digital age. *Journal of Interactive Marketing*, *27*(4), 257–269. doi:10.1016/j.intmar.2013.09.002

Li, L. P., Juric, B., & Brodie, R. J. (2017). Dynamic multi-actor engagement in networks: The case of United Breaks Guitars. *Journal of Service Theory and Practice, 27*(4), 738–760. doi:10.1108/JSTP-04-2016-0066

Li, L. P., Juric, B., & Brodie, R. J. (2018). Actor engagement valence: Conceptual foundations, propositions and research directions. *Journal of Service Management, 29*(3), 491–516. doi:10.1108/JOSM-08-2016-0235

Lu, A. S., Baranowski, T., Thompson, D., & Budday, R. (2012). Story Immersion of Videogames for Youth Health Promotion: A Review of Literature. *Games for Health Journal, 1*(3), 199–204. doi:10.1089/g4h.2011.0012 PMID:24416639

Lyotard, J. F. (1984). *The postmodern condition: A report on knowledge.* Minneapolis: University of Minnesota Press.

Malay Mail. (2019). Survey shows majority support "no single-use plastic" campaign.

McKee, R. (1997). *Story, substance, structure, style and the principle of screenwriting.* New York: HarperCollins.

Mei, N. S., Wai, C. W., & Ahamad, R. (2016). Environmental Awareness and Behaviour Index for Malaysia. *Procedia: Social and Behavioral Sciences, 222*(07), 668–675. doi:10.1016/j.sbspro.2016.05.223

Miniwatts Marketing Group. (2018). Internet World Stats.

Morschheuser, B., Hamari, J., Koivisto, J., & Maedche, A. (2017). Gamified crowdsourcing: Conceptualization, literature review, and future agenda. *International Journal of Human-Computer Studies, 106*(April), 26–43. doi:10.1016/j.ijhcs.2017.04.005

Muniz, A. M. J. Jr, & O'Guinn, T. C. (2001). Brand Community. *The Journal of Consumer Research, 27*(4), 412–432. doi:10.1086/319618

BBC News. (2018). PubG: The story behind one of the world's most popular games. Retrieved from https://www.bbc.com/news/av/newsbeat-42660502/pubg-the-story -behind-one-of-the-world-s-most-popular-games

Payne, A. F., Storbacka, K., & Frow, P. (2008). Managing the co-creation of value. *Journal of the Academy of Marketing Science, 36*(1), 83–96. doi:10.100711747-007-0070-0

Petty, R., & Cacioppo, J. T. (1981). *Attitudes and Persuasion: Classic and contemporary approaches.* Iowa: Brown.

Piligrimiene, Z., Dovaliene, A., & Virvilaite, R. (2015). Consumer engagement in value co-creation: What kind of value it creates for company? *The Engineering Economist, 26*(4), 452–460. doi:10.5755/j01.ee.26.4.12502

Revees, B., & Read, J. L. (2009). *Total Engagement: Using Games and Virtual Worlds to Change the Way People Work and Businesses Compete.* Boston: Harvard Business School Press; doi:10.1016/j.chb.2010.03.035

Rezadoost, A., & Charvadeh, B. K. (2013). Studying narrative structure of one thousand and one night tales based on Labov's diamond- shaped model. *International Research Journal of Applied and Basic Sciences, 4*(11), 3324–3327.

Riessman, C. K. (2008). *Narrative Methods for Human Sciences*. London: Sage Publications.

Rubio-Tamayo, J. L., Barrio, M. G., & García, F. G. (2017). Immersive Environments and Virtual Reality: Systematic Review and Advances in Communication, Interaction and Simulation. *Multimodal Technologies and Interaction, 1*(4), 21. doi:10.3390/mti1040021

Saarijärvi, H., Kannan, P. K., & Kuusela, H. (2013). Value co-creation: Theoretical approaches and practical implications. *European Business Review, 25*(1), 6–19. doi:10.1108/09555341311287718

Sailer, M., Hense, J. U., Mayr, S. K., & Mandl, H. (2017). How gamification motivates: An experimental study of the effects of specific game design elements on psychological need satisfaction. *Computers in Human Behavior, 69*, 371–380. doi:10.1016/j.chb.2016.12.033

Schau, J. H., Muniz, A. M. Jr, & Arnould, E. J. (2009). How brand communities create value. *Journal of Marketing, 73*(September), 30–51. doi:10.1509/jmkg.73.5.30

Slater, M. D., & Rouner, D. (2002). Entertainment-education and elaboration likelihood: Understanding the processing of narrative persuasion. *Communication Theory, 2*(12), 173–191.

Storbacka, K., Brodie, R. J., Böhmann, T., Maglio, P. P., & Nenonen, S. (2016). Actor engagement as a microfoundation for value co-creation. *Journal of Business Research, 69*(8), 3008–3017. doi:10.1016/j.jbusres.2016.02.034

The Star. (2017). Malaysia has the most Wazers.

The Star. (2018). Make green growth a priority. Retrieved from https://www.thestar.com.my/news/nation/2018/10/19/make-green-growth-a-priority-we-must-focus-on-making-sustainable-development-a-mainstream-goal/

Topu, F. B., Reisoğlu, İ., Yılmaz, T. K., & Göktaş, Y. (2018). Information retention's relationships with flow, presence and engagement in guided 3D virtual environments. *Education and Information Technologies, 23*(4), 1621–1637. doi:10.100710639-017-9683-1

Vargo, S. L., & Lusch, R. F. (2004). Evolving to a New Dominant Logic for Marketing. *Journal of Marketing, 68*(1), 1–17. doi:10.1509/jmkg.68.1.1.24036

Vargo, S. L., & Lusch, R. F. (2008). Service-dominant logic: Continuing the evolution. *Journal of the Academy of Marketing Science, 36*(1), 1–10. doi:10.100711747-007-0069-6

Vargo, S. L., & Lusch, R. F. (2016). Institutions and axioms: An extension and update of service-dominant logic. *Journal of the Academy of Marketing Science, 44*(1), 5–23. doi:10.100711747-015-0456-3

Vega-Vazquez, M., Revilla-Camacho, M. Á., Cossío-Silva, F. J., & Cossı, F. J. (2013). The value co-creation process as a determinant of customer satisfaction. *Management Decision, 51*(10), 1945–1953. doi:10.1108/MD-04-2013-0227

Waze. (2018). Data, Driven. Retrieved from https://www.waze.com/brands/drivers/

Werbach, K., & Hunter, D. (2012). *For win: How game thinking can revolutionize your business*. Philadelphia: Wharton Digital Press.

Zhao, Y., & Zhu, Q. (2014). Effects of extrinsic and intrinsic motivation on participation in crowdsourcing contest. *Online Information Review*, *38*(7), 896–917. doi:10.1108/OIR-08-2014-0188

Zheng, H., Li, D., & Hou, W. (2011). Task Design, Motivation, and Participation in Crowdsourcing Contests. *International Journal of Electronic Commerce*, *15*(4), 57–88. doi:10.2753/JEC1086-4415150402

Chapter 60
The Use of Gamification in Social Phobia

Vitor Simões-Silva
https://orcid.org/0000-0003-2831-9729
School of Health, Polytechnic of Porto, Portugal

Vanessa Maravalhas
School of Health, Polytechnic of Porto, Portugal

Ana Rafaela Cunha
School of Health, Polytechnic of Porto, Portugal

Maria Inês Soares
School of Health, Polytechnic of Porto, Portugal

António Marques
https://orcid.org/0000-0002-8656-5023
School of Health, Polytechnic Institute of Porto, Portugal

ABSTRACT

Social phobia usually starts in adolescence. Social situations that include meeting people, talking in groups, or in more specific situations are going to be avoided by individuals. Therefore, this condition has the consequence of significant impairment in different occupations. Recent studies show that gamification is commonly applied to interventions for the treatment of chronic diseases, and although there are interventions concerning mental health, these are few and there is evidence that these interventions have positive effects on mental health, particularly among young people. The desensitization therapy program using gamification consisted of 15 sessions: an initial assessment session, 13 biweekly exposure therapy sessions, and the last reevaluation session corresponding to a total duration of the program of seven weeks. Each session, lasting approximately 50 minutes, is followed a formal structure consisting of the following phases. The intervention focused on shaping appropriate approach behaviors through a process of successive approximations.

DOI: 10.4018/978-1-6684-7589-8.ch060

SOCIAL PHOBIA

Social phobia, also called social anxiety disorder, is the third most common neuropsychiatric disorder after depression and substance abuse, with a prevalence of approximately 12% throughout life in Western societies and which increases with age, and generally starts in childhood or adolescence (Bas-Hoogendam et al., 2017; Cabral & Patel, 2020; Erin et al., 2017; Hirsch, 2018; Kampmann, Emmelkamp, & Morina, 2016; Kishimoto & Ding, 2019; Lange & Pauli, 2019; Leichsenring & Leweke, 2017; Leigh & Clark, 2018; Miloff et al., 2015; Morrison et al., 2016; Rose & Tadi, 2020; Serlachius et al., 2019). Social phobia refers to the fear of exposure to one or more social situations, as well as excessive concern about your social performance and the focus is on fear of being negatively assessed (American Psychiatric Association, 2014; Apolinário-Hagen et al., 2020; Bas-Hoogendam et al., 2017; Clauss et al., 2019; Emmelkamp et al., 2020; Erin et al., 2017; Felnhofer et al., 2019; Hirsch, 2018; Kampmann, Emmelkamp, Hartanto, et al., 2016; Kampmann, Emmelkamp, & Morina, 2016; Kampmann et al., 2019; H. Kim et al., 2018; Lange & Pauli, 2019; Leichsenring & Leweke, 2017; Miloff et al., 2015; National Collaborating Centre for Mental Health, 2013; Perna et al., 2020; Rose & Tadi, 2020; Serlachius et al., 2019; Wechsler et al., 2019). It should be noted that social phobia is characterized by anticipated anxiety and hypervigilance to social stimuli and the fact that individuals with this pathology are concerned with social judgment, creates an ambiguous and unpredictable situation (Clauss et al., 2019). Thus, social phobia is associated with a high intolerance to uncertainty which suggests that ambiguous or uncertain situations are critical for the disorder (Clauss et al., 2019). It is possible to mention that this pathology affects more females than males (Cabral & Patel, 2020; Rose & Tadi, 2020).

Therefore, social phobia represents a continuum of several feared social situations (Leichsenring & Leweke, 2017). In these situations, individuals who have a social phobia avoid eye contact, divert their attention from external suggestions and focus on internal ones, which contributes to the persistence of fear (H. Kim et al., 2018; Lange & Pauli, 2019). Studies have shown that individuals with this pathology show less fixation on the face, especially avoiding the eye region, which is perceived negatively by other people, as well as this type of behavior becomes more evident as the emotional intensity increases (H. Kim et al., 2018). People with angry or irritated facial expressions are more avoided compared to people with neutral or sad facial expressions (Lange & Pauli, 2019).

Social situations can be grouped into different groups that involve observation, interaction, and performance (National Collaborating Centre for Mental Health, 2013; Wechsler et al., 2019). As such, these include meeting people, talking in groups or more specific situations, such as at meetings, talking to authority figures or giving presentations, starting conversations, being seen in public, eating or drinking while being watched, working, going shopping, among others (Emmelkamp et al., 2020; National Collaborating Centre for Mental Health, 2013; Wechsler et al., 2019). Individuals with social phobia will try to avoid the above situations, which is not always feasible (Hirsch, 2018; Miloff et al., 2015; National Collaborating Centre for Mental Health, 2013; Pepper et al., 2019; Perna et al., 2020). Consequently, this condition results in significant impairment in different occupations, which, consequently, translates into a decrease in quality of life (Ahmed-Leitao et al., 2019; Bas-Hoogendam et al., 2017; Cabral & Patel, 2020; Kampmann, Emmelkamp, & Morina, 2016; Kampmann, Emmelkamp, Hartanto, et al., 2016; Kishimoto & Ding, 2019; Leichsenring & Leweke, 2017; Miloff et al., 2015; National Collaborating Centre for Mental Health, 2013). Individuals with social phobia are more likely to have a low level of education, to be single, and to have a lower socioeconomic level (Cabral & Patel, 2020; Perna et al., 2020;

Rose & Tadi, 2020). Social phobia also has implications for society, particularly at the economic level, due to the loss of productivity and the costs of using healthcare (Miloff et al., 2015; Perna et al., 2020).

The course of social phobia tends to be chronic with the recovery rate being low (Canton et al., 2017; Clauss et al., 2019; Leichsenring & Leweke, 2017; Rose & Tadi, 2020). It is important to note that there are coexisting conditions such as other anxiety disorders, avoidant personality disorders, hyperactivity and attention deficit disorders, depressive disorders, and substance use disorders (Cabral & Patel, 2020; Leichsenring & Leweke, 2017). Therefore, social phobia is associated with an increased risk of behavioral problems, depressive and substance use disorders, as well as cardiovascular disease and increased risk of suicide (Bas-Hoogendam et al., 2017; Cabral & Patel, 2020; Leichsenring & Leweke, 2017).

About the etiology of social phobia, it is understood that it results from the interaction between several biopsychosocial factors, as in most psychiatric disorders that often lead to cognitive changes, such as the tendency to interpret most social situations negatively and to a propensity to inaccurately infer about the attitudes of peers, as well as the feeling and fear of being evaluated by others (Erin et al., 2017; Gray et al., 2019; Lange & Pauli, 2019; National Collaborating Centre for Mental Health, 2013; Serlachius et al., 2019).

Recent studies suggest that genetic and environmental factors explain most of the individual differences of people with this pathology (Leichsenring & Leweke, 2017; Rose & Tadi, 2020). Therefore, risk factors may include behavioral inhibition in childhood, family history of anxiety or other psychopathological conditions, the presence of negative life experiences, separation from parents, disturbed family environment, reduced academic performance, low self-esteem, sociodemographic characteristics, and physiological, genetic, and environmental factors (Ahmed-Leitao et al., 2019; Cabral & Patel, 2020; Leichsenring & Leweke, 2017; Rose & Tadi, 2020; Wang et al., 2020).

Exposure to phobic stimulus, in most cases, causes an immediate response to anxiety that can take the form of a panic attack linked to or predisposed to the situation (Paschali & Tsitsas, 2014). The phobic situation is usually avoided or is supported with intense anxiety or distress (Paschali & Tsitsas, 2014). Consequently, prevention often interferes with the person's routine occupational functioning, social activities, or relationships (Paschali & Tsitsas, 2014).

Several neuroimaging studies have supported that the amygdala and its connections play an important role in attributing emotional salience to stimuli and in the downward modulation of associative, attentional, and interpretive processes (Freitas-Ferrari et al., 2010). In anxiety disorders, an anomaly in the normal functioning of this circuit impairs communication with prefrontal areas responsible for inhibitory responses, which, consequently, causes an increase in amygdala responsiveness and a consequently sustained processing bias related to the threat in anxious individuals (Freitas-Ferrari et al., 2010). Some authors point out that, in this pathology, there is an increase in the activation of prefrontal areas to regulate (Bas-Hoogendam et al., 2017; Bruhl et al., 2014). However, this regulatory effect is not effective for controlling and regulating amygdala hyperactivation in individuals with social phobia (Bruhl et al., 2014). Other authors defend the reverse and ascending process, that is, that there is an increase in the activation of the prefrontal structures resulting from hyperactivation of the amygdala (Bruhl et al., 2014).

In turn, the insula plays a key role in the detection and interpretation of internal body states (Freitas-Ferrari et al., 2010). Furthermore, the insular cortex is involved in the recognition and experience of aversive states, such as disgust, fear, and pain (Freitas-Ferrari et al., 2010).

The hippocampus has been referred to in terms of emotional processing and regulation and response to positive stimuli, including autobiographical memories (Ahmed-Leitao et al., 2019; Zhu et al., 2019).

Several studies have suggested that, in social phobia, there is an increase in brain activation in the hippocampus (Bas-Hoogendam et al., 2017).

Thus, structural and activity changes in the amygdala, hippocampus, and insula have been proposed as biomarkers of social phobia (Cosci & Mansueto, 2020). People with this pathology show differences in the level of cerebral blood flow, which is increased specifically in the amygdala-hippocampus region, right dorsolateral prefrontal cortex, left inferior temporal cortex, and decreased in the cerebellum (Cosci & Mansueto, 2020). Since social phobia is associated with a high intolerance to uncertainty and unpredictability, as previously mentioned, studies show that social phobia moderates the relationship between the bed nucleus of the stria terminalis (BNST) and other brain regions in response to unpredictability (Clauss et al., 2019). Social phobia is associated with BNST connectivity and BNST-amygdala dissociation, thus moderating BNST's connectivity with the amygdala (Clauss et al., 2019). Individuals with low or medium social phobia had a stronger amygdala response to threat images, while individuals with high social phobia had an increased BNST response (Clauss et al., 2019).

Besides, multiple neurotransmitter systems, such as serotonin, dopamine, and glutamate, may be implicated in the pathogenesis of social phobia (Bas-Hoogendam et al., 2017; Cosci & Mansueto, 2020; Leichsenring & Leweke, 2017; Perna et al., 2020; Rose & Tadi, 2020). Neurobiological research also suggests that there is a dysfunction in the regulation of serotonin and dopamine, since there is a greater synthesis of serotonin and a lower striatal density of dopamine in individuals with social phobia (Bas-Hoogendam et al., 2017; Cosci & Mansueto, 2020; Leichsenring & Leweke, 2017).

Regarding the diagnosis, psychiatric disorders are commonly diagnosed in a clinical context and not through exams, through the reporting of symptoms and the completion of evaluation scales (Allsopp et al., 2019).

As for the diagnostic criteria, these include the fear of acting in a way or showing symptoms of anxiety that offend other people or lead to rejection, in addition to the fear of humiliation and of being assessed negatively; fear or anxiety is almost always caused by social situations and are disproportionate to the real threat posed by the social situation; fear, anxiety or avoidance are not attributable to the physiological effects related to substance abuse or other medical conditions, cause clinically significant distress or occupational impairment, are persistent for about six months or more, and are not best explained by symptoms of other mental disorder, among others (American Psychiatric Association, 2014; Leichsenring & Leweke, 2017; Park & Kim, 2020; Perna et al., 2020; Rose & Tadi, 2020). However, if fear or anxiety is restricted to speaking or acting in public, social phobia should be specified as performance anxiety (American Psychiatric Association, 2014; Leichsenring & Leweke, 2017). To assess the disproportion between fear or anxiety and real risk, the sociocultural context is recommended as a method of judgment, since the influences of culture may be important (Park & Kim, 2020).

As for its evaluation, an instrument used is the Anxiety and Avoidance Scale in Performance and Social Interaction Situations (AESDIS), being a self-answer questionnaire that measures the level of anxiety and avoidance in various situations of social interaction (Gouveia et al., 2003; Pinto-Gouveia, 1997). This scale is derived from the Liebowitz Social Anxiety Scale (LSAS) which assesses the degrees of anxiety in 24 situations (11 of social interaction and 13 of social performance) (Gouveia et al., 2003; Pinto-Gouveia, 1997). Pinto-Gouveia, Cunha, and Salvador (2003) added 34 new situations selected through clinical interviews with patients with social anxiety. AESDIS is composed of two subscales: the anxiety subscale and the avoidance subscale (Gouveia et al., 2003; Pinto-Gouveia, 1997). Answers to each of the items (58 items) are given on a 4-point Likert scale (Gouveia et al., 2003; Pinto-Gouveia,

1997). In addition to the items mentioned, five blanks are provided for the five situations that cause the highest levels of anxiety (Gouveia et al., 2003).

TREATMENT

The National Institute for Health and Care Excellence (NICE) and the Canadian Psychiatric Association present evidence-based clinical guidelines that allow for reliable recommendations regarding approaches to be taken in various health conditions (Leichsenring & Leweke, 2017; NICE Clinical Guidelines, 2013). NICE guidelines recommend using cognitive-behavioral therapy instead of drug therapy, while the Canadian Psychiatric Association considers both first-line pharmacological and non-pharmacological treatments (Leichsenring & Leweke, 2017).

Psychotherapeutic and pharmacological interventions that are effective in treating anxiety appear to specifically alter brain activation patterns in the brain structures mentioned above (Holzschneider & Mulert, 2011; Irle et al., 2010).

Regarding the treatment of phobias, several therapeutic approaches are applied, the most used being desensitization therapy, exposure therapy in vivo, exposure therapy using virtual reality, applied relaxation, cognitive-behavioral therapy, training of social skills, cognitive restructuring, mindfulness, and drug therapy in association or not with one of the previous interventions (Arroll et al., 2017; Donker et al., 2018; Felnhofer et al., 2019; Fernández-Álvarez et al., 2020; Gebara et al., 2016; Geraets et al., 2019; Hirsch, 2018; Kampmann, Emmelkamp, & Morina, 2016; Kampmann, Emmelkamp, Hartanto, et al., 2016; Kishimoto & Ding, 2019; Leichsenring & Leweke, 2017; Lindner et al., 2017; Miloff et al., 2015; National Collaborating Centre for Mental Health, 2013; Paschali & Tsitsas, 2014; Perna et al., 2020; Serlachius et al., 2019; Wechsler et al., 2019).

As for drug therapy, it appears to have an efficacy similar to cognitive-behavioral therapy in the short-term treatment of social phobia (Leichsenring & Leweke, 2017). Several drugs have been used, the selective serotonin reuptake inhibitors (SSRIs) being considered the first line (Emmelkamp et al., 2020; Leichsenring & Leweke, 2017; Perna et al., 2020; Rose & Tadi, 2020). These drugs have a low risk of side effects and have the advantage of beneficial effects in the treatment of depression and other anxiety-related disorders, which may be coexisting with social phobia (Leichsenring & Leweke, 2017). The continued use of this therapy after short-term treatment, about 14 weeks, has been associated with lower rates of relapse (Leichsenring & Leweke, 2017). Evidence suggests that treatment should be continued for at least about 3 to 6 months after an individual responds (Leichsenring & Leweke, 2017). Thereafter, the use of the drug can be gradually decreased (Leichsenring & Leweke, 2017). Benzodiazepines, such as clonazepam and bromazepam, and beta-blockers, such as propranolol, have also been considered for treatment (Leichsenring & Leweke, 2017; Perna et al., 2020; Rose & Tadi, 2020). These drugs are used in individuals with performance anxiety (Leichsenring & Leweke, 2017). However, benzodiazepines can cause sedation and present risks of physiological dependence and withdrawal symptoms and are not considered in individuals with depression or a history of substance abuse (Leichsenring & Leweke, 2017). It is important to add that tricyclic antidepressants are not considered in the treatment of people with social phobia (Leichsenring & Leweke, 2017).

In vivo exposure consists of building a hierarchy of feared situations (from the least to the most feared) and encouraging the individual to repeatedly expose themselves to situations, starting with less anxiogenic situations and gradually moving on to situations that trigger greater anxiety and insecurity as confidence develops (Donker et al., 2018; Erin et al., 2017; National Collaborating Centre for Mental Health, 2013). Exposure exercises involve confronting real-life social situations through role-plays (National Collaborating Centre for Mental Health, 2013). It is noteworthy that this technique is based on the assumption that avoiding fearful situations promotes the maintenance of social anxiety and is one of the most effective methods for the treatment of social phobia (Donker et al., 2018; Gebara et al., 2016; Kishimoto & Ding, 2019; Lindner et al., 2017; National Collaborating Centre for Mental Health, 2013). However, the traditional aspect of this therapy has some disadvantages, namely the fact that phobic stimuli may not be easily accessible, difficult to acquire or maintain, or difficult or impossible to manipulate and control during the exposure session (Lindner et al., 2017).

As for applied relaxation, it is a specialized form of relaxation that aims to teach individuals to be able to relax in common social situations (National Collaborating Centre for Mental Health, 2013). It starts with progressive muscle relaxation training that allows a series of steps for individuals to apply relaxation in everyday anxiogenic situations (National Collaborating Centre for Mental Health, 2013). The final phase of treatment involves the intensive practice of using relaxation techniques in social situations in a real context (National Collaborating Centre for Mental Health, 2013).

Mindfulness in this pathology aims to encourage individuals to psychologically distance themselves from negative emotions and thoughts, having two aspects: stress reduction and cognitive therapy based on mindfulness (Leichsenring & Leweke, 2017; National Collaborating Centre for Mental Health, 2013). Treatment begins with therapeutic education about stress, social anxiety, and meditation techniques (Leichsenring & Leweke, 2017; National Collaborating Centre for Mental Health, 2013). Individuals must participate in therapeutic groups weekly where they learn meditation techniques, and formal meditation practice is also encouraged for at least 30 minutes daily (Leichsenring & Leweke, 2017; National Collaborating Centre for Mental Health, 2013).

In turn, social skills training is based on the assumption that people are unable to deal with anxiety in social situations, partly because they have deficits in terms of their social skills, need to improve them to regulate their emotions and behaviors in their interactions with others (National Collaborating Centre for Mental Health, 2013). This technique involves systematic training of non-verbal social skills (for example, increased eye contact, caring and friendly posture, etc.) and verbal social skills (for example, how to start a conversation, how to give positive feedback to other people, how to ask questions that promote conversation, and so on) through role-plays in sessions and homework (National Collaborating Centre for Mental Health, 2013).

Concerning cognitive-behavioral therapy (CBT), it assumes that it is not the context or the circumstances that make a person suffer emotionally, but rather the perceptions, beliefs, and assumptions about the situation (Apolinário-Hagen et al., 2020). Thus, this therapy aims to modify non-adaptive cognitions and behaviors, challenging dysfunctional thoughts and beliefs, through the use of cognitive and behavioral strategies, including cognitive restructuring and exposure, for example (Apolinário-Hagen et al., 2020; Gebara et al., 2016; Kampmann, Emmelkamp, & Morina, 2016; Kampmann, Emmelkamp, Hartanto, et al., 2016). Cognitive-behavioral therapy has been indicated as the most effective non-pharmacological approach in the treatment of social phobia, is considered a first-line treatment (Apolinário-Hagen et al., 2020; Emmelkamp et al., 2020; Erin et al., 2017; Leichsenring & Leweke, 2017; Perna et al., 2020; Rose & Tadi, 2020).

Regarding cognitive restructuring, it does not have a clear and universal definition, it is rather a set of techniques, procedures, and psychotherapeutic approaches (Cebrián et al., 2017). There is little precision regarding its definition, the most mentioned being the importance of following a procedure that must specify the when and where of its application (Cebrián et al., 2017). It is one of the most used techniques in psychological intervention in clinical practice and is commonly associated with cognitive behavioral therapy and presupposes a change in the client's thinking (Cebrián et al., 2017; Larsson et al., 2015). The literature considers a technique difficult to apply due to the lack of structure (Cebrián et al., 2017).

Systematic desensitization is a therapeutic approach based on the principle of reciprocal inhibition that comprises three stages of deep muscle relaxation training, building a hierarchy of fear and presenting the signs of anxiety, bringing them closer to the relaxation experience so that relaxation inhibits the anxiety (Janardhan Reddy et al., 2020).

Finally, in exposure therapy using virtual reality (VRET), individuals are confronted with stimuli that are generated through the computer, such as virtual social interaction, and these stimuli can cause high levels of social anxiety (Erin et al., 2017; Felnhofer et al., 2019; Kampmann, Emmelkamp, Hartanto, et al., 2016). Virtual Reality emerged as a more fascinating alternative to conventional treatment and consists of a simulation system through the use of a computer, which allows creating virtual environments and the feeling of presence in these environments, presenting an immersive visual and auditory experience (Ben-Moussa et al., 2017; Donker et al., 2018; Fernández-Álvarez et al., 2020; Kishimoto & Ding, 2019; Lindner et al., 2017). The virtual environments can be personalized and controlled, to trigger specific stimuli that allow practicing social behavior in various environments, which can be repeated to achieve therapeutic goals and the therapist can provide feedback on the same (Donker et al., 2018; Fernández-Álvarez et al., 2020; Gebara et al., 2016; Geraets et al., 2019; Kishimoto & Ding, 2019; Lindner et al., 2017). Studies have suggested that this therapy has positive effects on psychiatric illnesses, namely in the treatment of social phobia, reducing its symptoms (Donker et al., 2018; Erin et al., 2017; Felnhofer et al., 2019; Gebara et al., 2016; Geraets et al., 2019; Kampmann, Emmelkamp, & Morina, 2016; Kampmann, Emmelkamp, Hartanto, et al., 2016; Kampmann et al., 2019; H. Kim et al., 2018). This therapy associated with cognitive-behavioral therapy has the consequences of reducing social anxiety and depressive symptoms and increasing quality of life (Erin et al., 2017; Geraets et al., 2019). VRET has advantages compared to in vivo exposure, such as the possibility of performing therapy within a physical space, without having to leave, offering more flexibility as to the intensity of treatment and grading of exposure, the control of phobic stimuli, greater acceptability of exposure by individuals being treated, among others (Donker et al., 2018; Emmelkamp et al., 2020; Fernández-Álvarez et al., 2020; Lindner et al., 2017).

GAMIFICATION

Currently, special attention has been paid to computerized and mobile interventions due to their potential to reduce costs and increase treatment accessibility (Dennis & O'Toole, 2014; Miloff et al., 2015). Therefore, cognitive-behavioral interventions have been used through the computer, using virtual reality, instead of traditional techniques, which were based on imagination (Christie et al., 2019; Felnhofer et al., 2019; Kampmann, Emmelkamp, Hartanto, et al., 2016; Kishimoto & Ding, 2019; Miloff et al., 2015). According to the American Psychological Association, virtual reality would be preferable for realizing the preferences of individuals being treated, which is one of three aspects in providing adequate evidence-based practices, in addition to presenting itself as a more attractive exposure tool. compared to in vivo exposure, as previously mentioned (Fernández-Álvarez et al., 2020). In addition to this, virtual reality has shown to play an important role in treatment satisfaction (Fernández-Álvarez et al., 2020).

However, there is some difficulty in implementation due to the difficulty of access caused by the cost, the lack of specific training, technical obstacles, as well as the limited accessibility (Christie et al., 2019; Donker et al., 2018; Fernández-Álvarez et al., 2020).

The concept of gamification has been defined by several authors as the use of game design elements in non-game contexts or considered as a process of improving service with resources for gaming experiences, to support the user in creating global value (Brown et al., 2016; Cheng et al., 2019; Fleming et al., 2017; Lindner et al., 2017; Pham et al., 2016; Sánchez & Gómez Trigueros, 2019; Sardi et al., 2017). It is based on the principles of serious games, not having the purpose of having fun in the game, but working on skills that can be applied in the daily situations of the player (Cheng et al., 2019). This means that instead of creating immersive and complete games as in "serious games", gamification aims to change users' behavior and motivation through remaining gaming experiences (Brown et al., 2016; Cheng et al., 2019; Fleming et al., 2017; Lindner et al., 2017; Sardi et al., 2017). In the literature, the term "serious games" refers to games designed and created specifically for education, training, or behavioral modification (Lau et al., 2017; Zhang et al., 2018). One of the frequent uses of serious games is to solve social problems (Floryan et al., 2019).

Health-centered gamification involves the intersection of persuasive technology, serious games, and personal computing, as it requires the application of specific design principles or resources capable of inducing changes in targeted behaviors and experiences, based on intrinsically motivating qualities of well-played games simultaneously tracking individual behaviors through goal setting and feedback on individual progress (Johnson et al., 2016).

Thus, gamification aims at a double improvement, which consists of making activities more pleasant, while ensuring the involvement of people in tasks that seem demotivating (Lindner et al., 2017; Pham et al., 2016; Sardi et al., 2017; Turan et al., 2016). Also, it has emotional, cognitive, and social benefits as it stimulates various cognitive functions such as decision making and problem-solving, promotes knowledge acquisition, and develops positive social relationships (Abu-dawood, 2016; Pham et al., 2016; Sardi et al., 2017; Turan et al., 2016). Concerning the social benefits related to gamification, the main ones are to develop positive social relationships and promote a feeling of integration (Fleming et al., 2017). Social influence can also invoke a sense of competition to achieve a higher status on the leaderboard, resulting in numerous emotional competencies, such as self-satisfaction, self-esteem, and pride (Abu-dawood, 2016; Sardi et al., 2017).

In addition to what was previously mentioned, gamification also develops strategic players' skills, improving working memory, visual attention, and processing speed (Lumsden et al., 2016). Typically, the various game mechanics potentially involved in gamification are considered an anchor point for players to ensure a flow of cognitive skills, such as achieving a state of concentration, developing problem-solving skills, and acquiring a sense of goal orientation (Ruhi, 2015; Sardi et al., 2017).

As for the player's involvement, this can be explained by a motivational model derived from the theory of self-determination (Lee, 2016). This model stipulates that the satisfaction, immersion, and enjoyment of a game are mediated by how the game meets the psychological needs of autonomy, competence, and relationship (Lee, 2016).

It is also noteworthy that there are several gamification resources namely history/theme, progress, feedback, leaderboards, setting goals, rewards, challenges, badges/trophies, points, and levels or game leaders (Brown et al., 2016; Fleming et al., 2017; Lindner et al., 2017; Pham et al., 2016).

Gamification is a cognitive-behavioral technique that has been widely studied (Cheng et al., 2019). As previously mentioned, this type of intervention has been widely used in the health area, since it increases motivation and involvement in interventions (Cheng et al., 2019; Lindner et al., 2017; Linke et al., 2019; Sardi et al., 2017).

GAMIFICATION AND EXPOSURE THERAPY USING VIRTUAL REALITY

Combining gamification with VRET has advantages since gamification can reduce negative treatment experiences, gamified scenarios can be reproduced regularly, which consequently allows the individual to continue to face phobic stimuli, even after treatment (Lindner et al., 2017). The fact that it allows you to continue to face phobic stimuli after treatment can reduce the risk associated with returning to fear (Lindner et al., 2017). To ensure the effectiveness of gamification, so that it does not deviate from the therapeutic objectives outlined, the culture, gender, socioeconomic level, and age group of individuals must be considered (Lindner et al., 2017). Virtual Reality, like gamification, also allows to increase the participation and adhesion of individuals in the treatment (Cheng et al., 2019; Fernández-Álvarez et al., 2020; Lindner et al., 2017; Linke et al., 2019; Sardi et al., 2017). In this sense, the development of applications and interventions using gamification and virtual reality has been increasingly developed (Fernández-Álvarez et al., 2020).

GAMIFICATION AND SOCIAL PHOBIA

Recent studies show that gamification is commonly applied to interventions for the treatment of chronic diseases and although there are interventions to mental health, these are few (Cheng et al., 2019; Hopia & Raitio, 2016). However, although there are few studies in this regard, there is evidence that these interventions have positive effects on mental health (particularly depression and anxiety), particularly among young people, especially those who require internet access (Christie et al., 2019). In young people and young adults, in particular, gamified interventions have several advantages such as being more appealing, reducing stigma, and increasing compliance (Dennis & O'Toole, 2014). Considering the conclusions drawn from the studies presented, gamification can have positive effects on social phobia.

ARTIFICIAL INTELLIGENCE

Artificial Intelligence, it was defined as the science and engineering of making intelligent machines (Graham et al., 2019). Although intelligence is defined as a human characteristic, the associated artificial word refers to a form of computerized intelligence (Graham et al., 2019). The use of AI has been studied, particularly in mental health, despite being an area in which health professionals tend to take a more personal approach (Davenport & Kalakota, 2019; Graham et al., 2019; Weisel, 2018). Artificial Intelligence has great potential for a greater understanding of the client's status since, through this tool, it is possible to observe the client's profile and thus holistically understand their mental health (Graham et al., 2019). The positive result of the application of AI to mental health intervention is the adherence that individuals have to the use of mobile phones for this purpose (Davenport & Kalakota, 2019). The greater the involvement of individuals in their rehabilitation, the better the results, and the AI is believed to provide this involvement (Davenport & Kalakota, 2019).

OTHER STUDIES

As mentioned earlier, there are few studies on the use of virtual reality and gamification in social phobia (Emmelkamp et al., 2020). From the studies carried out, the main conclusions were that the use of virtual reality in the treatment of individuals with social phobia has positive effects (Anderson et al., 2013; Ben-Moussa et al., 2017; Kampmann, Emmelkamp, & Morina, 2016; Klinger et al., 2005; Opriş et al., 2012; Wallach et al., 2009). In a study by Klinger et al., individuals participated in virtual conversations in a meeting room and at a dinner table, and they were being analyzed and needed to assert themselves against the virtual agents (Klinger et al., 2005). The conclusions drawn were that this treatment is similarly effective compared to group CBT (Klinger et al., 2005). In turn, Wallach et al. also found similar effects to CBT in a public speaking task in a virtual reality setting (Wallach et al., 2009). In addition, another conclusion drawn was that dropout rates were lower (Wallach et al., 2009). Likewise, Anderson et al. they also concluded that there was a significant improvement in a public speaking task in a virtual reality setting and found no difference between VRET and *in vivo* (Anderson et al., 2013). In addition, they concluded that the effect is stable over 1 year after treatment (Anderson et al., 2013). Finally, Kampmann et al. reported that preliminary evidence indicates that VRET may have effects comparable to active treatments and that it has reduced the symptoms of individuals with social phobia (Kampmann, Emmelkamp, & Morina, 2016). In this study, individuals with social phobia were exposed to situations of virtual speech, job interviews, conversations with strangers, product returns in a supermarket, among others (Kampmann, Emmelkamp, & Morina, 2016). The therapist could adjust the number, gender, and gestures of the avatars, the friendliness, and, to some extent, the content of the dialogs depending on the needs of the individuals, the anxiety, and the progress of the treatment. Like Opris et al., Kampmann et al. they also concluded that VRET is just as effective as classic evidence-based interventions (Kampmann, Emmelkamp, & Morina, 2016; Opriş et al., 2012). Several studies also report that virtual social environments can be used successfully for therapeutic purposes (Emmelkamp et al., 2020; Felnhofer et al., 2019; Hartanto et al., 2014; H. Kim et al., 2018; Kishimoto & Ding, 2019; Lange & Pauli, 2019). Another study found that VRET was as effective as group CBT (Emmelkamp et al., 2020). Bouchard et al. concluded that CBT and VRET together were more effective compared to CBT and *in vivo* exposure (Bouchard et al., 2011). It is important to refer that most studies used virtual reality systems with immersive headsets (Emmelkamp et al., 2020).

Although studies carried out to date document positive effects regarding the use of virtual reality in the treatment of social phobia, most focus on the fear of public speaking, neglecting other contexts in which symptoms of social phobia may occur (Ben-Moussa et al., 2017). Besides, the majority of studies were carried out with people between 13 and 16 years old (Emmelkamp et al., 2020). Therefore, it is recommended to establish a treatment program that involves various symptoms of social phobia and that allows specific adaptations to the individual (Ben-Moussa et al., 2017; Emmelkamp et al., 2020).

PROPOSAL OF A TREATMENT PROGRAM

In this line of thought, the authors' main objective is to create a gamification program associated with the development of social skills, to bridge deficits in individuals with social phobia. In this program, each user will be able to create an avatar and there will be a table of classifications, as well as psycho-educational tips.

Individuals with social phobia have low levels of social interaction and high levels of negative affect associated with these interactions, that is, a set of negative emotions such as fear associated with social interactions (Morrison et al., 2016). Given these difficulties, it is possible to state that individuals with social phobia have unregulated empathic experiences (Morrison et al., 2016). These empathic difficulties can explain a large part of the social changes of these individuals (Morrison et al., 2016).

Regarding empathy, this is the set of cognitive and affective components, with cognitive empathy being the perception of the emotional state of the other, while emotional empathy is the response given with the same emotion, to the emotion perceived in the other (Morrison et al., 2016). These individuals show difficulties mainly in terms of cognitive empathy, showing difficulties in the theory of mind, that is, in the ability to perceive the emotions expressed by others (Morrison et al., 2016). In this sense, the literature refers that individuals with social phobia tend to perceive the verbal and non-verbal behavior of others as negative, increasing their levels of anxiety (Morrison et al., 2016).

Thus, considering the empathic deficits, it is proposed to create avatars at the beginning of the game. In this way, players will be able to express what they are feeling more clearly so that participants with social phobia can interact more efficiently and with lower levels of anxiety. This program will have a classification table in which each user can consult his classification. To be better classified in the table, extra social tasks will be available which, after completing, correspond to points which, consequently, allows the gain of more points.

To increase positive reinforcement, there will be notifications of psychoeducation that consist of providing support to each person using tips regarding their pathology and the treatment in which they are inserted. In the same sense, there will be notifications of motivational phrases with associated positive reinforcement. Each person will also be able to communicate with the therapist or with other users, through a chat, which will allow them to talk about their experience, how they felt during the sessions, or during the week, as well as about their progress/evolution. If they communicate with other users, the person can choose to send the message anonymously, to reduce their exposure.

Regarding these notifications, they must be presented as messages throughout the games and adjusted to the player's performance and needs, adopting an Artificial Intelligence (AI) system, which will be programmed for the different possible performances. This program must be associated with an application on the customer's mobile phone so that the customer can receive messages throughout the week, to keep in touch with progress and maintain involvement in rehabilitation.

It is important to note that this program will ensure the protection of each individual's data, with no sharing of personal and confidential information, both during sessions, as well as in conversations between the client and the therapist, or between the client and other players. In the same vein, the application associated with the program meets all confidentiality requirements.

Through the non-probabilistic convenience technique, as individuals voluntarily agreed to participate in the study, they would be selected according to inclusion and exclusion criteria, and to the more accessible contact. Inclusion criteria to participate in the study would be social phobia (more than 115 points on the AESDIS) and over the age of 18 years, motivation, and willingness to participate in the study. Exclusion criteria were individuals with health problems that prevented exposure to virtual reality, namely labyrinthitis, and have no smartphone.

The participation of individuals in the study would be formalized by completing the informed consent form, to ensure their rights and access to all information relevant to the decision to participate in the study. The privacy and confidentiality of the collected data would be also attested. In this study would be utilized a Clinical Interview, Demographic Characterization Questionnaire, and AESDIS. Collected data would be analyzed using the IBM SPSS Statistics 26 software. In terms of sociodemographic characterization of the participants, descriptive statistics would be used and taking into account the variables used, the mean and mode would be calculated as a measure of central tendency, the standard deviation as a measure of dispersion, and the absolute frequencies and frequency of each characteristic under analysis. Regarding the verification of significant changes before and after the implementation of the intervention protocol, inferential statistical analysis procedures would be used, assuming for all statistical tests a significance value (α) of 0.05 (Marôco, 2014; Pereira, 2008; Pestana & Gageiro, 2014).

The objective of the program is to check the impact of gamification in the treatment of social phobia. The hypotheses raised would be (1) gamification has an impact on the treatment of individuals with social phobia and (2) gamification has no impact on the treatment of individuals with social phobia.

PROGRAM

Therefore, a seven-level program was structured. In this program, the individual will have to perform various social tasks to pass the game levels, solving challenges alone and in a group.

The desensitization therapy program using gamification and virtual reality consisted of 15 sessions: an initial evaluation session, 13 biweekly exposure therapy sessions, and the last reevaluation session corresponding to a total program duration of 7 weeks. At the beginning of each session, an abdominal breathing exercise will be carried out to reduce anxiety levels. It is important to note that an initial and final evaluation will be carried out to understand the impact of the program on individuals with social phobia.

Each session, lasting approximately 50 minutes, follows a formal structure consisting of the following phases: Preparation and Warm-up of the Participant; Personalized and progressive exposure to social interaction associated with systematic desensitization games; and Relaxation and Feedback. This treatment strategy, therefore, consists of a combination of therapeutic ingredients, which includes exposure to fear-triggering stimuli, therapeutic instructions, monitoring client progress, performance feedback, and contingent performance enhancement.

The intervention focused on shaping appropriate approach behaviors through a process of successive approximations. The treatment was achieved by reducing the flight from the feared situation, assuming that the absence of consequences results in the extinction of fear, a common ingredient of exposure therapies. (Landowska et al., 2018; Verkuyl et al., 2018). The performance of approaching behaviors was facilitated by strengthening approaches and removing the negative reinforcement of avoidance. The grading of the exhibition was based on a duration of time (between 15 and 30 minutes) or several practical exhibitions with different levels of complexity and intensity.

The proposed plan involves several games, with each level gradually increasing the social interaction necessary to overcome it, making it possible to adapt the game to the difficulties presented.

The main objectives are to improve verbal communication with peers and social interaction, deal with their own emotions, understand and interpret non-verbal communication, manage anxiety and crises, reduce disruptive thoughts, decrease social isolation, encourage the use of coping strategies.

First Level

The player must be in a quiet place and must be alone. At this level, the individual must play Packman, and if he is eaten by the ghost, he must go to the supermarket to recover his life. At the end of the game, he must perform another social task, such as communicating with the employee. It is important to emphasize that in the supermarket there will be more players who will be able to communicate with him and may also express different emotions through facial expression.

Second Level

At this level, the individual must continue to play Packman, and if he is eaten by the ghost, to recover his life, the individual communicates with someone in the game, that is, he will have to talk to his virtual partner for a minute about his favorite food.

Third Level

The player will continue to play Packman, and if he is eaten by the ghost, to recover his life, have a conversation with the other person, for two minutes, without showing emotional, behavioral, and physiological symptoms inherent to the behaviors observed in social phobia (such as fear that the other person will notice that he is nervous, shortness of breath, increased sweating). You must make eye contact and be able to ask a question. It is important to note that this level will be carried out using virtual reality.

Fourth Level

The participant will continue to play Packman, and if he is eaten by the ghost, should go for coffee with the same partner on the second level, since you have already had contact with them, this will help to reduce anxiety levels, to recover his life.

Fifth Level

The individual will continue to play Packman, and if he is eaten by the ghost will have to mimic in trios, to recover his life. Therefore, the player will have to represent, through mimicry, a phrase that the other participants will have to guess. With the level increase, you will have to mimic, first, with one more person and then with 2 people, and in these cases, each element can only use one arm, the other arm being attached to the partner's arm of play.

Sixth Level

The individual will continue to play Packman, and if he is eaten by the ghost will have to participate in a quiz with a group of five people, in which you have to communicate and agree on the final answer with everyone agreeing, to recover his life.

Seventh Level

The player will continue to play Packman, and if he is eaten by the ghost, to recover his life, should perform a role play that consists of participating in a debate on a subject with another person, having to defend your point of view, presenting your arguments with the minimum of emotional, behavioral, or physiological symptoms inherent to the pathology.

Figure 1.

Nº	Tasks
Session 1	Task 1. Informed consent with authorization for filming
	Task 2. Demographic Characterization Questionnaire and Clinical Interview
	Task 3. Anxiety and Avoidance Scale in Performance and Social Interaction Situations
	Task 4. Teaching Breathing Exercise
	Task 6. Exposure **(adjusted to the reported level)**
	Task 8. *Feedback*, Scheduling Sessions
Session 2	Task 1. Breathing exercise/relaxation
	Task 2. Preparation for exhibition
	Task 3. Exposure **(adjusted to the reported level)**
	Task 4. *Feedback*, Scheduling Sessions
Session 3	Task 1. Breathing exercise/relaxation
	Task 2. Preparation for exhibition
	Task 3. Exposure **(adjusted to the reported level)**
	Task 4. *Feedback*, Scheduling Sessions
Session 4	Task 1. Breathing exercise/relaxation
	Task 2. Preparation for exhibition
	Task 3. Exposure **(adjusted to the reported level)**
	Task 4. *Feedback*, Scheduling Sessions
Session 5	Task 1. Breathing exercise/relaxation
	Task 2. Preparation for exhibition
	Task 3. Exposure **(adjusted to the reported level)**
	Task 4. *Feedback*, Scheduling Sessions
Session 6	Task 1. Breathing exercise/relaxation
	Task 2. Preparation for exhibition
	Task 3. Exposure **(adjusted to the reported level)**
	Task 4. *Feedback*, Scheduling Sessions
Session 7	Task 1. Breathing exercise/relaxation
	Task 2. Preparation for exhibition
	Task 3. Exposure **(adjusted to the reported level)**
	Task 4. *Feedback*, Scheduling Sessions.

It is important to emphasize that, since it is an individualized program and adapted to each person, the order of the levels can be changed, depending on the results obtained from the evaluation carried out in the first session through the interview and the Anxiety and Avoidance Scale in Situations of Performance and Social Interaction, that is, according to the most exacerbated difficulties of each person.

Regarding the continuation of the game, it only continues after all the social tasks corresponding to the level in question have been completed. All topics for debate, mime, and quiz will be selected by the game's program, depending on the player's rating.

SOLUTIONS AND RECOMMENDATIONS

It is important to refer that this program was not applied, so the authors don't have any solution for vies in the program.

REFERENCES

Abu-dawood, S. (2016). The Cognitive and The Social Motivational Affordances of Gamification in E-Learning Environment. International Conference on Advanced Learning Technologies. doi:10.1109/ICALT.2016.126

Ahmed-Leitao, F., Rosenstein, D., Marx, M., Young, S., Korte, K., & Seedat, S. (2019). Posttraumatic stress disorder, social anxiety disorder and childhood trauma: Differences in hippocampal subfield volume. *Psychiatry Research: Neuroimaging*, *284*, 45–52. doi:10.1016/j.pscychresns.2018.12.015 PubMed

Allsopp, K., Read, J., Corcoran, R., & Kinderman, P. (2019). Heterogeneity in psychiatric diagnostic classification. doi:10.1016/j.psychres.2019.07.005

de Almeida, M. C. (2018). *A saúde mental dos portugueses*. Academic Press.

American Psychiatric Association. (2014). 5th ed.). DSM-V. Diagnostic and Statistical Manual of Mental Disorders., doi:10.1176/appi.books.9780890425596.744053

Anderson, P. L., Price, M., Edwards, S. M., Obasaju, M. A., Schmertz, S. K., Zimand, E., & Calamaras, M. R. (2013). Virtual reality exposure therapy for social anxiety disorder: A randomized controlled trial. *Journal of Consulting and Clinical Psychology*, *81*(5), 751–760. Advance online publication. doi:10.1037/a0033559 PubMed

Andreatta, M., Neueder, D., Glotzbach-Schoon, E., Mühlberger, A., & Pauli, P. (2017). Effects of context preexposure and delay until anxiety retrieval on generalization of contextual anxiety. *Learning & Memory (Cold Spring Harbor, N.Y.)*, *24*(1), 43–54. doi:10.1101/lm.044073.116 PubMed

Apolinário-Hagen, J., Drüge, M., & Fritsche, L. (2020). Cognitive Behavioral Therapy, Mindfulness-Based Cognitive Therapy and Acceptance Commitment Therapy for Anxiety Disorders: Integrating Traditional with Digital Treatment Approaches. In Y. Kim (Ed.), *Anxiety Disorders Rethinking and Understanding Recent Discoveries* (pp. 291–330). Advances in Experimental Medicine and Biology., doi:10.1007/978-981-32-9705-0_17.

Arroll, B., Henwood, S. M., Sundram, F. I., Kingsford, D. W., Mount, V., Humm, S. P., Wallace, H. B., & Pillai, A. (2017). A brief treatment for fear of heights : A randomized controlled trial of a novel imaginal intervention. doi:10.1177/0091217417703285

Bas-Hoogendam, J. M., van Steenbergen, H., Nienke Pannekoek, J., Fouche, J. P., Lochner, C., Hattingh, C. J., Cremers, H. R., Furmark, T., Månsson, K. N. T., Frick, A., Engman, J., Boraxbekk, C. J., Carlbring, P., Andersson, G., Fredrikson, M., Straube, T., Peterburs, J., Klumpp, H., Phan, K. L., ... van der Wee, N. J. A. (2017). Voxel-based morphometry multi-center mega-analysis of brain structure in social anxiety disorder. *NeuroImage. Clinical, 16*, 678–688. doi:10.1016/j.nicl.2017.08.001 PubMed

Ben-Moussa, M., Rubo, M., Debracque, C., & Lange, W. G. (2017). DJInnI: A novel technology supported exposure therapy paradigm for SAD combining virtual reality and augmented reality. *Frontiers in Psychiatry, 8*, 26. Advance online publication. doi:10.3389/fpsyt.2017.00026 PubMed

Bouchard, S., Dumoulin, S., Robillard, G., Guitard, T., Klinger, E., & Forget, H. (2011). A randomized controlled trial for the use of in virtuo exposure in the treatment of social phobia. *Journal of Cyber Therapy and Rehabilitation, 4*(2), 197–199.

Brown, M., O'Neill, N., van Woerden, H., Eslambolchilar, P., Jones, M., & John, A. (2016). Gamification and Adherence to Web-Based Mental Health Interventions: A Systematic Review. JMIR Mental Health, 3(3), e39. doi:10.2196/mental.5710 PubMed

Bruffaerts, R., Villagut, G., & Demyttenaere, K. (2011). The Burden of mental disorders in the European Union. The EU Contribution to the World Mental Health Surveys.

Bruhl, A. B., Delsignore, A., Komossa, K., & Weidt, S. (2014). Neuroimaging in Social Anxiety Disorder–a meta-analytic review resulting in a new neurofunctional model. *Neuroscience and Biobehavioral Reviews, 47*, 260–280. doi:10.1016/j.neubiorev.2014.08.003 PubMed

Cabral, M. D., & Patel, D. R. (2020). Risk Factors and Prevention Strategies for Anxiety Disorders in Childhood and Adolescence. In Y.-K. Kim (Ed.), *Anxiety Disorders Rethinking and Understanding Recent Discoveries* (pp. 543–559). Advances in Experimental Medicine and Biology., doi:10.1007/978-981-32-9705-0_27.

Canton, J., Scott, K. M., & Glue, P. (2017). Optimal treatment of social phobia: Systematic review and meta-analysis. Neuropsychiatric Disease and Treatment. PubMed

Carnevali, L., Sgoifo, A., Trombini, M., Landgraf, R., Neumann, I. D., & Nalivaiko, E. (2013). Different Patterns of Respiration in Rat Lines Selectively Bred for High or Low Anxiety., 8(5). Advance online publication. PubMed doi:10.1371/journal.pone.0064519

Carvalho, Á. (2017). *Depressão e outras Perturbações Mentais Comuns: enquadramento global e nacional e referência de recurso em casos emergentes*. Academic Press.

Cebrián, R. P., Elvira, A. C., & Elvira, A. N. A. C. (2017). Applying cognitive restructuring in therapy : The clinical reality in Spain Applying cognitive restructuring in therapy : The clinical reality in Spain. doi:10.1080/10503307.2017.1341655

Cheng, V. W. S., Davenport, T., Johnson, D., Vella, K., & Hickie, I. B. (2019). Gamification in apps and technologies for improving mental health and well-being: Systematic review. *Journal of Medical Internet Research*. Advance online publication. doi:10.2196/13717

Christie, G. I., Shepherd, M., Merry, S. N., Knightly, S., & Stasiak, K. (2019). Gamifying CBT to deliver emotional health treatment to young people on smartphones. *Internet Interventions : the Application of Information Technology in Mental and Behavioural Health, 100286*, 100286. Advance online publication. doi:10.1016/j.invent.2019.100286 PubMed

Clauss, J. A., Avery, S. N., Benningfield, M. M., & Blackford, J. U. (2019). Social anxiety is associated with BNST response to unpredictability. *Depression and Anxiety, 36*(8), 666–675. doi:10.1002/da.22891 PubMed

Cosci, F., & Mansueto, G. (2020). Biological and Clinical Markers to Differentiate the Type of Anxiety Disorders. In Y. Kim (Ed.), *Anxiety Disorders Rethinking and Understanding Recent Discoveries* (pp. 197–218). Advances in Experimental Medicine and Biology., doi:10.1007/978-981-32-9705-0_13.

Davenport, T., & Kalakota, R. (2019). *The potential for artificial intelligence in healthcare*. Academic Press.

Dennis, T. A., & O'Toole, L. J. (2014). Mental health on the go: Effects of a gamified attention-bias modification mobile application in trait-anxious adults. *Clinical Psychological Science, 2*(5), 576–590. Advance online publication. doi:10.1177/2167702614522228 PubMed

DGS. (2015). *Saúde mental em números*. Direção Geral Da Saúde.

Donker, T., Van Esveld, S., Fischer, N., & Van Straten, A. (2018). 0Phobia - towards a virtual cure for acrophobia: Study protocol for a randomized controlled trial. *Trials, 19*(1), 433. Advance online publication. doi:10.1186/s13063-018-2704-6 PubMed

Eaton, W. W., Bienvenu, O. J., & Miloyan, B. (2018). Specific phobias. *The Lancet. Psychiatry, 5*(8), 678–686. doi:10.1016/S2215-0366(18)30169-X PubMed

Emmelkamp, P. M. G., Meyerbröker, K., & Morina, N. (2020). Virtual Reality Therapy in Social Anxiety Disorder. *Current Psychiatry Reports, 22*(7), 32. Advance online publication. doi:10.1007/s11920-020-01156-1 PubMed

Erin, H., Hong, Y., Kim, M., Hoon, Y., Kyeong, S., & Kim, J. (2017). Computers in Human Behavior Effectiveness of self-training using the mobile-based virtual reality program in patients with social anxiety disorder. *Computers in Human Behavior, 73*, 614–619. doi:10.1016/j.chb.2017.04.017

Felnhofer, A., Hlavacs, H., Beutl, L., Kryspin-Exner, I., & Kothgassner, O. D. (2019). Physical Presence, Social Presence, and Anxiety in Participants with Social Anxiety Disorder during Virtual Cue Exposure. *Cyberpsychology, Behavior, and Social Networking, 22*(1), 46–50. Advance online publication. doi:10.1089/cyber.2018.0221 PubMed

Fernández-Álvarez, J., Di Lernia, D., & Riva, G. (2020). Virtual Reality for Anxiety Disorders: Rethinking a Field in Expansion. In Y.-K. Kim (Ed.), *Anxiety Disorders Rethinking and Understanding Recent Discoveries* (pp. 389–414). Advances in Experimental Medicine and Biology., doi:10.1007/978-981-32-9705-0_21.

Fleming, T. M., Bavin, L., Stasiak, K., Hermansson-Webb, E., Merry, S. N., Cheek, C., Lucassen, M., Lau, H. M., Pollmuller, B., & Hetrick, S. (2017). Serious games and gamification for mental health: Current status and promising directions. Frontiers in Psychiatry, 7. Advance online publication. doi:10.3389/fpsyt.2016.00215 PubMed

Floryan, M. R., Ritterband, L. M., & Chow, P. I. (2019). Principles of gamification for Internet interventions. doi:10.1093/tbm/ibz041

Freitas-Ferrari, M. C., Hallak, J. E. C., Trzesniak, C., Filho, A. S., Machado-de-Sousa, J. P., Chagas, M. H. N., Nardi, A. E., & Crippa, J. A. S. (2010). Neuroimaging in social anxiety disorder: A systematic review of the literature. *Progress in Neuro-Psychopharmacology & Biological Psychiatry*, *34*(4), 565–580. doi:10.1016/j.pnpbp.2010.02.028 PubMed

Galderisi, S., Andreas, H., Marianne, K., Julian, B., & Norman, S. (2017). *A proposed new definition of mental health.* Academic Press.

Gebara, C. M., de Barros-Neto, T. P., Gertsenchtein, L., & Lotufo-Neto, F. (2016). Virtual reality exposure using three-dimensional images for the treatment of social phobia. *The British Journal of Psychiatry*, *38*(1). Advance online publication. PubMed doi:10.1590/1516-4446-2014-1560

Geraets, C. N. W., Veling, W., Witlox, M., Staring, A. B. P., Matthijssen, S. J. M. A., & Cath, D. (2019). Virtual reality-based cognitive behavioural therapy for patients with generalized social anxiety disorder: A pilot study. *Behavioural and Cognitive Psychotherapy*, *47*(6), 745–750. doi:10.1017/S1352465819000225 PubMed

Goessl, V. C., Curtiss, J. E., & Hofmann, S. G. (2018). The effect of heart rate variability biofeedback training on stress and anxiety : a meta-analysis. doi:10.1017/S0033291717001003

Gouveia, J. P., Cunha, M., & Salvador, M. do C. (2003). Assessment of Social Phobia by Self-Report Questionnaires: The Social Interaction and Performance Anxiety and Avoidance Scale and the Social Phobia Safety Behaviours Scale. In Behavioural and Cognitive Psychoterapy (pp. 291–311). Academic Press.

Graham, S., Depp, C., Lee, E. E., Nebeker, C., Tu, X., Kim, H., & Jeste, D. V. (2019). *Artificial Intelligence for Mental Health and Mental Illnesses : an Overview.* Academic Press.

Gray, E., Beierl, E. T., & Clark, D. M. (2019). Sub-types of safety behaviours and their effects on social anxiety disorder. *PLoS One*, *14*(10), e0223165. Advance online publication. doi:10.1371/journal.pone.0223165 PubMed

Hartanto, D., Kampmann, I. L., Morina, N., Emmelkamp, P. G. M., Neerincx, M. A., & Brinkman, W. P. (2014). Controlling social stress in virtual reality environments. *PLoS One*, *9*(3), e92804. Advance online publication. doi:10.1371/journal.pone.0092804 PubMed

Hirsch, J. A. (2018). Integrating Hypnosis with Other Therapies for Treating Specific Phobias: A Case Series. *The American Journal of Clinical Hypnosis*, *60*(4), 367–377. doi:10.1080/00029157.2017.132 6372 PubMed

Holzschneider, K., & Mulert, C. (2011). Neuroimaging in anxiety disorders. Translational Research; the Journal of Laboratory and Clinical Medicine. PubMed

Hopia, H., & Raitio, K. (2016). Gamification in Healthcare: Perspectives of Mental Health Service Users and Health Professionals. *Issues in Mental Health Nursing*, *37*(12), 894–902. Advance online publication. doi:10.1080/01612840.2016.1233595 PubMed

Irle, E., Ruhleder, M., Lange, C., Seidler-Brandler, U., Salzer, S., Dechent, P., Weniger, G., Leibing, E., & Leichsenring, F. (2010). Reduced amygdalar and hippocampal size in adults with generalized social phobia. *Journal of Psychiatry & Neuroscience*, *35*(2), 126–131. doi:10.1503/jpn.090041 PubMed

Janardhan Reddy, Y. C., Sudhir, P. M., Manjula, M., Arumugham, S. S., & Narayanaswamy, J. C. (2020). Clinical Practice Guidelines for Cognitive-Behavioral Therapies in Anxiety Disorders and Obsessive-Compulsive and Related Disorders. *Indian Journal of Psychiatry*, *62*(8), S230–S250. doi:10.4103/psychiatry.IndianJPsychiatry_773_19 PubMed

Johnson, D., Deterding, S., Kuhn, K. A., Staneva, A., Stoyanov, S., & Hides, L. (2016). Gamification for health and wellbeing: A systematic review of the literature. In Internet Interventions (Vol. 6, pp. 89–106). doi:10.1016/j.invent.2016.10.002

Kampmann, I. L., Emmelkamp, P. M. G., Hartanto, D., Brinkman, W. P., Zijlstra, B. J. H., & Morina, N. (2016). Exposure to virtual social interactions in the treatment of social anxiety disorder: A randomized controlled trial. *Behaviour Research and Therapy*, *77*, 147–156. Advance online publication. doi:10.1016/j.brat.2015.12.016 PubMed

Kampmann, I. L., Emmelkamp, P. M. G., & Morina, N. (2016). Meta-analysis of technology-assisted interventions for social anxiety disorder. *Journal of Anxiety Disorders*, *42*, 71–84. Advance online publication. doi:10.1016/j.janxdis.2016.06.007 PubMed

Kampmann, I. L., Emmelkamp, P. M. G., & Morina, N. (2019). Cognitive predictors of treatment outcome for exposure therapy: Do changes in self-efficacy, self-focused attention, and estimated social costs predict symptom improvement in social anxiety disorder? *BMC Psychiatry*, *19*(1), 80. Advance online publication. doi:10.1186/s12888-019-2054-2 PubMed

Kim, H., Shin, J. E., Hong, Y. J., Shin, Y., Shin, Y. S., Han, K., Kim, J.-J., & Choi, S.-H. (2018). Aversive eye gaze during a speech in virtual environment in patients with social anxiety disorder. *The Australian and New Zealand Journal of Psychiatry*, *52*(3), 279–285. doi:10.1177/0004867417714335 PubMed

Kishimoto, T., & Ding, X. (2019). The influences of virtual social feedback on social anxiety disorders. *Behavioural and Cognitive Psychotherapy*, *47*(6), 726–735. doi:10.1017/S1352465819000377 PubMed

Klinger, E., Bouchard, S., Légeron, P., Roy, S., Lauer, F., Chemin, I., & Nugues, P. (2005). Virtual reality therapy versus cognitive behavior therapy for social phobia: A preliminary controlled study. *Cyberpsychology & Behavior*, *8*(1), 76–88. Advance online publication. doi:10.1089/cpb.2005.8.76 PubMed

Landowska, A., Roberts, D., Eachus, P., Barrett, A., & Pauli, P. (2018). Within- and Between-Session Prefrontal Cortex Response to Virtual Reality Exposure Therapy for Acrophobia. doi:10.3389/fnhum.2018.00362

Lange, B., & Pauli, P. (2019). Social anxiety changes the way we move— A social approach-avoidance task in a virtual reality CAVE system. *PLoS One*, *14*(12), e0226805. Advance online publication. doi:10.1371/journal.pone.0226805 PubMed

Larsson, A., Hooper, N., Osborne, L. A., Bennett, P., & Mchugh, L. (2015). Using Brief Cognitive Restructuring and Cognitive Defusion Techniques to Cope With Negative Thoughts. doi:10.1177/0145445515621488

Lau, H. M., Smit, J. H., Fleming, T. M., & Riper, H. (2017). Serious Games for Mental Health: Are They Accessible, Feasible, and Effective? A Systematic Review and Meta-analysis. Frontiers in Psychiatry, 7. Advance online publication. doi:10.3389/fpsyt.2016.00209 PubMed

Lee, M. D. (2016). Gamification and the Psychology of Game Design in Transforming Mental Health Care. *Journal of the American Psychiatric Nurses Association*, *22*(2), 134–136. doi:10.1177/1078390316636857 PubMed

Leichsenring, F., & Leweke, F. (2017). Social anxiety disorder. *The New England Journal of Medicine*, *376*(23), 2255–2264. doi:10.1056/NEJMcp1614701 PubMed

Leigh, E., & Clark, D. M. (2018). Understanding Social Anxiety Disorder in Adolescents and Improving Treatment Outcomes: Applying the Cognitive Model of Clark and Wells (1995). *Clinical Child and Family Psychology Review*, *21*(3), 388–414. doi:10.1007/s10567-018-0258-5 PubMed

Lindner, P., Miloff, A., Hamilton, W., Reuterskiöld, L., Andersson, G., Powers, M. B., & Carlbring, P. (2017). Creating state of the art, next-generation Virtual Reality exposure therapies for anxiety disorders using consumer hardware platforms: Design considerations and future directions. *Cognitive Behaviour Therapy*, *46*(5), 404–420. Advance online publication. doi:10.1080/16506073.2017.1280843 PubMed

Linke, J. O., Jones, E., Pagliaccio, D., Swetlitz, C., Lewis, K. M., Silverman, W. K., Bar-Haim, Y., Pine, D. S., & Brotman, M. A. (2019). Efficacy and mechanisms underlying a gamified attention bias modification training in anxious youth: Protocol for a randomized controlled trial. *BMC Psychiatry*, *19*(1), 246. Advance online publication. doi:10.1186/s12888-019-2224-2 PubMed

Lumsden, J., Edwards, E. A., Lawrence, N. S., Coyle, D., & Munafò, M. R. (2016). Gamification of Cognitive Assessment and Cognitive Training: A Systematic Review of Applications and Efficacy. JMIR Serious Games, 4(2), e11. Advance online publication. doi:10.2196/games.5888 PubMed

Marôco, J. (2014). Análise estatística com o SPSS Statistics. In Análise e Gestão da Informacão.

Miloff, A., Marklund, A., & Carlbring, P. (2015). *The challenger app for social anxiety disorder: New advances in mobile psychological treatment*. Internet Interventions., doi:10.1016/j.invent.2015.08.001

Morrison, A. S., Mateen, M. A., Brozovich, F. A., Zaki, J., Philippe, R., Heimberg, R. G., & Gross, J. J. (2016). Empathy for Positive and Negative Emotions in Social Anxiety Disorder. *Behaviour Research and Therapy*, *87*, 232–242. Advance online publication. doi:10.1016/j.brat.2016.10.005 PubMed

National Collaborating Centre for Mental Health. N. C. G. (2013). Social Anxiety Disorder. Recognition. Assessment and Treatment. *The New England Journal of Medicine*. Advance online publication. doi:10.1056/NEJMcp1614701

NICE Clinical Guidelines. (2013). *Social Anxiety Disorder: Recognition*. Assessment and Treatment.

Opriş, D., Pintea, S., García-Palacios, A., Botella, C., Szamosközi, Ş., & David, D. (2012). Virtual reality exposure therapy in anxiety disorders: A quantitative meta-analysis. *Depression and Anxiety*, *29*(2), 85–93. Advance online publication. doi:10.1002/da.20910 PubMed

Park, S.-C., & Kim, Y.-K. (2020). Anxiety Disorders in the DSM-5: Changes, Controversies, and Future Directions. In Y. Kim (Ed.), *Anxiety Disorders Rethinking and Understanding Recent Discoveries* (pp. 187–196). Advances in Experimental Medicine and Biology., doi:10.1007/978-981-32-9705-0_12.

Paschali, A. A., & Tsitsas, G. (2014). A cognitive-behavior therapy applied to a social anxiety disorder and a specific phobia, case study. Health Psychology Research. PubMed

Pepper, K. L., Demetriou, E. A., Park, S. H., Boulton, K. A., Hickie, I. B., Thomas, E. E., & Guastella, A. J. (2019). Self-reported empathy in adults with autism, early psychosis, and social anxiety disorder. *Psychiatry Research*, *281*, 112604. Advance online publication. doi:10.1016/j.psychres.2019.112604 PubMed

Pereira, A. (2008). *SPSS - Guia prático de utilização*. Edições Sílabo.

Perna, G., Alciati, A., Sangiorgio, E., Caldirola, D., & Nemeroff, C. B. (2020). Personalized Clinical Approaches to Anxiety Disorders. In Y.-K. Kim (Ed.), *Anxiety Disorders Rethinking and Understanding Recent Discoveries* (pp. 489–521). Advances in Experimental Medicine and Biology., doi:10.1007/978-981-32-9705-0_25.

Pestana, M. H., & Gageiro, J. N. (2014). *Análise de dados para ciências sociais a complementaridade do spss 6 a edição Revista*. Atualizada e Aumentada., doi:10.13140/2.1.2491.7284

Pham, Q., Khatib, Y., Stansfeld, S., Fox, S., & Green, T. (2016). Feasibility and Efficacy of an mHealth Game for Managing Anxiety: "Flowy" Randomized Controlled Pilot Trial and Design Evaluation. *Games for Health Journal*, *5*(1), 50–67. Advance online publication. doi:10.1089/g4h.2015.0033 PubMed

Pinto-Gouveia, J. A. (1997). *Modelos cognitivos de fobia social: conceptualizações teóricas, apoio empírico e implicações terapêuticas*. Psiquiatria Clínica.

Rose, G. M., & Tadi, P. (2020). Social Anxiety Disorder. StatPearls Publishing. https://www.ncbi.nlm.nih.gov/pubmed/32310350

Ruhi, U. (2015). *Level Up Your Strategy: Towards a Descriptive Framework for Meaningful Enterprise Gamification*. Technology Innovation Management Review.

Sánchez, D. O., & Gómez Trigueros, I. M. (2019). Gamification, social problems, and gender in the teaching of social sciences: Representations and discourse of trainee teachers. PLoS One. Advance online publication. PubMed doi:10.1371/journal.pone.0218869

Sardi, L., Idri, A., & Fernández-Alemán, J. L. (2017). A systematic review of gamification in e-Health. Journal of Biomedical Informatics. doi:10.1016/j.jbi.2017.05.011

Serlachius, E., Kleberg, J. L., Högström, J., Nordh, M., Lindal, M. L., & Taylor, E. (2019). Visual attention to emotional faces in adolescents with social anxiety disorder receiving cognitive behavioral therapy. *PLoS One*, *14*(11). Advance online publication. PubMed doi:10.1371/journal.pone.0225603

Turan, Z., Avinc, Z., Kara, K., & Goktas, Y. (2016). Gamification and Education: Achievements, Cognitive Loads, and Views of Students. International Journal of Emerging Technologies in Learning.

Verkuyl, M., Romaniuk, D., & Mastrilli, P. (2018). Virtual gaming simulation of a mental health assessment: A usability study. *Nurse Education in Practice*, *31*, 83–87. doi:10.1016/j.nepr.2018.05.007 PubMed

Wallach, H. S., Safir, M. P., & Bar-Zvi, M. (2009). Virtual reality cognitive behavior therapy for public speaking anxiety: A randomized clinical trial. *Behavior Modification*, *33*(3), 314–338. Advance online publication. doi:10.1177/0145445509331926 PubMed

Wang, H., Zhao, Q., Mu, W., Rodriguez, M., Qian, M., & Berger, T. (2020). The Effect of Shame on Patients With Social Anxiety Disorder in Internet-Based Cognitive Behavioral Therapy: Comparison Clinical Trial in China. JMIR Mental Health. Advance online publication. doi:10.2196/15797 PubMed

Wechsler, T. F., Kümpers, F., & Mühlberger, A. (2019). Inferiority or Even Superiority of Virtual Reality Exposure Therapy in Phobias? — A Systematic Review and Quantitative Meta-Analysis on Randomized Controlled Trials Specifically Comparing the Efficacy of Virtual Reality Exposure to Gold Standard in vivo. *E (Norwalk, Conn.)*, *10*(September). Advance online publication. PubMed doi:10.3389/fpsyg.2019.01758

Weisel, K. K. (2018). Standalone smartphone apps for mental health— A systematic review and meta-analysis. NPJ Digital Medicine, 1–10. PubMed doi:10.1038/s41746-019-0188-8

World Health Organization. (2018). *Mental health: strengthening our response*. WHO.

Zhang, M., Ying, J., Song, G., Fung, D. S., & Smith, H. (2018). Gamified Cognitive Bias Modification Interventions for Psychiatric Disorders [Review]. JMIR Mental Health, 5(4), e11640. doi:10.2196/11640 PubMed

Zhu, Y., Gao, H., Tong, L., Li, Z., Wang, L., Zhang, C., Yan, B., & Yang, Q. (2019). Emotion Regulation of Hippocampus Using Real-Time fMRI Neurofeedback in Healthy Human. *Frontiers in Human Neuroscience*, *13*, 242. doi:10.3389/fnhum.2019.00242 PubMed

Chapter 61
Online Simulations and Gamification:
A Case Study Across an Emergency and Disaster Management Program

Terri L. Wilkin

ⓘ https://orcid.org/0000-0003-4443-3521

American Public University System, USA

ABSTRACT

Higher education has seen a dramatic increase in the number of courses and programs offered in an online environment over the past two decades. As most online educational courses are asynchronous in nature, ensuring that applied learning happens in scenarios that replicate real-life events is of utmost importance especially in certain disciplines such as emergency and disaster management. With the advent of newer and advanced technologies, online gamifications and simulations offer a learning method that requires the students to use decision-making, problem solving, and critical thinking skills in a fictional scenario that imitates events that individuals in the particular career field will experience. This chapter is an examination of the use of gamifications and simulations in online higher education highlighting a holistic approach to gaming and simulations designed and implemented across an undergraduate emergency and disaster program.

INTRODUCTION

A vital role for individuals in the emergency management field is protecting a community before and after a disaster strikes. This role requires the completion of an emergency operations plan (EOP) that identifies possible vulnerabilities and hazards that pose a risk to the community. A first critical step in the process is completing a hazard vulnerability assessment (HVA) that identifies those hazards posing the most threat to a community. Consider an individual who steps into an incident commander's role and is responsible for coordinating the information from critical infrastructure resources to secure and

DOI: 10.4018/978-1-6684-7589-8.ch061

protect the community during a disaster. Decisions and activities carried out during emergencies must be appropriately coordinated as failure to do so may cause additional loss of life, injury, and/or damage to the community. Proper coordination requires understanding key actors' roles and responsibilities in the emergency and disaster management space. The question for curriculum leadership, be it a Department Chair or Program Director then becomes how to teach these skills to students in online classrooms allowing them to learn from their mistakes in a learning environment where a wrong decision in real-life could cause harm to life and/or property. Experential learning not only helps students to succeed on the job but also helps when they are in the job market. For programs with adult learners, students are often looking to up-skill, learn new skills, or looking to transition to a new field. Therefore, higher abilities such as experiential learning is a key concern for program directors. This is why programs engage with an Industry Advisory Council (IAC) to ensure that upon graduation, students have the skills they need to be successful in the workforce. How can online classrooms replicate real-life events allowing the students to make decisions, solve problems, and think critically in a high-energy and emotive environment? The answer is to teach students what it is like by making them do it themselves within a safe and well-controlled environment. The addition of simulations and games in the online classroom allows the students to play an EOP, among other true-to-life tasks.

LITERATURE REVIEW

There are many articles on simulations and gamification in online higher education; however, few exist that focus on the emergency and disaster management discipline. A few books on the market cover simulations and gamification and are specific to nursing and science subjects. However, few books exist that are specific to the field of emergency and disaster management (Aldrich, 2009; Bursens, Donche, Gijbels, & Spooren, 2018; Cai, van Joolingen, & Walker; Carnes, 2014; 2019; Information Resources Management Association, 2018; Nygaard, Courtney, & Lee, 2012). One book on the market includes different types of simulations, applications for gaming and simulations, and design and evaluation of interactive training methodologies (Rolfe, Saunders & Powell, 2013). Adding simulations into online courses such as emergency and disaster management ensures that students can apply the skill-sets needed to succeed within the discipline.

Education

There are many notable examples of simulations in training and education classrooms across the globe. Sections within conferences dedicate much time to active learning, such as within the International Studies Association, "Active Learning in International Affairs Section (ALIAS)," that was established to promote the use of active learning and simulations in the classroom (Lantis 1998). Across the globe and in many different fields, higher educational institutions design and use simulations in the classroom (Kempston & Thomas, 2014). Online higher educational institutions need to take advantage of technology advancements and add simulations and gamification to the classroom to ensure students are equipped with the requisite skills, especially in specific disciplines such as emergency and disaster management, to succeed in the workplace.

Experiential Learning

Simulations and gamification are methods whereby students can learn by applying critical thinking, decision making, and problem-solving followed by a reflective piece to close the gap in required experiential skills and enhance learner digital literacy. Games have moved beyond being only used for entertainment purposes and have moved to the online classroom as immersive, experiential educational learning applications (Zemliansky, & Wilcox, 2010). Besides using simulations and games as a learning tool, digital literacy is a vital skill set that is becoming more of a requirement in the workplace and everyday life (Bond, Marin, Dolch, Bedenlier, & Zawacki-Richter, 2018). Many employers complain about the lack of digital skills graduates of higher education have (Azmi, Iahad, & Ahmad, 2015). An estimated 90% of the skills required in the workplace are experiential - learning by actually doing it (Beckem & Watkins, 2012). Within simulations, students gain the digital literacy and practical skills needed for use in the workforce or their careers.

Simulations in the Classroom

The use of simulations and gamification within higher education offers the student the opportunity to control their learning by applying the knowledge in scenarios that replicate real-life events. Simulations and gamification move the learning from complete forms such as an HVA using a fictitious town, prepare an instructor-centered approach to a student-centered approach letting the students be in charge of and responsible for their learning (Beckem & Watkins, 2012). Instead of memorizing course material, students can move beyond this by applying concepts, analyzing, evaluating, and synthesizing information formulating new knowledge in the process (Beckem & Watkins, 2012). Simulations and gamification allow the learner to make mistakes in practice instead of making these mistakes in real-life events where persons and/or property could be damaged (McCallum, 2006). One study specific to emergency management found that simulations were critical in higher education as the students need to have specific skills and not just the knowledge to be successful (Fortino, Kanjanabootra & von Meding, 2017). Just knowing the course material is not enough, as the ability to apply the material is a critical goal for students to take these skills with them into the workplace. Ultimately, simulations create a safe environment where learners can experiment with their application of content knowledge. EOP, and etc.

Learning Theories

Studies on how different individuals learn are essential considerations when designing an online course and considering simulations and gamification. Several learning theories revolve around the experiential learning involved in simulations and games. Increasing student performance and participation can be explained by social learning, self-efficacy, and self-determination theories that involve intrinsic and extrinsic motivations (Azmi, Iahad, & Ahmad, 2015; Banfield & Wilkerson, 2014). Gamification and simulations also relate to the motivational theory that encourages students' intrinsic motivation by offering challenging and socially interacting learning tools (Alabbasi, 2017). Social interaction within online courses has been problematic, with the lack of physical interaction that frequently leads to lonely and disconnected students leading to higher attrition rates (Alabbasi, 2017). Simulations and games within online courses help motivate the student to learn and decrease the online student from feeling detached from the learning environment.

Learning by Doing

The learning theories associated with simulations and gamification focus primarily on the learner's interaction with the presentation of the information. Several learning theories support the proposition that learning with simulations and gamification offers the learning by doing construct that has been missing in online courses. There is ample research on the effectiveness of learning by doing instead of merely memorizing information tracing back to 1899 in the work of John Dewey, which has been followed by others throughout the years (Zemliansky & Wilcox, 2010). Social constructivism learning theory revolves around each student being a unique learner, with each learner being involved actively in the process of learning (Beckem & Watkins, 2012). In constructiveness learning theory, the learning is transformational, experiential, reflective, and situated (Rutherford-Hemming, 2012). In situated cognition, learning theory applies to an immersive learning design, whereby learning focuses on real-life events (Becken & Watkins, 2012; Rutherford-Hemming, 2012). Simulations create an environment whereby students can process the knowledge and skills being mastered with those they may need additional practice or instructor that facilitates cognitive learning (Rutherford-Hemming, 2012). Games and simulations offer the student the opportunity to revisit the material at different times in different contexts, for different purposes and perspectives essential to acquire advanced knowledge (Zemliansky, & Wilcox, 2010). To produce usable knowledge, the student needs to also reflect about what they did and what it meant to them (Zemliansky, & Wilcox, 2010). Jin, Jiong, Yang, Huaping, and Wei (2014) found that simulations help students with complex networks theory, as disasters are dynamic with effects that avalanche requiring quick decisions. These learning theories center on the learner and the need for an engaging and meaningful learning environment where the transfer of learned skills to real-life occurs.

Design of Simulations and Gamification

Within the literature, a clear debate arises over the integration and use of simulations and games within the classroom. Besides the studies that found a minimal number of instructors and students who thought that simulations and games within the online course had adverse effects as a learning tool, most disadvantages concerned the actual simulation design. In one camp, researchers caution that simulations and games are a supplemental tool. Hallyburton and Lunsford (2013) recommend that simulations in online courses should only be a supplemental tool and not replace the traditional makeup of a course, such as reading materials, discussions, assignments, and other content customarily within a course. The choosing of simulations is a critical step as some computer simulations can be expensive and flashy yet are ineffective in building needed skills (Hallyburton & Lunsford, 2013). Laxman and Chin (2011) advise that simulations by themselves do not bring about learning or results, as an exploitation of the tools to meet the educational setting's needs in significant ways if enhanced learning is the goal. Studies have found that the most effective simulations and games are those where the student faces a scenario based on real-life events where cooperative learning takes place among the students and instructors, allowing for the reflection and discussion of how they might have done something differently (Rutherford-Hemming, 2012). With simulations and gamification, as with any course materials, caution is required in the planning stages, with a holistic approach to ensure that the course is comprehensive and is still a learning environment achieving the course objectives.

Importance of Design

The design of simulations and gamification is one of the most essential parts in ensuring that an appropriate and productive learning environment happens. The design of simulations and games is essential. If the research about suitable simulation and game design with a faulty rationale and poor design of a game, then the simulations and games will not be effective learning tools (Chang & Wei, 2016). In designing simulations and games, one of the most important aspects is to ensure that they align with the desired learning objectives and outcomes of the course (Ahmed & Sutton, 2017). According to one study, another problem is that there is a general lack of information available related to the systematic planning, designing, and implementation of simulations and gamification in higher education (Lockley & Darwin, 2014). It is also essential to consider the relationship between different students and their learning styles when designing simulations (Abdollahzade & Jafari, 2018). Students want simulations and gamification that are easy to navigate and flexible to use (Alabbasi, 2017). The design of simulations and gamification is important because they need to be reusable at any time in any course with ease of modification, including revisions and improvements over time (Beckem & Watkins, 2012). The development of a comprehensive strategy is required before designing and implementing simulations and games within the online classroom to ensure that they meet the requirements of the course, the student, and the instructor.

BEFORE SIMULATIONS

Before the adoption of simulations and games in the online asynchronous courses, the content within the courses consisted of the traditional online teaching processes such as assignments, discussion forums, reading materials, videos, etc. These traditional teaching methods do not provide for experiential learning or the hands-on application of the material to gain the much-needed skills in the workplace, with 90% of the workforce's skills being experiential (Beckem & Watkins, 2012). From a program director's perspective, these teaching methods achieve institutional learning objectives, program objectives, and course objectives which ensure that student learning is mapped across the institution and curriculum. Experiential learning, however, comprises a small component in meeting these objectives. Typically program directors try to have a few assignments across the curriculum that demonstrate where in the program students carry out applied learning. The addition of simulations takes applied learning to another level. In emergency and disaster management, students need to develop hands-on skills and apply their knowledge because they need to know how to deal with real-life situations that involve death, injury, and property damage. Traditional brick and mortar institutions teach these skills, and to remain competitive, online institutions that offer these types of programs also need to ensure that the application of the student's knowledge and skills happens.

WHY SIMULATIONS

To ensure that students can apply learning in an online course, simulations and gamification are required. Simulations and gamification expand the students' skills by putting the material learned into actual practice. Adding simulations and games to the online EDMG courses allows the students to improve their decision-making, critical thinking, and problem-solving skills. These are the skills required in the workplace today and in the future. Simulations and games allow students to practice their skills and make mistakes that could be disastrous in real-life. The students will learn from their mistakes without endangering life and property and will practice what they will encounter in their day-to-day operations and actual incidents out in the field. Besides offering students the opportunity to apply what they have learned in simulations and games, using these types of scenarios based on real-life events increases the students' digital literacy skills, which are much-needed in an ever-advancing technological society. Today's technology has allowed online instruction to provide real-life simulated events using various platforms and methodologies.

ADOPTION OF SIMULATIONS

In July 2018, the American Public University System (APUS) selected the undergraduate Emergency and Disaster Management (EDMG) program to systematically plan, develop, and implement simulations and games holistically across the program. A review of the undergraduate emergency and disaster management courses revealed that courses had required reading materials, followed by writing about the material covered. There was no application of the material, only reading the material followed by regurgitation of that material. The students did not complete the actual forms and assessments used in the field as applied to a scenario that replicated real-life events. The courses did not have a fictional town whereby students could make decisions and problem solve, putting their skills into action similar to what they would be required to do in real-life. After this assessment, it was decided to revise the courses to add simulations in them. While most universities and colleges have incorporated simulations in select courses within the undergraduate Emergency and Disaster Management (EDMG) program, adding simulations was different. The Emergency and Disaster Management program sought to incorporate simulations that would build upon one another across the program curriculum. The initial plan for the addition of simulations and games included all of the courses in the emergency and disaster management undergraduate program. After completing this project, the next phase of the simulation plan included incorporating simulations into other courses related to the discipline, such as homeland security, public health, transportation, and logistics management. In this fashion, the simulation project will start to cross over into other programs and disciplines throughout the university. An important consideration taken into account during the beginning stages of the simulation project included ensuring the simulations fit into the program and course objectives and not chosen solely because they are flashy and expensive as student skill-building is the overall goal (Hallyburton & Ludsford, 2013). The differentiation project does not focus solely on integrating technology, which is important, but on the technology's appropriate use to support the course's existing course material and requirements.

THE SIMULATION TEAM

To accomplish the task of adding simulations and games within the undergraduate courses, a team (Team) was developed and comprised of the Program Director, subject matter experts (SMEs) teaching within the program, and eLearning Architects from Academics and Instructional Technology (A&IT). A&IT hosts a select group of individuals who have unique skills that believe in thinking outside the box and taking technology to the next level. These individuals include a storyteller (scenario designer), a simulation designer (storyboard development and decision designer), and a senior multimedia programmer who understands the use of multimedia, 3D modeling, and digital artistry. The selection of different Team members includes individuals with subject matter expertise in each course, along with instructors who regularly teach the course, to ensure the simulations' authenticity to actual real-life events. The eLearning Architects ensure the Team has the best technology tools to support the simulation development for each course, designing and developing the simulation for each course. The Team works together from the beginning stage to the final incorporation of simulations into the classrooms with regular scrum meetings to accomplish key milestones in the process. The solicitation of feedback from all Team members helps ensure that the students get as real of an experience as possible. The Program Director is part of the Team during the entire process. Working with the Team, the Program Director is the person who is responsible for approving the simulation from the planning phase through the implementation of the simulation into a course. Ensuring that the content is appropriate for each course and that the program and course objectives are met is the responsibility of the Program Director. As the final approval for the simulation during each phase, the Program Director plays an integral role in ensuring the simulation provides the learning outcomes needed by the student to be successful.

The best approach for a differentiated program begins with an evaluation of the program. The logical progression of the required course and program outcomes needed by the student and the learning in an experiential learning environment or simulation determined the courses' progression that built upon each other. The first step in any simulation project is to ensure the course and program's educational objectives are met (Smith & Boyer, 1996). To complete this, the first part of the simulation project consisted of reviewing each course in the context of the entire emergency and disaster management program since the differentiation targeted the entire program as opposed to just one or two courses. Each class underwent an in-depth evaluation to include the learning objectives, assignments, Forums, and exams. The Team took a holistic approach to gain a competitive advantage with each proposed simulation and game approved by the SMEs and course owners, with final approval granted by the Program Director. The A&IT team developed the simulations using an agile approach in the differentiation components reviewed and approved regularly at the Scrum meetings.

The Team also reviewed industry standards, technology, and other comparable and competitive courses for inclusion in the project. In designing the simulations, the Team used the Federal Emergency Management Agency (FEMA) Emergency Support Function Annexes (ESFs) to ensure the students obtained the skills required in the field. The mapping of the fifteen ESFs to each of the simulations ensures that they learn the required skills needed within emergency and disaster management. The ESFs are essential in the emergency management field. They are the overlying structure of the functions regularly used during a disaster and emergency that coordinates the support between federal and state agencies and the response to an incident and follows the National Response Framework (NRF) (DHS, 2008). The ESFs and the NRF provide guidance to ensure all agencies nationwide practice the guidelines for an effective response to a disaster.

WORK-PLAN

Several tasks were involved in the simulation project plan. An eLearning Architect evaluates the courses to include the program and learning objectives, content, and assessment of how the content may or may not relate to the possible scenario event. The Program Director reviews and approves the proposal. After the evaluation and gap analysis, the eLearning Architect develops the scenario and media modality with an overarching storyline based on the alignment of the objectives. The proposed scenario and modality are discussed with the Program Director who will either approve it or make suggestions for improvement. Next, determining the pedagogical approach in the design document provides the descriptions of the elements required to design the scenario events. This includes the objectives, competencies, instructional strategies, and sequencing of instruction, assessment strategy, and technical specifications. The Program Director reviews and approves this to ensure that it meets the needs of the program courses. The next step entails determining the fit for the scenario within the emergency and disaster management courses to ensure it enhances and provides the students with a learning experience that supplements the ordinary course of instruction. The Program Director reviews the scenario to ensure it is based on real-life scenarios and that they are appropriate for each suggested course. The program starts with introducing skill-sets to the students then provides further development and mastery of the material as the student progresses through the program. Consideration of the sequencing of the courses within the emergency and disaster management program with each course building upon the previous course/s ensures the right type of event is in the right course. A review of the whole program, the courses, and the learning objectives inform the decision on selecting the appropriate courses to incorporate the different simulations. The scheduling of weekly brainstorming meetings serves to collect information from SMEs, A&IT personnel, and the Program Director to inform the planning, analysis, design, development, implementation, and evaluation products. The storyboards are designed and developed with the following elements; event setting, event title, time, emergency management cycle phase, event storyline, roles involved, pre-scripted avatars, complexity, interactive elements, and the deliverables from each scenario. The next phase consists of faculty training that includes a systematic approach to managing the scenario from the beginning to the evaluation stage. The Program Director is the final approval for each stage in the simulation project plan.

Besides these particular phases within the work plan, the plan includes additional tasks supporting the project to ensure the project's overall success. Internal quality assurance of each simulation's storyboards and storylines will likely require modification and embellishment throughout the differentiation project. The Program Director is responsible to ensure that the storyboards and storylines are a fit for each course. Workshops discussing storyboards and storylines for each course will occur with the Team. The Program Director and the identified SME for each course discusses the storyboards and storylines to ensure that they are equivalent to real-life events and that they are suitable to the course content and objectives. If the simulation requires, the development of virtual environment models might need to happen. The responsibility for the virtual environment and any logging tools rests with the programmers who write the scripts and program the attributes, methods, and properties of 3D objects built for the prototype. An internal quality review is required before any presentation at Team meetings or workshops. Prototypes upon finalization are then delivered to the appropriate course.

PROJECT DESIGN

By applying neuroscience learning principles, more extensive simulations were compartmentalized and connected across various modules that built upon one another. The mini simulations specifically target the outcomes within each course and map back to the outcomes required for the entire program. Chaining and cascading simulations from one course to the next is a cost-effective way to use the existing developments in technology. A main focal point is to address the concept of command in each simulation and that the continuity in the use of simulations from course to course enhances learning leading to a higher level of cognition. The program's design consisted of focusing on the authentic application by changing assignments from merely writing about a topic to constructing authentic documents and performing authentic tasks. Specific skills and not just knowledge are essential in higher education (Fortino, Kanjanabootra, & von Meding, 2017). The simulations specifically targeted the learning outcomes in each course and mapped back to the entire program's outcomes. In this fashion, students create a comprehensive portfolio of all standard professional documents by graduation. The students build upon the portfolio documents created in prior courses allowing for course sequencing and transfer.

BOBSVILLE

One of the first things that the simulation project needed was a fictional town whereby students would use in the simulations. The Team created the fictional location of Bobsville that students consistently revisit in all simulation assignments throughout all of the courses. Bobsville consists of a seven-plus page description and map of a fictional town. It includes a brief description of the area, its geography, and City Council information. The document has In Town and Out of Town information that highlights everything about and surrounding the location. Festival events are included, as well as the natural disasters Bobsville has incurred in the past. There is a detailed map of Bobsville and its surrounding area with a detailed map of downtown Bobsville.

EDMG DIFFERENTIATION EFFORTS

The Team differentiated many courses within the emergency and disaster management program from July 2018 through September 2019. A recommended course progression encourages students to take the undergraduate courses in a specific order to ensure that the learning builds upon skills based on where they are first introduced, developed, and finally, where they should be mastered. The course progression is now imperative as the incorporated simulations build upon each other from the introductory courses to the final mastery courses. In this fashion, the courses build the learners' cognition skills. Over the next couple of years, the implementation of simulations are scheduled for the remaining undergraduate emergency and disaster management courses are planned to occur, including the end-of-program requirement.

EDMG101 Introduction to Emergency Management

The first course to undergo the differentiation effort was EDMG101 Introduction to Emergency Management. EDMG101 provides students with foundational knowledge to understand the inner workings in the emergency and disaster management field. Before the simulation was incorporated into this course, students read about hazard vulnerabilities and participated in discussions and assignments about the course material. There was no direct application of the material, and students were tested on their knowledge retention through traditional means. The first phase of simulation incorporated into the EDMG101 course consisted of creating a Hazard Vulnerability Assessment (HVA). The HVA exercise replaced all assignments and some discussion forums and consisted of three discussion Forums and five assignments. Instead of students merely writing about an HVA, the students create the artifact. The course introduced the fictional location of Bobsville used throughout the program courses in all phases of emergency and disaster management scenarios that replicate real-life events. The students complete a comprehensive risk assessment of Bobsville and apply the assessment results to the Hazard Vulnerability Assessment. The HVA assesses the different human-made, technological, and natural hazards, and the students work to identify the hazards that pose the greatest threat to the fictional town of Bobsville. The HVA simulation combined several small assignments that lead to a full course project in EDMG101. Students utilized Google Crisis Maps and Federal Emergency Management Agency's (FEMA) historical data to complete the HVA. As the students complete the actual industry-standard HVA form, they engage in an authentic activity and use field-based material. In this manner, the students used the tools to apply the theory and the lecture material, instead of merely writing about an HVA. Students evaluate each other's work during this exercise and provide feedback on the HVAs completed by their peers. The students retain their HVA assessments for EDMG220 Emergency Planning as the simulations within the courses build upon each other.

EDMG220 Emergency Planning

The second course of the differentiation project consisted of EDMG220 Emergency Planning and creating an Emergency Operations Plan (EOP) based on the HVA created in EDMG101 Introduction to Emergency Management. Students build upon their knowledge from EDMG101 and carry the HVA forward, using their prior work to develop an Emergency Operations Plan section. Before the incorporation of the simulation exercises, the students wrote about the different parts of an EOP. With the incorporated simulation, the students now apply the material to a fictional location. Throughout the institution, this course is offered where EDMG101 is not a required course; therefore, the student would not have a created an HVA. For those students who did not create this, the Team created a generic HVA that could be used to complete the simulation. These students can also work through a self-paced optional refresher module on creating an HVA to ensure that all students have the requisite skills needed to participate successfully in EDMG220. The fictional location, Bobsville, provided more detail, organization, and a visual map to assist the students in detailed planning. The EOP replaced all of the previous assignments and some of the discussions in the course. In addition to the EOP, students create annexes to the document and will continue to create additional annexes throughout the other program courses. These assessments then lead to the production of a complete portfolio. Collectively, the simulation exercises consist of three assignments and one discussion within this course.

EDMG230 Emergency and Disaster Incident Command

Following EDMG220, the next course in the progression, EDMG230 Emergency and Disaster Incident Command, added a 2D/3D simulation that involves a branching decision scenario. Before the incorporation of the simulation, the students learned and discussed the Incident Command System. With the simulation, students apply their knowledge by transitioning from an information producer to an information consumer and decision-maker. The simulation uses a terrorist event at a university graduation that requires them to activate their incident command system. The students work the scenario through to a conclusion using decision-making points throughout. The scenario allows students to take the position of an emergency manager who advises the Incident Commander on handling the incident during the event's development. The scenario is similar to a video game whereby the student goes in and makes decisions that branch and vary according to the student's decision. In this manner, the students see the consequences of the choices made during the simulation. While this simulation is placed towards the end of the course, students are prompted to practice with it starting in week one. The simulation exercise expands across two discussions over two weeks. Within the discussion, students evaluate and reflect on the scenario and their performance. The literature reveals that simulations increased discussion board participation, increasing the student's sense of belonging and decreasing the disconnectedness that some experience in an online course (Alabbaasi, 2018). The discussion board participation in this course with the added simulation has proven this to be true. Allowing students to partake in the simulation as often as possible allows them to make mistakes in a setting where there are no harmful consequences to life or property. Studies show that the ability for students to apply their knowledge without any real-life consequences is a safe way for students to practice (Dubovi, 2018), and the allowing of the students to make mistakes replaces failure with the chance to improve by allowing the student to continually practice (Alabbasi, 2017). The simulation exercise prepares the student for the final written project where students create a scenario. The EDMG101, 220, and 230 courses serve to provide the students with key skill-sets utilized by emergency managers in the field.

EDMG259 Hazard Mitigation and Preparedness

In EDM259 Hazard Mitigation and Preparedness, students create mitigation ideas for the fictional location's top hazards. Before implementing the simulation exercises, the students learned about and discussed the mitigation and preparedness of hazards. With the simulation's incorporation, students now directly apply their learning to an event within the fictional town. The students create Public Service Announcements using various media tools that promote preparedness using text, images, and video. Both the HVA and the EOP from the previous courses are used. The simulation exercise replaces all of the assignments and some of the Forums and consists of three assignments and one discussion Forum. The students continue to create annexes to the EOP and continue to do so in other courses throughout the program until a complete portfolio exists.

EDMG320 Natural Disaster Management

In EDMG320 Natural Disaster Management, the students participate in a tornado roleplaying scenario. Before incorporating a simulation, students read and wrote about different natural disasters and the emergency management cycle, whereas students now apply the information to an event within the simulation. The simulation exercise covers two weeks of discussion within the online discussion forums and requires that the student complete seven responses. The simulation provides a series of weather-related information about a natural disaster that progresses across a series of weeks, with each student assigned to a specific role. Based on the student's role and the weather information, the student makes leadership decisions on how to utilize their resources, regularly responding to the Incident Commander (the course instructor) explaining what actions need to be taken and their rationale for their actions. The development of a series of snippets requires that students react to this information in the discussion Forum. The looming tornado simulation provides situational updates every two days requiring regular responses from the students during the tornado's unrelenting progress. The reports provide information that conditions will deteriorate, requiring more precise and informative decisions by the students, especially after the disaster. Students provide an assessment for the Incident Command Team on the damage they have encountered. Students also draft a series of Twitter announcements with locked down accounts for use by the students to the fictitious community under threat based on their roles. Each communication must begin and end with "EXERCISE, EXERCISE, EXERCISE" to emulate exercise participation within the field and prevent any communications from being perceived as a real emergency. However, they are posted within a locked-down account accessible only by the students and instructor. Students who fail to follow these protocols can incur steep penalties to include possible failure of the course, mirroring the severity such an infraction would earn them in the field. The students complete an Incident Action Plan using FEMA's ICS Form 202 Incident Objective Form. A lesson learned phase at the end of the course allows students to exchange information on where they performed well and what needed improvement, providing them with an opportunity to reflect on how they can improve their skills for the next disaster. The simulation based on the Homeland Security Exercise and Evaluation Program attempts to place students in a true high-stakes decision-making role. The simulation in EDMG320 allows the students to gain familiarity with a real-life disaster scenario and utilize the tools used in the field to carry out their actions. The student will take the damage assessment they created into EDMG259 Hazard Mitigation and Preparedness, where they will determine from the assessment how the town can mitigate some of the damage and prepare for the next event.

EDMG321 Social Media Application to Emergency & Disaster Management

The EDMG321 Social Media Application to Emergency & Disaster Management course makes the students use Twitter and Facebook to roleplay their responses to a mock terrorist event and natural disaster scenario. The students experience another vital role within emergency and disaster management that of a Public Affairs Officer. The students explore the utility and challenges of using social media as an emergency management communication tool to support homeland security and public health emergency operations. The social media simulation posts replaced four weeks of regular Forum posts as previously the course had students create two posts for Facebook and Twitter with no student interaction. The simulation expands across four discussion Forums with roleplaying on social media. The creation of private locked-down Twitter and Facebook pages for each course allows access only to the students in the course. Students assume a specific role providing Tweets and Facebook postings based upon what they need to convey to the town. Students are encouraged to explore Facebook and Twitter sites set-up by real organizations during a disaster. Students must create posts that provide accurate and truthful estimates on damages and how the fictitious town under threat will move forward from the disaster. The intent is for students to learn the social media's ins and outs and use the Center for Disease Control (CDC) Social Media Toolkit to improve their communications within social media. Also, the intent during the roleplay is to have one student play the antagonist on social media and attack and dispute the sent out claims or messages, as well as having one individual who is a myth/rumor/misinformation spreader to emulate some of the critical challenges that emergency management personnel encounter regularly. During the Boston Marathon, there was a significant amount of misinformation, especially regarding the whereabouts of the terrorists. During the course, safety protocols are maintained as each posting requires EX, EX, EX. By adding this simulation, the students spent much more time on the roleplay and demonstrated more ability than prior to the differentiation.

EDMG420 Risk Communications

In EDMG420, students create a Communication Plan for top hazards within the fictional town. This course is a culminating experience as it brings all of the concepts learned in the other courses together. The simulation is larger than those carried out in the earlier courses and includes a virtual press conference experience. The students also draw from the HVA and EOP exercises completed in prior courses. Before incorporating a simulation exercise, the students read the material and wrote about risk communications in discussion forums and assignments. Within the simulation, the students prepare and record a mock press release video to demonstrate their verbal skills in response to a terrorist disaster scenario. The students also respond to community feedback and rumors regarding the simulated terrorist attack. The simulation exercise spans two discussion forums, six assignments, and students continue to create annexes to the EOP they began in the prior course.

EDMG340 Consequence Management

EDMG340 Consequence Management is currently being worked on in reference to adding a simulation to the course. This course relates to Weapons of Mass Destruction (WMD), and Chemical, Biological, Radiological, and Nuclear (CBRN) threats. The students will continue from EDMG230 Emergency and Disaster Incident Command with the terrorist chemical attack moving through the response, recovery, and mitigation phases of emergency management. This exercise will replace an assignment where students analyzed an event to have the students respond and recover from a mock event that is a WMD scenario. The students will continue to create annexes to their EOPs.

EDMG240 Chemistry of Hazardous Materials

EDMG240 Chemistry of Hazardous materials is also being worked to add a simulation. The scenario will consist of a hazardous chemical release from a tanker crash, and students will identify the chemical/s and evaluate possible reactions and hazards. The students will propose an approach to the containment and neutralization of the chemical/s. This simulation exercise will replace the final exam and include a discussion Forum whereby the student regurgitated in writing the material provided in the course about hazardous materials with no application involved.

EDMG330 Managerial Issues in Hazardous Materials

EDMG330 Managerial Issues in Hazardous Materials is currently being worked on to add a simulation to the course. The simulation exercise will continue the hazardous chemical release scenario with the tanker crash in EDMG240 Chemistry of Hazardous Materials. Students will implement a response, recovery, and mitigation effort to include an evacuation of the Fictional location. The simulation will replace the research paper and include a discussion Forum. In the prior course, the student selected a topic related to the course subject matter and wrote a paper about it, whereas in the simulation, the students will apply the learning to an event. The students will also continue to create annexes to their EOP.

EDMG498 Senior Seminar in Emergency & Disaster Management

The EDMG498 Senior Seminar in Emergency & Disaster Management is the end of the program course. It is the last course the student takes for their bachelor's degree in emergency and disaster management. A simulation will be added to EDMG498 once all of the other undergraduate courses have been completed. The proposed simulation consists of a fully functional 3D exercise that will evaluate students on all phases in the emergency management cycle. The simulation will consist of an earthquake that is a lower-risk environmental hazard with less mitigation and preparation done before the incident. The earthquake will compound with a high-risk human hazard such as a festival. The student will progressively move through the simulation spanning over 16 weeks with multiple progressive interactions. This simulation replaces a research paper whereby the student selected and wrote on a topic related to emergency and disaster management.

Next Steps for the EDMG Program

As EDMG was the pilot program within APUS to differentiate itself based on simulations, the simulation project will move to other courses and programs, including the master's degree in EDMG. The way simulations and games were incorporated into the EDMG program was done to allow for other programs to make use of the resources in place and build them out specific to their own needs. For example, with the fictitious town built, the groundwork is set to establish a fictitious hospital where simulations could be run within a nursing home, or with a city hall, a public administration program could incorporate simulations suited to their needs as well. In this fashion, the simulation project will move into other disciplines within the university. The proposed simulations for these courses will use similar tools as those in the EDMG courses but with a change in the scenario all depending on the course subject matter.

COURSE ASSESSMENT

Student Assessment

In every course where a simulation was added, a Hotwash was added not only for student learning but also for data collection. The Hotwash is completed by the student at the end of the course to reflect the simulation results. The Hotwash replicates the after-action review that is industry practice in the emergency and disaster field. The Hotwash requires students to reflect on their experiences and decisions in the simulations and assess what they did well and what areas need improvement. The Hotwash discussion has the students evaluate their experience in the simulation with a series of positive and negative comments for the Incident Commander to ensure improvement in handling the next disaster. These reflections are in the last week of the course and require students to interact with one another, allowing for critical reflection and learning by sharing different perspectives. This also helped to serve feedback used in fine-tuning the simulations and identify where improvement was needed. Additionally, these discussion sessions provide additional insight into where continuous course improvements can be made.

Simulation Assessment

A voluntary end-of-course evaluation asks students for their thoughts and perspectives on the simulation and their experiences in each simulation course. The Team reviews the feedback at the end of each course and discusses it at the weekly meetings. Students voluntarily participate in telephone conferences with the Team to discuss the simulations looking for ways to improve and tweak them as necessary. The Team decides whether the feedback requires action within the course and if so, the feedback drives the revision/s. Instructors who regularly teach the courses also provide recommendations and suggestions for improvement, thus making the simulation project an ongoing continual improvement cycle. This data could also be useful in programs across the institution seeking to incorporate simulations into their courses.

Persistence and Retention

Besides evaluations, a key indicator that the Team uses in assessing the success of simulations in the learning environment is the drop, failure, withdrawal, and incomplete (DFWI) rates and the final grades breakdown in each course. The DFWI rates assess students' persistence and retention that reflects the effects on the students based on changes within a course. DFWI rates are important to all colleges and universities as institutions want to retain their current students. Many reasons exist why students withdraw, drop, fail, or do not complete the course. Two of the major reasons for high DFWI rates are the instructor and/or the curriculum. An overarching goal of the simulation project included adding experiential or hands-on learning into the classroom and curriculum improvement.

The Team gathers the DFWI and final grades breakdown data to compare courses before the simulation to those courses after implementing the simulations. To ascertain the effect, if any, on the DFWI rates and final grades breakdown data before and after the addition of a simulation to a course, the Team gathered and reviewed the DFWI and final grades breakdown data from four courses. Since studies have shown that simulations increase the academic performance of the students (Becken & Watkins, 2012; Looyestyn et al., 2017), over the next three years, DWFI data will be used to compare academic performance, which will aid in future decision making on the incorporation of simulations into university curricula.

CONCLUSION

The use of simulations and gamification in online courses allows students to apply their learning to real-life events. The ability for the learner in an educational setting to cognitively store and recall learning when faced with real-life experiences is an essential element in a learning environment (Collins, 2015; Zull, 2011). To ensure learning occurs, simulated practices help ensure that memory and retention of these events or tasks transpire. Learned skills are essential in disciplines such as emergency and disaster management as students need to have decision-making, problem-solving, and critical thinking skills if they are going to succeed in the field.

The American Public University System (APUS) developed a framework within the undergraduate Emergency and Disaster Management program to implement simulations within the courses holistically recreating events that students will face in the field. The simulation project is a framework for active, experiential learning based on game theory to enhance the classroom experience further and propel students into a competitive marketplace. The project developed real-life simulations that helps students put their classroom skills to the test in a gamified environment where they work to resolve real-world problems requiring real-time decision making. Simulations within emergency and disaster management require an understanding of the functions and theories involved in the field and the hands-on skills needed to handle an actual event. The simulation project at APUS is an ongoing effort as the project continues to design and implement simulations within other courses in the undergraduate emergency and disaster program and other programs throughout the university. In this fashion, the simulations that consist of experiential learning and knowledge application will enhance the traditional teaching methods of reading resources, writing assignments, and discussions and will further enhance the missing teaching component needed for student learning. Other universities and colleges can use the framework outlined in this project to develop their own simulations, especially in fields where there is a need to apply skills. With the continued advancements within technology, online universities and colleges can provide the skills necessary via simulations and gamification within fields such as EDMG to provide an enhanced learning experience similar to what occurs in face-to-face experiences. Online universities and colleges need to ensure that their students have the requisite skills, digital literacy, and the application of knowledge needed in the workforce.

REFERENCES

Abdollahzade, Z., & Jafari, S. M. B. (2018). Investigating the relationship between player types and learning styles in gamification design. *Iranian Journal of Management Studies*, *11*(3), 573–600. doi:10.22059/ijms2018.256394.673107

Ahmed, A., & Sutton, M. J. D. (2017). Gamification, serious games, simulations, and immersive learning environments in knowledge management initiatives. *World Journal of Science. Technology and Sustainable Development*, *14*(2), 78–83. doi:10.1108/WJSTSD-02-2017-0005

Alabbasi, D. (2017). Exploring graduate students' perspectives towards using gamification techniques in online learning. *Turkish Online Journal of Distance Education*, *18*(3), 180–196. doi:10.17718/tojde.328951

Aldrich, C. (2009). *Learning online with games, simulations, and virtual worlds: Strategies for online instruction*. Jossey-Bass.

Azmi, S., Iahad, N. A., & Ahmad, N. (2015). Gamification in online collaborative learning for programming courses: A literature review. *Journal of Engineering and Applied Sciences (Asian Research Publishing Network)*, *10*(23), 18087–18094. https://search.proquest.com/docview/1808124406/

Banfield, J., & Wilkerson, B. (2014). Increasing student intrinsic motivation and self-efficacy through gamification pedagogy. *Contemporary Issues in Education Research*, *7*(4), 291–298. doi:10.19030/cier.v7i4.8843

Beckem, J., & Watkins, M. (2012). Bringing life to learning: Immersive experiential learning simulations for online and blended courses. *Journal of Asynchronous Learning Networks*, *16*(5), 61–70. https://eric.ed.gov/?id=EJ1000091

Bond, M., Marín, V. I., Dolch, C., Bedenlier, S., & Zawacki-Richter, O. (2018). Digital transformation in German higher education: Student and teacher perceptions and usage of digital media. *International Journal of Educational Technology in Higher Education, 15*(1), 1. doi:10.118641239-018-0130-1

Bursens, P., Donche, V., Gijbels, D., & Spooren, P. (2018). *Simulations of decision-making as active learning tools: Design and effects of political pcience simulations (Professional and Practice-based Learning)*. Springer Nature. doi:10.1007/978-3-319-74147-5

Cai, Y., van Joolingen, W., & Walker, Z. (2019). *VR, simulations and serious games for education (Gaming Media and Social Effects)* (1st ed.). Springer Nature. doi:10.1007/978-981-13-2844-2

Carnes, M. C. (2018). *Minds on Fire: How Role-Immersion Games Transform College*. President and Fellows of Harvard College.

Chang, J. W., & Wei, H. Y. (2016). Exploring engaging gamification mechanics in massive online open courses. *Journal of Educational Technology & Society, 19*(2), 177–203. https://www.jstor.org/stable/jeductechsoci.19.2.177

Collins, S. (2015). *Neuroscience for learning and development: How to apply neuroscience & psychology for improved learning & training*. Kogan Page Limited.

Department of Homeland Security (DHS). (2008, January). *Overview: ESF and Support Annexes Coordinating Federal Assistance in Support of the National Response Framework*. Retrieved from https://www.fema.gov/media-library-data/20130726-1825-25045-8535/overview_esf___support_annexes_2008.pdf

Dubovi, I. (2018). Designing for online computer-based clinical simulations: Evaluation of instructional approaches. *Nurse Education Today, 69*, 67–73. doi:10.1016/j.nedt.2018.07.001 PMID:30007150

Fortino, G., Kanjanabootra, S., & von Meding, V. (2017, August). Critical dimensions for the effective design and use of simulation exercises for emergency management in higher education. *Journal of Applied Research in Higher Education, 9*(4), 530–549. doi:10.1108/JARHE-11-2016-0086

Hallyburton, C. L., & Lunsford, E. (2013). Challenges and opportunities for learning biology in distance-based settings. *Bioscene, 39*(1), 27–33. Retrieved from https://eric.ed.gov/?id=EJ1020526

Information Resources Management Association. (2018). *Gamification in education: breakthroughs in research and practice*. IGI Global.

Jin, L., Jiong, W., Yang, D., Huaping, W., & Wei, D. (2014). A simulation study for emergency/disaster management by applying complex networks theory. *Journal of Applied Research and Technology, 12*(2), 223–229. doi:10.1016/S1665-6423(14)72338-7

Kempston, T., & Thomas, N. (2014). The drama of international relations: A South China Sea simulation. *International Studies Perspectives, 15*(4), 459–476. doi:10.1111/insp.12045

Lantis, J. S. (1998). Simulations and experiential learning in the international relations classroom. *International Negotiation, 3*(1), 39–57. Advance online publication. doi:10.1163/15718069820848094

Laxman, K., & Chin, D. Y. K. (2011). Impact of simulations on the mental models of students in the online learning of science concepts. *I-Manager's Journal on School Educational Technology*, *7*(2), 1–12. doi:10.26634/jsch.7.2.1647

Lockley, A., & Boyle, A. (2014). Towards a game-based learning ecosystem: An institutional strategy. *Proceedings of the European Conference on Games Based Learning, 1*, 312–320. Retrieved from https://search.proquest.com/docview/1674172734/

Looyestyn, J., Kernot, J., Boshoff, K., Ryan, J., Edney, S., & Maher, C. (2017). Does gamification increase engagement with online programs? A systematic review. *PLoS One*, *12*(3), 1–19. doi:10.1371/journal.pone.0173403 PMID:28362821

Mccallum, J. (2007). The debate in favour of using simulation education in pre-registration adult nursing. *Nurse Education Today*, *27*(8), 825–831. doi:10.1016/j.nedt.2006.10.014 PMID:17150284

Nygaard, C., Courtney, N., & Lee, E. (2012). Simulations, games and role play in university education. *Libri*.

Rolfe, J., Saunders, D., & Powell, T. (n.d.). *Simulation & gaming research yearbook (The international simulation and gaming uearbook series, vol 6)*. Routledge.

Rutherford-Hemming, T. (2012). Simulation methodology in nursing education and adult learning theory. *Adult Learning*, *23*(3), 129–137. doi:10.1177/1045159512452848

Smith, E. T., & Boyer, M. A. (1996). Designing in-class simulations. *PS, Political Science & Politics*, *29*(4), 690–694. doi:10.1017/S1049096500045686

Zemliansky, P., & Wilcox, D. (2010). *Design and implementation of educational games theoretical and practical perspectives*. Information Science Reference. doi:10.4018/978-1-61520-781-7

Zull, J. E. (2011). *From brain to mind: Using neuroscience to guide change in education*. Stylus Publishing.

ADDITIONAL READING

Abrandt Dahlgren, M., Fenwick, T., & Hopwood, N. (2016). Theorising simulation in higher education: Difficulty for learners as an emergent phenomenon. *Teaching in Higher Education*, *21*(6), 613–627. doi:10.1080/13562517.2016.1183620

Braithwaite, G. (2017). The Use of High-Fidelity Simulations in Emergency Management Training. In *Forensic Science Education and Training* (pp. 235–252). John Wiley & Sons, Ltd., doi:10.1002/9781118689196.ch15

Chernikova, O., Heitzmann, N., Stadler, M., Holzberger, D., Seidel, T., & Fischer, F. (2020). Simulation-Based Learning in Higher Education: A Meta-Analysis. *Review of Educational Research*, *90*(4), 499–541. doi:10.3102/0034654320933544

Danko, T. T. (2020). Perceptions of gains through experiential learning in homeland security and emergency management education. *Journal of Homeland Security Education*, *9*, 1–31. https://search-proquest-com.ezproxy1.apus.edu/scholarly-journals/perceptions-gains-through-experiential-learning/docview/2431215252/se-2?accountid=8289

Hertel, J., & Millis, B. (2002). *Using Simulations to Promote Learning in Higher Education: An Introduction*. Stylus Publishing LLC.

Juan, A. A., Loch, B., Daradoumis, T., & Ventura, S. (2017). Games and simulation in higher education: Revista de universidad y sociedad del conocimiento. *International Journal of Educational Technology in Higher Education, 14*, 1-3. doi:http://dx.doi.org.ezproxy1.apus.edu/10.1186M1239-017-0075-9

Morley, D., & Jamil, M. (2021). *Applied Pedagogies for Higher Education Real World Learning and Innovation across the Curriculum* (1st ed. 2021). Springer International Publishing., doi:10.1007/978-3-030-46951-1

Vlachopoulos, D., & Makri, A. (2017). The effect of games and simulations on higher education: A systematic literature review: Revista de universidad y sociedad del conocimiento. *International Journal of Educational Technology in Higher Education, 14*, 1-33. doi:http://dx.doi.org.ezproxy1.apus.edu/10.1186/S41239-017-0062-1

KEY TERMS AND DEFINITIONS

Asychronous Learning: Allows students to access learning flexibly on their own time at anyplace without real-time interaction.

Experiential Learning: Learning by doing followed by a reflection on the experience.

Hot Wash: A review and reflection following a training session that discusses and assesses the performance of an individual or agency.

Industry Advisory Council (IAC): A committee of individuals who are professionals in a specific discipline who collaborate to advice on academic programs and aid in the future direction of the program to ensure that the program is offering students the skills necessary for the workforce.

Program Director: An individual who leads a program and is responsible for managing and developing curriculum.

Simulation: A scenario based on real-life events that is created for learning.

Subject Matter Expert (SME): An individual who is considered an authority in a particular topic based on their work and/or educational experiences.

This research was previously published in Simulation and Game-Based Learning in Emergency and Disaster Management; pages 237-261, copyright year 2021 by Information Science Reference (an imprint of IGI Global).

Chapter 62
Is the News Cycle "Real"?
A Case Study of Media "Phandom" and Agenda Setting in Persona 5

Emory S. Daniel, Jr.
Appalachian State University, USA

Gregory P. Perreault
https://orcid.org/0000-0002-6645-1117
Appalachian State University, USA

Michael G Blight
North Central College, USA

ABSTRACT

This chapter features a game from the Shin Megami Tensei series called Persona 5. This chapter examines how the case of role playing video game Persona 5 depicts agenda setting through the use of an in-game audience-oriented polling systems and comment system in order to understand to a greater degree the ways in which games contribute to our understanding of media processes and explores the idea of fandom as integral to the agenda setting process. The case chapter addressed in this manuscript represents a unique narrative featuring a daily life simulator, a turn-based Japanese role-playing game (JRPG), and complex in-game media vehicles to drive the story.

INTRODUCTION

Persona 5

As video games have become increasingly more accepted into the mainstream, so have the complexity of the stories that are presented in them (Tucker, 2012). Gaming has addressed complex topics within Universalizability, Utilitarianism, Game Theory, amongst many other theories that exist within the visual and interactive narrative of a video game. Additionally, Bogost (2008) has indicated that video

DOI: 10.4018/978-1-6684-7589-8.ch062

game narratives have more complexity than any other medium due to their interactivity. The case study addressed in this manuscript represents a unique narrative featuring a daily life simulator, a turn-based Japanese role-playing game (JRPG), and complex in-game media vehicles to drive the story.

This chapter features a video game from the Shin Megami Tensei series called *Persona 5 (Atlus, 2017)*. It is the fifth installment of the *Persona* series, which contrasts dark and disturbing themes with tales of developing friendships and light-hearted banter among Japanese high school students. While the tone has lightened in the last two entries in the series, the *Persona* series also includes the eponymous "Personas," summoned creatures, like Pokemon, that grant the characters special powers to battle enemies in an alternate world (known in *Persona 5* as the "metaverse"). All of this terminology and worldbuilding only indicates the degree to which this is a constructed world that depicts a highly mediated Tokyo and in which the high school students featured a constantly working to assess the reality around them. Central in Persona 5, is the social media in the game's world. As the protagonist group, known as the "Phantom Thieves," defeats the first antagonist, a student and fan submit a blog which has a poll regarding the approval of the group. As the Phantom Thieves defeat more antagonists, media exposure and fandom grow as does the approval on the "Phansite." The Phansite is an in-game blog that fictional fans interact with each other concerning the Phantom Thieves actions, the Phantom Thieves justifiability for their in-game actions, and a poll discussing the existence of the Phantom Thieves. As the game states, you are allowed to progress through the narrative as you become more prevalent in the general public's cognition. Therefore, the theme of this chapter is to determine how *Persona 5* uses its in-game narrative to illustrate agenda setting as the Phantom Thieves grow in popularity.

Research indicates increasingly that media literacy is at a disturbingly low level (Potter & Christ, 2007). People draw knowledge of media processes from a variety of sources, including entertainment media artifacts such as *Persona 5* (Ferrucci, 2018). This chapter would like to argue that as a result of *Persona 5*'s popularity and widespread appeal (Romano, 2018, May 14), it serves as an ideal case to understand how the media process of agenda setting is communicated. It showcases a fictional array of happening, reported by fictional news and interpreted by fictional fans. Prior research has shown that such popular culture artifacts accomplish a great deal in modeling our relationship with institutions in society (Ferrucci, 2018).

Agenda setting is a vital concept in media literacy as helps explain the natural operations within journalism and distinguishes a shared set of news values from the more troubling concept of collusion. This chapter proposes to examine how the case of *Persona 5* depicts agenda setting through the use of an in-game audience-oriented polling systems and comment system in order to understand to a greater degree the ways in which games contribute to our understanding of media processes. Largely, the chapter finds that the nature of *Persona 5* reflects the agenda setting process, with the in-game poll and comments helping identify the relationship between news media and not just what fans think about but also what they think.

Theoretical Framework - Fandom

Being a "fan" means participating in a range of activities that extend beyond private personal involvement and extending into public displays of emotional involvement. There are a plethora of ways that fans can be involved including in participating in dialogue about the subject, buying merchandise, subscribing to publications, joining fan clubs, etc. (Bielby, Harrington, & Bielby, 1999). This involvement with discussion makes fan groups to be incredibly social, especially considering the advent of technology to foster fan group conversations (Jenkins, 1992; Perreault, 2015). As online involvement has influenced fan communities, it has dissolved space and time as asynchronous computer mediated communication fandoms form (Bury, 2005). Within *Persona 5*, the Phantom Thieves use their fans as resources for their investigation and acknowledge their help throughout the process of apprehending criminals.

Fandom through means of CMC can create levels of public involvement. Specifically, Former U.S. President Barack Obama published his first book that developed a strong social media following. Fans had an emotional investment in his beliefs and campaign, which helped grassroot support towards his candidacy. While fans can often contribute to importance for a figure (i.e., build a community surrounding the figure), they can also impact on the figure's narrative. Gaming, for instance, has become an example of fans creating content (e.g., user-generated content), which has changed the overall production and business models (Lotz, 2014). More specifically, in games such as Skyrim, fans play an integral role in the production process of the game through game modifications. Jenkins (2014) mirrored the sentiment that new communication technologies have created a need to not only work with fans, but collaborate and cooperate with fan cultures. Fandom in *Persona 5* exemplifies much of this alliance as throughout the story, the PT are often torn about their desire for what is the ethical decision, versus adhering to the fans. Moreover, it also demonstrated an ideology that fan cultures, in the case of *Persona 5*, might have an influence as public agenda, to media agenda.

Agenda Setting

Agenda setting theory focuses on how the media creates, adjusts, and alters coverage of newsworthy items. In short, news media does not inherently influence audiences about what to think (i.e., which political candidate to support for presidency), but instead what to think about (i.e., which political candidate may be suitable for presidency) (Lasorsa, 2008). In that way, agenda setting focuses more specifically on the transfer of salience from one agenda to another (McCombs, 2006). As stories progress and develop, different agendas are promoted based on the respective goals of each individual media outlet.

Agenda setting is one media tool of many that can be used to build consensus among individuals in communities, as reflected in the original chapter by Shaw and McCombs (1997). Much of agenda setting is hinged upon topics that become visible to the public eye. Weaver and Elliot (1985) argue that agendas originate or are built by the press. As these topics build, so do the foci of audience members to shift attention to the agendas that are presented at any given moment. Access to modern technologies (e.g., traditional television, smartphones, tablets, etc.) provides an around-the-clock news cycle that may be hard to break. Moreover, the public's agenda (e.g., salience) is a byproduct of different forces (e.g., personal and social) that direct the attention of the viewer (McCombs, 2006).

First-level agenda setting focuses on the media's process (i.e., frequency of representation and emphasis placed on the agenda) of presenting information to different publics (Coleman, McCombs, Shaw, & Weaver, 2009). In short, the media has a profound say in how often an agenda is promoted as well as the underlying importance that is presented.

Second-level agenda setting focuses more closely on the two dimensions that the media covers. First, the substantive dimension underscores the way that individuals' structure and make sense of agendas that are being promoted. Second, the affective attributes refer to the tone of how media presents the attributes (e.g., positively, negatively, or indifferently). The controlling forces of second-level agenda setting plays on the emotions of the audience members and how they discern these notions within communal spaces.

In the years since the postulating of agenda setting theory, scholarship has sought to address Lippman's (1922) concern regarding the "pictures in our head" created by news media. In summary, first-level agenda setting addresses "what are these pictures about?", second-level agenda setting addresses "What are the dominant characteristics of these pictures?", and, in recent years, scholars Guo, Vu, & McCombs (2012) have postulated a third-level of agenda setting which addresses "What are the pictures in our heads?" (p. 54). Guo, Vu & McCombs argue that in the third-level "the news media can actually bundle different objects and attributes and make these bundles of elements salient in the public's mind simultaneously" (p. 54); a concept addressed in part through the idea of agenda melding.

Agenda melding argues that "individuals join groups, in a sense, by joining agendas" (Shaw et al, 1999, p. 2). Individual agendas are inherently melded with those of their community and group affiliations (McCombs, 2006). Agenda setting and melding is relevant to this chapter in that increasingly knowledge of how media operates come from a variety of sources. *Persona 5* serves as a unique video game case that illustrates not only the media in operation but more specifically the agenda setting role of the media in operation. Further, work by Longhurst (2007) notes that individuals understand themselves and social interactions through the media. Moreover, Crawford and Gosling (2009) expand upon Longhurst's idea by suggesting that exposure to the media influences the way individuals socialize and communicate with others - often within online communities.

Procedural Rhetoric in Gaming

Procedural rhetoric is the procedural practice of persuasive argumentation (Bogost, 2008). Video games are innately procedural media and as such meaning in a game is understood because the player enacts with the rule system presented to them (Treanor & Mateas, 2009). This rhetorical process operates under the assumption that games mechanics or the narrative cannot be separated (Harper, 2011) in order to understand how communication occurs through the game. "The stock tools of visual rhetoric are inadequate" given that "images are frequently constructed, selected and sequenced in code" (Bogost, 2008, p. 124). Hence games use procedure in order to make claims about human existence cultural, social or material aspects."

Procedural rhetoric also acknowledges that video games are by no means a neutral medium. The nature of how a game is constructed "may be less deliberate in their rhetoric, but they are not necessarily free from ideological framing. Such games may imply complex procedural rhetoric with or without the conscious intention of the designers" (Bogost, 2006, p. 181). That said, largely the public has little understanding of the "moral conceptual systems that underwrite verbal and written...utterances" (p. 181).

The locus of the present chapter is in underscoring how the concept of agenda setting is illustrated in the case of *Persona 5*--in contemporary society, we would argue that this is material to understanding the larger public problems in media literacy. The concept of media operations is no longer solely a theoretical issue but also a political one in the United States in particular. Bogost (2006) argues that "video games might offer the most salient locus for discussions of how we think about political problems" even as "games have been a part of public political discourse all along) (Bogost, 2006, p. 182).

This leads us to pose the following research questions:

RQ1: "In the video game *Persona 5*, how does the audience poll illustrate the process of agenda setting?"

RQ2: "In the video game *Persona 5*, how do comments associated with the audience poll illustrate the nature of agenda setting?"

METHOD

In order to address these research questions, this particular chapter uses a case study approach through "examining one or more cases in a bounded system" (e.g. both the audience poll itself and the comments associated with the poll in *Persona 5*) (p. 73). This approach to trying to understand the broader systems in play with agenda setting helps address the common agenda setting criticism that in many studies.

"The emphasis placed on an element in a communicator's message(s) -- as measured by the frequency with which the statement was mentioned in the message(s) -- was a valid indicator of the importance of that element in the communicator's mind" (Edelstein, 1993, p. 86).

Such critique can be addressed through qualitative analysis that considers the broader social context in which agenda setting research operates (Robinson, 1998). Hence, why this chapter will look at persona from the perspective of a thematic analysis. Based on the comments of the fans in the Phan-site and the overall approval rating.

Sample

In order to address the research questions asked in this chapter, the in-game mechanic of the poll and the comments associated with the poll were analyzed. The unit of analysis was the approval bar for each day and the story related feedback from non-playable commenters. *Persona 5* has an in-game calendar spanning 345 days and it provides specific times of the day labels where the user may play the game during the week[1] and on Sundays[2]. The game will occasionally skip entire days where the Phan-site is inaccessible and specific days that will not give the player the option to interact during a normally accessible time of day. Thus, there were 810 coded instances of each mention of the days change, and there were 86 instances where the poll was not available due to the beginning of the narrative where the Phantom Thieves actions were unknown to anyone else, thus there were no polls that day because it had not yet been created within the game. Therefore, the final coded total sample was 724 coded instances that the poll was made available. In addition, there were five questions associated with the approval poll[3] and 289 comments that corresponded with the question[4].

Coding Categories and Procedure

Given the episodic and exploratory nature of this chapter, the coding was done specifically for the in-game poll when it was available for the player to view. The coder created an excel spreadsheet and accounted for several categories specific to the game's narrative. Each of the 724 entries included the Date, Day of the Week, Time of Day (See Footnotes 1 & 2), Approval Percentage (Between 0% and 100%), and any canon event (any section that does not involve player choice). While the narrative of the game began on April 9th, the poll is not adopted in the game until May 5th. However, the poll's absence was still accounted for as it created for greater impact of the first breaking story.

The coder played through the entire game working towards the "true ending." The true ending was essential because this contained all of the poll results, otherwise the game would have ended prematurely. Moreover, each time of day (see footnotes 1 & 2) was coded for the percentage in the poll. If the poll did not show up during a specific time of the day on the loading screen, the coder paused the game and coded from the poll within the menu selection screen. Lastly, the poll fluctuated several percentage points back and forth, so the coder recorded the first number that appeared on screen with one exception.[5] The coder proceeded with this procedure until the true endings' completion on March 20th.

The comments were also coded for agenda setting illustration. The researchers retrieved the comments from the Megami Tensei Wiki, which features all the comments and when they exist based on the question of the poll and the date range where it might be found. The reason it was recorded this way is because the comments are randomly generated each time the loading screen is on screen. Therefore, there might have been a comment missed if we recorded it on a normal playthrough. The coder created an excel spreadsheet and recorded the question asked during the date range, the range of the approval percentage, and the comments that occur during a specific question and approval range.

Comments were examined multiple times via a method of discourse analysis. Discourse analysis brings to the foreground the discursive strategies and techniques used by writers to create meaning: it seeks to interrogate word choice, metaphors, and lines of argument (Hall, 1980; van Dijk, 1988). Discourse analysis locates discourse within social and institutional contexts which is particularly valuable for understanding how the nature of agenda setting is constructed. In this case, researchers were most interested in discourse on the audience poll comments as it reciprocally responded to happenings in the in-game news media. In short, the game presents a microcosm of our world: the news media present a strong ability at "telling us what to think about" (Cohen, 1977, p. p. 13) and the comments demonstrate not just that they are thinking about what has been presented but also their sentiment toward the topic.

In initial reads, the researcher made note of common discursive traits (short length, abbreviations, misspellings, capitalization, punctuation, and use of sentiment text images such as hearts). In the reads that followed, the researcher examined the discursive strategies that emerged throughout the discourse as a whole--noting the common traits associated with the nature of agenda setting. Finally, those themes were reconnected with the date/news media events and the discursive traits of the comments.

Results

The Agenda Setting Process According to Persona 5

As Chyi and McCombs (2004) argue, the news cycle typically emerges and dies out within 30 days. The narrative of *Persona 5*'s in game news coverage accounts for this as the story updates almost every month. In order to answer RQ1, this chapter will report the percentages based on the incident, the dates that coincided with the incident, the question asked in the poll, and what topics were discussed in the in-game news media agenda.

Act 1 of the *Persona 5* story saw the beginning of the Phansite poll (See Appendix A). The poll began on May 5th when a local high school gym teacher confessed publicly that he had assaulted and sexually harassed members of the school's volleyball team. This marked the first instance of agenda setting for the Phantom Thieves as they sent a calling card to the teacher indicating that he would confess his crimes. Since that is exactly what happened, members of the high school made the connection that the Phantom Thieves existed and enacted justice on the corrupt teacher. The poll began with the question: "Do you believe in the Phantom Thieves?" The poll is a yes/no question, and given the local story, the percentage of audience members who say "Yes" Begin at 6.6%, rise as high as 6.7%, and concluded at 6%. While this was a local event, there was some in-game mentions that national media outlets were covering the case.

As the poll began to drop slightly, Act 2 saw a resurgence in the attention from national news media to attention within the poll. The poll increased to 16.8% in salience on June 5th as a nationally renowned artist confessed crimes of plagiarizing and abusing pupils on a nationally televised press conference. The poll percentage jumps to 16.8% for who people who believe in the Phantom Thieves. After a public figure opposes the Phantom Thieves, the question changes on 6/10 to "Are the Phantom Thieves Just?" This question prompts another small increase in the poll to as high as 19.5% and ends with 19.7% before Act 3 of the story.

Act 3 indicated yet another resurgence in the poll and national media attention. The poll increased slightly to 23.7% until a national news report covered a story of a mafia boss confessing crimes of drug and human trafficking. The poll percentage increased in salience again to 35.7%. Through the lens of second-level agenda setting, the question of whether or not the Phantom Thieves motives are justified continue to increase as the poll question did not change.

Act 4 continues with the increase in justification for the Phantom Thieves actions. This time, instead of a morally evil public figure confessing their crimes, a third-party hacker group (Medjed) set major media outlets' agenda by declaring war against the Phantom Thieves. They threaten to expose the Phantom Thieves identities and threaten to attack Japan's economy if the Phantom Thieves do not reveal themselves. The Phantom Thieves gain a new character that is talented in computer hacking and she is able to shut Medjed's site down, making the Phantom Thieves emerge victorious. This acts as a monumental shift in coverage as the percentage jumps from 38.5% to 60.4% in a matter of hours from the news report of Medjed's site being shut down. The fanbase roars in approval as the Phansite's approval dramatically increases from 60.4% on 8/22 to 92.2% on October 11.

Act 5 sees continued salience in the Phantom Thieves, but sees valence suffering tremendously. On the evening of October 11, the next target (a CEO) confesses his wrongdoings of overworking employees, forcing his daughter into an arranged marriage, and contributing to the "mental shutdowns" --a deadly mental breakdown that occurs as a result of metaverse activity. However, this time the target suffers his own "mental shutdown," dying on live television. This leaves the public to believe it was the Phantom Thieves' fault. While the Phantom Thieves are still salient in news coverage, the approval numbers that reached 92.2% before the in-game press-conference plummeted overnight to 79.7% and continued to drop dramatically over the courses of Acts 5 and 6. It is because of this negative press coverage and perceived wrongdoing that the question on the Phansite changes to "Are the Phantom Thieves Innocent?" The act ends at an approval of 18.5% after a public "mental shutdown" and subsequent death.

Act 6 sees much of the same decline, as the popularity of the Phantom Thieves grows but with a negative valence despite the mission to save a special prosecutor and sister to one of the members of the Phantom Thieves. Per the story, the Phantom Thieves ultimately fail to change her cognition and the news coverage indicates that the protagonist in the story has been arrested and eventually committed suicide while under custody. The percentage of the Phansite continues to plummet to 3% approval on November 23.

Act 7 sees two mild resurgences of salience and valence as it is revealed that the protagonist did not commit suicide (and was alive), was framed into multiple crimes he did not commit, and the real culprit(s) were revealed per a nationally televised calling card. The proclamation of innocence and the attack on the real perpetrator saw the poll to increase from 2.9% to 9.8% on November 26 The question also changed to "Do you support the Phantom Thieves" as approval took another small spike in salience in on 19.7% as the politician primed to be Japan's next prime minister confessed publicly to the murder of the CEO the Phantom Thieves were accused of murdering earlier. While the Phantom Thieves were vindicated, the perception from the public was largely unchanged.

The final Act 8 sees some bizarre shifts in the poll as the narrative shifts to the public refusing to accept the guilt of the previous victims and forgetting the Phantom Thieves all together. The Phansite reflects this notion by changing the question again to "Do the Phantom Thieves exist?", the poll drops to 0% on December 24 only to ludicrously increase to 100% as the Phantom Thieves attempt to save the world. The Phantom Thieves are successful, but the protagonist is once again arrested for different charges. He remains in juvenile hall for three months until the final scenes in the game where he was released with the help of his friends and the politician's confession in court. While that occurs, the poll drops over that time to 50% for the final scene of the game.

The Nature of Agenda Setting According to Persona 5

In RQ 2, the question was posed "In the video game *Persona 5*, how do comments associated with the audience poll illustrate the nature of agenda setting?" Analysis found that the nature of first-level agenda setting was illustrated very clearly with topics discussed in the in-game news commonly being reflected in comments on the audience poll. Furthermore, second-level agenda setting was illustrated predominantly by discursively constructing the agenda as inappropriate either as a result of topic or because of the level of emphasis placed on the topic.

In many ways, the comments from the *Persona 5* audience poll narrate the entirety of the game by reflecting the major news events depicted within the game. When the Phantom Thieves steal their first heart--in-game parlance for forcing criminals to admit their crimes--comments indicated the novelty of the group. Commenters questioned "is this a prank?" and "is this a cult?" And the commenters noted that, in reference to stealing hearts, "even kids aren't that dumb." When the detective Akechi is interviewed via in-game media, he notes that while he appreciates the outcome, he views the Phantom Thieves as criminals. Commenters immediately echo Akechi's sentiments noting that "This is the police's job," "Akechi-kun is right!" and "they're still thieves…" Not all commenters backed Akechi, yet they nevertheless responded discursively to the agenda presented in that the Phantom Thieves were simultaneously "allies of justice" and yet simultaneously both the Phantom Thieves and Akechi were "crossing the line."

As the Phantom Thieves enjoy a string of successes, there is a brief period in which the comments almost-universally praise the Phantom Thieves' actions. These respond in tandem with the targeted criminals. This collapses quickly when a targeted individual dies during his confession. This leads the news to speculate--and by extension the audience on the audience poll--that the Phantom Thieves committed murder. In the same manner, the audience mirrors the agenda presented in the news with "well, that was disturbing" and "whoa wtf." In the same manner that a news agenda builds, gradually sentiment shifts in the midst of the agenda because "they went overboard" and forgot that "killing ppl's a no-no." All this together indicates the degree to which first-order agenda setting is illustrated as being pervasive--with government officials (denoted here through the character Akechi) largely given the opportunity to be agenda-setters.

Second-order agenda setting however was illustrated by indicating that while news media were remarkably successful in indicating what people should "think about" (Cohen, 1977), news media were less successful in adjusting their sentiment. For example, while comments illustrated that commenters were responding to a media agenda, they simultaneously questioned the media agenda, noting "gtfo with that shit LOL" because the story seemed like a piece of "viral marketing." And while Akechi-kun was largely given the right to set the agenda for discussion, that didn't keep sentiment from being negative toward him as an individual in that, as one commenter noted, the Phantom Thieves were just because "i hate Akechi" as Akechi seemed to be on a "high horse" and "immature." In this way, audience members on the fan site largely questioned the agenda and even the illustrated agenda-setter Akechi. In fact, over time, the attitude even toward the fan site itself shifts in sentiment; that is fan site is questioned for even providing a forum for news and discussion on the media agenda. Commenters noted that they "reported this website," questioned whether the "admin is an accomplice," and even argued that they should "kill this website." The comments also indicate that commenters at times found the agenda to be overblown for the news presented. For example, near the conclusion of the game, after the Phantom Thieves have successfully coerced confessions from numerous criminals, one comment noted "why this. even now???" and yet another noted that the continued support from some was because "ppl are desperate." The reports on the Phantom Thieves seemed so supernatural that commenters rightly questioned "Isn't this just a prank?" and "they're just making threats."

In short, the nature of first-order agenda setting was illustrated with news media largely setting the stage for what was discussed in the comment threats on the fan site. That said, audience sentiment often contrasted fiercely with that presented by news media. Commenters questioned the authenticity of the agenda setter (Akechi), the veracity of the news, and value of the fan site itself in that it seemed to play a role in propagating the news media agenda.

Discussion

Through the visual narrative, *Persona 5* builds a universe around the coverage concerning the importance of the Phantom Thieves. The coverage is central to the plot as it is a common theme amongst the members of the Phantom Thieves to be recognized. Popularity is embedded in the plot as increasing coverage of the Phantom Thieves is the only way the plot progresses into the true ending. The game is divided into eight acts that focus on the popularity of the Phantom Thieves, the fall, and the vindication of their existence and deeds. Even as their perceptual valence fluctuates, the narrative indicates that they are very much central to the world around them. It is important to note though that the majority of the game explains themes of agenda setting and other mass communication related theories throughout the story of the game, and thus the game communicates through visual and interactive storytelling how media theories are explained.

In order to answer RQ1, each act of the game must be dissected for mentions of agenda setting throughout the narrative. Salience begins from the first act of the story with the traditional hypothesis of agenda setting regarding media and public agenda. While the story is central to the school and those that live in the game's version of Tokyo, there are scenes in the game where people outside the school begin to talk about scandal regarding the gym teacher. This proposes the second-hand reality in which the folks who are unaware of the crime become immersed based on the coverage of the event (McCombs & Shaw, 1972). The first act also addresses the importance of the Phantom Thieves and thus the need to cover the scandal, but also mention the group. First level agenda setting helps explain this by stating media outlets focus a specific amount of coverage on the issue reported (Wu & Coleman, 2009).

Thus, the public brings in their own experiences and considers the topic salient as well. The public also plays an important role as agenda melding plays a role as a community around the Phansite emerges. These individuals shape their own agenda based on shared values, attitudes, or opinions (Ragas & Roberts 2009). The Phansite reoccurs with this consistent mentality of the belief, practices, and innocence of the Phantom Thieves both positively and negatively.

Not until the second act does the narrative address second level agenda setting, which states this is what media outlets want the public to "think about" (Wu & Coleman, 2009). They also state that this is more important to the public as the public will translate what they see in a media story regarding the issue. This occurs in the narrative as well when the famous artist confesses his crimes on a national press conference. The Phantom Thieves are a causal link between the corrupt deeds and the subsequent mortification for those deeds. This is largely seen through positive valence, as emotions are attached to a new story (McCombs, Llamas, Lopez-Escobar & Rey, 1997). However, the public figure detective introduced at this part in the story refutes the claims and presents a negative devil's advocate for the group.

This does resonate in the comments as well; the comments largely indicate a vigilante framing of the group at this point--fan site commenters bought into the agenda presented by the public figure detective Akechi while simultaneously championing the downfall of a corrupt figure. Commenters backed Akechi noting that "isn't it a crime?" and "they've always been fishy." One commenter even dismissed the group as being "fukkin hypocrites"--a reference to them committing a perceived criminal action in order to stop criminals. This vigilante framing is presented vis-a-vie the news media interview with the detective in which the Phantom Thieves are transgressive, yet the results of their actions are lauded. Comments indicate that this is to some degree a result of the anonymous nature of the group, as one commenter puts it "if ur so just, show ur face."

This is also apparent within Act 3 and Act 4 as the audience continuously submits comments for a need for orientation (NFO). Audiences want to understand the surrounding environment, as they are uncomfortable without knowing (McCombs, 2006). While the detective continuously tries to attack the morals of the Phantom Thieves, the group helps students by making an un-apprehended mob boss confess his crimes, and shutting down a hacker site that is determined to destroy Japan's economy is the Phantom Thieves do not unmask themselves. Audience members overcome any negative emotions concerning the group because the Phantom Thieves only apprehended villains, and thus any cognitive dissonance was removed because of the positivity of the deeds superseding any negative coverage.

The comments here denote a heroic frame for the group in that in the dropping of the calling cards, the fan site for the Phantom Thieves are quickly followed with comments like "Calling card! YAAAAAAS!" and "Here comes the apology rofl." The group is lauded for their work, even if the support is at times extreme, as seen in the comment "Exterminate his family too!" The audience is familiar with the Phantom Thieves' mode of attack: dropping a calling card before following up with their theft of the criminals' heart, and then the inevitable public apology from the criminal that follows. Hence, when the card is dropped, comments cast a negative valence on the criminal in question in comments like "Yeah, get that greedy CEO" and even "an apology isn't enough."

The certainty of the goodwill of the Phantom Thieves amongst the public makes the 5th act unusual within the narrative. Unlike all the other acts, the Phantom Thieves do their job, the villain confesses, and they continue to gain popularity. This time, the story's salience is still high, but the emotional valence has switched dramatically as the CEO dies during his confession, thus placing the blame on the Phantom Thieves. This is also the beginning of what scholars Guo, Vu, & McCombs (2012) have described as "third-level agenda setting"--the ability to build information regarding salient events in the publics' minds simultaneously (p. 54). Since Act 2, there has always been a defeated dissenting voice about the Phantom Thieves taking the law into their own hands. Now that a death is linked to this negative emotional frame, the previous dissenting voice prevails from Acts 5 to 7. This is also the time where the agenda melding shifts in the opposite direction with regards to valence as the comments with the fan site presenting the Phantom Thieves in an explicitly criminal frame. This is a clear transition from the prior frames of a vigilantism and heroism--there is no longer anything laud-worthy in the action of the Phantom Thieves. The Phantom Thieves now were "bloodthirsty killers" who needed to be "punished" and "executed." Comments indicate that the audience commenters also felt betrayed, with one commenter asking "were we deceived?" and "'justice' sounds hollow now."

Act 6 is largely uneventful as it just sees the Phantom Thieves Phansite decrease progressively through approval and now dissenting comments. Even when the report of the protagonist's apprehension, subsequent arrest and suicide are reported, the agenda melding is still apathetic and dissenting as comments state given that commenters believed the "kid had it coming." The protagonist's death was seen as a "worthy end for a villain" since "evil is destined to perish." Commenters saw the death of the protagonist as bringing the story to a close and bringing equilibrium in the turbulent media environment that emerged from the Phantom Thieves' actions. Commenters hope that "things are safer now" and that "we'll finally have peace."

However, the climax of the narrative in Act 7 shows the Phantom Thieves actually setting the media agenda by hacking into satellite feeds and broadcasting their message across Japan claiming the protagonist is alive, they had been framed, and the real culprit(s) behind the CEO's death are now revealed. This message coincides with apologia tactics such as denial and evasion of responsibility, as well as kategoria based apologia such as attack on character (Benoit, 1995). While this does boost the agenda melding amongst those on the Phansite, the reputation is too tarnished at that point in time for the Phantom Thieves to gain back their reputation. Even when the politician confesses his crimes absolving all guilt away from the Phantom Thieves, the percentage does not increase much. Commenters indicated a degree of confusion in seeing the media agenda shift so significantly with "so wait, who do we hate?" and "we need answers."

Actions do speak louder than words with regards to image restoration, and a corrective action strategy can build a reputation back from the depths of negativity (Frederick, Burch, Sanderson, & Hambrick, 2014). Such is the case of the final act where the Phantom Thieves save the world. While the conclusion is outlandish and unrealistic, it does demonstrate the Phantom Thieves' ability to repair their image. Hoaxes mirror this concept as organizations who are not at fault for their poor image can actually see some turnaround, but can still receive an amount of skepticism from the public (Frederick, Burch, Sanderson, & Hambrick, 2014). This is the focus of the final act, and it is not until the conclusion of the game that the attention subsides, no new reports occur, and the news cycle finally stops and the Phantom Thieves are largely forgotten by the media and public agenda. The story doesn't end with the Phantom Thieves at the center of the media agenda but with the agenda having moved on.

Largely, this game tends to reflect on social media fandom and how members communicate with one another. It also expresses a rhetorical frame for how fandom can change based on the actions of the public figures. As public figures become more interactive with their fans, more fans will perceive the public figures as social contacts. This means that any interaction, activity, or issue that a public figure is facing, the audience acts as a stakeholder as a fan. The in-game narrative not only provides an opportunity to understand fandom as it relates to their contact with public figures; but it also can address the long-term relationships that exists in fandom.

Implications and Future Directions

As game narratives offer salient viewpoints on how individuals view political problems, *Persona 5*'s story also conceptualizes the larger spectrum of societal issues and trends. As the *Persona* series has evolved over the years, so has its view on current society. For example, In *Persona 4*, players enter the alternate reality by means of a television set, but this changes in *Persona 5* as players enter the metaverse by means of an application on a smartphone.

This also is apparent in the way agenda setting is conveyed as the group progresses through the game. Each time the Phantom Thieves alter the cognition of an antagonist, their salience on mainstream media grows, and thus those interested in the group create a niche collective in support of the Phantom Thieves. The Phansite emerges because a tech-savvy classmate decides to create a blog/forum/poll in support of one of his interests. The website and the administrator ultimately become the face of credibility for the group (Booth & Matic, 2011). The game also projects a realistic view for how fan-oriented blogs and mass media outlets communicate with one another (Meraz, 2009; Williams and Deli Carpini, 2004). This provides another outlet for gaming narrative research for how in-game fans react to deeds by the protagonist and how the fans communicate with each other. Lastly, with availability of fandom on social media and blogging, this study provides an alleyway for future studies to see how agenda setting and fandom rhetoric coincide with one another.

Due to the connection with the source material and the credibility the blogs convey, traditional media often cites these blogs (Messner & Distaso, 2008). Blogs rely on traditional media as well (Messner & Distaso, 2008), which is represented in game as the website's administrator conveys what has been seen on mainstream media outlets, how viewers have communicated their take on the media reports, and how the phan-site eventually responds towards the often-negative valence of the Phantom Thieves. It is clear both in reality and in game that both media outlets, active viewers, and the fans who have a stake in the story all have the opportunity to set an audiences' agenda. Future studies could look into how other games communicate media coverage as a protagonist gains popularity in the game (e.g. Mass Effect, FIFA).

The reflection and communication of societal problems supports Bogost's (2006) argument and has become so important within the gaming community, that the community has actually created an actual "phan" site (https://phansite.net/) that features a question, comments, and even a "phorum." The topics within the "phorum" range from fan theories concerning a new *Persona* game, fan fiction games to change the hearts of fake antagonists that fans of the game have come up with, to seeking help for real problems and asking anonymously for help. This is a real time example for how individuals handle the end of a series by means of staying in touch with it (Schmid & Klimmt, 2010). Also the intention of the in-game forum has translated to reality by means of computer mediated communication (CMC) acting as an effective social support group for people in search of help. The in-game Phansite embodied anonymity, community, and outlet to call for help when no one else would. Future research could not only look at how gamers continue relationships with characters and games when a game has been concluded by means of fanfiction, the later installment of the new game *Persona 5, The Royal* or downloadable content (DLC). Also, future research could look into fan communities of a specific game and analyze CMC potential mental advice given amongst group members. Moreover, studies could also look into fan related content through other social media outlets like Tumblr and Facebook groups. These fandoms often post art, fan fiction, and "shipping" character support through art, in-game canon text, and even things like cosplay.

Limitations

Due to the exploratory and case chapter direction that this chapter took, the focus was making the internal validity as strong as possible. Games will have a different narrative and even games within the *Persona* series differ so drastically in terms of in-game narrative, it would be difficult to replicate this chapter. Additionally, the goal was to follow the in-game story as closely as possible, but there were gaps within the dates between December 25 and February 13. That said, the poll did not change drastically between those dates, and were limited in their use for the overall chapter. Lastly, the final boss battle saw an unrealistic increase from 0% to 100% in the same day. While that created an odd spike in the data, it was mostly unrelated to the overall findings.

CONCLUSION

The narrative of *Persona 5* was lengthy and complicated. The appeal of a massive game allowed for many rhetorical themes to emerge. While some themes appeared across multiple *Persona* games in the franchise, this chapter found themes that were exclusive to one game's story. It is important that the game not only tells an accurate story that reflects issues and patterns outside of its story line, but how it transcends into other outlets that their fans created. Moreover, this chapter and *Persona 5* reinforces the Bogost (2006) chapter when referencing that games can offer the salient locus for discussions about how we think about problems. As Agenda Melding would help explain, the public opinion often can lead the charge for this discussion.

REFERENCES

Benoit, W. (1995). *Accounts, Excuses, and Apologies: A Theory of Image Restoration Strategies*. New York: State University of New York Press.

Bielby, D. D., Harrington, C. L., & Bielby, W. T. (1999). Whose stories are they? Fans' engagement with soap opera narratives in three sites of fan activity. *Journal of Broadcasting & Electronic Media, 43*(1), 35–51. doi:10.1080/08838159909364473

Bogost, I. (2006). Comparative video game criticism. *Games and Culture, 1*(1), 41–46. doi:10.1177/1555412005281775

Bogost, I. (2008). The rhetoric of video games. In K. Salen (Ed.), *The Ecology of Games: Connecting Youth, Games, and Learning. The John D. and Catherine T. MacArthur Foundation Series on Digital Media and Learning* (pp. 117–140). Cambridge, MA: The MIT Press.

Booth, N., & Matic, J. A. (2011). Mapping and leveraging influencers in social media to shape corporate brand perceptions. *Corporate Communications, 16*(3), 184–191. doi:10.1108/13563281111156853

Bury, R. (2005). *Cyberspaces of their own: Female fandoms online* (Vol. 25). New York, NY: Peter Lang.

Chyi, H. I., & McCombs, M. E. (2004). Media salience and the process of framing: Coverage of the Columbine school shootings. *Journalism & Mass Communication Quarterly*, *81*(1), 22–35. doi:10.1177/107769900408100103

Cohen, B. J. (1977). *Organizing the world's money: the political economy of international monetary relations* (Vol. 1). New York: Basic Books. doi:10.1007/978-1-349-04006-3

Coleman, R., McCombs, M., Shaw, D., & Weaver, D. (2009). Agenda setting. In K. Wahl-Jorgensen & T. Hanitzsch (Eds.), *The handbook of journalism studies* (pp. 147–160). New York, NY: Routledge.

Crawford, G., & Gosling, V. K. (2009). More than a game: Sports-themed video games and player narratives. *Sociology of Sport Journal*, *26*(1), 50–66. doi:10.1123sj.26.1.50

Edelstein, A. S. (1993). Thinking about the criterion variable in agenda setting research. *Journal of Communication*, *43*(2), 85–99. doi:10.1111/j.1460-2466.1993.tb01264.x

Ferrucci, P. (2018). Mo "Meta" Blues: How Popular Culture Can Act as Metajournalistic Discourse. *International Journal of Communication*, 12.

Frederick, E., Burch, L., Sanderson, J., & Hambrick, M. (2014). To invest in the invisible: A case chapter of Manti Te'o's image restoration strategies during the Katie Couric interview. *Public Relations Review*, *40*(5), 780–788. doi:10.1016/j.pubrev.2014.05.003

Guo, L., Vu, H., & Mccombs, M. (2012). An expanded perspective on agenda setting effects: Exploring third level agenda setting. *Revista de Comunicación.*, *11*, 51–68.

Hall, S. (1980). Encoding/decoding. Culture, Media, Language: Working Papers in Cultural Studies, 79, 128-38.

Harper, T. (2011). Rules, rhetoric, and genre: Procedural rhetoric in *Persona 3*. *Games and Culture*, *6*(5), 395–413. doi:10.1177/1555412011402675

Jenkins, H. (1992). *Textual poachers: Television fans and participatory culture.* New York, NY: Routledge.

Jenkins, H. (2014). Participatory culture: From co-creating brand meaning to changing the world. *GfK Marketing Intelligence Review*, *6*(2), 34–39. doi:10.2478/gfkmir-2014-0096

Lasorsa, D. L. (2008). Agenda Setting. In L. L. Kaid & C. Holtz-Bacha (Eds.), *The encyclopedia of political communication*. Thousand Oaks, CA: Sage. doi:10.4135/9781412953993.n11

Lippmann, W. (1922). *The world outside and the pictures in our heads.* New York, NY, US: MacMillan Co.

Longhurst, B. (2007). *Cultural change and ordinary life*. Maidenhead: McGraw Hill.

Lotz, A. D. (2014). *The television will be revolutionized*. New York, NY: NYU Press.

McCombs, M. (1997). Building consensus: The news media's agenda setting roles. *Political Communication*, *14*(4), 433–443. doi:10.1080/105846097199236

McCombs, M. (2006). *Setting the agenda: The mass media and public opinion.* Malden, MA: Policy Press.

McCombs, M., Llamas, J. P., Lopez-Escobar, E., & Rey, F. (1997). Candidate images in Spanish elections: Second-level agenda setting effects. *Journalism & Mass Communication Quarterly*, *74*(4), 703–717. doi:10.1177/107769909707400404

McCombs, M., & Shaw, D. L. (1972). The agenda setting function of mass media. *Public Opinion Quarterly*, *36*(2), 176–187. doi:10.1086/267990

Meraz, S. (2009). Is there an elite hold? Traditional media to social media agenda setting influence in blog networks. *Journal of Computer-Mediated Communication*, *14*(3), 682–707. doi:10.1111/j.1083-6101.2009.01458.x

Messner, M., & Distaso, M. (2008). How traditional media and weblogs use each other as sources. *Journalism Studies*, *9*(3), 447–463. doi:10.1080/14616700801999287

Perreault, G. (2015). Not Your Average Church: Communal Narratives in an Evangelical Video Game Guild. The Electronic Church in the Digital Age: Cultural Impacts of Evangelical Mass Media: Cultural Impacts of Evangelical Mass Media, 151.

Potter, W. J., & Christ, W. G. (2007). *Media literacy*. The Blackwell Encyclopedia of Sociology.

Ragas, M., & Roberts, M. (2009). Agenda setting and agenda melding in an age of horizontal and vertical media: A new theoretical lens for virtual brand communities. *Journalism & Mass Communication Quarterly*, *86*(1), 45–64. doi:10.1177/107769900908600104

Robinson, V. M. (1998). Methodology and the research-practice gap. *Educational Researcher*, *27*(1), 17–26. doi:10.3102/0013189X027001017

Romano, S. (2018, May 14). *Persona 5* worldwide shipments top 2.2 million. *Gematsu*. Available online: https://gematsu.com/2018/05/persona-5-worldwide-shipments-top-2-2-million

Schmid, H., & Klimmt, C. (2010) *Goodbye, Harry? Audience Reactions to the End of Parasocial Relationships: The Case of Harry Potter.* Paper presented at the annual meeting of the International Communication Association, Suntec Singapore International Convention & Exhibition Centre, Suntec City, Singapore. http://citation.allacademic.com/meta/p404037_index.html

Shaw, D. L., McCombs, M., Weaver, D. H., & Hamm, B. J. (1999). Individuals, groups, and agenda melding: A theory of social dissonance. *International Journal of Public Opinion Research*, *11*(1), 2–24. doi:10.1093/ijpor/11.1.2

Shaw, D. L., McCombs, M. E., & Keir, G. (1997). *Advanced reporting: Discovering patterns in news events*. Fulcrum Publishing.

Treanor, M., & Mateas, M. (2009, September). News games-Procedural Rhetoric Meets Political Cartoons. *DiGRA Conference*.

Tucker, A. (2012) The art of video games. *Smithsonian Magazine*. https://www.smithsonianmag.com/arts-culture/the-art-of-video-games-101131359/

Van Dijk, T. A. (1988). News analysis. *Case Studies of International and National News*.

Weaver, D. H., & Elliott, S. (1985). Who sets the agenda for the media? A chapter of local agenda building. *The Journalism Quarterly*, *62*(1), 87–94. doi:10.1177/107769908506200113

Wu, H. D., & Coleman, R. (2009). Advancing agenda setting theory: The comparative strength and new contingent conditions of the two levels of agenda setting effects. *Journalism & Mass Communication Quarterly*, *86*(4), 775–789. doi:10.1177/107769900908600404

ADDITIONAL READING

Bantimaroudis, P. (2017). *Setting agendas in cultural markets : organizations, creators, experiences*. New York, NY: Routledge. doi:10.4324/9781315671734

Burch, L. M., Frederick, E. L., Zimmerman, M. H., & Clavio, G. E. (2011). Agenda-setting and La Copa Mundial: Marketing through agenda-setting on soccer blogs during the 2010 World Cup. *International Journal of Sport Management and Marketing*, *10*(3-4), 213–231. doi:10.1504/IJSMM.2011.044791

Dearing, J. W., & Rogers, E. M. (1996). *Agenda-setting*. Thousand Oaks, CA: Sage.

Johnson, T. J. (2014). *Agenda setting in a 2.0 world*. New York, NY: Routledge.

Mohn, E. (2018). *Agenda-setting theory. Salem Press Encyclopedia*. Hackensack, NJ: Salem Press.

Skogerbø, E., Bruns, A., Quodling, A., & Ingebretsen, T. (2016). Agenda-Setting Revisited. In *The Routledge Companion to Social Media and Politics*. New York, NY: Routledge.

Zimmerman, M. H., Clavio, G. E., & Lim, C. H. (2011). Set the agenda like Beckham: A professional sports league's use of YouTube to disseminate messages to its users. *International Journal of Sport Management and Marketing*, *10*(3-4), 180–195. doi:10.1504/IJSMM.2011.044789

KEY TERMS AND DEFINITIONS

Computer-Mediated Communication: Human communication via computers.

Media Literacy: An understanding of how media works and why media works the way it does.

Need for Orientation: When audiences express discomfort not understanding something regarding the surrounding environment.

Personas: Grants the characters special powers to battle enemies in an alternate world (known in *Persona 5* as the "metaverse")

Phantom Thieves: The heroes of the *Persona 5* video game, who travel to an alternate world (the metaverse) in order to address real world problems.

Procedural Rhetoric: Term is often used in reference to gaming to describe the ways in which electronic processes can be used to persuade.

Shin Megami Tensei "Persona": A series of Pokemon-style, role-playing video games in which players collect demons that can be used in battle sequences.

ENDNOTES

[1]   Times of Day (Mon-Sat): Early Morning, Morning, Lunchtime, Afternoon, After School, Evening.

[2]   Times of day (Sun): Early Morning, Daytime, Evening.

[3]   Q1: "Do you believe in the Phantom Thieves?", Q2:" Are the Phantom Thieves Just?", Q3: "Are the Phantom Thieves Innocent?", Q4: "Do you Support the Phantom Thieves?", and Q5: "Do the Phantom Thieves Really Exist?"

[4]   Q1: 28 comments, Q2: 143 comments, Q3: 36 comments, Q4: 39 comments, Q5: 39 comments.

[5]   The key exception is when the poll took a popularity spike (e.g. see 5/5 in Appendix A). Then the coder would record the first percentage that appeared in the spike.

This research was previously published in Multidisciplinary Perspectives on Media Fandom; pages 270-286, copyright year 2020 by Information Science Reference (an imprint of IGI Global).

Chapter 63
On Computerizing the Ancient Game of Ṭāb

Ahmad B. Hassanat
Mutah University, Karak, Jordan

Mahmoud B. Alhasanat
Al-Hussein Bin Talal University, Maan, Jordan

Ghada Altarawneh
Mutah University, Karak, Jordan

Alex de Voogt
Drew University, Madison, USA

Ahmad S. Tarawneh
Eotvos Lorand University ELTE, Budapest, Hungary

Baker Al-Rawashdeh
Mutah University, Mutah, Jordan

Hossam Faris
The University of Jordan, Amman, Jordan

Mohammed Alshamaileh
Mutah University, Mutah, Jordan

Surya V. B. Prasath
Cincinnati Children's Hospital Medical Center, Cincinnati, USA

ABSTRACT

The ancient game of ṭāb is a war and race game. It is played by two teams, each consisting of at least one player. In addition to presenting the game and its rules, the authors develop three versions of the game: human versus human, human versus computer, and computer versus computer. The authors employ a Genetic Algorithm (GA) to help the computer to choose the 'best' move to play. The computer game is designed allowing two degrees of difficulty: Beginners and Advanced. The results of several experiments show the strategic properties of this game, the strength of the proposed method by making the computer play the game intelligently, and the potential of generalizing their approach to other similar games.

DOI: 10.4018/978-1-6684-7589-8.ch063

INTRODUCTION

The game of ṭāb (Arabic: باط) is a board game, played by two teams, each of which consists of at least one player. It uses a game board of four rows of holes, which are normally impressed in the sand, with typically 8 to 12 holes per row. The rows of holes are used to host the players' pieces while playing. The pieces, also referred to here as soldiers, are moved based on the throws of four two-sided stick dice. The game ends by capturing all soldiers of the opponent and in this game a tie is not possible. Figure 1 shows two teams of two players enjoying the game of ṭāb in Petra, Jordan.

Figure 1. Two teams of two players playing the game of ṭāb in Petra. Four stick dice are used and the board is impressed in the sand. Photograph: Alex de Voogt 2009.

This game is one of the most popular board games in the Middle East and attested particularly in Jordan, Palestine, Sudan and some places in Egypt. The history of this game can be traced back to several hundred years. A recent survey of the archaeological region of Petra in Jordan revealed an unusually large number of ṭāb playing boards carved in rock surfaces distributed over two major sites in the ancient city (De Voogt, Hassanat, & Alhasanat, 2017). See Figure 2 for examples of these game boards. The survey study suggests a connection to the ancient city of Petra, but there was no evidence to date this game back to the Nabataeans (about 2000 years ago). The game has not been mentioned in Roman sources and no excavation has revealed such game boards even though several such game boards were found near archaeological sites. In addition, there is little evidence that can date the origin of the game of ṭāb to any specific period so that the birth date of the game of ṭāb remains elusive.

A nineteenth century description of this game is almost identical to what it is found today (Murray, 1952). Murray reports on sources that show that this game was played in Turkey, Egypt, and Persia, so that its presence in Jordan is not necessarily surprising. The majority of the ṭāb players in Jordan seem to be elderly people. It is hard to find a young man in the area who knows how to play ṭāb, or who even knows what the game of ṭāb is. Therefore, at least in Jordan, the gaming practice is slowly disappearing in the absence of a new generation of players.

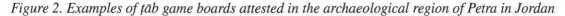

Figure 2. Examples of ṭāb game boards attested in the archaeological region of Petra in Jordan

The main goal of this work is to develop an intelligent computerized version of the game of ṭāb that allows the game to be acquired and enjoyed by a younger generation in Jordan and beyond. In addition, the unique properties of the game as described in section 2 may serve the research community for allowing further comparisons and analysis. This may provide the necessary momentum to ensure its cultural survival as well.

The literature is rich with attempts to computerize board games such as Sega (Abdelbar, Ragab, & Mitri, 2003), Chess (Simon & Schaeffer, 1992), Go (Jagiello, et al., 2006), Backgammon (Tesauro, 2002), etc. In addition, there are attempts to program proprietary games, such as Human Pacman (Cheok, et al., 2004) and several computing games (Björk, Holopainen, Ljungstrand, & Åkesson, 2002) and other ancient Egyptian games (Crist, Dunn-Vaturi, & de Voogt, 2016). The current research introduces the first computerized version of the game of ṭāb, a game that has properties not found in the games analysed in previous studies.

We have developed three versions of the game: Human against Human, Human against Computer, and Computer against Computer. The heuristic developed for this game chooses the "best" or "near optimal" move, and is designed with two levels of competency, Beginners and Advanced.

The remainder of this paper is organized as follows: Section 2 provides the basic descriptions, components and rules of the game of ṭāb; Section 3 details the computerization of the game using a genetic algorithm approach; Section 4 provides some experimental results using the developed computerized program; and, Section 5 summarizes the main conclusions that can be drawn from this work.

GAME COMPONENTS AND RULES

The game has three main components: a board, pieces and four stick dice. First, the game of ṭāb uses a game board that consists of a fixed number of rows (4) but a varying number of holes per row, referred to here as columns. The first row is home to the soldiers of the first team, and the fourth row to the opposing team. The in-between rows represent the battlefield. The soldiers move in a specified direction along the board. Figure 3 depicts the game board and the move directions.

Figure 3. A sketch of the ṭāb game board representing the starting position of the game. The numbers and letters were added to give an address to each location in order to encode the moves.

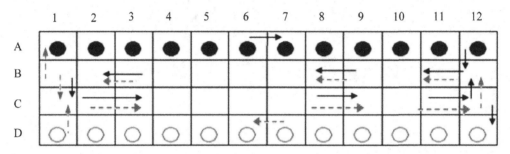

Second, the game features playing pieces commonly referred to soldiers or puppies by local players. They are represented by white and black circles in Figure 3. Players commonly use stones of two distinct colours, preferably black and white. The number of soldiers for each team is identical to the number of columns on the board.

The red-dotted arrows shown in Figure 3 depict the moves of the white soldiers, while the black arrows show the moves of the black soldiers. Each player starts with one soldier on their left-hand side —D1 for white, and A12 for black. Soldiers cannot return to their home row, however, they can enter the opponent's home row. When they do so, they remain frozen until all the soldiers in the other rows have been captured. Some players prefer to protect some of their soldiers from capture this way, since the opponent's soldiers cannot reach this row once they are in play.

Third, four stick dice are used to get a value with which a player can move their soldiers. These sticks are rectangular in shape and identical in size. They are commonly taken from Oleander trees, then cut horizontally to get a half cylinder shape with one flat side, represented here with a white colour, and one convex side, shown here as a dark green or brown colour. An overview of the values and the probabilities of each throw is presented in Table 1.

Stick dice are used instead of cubic dice. The latter are common in previously programmed games such as backgammon (Tesauro, 2002), Yahtzee (Glenn, 2006) and Monopoly (Yasumura, Oguchi, & Nitta, 2001). All six numbers on a cubic die have an equal probability. When using stick dice, players get five different numbers (1, 2, 3, 4, or 6), but each number has a different probability as shown in Table 1.

When a player throws the sticks, the number of flat or white sides determine the moves the player may play. If just one of the four sticks show its flat side, the player may move one piece one square further along the board. This score of one is called ṭāb. Ṭāb is considered the best move in the game; first, it is not allowed to jump over opponent's soldiers, so that this move allows for capturing soldiers directly in front of one's own piece; second, it allows the player to play again, i.e., the player throws the sticks again after completing this first move of one square; finally, it is the only throw that allows a soldier to move from its home row. The game and the throw are named after each other.

Table 1. The sticks' shape, value and the probability for each possible throw

Sticks side	Value	Probability to Occur
	1 (ṭāb)	25%
	2	37.5%
	3	25%
	4	6.25%
	6	6.25%

If any two sticks show their flat sides, the player gets to move two squares. If three sticks show their flat sides, the player gets to move three and four when four sticks show their flat sides. The player gets six when no flat side is shown. There is no value of "five" that can be thrown with these sticks.

The probabilities of getting 1, 4 and 6 are relatively small and if thrown the player is allowed to throw the sticks again just as with the throw of ṭāb. In contrast, the player stops playing and gives the sticks to the opponent after throwing 2 or 3.

At the beginning of the game, each player throws the sticks once; the one who gets the largest number starts playing the game. Each player needs to throw a ṭāb to free their first soldier; if not, the other player takes their turn to play. After a soldier is freed by one ṭāb move, it can be moved with all other throws as well. Players may agree to relax this rule in order to speed up the game. The players move their soldiers from the home row in a specific order, from the rightmost piece to the leftmost piece.

As indicated above, one turn may consist of multiple throws of the sticks. A player may choose to play a soldier directly or the player can wait until all the throws in one turn are completed. In the latter case, the player is allowed to move one or more of the pieces using their throws in any sequence they wish.

If a player's piece lands on any hole occupied by an opponent's piece, the opponent's piece is captured and removed from the game. A player may move one or more of their own soldiers onto the same square, creating a set. The set then moves as a whole and is potentially captured as a whole. To disassemble a set, a ṭab throw is needed to remove one piece to the next position. A set is not allowed to move around in the back row of the opponent. Once it reaches this row or is created there, it stays put. Only if no other moves are possible can a set on an opponent's home row be moved.

After a soldier reaches the right end of the home row, it proceeds up one hole and begins moving clockwise in the two center rows. Here the soldier will circle in the center two rows until it is captured or moved into the opponent's home row. In other words, the game of ṭab has a race and a war game component, which is known as a running-fight game. The options for moving pieces that a dice throw affords suggest that the game should be considered a competitive strategic game rather than a gambling game. In addition, the player is allowed to wait until all the throws have finished, after which the optimal order of moves is determined. This adds further strategy to the game.

Two of the co-authors video recorded and discussed (in Arabic) a complete ṭab game to illustrate the game rules, see https://youtu.be/wIF86O-EgMw. For alternates description of the rules see (Murray, 1952) and (De Voogt, Hassanat, & Alhasanat, 2017).

The Ṭāb Game Application

We used VC++.NET 2008 to develop the game application. We selected a board of four rows with eight holes per row. The main screen developed for this application shows boxes that provide information about the current state, stick values, history of moves, etc. Figure 4 shows the main screen of this ṭab application.

Figure 4. The main screen developed for the ṭab game

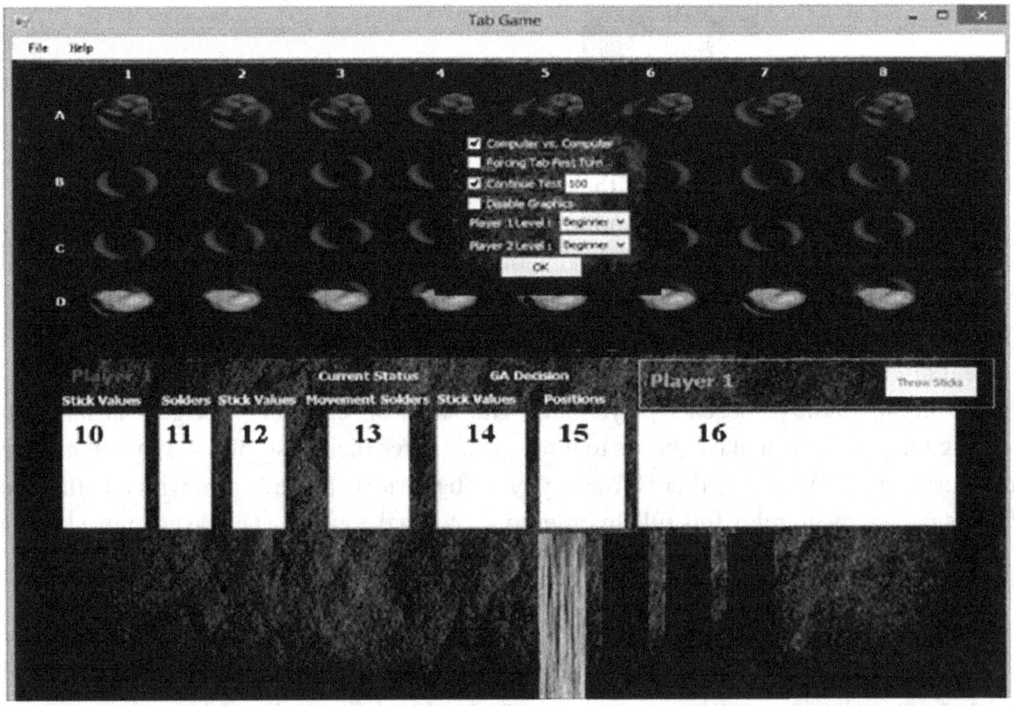

As shown in Figure 4, there are 18 elements numbered from 1 to 18 that represent the following options:

1. This element represents a soldier. Each player has eight soldiers; instead of black and white, we used silver and gold for the two sides;
2. This shows an options menu that contains settings used in the game;
3. This option allows two computer agents to play against each other;
4. Checking this option forces soldiers to make their first move using a ṭāb throw;
5. This option regulates the number of games that the computer agents will play against each other (for research purposes);
6. This option disables the visualization of the moves to save time, particularly when two computer agents play many games for research purposes;
7. This option sets the level of the first player if it is a computer agent, which can be a beginner or advanced;
8. This option sets the level of the second player if it is a computer agent, which can be beginner or advanced;
9. This option shows the board coordinates, which help the players to identify the positions of their soldiers;
10. This option provides the value list of the stick dice. It also shows all the values that the player obtained during the current turn, so that the player can choose which one to use first with which soldier;
11. This option lists the soldiers that a player can move, each soldier is represented by its initial index (from 1 to 8 for player 1, and 25-32 for player 2);
12. This option also shows the history of stick dice throws but here the system has removed the ṭāb throws that moved the frozen soldiers;
13. This option ensures that a soldier is automatically freed after playing ṭāb;
14. This option lists the stick dice throws that have automatically freed a soldier;
15. This option shows the position of each soldier after automatically freeing the soldiers with a ṭāb throw. Also, this list shows the cost of the decision that will be used by GA, which will be discussed later;
16. This option shows the history of each move for each player showing the coordinates of old and new positions of soldiers;
17. This option is used to throw the sticks and get new values; this option is available for human players only;
18. This figure provides a graphic view of the stick dice that shows the sides of the sticks for each throw.

Figure 5 shows a snapshot of the ṭāb game application, in this snapshot some of the soldiers have moved from initial positions to the active positions on the board.

As shown in Figure 5 there is a group of soldiers on D8; grouped soldiers can only be separated by throwing ṭāb, otherwise they remain as a set; soldiers in D8 cannot move because they are in the opponent's area, also A1 cannot move until B2 is captured or gets into row 1. The snapshot shows how the silver soldier moves from C5 to C6. Algorithm 1 shows how the soldiers are moved over the board.

Figure 5. A snapshot while the game is played between two computer agents

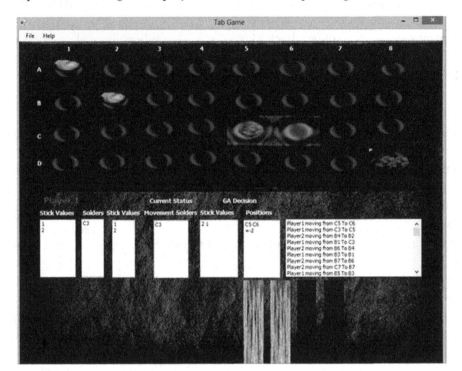

Algorithm 1: *The Moves of Soldiers on the Board*

```
Start
throw_again:
Value = Throw_the_sticks()
IF value ==1
IF frozen soldiers then
Move frozen soldier 1 move
End if
End if
Sticks_values_array.add(value)
If Value == 1 OR Value == 4 OR Value == 6
Go to throw_again;
End if
Selected_soldier_ position = get_soldier_position(mous_click)//reject
Oldnumberofsoldiers= Selected_soldier_ position.getsoldiersnumber();
Selected_move_ position = get_position(mous_click)
Distance = |Selected_move_ position - Selected_soldier_ position|
Value_index = Sticks_values_array.find (Distance)
New_ position = Selected_soldier_ position+ Distance
Move_soldier_to(New_ position)
Sticks_values_array.remove_at(Value_index)
```

```
Snumber = Number_of_soldiers(New_ position)
S_team= type_of_soldiers(New_ position)
If S_team==our_team
Snumber= Snumber+ Oldnumberofsoldiers
New_ position_soldiers.add(Snumber, New_ position)
Else
position_soldier(Oldnumberofsoldiers, New_position)//kill any opponent sol-
diers in a new positions
End if
Team1_soldiers=team1.numb_of_soldiers()
Team2_soldiers= team2.numb_of_soldiers()
If Team1_soldiers==0
winner= Team2
Else if Team2_soldiers==0
Winner= Team1
Else
Change_player();
Goto throw_again;
End if
End
```

A Game of Probabilities

Winning a ṭāb game is decided by choosing the "best" soldiers to move and by selecting which value to use for each soldier at each turn. This is a nontrivial task even for the most expert players. The difficulty stems from the number of possible solutions (moves) that may be available to the players, especially when the player gets a larger sequence of values of 1s, 4s and 6s (the throws that allow the player to throw again) in combination with a large number of free soldiers. Thus, the number of available solutions in ṭāb increases dramatically when the throw sequence increases and when the number of free soldiers increases.

For example, suppose that there are M free soldiers and N throw values. Any soldier can be moved by any number in the sequence, or one soldier or sub-group of soldiers can be moved by all the values. In addition, the player can start with any value in the sequence, so the sequence is not sorted. The number of these solutions can be defined by:

$$\text{Number of solutions} = \frac{(N + M - 1)!}{(M - 1)!} \tag{1}$$

Table 2 illustrates how an increasing number of free soldiers with specific values for the stick dice creates an increasing number of possible solutions for a player.

As shown in Table 2 there are a large number of solutions even with small sequences. When there are 5 or more free soldiers, which is statistically common; we get particularly large numbers of different solutions that complicate decision-making. Due to time constraints, a brute-force search algorithm is not practical to find the optimal move. Instead, we opt for the genetic algorithm (GA) as a meta-heuristic search tool to find a near-optimal, but possible, move. GA is not the only method that can solve this problem; other optimization methods can too, these include particle swarm optimization (Kennedy & Eberhart, 1995), cuckoo search (Yang & Deb, 2009), Ant colony optimization (Dorigo & Birattari, 2011), etc. However, GA is a well-established optimization method and has been used extensively in the computer science literature for the optimization of game play, such as Tetris (Böhm, Kókai, & Mandl, 2005), Seega (Abdelbar, Ragab, & Mitri, 2003), Checkers (Chellapilla & Fogel, 1999), (Chellapilla & Fogel, 2001), War Game Strategies (Revello & McCartney, 2002), Othello (Sun, Liao, Lu, & Zheng, 1994), first-person shooter game (Cole, Louis, & Miles, 2004), etc. Since this presents the first computerization of the ṭāb game, a comparison of these other optimization methods is outside the scope of this study.

Table 2. The possible number of solutions that can be generated from a different number of free soldiers (M) and stick dice values (N)

M	N									
	1	2	3	4	5	6	7	8	9	10
1	1	2	6	24	120	720	5040	40320	362880	3628800
2	2	6	24	120	720	5040	40320	362880	3628800	4E+07
3	3	12	60	360	2520	20160	181440	1814400	2E+07	2.4E+08
4	4	20	120	840	6720	60480	604800	6652800	8E+07	1E+09
5	5	30	210	1680	15120	151200	1663200	2E+07	2.6E+08	3.6E+09
6	6	42	336	3024	30240	332640	3991680	5.2E+07	7.3E+08	1.1E+10
7	7	56	504	5040	55440	665280	8648640	1.2E+08	1.8E+09	2.9E+10
8	8	72	720	7920	95040	1235520	1.7E+07	2.6E+08	4.2E+09	7.1E+10

Genetic Algorithm

GA is an evolutionary computing algorithm that is based on evolution and natural selection theory (Holland, 1992). It is an efficient tool for solving optimization problems. Particularly, it helps with combinatorial problems that cannot be solved in polynomial time, such as the one that we have with ṭāb (Hassanat A. B., et al., 2016).

Typically, GA consists of four major components: Initial Population, Crossover, Mutation and Selection based on fitness function (Hassanat & Alkafaween, 2017).

Initial Population

The initial population seeding is the first phase of any GA application. It generates, randomly or systematically, a population of feasible solutions or individuals (Hassanat, Prasath, Abbadi, Abu-Qdari, & Faris, 2018). Here, we create the initial population by allocating the stick values that move free soldiers randomly. This generates different random solutions where each soldier may or may not move.

Suppose that a player throws the sticks and gets the following sequence of values (moves): 6, 6, 4, 4, 4 and 2, and having 3 free soldiers. One possible solution can be created by allocating (6 and 4) to move soldier (1), (6, 4 and 4) to move soldier (2), and, finally, (2), to move soldier (3) two steps ahead, or any other combination from 20160 different solutions, since we have M=3 and N=6, see Table 2. Table 3 shows some of these possible solutions.

Table 3. Some of the possible random solutions to move 3 free soldiers ahead when throwing a sequence of 6, 6, 4, 4, 4 and 2 with the sticks dice

Soldier	Moves				
	Solution 1	Solution 2	Solution 3	Solution 4	Solution 20160
1	6,6	6,4,4,4	4,6	6,6,4,4,4,2	2
2	4,4	6	6,4,4	-	-
3	4,2	2	2	-	6,6,4,4,4

Crossover

Typically, the crossover is a binary process that operates on two solutions (chromosomes) called parents in order to generate new offspring solutions. This process attempts to create better solutions from existing in-hand solutions (Hassanat, Prasath, Abbadi, Abu-Qdari, & Faris, 2018). Here, we opt for the traditional one-point crossover process. In this process, it is essential to choose a random separation point that allows the parents' chromosomes to form new offspring, or solutions containing genes from both parents. Figure 6 shows the new offspring that result from the crossover process.

Figure 6. Crossover process of Solutions (1 and 2 from Table 3)

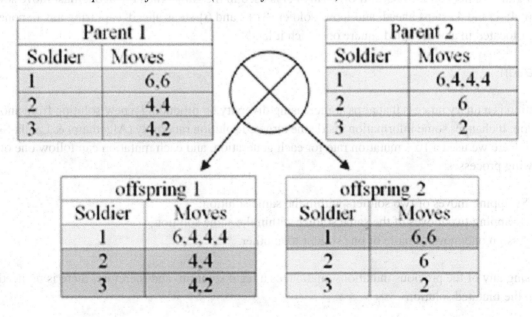

Fixing Chromosome Size and Content

As can be seen from Figure 6 there are some missing values in offspring (2), and more but also incorrect values in offspring (1). These errors occur because of the nature of one-point crossover used. Therefore, we need to correct each new offspring to get a legal solution. To solve this problem, we create a histogram for the stick values with the length of the histogram having five values: 0, 1, 2, 3 and 4. These values represent one of the possible values of the stick dice (1, 2, 3, 4 or 6) to which we add the frequencies of the sticks values. The histogram of the previous example (shown in Figure 6) is shown in Table 4.

Table 4. The histogram of sticks values of the example shown in Figure 6

Values	1	2	3	4	6
Frequencies	0	1	0	3	2

New offspring can be determined based on this histogram. Each offspring gets a copy of this histogram; we scan each solution and decrease the frequency of the found value. If we find a value that has a 0 frequency, this means it is an illegal move, so we can delete it from the chromosome. If the chromosome scanning has finished and there are still frequencies in the histogram, we add them randomly with random soldier(s) in the chromosome. Figure 7 shows the correction of offspring (1) from Figure 6.

As shown in Figure 7, all extra values are removed, but the final histogram shows that there is still a missing value, which is 6. We add this number to a random soldier. If we randomly choose soldier (3), the final solution and histogram is given in Figure 8.

All new offspring are checked in the same way to guarantee legal solutions, which are used later for moving the soldiers on the board. If offspring (1) is used in the game, then the agent must move soldier (1) {6; 4; 4; and 4} steps ahead, and move soldier (3) {2 and 6} steps ahead, capturing any opponent's soldier located in any occupied square on which it lands.

Mutation

Mutation is a unary process that aims at increasing diversity by producing a new solution from another solution. It changes some information inside the targeted solution randomly (Algethami & Landa-Silva, 2017). Here we used a 10% mutation rate for each generation, and each mutation can follow one of the following processes:

1. Swapping moves of two soldiers within the same solution;
2. Swapping two moves of the same soldier within the same solution;
3. Assign one move or more of one soldier to another.

Using any of the previous mutations guarantees a legal solution, and therefore, there is no need for fixing the mutated solutions.

Figure 7. Fixing chromosome's size and content offspring (1) from Figure 6, with stick values {6; 6; 4; 4; 4; 2}, and histogram {0; 1; 0; 3; 2}

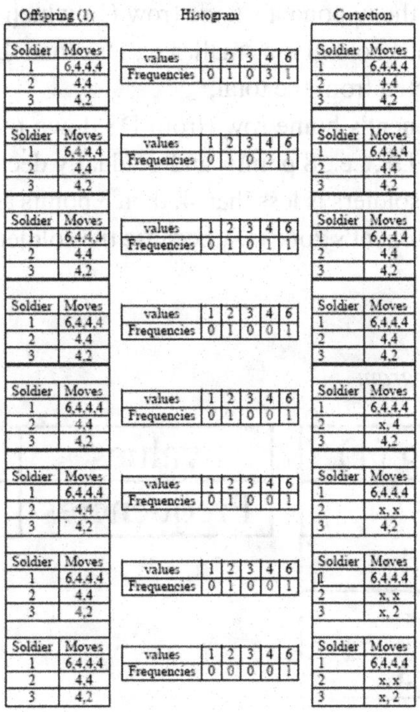

Fitness Function

Fitness function is used with GA to evaluate solutions. It uses calculations that depend on the problem in hand. In our application, the fitness function depends on finding a weight for each solution. Each square on the board is given a value that is affected by one or more soldiers occupying that square. The board contains dangerous squares, which expert players try to avoid occupying. These squares are the ones located in the way of the opponent's soldiers. There are also safe or safer squares, namely, those which are located farther from the reach of the opponent's soldiers. Both dangerous and safe squares are given high weights (points); however, the points of the dangerous ones have negative values. The remainder of the squares have neutral values. Both dangerous and safe squares are identified in Figure 10.

There is no completely safe place on the board with the exception of the home row of the opponent. But as soon as the soldiers get there, they cannot move unless there are no other moves left. There are other factors affecting the weight of each solution, and they can be summarized as follows:

1. For each soldier staying in the home row 4 points are added to the solution. For each soldier moving to the playing area or the middle rows, 2 points are added;
2. For each soldier moving to the strategic area (from B1-B4) 2 points are added;
3. The presence of more than one soldier in the same square deducts 4 times the number of the merged soldiers from the total number of points. The deduction process is maintained by adding negative points to the total weight of a solution;

4. If there are enemy soldiers located 4 squares or less behind the square proposed by the solution, then 2 points per opponent's soldier in such a position are deducted from the total;

5. If the proposed square is in the opponent's zone (row C), which is part of the dangerous squares, and the number of opponent's soldiers is small, i.e., less than 4, then 3 times the number of the opponent's soldiers is deducted from the total;

6. Putting soldiers in the opponent's home row (from D8 down to D1) gives additional points; the largest value goes to square D8, i.e., 8 points, and gradually decreases to 1 point for square D1;

7. If the number of the agent's soldiers is less than 4, then 3 points are deducted from the total weight if the soldier entered the opponent's zone (D), because the soldier becomes frozen and cannot play and capture.

Figure 8. Final solution and histogram

Legal Offspring (1)	
Soldier	Moves
1	6,4,4,4
2	-
3	2,6

values	1	2	3	4	6
Frequencies	0	0	0	0	0

Choosing the previous points (parameters) was based on pilot experiments. They were conducted and programmed by expert players that include the first author and three of the co-authors. The pilot experiments were based on trial and error, as the parameters were chosen, and the game was then tested by four of the authors who are already expert ṭāb players. The GA is used to generate solutions with the highest number of points (weight). The following is an example of a real status of the game showing the calculations of the fitness function.

Assuming the current state is as shown in Figure 11, and that it is the turn of the computer (the silver stones) to play, and it threw (4), (4), (1) and (2) with the stick dice, then the GA gives the following solutions:

Solution 1: This solution proposes moving the silver soldier from A8 to B2 using (1), (2), and (4), in addition to moving the other soldier from C1 to C5 using (4). The fitness function is calculated as follows: 2 points are added for each soldier in the playing area. In addition to 2 points for moving to a strategic square (B2), this makes the total number of points equal to 6. But 6 points are deducted because we have 3 opponent soldiers of which none have been captured. Four more points are deducted because of the threat of these soldiers at B1 and D1 (two for each), making the final weight of this solution -4. Figure 9 shows an example for each of these mutations. Figure 10 shows dangerous and safe areas. Figure 12 shows the solution for the game state in Figure 11.

Figure 9. Examples of the 3 mutation types adopted

Type 1		Type 2		Type 3	
Legal Offspring (1)		**Legal Offspring (1)**		**Legal Offspring (1)**	
Soldier	Moves	Soldier	Moves	Soldier	Moves
1	6,4,4,4	1	6,4,4,4	1	6,4,4,4
2	-	2	-	2	-
3	2,6	3	2,6	3	2,6

After mutation

Type 1		Type 2		Type 3	
New offspring		**New offspring**		**New offspring**	
Soldier	Moves	Soldier	Moves	Soldier	Moves
1	2,6	1	4,4,4,6	1	6,4,4,4
2	-	2	-	2	6
3	6,4,4,4	3	6,2	3	2

Figure 10. Dangerous area (red), safe or strategic area (blue), and neutral area (uncolored)

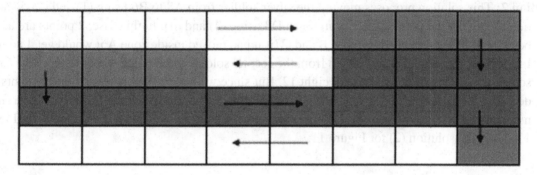

Figure 11. An assumed state of the game

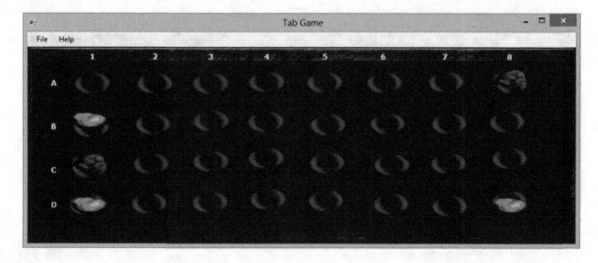

Figure 12. Solution (1) for the game state in Figure 11

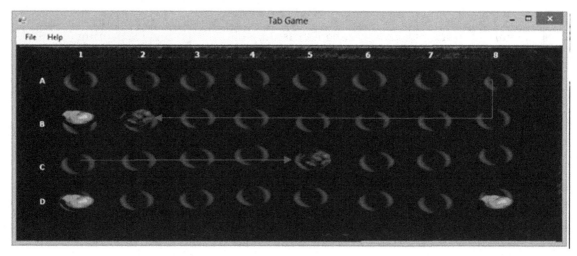

Solution 2: This solution proposes moving the silver soldier from A8 to B6 using (1) and (2), in addition to moving the other soldier from C1 to D8 using (4) and (4). In this case, 2 points are added because of moving to playing zones B and C (if it had moved inside zone A it would get 4 points). In addition, there are 2 points added from the second soldier and 8 points for moving to the safest square (D8). This makes the total weight 12. But since we have 2 opponent soldiers, 2 points are deducted for each of them. Finally, because of entering the opponent's zone (D) and having a small number of soldiers (less than 4), 3 points are deducted making the final weight equal to 5. Figure 13 shows the solution (2) for Figure 11.

Figure 13. Solution (2) for the game state in Figure 11

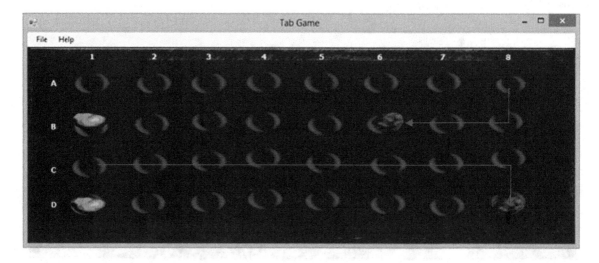

Solution 3: This solution proposes moving the silver soldier from A8 to B5 using (4), in addition to moving the other soldier from C1 to C8 using (1), (2) and (4). There are 2 points added for each soldier moving to the playing zone, and 6 points are deducted because of the 3 opponent's soldiers, making the final weight equal to -2. Figure 14 shows the solution (2) for Figure 11.

Figure 14. Solution (3) for the game state in Figure 11

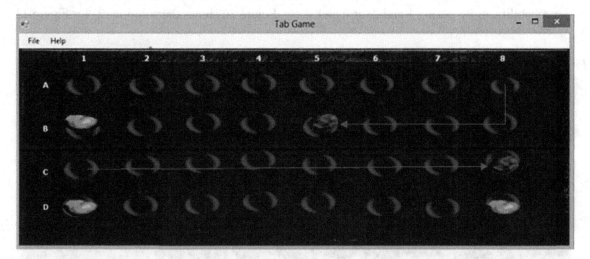

Solution 4: This solution proposes moving the silver soldier from A8 to B1 using (4) and (4) to capture an opponent's soldier on B1 and carrying on moving using (2) and (1), but without moving soldier at C1. This adds 4 points for deploying 2 soldiers to the playing zone. It deducts 4 points for having an opponent's soldier at D1 threatening both of the computer's soldiers and 4 more points are deducted for having 2 opponent's soldiers. This makes the final weight equal to -4. Figure 15 shows the solution (2) for Figure 11.

Figure 15. Solution (4) for the game state in Figure 11

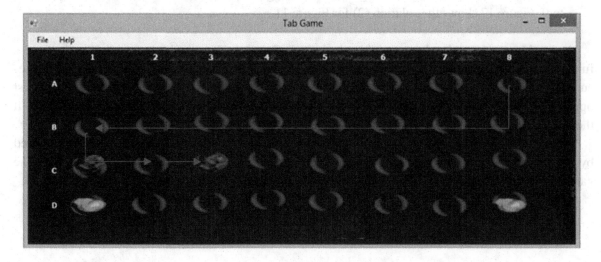

Solution 5: This solution proposes moving the silver soldier from A8 to B1 using (4) and (4) to capture the opponent's soldier on B1 and carrying on moving using (1) to merge with another soldier at C1. Then both are moved to C3 using (2). There are 4 points added for deploying 2 soldiers to the playing zone, 4 points are deducted for having 2 opponent soldiers, 2 more points are deducted for having a threat coming from D1, and in addition, 8 points are deducted from merging 2 soldiers into a set (-4 points for each merged soldier). This makes the final weight equal to -10. This might be the worst solution as the opponent can easily end the game by throwing 3, which has a 25% probability, or by getting 1 and 2, or 6 and 4, etc. Figure 16 shows the solution (2) for Figure 11.

Figure 16. Solution (5) for the game state in Figure 11

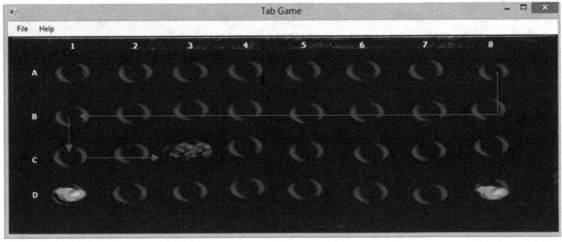

Solution 6: This solution proposes moving the silver soldier from A8 to B1 using (4) and (4) to capture an opponent's soldier on B1, and moving the other silver soldier from C1 to C3 using (2) and (1). This adds 4 points for deploying soldiers to a playing zone, in addition to 2 points for having one soldier on a strategic square (B1). Then 4 points are deducted for having 2 opponent soldiers, 2 more points are deducted for having a threat coming from D1. This makes the final weight equal to 0. Figure 17 shows the solution (2) for Figure 11.

As can be seen from the above weight calculations, Solution (2) is the best according to the fitness function, and this would be a logical conclusion, as the computer can now capture one soldier and secured one of its soldiers in the D zone, while it keeps one of its soldiers 5 squares away from the nearest opponent's soldier. This makes it difficult to be captured in the opponent's turn. Table 5 summarized all the probabilities for capturing the soldier on B6 from B1 in Solution (2).

As can be seen from Table 5, it is not likely (3.8%) that the computer's soldier B6 will be captured by the opponent's soldier located five squares behind. Also, it should be noted that there is no 5 in the game. The table shows the strength of solution (2) as proposed by the fitness function.

Figure 17. Solution (6) for the game state in Figure 11

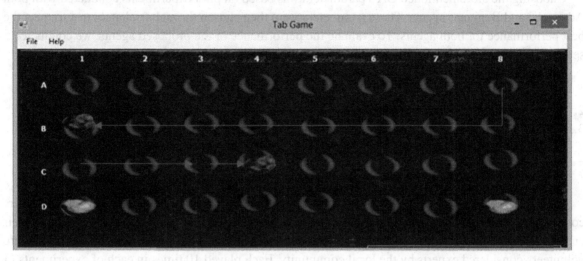

Table 5. All possible situations where the opponent captures the computer's soldier on B6 from B1 in Solution (2)

Which Throw is Needed to Capture a Soldier Located 5 Squares Ahead?	Probability*	
5 ones	0.25×0.25×0.25×0.25×0.25	0.000977
3 ones and a two	0.25×0.25×0.25×0.375	0.005859
2 ones and a three	0.25×0.25×0.25	0.015625
a one and a four	0.25×0.0625	0.015625
Sum		0.038086

* Probability for each number to occur is taken from Table 1

Experimental Results

In this study, we programmed the game using 2 degrees of difficulty, i.e., using 2 agents, Advanced and Beginner. The Beginner agent is almost the same as the Advanced, with the following exceptions: a) the number of generations of the GA; we used 200 generations for each solution for the Advanced agent, while we used only 50 generations for the Beginner agent, as it is well-known that more generations for GA provides better solutions (Oh, 2017), (Amirjanov & Sobolev, 2017). b) The Beginner agent does not include values for grouped soldiers. The other parameters of the GA are the same for both agents, which are:

- Crossover rate = 80%;
- Mutation rate = 10%;
- Size of population = 500 chromosomes (solution);
- The selection operation chooses the best 500 solutions at each generation.

Choosing the aforementioned GA's parameters was based on pilot experiments conducted with both Advanced and Beginner agents. These parameters were then chosen through trial and error to meet the best performance for both agents. To evaluate the performance of the proposed agents, we conducted 5 sets of experiments, which are based on playing the game as follows:

1. Advanced vs. Advanced
2. Advanced vs. Beginner
3. Beginner vs. Beginner
4. Human vs. Advanced
5. Human vs. Beginner

Each set of experiments was repeated 100 times before drawing any conclusion. The human players consist of 10 expert players, who have been experience with playing the game for at least 4 years. Their ages range from 24 to 65 years. Four of these players are the authors of this paper, while the rest are volunteers considered experts by the local community. Each played 10 times in each of experiments (4 and 5). The results of the 5 sets of experiments are listed in Table 6.

Table 6. Experimental results

Experiments	# of Wins	Largest Sequence (Sticks Value)	Largest Number of Free (Movable) Soldiers
Player1 = Advanced Player2 = Advanced	47 / 53	5	5
Player1 = Advanced Player2 = Beginner	79 / 21	4	6
Player1 = Beginner Player2 = Beginner	43 / 57	5	8
Player1 = Beginner Player2 = Human	38 / 62	6	7
Player1 = Advanced Player2 = Human	60 / 40	7	7

As can be seen from Table 6 the Advanced agents compared to the Beginner won most of the games, 79%. Compared to a human agent, it won 60% of the played games. These results support the strength of the proposed heuristic, particularly, when we give the GA enough time (200 generations) to find the 'best', i.e., near optimal, move. In addition, these results stress the importance of playing strategically with the grouped-soldiers, knowing that the GA of the beginner agent has not enough time to evaluate solutions and ignores the grouped-soldiers strategy. Moreover, the human brain cannot compete with machines when there is a very large number of possibilities to consider (Bushko, 2005).

When human players played against a beginner agent, they won most of their games (62%). This is explained by the weakness of the beginner agent for the above-mentioned reasons. The advanced agent when playing another advanced agent, both performed almost the same (47% vs. 53%), there was no fifty-fifty result because a larger number of simulations would be needed to have a near equal distribution of advantageous dice throws. Statistically speaking the probability to get advantageous ṭāb throws is such that players should count on strategies more than luck when playing ṭāb.

For each experiment, we recorded the number of stick dice values for each throw (the number of times a player was allowed to play before handing the sticks to the opponent), in addition to the number of "Free" (or movable) Soldiers. Those two numbers (N and M from Table 2) are crucial to the number of possible solutions, as the number of these solutions is calculated by a factorial function as shown in Equation (1). A closer look at the data in Table 6, specifically the third and fourth columns, we see that one of the experiments has 5 numbers in sequence in one turn, and 8 free soldiers (maximum). This gives according to Equation (1) 2E + 07 possible solutions. Therefore, it is a rational decision to use an optimization method such as the GA to optimize such a large number of solutions.

The aforementioned experiments used three versions of the game, which were designed for a beginner agent, an advanced agent and a human. Table 7 summarizes the differences between these versions.

Table 7. Summary of different versions of the game

Game Version	#Generations	Grouped Soldiers Used	GA Parameters	Throw Sticks Button
Beginner agent	50	No	Crossover rate = 80%, Mutation rate = 10%, Size of population = 500	NA
Advanced agent	200	Yes	Crossover rate = 80%, Mutation rate = 10%, Size of population = 500	NA
Human player	NA	Yes	NA	Yes

CONCLUSION

In this work, we have presented the game of ṭāb and computerized it for the first time to be played by humans and/or machines. We used a GA approach to create the best (near optimal) solution for two agents (Advanced and Beginner). Several experiments were conducted to evaluate the performance of the agents. Due to the large number of different solutions presented to a player, the agent designed on the advanced level can beat human players in most of the played games, proving the strength of our proposed GA approach for this game. In addition, we show that for human players the game of ṭāb is a strategic game as opposed to a game of chance. This claim is further supported by the experiments conducted.

One of the limitations of this study is the lack of comparisons of our agent with agents from other studies due to the absence of previous studies for the game of ṭāb. For this reason, the first version of the game is made freely available on Google drive at (https://drive.google.com/drive/folders/0B6f_uK dnLbrlcjNxMHkwa2REM2s?usp=sharing). It allows researchers from the computer game community to contribute to better versions of this historical game. Other limitations of this work include the use of probabilities for the throws. For example, we added penalties to the moves that put a soldier in a location less than 5 squares ahead of an opponent's soldier. We did not distinguish between these 4 squares. However, statistically, one square ahead is different from 2 squares ahead, as the probability of getting

1 (25%) is less than the probability of getting 2 (37:5%). The same applies to 3 and 4 squares ahead. This issue needs to be further investigated in future work in order to enhance the performance of the heuristic used. Finally, the fitness function used in this paper depends heavily on expert knowledge. Future research may explore a fitness function that allows the algorithm to discover its own strategies, for instance, by using a form of deep learning.

We aim not only to address the limitations mentioned above in future research but also to develop mobile and web-based versions. The latter are instrumental in facilitating the spread of the game and raising awareness of the game for both general and academic audiences.

ACKNOWLEDGMENT

The authors would like to thank Jose Brox with University of Coimbra, Portugal; And Ioulia N. Baoulina with Moscow State Pedagogical University, Russia, for their help and valuable discussions to formulate Equation (1).

REFERENCES

Abdelbar, A. M., Ragab, S., & Mitri, S. (2003). Applying co-evolutionary particle swam optimization to the Egyptian board game seega. In *Proceedings of the first Asian-Pacific workshop on genetic programming* (pp. 9-15).

Algethami, H., & Landa-Silva, D. (2017). Diversity-based adaptive genetic algorithm for a Workforce Scheduling and Routing Problem. In *2017 IEEE Congress on Evolutionary Computation (CEC)* (pp. 1771-1778). IEEE.

Amirjanov, A., & Sobolev, K. (2017). Scheduling of directed acyclic graphs by a genetic algorithm with a repairing mechanism. *Concurrency and Computation*, *29*(5), 1–10. doi:10.1002/cpe.3954

Björk, S., Holopainen, J., Ljungstrand, P., & Åkesson, K. P. (2002). Designing ubiquitous computing games–a report from a workshop exploring ubiquitous computing entertainment. *Personal and Ubiquitous Computing*, *6*(5), 443–458. doi:10.1007007790200048

Böhm, N., Kókai, G., & Mandl, S. (2005). An evolutionary approach to Tetris. In *The Sixth Metaheuristics International Conference (MIC2005)* (pp. 5-11).

Bushko, R. (Ed.). (2005). *Future of Intelligent and Extelligent Health Environment*. Amsterdam: IOS Press.

Chellapilla, K., & Fogel, D. B. (1999). Evolving neural networks to play checkers without relying on expert knowledge. *IEEE Transactions on Neural Networks*, *10*(6), 1382–1391. doi:10.1109/72.809083 PMID:18252639

Chellapilla, K., & Fogel, D. B. (2001). Evolving an expert checkers playing program without using human expertise. *IEEE Transactions on Evolutionary Computation*, *5*(4), 422–428. doi:10.1109/4235.942536

Cheok, A. D., Goh, K. H., Liu, W., Farbiz, F., Fong, S. W., Teo, S. L., ... Yang, X. (2004). Human Pacman: A mobile, wide-area entertainment system based on physical, social, and ubiquitous computing. *Personal and Ubiquitous Computing, 8*(2), 71–81. doi:10.100700779-004-0267-x

Cole, N., Louis, S. J., & Miles, C. (2004). *Using a genetic algorithm to tune first-person shooter bots. In Congress on Evolutionary Computation, CEC2004. 1* (pp. 139–145). IEEE.

Crist, W., Dunn-Vaturi, A. E., & de Voogt, A. (2016). *Ancient Egyptians at Play: Board Games Across Borders*. London: Bloomsbury Publishing.

De Voogt, A., Hassanat, A. B., & Alhasanat, M. B. (2017). The History and Distribution of ṭāb: A Survey of Petra's Gaming Boards. *Journal of Near Eastern Studies, 76*(1), 93–101. doi:10.1086/690502

Dorigo, M., & Birattari, M. (2011). Ant colony optimization. In Encyclopedia of machine learning (pp. 36-39).

Glenn, J. (2006). *An optimal strategy for Yahtzee. Loyola College*. Maryland: Loyola College in Maryland.

Hassanat, A. B., & Alkafaween, E. (2017). On enhancing genetic algorithms using new crossovers. *International Journal of Computer Applications in Technology, 55*(3), 202–212. doi:10.1504/IJCAT.2017.084774

Hassanat, A. B., Alkafaween, E., Al-Nawaiseh, N. A., Abbadi, M. A., Alkasassbeh, M., & Alhasanat, M. B. (2016). Enhancing Genetic Algorithms using Multi Mutations: Experimental Results on the Travelling Salesman Problem. *International Journal of Computer Science and Information Security, 14*(7), 785–802.

Hassanat, A., Prasath, V., Abbadi, M., Abu-Qdari, S., & Faris, H. (2018). An Improved Genetic Algorithm with a New Initialization Mechanism Based on Regression Techniques. *Information, 9*(7), 167–197. doi:10.3390/info9070167

Holland, J. H. (1992). *Adaptation in natural and artificial systems: an introductory analysis with applications to biology, control, and artificial intelligence*. MIT press.

Jagiello, J., Eronen, M., Tay, N., Hart, D., Warne, L., & Hasan, H. (2006). Simulation Framework as a Multi-User Environment for a Go*Team game. In *37th Annual Conference of the International Simulation and Gaming Association*, St Petersburg, Russia (pp. 3-7).

Kennedy, J., & Eberhart, R. (1995). Particle Swarm Optimization. In *IEEE International Conference on Neural Networks IV* (pp. 1942–1948). IEEE. doi:10.1109/ICNN.1995.488968

Murray, H. J. (1952). *A history of board-games other than chess*. Clarendon press.

Oh, D. Y. (2017). Experiments to Parameters and Base Classifiers in the Fitness Function for GA-Ensemble. *International Journal of Statistics in Medical and Biological Research, 1*(1), 9-18.

Revello, T. E., & McCartney, R. (2002). *Generating war game strategies using a genetic algorithm. In Evolutionary Computation, CEC02. 2* (pp. 1086–1091). IEEE.

Simon, H. A., & Schaeffer, J. (1992). The game of chess. Handbook of game theory with economic applications, 1(1), 1-17.

Sun, C. T., Liao, Y. H., Lu, J. Y., & Zheng, F. M. (1994). Genetic algorithm learning in game playing with multiple coaches. In *IEEE World Congress on Computational Intelligence* (pp. 239-243). IEEE.

Tesauro, G. (2002). Programming backgammon using self-teaching neural nets. *Artificial Intelligence*, *134*(1), 181–199. doi:10.1016/S0004-3702(01)00110-2

Yang, X. S., & Deb, S. (2009). *Cuckoo search via Lévy flights. Nature & Biologically Inspired Computing* (pp. 210–214). IEEE.

Yasumura, Y., Oguchi, K., & Nitta, K. (2001). Negotiation strategy of agents in the Monopoly game. In *IEEE International Symposium on Computational Intelligence in Robotics and Automation* (pp. 277-281). IEEE. 10.1109/CIRA.2001.1013210

This research was previously published in the International Journal of Gaming and Computer-Mediated Simulations (IJGCMS), 10(3); pages 20-40, copyright year 2018 by IGI Publishing (an imprint of IGI Global).

Section 5
Organizational and Social Implications

Chapter 64
Institutions as Designers of Better Social Games

Albena Antonova
Sofia University, Bulgaria

ABSTRACT

Institutions predefine and make possible development of many social processes. As already discussed, institutions define "the rules of the game," encouraging further social and organizational transformations. The aim of Chapter 6 is to propose an alternative approach for shaping the future institutions. By assuming institutions to be game-designers of complex social systems, there are explored the main mechanisms and elements of the game-design. Following this approach, the author discusses how institutions can transform to designers of new types of rules and social arrangements that will be more just and efficient for all. The structure of the chapter is as follows: In the first part there are identified the main elements of the game design, including game-mechanics, game-play, and game-word. The second part makes analysis of social ecosystems, where the new types of rules and regulations can stimulate creativity and innovations. Finally, an analysis is made about how institutions can figure out the gamification models and transform in order to promote new type of development and social cohesion. In this respect, Chapter 6 aims to propose an experiment of thought, discussing how to design more efficient and more socially just rules and regulations that can further ensure our sustainable development.

INTRODUCTION

The digital transformation processes under the paradigm of Industry 4.0 are expected to have a tremendous impact on the economic and social development. All stakeholders: businesses, private organizations, NGOs and public authorities have a role to play for shaping the next "robotic era". Even more, many new rules have to be defined and many new models for economic and social long-term development have to be discussed, taking into account the increased number of new machines on the job. Technologies cannot decide how our societies and how our personal life will change. Technologies provide us with tools and instruments, extending our abilities to cope more efficiently with the new coming challenges and future problems. Current digitalization trends focus to further improve human capacity to understand

DOI: 10.4018/978-1-6684-7589-8.ch064

more complicated dynamic processes, switching the gap between virtual and real with sophisticated cyber-physical systems. The promise for better manufacturing processes can improve resource efficiency, customization, supply chain reorganization and product life-cycle management patterns. More advanced robots on the work can lead to increased service and production functions, confirming that digitalization processes come for more rational and data-based decision-making in order to better forecast, plan and implement the next models of development.

However, technologies cannot resolve our social and human problems and cannot make our societies more sustainable and future-oriented. The data all over the world continue to show accumulating waste, based on overproduction, neglected environmental and ecological balances, impermissible abuse of social and human rights and political oppression, short-focused and unsustainable global development movements. People increasingly feel excluded and unrepresented in main political and governance processes. Power distribution polarizes and inequalities intensify both internally in the countries and in the regions and internationally. New impactful Internet phenomena raise including fake news, social-network propaganda and intensified misinformation, using artificial intelligence applications to modify behavior patterns and social preferences. All this come to show that new technologies do not offer a "magic key" for the better future. Thus in the next robotic era there is a clear need for new social contract renegotiation. This means designing new institutions and defining new rules for making the "game" again more efficient and fair for all. Social exclusion, inequality, future of work and sustainable development are among the number of challenges that the new rules have to address.

Today is the moment to open the debate about the future of institutions. In order to "unlock" the potential of the next growth people should reach new common understanding for the next types of social arrangements and power distribution. Discussing the future of work and the new roles of humans in the labor force raise two main questions. On one side there should be redefined the new skillsets and new competences needed in the years to come. On the other side, much more attention should be paid on the issues of inclusive models of growth, encouraging and supporting people for cultivating and expressing talents and gifts in a socially enriching and responsible-for-the future way.

However, we have to admit that in the framework of the current institutionalized market-dominated, consumer-oriented and growth-based economic models, little attention is paid to many of the inherent human capacities. Due to the lack of monetization mechanisms and social support, many of the human gifts and dispositions remain undervalued and underestimated on the labor market, as for example the ability to take care, to protect, to persist, to share knowledge and competences, to artistically express, to encourage and motivate, to cooperate altruistically for a common cause. Thus, technically, human have the capacity and the potential to cope with the pressing problems of the future. However, in the current settings, many of the activities, ensuring sustainable development, environmental and social protection, crisis relief and poverty alleviation are just downsized to short-term campaigns, leaded by NGOs and volunteers. Thus in order to have much larger impact in the future, more efforts will be necessary to put all this hidden human capital to work. Meanwhile the existing institutional arrangements still widen the gap, measuring skills, personal success and organizational future perspectives only in economic terms.

All this come to show that the debates for the future of work can open the floor for the design and experimentation with new institutional arrangements. This way, by revising the main common principles, we can reevaluate the basic human rights and regulations, giving a chance for emerging more socially just and efficient institutions. Only adopting new forms of governance paradigms will help us to raise new informal institutions, ideologies (by North, 1990) and mental models, unlocking the potential for new types of personal and social development. In order to figure out on practice how institutions and organizations can further transform in the robotic era, we will analyze how rules and regulations can potentially evolve. Conceptualizing the models of (computer) games design, we will test the idea whether and how "rules of the game" can create enjoyable social interactions and fulfilling experiences.

The aim of the chapter six is to propose an alternative approach for shaping institutions in the future, discussing their role as game-designers of complex social systems. Exploring the game-design approach we will further investigate how institutions can design new types of rules and social arrangements that will be more just and efficient for all.

In the first part of the chapter there will be identified the main elements of the game design, including game-mechanics, game-play and game-word. By developing the main game design elements, there will be explored the elements of the social ecosystems that apply new types of rules and regulations in order to stimulate creativity and innovations. Finally, an analysis is made about how institutions can figure out the gamification models and transform, in order to promote new type of development and social cohesion. In this respect, chapter six aims to propose an experiment of thought, discussing how to design more efficient and more socially just rules and regulations, that can further ensure our sustainable development.

DEFINING THE GAME

The games design and game development started in antiquity and spread in a large continuum of ideas and directions, covering different aspects of the social subjects as philosophy, pedagogy, psychology, and others (Dixon, 2009). Based on the classification of Caillois (1961) play and games differentiate in a way that "ludus" represents a rule-based games and "paidia" is an anarchic playing. A game can be broadly defined *as a structured or rule-based social system in which players engage in a safe environment, resolving different challenges and leading to a quantifiable outcomes* (Huotari & Hamari, 2012). The game can be considered as a dynamic process and social activity rather than a simple object. Any game's primary objective and meaning is to motivate the player to perform well and to win. Therefore, he needs to have the ability and freedom to explore various strategies for success, experimenting with different techniques and analysing the feedback of the results. There are three main dimensions that characterize almost every game (Aerseth, 2003). The gameplay (the set of problems and challenges requiring the players' actions, strategies and motives); the game-structure (the rules of interaction in the game); the game-world or the game story (all plot and character fictional content, topology design and others). "Game mechanics" or the design of the rules and models of interactions within games, gained the researchers' interest in respect to the rise of the computer and video games. There game mechanics, game-structuring and the "rules of the game" include a general framework of rules that determine how a players can advance in a specific computer-generated game context. Without rules, the players' actions cannot be structured and there cannot be a gameplay (Aerseth, 2003). Thus game rules play a substantial role for the player's experiences. It is interesting to note as well that game mechanics are "second order designs", meaning that game designers can only indirectly design and influence the players' experiences by defining the rules of the game (Kultima, 2009).

GAME-STRUCTURE (RULES)

In order to identify the structure and the common characteristics and elements of the rules in the game-mechanics, there are identified two main approaches: studying casual games mechanics and investigating findings from gamification approaches.

Focusing to identify what triggers the casual games design, Kultima (2009) make an in-depth study of the main characteristics and common elements. It is important to stress that casual games are designed for heterogeneous groups of players with different backgrounds, skills, cultural settings and interests, and they are actually played by millions of people daily across different contexts and countries. The casual games are the most popular digital games and the current statistics prove that the overall playing time worldwide is gradually increasing at the expense of other media.

Casual games are designed mainly for entertainment and there is a huge Game industry, involved in its development and delivery. Casual games can play on different hardware platforms and devices. However, Kultima (2009) derived to main four common characteristics of the game mechanics that most of the casual games possess. They are: acceptability (of the content), accessibility (of the form), simplicity (of the use) and flexibility (in the context). Thus on Table 1 there are summarized the main aspects of these characteristics.

Gamification is a new rising phenomenon designating *the use of the game mechanics and applying them to other (web) properties to increase engagement,* or in general *the use of game design elements in non-game contexts* (Deterding, Dixon, Khaled, & Nacke, 2011). In the general aspect, gamification refers to a process of enhancing a service with affordances for game experiences in order to support user's overall value creation (Huotari & Hamari, 2012). Some other in-depth studies suggest that gamification is a developing approach for encouraging user motivation, engagement and enjoyment in non-gaming, computer-mediated environments with an early collection of empirical work supporting its potential for beneficial effects in certain contexts (Seaborn & Fels, 2015).

Robinson and Belotti (2013) proposed a model of general gamification framework. It consists of six main categories of elements including: general framing (context and motivation for participation, back story or relevant information); general rules and performance framing (what is expected), social features (permit the user to interact with others), incentives (both intrinsic and extrinsic), resources and constraints, feedback and status information (allow user to understand what is going on). Making a review of different gamification applications, (Seaborn & Fels, 2015), find out that end-users mostly preferred strategies for collection (badges, points, and others), competition, status achievements, challenge and others.

In summary, among the main elements of the gamification approaches can be identified:

- Motivation (the ultimate reasons and conditions for taking certain actions and the observance of certain rules or behavior);
- Freedom of choice (the player must have the freedom to make decisions and to undertake his own strategies);
- Rules (The rules must be clear, honest, shared by the participants and easy to implement.);
- Risk-taking (ability to take risks and to make mistakes)

Table 1. Analysis of Game mechanics characteristics in casual games adapted from Kultima (2009)

Acceptability	Accessibility	Simplicity	Flexibility
Content matches the norms of the players' social context.	Game is mentally or cognitively easy to access.	Player's cognitive load is alleviated by simplifying the design.	The game supports spatial, temporal and social pervasiveness and can be easily restarted.
Game avoids offensive topics.	Concise information is provided in the adoption phase, such as descriptive game title.	Functions are combined into one activity, as one-button interfaces.	Flexible intensity level.
Game uses abstract topics and game mechanics such as puzzles.	The design is simplified: players are not required to learn the rules before they start to play.	Some of the activities in the game are automated.	The game can be used for (many) different functions.
Game uses already accepted and established game designs, such as solitaire, chess etc.	Game is physically or materially easy to access.		Options for instrumental functions, for example, sports games.
Games are based thematically on topics with a universal appeal such as gardening, travelling, nature, cooking and other activities that a large population may already have as a common interest.	Game is accessible in environments that players use otherwise, for example, games in social media.		The game is error-forgiving: a player can make mistakes without punishment.
Game endorses positive emotions and values	Low price: the game is designed in a way to be accessible with low investments.		Options for user-created content: the player can adjust the functions of the game to his preferences.
Game uses mechanics, such as building, collecting, nurturing, exploration and collaboration instead of destruction, killing, fighting or survival.	Content of the game suits the norms of the players' social context.		Feedback can be provided, allowing users to decide what of the mistakes are decisive.
Investments of the game do not engage the player excessively and/ or do not provide useful function outside the game			
Games can include instrumental functions, such as learning, mental exercise, measuring, losing weight, social interaction and physical prizes.			

GAME-WORLD (INNOVATION ECOSYSTEMS)

The interest toward various forms of ecosystems raised in the recent years, based on their positive role for nurturing innovations and entrepreneurship and successful cultural mind-set transformation.

The term 'ecosystem' is built on biomimetic thinking, transposing it to economic development (Oh, Phillips, Park, & Lee, 2016). The ecosystem metaphor makes a parallel to the biological ecosystem, which can be defined as a complex set of relationships among people and animals, habitat and resources, whose function is to maintain an equilibrium (Frenkel & Meital, 2014). The ecosystem approach aims to explain and measure the ability of the local stakeholders to stimulate economic development and foster innovations. Jackson (2011) sets that *innovation ecosystem* is composed by *the complex relationships (intangibles) that are formed between actors or entities whose functional goal is to enable technology development and innovation*. Thus innovation ecosystem reflects the relationships between entities (such as firms, government bodies, universities) and individuals (such as researchers, entrepreneurs, consumers and investors), whose goal is to drive technology development and innovation. Recently the use of terms innovation/ business/ start-up or entrepreneurial ecosystem overlap, and de Vasconcelos Gomes et al. (2016) conclude that different labels, meanings and purposes combine: *digital innovation ecosystem, hub ecosystem, open innovation ecosystem, platform-based ecosystem*. It is important to mention, that *innovation ecosystems* differ from other networking constructs such as Science and technology parks, science cities, or innovation clusters, as innovation ecosystem is set for value co-creation. It is composed of interconnected and interdependent networked actors and include firms, customers, suppliers, complementary innovators and other agents as regulators both cooperating and competing de Vasconcelos Gomes et al. (2016). From practitioner's perspective, recently innovation ecosystems and creative hubs become a world-phenomena (Dovey, Pratt, Moreton, Virani, Merkel, & Lansdowne, 2016), defining "creative hubs" as various forms of platforms: *co-creation open (innovation) spaces, ecosystems, co-working spaces, accelerators and incubators, start-up or innovation spaces*.

The innovation ecosystem typology can cover the following models:

- **Geographic-Based:** Regional and national ecosystem, innovation districts and city-based innovation ecosystem, hyper-local innovation ecosystem (hosted and developed by specific incubators and accelerators) and others (Oh, Phillips, Park, & Lee, 2016).
- **Owner-Oriented:** Corporate-organized (open innovation) ecosystems, digital innovation ecosystem, high-tech ecosystems (consisting of digital platforms, apps, mobiles technologies etc.), university-based ecosystems, entrepreneurial ecosystems and others (Oh, Phillips, Park, & Lee, 2016).
- **Value-Based:** Focusing on innovation (value creation) ecosystem or business (value capturing) ecosystem (de Vasconcelos Gomes, Facin, Salerno, & Ikenami, 2016).

The successful innovation ecosystem leads to market innovations and increased economic activity: new jobs, new products and services, fuelling economic growth. Further impacts can include: start-up ventures, future investment (public and commercial), talent development, regional talent retention, informal education and engagement, training, urban regeneration, research and development, new networks, innovative models of organisation, quality of life enhancements and resilience (Dovey, Pratt, Moreton, Virani, Merkel, & Lansdowne, 2016). While public-funded ecosystem purposes are to encourage jobs creation, exports, environmental protection and local quality of life; privately funded focus on more efficient value chain and superior returns on investments (Luo, 2017). More generally Jackson (2011) states that the innovation ecosystem is successful when "intangibles" or the complex relationships between actors and entities can effectively influence the slope of the "valley of death" by decreasing the investor's risk, lowering the negative impact of entrepreneurial failure, decreasing the entry costs and increasing the success rate by increasing the number of attempts. Further, successful creative hubs are embedded in local cultural and economic ecosystems and are sustained by the respect of participants and audiences.

Some other studies show that the main success factors for the innovation ecosystems are: *talent; density of researchers, entrepreneurs and facilitating institutions; entrepreneurial culture, access to capital, and a supportive regulatory environment* (Oh, Phillips, Park, & Lee, 2016).

The main characteristics of the innovation ecosystem, as summarized by (de Vasconcelos Gomes, Facin, Salerno, & Ikenami, 2016) are identified as follows: *members' interconnectedness and interdependency; co-evolution; symbiosis, common platform, common set of goals and objectives and shared set of knowledge and skills.* The members play both cooperation and competition strategies; furthermore, the ecosystem follows a five-phase lifecycle model: emerging, diversifying, converging, consolidating and renewing.

The main actors can take the following role: keystone organizations, dominators and niche players; focal firms, customers, suppliers or complementary innovators (regulatory agencies and media). Thus ecosystem actors may be: bridge, hub or broker. Besides, the actors can have one of the following functional roles: initiators (who builds the ecosystem and set up the platform); specialists, (who add value to the central platform); or adopter, (who develops products following the initiator and co-designs the platform with the specialist) (de Vasconcelos Gomes, Facin, Salerno, & Ikenami, 2016).

The innovation ecosystems usually have an architecture, identified by the interfirm diversity, density and cyclicality. Its boundaries are porous and often nurture open innovations. The main four organizing problems in the ecosystem designs that commonly exist in innovation networks, innovation clusters, ecosystems and self-organizing groups, include four universal problems: task division, task allocation, reward distribution and information flow (Li, Du, & Yin, 2017). The management and operation of a hub is primarily about the careful selection and compatibility of tenants and the 'animation' of the interaction between the actors and activities based on a clear understanding of the values of the hub.

Further Li et al. (2017) identify that digital ecosystem is an organizational form or platform enabling individual actors to absorb (acquire) resources and knowledge. Unlike a traditional organization, an ecosystem lacks the formal authority that is needed for coordination. Thus a healthy and productive digital entrepreneurship ecosystem possesses a relatively stable organizing form whereby its stakeholders can effectively achieve a division of labor and integration of effort, without a hub or a central authority, while an ill organized digital entrepreneurship ecosystem is bound to fail. In this respect platforms help to aggregate various resources and facilitate collaboration. Because of the limited resources and knowledge available within individual firms, many firms seek to leverage external resources to generate innovations, and that is why digital innovation often takes place outside the boundary of firms through collective collaboration, which overcomes the resource limitations of a single firm (Adner & Kapoor, 2010).

In the report of (Dovey, Pratt, Moreton, Virani, Merkel, & Lansdowne, 2016) there are summarized the six possible innovation ecosystems/ creative hubs architectures:

- **Studio:** Small collective of individuals and/or small businesses in a co-working space.
- **Centre:** Large-scale building which may have other assets such as a cafe, bar, cinema, maker space, shop, exhibition space.
- **Network:** Dispersed group of individuals or businesses – tends to be sector or place specific.
- **Cluster:** Co-located creative individuals and businesses in a geographic area.
- **Online Platform:** Uses only online methods – website/social media to engage with a dispersed audience.
- **Alternative:** Focused on experimentation with new communities, sectors and financial models.

GAME-PLAY (MAIN CHALLENGES AND PROBLEMS)

As early discussed, in the framework of the game design, the game-play usually describes the set of the problems and challenges requiring the players' actions, strategies and motives. In order to design future-oriented and responsible institutions, focusing on the real humanity problems and outstepping the single market dynamics, we will discuss the approach of Ferraro et al. (2015).

In their work, the authors propose a pragmatic perspective, covering three robust strategies that can be applied for tackling with "grand challenges". Grand challenges are defined as complex, uncertain, evaluative events, difficult to predict and to address individually even by large organizations. Considering climate change and social inclusion as grand challenges, we can further mention digital transformation and institutional shift. The model of Ferrero et al. (2015) includes three main components: participatory architecture, multivocal inscriptions and distributed experimentations. The model claims to propose working pragmatic, distributed, and processual approach enhancing problem solving.

Thus on a structural level, it is needed a participatory architecture or a network of rules of engagement that allow diverse and heterogeneous actors to interact constructively over prolonged timespans. On interpretative level, multivocal inscription consists of defining common actions among various audiences with different evaluative criteria and different interpretations, in a manner that promotes coordination without requiring explicit consensus. There, the pragmatist approach is needed to facilitate the articulation, discussion, and negotiation of meaning across different actors, times and places. Finally, on the practice level, distributed experimentations can be planned by providing iterative action that will generate small wins, promoting evolutionary learning, and increasing engagement, while allowing unsuccessful efforts to be abandoned. By prolonging the ongoing local experimentation will encourage actors to solve not only one particular problem or another, but also improve their capacity for subsequent problem solving.

In summary, by putting together the three components: cooperating heterogeneous actors, common guidelines, shared inscriptions, and large-scale experimentations, Ferrero et al., (2015) expect to tackle the big challenges. One of the critical issues in the model is that usually "grand challenges" cover large scale and complex phenomena that can have be difficult to tackle by small-scale experimentations. However, this approach explore the design-thinking methodology, focusing on the fast and experienced based learning, reflections and experimentations.

PUTTING THE GAME TOGETHER: INSTITUTIONS AS GAME DESIGNERS

Since institutions define the rules of the game, their role as social "game designers" is substantial. Based on the elements and methods of the game design, as discussed above, we will analyse the role of institutions as "designers" and regulators of complex social systems and social relations. In order to model the processes in which institutions lay down the rules of the game, we will briefly look at the principles and patterns of gamification approaches and will attempt through the system approach to identify the key features that define

Gamification techniques, as thoroughly discussed, are gradually entering organizational practice, changing different organizational functions such as: marketing, customer relationships, career development and human resource management. Gamification and game playing recently became an important part of the culture of the modern society and its elements have been implemented in different directions. Furthermore, gamification techniques avoid the patterns of pure coercion and seek to achieve long-lasting results and more satisfying relationships that bring benefits (internal and external) both to the community and to individuals. Thus, different indications confirm that games improve social environment, lead to higher results, develop creativity, innovation, and improve players' competencies. That is why, by implying different gamification approaches methodologies, we will further discuss how institutions can shape relationships in the social environment through non-violent, internally motivating and satisfying way.

By summarizing the findings above, in Table 2 there are provided different elements and suggestions for performance indicators, that can help institutions to improve its processes of "setting the rules".

Table 2. Elements and indicators for evaluating game systems

	Elements	Performance Indicators
1. Motivation General factors	Goals Difficulty Feedback Challenges	Clarity of the goals Internal interest in the challenge Achievement level, level of success Internal motivation for taking part in the system
Motivation Internal factors	Autonomy Choosing own strategy Decision making	Degree of freedom in the system Alternative paths Options for implementing own strategies
Motivation External factors	Prize Competition Collaboration	Type of awards Competitive relations Cooperative relations
2. Content	Relevant content Adaptation to participants Internal motivation	System elements meet the objectives Level of adaptation and personalization Level of internal motivation to explore the content
3. Freedom, rules and feedback	Freedom to take decisions Level of control Clear feedback Acceptable rules Clear rules Relevant rules	Degree of freedom Control patterns Feedback models Socially acceptable rules Complexity of rules Linking rules to system goals
4. Errors, risks and emotional aspects	Recognition of errors A sense of security Identity Humor Attractive environment Friendly environment Presence of "fantasy" elements	Degree of freedom of error and risk taking Models for exploration and risk Opportunity for self-expression Creating a positive environment Stimulating creative thinking Collaboration Elements of Innovation
5. Integration of the game	Easy access and start of the game Easy way out of the game Awareness and reflection of experience	Intuitive and easy to use Easy way out of the game Analysis of experience and opportunities for reflection

In this context, various elements of the "social game" can be measured by a set of quantitative and qualitative criteria and indicators. That is how, institutions can further lead social regulations setting processes, providing new models of games within holistic social system.

DISCUSSION: DEMYSTIFYING THE ANATOMY OF INSTITUTIONAL CHANGE

When discussing institutions and institutional change, we have to admit that all social structures and all social transformations are subject of purposeful individuals' actions. Therefore, the main change agents inducing social and institutional change are individuals, who pursue their specific personal or group goals and objectives. In this respect, institutional entrepreneurs (or change agents) are individuals who can break the rules and practices associated with the dominant institutional logic and can develop and implement alternative rules and practices. Furthermore, a norm is not just an institutional paradigm, but this is the result of the purposive actions of discrete individuals. Both those who are particularly suited to providing new rule and those who are particularly eager to have it adopted play the role in the processes. Thus undertaking adoption or change of norms and rules is a human and social process.

In revolutionary times, the dominating institutional logic gradually loose its basic role to provide economic effectiveness and social coherence. Therefore, the new coming social rules follow the inherent logic of the emerging technologies and spontaneously transfer to new mental models. Starting to be promoted and admitted to be more effective, the new social logic gain further supporters, who gradually expand and become the new emerging social rules.

New technologies implementation is always a function of adaptation of the economic, cultural and institutional environment to the requirements of new technology systems. The social environment becomes a powerful selection mechanism for the inclusion or exclusion of particular innovations.

Furthermore, the deployment of each technology system involves several interconnected processes of change and adaptation. First, technologies and innovation require development of surrounding services (infrastructure, suppliers, distributors, maintenance services. Next, a "cultural" adaptation is needed, in order to transfer it with the logic of the interconnected technologies involved (among engineers, managers, service people, consumers, etc.). Finally, there should be set up institutional facilitators (rules and regulations, specialized training and education, etc.).

CONCLUSION

During the last years, it became clear that new disruptive technologies could not provide adequate response to the pressing social problems and larger institutional transformations have to be defined. Lack of efficiency and fairness are omnipresent. Rent-seeking became again a factor of success, as public institutions fail to impose appropriate rules to the fast changing environment. Moreover, the wealth accumulation in the top of the social pyramid accelerates. The social divide, inequality and disintegration intensify. It has to be underlined, that as previously discussed in chapters three and four, institutions strongly affect the socio-economic mechanisms and political models of wealth generation and wealth distribution. Furthermore, institutional arrangements reflect the social balance of power distribution, which is legalized, publicly recognized and protected by force within internal and international regulations. Therefore, any movement for revolutionary change in institutional arrangements should take in consideration the resources needed to oppose, the inherent reason behind the proposed change and the alternatives that can be proposed. As thoroughly discussed in chapter four, the successful revolutionary changes occur to oppose to rulers that are both inefficient and unjust. That is why, the main shifts in institutional settings that can overcome the social resistance need to address the changing dominant cultural mindset and the new coming shared mental models. This means that revolutions in institutional settings need to provide new set of alternative rules and regulations that provide more socially just, commonly acceptable and efficient rules, corresponding to the changed ideologies and mindsets.

REFERENCES

Aarseth, E. (2003, May). Playing Research: Methodological approaches to game analysis. In *Proceedings of the digital arts and culture conference* (pp. 28-29). Academic Press.

Adner, R., & Kapoor, R. (2010). Value creation in innovation ecosystems: How the structure of technological interdependence affects firm performance in new technology generations. *Strategic Management Journal*, *31*(3), 306–333. doi:10.1002mj.821

Caillois, R. (1961). *Man, play, and games*. University of Illinois Press.

de Vasconcelos Gomes, L. A., Facin, A. L. F., Salerno, M. S., & Ikenami, R. K. (2016). Unpacking the innovation ecosystem construct: Evolution, gaps and trends. *Technological Forecasting and Social Change*.

Deterding, S., Dixon, D., Khaled, R., & Nacke, L. (2011, September). From game design elements to gamefulness: defining gamification. In *Proceedings of the 15th international academic MindTrek conference: Envisioning future media environments* (pp. 9-15). ACM. 10.1145/2181037.2181040

Dixon, D. (2009). *Nietzsche contra Caillois: Beyond play and games*. Academic Press.

Dovey, J., Pratt, A., Moreton, S., Virani, T., & Merkel, J. L. (2016). *Creative Hubs, understanding the new economy*. Retrieved from https://creativeconomy.britishcouncil.org/media/uploads/files/HubsReport.pdf

Ferraro, F., Etzion, D., & Gehman, J. (2015). Tackling grand challenges pragmatically: Robust action revisited. *Organization Studies*, *36*(3), 363–390. doi:10.1177/0170840614563742

Frenkel, A., & Maital, S. (2014). *Mapping National Innovation Ecosystems: Foundations for Policy Consensus*. Edward Elgar Publishing. doi:10.4337/9781782546818

Huotari, K., & Hamari, J. (2012, October). Defining gamification: a service marketing perspective. In *Proceeding of the 16th International Academic MindTrek Conference* (pp. 17-22). ACM. 10.1145/2393132.2393137

Jackson, D. J. (2011). What is an innovation ecosystem. *National Science Foundation, 1*.

Kultima, A. (2009, September). Casual game design values. In *Proceedings of the 13th international MindTrek conference: Everyday life in the ubiquitous era* (pp. 58-65). ACM.

Li, W., Du, W., & Yin, J. (2017). Digital entrepreneurship ecosystem as a new form of organizing: The case of Zhongguancun. *Frontiers of Business Research in China*, *11*(1), 5. doi:10.118611782-017-0004-8

Luo, J. (2017). Architecture and evolvability of innovation ecosystems. *Technological Forecasting and Social Change*. doi:10.1016/j.techfore.2017.06.033

Oh, D. S., Phillips, F., Park, S., & Lee, E. (2016). Innovation ecosystems: A critical examination. *Technovation, 54*, 1–6. doi:10.1016/j.technovation.2016.02.004

Robinson, D., & Bellotti, V. (2013, April). A preliminary taxonomy of gamification elements for varying anticipated commitment. *Proc. ACM CHI 2013 Workshop on Designing Gamification: Creating Gameful and Playful Experiences.*

Seaborn, K., & Fels, D. I. (2015). Gamification in theory and action: A survey. *International Journal of Human-Computer Studies, 74*, 14–31. doi:10.1016/j.ijhcs.2014.09.006

Suseno, Y., & Standing, C. (2017). The Systems Perspective of National Innovation Ecosystems. *Systems Research and Behavioral Science*. doi:10.1002res.2494

This research was previously published in Institutional and Organizational Transformations in the Robotic Era; pages 137-152, copyright year 2019 by Business Science Reference (an imprint of IGI Global).

Chapter 65

Balancing Entertainment and Educational Objectives in Academic Game Creation

Christopher A. Egert

https://orcid.org/0000-0001-6087-3450

Rochester Institute of Technology, USA

Andrew M. Phelps

University of Canterbury, New Zealand & American University, USA

ABSTRACT

Production experiences are important to the educational progression of game design and development students. Coursework that leads to a quality deliverable is highly desirable by students, faculty, and industry for both pedagogical and portfolio purposes, including a focus on multi-disciplinary teamwork, and professional practice at scale. Despite the impetus to provide meaningful production experiences, successful execution within an academic context can be difficult. The situation is further exasperated when the result of the production experience is more than just an entertainment product – i.e. a game that embodies and facilitates a learning outcome. This chapter presents the successes, challenges, and lessons learned from two cases in which the authors created a production-oriented classroom experience utilizing a game studio model. The authors also address the balance between entertainment goals and learning outcomes in educational game production, including how such balance influences faculty and learner comprehension of design and process techniques.

INTRODUCTION

Game design and development academic programs have a strong presence on the collegial landscape, and such programs approach the field from a number of perspectives. Some stress development, others emphasize game art, while others focus directly on design in a variety of contexts. No matter the emphasis, these programs all share a common characteristic in they provide students the opportunity

DOI: 10.4018/978-1-6684-7589-8.ch065

to study and prepare for careers creating entertainment products to varying degrees, and they typically engage students in creating such applications either in whole or in part.

While programs strive to impart the fundamental knowledge and skills that would ensure success in the field, they also recognize that students must be able to synthesize their various skills to create novel game applications. Both students and faculty want curricular experiences that illustrate the student's ability to create complex games, thereby demonstrating such students are able to work productively in their field of practice, which often manifests in a production course or capstone experience. In addition to synthesizing knowledge across numerous preparatory experiences, such courses are often compounded and complicated by the fact that such applications are typically produced in teams, necessitating the application of strong communication and collaboration skills. Such experiences also demonstrate the students' ability to perform effective time management and manage a production workflow, and such experiences are seen as appropriate preparation for professional work.

Despite all of the positive characteristics of production courses, there are still many potential hazards, especially when the production course moves away from passion-based student projects and moves toward outcomes that are not simply measured by their entertainment value alone. Games that have a learning outcome must create a balance between an entertaining experience that captures the player's attention and an experience that makes the player think and reflect. These designs are a compound problem not only of entertainment product design, but also of pedagogical complexity. Thus, the difficulty lies in balancing competing concerns: an educational game must be both fun *and* effective in an educational context, and this often creates tension as students will focus on one area or another instead of the relationship between the two.

This chapter begins with an exploration of production courses in the technologies and the arts, and depicts how students in game design and development programs may approach production experiences. The chapter then focuses on the configuration of a hybrid approach employed by the authors, which combined a collegiate course with a semi-commercial game studio on campus. The chapter continues by exploring two cases in which students published educational games with a learning outcome, one at the formation of the hybrid model and one after a few offerings. The authors then conclude by proposing solutions and recommendations that can be utilized in other production-oriented experiences. It should be noted that this chapter covers the period of time when both authors worked at the same institution, and were both instrumental in the construction of academic games program and a campus-based, commercial games studio that operated in tandem with a university-wide games research center.

BACKGROUND

The concept of production-oriented coursework, especially for capstone experiences, is not new in the computing disciplines or in the studio arts. The literature is full of examples of such offerings for computer science (Chamillard & Braun, 2002; Engelsma, 2014; Vanhanen, Lehtinen, & Lassenius, 2012), information technology (Gorka, Miller, & Howe, 2007), and software engineering (Reichlmayr, 2006). Similarly, most undergraduate degrees in studio art conclude with a capstone or senior show of some form. These experiences share common themes through their desire to synthesize knowledge and skills from prior courses and apply that ability towards a particular project or theme (Umphress, Hendrix, & Cross, 2002).

The literature also depicts a number of educational variations, from efforts to distribute production concepts throughout the curriculum (Goold, 2003), to providing authentic experiences with industry partnership (Engelsma, 2014; Gorka, Miller, & Howe, 2007; Vanhanen, Lehtinen, & Lassenius, 2012), and to providing cooperative education opportunities for real-world experience (Reichlmayr, 2006). Games have also become a focus of interest for production experiences due to their complexity and their motivating qualities for students (Jones, 2000; Kanode & Haddad, 2009; Linhoff & Settle, 2009; Parberry, Roden, & Kazemzadeh, 2005), as well as their multi-disciplinary nature in engaging teams of students from multiple fields of study such as computing, design, communication, art, and other disciplines. As such, the literature presents many examples of where games have been used to motivate the production experience (Smith, Cooper, & Longstreet, 2011). Production experiences rooted in the technical fields are often (although not always) evaluated by the degree of completeness or the level of conformance to an original specification (Delaney & Mitchell, 2002), or a degree of product satisfaction with an industry client (Engelsma, 2014; Vanhanen, Lehtinen, & Lassenius, 2012).

In the arts, senior studio courses are used as a means for students to explore a particular technique or subject matter (Hetland, Winner, Veenema, & Sheridan, 2013; Sommer, 1999), and to demonstrate both proficiency in a given medium as well as the communication and professional skills needed to frame their work effectively and engage a an audience and the critical community. The art studio course often relies on a process of critique where a student works with a faculty mentor to refine a technique or approach. Through a series of critiques, repetition, and iterative refinement, the student hones the work into a viable artistic expression.

Because of the hybrid nature of game design and the fact that it relies on many disparate fields and practices to flourish, successful strategies for production often borrow from disciplines ranging across software development, engineering, social science, art, music, and more. Materials and documentation in game design often relay the need for production process as part of the overall game development cycle (Chandler, 2014; Merritt, 2010) and often refer to software engineering models for teamwork and communication while contextualizing the process in the steps employed by game production houses to deliver a game title. Such materials refer to the study and exploration of production processes as an important part of understanding the game industry.

Production in this context can also refer to the culminating experiences that define the capabilities of the student beyond their coursework. These experiences set students apart from their peers and distinguish their potential in the field. Throughout game design and development programs, students take several approaches to find these production experiences.

First, students may elect to take a production course or an independent study in which they can explore a topic of their own choosing. In the authors' academic program, students often choose these paths to explore passion projects while achieving the goals of the program. While such experiences can be highly motivating, the students often find themselves too attached to the material and are unable to make the difficult choices that would help refine the quality of the deliverable. In essence, scope often exceeds capability, which can be a credible learning opportunity in its own right, but can also undercut learning other aspects of the production process.

Second, students may elect to participate in outside activities such as game jams (Fowler, Khosmood, & Arya, 2013; Smith & Bowers, 2016). While such activities are now mature enough to include entertainment as well as educational themes (Johnson, Smith, Dombrowski, & Buyssens, 2017; Preston, 2014), they do not always fully realize a production experience. Many game jams focus on the ideation and the prototype over a short one to two-day span, including non-stop development, rapid iteration, and a game application that may show a concept but is far from a final deliverable. There is also the challenge that many game jam ideas are never refined or revisited after the game jam is complete.

Third, students may obtain production experiences from cooperative education opportunities. The authors' program mandates that all students must engage in multiple cooperative education experiences to satisfy graduation requirements. While these experiences are extremely valuable, the student is working for a company whose scale and process can vary widely from one to the next. Thus, the student may only be exposed only to a particular slice of the production experience, if at all.

THE PRODUCTION-ORIENTED VENUE

The authors employed a different approach when addressing the production course. Rochester Institute of Technology (RIT) is home of a strong Game Design and Development program with curricula supporting a Bachelors and Masters of Science in the field. RIT also invested in the creation of the Center for Media, Arts, Games, Interaction, and Creativity (MAGIC) that supports multidisciplinary research, entrepreneurial activities, industry collaborations, and an associated games and media studio, MAGIC Spell Studios. The studio and center work together to create experiences that are beyond the typical classroom and program experience. To make this hybrid academic and studio experience work, the authors reengineered the experience of a production course to best leverage the possibilities of a sustainable production effort.

The first component to this approach is in the classroom. The academic program has a generic production studio course that has been available since 2013. The course prescribes that students will engage in a production experience, but does not define a particular subject matter or approach. Rather, the course's flexibility makes it adaptable for any design and development scenario within the program. The learning objectives for the course itself focus largely on students' ability to apply their professional skills learned earlier in the program in context, and to demonstrate multi-disciplinary communication and collaboration skills in a role-based setting.

Unlike other courses in the curriculum, a student can take the production studio experience multiple times. Similarly, subsequent offerings of the course can extend a project beyond a single semester. This allows for student involvement with a project over an extended period and provides a longer-term commitment to efforts that fall between a course and a scholarly or research exploration. This activity is not without risk, and students must carefully plan with their academic advisors to ensure their involvement meets graduation requirements and provides the best opportunities for a career path, as various students define their professional goals and objectives very differently from one another.

The second component is the research center itself. As described above, MAGIC is a different model as it is a fully functioning studio. Along with providing a physical space that is not owned by any particular program or college, the center provides access to a range of technologies. Because of the various activities happening in the center, those involved see a clearly articulated range of backgrounds, skills, and perspectives as part of everyday operations. In addition, the studio portion of the center gives students access to workstations and servers as well as educational and commercial software technologies as needed.

The third component is the support team related to the studio model. Some roles were based on dual responsibility - personnel with both a faculty and studio commitment. For example, the CEO of the studio was the course lead. The CTO served in a faculty capacity but also assured that the systems, software, technologies, and workflow processes were appropriate for the students. Other roles were specific to the studio: the Creative Director, who was responsible for the studio perspective on the design and development of the games, and the Chief Communications Officer assisted students with their branding and messaging related to their project. The Operations Manager ensured students had access to the resources they needed and resolved problems with the distribution channels related to the production and upkeep of games, and provided support to the accounting and financial services related to product offerings. It is important to note that each of these roles, both those filled by faculty and those filled by professional staff, were mandated to operate in an 'open book' context to students in the production course and beyond, thus providing students with numerous resources for mentorship throughout their experience. Along with the studio principals, there were also other faculty, student employees, and studio affiliates engaged in the production experience.

The last component was the pre-production work. Because the authors have worked with numerous students over the years developing educational game systems and technologies, they realized the inherent difficulties of balancing entertainment and learning goals, as well as the time constraints of realizing even a suitable prototype project in any given semester. The pre-production work created the context such that students could quickly ramp up with the project idea as well as the materials to support the educational goals. With these constructs in place, the authors embarked on their first entry into a hybrid model for a production-oriented course.

CASE STUDY 1: SPLATTERSHMUP: A GAME OF ART AND MOTION

The first case the authors wish to present is Splattershmup (Decker, Egert, & Phelps, 2016; Decker, Phelps, & Egert, 2017; MAGIC Spell Studios, 2015). Splattershmup was the first game produced under the hybrid classroom and game studio model. Entering the experience, the authors did not know what to expect, but knew they wanted to work with students to create a game with an educational component. Development of Splattershmup started in 2013 and continued until its release in 2015.

The Entertainment Experience

Splattershmup is a synthesis of two primary modes of interaction. The first part of the name "Splatter" refers to the game's ability to create works of art representative of action painting popularized by artist Jackson Pollock (Kleiner, 2010). The second part of the name "Shmup" refers to a specific genre of shoot-'em-up games typified by overwhelming waves of opponents firing complex waves of projectiles that the player must deflect or avoid (Rojas, 2012).

Splattershmup starts on an open, blank canvas. The player controls a space ship avatar, which has the ability to move and fire. Along with these controls, the player has the ability to select from a set of secondary offensive and defensive characteristics. Three of the secondary characteristics provide attack capabilities, including a multi-shot fire, a beam weapon, and a tracking missile system. The fourth secondary system provides a defensive shield that can also destroy enemies. All secondary systems are resource limited, requiring power-ups to refuel their capabilities when exhausted by the player.

When the player begins the game, he or she has the ability to travel throughout an empty world. The player can move in any direction and the world is larger than the players screen. As the player moves, he or she will leave a paint trail signifying prior position and the quality of player motion. As the player explores the game, he or she quickly realizes that although the world is expansive, it is finite.

After a brief interval, the player begins to encounter waves of enemies. The player must evade collisions with enemies and must avoid enemy weapons fire. Collisions with ships and weapons fire will degrade the player's health, and when the health bar reaches zero, the game will end. As the player destroys enemy targets, a record of the encounter is signified by a paint expression on the canvas. After each wave, the enemy quantity, type of enemy, enemy movement pattern, and enemy weapons profile changes. Figure 1 illustrates the nature of gameplay and the interactions between the player and the enemy opponents.

As play continues, successful encounters with enemy ships reveal power ups. Some power-ups can rejuvenate shields and weapons while others change the paint color exuded by the player and enemies. When the game is complete, the player has an artistic expression of the experience in which every movement and every battle is transformed into a stroke and blot on the canvas. The player has the option of saving the canvas locally or sharing the canvas and related artwork on popular social media platforms.

The Learning Outcome

When Splattershmup was created, there was not any particular learning outcome related directly to action painting. There was no desire to use the game to provide a history of Jackson Pollock or specific techniques used by artists to create action painting experiences. Rather, the authors desired a subtle learning experience based upon Jackson Pollock's account of the process of action painting, one that was emotionally and physically resonant, that relied less on overt 'facts' and much more on the core nature of gestural abstraction as a movement. They wanted players to *feel* what it was to engage with gestural abstraction.

As Pollock described the process of action painting, he noted his relationship to the work by stating, "When I am in my painting, I'm not aware of what I'm doing. It is only after a sort of "get acquainted" period that I see what I have been about. I have no fears about making changes, destroying the image, etc., because the painting has a life of its own. I try to let it come through. It is only when I lose contact with the painting that the result is a mess. Otherwise there is pure harmony, an easy give and take, and the painting comes out well" (Karmel, 1999, p.18).

Splattershmup endeavored to preserve this ideal in its construction. By working with the connection between the gameplay as both a producer of entertainment and creative expression, less emphasis is placed on the overt act of creating the work. Rather, the player's attention on the gameplay allows the art to unfold in a manner that takes on a life of its own. Figures 2 and 3 provide examples of the artworks created within Splattershmup, ranging from simple as depicted in Figure 2 to intricate in Figure 3.

Over multiple play sessions with Splattershmup, the player quickly develops a portfolio of works. For those merely interested in gameplay, the works can be discarded. For others, the works can be saved and reflected upon, or shared with a broader community. In user testing, nearly all of the play testers, and later after release the audience members, would reflect on the work they had created, and its relationship to different styles and personalities of players and their strategies for engaging with the game.

The Production Experience

Leading up to the production course, the faculty and studio staff worked to create a framework for both the entertainment and learning outcomes. The team selected the topic of action painting and started to develop the artist statement and preliminary sketches and renders for previsualization. The team also pulled reference materials related to the learning outcomes describing Jackson Pollock, gestural abstraction and the form of action painting. The materials also included recent articles that revealed greater information about Jackson Pollock's process (Phaidon, 2013; Vogel, 2013).

During the preliminary phase, the team was very open about the process, posting previsualization and concept art where students could access the images, and discussing the new production course with the students. The team was very honest with the students, balancing the message of creating a distribution-worthy deliverable with the time and dedication it would take to be involved with the project.

Figure 1. A screen capture of Splattershmup gameplay

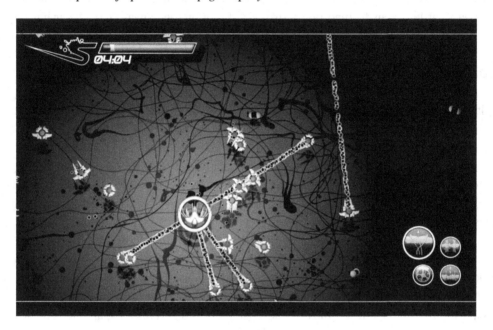

Figure 2. Example of art generated from a simple play session in Splattershmup

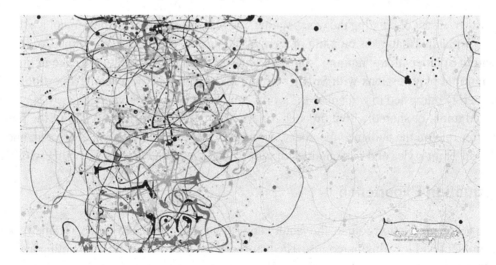

Figure 3. An intricate expression representing a higher degree of interaction and time engaged with play

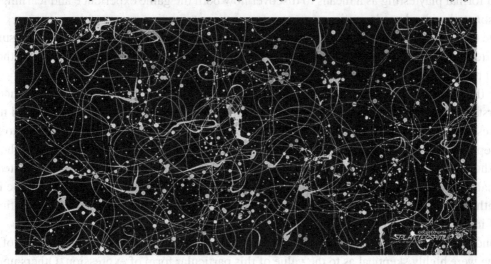

When the production course started, the first day consisted of an overview of the game, including the entertainment and learning outcomes expected in the deliverable. Time was also spent discussing how the combined classroom and studio model would work. This included a discussion of the resources as well as an introduction to the personnel who would be part of their experience. A discussion of team roles framed the expectation of how students would participate and the intellectual property aspect was addressed.

One of the more challenging aspects of the course from an administrative aspect was the intellectual property agreement. This concept is now new at the authors' institution, as many industry partnerships with classroom activities require a signed intellectual rights transfer form to participate. In this case, all members of the team, students and faculty alike, transferred their rights to the studio. Not only did the authors' feel this would dissipate any arguments of ownership, but it could help protect the students and faculty throughout the process. For those not wishing to sign the agreement, other production options were available in different courses.

Early in the execution of the class, the students divided into teams and roles with the guidance of the faculty lead. The class designated a student lead. The lead was the main interface between the production groups and the faculty and studio leads. For faculty who held positions in the studio, they would move back and forth between the in-course educational objectives and the needs of publication. Faculty were brought in for their expertise when needed and studio employees were brought in to advise on production topics and goals.

Each week, the student team leads would present their status, discuss their challenges, and plan the activities for the next week. Milestones were set to correspond with university events and opportunities to interact with guests or the community. Each week, the faculty would institute conversation around techniques related to critique and introspection on what had been done and both the quantity and the quality of the contribution.

The students were responsible for communicating with a range of stakeholders, including visitors from industry, to refine their ideas as well as the aesthetic and feel of the game. The experience also included formal playtesting as a means to discover how both the game experience and learning interactions resonated with a broader audience.

While the students created a product by the end of the semester, the work continued for a substantial period afterwards. Students utilized the intersession break and the following semester to hone the experience and to ensure the application could be delivered on the Windows Store platform.

Over the course of the semester, there were several challenges encountered in the production process. First, despite providing treatment for the learning objectives of the game, students did not know how to respond in a situation where entertainment was not the only factor. Their intent was to focus on the gameplay elements, with the idea that the educational components would integrate into the product later in the process. Furthermore, when students did envision education games, they gravitated toward traditional skill-and-drill experiences that could be easily separated from the game itself. The idea of a game with intrinsic learning outcomes was not familiar, and the students had difficulties relating to this mode of interaction.

Second, the student designers and developers found it difficult to connect to the concept of abstract art. Some were highly skeptical as to the value of this particular form of expression. Others understood the concept, but did not necessarily see the value in participating in an analog experience for constructing such works. Both challenges led students to feel disengaged with the overall content to the point where many felt that the educational content was holding back the development of the game.

Luckily, the faculty and studio personnel were able to help guide the students back to the path, demonstrating through both art and gameplay the connection between play and entertainment intent and play as creative expression. Although this journey was not easy, it was deemed one of the most important components of the course offering.

Another challenge during the production process was the tenuous relationship between the students' perception of representational elements for the art process and the elements for player engagement. The duality that enemy ships contributed to play and also helped in the creative process proved especially vexing to the designers in that the duality of destroying the opponent resulted in a creative gesture. This was an area in which attention to detail proved extremely important. Engaging the enemy had to result in an entertainment award in which the visuals and sound clearly indicated the results of the engagement and provided a level of satisfaction when the enemy was defeated. Similarly, the resulting artistic impact on the canvas had to convey the proper look, including the capture of properties of the engagement between the player and opponent. Students gravitated to the gameplay visuals, but did not always see why there was equal emphasis to both processes. This was partly due to the complexities of the visual representation and its relationship to the underlying artistic reference, and partially due to students' tendency to mimic other games they were familiar with in the general 'shmup' genre.

To provide further balance, faculty and studio affiliates worked with a combination of outside guests and playtest scenarios. The outside guests were from companies and studios and were known experts in game design and development. These visits provided the student teams with valuable feedback. Guests also provided deeper critique and suggestion, providing students with analogs to their processes. Unfortunately, an unanticipated side effect was that some of the students felt demoralized as they did not know how to process the interactions in a meaningful way. Again, the faculty had to provide guidance and help reframe the engagement such that motivation could be restored.

Playtesting also provided a great deal of information once the team learned to ask and observe non-superficial aspects of gameplay and learning. Faculty worked with the team to link playtest opportunities to the iterative process, coaching students as to how to interpret feedback and how to change playtest data into actionable methods.

The Result

As a first endeavor with a hybrid course and studio experience, Splattershmup was a reasonable success. The game was self-published through the MAGIC website and was available through the Windows Store. Locally, Splattershmup was shown at Imagine RIT (Dawson, 2015; Rochester Institute of Technology, 2019), an annual exhibition for the region demonstrating RIT's creativity and innovation. It was also featured the retirement party for RIT President Emeritus Dr. William Destler. Furthermore, the game had a strong presence at the West Coast Board of Trustees meeting to highlight the output of the semi-commercial studio model. Nationally, the game was featured in the Blank Arcade at DiGRA (Grace, 2015) and was a finalist for Best Learning Game at the Games, Learning, and Society eleventh annual conference (Games, Learning, and Society, 2015). Most famously, the game was shown by juried selection at the Indie Arcade at the Smithsonian American Museum of Art in January of 2016. Some of the students involved in the project used their experiences to help secure strong jobs in the industry.

After the project was completed, a teacher from a regional school system created a guide to help primary and middle school instructors use Splattershmup in the exploration of action painting and modern art (Cometto, n.d.). This work provided some of the linkages between the game as a work focused on experiential education with the formal learning outcomes typically associated with primary and secondary art education.

CASE STUDY 2: FRAGILE EQUILIBRIUM: AN ACTION GAME OF MELANCHOLIC BALANCE

Fragile Equilibrium (MAGIC Spell Studios, 2018) represents the latest attempt at the hybrid model. Between Splattershmup and Fragile Equilibrium, the hybrid model supported the production of another commercial game, and two more research-oriented production experiences. Fragile Equilibrium represents the culmination of prior experiences and is probably the last game that will be developed under this model by the authors given new academic directions, projects, and focus. Fragile Equilibrium was developed over two and a half years, from summer 2016 to late 2018.

The Entertainment Experience

Fragile Equilibrium is a fast-paced side scrolling shooter game. The player is introduced to a visually splendid world created in an artistic style reminiscent of Roger Dean album covers (Dean, 1975) and other similar works of the early 1980s fantasy art and music scene. The player has a number of weapons available to assist in gameplay, and must proceed forward through waves of enemies to a culminating boss battle at the end of each level. Figure 4 depicts the player interacting with the game.

The game supports four different levels that are unique in their visual appeal but connect to the overall experience of the game. What makes Fragile Equilibrium truly interesting is that as the player engages enemies and lets some slip past, the beauty of the landscape is fractured and replaced by emptiness. Not only is this process visually disrupting, but also impacts gameplay as the player is no longer able to move into the areas of fractured space. Thus, the compression of the space by having things 'get by' the player reduces the area they can then use to weave and dodge additional obstacles.

As gameplay unfolds, the player has the option to repair damaged space, restoring the empty void a section at a time. This is also how players recharge their weapons, and thus as a strategic element players need to masters a balance of letting portions of the world fracture and repair them. However, the decision to repair space must be carefully balanced against the continuing waves of enemies – a player facing 'backwards' (left) to repair the screen cannot engage with enemies facing 'forwards' (right). Timing, nuance, and pattern all play important roles in this feeling of balance and decay. A simple misstep can lead to the world unraveling, thus ending the game.

Figure 4. An example of Fragile Equilibrium gameplay

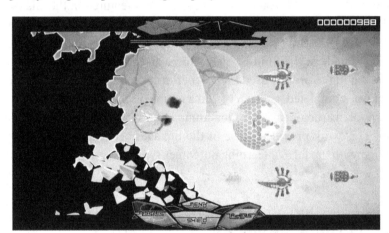

The Learning Outcome

Fragile Equilibrium's learning outcomes were even more subtle than Splattershmup. The game exists as a visual and experiential metaphor for living and struggling with depression and anxiety. In this vein, it is intended directly as an experiential 'deep' game in the context as presented by Rusch (2017) and the work at DePaul (Conboy, 2018), among others. As the player progresses through a level, there is a sense of restricting the possibilities through the deconstruction of the playable space. Simultaneously, each time an enemy slips past the player's guard, the world crumbles and falls away, reducing the beautiful visage to an empty void of no possibility and no existence. The combination of feeling squeezed and deconstructed is balanced against the player's ability to recreate the space through a process of willful struggle against the primary game mechanic to destroy the enemy ships. Figure 5 illustrates what the player encounters as the world deconstructs and the playable options reduce in quantity and impact.

The idea is for players to find balance in their own form of play, constructing the equilibrium as a conscious act of gameplay while still taking time to reflect of the symmetry and eventual renewal in an unstable system.

Great effort was directed towards the visuals in order to connect the sense of beauty and serenity to a graphical notion of the world cracking and breaking. The world has a feeling of brittleness and decay that is obvious in that it transcends the two dimensional playing field. When the world first fractures, the effect is simple and hardly recognizable, but as gameplay progresses, the shards of the world falling apart seem to pop out of the screen. As this transition continues, the gameplay becomes more frantic and erratic, requiring the player to make a concerted effort to recognize and correct the situation.

Figure 5. Fragile Equilibrium screen capture that depicts a crumbling world and the player's attempt to reconstruct the visual facade

The Production Experience

While the faculty and studio personnel learned and adapted from the prior course offerings, Fragile Equilibrium represented a level of refinement that had not been attempted before. Fragile Equilibrium had greater technical and art requirements. Gameplay logic proved to be more sophisticated than prior efforts, and there were a number of open challenges related to the presentation and interaction of game assets, particularly around the 'cracking' mechanic. The art side also proved to be challenging with an aesthetic for the world and the deconstructed experience that had to embody a particular visual quality. Simply speaking, the art had to convey strong emotion and had to create a reaction in the player as the world started to deconstruct. There was also the new technical challenge of a new distribution platform through the Xbox One Creators Program that was new and unfamiliar to all participants.

Similar to prior offerings, the course started with pre-production materials and presentation of learning outcomes for the game. In some ways, the learning outcome proved to be approachable to students. Many had either first-hand knowledge or associative knowledge of the effects of depression and anxiety, and could relate to the feelings and thoughts that surround the issue. While this seemed to put the team in a better position at the start, it was quickly realized that students still struggled with the nuances of a game whose learning outcome was not direct and obvious in its execution.

One of the results from the production course was that the studio decided not to continue development with the initial product. While both students and faculty learned a great deal, shelving the project gave all parties time to reflect upon what went right or wrong, and whether or not it was appropriate to continue forward with the product.

After a period of reflection, the faculty and staff at the studio decided to try again, and indeed some of the students who had engaged with the prior offering of the course either repeated the course to engage with it a second time, or recommended the experience to their peers. The progress throughout the second iteration ran into some familiar problems in balancing gameplay with the learning outcomes. The faculty and studio personnel were more deliberate and methodical in adjusting the expectations. However, the students desire to focus on new gameplay features over enhancing the learning outcomes became a continual struggle in this attempt.

One key area where the development of Fragile Equilibrium struggled was in the balanced utilization of resources. Students were disproportionate in their use of faculty and studio resources, gravitating to those whose ideas and opinions best matched their desired gameplay strategy. The students also struggled to appropriately use playtest opportunities to reflect upon their choices. Part of the failure in the playtest was the sense of familiarity with the genre that interfered with the ability to surrender control to the observation of outsiders.

The Result

Fragile Equilibrium was an overall success in terms of the production experience. Fragile Equilibrium represented the authors' first exposure to the Xbox One Creators Program. In addition, the product was delivered through a number of distribution channels, including the Windows Store, Steam, and itch.io. The product was an official selection for Miami@Play (Filmgate Miami, 2018) and was shown at the ICA Games "Ante-Conference" (International Communication Association, 2019). The game is currently the focus of additional publications regarding its representation of mental health issues, and has been presented at Adobe MAX (Adobe, 2018) for its innovative use of the Adobe XD product during portions of the design process. It has also been selected by an independent jury for inclusion in the Open World Arcade event in collaboration with the Open World: Video Games & Contemporary Art exhibit at the Akron Art Museum in December of 2019. It has amassed numerous popular and critical reviews on Steam, itch.io, YouTube and Twitch. It was also used as the basis for a talk at the 'Ruins in Games' workshop at the 2019 international conference of the Digital Games Research Association (DiGRA) in Kyoto, Japan, and is the basis of a forthcoming journal article on abstract representations of mental health topics in games and interactive media. Thus, to the extent that students learned professional practice through the creation and production of the game, it was one of the most successful offerings of the production experience.

SOLUTIONS AND RECOMMENDATIONS

The case examples described above represent the two extremes of production-oriented course offerings utilizing a hybrid classroom and game studio model. While the cases outline some of the challenges associated with the execution of a production experience, they also allow the authors to provide solutions and recommendations for others to follow. This section provides an overview for some of these challenges and presents the reader with possible approaches to utilize in their own courses.

Accentuating Learning Outcomes

As described in both cases, one of the major challenges involved reconciliation of the entertainment value of the game experience with the learning objectives of an educational game. Students were not always motivated by the learning objectives embedded within the game. Instead, the students focused on the gameplay issues, substituting game augmentation for authentic learning possibilities. This problem arises from the duality of games with multiple outcomes, often those designed for educational purposes. Some less than desirable approaches lean toward the creation of an entertainment product where the learning outcome occurs by happenstance or, worse yet, the educational material is bolted onto the game at the culmination of the development process. Conversely, some educational approaches profess to meet the educational goals, but result in experiences that are not always fun or engaging in ways that are likely to engage a typical public audience.

The creation of game experiences that exhibit *both* entertainment and learning qualities is a difficult balance, especially if the goal is to create learning experiences that require thought and reflection as to the experience and where interacting with the game could eventually transform the mindset of the player. These 'experiential learning games' have particular appeal in their approach to learning through engagement, but are less traditional in context and approach either as games or as learning tools. In the case examples, it was clear that students were not able to continually focus on the duality of entertainment and learning approaches to the deliverable. As such, faculty and other stakeholders had the continual task of guiding students back to what was important and essential for a successful product. Questions such as 'how does this engage the player in the learning objective?' and 'how does this engage the player?' and 'how does this reinforce the core purpose of the game?' were repeatedly used to refocus the team.

The recommendation for faculty is not to allow this disconnect to overwhelm the process. Start by showing students great examples of games that are successful in their balance in entertainment and educational outcome (Schrier, 2014, 2016). Continue by exposing students to the range of games that support learning, from blatant skill and drill exercise games (Egenfeldt-Nielsen, 2006) to those that create an implicit and non-directed learning environment (Carnegie Mellon University, 2019; Mojang, 2019). However, all of the games selected should represent the best of each educational approach. When the inevitable process of drift occurs in the classroom, refer back to a solid exemplar. The purpose should not be to emulate the example, but to illustrate how the example's approach addressed similar issues. Whenever possible, ensure that students have access to people who have been successful in creating educational game experiences and have the students hear their stories.

Combating Lack of Student Preparedness

Faculty always hope that their students are prepared for production-level and capstone courses. Such courses occur late in the program, and assume students have a range of skills and abilities from their prior coursework and a sense of educational balance from their other work in math, liberal arts, science, and other academic areas of inquiry. In the case of the authors, many of the students entering production studio also had prior industrial experience, as cooperative education is a requirement toward degree completion. However, the authors were quick to find that such prior exposure was not enough to prepare students for the production experience.

Students in game programs often have repeated exposures to group projects, for better or worse. Such experiences are littered with stories of team inequity, breakdowns in execution, last minute panic development, and other calamities, although there is also often cause for optimism as overall these experiences would seem to prepare students for successful careers later on (Higher Education Video Game Alliance, 2019). While the students may have specific skills, simple team projects do not lend themselves toward emulating longer-term and higher-stake outcomes, especially across multi-disciplinary boundaries. Similarly, students engaged in cooperative education have wildly different experiences, with few experiencing work environments that can regulate industry and academic outcomes.

While it is impossible to change the entering skills and impractical to change the prior experiences, the recommendation is to leverage the studio model to help shore up these shortcomings. The advantage of an academic studio model includes the reasonable expectation that there are many participants engaged in development activities. Some of these are the students engaged in the production course, but others include students engaged in entrepreneurial activities, faculty affiliates involved in research and commercial activities, as well as industry partners working with students within the studio. If the studio culture is healthy, students can easily recognize weaknesses in their abilities from skill deficiencies to team dynamics and can work with those willing to help.

Managing Faculty Workload Expectations

Students in production-oriented courses may rely on a lead instructor as producer, but also rely on other faculty throughout the process. Faculty can provide occasional guidance or maybe involved with the project on a daily basis. Unfortunately, faculty often underestimate the time investment of production courses.

On the surface, there is an allure that production courses require little preparation. For some courses, the role of the faculty is to apply gentle guidance to the team and individual students when appropriate, instead of daily lecture and presentation. However the authors' experiences are quite the opposite as production courses require much more preparation and ongoing engagement and mentorship to execute successfully, particularly at the scale of the case examples presented here.

The recommendation in this case is twofold. First, when involving faculty, it is important to clearly define their role and expectation. For example, one of the authors has extensive experience playtesting educational games. When needed, he delivered content, performed critique, and made recommendations for instrumentation and question formulation. In this case, the particular role and the expectations surrounding that role was abundantly clear to all parties involved and was therefore successful. Second, when a faculty leads a production-oriented course, especially when dealing with a game designed for learning, he or she must be realistic regarding the time expenditure. In the authors' case, a great deal of time was given toward pre-production activities, including the formulation of the game and art statements and well as preliminary staging of the processes required for the production cycle, and then a near-constant monitoring of the production process, team dynamics, and various production activities (development, testing, integration, marketing, certification, etc.)

Investing in Co-Created Work

The prior section hints to another common problem when a work is co-created. Banks and Potts (2010) discussed this approach, but at the heart of the issue is a notion that no one party is the complete owner of a work. In the authors' case, the overarching themes and approach originated with the faculty and the Creative Director of the studio. Students also had input to the experience, their choices adding to the aesthetics and gameplay context. The challenge was how to get students to invest in a co-created work where they were no one party had complete creative control.

In some cases, students wanted a production experience in which their sole purpose was to create a work of passion. As such, these students wanted to control all aspects of the experience including the visuals, play experience, and the overall outcomes, often with little to no input from others (and in some cases even challenged the validity of feedback from outside play testers and audience participants at shows and festivals as being incongruent with their vision). In other cases, the students believed that co-created work meant either they had no input or that any input would be trivial, that work that was not wholly 'theirs' was not of value.

The solution utilized in both cases was to utilize the studio mechanism. Co-creation for the faculty and studio members provided a robust and complete set of requirements. The students were able to provide creative input under the realization that the studio as an entity had to sign off any particular direction, and that expectations were balanced across student feedback, faculty input, feedback from professional staff and industry partners, and data from playtests and limited early-audience sneak-peak style events. The intellectual property of the game was held by the studio to mitigate feelings that any particular faculty, staff, or student had exclusive rights to the work.

Creating a Production Focused Experience

Another misunderstanding that can occur in a game production course involves the relationship between design and production process. This occurs because sometimes curricula does not accommodate a specific experience on production, relegating the experience to a course in software engineering. Sometimes this is an issue related to trade books, which can include some treatment of production in a design context (Crawford, 2003; Fullerton, 2008). However, when students apply motivation and passion to a project, a blurred line between design and production process can be a disadvantage and can quickly demoralize a production team. It also creates pedagogical ambiguity: a design and prototyping course and a production course are not the same thing!

In practice, students will often attempt to use a particular process to justify a particular design choice, insinuating the decision was made to accommodate process instead of being a personal decision. The authors advocate the separation of design from production process, and encourage other faculty to find ways to identify and diffuse personal design desire when it intersects with process. While it may seem this could cause a level of discouragement, the authors found that by creating this separation, choices were not deemed as personal attacks against other team members. Instead, the separation served as a catalyst to encourage dialog when necessary and to focus on the design elements and production process elements in an appropriate context. In addition, because the experience was very directly and openly focused on the production of a shipped product, this led both students and faculty to focus on the relationship between design and process issues, and to reconcile them quickly.

Attention to Detail

Because production focuses on a tangible product, there is the inevitable challenge of dealing with the myriad of details and issues inherent in pushing a product beyond the prototype level. These details spanned the gameplay, aesthetic, technical, and learning elements inherent in all of the works discussed. For example, in Splattershmup, the detail of balancing enemy waves against the ability to gather power-ups had to be finely tuned. If that balance was too simplistic, players would not remain engaged. If it was too difficult, players would give up in frustration.

This may seem like a simple and obvious type of 'game balancing' but it was compounded by the need to think carefully about these issues in the context of the art the player was creating, and what felt like the most representational form relative to the underlying learning objective. The fluidity of the controls, particularly on the gamepad version, took months to resolve into a workable solution. Tuning the look and the interactivity to emulate the visceral experience of action painting proved incredibly difficult. Not only did the interactions have to translate in to changes of stroke, thickness, and color, but the paint had to embody the visual expectation of the medium. Designers and developers found the process of tuning this level of detail incredibly intricate and exhausting.

As students are seldom exposed to this level of detail and the time and effort that it takes for such refinement, the authors recommend continued and iterative treatment to detail-oriented exercises throughout the production lifecycle.

Pushing Beyond the Comfort Zone

On the production team, not every student can work in the role he or she desires. Unlike the real world where companies match applicant skills with available roles, students are free to register for production courses provided they have the necessary pre-requisites. This can result in a differing mix of skills across various specialties and an unknown balance of skills from offering to offering.

The authors recommend that each student embody multiple roles when possible, and should go through a process similar to industry to match skills to the roles available. Even though the authors know there will never be a perfect match and even if students are asked to take on responsibilities outside their comfort, the situation can still be beneficial to the students involved from an educational perspective. In some cases, faculty can work with students to demonstrate how their skills can actually transfer to other roles. In other cases, with careful guidance, such repurposing can increase confidence and demonstrate the student can do more than she or he believed they were capable of.

Critique Culture

For students entering a game program from an art perspective, critique culture is nothing new. However, for technologically centered students, critique culture is often a mystery. Some students focus too much on the word critique, relegating the experience to a process that must be endured. They feel that if they can ride out the storm of faculty and outside voices they can see their vision through. However, the real focus should be the second word, culture. The idea is to create an atmosphere of continued reflection and refinement, in which choices can be challenged in a positive way, complete with suggestions and recommendations that allow all constituents to explore or challenge a particular treatment or approach.

The recommendation is for faculty in production-oriented experiences to provide a positive atmosphere for critique culture. This is in part an educational process, as students must learn how such systems work. When critique goes wrong, the instructor must guide the students and the teams back on course. Furthermore, it is imperative that critique focus on the *work*, not the *designer*.

Playtest Culture

Playtest culture can also be an elusive part of the production experience. Students often employ playtests as a means to verify their design choices. Questions asked during playtest often speak to the issue of fun when evaluating the entertainment experience. When the focus shifts to education, the playtest is sometimes used to address the most basic level of learning. Playtests need to be carefully designed and considered as part of the production process. Questions need to be tailored to specific elements of the entertainment experience. Learning must be measured through capture or observation of specific outcomes. Furthermore, playtest may extend beyond questions and observation and may need to delve into game instrumentation and in-situ capture of interactions, decisions, and experiences.

The solution is to start early with exposing students the role and extent of playtesting for entertainment and educational outcomes, and work with the students to explore when and where to add instrumentation capabilities that can help analyze player traits and behaviors at a deeper level. In cases where students have a prior course in research methods or analytics, leveraging these skills as a part of the play test process is ideal.

Studio Culture

The game studio model provides students with a cultural perspective that is external to the academic experience. While some members of the studio have overlapping faculty and studio responsibilities, others are solely responsible for the operation of the studio.

The authors' recommendation is to have the students get involved in the studio and encourage direct interaction with those employees who have studio-only roles. In the case of MAGIC, students had to interact with the Chief Communications Officer, Operations Manager, and the Creative Director, in addition to the CEO and CTO roles that the authors served in during this context. Each of these key personnel had roles that were not situated in the classroom or that extended beyond it.

Classroom Culture

Production-based courses are often constrained by their academic expectations, and this is one of the biggest problems facing such experiences as parts of successful curriculum. Students and faculty alike often misjudge the amount of effort required for the successful completion of a production experience, as most work in creating games inside academic contexts, either pedagogical or research focused, ends at the creation of a prototype, or occasionally with a polished vertical slice. Similarly, constraint of the production class to a single semester often means that once the course is completed, the project is delivered regardless of the state of implementation, for good or for ill.

The recommendation is to change the nature of production-oriented courses when allowed through curricular process. As discussed earlier, the case study production course allows for a project to extent across multiple offerings of the production course, and for students to take the production course more than once. This allows a project to continue for multiple semesters and allows students to continue to be engaged if they so choose. Of course, the faculty challenge is to ensure that with each retake, the student has greater exposure to a range of roles and topics. This approach also emulates industry where members of a design and development team can change during the development of a project, and where designers and developers may be asked to join a project mid-stream. There are other emerging curricular practices that may also be of benefit here: capstone designs that draw from multiple schools or programs are becoming more common, as are team-taught experiences where groups of faculty engage with groups of students to better serve as a collaborative mesh of expertise in the support of these kinds of experiences.

Tools for Creation, Communication and Culture Pipeline

Tools play an important part in production courses. During development, students need an array of tools to succeed. Some students utilize commercially available games platforms such as Unity3D and Unreal to build their experiences. Other students utilize compilers and development environments such as Visual Studio and XCode to create game systems. Asset creation software for models, images, audio, interfaces, and other game content are also important in the construction process. However, for production teams, numerous tools help with communication and workflow management. This includes messaging applications to keep the team connected and to log design and development decisions. Student teams also utilize tools to address issues of task assignment, version control, development branches, asset classification, and continuous integration.

The authors recommend that faculty in production-oriented courses explore the range of tool choices available, not just for game creation, but also for maintaining communication and workflow within the team. While particular tools change over time, it is important to select tools that best fit with teamwork styles while creating a record that can be explored, critiqued, and reflected upon by students and faculty alike.

Setting the Bar

Academics often provide a dual message to students, with one part of the message conveying consequences if the team does not perform and the other part of the message creating a safety net if the situation degrades. The grade in the course does not always match a production mentality as faculty are seldom motivated to create bimodal 'A' and 'F' grades equivocal to success and failure in the industry. Rather, they separate the deliverable from the rubric that enumerates how the team and individuals engage with the project.

The solution to this dilemma in the case study was to fully separate the grade from the deliverable. The result was that in some cases, the faculty and studio team decided that a product was not ready for distribution. In such cases, the work was not published, and the faculty along with the studio decided whether to continue development in another course or to bench the product altogether. While this may seem harsh, the recommendation of setting the bar early and tuning the expectation that not everything is of high enough quality to publish helped refine the conversation and expectation within the classroom.

Similarly, faculty worked to create the expectation that students could engage with a 'successful' product that shipped, but that it might still be the case that their contribution, style, and engagement with their role was lacking or ineffective. Students were evaluated by faculty after contributions from both the professional staff and their peers, and the overall workflow, communication tools, adherence to Scrum-style scheduling, in-class critique, and designated individual roles and objectives made it exceedingly clear which students had demonstrated effective mastery of the course outcomes and which had struggled. Thus, the grade students received was divorced from a simple consideration of whether or not the overall product was a success.

Distribution Channel Publication

Distribution was another essential part of the production experience. Faculty expressed a requirement that students must prepare for more than one distribution channel. Students had to be ready for delivery on Xbox, Steam, itch.io and other mainstream distribution venues. Students had to explore the requirements of each distribution platform. As part of the process, the team had to determine how distribution delivery requirements could change the nature of assets, game logic, and overall gameplay.

The authors strongly recommend that production-oriented experiences contain a publication requirement beyond web self-publication. Students can gain valuable insight on processes and procedures related to platform and delivery conformance. From a faculty perspective, authentic distribution requirements allow for a great educational opportunity. Faculty can work with students to address issues in how to read and process distribution requirements and the steps needed to ensure conformance with the rules and obligations of the delivery mechanism.

Certification Process

Another important aspect of the publication process is certification. When faculty address the topic of certification in the classroom, it often warrants superficial treatment as one additional step on the road to a successful launch. However, in game studio culture, certification can be a grueling part of the release process.

The recommendation is to expose students to real and authentic certification processes whenever possible. Many times, faculty have to jump through a number of hoops to start the certification process, reading through agreements and making sure what is under NDA for the process. This is one aspect where having a connection to an academic game studio proved advantageous. The studio entity could address the issues around setting up the certification process allowing the students to participate in the process. Those students who dealt with certification gained knowledge that not only benefited the project but also helped in additional experiences within the curriculum.

Post-Publication Lifecycle

When students learn about the game development lifecycle, they often learn of the importance of maintenance. Unfortunately, academic treatment of after publication processes are often treated as an afterthought, and certainly are not promoted as a desirable aspect of the field. Students here stories about cuts and reassignments after publication, and often to their horror feel that if one is stuck on the maintenance team, his or her career is over.

However, reality diverges from this perception. Once a game reaches publication, players expect the experience will be available and will continue to work as situations change. Challenges such as platform API modification, changing hardware platforms, systems upgrades, user configuration changes, and much more can influence the quality of the experience. Furthermore, specific platform distribution channels may change their distribution agreements and requirements. In such cases, the developer often has to go back and work through the certification process again.

The impact of not embracing a maintenance culture can be catastrophic especially when production experiences reside on commercial channels. However, the community is often quick to react. Players will demand refunds for their game and will leave negative reviews for the world to read. When the rules for certification change, developers will find access to their game disabled, potentially enabling large-scale disruption to the player community. Even in cases where the game is self-published to a web site, the degree of maintenance can send the wrong message to potential players and to industry.

The solution is to encapsulate maintenance process from the very beginning of the production experience. When faculty leave this process to the end, the subject can be deemphasized in the process. Instead, faculty should address the topic early and focus the attention of the class towards maintenance issues often in the process. Such focus enables students to see how early choices can greatly affect the process of maintenance as well as its overall sustainability for years to come.

Promoting Success

One of the challenges that was not anticipated involved how students presented their involvement with the project. As part of the educational process, all students in the production course had experiences in resume writing. The students also had multiple exposures to the use and power of the web and social media to propagate their message to a wider community. However, at the end of the project, the authors found that students separated into two groups. The first, and much smaller, group was able to use their production experience effectively in a job search. These students were able to demonstrate their role in the process as well as their individual contribution to the work. In addition, they were able to utilize the success of a game distributed on a major platform as a positive experience.

Unfortunately, the other group of students struggled to represent their contributions on their resumes and on their social media presence. One of the reasons students struggled was the perceived lack of connection to the theme of the game. Some felt that if the game was not entirely their idea or vision, their contribution was minimal or inconsequential to the successful delivery of the project. Other students had difficulties formulating a way to balance individual and group contribution to the project experience. Others placed artificial values on the need to embrace multiple roles throughout the project. Some students even decided that because the experience co-existed in a classroom setting, it was of similar value of any other course, and would present their work on a senior, multi-disciplinary capstone side-by-side with introductory work in a beginning programming course or gam jam weekend event.

The authors recommend that faculty in production-oriented courses start early with methods of promoting success. One way to start this process is to require that students submit a resume at the beginning of the course. Such action provides a framework to discuss what a resume says about a student. Faculty can also use the resume to demonstrate the assignment of roles and responsibilities. Using the existing student resumes, the faculty has the ability to provide guidance. The faculty can share tips and techniques for disseminating the contributions to the project. The faculty can also use the process to demonstrate issues of motivation in the project goals, connecting the meaning of experience directly to the deliverable.

It is also important to note that the studio model also provides input to students in constructing their messages to potential employers and the world at large. In the cases presented in this chapter, personnel assigned to MAGIC had extensive experience reviewing resumes and working with individuals to craft social media and web presence messages. Some of the students realized these individuals were of great value and utilized their time in resume review and the construction of online presence. The most successful students engaged in the early case studies also created online galleries and professional materials for conferences and workshops that described their role in the production process. They also worked with the faculty and staff involved to review and strengthen these materials over multiple iterations.

FUTURE RESEARCH DIRECTIONS

There are a number of aspects as to how the future of production-oriented experiences will play out in game design and development. As the number of game design and development programs increase and as existing programs mature, students entering the workforce will be expected to show skills beyond those acquired in subject-level coursework. The production course that creates a strongly designed and precisely executed deliverable is rapidly becoming a means to separate average workforce candidates from strong ones.

In addition, as the field matures, there is greater emphasis on the game crafter's ability to move beyond merely entertaining experiences. Once of the fallacies shared by students and programs alike is that the only road to success is entry into the AAA industry. However, the global perspective is quite different. Metrics provided by game analytic organizations (Entertainment Software Association, 2019; Newzoo, 2019) demonstrate that from a global perspective, traditional console and computer workstation games are only one aspect of success. There are numerous platform and delivery choices that are atypical of what people believe constitutes success.

The field is also reinvesting in games that exceed the single dimension of entertainment. Games for health, humanities education, economic exploration, and simulation (Bergeron, 2006) all play an important role. There is increased interest in games that can be engines for social good. The global focus on such experiences is increasing and there are new ways to package educational outcomes in games that are balanced and subtle. Students entering the game design and development workforce should have an enlightened view regarding the possibilities of the field.

There are also a number of new opportunities on the horizon as organizations and industry see the value of games and games technologies. While such employment options are not the same as working for a commercial game studio, they will each have their own processes and production procedures that game students will have to embrace. This future will continue to play out on the global stage as simulation and visualization tasks increasingly rely on people with games backgrounds. Such people bring an understanding of information balance, goal-oriented design approach, and interactive mechanisms to the table when fusing game technologies with other domains.

This of course leads to the fact that there are a number of research and exploration possibilities that remain open challenges and areas of exploration for the production-oriented approaches. One of the future research opportunities consists of how to enhance and monitor motivation as it applies to production experiences. Faculty often find themselves in a dilemma in that projects of passion created by students create a level of motivation, but are atypical of what most students will encounter in their initial employment scenarios. It is important to research what constitutes meaningful, consistent motivation strategies that help students stay on target with the themes and motivations of their game experiences while regulating personal gratification for the work with the general expectation of the deliverable.

A pedagogical research possibility involves further understanding of how to incorporate production-oriented experiences within different levels of the curriculum. There are clearly examples of other institutions that have started to investigate this approach (Mikami et al., 2010), but such curricular modification is from the perspective of an entertainment outcome approach. If faculty want students to embrace the notion that games can be motivators for learning outcomes and other possibilities, they must start providing production style experiences earlier to allow time for incorporation and reflection. The authors believe there are tremendous opportunities in the research of pedagogy to explore how curricular design can manifest new approaches and opportunities to this problem.

Another research direction is the study of how to further separate design perspective from process in production environments. Faculty should explore this line of inquiry from the aspect of different disciplines including technology, design, and art. The act of exploring this separation can help students separate the emotion and passion for a particular project from the tasks and activities needed to ensure a successful implementation of the project.

There is also the need to investigate whether the tools and instrumentation currently available to production are appropriate for the changing needs of production-oriented approaches. In many cases, students have figured out how to adapt a range of tools to their needs. They select from communication software, workflow management, content creation, and documentation systems. Similarly, students often have a simplistic view when looking at issues like playtesting and instrumentation of their systems to collect data, whether for entertainment or for learning. Instrumentation and process have to delve deeper than questions of if something is fun or something is learned.

Finally, there is the open challenge on how to incorporate studio like mechanisms and procedures into the production-oriented classroom. The authors realize they have been fortunate in that they had the ability to merge an academic experience with a studio experience. Since both entities existed on a college campus, there was always the expectation that studio encompassed both production and educational goals. As most institutions and faculty do not have immediate access to such models, there is the question on how to adapt studio culture in meaningful and non-trivial ways. There should be particular interest in approaches that provide the range of resource and personnel access that provides students with a balance of academic and industrial input into the entertainment experience as well as the learning potential of their games.

CONCLUSION

Production courses and capstone experiences are an important part of game design and development curricula. As the field continues to evolve, production-oriented experience will provide new ways for students to convey their expertise with entertainment products as well as their ability to adapt game concepts to a variety of domains. These courses demonstrate the students' ability to work in teams and manage complex problems in an effective manner.

With higher expectations of what it means to be a designer and developer, production-oriented experiences must strive to create authentic, meaningful experiences that result in a polished deliverable that promotes completeness and quality. For faculty, this means a change in the focus and expectations for these educational experiences, and it means moving the students experience from one of passion projects to one where the student can find intrinsic motivation in any design and development task.

As faculty reconsider approaches to production, it is important that they separate design considerations from production processes, moderating expectations and maintaining a critique culture based on playtest and iterative refinement. Process should reinforce, and not negate intuitive design when done properly.

For games with an entertainment and educational outcome, production balance must consider both outcomes carefully, providing the appropriate educational scaffolding to guide students towards the worth and value of such efforts while not destroying the motivation and connectedness with the game and the learning outcomes. Such efforts must also resist the urge to address both outcomes in a sequential manner, and should not succumb to the ideas that educational outcomes can be added at the end of a game development process.

ACKNOWLEDGMENT

The authors would like to thank all of the students, staff, faculty, and industry participants involved in the design, development, critique, and deployment of both Splattershmup and Fragile Equilibrium. The success of these titles was truly a team effort and the products demonstrate that it is possible for academic programs to produce works of true quality. In addition, the authors would like to thank Mr. Aaron Cloutier specifically for his passion and engagement as the creative director for the studio, and President Emeritus Dr. William Destler for his support of the MAGIC Center and MAGIC Spell Studios during the period in which these games and experiences were developed.

REFERENCES

Adobe. (2018). *Adobe MAX – The creativity conference.* Retrieved from https://max.adobe.com

Banks, J., & Potts, J. (2010). Co-creating games: A co-evolutionary analysis. *New Media & Society*, *12*(2), 253–270. doi:10.1177/1461444809343563

Bergeron, B. (2006). *Developing serious games.* Hingham, MA: Charles River Media.

Carnegie Mellon University. (2019). *Alice – tell stories. Build games. Learn to program.* Retrieved from https://www.alice.org/

Chamillard, A. T., & Braun, K. A. (2002). The software engineering capstone: Structure and tradeoffs. In *Proceedings of the 33rd SIGCSE Technical Symposium on Computer Science Education* (pp. 227-231). New York, NY: ACM Press. 10.1145/563340.563428

Chandler, H. M. (2014). *The game production handbook* (3rd ed.). Burlington, MA: Jones & Bartlett Learning.

Cometto, S. (n.d.). *Splattershmup: An interdisciplinary teacher's guide.* Retrieved from http://splattershmup.edu/downloads/Splattershmup_Teacher_Guide.pdf

Conboy, B. (2018, Jan. 16). Deep games lab builds video games to treat mental illness. *The DePaulia*. Retrieved from https://depauliaonline.com/31309/news/deep-games-lab-builds-video-games-to-treat-mental-illness/

Crawford, C. (2003). *The art of interactive design: A euphonious and illuminating guide to building successful software.* San Francisco, CA: No Starch Press.

Dawson, E. (2015, April 21). Connections: Imagine RIT 2015. *WXXI News*. Retrieved from https://www.wxxinews.org/post/connections-imagine-rit-2015

Dean, R. (1975). Views. London, UK: A Dragon's Dream Book.

Decker, A., Egert, C. A., & Phelps, A. (2016). Splat! er, shmup? A postmortem on a capstone production experience. In Proceedings 2016 IEEE Frontiers in Education Conference (FIE) (pp. 1-9). IEEE Press.

Decker, A., Phelps, A., & Egert, C. (2017). Trial by a many-colored flame: A multi-disciplinary, community-centric approach to digital media and computing education. In S. Fee, A. Holland-Minkley, & T. Lombardi (Eds.), *New directions for computing education: Embedding computing across disciplines* (pp. 237–257). Cham, Switzerland: Springer. doi:10.1007/978-3-319-54226-3_14

Delaney, D., & Mitchell, G. G. (2002). PBL applied to software engineering group projects. In *Proceedings of the International Conference on Information and Communication in Education* (pp. 1093-1098).

Egenfeldt-Nielsen, S. (2006). Overview of research on the educational use of video games. *Digital Kompetanse, 3-2006, 12*(2), 184-213.

Engelsma, J. R. (2014). Best practices for industry-sponsored CS capstone courses. *Journal of Computing Sciences in Colleges, 30*(1), 18–28.

Entertainment Software Association. (2019). 2019 essential facts about the computer and video game industry. *The Entertainment Software Association (ESA).* Retrieved from https://www.theesa.com/wp-content/uploads/2019/05/ESA_Essential_facts_2019_final.pdf

Fowler, A., Khosmood, F., & Arya, A. (2013). The evolution and significance of the Global Game Jam. In *Proceedings of the Foundations of Digital Games Conference* (vol. 2013).

Fullerton, T. (2008). *Game design workshop: A playcentric approach to creating innovative games.* Burlington, MA: Morgan Kaufmann Publishers. doi:10.1201/b13172

Games, learning, and society. (2015). *2015 schedule – GLS11.* Retrieved from http://glsstudios.com/gls11/2015-schedule/

Goold, A. (2003). Providing process for projects in capstone courses. In *Proceedings of the 8th Annual Conference on Innovation and Technology in Computer Science Education* (pp. 26-29). New York, NY: ACM Press. 10.1145/961511.961522

Gorka, S., Miller, J. R., & Howe, B. J. (2007), Developing realistic capstone projects in conjunction with industry. In *Proceedings of the 8th ACM SIGITE Conference on Information Technology Education* (pp. 27-32). New York, NY: ACM Press. 10.1145/1324302.1324309

Grace, L. (2015). 2015 blank arcade: Games out of joint. *The Blank Arcade @ Digra 2015.* Retrieved from http://www.lgrace.com/blankarcade2015/

Hetland, L., Winner, E., Veenema, S., & Sheridan, K. M. (2013). *Studio thinking 2: The real benefits of visual arts education* (2nd ed.). New York, NY: Teachers College Press.

Higher Education Video Game Alliance. (2019). 2019 survey of program graduates. *Higher Education Video Game Alliance.* Retrieved from https://hevga.org/wp-content/uploads/2019/03/HEVGA_2019_Survey_of_Program_Graduates.pdf

International Communication Association. (2019). *Games + Communication Ante-Conference.* Retrieved from https://icagamesanteconf.info/

Johnson, E. K., Smith, P. A., Dombrowski, M., & Buyssens, R. (2017). Superjam: Participatory design for accessible games. In S. Lackey & J. Chen (Eds.), Lecture Notes in Computer Science: Vol. 10280. *Virtual, Augmented and Mixed Reality (VAMR 2017)* (pp. 339–348). Cham, Switzerland: Springer. doi:10.1007/978-3-319-57987-0_27

Jones, R. M. (2000). Design and implementation of computer games: A capstone course for undergraduate computer science education. In *Proceedings of the 31st SIGCSE Technical Symposium on Computer Science Education* (pp. 260-264). New York, NY: ACM Press. 10.1145/330908.331866

Kanode, C. M., & Haddad, H. M. (2009). Software engineering challenges in game development. In *Sixth Annual Conference on Information Technology: New Generations* (pp. 260-265). IEEE Press.

Karmel, P. (Ed.). (1999). Jackson Pollock: Interviews, articles, and reviews. New York, NY: The Museum of Modern Art.

Kleiner, F. S. (2010). *Gardner's art through the ages: The western perspective* (13th ed., Vol. II). Boston, MA: Wadsworth Cengage Learning.

Linhoff, J., & Settle, A. (2009). Motivating and evaluating game development capstone projects. In *Proceedings of the 4th International Conference on Foundations of Digital Games* (pp. 121-128). New York, NY: ACM Press. 10.1145/1536513.1536541

Merritt, G. C. (2010). *People, planning, and production for video game development.* Orlando, FL: CelleC Games Publishing.

Miami, F. (2018, December). *Miami at play – Filmgate Miami.* Retrieved from https://www.filmgate. miami/miami-at-play

Mikami, K., Watanabe, T., Yamaji, K., Ozawa, K., Ito, A., Kawashima, M., ... Kaneko, M. (2010). Construction trial of a practical education curriculum for game development by industry-university collaboration in Japan. *Computer Graphics, 34*(6), 791–799. doi:10.1016/j.cag.2010.09.015

Mojang. (2019). *Minecraft official site.* Retrieved from https://www.minecraft.net/en-us/

Newzoo. (2019). Global games market report: Free Version 2019. *Newzoo.* Retrieved from https://resources.newzoo.com/hubfs/Reports/2019_Free_Global_ Game_Market_Report.pdf

Parberry, I., Roden, T., & Kazemzadeh, M. B. (2005). Experience with an industry-driven capstone course on game programming. In *Proceedings of the 36th SIGCSE Technical Symposium on Computer Science Education* (pp. 91-95). New York, NY: ACM Press. 10.1145/1047344.1047387

Phaidon. (2013, May 29). MoMA's Jackson Pollock mystery. *Phaidon.* Retrieved from http://www. phaidon.com/agenda/art/articles/2013/may/29/momas-jackson-pollock-mystery

Preston, J. A. (2014). Serious game development: Case study of the 2013 CDC games for health game jam. In *Proceedings of the 2014 ACM International Workshop on Serious Games* (pp. 39-43). New York, NY: ACM Press. 10.1145/2656719.2656721

Reichlmayr, T. J. (2006). Collaborating with industry – strategies for an undergraduate software engineering program. In *Proceedings of the 2006 International Workshop on Summit on Software Engineering Education* (pp. 13-16). New York, NY: ACM Press.

Rochester Institute of Technology. (2019). *Imagine RIT.* Retrieved from https://www.rit.edu/imagine/

Rojas, F. (2012). What is a shmup? *Game History 101.* Retrieved from http://gamehistory101.com/2012/02/29/shmup

Rusch, D. C. (2017). *Making deep games: Designing games with meaning and purpose.* Boca Raton, FL: CRC Press. doi:10.1201/9781315748986

Schrier, K. (Ed.). (2014). *Learning, education, and games: Vol. 1: Curricular and design considerations.* Pittsburgh, PA: ETC Press.

Schrier, K. (Ed.). (2016). *Learning, education, and games: Vol. 2: Bringing games into educational contexts.* Pittsburgh, PA: ETC Press.

Smith, P. A., & Bowers, C. (2016). Improving social skills through game jam participation. In *Proceedings of the International Conference on Game Jams, Hackathons, and Game Creation Events* (pp. 8-14). New York, NY: ACM Press. 10.1145/2897167.2897172

Smith, T., Cooper, K. M. L., & Longstreet, C. S. (2011). Software engineering senior design course: Experiences with agile game development in a capstone project. In *Proceedings of the 1st International Workshop on Games and Software Engineering* (pp. 9 – 12). New York, NY: ACM Press. 10.1145/1984674.1984679

Sommer, R. (1999). Paid to teach and …: Internal contradictions of studio art at a research university. *Change: The magazine of higher learning, 31*(1), 40-45.

Spell Studios, M. A. G. I. C. (2015). *Splattershmup: A game of art and motion [home page].* Retrieved from http://splattershmup.rit.edu

Spell Studios, M. A. G. I. C. (2018). *Fragile Equilibrium: An action game of melancholic balance [home page].* Retrieved from http://fragileequilibrium.net

Umphress, D. A., Hendrix, T. D., & Cross, J. H. (2002). September/October). Software process in the classroom: The capstone project experience. *IEEE Software, 19*(5), 78–81. doi:10.1109/MS.2002.1032858

Vanhanen, J., Lehtinen, T. O. A., & Lassenius, C. (2012). Teaching real-world software engineering through a capstone project course with industrial customers. In *Proceedings of the First International Workshop on Software Engineering Education Based on Real-World Experiences* (pp. 29-32). Piscataway, NJ: IEEE Press. 10.1109/EduRex.2012.6225702

Vogel, C. (2013, May 28). A Pollock restored, a mystery revealed. *The New York Times.* Retrieved from http://www.nytimes.com/2013/05/28/arts/design/jackson-pollocks-one-number-31-1950-restored-by-moma.html?pagewanted=2&=tw&_r=1

ADDITIONAL READING

Chandler, H. M. (2014). *The game production handbook* (3rd ed.). Burlington, MA: Jones & Bartlett Learning.

Crawford, C. (2003). *The art of interactive design: A euphonious and illuminating guide to building successful software*. San Francisco, CA: No Starch Press.

Fullerton, T. (2008). *Game design workshop: A playcentric approach to creating innovative games*. Burlington, MA: Morgan Kaufmann Publishers. doi:10.1201/b13172

Merritt, G. C. (2010). *People, planning, and production for video game development*. Orlando, FL: CelleC Games Publishing.

Phelps, A. (2018). Fragile Equilibrium: Extended artist's statement. *Medium*. Retrieved from https://medium.com/@andymphelps/fragile-equilibrium-extended-artists-statement-5f3d84548411

Rusch, D. C. (2017). *Making deep games: Designing games with meaning and purpose*. Boca Raton, FL: CRC Press. doi:10.1201/9781315748986

Schell, J. (2008). *The art of game design: A book of lenses*. Burlington, MA: Morgan Kaufmann Publishers. doi:10.1201/9780080919171

Schrier, K. (Ed.). (2014). *Learning, education and games: Volume one: Curricular and design considerations*. Pittsburgh, PA: ETC Press.

Schrier, K. (Ed.). (2016). *Learning, education and games: Volume two: Bringing games into educational contexts*. Pittsburgh, PA: ETC Press.

Schrier, K. (Ed.). (in press). *Learning, education, and games: Volume three: 100 Games to use in the classroom*. Pittsburgh, PA: ETC Press.

KEY TERMS AND DEFINITIONS

Action Painting: A particular mode of painting popularized by Jackson Pollock that deals with motion as part of the creative process. This form is characterized by the visceral nature of the paint's interaction with the canvas, as rapid motion of the artist's brush creates the visual representation of the form.

Game Design and Development Programs: Classification of academic programs that address both the overall selection and balance of creative elements that define a game experience and the act of constructing a viable experience. These programs are characterized by their primacy around the creation of an entertainment experience.

Game Entertainment Goals: Refers to a game's ability to engage the player in a combination of fun, engagement, and flow such that the player maximizes a sense of enjoyment and overall satisfaction.

Game Learning Outcome: Refers to both the measurable and intrinsic qualities of games that have an additional purpose of providing an educational treatment for a particular subject matter or domain of inquiry.

MAGIC: The RIT Center for Media, Arts, Games, Interaction, and Creativity. A multi-disciplinary unit consisting of a combined research unit and a semi-commercial game production studio.

Production Experience: A course or real-world situation in which the focus is the production of a working system or artifact, characterized by problems of reasonable complexity and that require more than a single person to implement the solution.

Shmup: A fast-paced action style of video game exemplified by waves of enemy ships, copious amounts of weapons fire by the player and enemies alike, and recognition of balance and strategy to navigate treacherous patterns.

This research was previously published in Global Perspectives on Gameful and Playful Teaching and Learning; pages 164-192, copyright year 2020 by Information Science Reference (an imprint of IGI Global).

Chapter 66
The Minecraft Aesthetics:
Interactions for Reflective Practices

Diali Gupta
University of Calgary, Canada

Beaumie Kim
iD https://orcid.org/0000-0001-6726-0040
University of Calgary, Canada

ABSTRACT

INTRODUCTION

Game-based learning environments adopt games' systematic and data-driven pedagogies to engage learners in problem-solving (Johnson, Adams-Becker, Estrada & Freeman, 2014; Gee, 2008). Some game studies elaborate on rhythmic immersion of games and how game aesthetics could be an inspiration for learners to comprehend academic content (e.g., Squire, 2011). Hunicke, Leblanc and Zubek (2004), in theorizing the game design and research approach, defined aesthetics as the "desirable emotional response evoked in the player as the player interacts with the game system" (p.2). In this paper, we connect gaming experience with how learning can be an aesthetic experience. An aesthetic experience "is marked by focused intent to resolve an indeterminate situation and becomes aesthetic" when someone is "deeply invested in the effort" (Parrish, 2009, p.513). Eisner (2005) defines aesthetic experience as a mode of knowing in two ways – through aesthetic experiences that allow for vicarious participation in situations beyond practical possibilities and through knowledge of or the developed ability to experience the subtleties of the engagement in the activity. We have previously argued that the game aesthetic reveals the core learning concepts and provides complexities for deeper engagement in digital games (Gupta & Kim, 2014). By the game aesthetic, we refer to the ways that different genres of games guide player interactions and experiences with its design elements such as rules, geography and representation, number of players, and time (Egenfeldt-Nielsen, Smith & Tosca, 2013). In this paper, we delve into the *Minecraft* aesthetic as a specific game genre to establish how interactions with its design elements help

DOI: 10.4018/978-1-6684-7589-8.ch066

create an aesthetic learning experience. Our analysis examines the process of students' finding design solutions for the problems they encounter as they proceed with their goals in *Minecraft*. *Minecraft* is an open sandbox-style game where the players are able to develop and showcase creativity (Nguyen, 2016) through experiments within the digital game environment. These creative experiments evolve out of the two key player activities within *Minecraft,* as in construction and survival. The interrelations and tensions between these two activities contribute to the play experience of *Minecraft* (Duncan, 2011). Researchers argue that learners identify and solve problems through critical thinking (Snyder & Snyder, 2008), but more specifically we suggest that learners engage in problem-solving through what Schön (1983) called "reflection-in-action" enabled by the *Minecraft* aesthetic. By interacting with the design elements of *Minecraft*, learners shape the problems through their perception, understanding and experience of the game, and then assess and act upon the problems both individually and collaboratively. Our research therefore examined: (1) how the learners interpret the problems contextually undergoing an aesthetic experience as they interact with Minecraft, and (2) how these interactions help them to engage in reflective practices and solve the problems. Our research was based in an arts immersion school in Canada where students started using *Minecraft* to achieve curricular outcomes in high school Social Studies.

AESTHETIC EXPERIENCE AND DIGITAL GAMES

Discussions around the term game aesthetics are mostly about the design concepts in connection with the mechanics and dynamics of game design (e.g. Aleven, Myers, Easterday & Ogan, 2010). Salen and Zimmerman (2004) used the term "aesthetic trappings" to clearly distinguish the visual design elements from game mechanics. Niendenthal (2009), on the other hand, emphasized how games are aesthetic, social and technological phenomena, and added three detailed perspectives to the game aesthetic as the ways that players experience (1) the visual, aural, haptic or embodied sensory phenomena in the game, (2) the forms that similarly emerge and shape as arts and (3) pleasure, emotion, form giving, sociability, and so forth (p. 2). On a similar note, Egenfeldt-Nielsen and colleagues' (2013) argued that the digital game aesthetic is not how a game sounds or looks but how all its characteristics contribute towards showcasing the experience of "how it plays" (p. 117). We agree with Egenfeldt-Nielsen and colleagues' (2013) contention and further argue that the experience of how a game plays is in itself an aesthetic experience that emerges through the interactions between the player and the game. Studies on the human-computer interactions have reiterated the pragmatics of human experience that arises through the interplay of user, context, culture and history and the relations between artifact and viewer, subject and object, user and tool (Wright, Wallace & McCarthy, 2008). This is based on the foundation that aesthetic experience is the lively integration of means and ends, meaning and movement involving sensory and intellectual faculties and each act or interaction relates meaningfully to the total action and is felt by the experiencer to have a unity or wholeness that is fulfilling (McCarthy & Wright, 2004).

In digital games, the rules, geography, representation, time and number of players as the design elements facilitate the players' experience of a game (Egenfeldt-Nielsen et al., 2013). Players interact with rules to have imaginary experiences within the fictional world of the game (Juul, 2011; Bateman, 2014) whereas geography and representation foreground the importance of aesthetic experiences of the play of games (Bateman, 2014). Play also works through the imaginative and cognitive faculties facilitating an aesthetic experience in digital games (Kirkpatrick, 2007). Hence, we propose that when players interact with the above design elements while playing, they may undergo an aesthetic experience.

AESTHETIC EXPERIENCES AND REFLECTIVE PRACTICES

An experience becomes aesthetic through the pervasive quality of whatever one is doing as whole, continuous, and meaningful (Dewey, 1980). Aesthetic quality is not a specific part of the experience but remains ingrained throughout the experience. In the overall consummatory experience, Dewey (1980) focused on the instrumental nature of the meaningful experience clarifying how it is creative, enlivening and expressive involving the sense and values in an inclusive and fulfilling activity that is worth engaging for its own sake. Cognitive psychologists, like Norman (2004), pointed out how aesthetic experiences are sensory phenomena that evoke behavioural and visceral responses in addition to the cognitive or reflective responses, understood in terms of the emotional design of various designed artifacts. Aesthetic learning experiences may be initiated by an interesting problem, which creates anticipation for consummation of learning and is heightened through a complication or conflict that entraps the learners (Eisner, 2005; Parrish, 2009). We therefore argue that aesthetic learning experience signifies a holistic and meaningful understanding of the problem mobilizing the cognitive powers and hence reflective practices become an inherent part of learners' aesthetic experience.

In this paper, we are focused on learners' solving problems through reflective practices (Schön, 1983). Snyder & Snyder (2008) claimed six phases to solving a problem (p. 96): (1) the problem is identified and evaluated within the context; (2) upon framing of the problem, the solutions are assessed based on available options; (3) the most effective solution is chosen after an in-depth analysis. When we engage learners in solving problems, they may utilize collaborative practices towards assessing and acting upon them (Snyder & Snyder, 2008). On the other hand, our work is more in line with the Deweyan notion of how learners actually learn by doing and reflecting in action while problem-solving (Schön, 1983). Reflection-in-action is described as an individual or collective response to a problem, which includes thinking on what is being done and how it could evolve towards a solution (Schön, 1983). "In such processes, reflection tends to focus interactively on the outcomes of action, the action itself, and the intuitive knowing implicit in the action." (Schön, 1983, p. 56). Jonassen (2000) argued that conceptualizing a problem can be multimodal, incorporating structural, procedural, reflective, and strategic knowledge as well as images and metaphors of the system of the problem. Identifying and learning the concepts, rules, principles or inputs in the process of the problem-solving process (i.e., in the action) enables learners to grasp the complexity of the problems and solve them (Jonassen, 2000). In addition, the problem can be further assessed with reference to the context of the problem. Stanton, Wong, Gore, Sevdalis and Strub (2011) asserted that adaptive problem solvers blend domain expertise and situational nuances with interpersonal traits of persistence, creativity, reasoning and organizational skills, all of which can be considered as a collective response to problem solving as per Schön's definition (1983). Creative work is cyclical and reflective practices of checking and rethinking of tentative solutions (Boden, 1998; Klein, 1993). Creative practices rooted in the arts with visual literacy goals also engage students in reflective practices in relation to real world issues (Kafai & Peppler, 2012).

AESTHETIC EXPERIENCE WITH MINECRAFT

As a digital game, players could undergo an aesthetic experience in *Minecraft* as they interact with the design elements of the game. As explained earlier, the design elements such as rules, geography and representation, time and number of players help create a unique playing experience for a particular game.

Here, we have analyzed students' interactions with the design elements of *Minecraft* as in its geography, representation and multiplayer facets using our theoretical framework to show how learner interactions and interpretations within the game involves reflective practices.

While geography represents the physical space within the game, representation refers to the audio-visual characteristics of *Minecraft*. Although the visual representation of *Minecraft* is blocky (Duncan, 2011), what is unique about the game is the random generation of the landscapes that the players get to reinterpret, recreate or change based on their creative endeavors. Researchers in fact assert that creativity is not something afforded by the game's elements but is something integral to its sandbox nature, i.e., for creating anything within the game (Duncan, 2011; Robertson, 2010). Creativity in *Minecraft,* as Nguyen (2016) points out, is formally and procedurally articulated as the process of arranging game blocks outside of the game's crafting recipes. Constructing new things in *Minecraft* often includes modding, remixing and hacking what already exists or is known. The game evolves simultaneously as the interaction between the creative and complex play involving construction and the simplistic individual components of game mechanics or the three modes of play (Duncan, 2011). The emergent gameplay of *Minecraft*, among other open sandbox games, extends the definition of a game, which involves being a platform with particular resources and constraints for creative works. It becomes an experiential platform for the development and design of various other games and virtual spaces. (Duncan, 2011; Nguyen, 2016). The geography and representation of *Minecraft* through their inherent positioning in the game become noticeable to the players. Hence players could undergo an aesthetic experience through game play as the geography and representation (visual) change or emerge in *Minecraft* depending on the interactions and reinterpretations of the learners based on how they choose to represent their ideas through their constructions.

Again, at all levels of play, *Minecraft* is both a complex system requiring the sharing of information and a platform for creative self-expression (Duncan, 2011; Pellicone & Ahn, 2015). This enables the multiplayer component to add dimension to the form of play (i.e., collaborative construction and sharing of information and skills), amplifying the aesthetic experience.

RESEARCH CONTEXT AND DESIGN

The research was carried out as a connective ethnography (Fields & Kafai, 2009) in an arts immersion school in Western Canada. In connection with the Grade 9 Social Studies curriculum, the project included working on *Minecraft* and various artistic platforms for creating artifacts to demonstrate their geographic and historical skills, communication skills as well as creative thinking skills. The learners illustrated their ideas about immigration laws and the process of immigration from a Canadian perspective while drawing connections to various forms of government and economic practices. For this project, the teacher created a *Minecraft* world *(Pixel Playground)* for the learners to show case their constructions. The teacher designed a *Land Rush* activity within *Pixel Playground* for each team to acquire a piece of land in *Pixel Playground*. The learners had to complete a quiz on Canadian immigration before they were allowed to claim a land that was still available. Learners then needed to construct an immigration booth along with a flag of a fictional country on their claimed land within *Pixel Playground*, based on the type of governance and economy they had imagined for this country. In other words, they had to elaborate upon the governance and economy through the immigration booth and flag in order to entice immigrants to their fictional country. Their booth could reflect any conceptual aspect of the type of government and/

or the economy of their country. The learners also had to create a point system based on the Canadian immigration policy or a set of requirements for the immigrants to fulfil in order to immigrate to their respective fictional countries. For the flag construction, they were asked to choose a provincial flag of Canada to draw inspiration from. Their flag had to be representative of their country and they could artistically borrow elements of or deviate from the flag of their chosen Canadian province. The learners also had to research actual immigrants to their chosen province within Canada and create a similar narrative. The narrative would portray the immigrant as a protagonist who would usher in changes to their country. After completing their booth and flag, each group would be given a physical country of their own (a generated space in *Minecraft*) to construct and expand upon their ideas.

It is however pertinent to mention that the learners were also gaming or interacting with other modes of *Minecraft* while working on the project. *Pixel Playground* was a world created within the *Paanaria* server where the students played other associated games. Hence they could explore in survival mode and their survival depended on some of their actions in the other games. For example, in order to raise capital for their country so as to bring in immigrants, the group had to collaboratively fight skeletons and zombies to collect enough *pancoins* before proceeding with their creative efforts (in creative mode) on *Pixel Playground*. To cite an example, one team member of the group we chose for this research, accidentally bought private healthcare for their country and ran into bankruptcy. He had to think of ways to regain the financial capacity before commencing with the construction in *Pixel Playground*.

For this paper, we chose to focus on the work of one group out of ten groups in the class. The group comprised four students from a Grade 9 social studies classroom. This group was selected for two main reasons. First, we wanted to choose a group that claimed their land early on and spent more time on their constructions to better understand their engagement in reflection-in-action through their constructions. They were the third group to complete the quiz for the Land Rush Activity. Compared to the first two groups, they had very well-formed ideas about what they were going to portray through their constructions. This particular group articulated to the teacher and the researcher that they were going to show their world through the lens of dictatorship. The first two groups, after claiming land, spent more time on deciding what they wanted to focus on. Second, we wanted to find a group that had members with different levels of expertise in *Minecraft*. One of the learners was an expert, two others had medium levels of expertise, and the other one was not too well-versed with *Minecraft*. We believed that the peer mentorship as well as organizing team work with different roles would enable us to hear more in-depth conversations on their interpretations in *Minecraft*. We analyzed how the learners interpreted and interacted with the design elements of *Minecraft* to reconstruct their understanding of the topic over a period of three weeks. As a connective ethnographer, the first author followed the group to understand learner interactions within *Minecraft* through the learners' activities and discussions both in the real world and in the virtual world. The learners worked on the Immigration project for a period of two weeks daily during their Social Studies class from planning for the project to completing their constructions in *Minecraft* and presenting to the class. The researcher was present in class three days a week. The video recordings were collected for five days, excluding the first day of planning.

The students were recorded at work on video along with selected screen captures of their work. Semi-structured one-on-one interviews were carried out with all members of both teams after the completion of the project to capture the essence of their gameplay. The group built welcome (immigration) booths and a flag for a fantasy world within the allocated area for building the booths in *Pixel Playground*. *They* opted to explicitly focus on the type of governance through their booth. Three of the group members (Tracy, Tim & Maya) worked on *Minecraft* construction while the fourth (Jennifer) was engaged in visualizing the concept of dictatorship through symbols, researching and building the narrative. The names used in this paper are pseudonyms to protect the identities of the learners.

Data Analysis Framework and Process

Our data analysis framework incorporates visualization of aesthetic for digital game-based learning environments highlighting how learners visualize the aesthetic of digital games. Our data analysis framework adopted visualization theory (Brodlie et al., 2005) which embeds a macro-cognitive model of sense making (Klein, Moon & Hoffman, 2006). We suggest that the process of visualization of aesthetic of digital games would help us understand the critical thinking process based on following principles:

1. Learners, while playing digital games interact with the design elements of the games as in the rules, the physical landscape, the representations, time and the multiplayer component of *Minecraft*. These interactions create the gaming experience that bring about or foster the aesthetic experience which help the learners to understand the context of the game. For example, when a player explores a world within *Minecraft,* the player interacts with its blocky representation of the physical landscape (e.g., mountains, water bodies) to understand this virtual environment and act upon it for their construction.
2. As the learners gather the information, they start making sense of it from a data frame perspective. The frame initially commences with some data or information that could be drawn from all or any of the design elements of the game and from that perspective other information starts making sense. For example, upon exploring the world, the player gains a better perspective on the choice of a location (e.g., base of a mountain) for constructing what he has in mind (e.g., better access).
3. As the learners make sense of the information using a data-frame perspective, they are able to reflect-in-action and frame the problem contextually for assessing, evaluating and acting upon the problem for solutions. Continuing with the previous example, as the player chooses the exact location at the base of the mountain, he decides on the material, the colour, the size and other factors. As he starts interacting with his construction, he re-assesses and re-evaluates his initial choices and accordingly modifies or adds details (e.g., brighter colour) to make it more meaningful towards his ultimate goal.

Visualization theory (Brodlie et al., 2005) refers to a process of extracting meaningful information from data and constructing a visual representation of the information. In the field of visualization, this process is generally understood in terms of three different yet interrelated semantic contexts. The first and second semantic contexts relate to the process of displaying the data through a digital environment and of specifying, depicting and conveying visual representations to the gamers. The third semantic context deals with the gamer's process and cognitive experience of interpreting received information in one's mind. In the process of analyzing our data we are primarily concerned with the third semantic context which we elaborate upon using a data frame perspective (Klein et al., 2006), and then how the first and second semantic contexts become part of the learners' iterative self-expressive process. Digital games therefore specify, depict and convey visual representations to the learners. As learners visualize the information about the game through the play experience arising out of the interaction with the design elements, they begin to understand the representation of the problem in the game. For example, after the learners claimed their land, they examined different information about the land, such as the proximity to the players' entry point, elevation and nature of the terrain to imagine and determine the location and appearance of the booth. As they continue to play and interact with the design elements of the game (i.e., rules, geography, representation, time and/or number of players), they form their own unique understanding of the game or problem. For example, after commencing the construction of the booth, the learners realize that they do not have enough space for the flag given the proximity to other booths in the area. Hence, they decide to place the flag on the roof of the booth. We argue that this sense making process in digital games occurs through a data frame perspective (Klein et al., 2006). The frame defines what counts as information or data and the frame changes as more and more information is acquired. They are then able to evaluate and act upon the problem by reflecting on their design solutions in context, i.e., they engage in reflective practices (Schön, 1983). For example, as the learners rebuild their flag on the roof of the booth, they realize that it is inconsistent with the size of the booth and as they reframe it they realize it has to be considerably larger to have an impact on the visitors to *Pixel Playground*. Hence, they opt to extend the outline of the flag even more. In other words, as the learners interpret the information through their interactions, they are able to identify the problem thereby creating the frame contextually through addition or modification of data or information.

To analyze the learners' reflective practices within *Minecraft*, we elaborated upon the third semantic context as discussed above. We started our analysis by looking at each of the symbols the group used to interpret and represent how dictatorship works in their country. Creating symbols within the flag and the booth were solutions to the problem of interpreting and representing their choice of the governance type, i.e., dictatorship. We examined how they iteratively engaged in creative practices and reflection-in-action to develop each of these symbols. We noted how the group referred to their initial plan, in particular a sketch of the flag they had created, how they collectively engaged in the constructions and their interpretations, and how they iteratively modified them based on their understanding of dictatorship. We specifically looked at the interactions with *Minecraft* design elements and how they interpreted and modified their constructions in order to meaningfully frame the bigger picture of their government of dictatorship. For this, we attended to the screen and video recordings to note their ongoing design changes, which helped us to understand how they were contextually rethinking the problem with reference to their *Minecraft* creations which served as their data for elaborating upon the frame (i.e., the coherent meanings and symbols of dictatorship). We also tried to connect their intentions (as stated in the post-interviews) to further clarify their actions or interactions with the design elements of *Minecraft*. Through this analysis, we addressed how their interactions affected their thinking process to gradually build all the symbols towards their final goal of representing the form of dictatorship in their country.

FINDINGS: REPRESENTING DICTATORSHIP BY ZLO

The group thought about the meanings of dictatorship and started creating their flag and booth considering the location of their group in *Pixel Playground*. We first provide a brief overview of how the group visualized the problem of representing dictatorship through their creations in *Minecraft* and then describe their problem-solving process (Jonassen, 2000; Snyder & Snyder, 2008; Stanton et al., 2011) commencing with their interactions with the design elements of *Minecraft*.

In the Land Rush activity, the group came in third and claimed their land not too far from the spawning area in *Pixel Playground*. Visually the landscape of *Pixel Playground* represented a cold physical space (geography) with vast areas filled with snow and water. Prior to commencing their project, the group had stated in class that they were going to represent governance and economy through the lens of dictatorship and that their country is called *ZLO*. They had chosen one of the Canadian provincial flags to artistically borrow and represent an aspect on their flag for *ZLO*. Some of their creations in the flag were also linked to the narrative of a political uprising involving an immigrant to their world who was going to usurp power and establish dictatorship in *ZLO*. The group commenced their work by sketching a flag for *ZLO* (Figure 1) and by placing the outline of the flag right in front of the welcome booth (Figure 2). However due to space constraints in *Pixel Playground,* they decided to place the flag on top of their booth and complete the exterior of the booth. The group began constructing the flag by creating the outline in black and then using the cross (of the provincial flag) to divide it into four quadrants. It was constructed as a tall dark grey structure with four sides for their booth. It had a flat roof with a red glass facade near the entrance (Figure 3). While some members of the group were working on the booth, the others were busy recreating the flag, based on the sketch they had drawn.

In this paper, we are examining the symbols the group specifically created to emphasize various notions of power and control associated with dictatorship. The most pronounced of these were on the flag and a few associated creations within the booth. These Include tentacle-like structures, a hand, an eye and a shrine on the flag along with tentacle-like structures within the booth. They also tried to symbolize dictatorship through the choice of colours and the sizes of the welcome booth and the flag.

Figure 1. Initial sketch of flag on paper

Figure 2. Initial placement of flag in front of booth (image derived from version 8 of Minecraft Edu gameplay)

The Dark and Intimidating "Welcome" Booth and Flag

The colours associated with all their constructions were made to signify various notions such as bloodshed, evil and control. The size of the booth and the flag were also used to signify over-powering presence of the governance within *ZLO*. As a group, they decided that the booth needed to be structurally imposing for it to command a presence in *Pixel Playground*. Tracy during her interview on March 14, 2016 explain the idea behind the creation of the booth.

…you can't escape the dictatorship that we have… and so we presented that into our building.

The following excerpts of conversation between Maya and Tracy show their decision-making process (from Dec 1, 2015, Video and screen recordings):

Maya: Tell me where the back of the booth is.

Tracy: Ok it is probably gonna be like…here ((walking around and showing the measurements))

Maya: Okie dokie. I don't think we have to make it very tall.

Tracy: We want to make it super tall so that it stands over everyone else's.

Maya: ((while choosing the building blocks)) What should I build it with? What colours?

Tracy: I was thinking we should go for black, red and maybe blue.

Maya: Our flag is black and blue.

Tracy: You have the drawing… look at the drawing

As seen in Tracy's comment (fourth turn, emphasized), they identified the problem as creating a presence in *Pixel Playground*. One of the solutions was to make their creations physically overwhelming by making them big and tall. As they continued working, Tracy explained to Maya how tall she wanted the booth to be and how they could place the flag on the roof of the booth.

Tracy: This is how tall it is going to be. The flag (showing Maya) …this is how we can have it …above it. I will try and make the roof first. We wanna make it big and intimidating.

Maya: That sounds good.

Figure 3. Flag above the welcome booth (image derived from version 8 of Minecraft Edu gameplay)

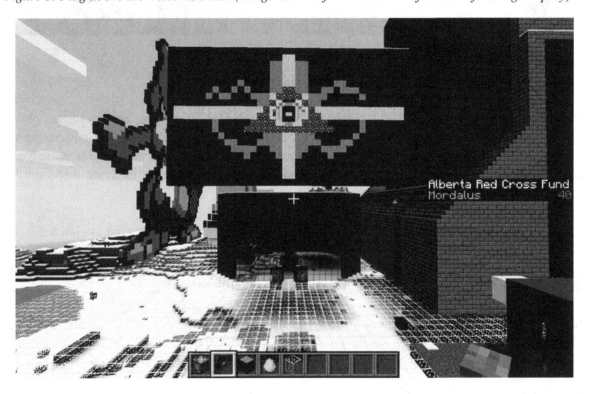

Figure 4. Final interior of welcome booth (image derived from version 8 of Minecraft Edu gameplay)

The representation of the booth was a major consideration in representing dictatorship in *ZLO*. The size and colour of the booth were both chosen to represent darkness and power as associated concepts of dictatorship. Tracy, Jennifer and Maya revealed during their interview that they chose dark colours to better represent evil. Tracy explained the choice of colours during their interview on March 14, 2016:

We used black and red. I think it is because when we were discussing we kind of thought of what colours do we think of when we think of … like a dictatorship? And you know evil was literally what we were talking about. And we decided that red and black were really interesting to go together because of course one is a shade instead of an actual colour and obviously darkness and then besides red might be blood-shed because if we did incite a war or something like that…they were just da::ark ((emphasis)) colours!

Others team members confirmed during their interviews on March 4, 2016 the purpose of using dark colours and the challenges they faced with finding darker colours.

Jennifer: We kind of used dark colours to give that sense of eeriness to it…. yeah

Maya: …We were looking for darker colours and Minecraft had only lighter colours…… We thought they ((referring to dark colours)) were more evil colours and better represented …(dictatorship).

Maya also mentioned how they tried to use less lighting in the inside of the booth to make it appear dark but replaced the façade with red stained glass so that the interior would be visible from the outside as a dark place to be in. This change was made as they were working on the interior of the booth. This exemplifies learners' reflection-in-action where the group was evaluating their experimentation with colours in a problem setting of representing dictatorship.

The group was also interacting with the representation and the geography of *Minecraft* for their design of the booth. In other words, the choice of colours and size of their booth depended on the choices they had on colours, the general sizes of other immigration booths within *Pixel Playground* and their ideas on representing dictatorship. These interactions created the initial data frame. Based on the frame, they began adding more data that they felt would better represent the form of dictatorship that *ZLO* possessed (and discussions on December 1 and December 2, 2015 clarify their choice of location and colours).

While working on the project on December 4, 2015, Tracy explained to the researcher who was observing.

We have a flag. Our theme is red, blue and black ((Jennifer interjects "with a hint of white")). It represents the dark side.

The group had decided that their flag would be the primary representation of *ZLO*'s type of governance. Tracy explained during her interview that they wanted the flag to be unique in order to attract the attention of the visitors to *Pixel Playground*. Tracy in her interview on March 14, 2016 explained:

I think we got closest one to the spawn point that we could, and when we looked around we realized ok... but we were far enough back that you would have to weave through some buildings to get there. So how do we fix that? We decided........ let's just make a big building with a big flag over top of it and then somebody is going to be like "what is that flag doing up there" and "why does it look so weird", and they're going to go and investigate so that was the thinking behind where we had put...

This quote shows how the group conceptualized the multi-modal problem of representing dictatorship incorporating the structural knowledge of the flag and booth, the procedural knowledge of the form of governance, and reflective knowledge to come up with the symbols and images of dictatorship to solve their problem. These goal-directed sequences of activities for problem solving reflect their thinking process (Jonassen, 2000). This also demonstrates the group's reflective conversation with the situation where they experimented with their stance towards inquiry on how to attract the visitors' attention to their flag and the booth (Schön, 1983).

The Power Grasping Tentacles on the Flag and Booth Interior

Based on their initial sketch of the flag for *ZLO* that bore the cross of the original flag, an eye and outreaching tentacle-like structures (Figure 1), the group started their *Minecraft* construction of *ZLO's* flag, beginning with the cross of the flag. It divided the flag into four quadrants. The cross also held the eye in the centre with a light blue hand at the back. The centre had the symbols of the illuminati, and each quadrant had a tentacle-like structure as seen on the sketch and final construction in Figure 1 and 3. The group's decision to use the flowing tentacle-like structures on the flag changed to the idea of clasping tentacle-like structures to better illustrate the grasping power of dictatorship.

The tentacle-like structures within the flag were symbols drawn from analogies with the clasp of an octopus. Although their initial idea was to represent long flowing tentacle-like structures, as seen on the sketch (Figure 1), they decided to make the tentacle-like structures converge into the hand and the cross in order to convey the notion of the powerful grasp of the tentacles. Tracy informed the researcher, who was observing their work on December 4, 2015, that they were interpreting and representing the dictatorship using symbols.

We have symbolism with these little tentacles here… like you can't escape the grasp of darkness.

Two of the group members (Maya and Tim) were working on the tentacles and their discussion on the representations in flag demonstrates their reflection-in-action on representing dictatorship. Maya looked at the sketch and Tim's tentacle-like structures to create hers and then realized that the tentacle-like structures were merging at the corner of the flag from the vertical section of the cross. Maya's representation of the tentacle-like structures on the flag revealed that she was unsure whether the tentacle-like structures should branch out in different directions. These data show how they were interrogating the representation of the tentacle-like structures in their initial sketch. The conversation that followed clarified how they were rethinking the representation to make sense of tentacle-like structures as a source of grasping power.

Figure 5. Tim looking at tentacles

Figure 6. Tim showing tentacles to Maya & Tracy

Dec 7, 2015 (Video recording):

Maya: ((to Tracy)) Do you want the tentacles to come up to the flag and then down below the thing?

Tracy: Yeah that would be great!

Tim: ((to Maya, Figure 5)) Hey Maya! Do you see this tentacle here? Should we have it the same way as that?

Maya: Ok I will change it.

Tim: It just kinda looks all flipped.

Maya: Yeah ...I was just wondering. I don't know if I should put it this way or.... ((pointing downwards towards the centre of the cross)) (Figure 6)

Tim: Alright.

The screen recordings (December 7, 2015) show that the tentacle-like structures were made to clasp in the middle section of the flag along the cross. Maya, Tim and Jennifer explained their ideas on the tentacle-like structures during the interview held on March 4 and March 14, 2016:

Maya: It was supposed to pull you into our planet and then you can never go back to where you came from and you keep living here and it is evil.

Tim: The tentacles represent… like they grab onto you and one can never escape…

Jennifer: Well a big theme in the art we created in Minecraft was like… the idea of tentacles …like kind of used long outreaching arms and there are so many and they can grab you so quickly. We wanted to kind of use that to represent the idea of like dictatorship and like violence and obsession …like grabbing onto someone and something ….and yeah …in our actual flag we incorporated that design of the tentacles.

These data reflect the thought process of the learners as they started working on the tentacles. As they had decided to represent the grasp of power through the tentacles, creating the outreaching tentacles as per the original decision (group decision on December 1, 2015) had to be improved to better represent violence and obsession. The frame of the flag along with the cross and outreaching tentacles in one quadrant of the flag served as the data for them to rethink their approach. Our video recording from December 7, 2015 showed us how they reinterpreted the representation of the tentacles. As Maya worked on the top right quadrant, Tim, who was collaborating with her on the tentacles in the bottom left quadrant, suggested after looking at the tentacles, that representing them in the outreaching way towards the corner of the flag made them appear flipped. Although the word flipped did not make much sense, as these were tentacle-like structures, both Maya and Tim looked at the sketch to reinterpret the meaning of the tentacle-like structures. Tracy, who was working alongside them clarified that the tentacle-like structures were being used as symbols of grasping power, and both Tim and Maya started working on getting the tentacle-like structures to grasp at the centre of the cross. This design change was a result of co-reflection to connect the notion of power structure within *ZLO*. In Schön's (1983) interpretation it could be understood as a "rigor in on-the spot experiment" (p.141) where Tim, questioning the flag design, decided to collaborate with his classmates and intuitively explored and tested the representation of the tentacle-like structures to create meaning. It arose as a situational problem as Maya inquired into the correct representation of the tentacles in the quadrant as she made the tentacles reach out and flow. Her *Minecraft* construction of the tentacles outwards from the cross made Tim rethink the approach. Their collaboration and conversation with Tracy finally clarified that making the tentacles grasp would be a more meaningful representation. Here the group attended to the situational problem while reflecting on their designs and reasoning through the suggested changes (Stanton et al, 2011).

As Tim and Maya worked on the tentacles in the flag, Tracy decided to create symbols to extend the notion of grasping power in all spheres of life within *ZLO*. To establish a sense of continuity, the group also decided to have tentacle-like structures inside the welcome booth, which were created to represent fluid movement that would symbolize extension of power and control over all spheres of life within *ZLO*. The screen recording on December 7, 2015 showed that Tracy was repeatedly going outside and returning to the booth in *Minecraft* after the conversation about the grasping quality of the tentacle-like structures. She was experimenting with the representation of two tentacle-like structures at the back wall of the booth. She later described this process during her interview on 14 March 2016.

It was just kind of like the movement that we had. We were trying the best to create…… an idea for it…… but it was really difficult because of course it's a square and it's not going to really get a fluid movement so…….

She came up with the idea of fluid movement of tentacle-like structures and reworked the shape of those (from square, to circle and then to left open and hanging in the back wall, see Figure 4) several times to represent her idea of fluid movement. The fluidity of the tentacle-like structures signified how evil power could control all aspects of life within *ZLO*. She was using the tentacles-like structures on the flag as a reference frame for her constructions and was trying to extend the connections of control and power over life within *ZLO*.

After finishing the tentacle-like structures, Tracy decided to work on the lighting within the booth. She placed redstone lamps behind the tentacle-like structures which she claimed during her interview was a reflection of hope. The rest of the booth as seen in Figure 4 had very dim lighting and she modified the façade by changing the grey exterior to a red stained glass, which made the booth see-through from the exterior (Figure 3). Tracy during her interview on March 14, 2016 explained the idea of using dim lighting in the interior of the booth.

We wanted to add different effects …we decided there couldn't be light behind the darkness (referring to the interior of the booth) as if you know it is barely peeking through. So, it really was just for us to work around. So, the final product …it wasn't bright. ((comments omitted)) Shows …we still have room for an uprising and to change.

Her emphasis on the lighting and fluidity of the tentacle-like structures inside the booth clarified her effort to symbolize various aspects of *ZLO's* governance. She was reflecting about the problem of conceptualizing the power structures within *ZLO*, in order to symbolically represent and emphasize the procedural control over every aspect of life in *ZLO*. She tried to strengthen this notion with dim lighting and brought in connections with uprisings or revolts (Jonassen, 2000) that are often associated with dictatorships. She also made efforts to convey how the power structures worked within *ZLO* by strategically placing the tentacles at the rear wall of the interior (Jonassen, 2000). *ZLO* team members' creativity towards the representation further illustrated how reflection-in action was a creative and iterative process involving problem solving, for determining what the symbols could signify, and then making decisions on the representation of the symbols (Boden, 1998; Kafai & Peppler, 2012).

Multiple Symbols of Power and Control on the Flag

The association of power and control using the basic tenets of dictatorship was signified not only through the representation of tentacles, but also through the hand, the shrine and the eye within the flag (Figure 3). This symbolization through their creations show how the group members were reflecting-in-action by evaluating various experiments in a problem setting of representing dictatorship in their flag (Schön, 1983). The eye was created to signify surveillance over *ZLO* and took on several new characteristics such as purple extensions to signify the octopus, the ability to see on all sides as a proper representation of surveillance. These symbols, which were modified iteratively, clarify how they were looking at the initial data and adding on more data to create the frame that was meaningful. The group also came up with the concept of using a hand in the background to signify the dictator as they worked on the tentacles. Collaboratively as they developed the narrative of the dictatorship they decided to illustrate the notion of power in the hands of few as a way of governance in *ZLO* by adopting the illuminati symbol.

The Surveillance Eye

An eye was created at the centre of the cross to signify surveillance over life within *ZLO*. The eye was first created by Jennifer as a sketch that Maya and Tim referred to while working on their construction in *Minecraft*. Association of the eye with dictatorship brought in connections to the notion of surveillance. Tim worked on the eye in *Minecraft* (December 4, 2015) and there were several edits on the size, the shape and the colour of the eye. He began constructing the eye by breaking the centre of the cross. However, he introduced changes to the initial sketch by using glass to make the eye appear as an eye on both the front and back of the flag. Then he experimented with coloured glass and changed it into purple stained glass which he claimed was an artistic alignment with the tentacles. He continued experimenting with the pupil of the eye finally settling on a white border with a black centre (Figure 7). As he worked, Jennifer who was looking at his screen commented that it did not look like an eye.

Jennifer: ((to Tim)) No! Make it shape like this in the corners. It looks like a square right now. Look at that ((pointing to the sketch)).

Screen recordings and video of December 4, 2015 subsequently show Tim modifying the centre of the cross into a shape of an eye with a dark centre. (Figure 8). Tim explained his work on the eye during his interview on 4 March 2016,

The eye is floating in the middle (of the illuminati) and can turn in all directions ... 360 degrees

Figure 7. Eye under construction

Figure 8. Eye takes a real shape

These interactions with the representation of the game in particular explain the decision to make the appearance of the eye realistic. There were also efforts as seen through Tim's edits to connect the eye to the tentacle to bring in unity to the overall conceptualization of the flag and the representation of dictatorship through the symbols. The interactions further illustrate their ideas on the notion of surveillance under dictatorship and how that could be represented through a 360 degree, rotation of the eye. Maya explained the function of the eye in her interview on March 4, 2016:

The eye …it sees all…

It is evident that the interactions with the design elements, specifically the representation of the game, made the group members think about how to frame the issue of surveillance within the context and choose and modify their solution upon reflection (Snyder & Snyder, 2008). They tried to shape the situation to the overall frame in order to achieve a coherence between the artifact and their ideas which were in congruence with the basic tenets of dictatorship. Hence, they were moving their inquiry forward by reflecting-in-action through rigor in on-the-spot experiment (Schön, 1983). The learners also solved the problem of framing the shape of the eye collaboratively to make it more meaningful so as to draw upon the analogy of surveillance (Jonassen, 2000).

The Controlling Hand

The hand was placed at the centre of the flag to symbolize the ruling of the dictator. The hand was created by Maya and was not in the original sketch (See Figure 1, 3 & 7). She created the hand (December 4 and 7, 2015) and ran it by Tim as well as Tracy who appreciated the idea (data from video recordings). She also discussed the colour of the hand, and Tracy stated that since they were using the provincial flag which uses light blue they would use the same. The hand was created on December 4, 2015 with reference to the cross and black frame/outline of the flag and was edited a number of times on December 7, 2015 for proper representation of the fingers. During her interview on March 4, 2016, Maya explained her ideas behind the creation of the hand.

We had a ruler... we all came together and decided we wanted to have ...a king... everyone else is just peasants... we kind of all decided that we have seen it from the other perspective a lot ... people are thinking they want to make their world all happy ... and we tried to go in the total opposite direction and tried to be more unique I guess in our idea ((speaking of the dystopian environment in ZLO)).

The interaction with the representation of *Minecraft* to create a hand demonstrated how Maya wanted to depict or symbolize the ruler/ dictator of *ZLO*. She reflected upon the form of governance and used symbols to signify the process (Jonassen, 2000). Although she came up with simple terms (king and peasants) to explain that the ruler held all the power, she emphasized how the world of *ZLO* was not exactly an ordinary or a happy place to be. This also emphasized her "stance towards inquiry" (Schön, 1983, p.163) as she shaped the situation through her own contribution to meaning making.

The Shrine/Illuminati of ZLO

The illuminati, as the group members explained, was to be the small group of power-hungry people chosen by the immigrant to rule *ZLO* (See Figure 3). The group members symbolized it using a gold triangle around the eye of the flag. The initial idea of the illuminati came through the notion of the shrine which the group members related with the notion of good versus evil and was used with reference to *ZLO*'s narrative of the immigrant. The immigrant usurped power and established a small and powerful group of people who dictated how life should run in *ZLO*. Their class discussion on December 4, 2015 explained their thinking on the symbol.

Jennifer: I don't know but in good versus evil should there be a temple?

Tracy: Some kind of shrine?

Jennifer: Yeah, which when he came he took over... ((referring to the immigrant in their narrative))

Tracy: ... and he showed us why be good when you can be ..."

Tim used this notion and created the triangle shaped symbol of the illuminati with reference to the eye, the cross and the four quadrants of the flag. In his interview on March 4, 2016, he explained

We just wanted to add it (the notion of the illuminati) because it was a popular image that a lot of people knew …that it meant evil …. it's like a triangle …like a pyramid with an eye in the middle …I used glow stone because I wanted a sandstone pyramid effect… I wanted to make it glowing ((referring to conversation about immigrant's powerful small group of people which they referred to as the illuminati)).

It is obvious that Tim was trying to tie in connections between their constructions and concepts that are well accepted or known. Tim was drawing from established concepts in real life and using representation that would add meaning to their construction. He was using his *Minecraft* expertise with the situational problem of representing the illuminati (Stanton et al. 2011). He also reasoned to connect the illuminati with the concept of dictatorship ("it meant evil") and representing it as the glowing light with direct references to the rhetoric.

Here the group members were primarily interacting with the representation of *Minecraft*, which showed how they were evaluating the experiment of tying in connections between the illuminati and the theme of dictatorship. As reflective designers and learners, the group members made efforts to solve the problem they had set by understanding the situation. They made connections to popular images and established notions of the illuminati in an effort to test their evolving understanding of dictatorship by drawing out new references to the immigrant (Schön, 1983). They were also interacting with the representation (colour and shape of tentacle-like structures or eye) to make the eye and tentacle-like structures as realistic as possible. These emerging issues of accurate representations were dealt with through their domain expertise and their interpersonal skills of creativity and reasoning towards problem solving (Stanton et al., 2011; Snyder & Snyder, 2008).

DISCUSSION AND CONCLUSION

Our findings indicated that the group working on representing dictatorship iteratively examined their work to represent and focus on certain aspects of dictatorship through their creations of the flag and the booth. Their interactions with the design elements of *Minecraft* triggered the development of ideas and hence there were modifications based on discussions or iterative trials to accurately represent their thoughts through the symbols. It is interesting to note how the group not only used multiple symbols on the flag to depict control and power as important facets of dictatorship but also used their main constructions of the booth and the flag to depict symbolism through their choice of colours, size, materials, lighting, shape, and style. These constructions were results of various interactions with the design elements of *Minecraft*, i.e., the virtual space or the geography, the representations or the audiovisual characteristics, and the multiplayer component present in the game (Bateman, 2014; Egenfeldt-Nielsen et al. 2013; Niendenthal, 2009). Through these interactions and interpretations, it became clear that the learners engaged in the process of problem solving, and the group's actions and interactions provided insights into the nature of those processes. One of the primary routes that the group used towards their problem solving was reflection-in-action or "design as a reflective conversation with the situation" (Schön, 1983, p.103).

To begin with, the group explored the landscape of *Pixel Playground* before deciding on the location of their booth (screen and video recordings of December 1, 2015). From their discourse on December 1 and the interview with Tracy (March 14, 2016 – reference to quote on dark flag), it became clear that understanding the geography played a crucial role in positioning and structuring the booth and the flag, which influenced their symbolization of dictatorship in the initial stage. It was also evident that the learners interacted with the representations of *Minecraft* to create and edit multiple symbols on the flag such as the eye, the tentacles, the hand and the illuminati. These symbols show the group's effort to revisit the concept of dictatorship and think through various notions associated with the concept. The thinking process in terms of design as a reflective practice through interactions with the representation was also highlighted in their subsequent effort to relate those associations (such the notion of surveillance) to their narrative and converting them into symbols within their flag.

It was also evident that their creation processes included their reflections on how each symbol could be made to signify meaning. Hence, we found that the iterative effort to design became a situational problem as the group reflected upon the representation of each symbol (Stanton et al. 2011). The group identified and evaluated the problem of representing the concept of surveillance and control in the hands of few within the context. As demonstrated through their discussions about the representation of the hand and the illuminati, the group assessed the problem collaboratively as well as individually, linked it with the narrative, and discussed the reasoning behind their changes (Schön, 1983; Snyder & Snyder, 2008; Stanton et al, 2011). We also see that the group focused on a multimodal problem (Jonassen, 2000) of representing the structural knowledge, procedural knowledge (e.g., surveillance through the eye, function or rule of the illuminati in *ZLO*) and reflective knowledge using images (e.g., the glowing illuminati with association to the shrine). In the case of the tentacle-like structures, the group members conceptualized a multimodal problem (Jonassen, 2000) of meaningful representation using structural knowledge (grasping shape and fluidity), procedural knowledge (the function of the tentacles for example), strategic knowledge (placement of the tentacle-like structures within the booth to signify control within *ZLO*) as well as images (drawing from the tentacles of an octopus) to solve the problem by assessing and acting upon it collaboratively (Snyder & Snyder, 2008). The group also symbolized the size and colour of the booth along with the lighting and façade changes to initiate interest in visitors and simultaneously make it appear "intimidating" so as to convey the notion of power structures in their country. Similarly, Tracy's iterative effort to create the shape of fluid tentacles were constant interactions with the representation in order to create curves given the blocky appearance of *Minecraft*. These interactions clarify how the geography and the representation in particular foregrounded the aesthetic experience of play (Bateman, 2014) within *Minecraft*.

As we have mentioned earlier, the group progressed with their construction collaboratively through the social interaction (i.e., being multiplayers in *Minecraft)* and the iterative design modifications (Duncan, 2011). This form of play (i.e., creative and collaborative) amplifies the aesthetic experience through the interplay of user, context, culture and history and the relations between artifact and viewer, subject and object, user and tool (Wright et al. 2008). As the learners were engaged in form giving (Niendenthal, 2009), the creative representation within their play became an intrinsic part of their aesthetic experience working through their cognitive faculties (Kirkpatrick, 2007) as well as through their design intuition. To further add to this, the group was constantly reflecting-in-action using their design of the booth and the flag as a reflective conversation with the situation (Schön, 1983). The work of this group of learners allows us to conclude that reflection-in-action as a means towards problem solving was an inherent part of the aesthetic experience that resulted from the interactions within *Minecraft*. The learning process was initiated through a problem of representing a dictatorship, and the constant interactions and interpretations of dictatorship through the creation of symbols within *Minecraft* engaged the learners and created anticipation for the consummation of their learning experiences (Parrish, 2009). The engagement was particularly visible through their thinking process where each interaction helped them to understand the context from a data-frame perspective. As the learners modified the frame, they were reflecting-in-action towards a meaningful solution tying in various associated notions of dictatorship to elaborate upon the governance in *ZLO*.

In this paper, we demonstrated how the interactions with, and the interpretations of design elements of *Minecraft* helped create an aesthetic experience for the learners and engaged them in creative and reflective conversation and practice with their designs. We discussed how learners in an arts immersion school visualized the *Minecraft* aesthetic and symbolized the theme of dictatorship within a digital game-based learning environment. Subsequently, we described how the learners identified and evaluated the problem of representing dictatorship contextually within *Minecraft*, and how the learners collectively reflected and assessed the options to find a solution through symbolic representations that elaborated upon the type of governance in their world. Their designs originated through visualization of the meaning of designs moving through an evolving data-frame sequence – the learners made sense of the design elements of and their own designs within *Minecraft*, which became their data to interpret for further modifications. This helped create a stronger frame that adequately represented their ideas on dictatorship. As they reinterpreted and interacted with their construction, the frame of representing dictatorship developed more and more, allowing the students to unify and present their ideas in a meaningful and holistic manner. We believe that such iterative design practices towards problem solving could be aesthetic experiences that lend to their reflection-in-action.

We, however, acknowledge that there needs to be further reflective practices with teachers and other students outside of this group, which we did not observe in this particular class as students were running out of time for this project. As one of the blind reviewers suggested, it is unclear how their choice of provincial flags and the particular government structure might be reflective of their prior perception of the particular province. There could have been a missed opportunity for them to question their own assumptions about the government structures. In order to have a deeper understanding of their changing (or not-changing) perspectives on such issues, we need to observe how the teacher engages them in conversations prior to and after this type of projects. There needs to be further research to explore how reflection-in-action could support learners' understanding of complex concepts and taking critical perspectives on what they are creating in a design environment, such as *Minecraft*.

REFERENCES

Aleven, V., Myers, E., Easterday, M., & Ogan, A. (2010). Toward a framework for the analysis and design of educational games. In *2010 IEEE International Conference on Digital Game & Toy Enhanced Learning,* (pp. 69-76). IEEE. 10.1109/DIGITEL.2010.55

Bateman, C. (2014). *Game aesthetics and diversity of play* [Doctoral Dissertation].

Brodlie, K., Riding, M., Jones, M. W., John, N. W., Hughes, C., Fewings, A., ... Roard, N. (2005). Visual supercomputing and technologies, applications and challenges. *Computer Graphics Forum*, 24(2), 217–245. doi:10.1111/j.1467-8659.2005.00845.x

Dewey, J. (1934/1980). *Art as experience*. New York, NY: Berkeley Publishing Company.

Duncan, S. C. (2011). Minecraft beyond construction and survival. *Well Played, 1*(1). 1-22. Retrieved from http://etc.cmu.edu/etcpress

Egenfeldt-Nielsen, S., Smith, J. H., & Tosca, S. P. (2013). *Understanding video games: The essential introduction*. New York, NY: Routledge. doi:10.4324/9780203116777

Eisner, E. W. (2005). *Reimagining schools: The selected works of Elliot W. Eisner*. London, UK: Routledge. doi:10.4324/9780203019078

Fields, D. A., & Kafai, Y. B. (2009). A connective ethnography of peer knowledge sharing and diffusion in a tween virtual world. *Computer-Supported Collaborative Learning*, *4*(1), 47–68. doi:10.100711412-008-9057-1

Hunicke, R., LeBlanc, M., & Zubek, R. (2004). MDA: A formal approach to game design and game research. In *Proceedings of the AAAI Workshop on Challenges in Game AI* (pp. 1–5). San Jose, CA: AAAI. Retrieved from https://aaai.org/Library/Workshops/ws04-04.php

Johnson, L., Adams-Becker, S., Estrada, V., & Freeman, A. (2014). *New Media Consortium Horizon Report K-12 Edition*. Austin, Texas: The New Media Consortium.

Jonassen, D. H. (2000). Towards a design theory of problem solving. *Educational Technology Research and Development*, *48*(4), 63–85. doi:10.1007/BF02300500

Juul, J. (2011). *Half-real: Video games between real rules and fictional worlds*. Cambridge, MA: The MIT Press.

Kafai, Y. B., & Peppler, K. A. (2012). Developing gaming fluencies with Scratch: Realizing game design as an artistic process. In C. Steinkuehler, K. Squire, & S. Barab (Eds.), *Games learning and society: Learning and meaning in the digital age* (pp. 355–380). New York, NY: Cambridge University Press. doi:10.1017/CBO9781139031127.026

Kirkpatrick, G. (2007). Between art and gameness: critical theory and computer game aesthetics. *Thesis 11, 89*(1), 74-93. Doi: doi:10.1177/0725513607076134

Klein, G., Moon, B., & Hoffman, R. R. (2006). Making sense of sense making 2: A macro-cognitive model. *IEEE Intelligent Systems*, *21*(5), 88–92. doi:10.1109/MIS.2006.100

Klein, G. A. (1993). A recognition primed model of rapid decision making. In G. A. Klein et al. (Eds.), *Decision making in action: Models and methods* (pp. 138–147). Norwood, NJ: Ablex Publishing Corporation.

McCarthy, J., & Wright, P. (2004). *Technology as Experience*. Cambridge, MA: The MIT Press.

Nguyen, J. (2016). Minecraft and the building blocks of creative individuality. *Configurations*, *24*(4), 471–500. doi:10.1353/con.2016.0030

Niendenthal, S. (2009). What we talk about when we talk about game aesthetics. In *Proceedings of Digital Games Research Association (DIGRA 2009). Breaking new ground: Innovation in games, play, practice and theory* (pp. 1-9). Retrieved from http://dspace.mah.se/handle/2043/13326

Norman, D. (2004). *Emotional Design: Why we love (or hate) everyday things?* New York: Basic Books. doi:10.1145/985600.966013

Parrish, P. E. (2009). Aesthetic principles for instructional design. *Educational Technology Research and Development*, *57*(4), 511–528. doi:10.100711423-007-9060-7

Pellicohn, A., & Ahn, J. (2015). Ethnography of play in Minecraft. *Games and Culture*, 1–19.

Robertson, M. (2010). Five minutes of… Minecraft. *Gamasutra*. Retrieved from http://www.gamasutra.com/view/feature/6179/five_minutes_of_Minecraft_php

Schön, D. (1983). *The reflective practitioner*. New York: Basic Books Inc.

Snyder, L. G., & Snyder, M. (2008). Teaching critical thinking and problem solving skills. *Delta Pi Epsilon Journal*, *50*(2), 90–99.

Squire, K. (2011). *Video games and learning*. New York, NY: Teachers College Press.

Stanton, N. A., Wong, W., Gore, J., Sevdalis, N., & Strub, M. (2011). Critical thinking. *Theoretical Issues in Ergonomics Science*, *12*(3), 204–209. https://www.ncbi.nlm.nih.gov/entrez/query.fcgi?cmd=Retrieve&db=PubMed&list_uids=20655632&dopt=Abstract doi:10.1080/1464536X.2011.564479 PMID:20655632

Wright, P., Wallace, J., & McCarthy, J. (2008). Aesthetics and experience-centered design. *ACM Transactions in Computer Human Interactions, 15*(4). 18.1 – 18.21.

This research was previously published in the International Journal of Gaming and Computer-Mediated Simulations (IJGCMS), 10(4; pages 20-41, copyright year 2018 by IGI Publishing (an imprint of IGI Global).

Chapter 67
Effect of Gaming Mode Upon the Players' Cognitive Performance During Brain Games Play:
An Exploratory Research

Faizan Ahmad

Research Center for Human-Computer Interaction (RC-HCI), COMSATS University Islamabad (CUI), Lahore, Pakistan

Zeeshan Ahmed

Institute of Software, Chinese Academy of Sciences, Beijing, China

Sara Muneeb

Research Center for Human-Computer Interaction (RC-HCI), COMSATS University Islamabad (CUI), Lahore, Pakistan

ABSTRACT

An improvement in cognitive performance through brain games play is implicit yet progressive. It is necessary to explore factors that potentially accelerate this improvement process. Like various other significant yet unexplored aspects, it is equally essential to establish a performative (fusion of accuracy and efficiency) insight about players' cognition (memory, vision, and analytics) among the different modes of brain games. This paper presents empirical research (n=117) that investigates the impact of different modes of brain games (single vs. multiplayer) upon the players' cognitive performance. An accumulated result of the research revealed that the cognitive performance in memory stimulating and visual activity-oriented brain games play significantly boosts during multiplayer mode. Similarly, cognitive accuracy in analytical brain gameplay also increases during the multiplayer mode; however, it's rather inefficient. In addition, both the components of cognitive performance in single-player mode are reported as negatively correlated, while in the multiplayer mode it's rather contrary.

DOI: 10.4018/978-1-6684-7589-8.ch067

1. INTRODUCTION

Cognitive performance (CP) is a mental capacity that is affected by inhibitory control and executive functions, which are factors responsible for the planning, intellectual organization and behavior control (Diamond., 2013; Ruiz-Ariza et al., 2017). Memory, visual acuity, concentration and numeric-linguistic reasoning abilities appear among the most important components of CP (Ruiz et al., 2010; Diamond., 2013; Esteban-Cornejo et al., 2015; Ruiz-Ariza et al., 2017). It has been observed that young people with high CP have greater self-esteem and self-concept (Fati-Ashtiani et al., 2007), and they show less risk of chronic widespread pain (Gale et al., 2012). However, low CP has been associated with anxiety disorder (Martin et al., 2007), depression (Jaycox et al., 2009), and psychological distress (Gale et al., 2008). Therefore, to ensure a better living of mankind, it's necessary to find an effective mean of CP improvement as well as rehabilitation.

Brain games (BGs) have been enormously being considered for a long time as one of the most cost-effective, entertaining and compelling means for the progressive improvement of CP (Lowery & Knirk., 1982; Dorval & Pepin., 1986; Drew & Waters., 1986; McClurg & Chaille., 1987; Dustman et al., 1992; Okagaki & Frensch., 1994; Subrahmanyam & Greenfield., 1994; Greenfield et al., 1996; Yuji., 1996). Recently, scholars also proposed several BGs that mostly offer single-player gaming mode in this regard (Chuang & Chen, 2009; Byun & Park, 2011; Foukarakis et al., 2011; Vasconcelos et al., 2012; Belchior et al., 2013; Navarro et al., 2013; Cecilia et al., 2014; Lopez-Samaniego et al., 2014; Matsushima et al., 2014). However, in order to achieve their ultimate goal, a challenge is to keep players committed to undertake BGs playing activity on regular bases for a longer period of time (Roschelle et al., 2000; Aison et al., 2002; Garris et al., 2002; Melenhorst., 2002; Eggermont at al., 2006; Ijsselsteijn et al., 2007; Pearce., 2008; O'Donovan., 2012). Single-player games, especially of serious nature such as BGs, normally lack in this regard. To overcome this issue, Faizan et al., 2017 designed a cooperative yet competitive multiplayer gaming environment for the BGs of *"BrainStorm"* game suite, which triggers the psychosocial factors of motivation among the players to achieve their long-term commitment with BGs playing activity. However, the proposed solution didn't delineate against the following contradictory facts about players' CP that potentially induce due to the psychosocial factors during the multiplayer mode of BGs play.

The multiplayer mode of videogames offers a competitive environment that motivates its players to aggressively engage in gaming activity, which consequently improves their efficiency in terms of response time during the gaming session (O'Donovan., 2012). Scientists recently started associating this phenomenon with the improvement of players' overall gaming performance (i.e. the fusion of accuracy as well as efficiency), and thus proposed numerous multiplayer video game solutions (Chen et al., 2016; Marin et al., 2017; Jason et al., 2018; Klopfenstein et al., 2018). On the contrary, it is equally evident that a continuous impel to respond quickly in such an extremely demanding environment often affects players' level of engagement that negatively reflects upon the accuracy of their gaming decisions; especially when rather than frequently performed natural stimulus-response tasks the nature of a particular activity explicitly involves memory and analytics for unanticipated circumstances (Matthias et al., 2005).

Based on the preceding facts, this paper presents empirical research that primarily validates the following two independent hypotheses: H_1 = "In comparison with single-player gaming mode, the competitive environment of multiplayer BGs play induces more arousal in CP" and H_2 = "In comparison with single-player gaming mode, the competitive environment of multiplayer BGs play generates more distraction in CP". A major objective of the presented research is to delineate the exact impact of both BGs mode (i.e. single vs. multiplayer) upon players' CP. The following section will provide a complete detail about the empirical research.

2. RESEARCH METHODOLOGY

2.1. Research Design

The presented empirical research includes two independent quantitative studies (QSs: QS_1 and QS_2). Every QS is a twofold activity that was undertaken by the different experimental groups (EGs) ($n_1=59$ and $n_2=58$), who initially went through the memorization phase for *"Picture Puzzle"* BG, and later they played three different BGs offered by *"BrainStorm"* game suite in a single (i.e. within QS_1) and multiplayer (i.e. within QS_1) gaming mode.

2.2. Participants and Experimental Setting

For both QSs, we invited children with their parent(s) from a nearby community school. The recruitment process of children was carefully carried out based on the adequate gaming experience of the participants, which is habitual to gameplay at least once a week. In both QSs, after a warm welcome to the arrived participants (65 male and 52 female Chinese children of age 9 to 10 years) in our department, we introduced the purpose of our ongoing research to them as well as provided them a basic guideline for the gaming activity. Both the QSs were conducted in an indoor environment. 19.5 inches touch screens were used for the activity of BGs play, which allowed each participant to interact with BGs with better visibility, unlike the tablet. However, to provide participants ease of use as a tablet does, we separated touch screens from their base and fixed them horizontally on the table (see Figure. 1).

2.3. Game Suite

To provide evidence of the findings from different game presentation and contexts, it is important that the participants undergo more than one videogame play as well as its different modes. Oftentimes, choosing only one game from a genre and limiting play styles to only one mode could generate biased results. Testing the association in more than one game and more than one mode provides clear evidence to reduce such bias (Ryan et al., 2006).

"BrainStorm" is a psychosocial game suite that offers single as well as multiplayer gaming environment for its all three BGs: i) *"Picture Puzzle"*, ii) *"Find the Difference"* and iii) *"Letter and Number"* (Faizan et al., 2017). These BGs respectively target players' memory, vision, and analytical abilities. A strategical design of *"BrainStorm"* BGs was elucidated by Faizan et al., 2017 in detail, which clearly differentiates the environment of its single-player mode from the multiplayer mode. Nonetheless, a general design of the employed BGs is as follows.

Figure 1. "BrainStorm" general environmental setting

2.3.1. Picture Puzzle

In *"Picture Puzzle"* BG, 15 images of famous and/or historical personalities or places appear one by one on the screen and player has to choose their correct name among the different options (see Figure. 2(a)). A core mechanism of this BG requires player's attention to receive the data from their visual source and pass it to the short-term memory (STM). STM then processes this data and retrieves related information by communicating with the long-term memory (LTM), which was established earlier during the memorization session.

An individual session of 5 to 10 minutes was organized for each participant, prior to the gaming activity, to memorize the names of famous and/or historical personalities or places that will be asked in *"Picture Puzzle"* BG; however, it is observed that only 10% (i.e. maximum on average) of the personalities or places were already known to the participants.

2.3.2. Find the Difference

In *"Find the Difference"* BG, 3 different pairs of similar images of famous and/or historical places appear one by one on the screen and every time a player has to find 6 differences between the paired images (see Figure. 2(b)). A core mechanism of this activity requires the player to hold visuospatial information of sample image for few seconds in its active memory so that it can be used to compare with a test image in order to detect differences in both visual frames (i.e. sample frame and test frame).

2.3.3. Letter and Number

In *"Letter and Number"* BG, 10 incomplete sequences of letters or numbers appear one by one on the screen and player has to analyze its pattern and complete the sequence by selecting a correct option from the given choices (see Figure. 2(c)). A core mechanism of this task requires the player to sequentially perform information visualization, articulation, analysis and decision making based on its personal understanding.

Figure 2. "BrainStorm" high fidelity prototype

(a). *"Picture Puzzle"*   **(b).** *"Find the Difference"*   **(c).** *"Letter and Number"*

2.4. Data Collection

In both QSs, the performative data was recorded noninvasively throughout the BGs playing activity. A consent about the data collection process was taken from the parent(s) of the participants at the time of recruitment. Every QS-intervention was 1 day in which computer aided BGs playing activity was conducted under the observation of psychologists in a silent room. The interactions were observed among the competitors during the activity of BGs play in QS_2. It is worth mentioning that most of the interactions were nothing but a casual exchange of feelings, thoughts, and updates regarding the ongoing gaming situation. Besides, to avoid bias risk as well as the possible influence of any strange variable in both QSs, we didn't allow participants who completed the gaming activity to interact with those who didn't start the activity. In every QS, each participant took 20 minutes on average to complete the whole gaming activity. A noninvasively recorded performative data of every QS was compiled separately for each BG in terms of their accuracy (i.e. the total number of correct attempts) as well as efficiency (i.e. the response time for each correct attempt) with respect to the memory, vision, and analytical abilities.

2.5. Data Analysis

A statistical analysis is performed on the compiled performative data to determine trends that exist between as well as within the QSs. During the initial phase of statistical analysis, two-sample paired t-test is applied between the data of same performative components received by the both QSs to determine the significance of their difference (i.e. separately for each BG activity). Whilst in the second phase, Pearson correlation (Cohen et al, 1988) is applied within the data of both performative components of every QS to determine their degree of correlation (i.e. separately for each BG activity), where r indicates the direction and strength of the correlation. Furthermore, the p-value is also calculated in this phase to demonstrate the significance of the findings (Cohen et al, 1988). It is well-known that the correlation doesn't imply causation, yet this approach has been used by the vast range of literature, which also includes a research *"StudentLife"* (Rui et al, 2014). It is nearly impossible in a real-world scenario to find the element(s) that has a causal relationship with the other element, as there always exists a un(known/addressed) factor(s) that affects causality between the associated elements. Therefore, the reason behind the use of the correlation technique is not to find a causal relationship but to understand the significance of one element in relation to the other(s), while acknowledging they are not causal.

3. RESULTS

A trend delineating the CP is demonstrated in Figure 3. The presented result comparatively summarizes the accuracy as well as the efficiency against memory, vision and analytical abilities of the players for both QSs.

Figure 3. CP results summary of both QSs

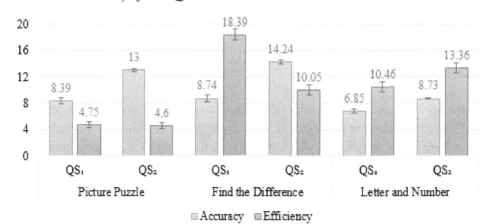

For *"Picture Puzzle"* BG, the result illustrates that in comparison with QS_1, the memorization-and-recalling performance in QS_2 was significantly more accurate (i.e. by 30.73%) ($t(116)= -17.828, p=0.05$) as well as slightly more efficient (i.e. by 3.16%) ($t(116)=2.052, p=0.05$). As while playing this BG, the players in QS_1 correctly attempted $\mu=8.39$ questions (i.e. out of 15) while taking $\mu=4.75$ seconds; whereas the players in QS2 correctly attempted $\mu=13$ questions while taking $\mu=4.60$ seconds. Similarly, for "Find *the Difference"* BG, in comparison with QS1, the visualization-and-searching performance in QS2 was significantly reported as more accurate (i.e. by 30.56%) (t(116)= -3.551, p=0.05) as well as efficient (i.e. by 45.35%) (t(116)=7.663, p=0.05). As while playing this BG, the players in QS1 correctly identified $\mu=8.74$ spots (i.e. out of 18) while taking $\mu=18.39$ seconds; whereas the players in QS2 correctly identified $\mu=14.24$ spots while taking $\mu=10.05$ seconds. On the contrary, for "Letters *and Number"* BG, *the* performative trend of players' analytical ability is relatively different. It was observed that in comparison with QS1, the analytical performance in QS2 was considerably more accurate (i.e. by 18.80%) (t(116)= -8.707, p=0.05); however, rather inefficient (i.e. by 21.71%) (t(116)= -4.913, p=0.05). As while playing this BG, the players in QS1 correctly attempted μ=6.85 questions (i.e. out of 10) while taking μ=10.46 seconds; whereas the players in QS2 correctly attempted μ=8.73 questions while taking μ=13.36 seconds.

A statistical analysis is performed on the above illustrated data to understand the precise trend of correlation among both performative components of the players within every QS (i.e. separately for each BG activity). It is worth mentioning that both the components of CP were reported as negatively correlated in QS1 (i.e. respectively as: [r= -0.27, p<0.001], [*r*= -0.74, p<0.001] an*d* [r= -0.57, p<0.001], whereas in QS2 their relationship was rather surprisingly contrary (i.e. respectively as: [r=0.20, p<0.001], [*r*=0.39, p<0.001] an*d* [r=0.36, p<0.001]).

4. DISCUSSION

To attain a clear insight about the preceding CP trend, it's important to simultaneously analyze the observations of the participants that were recorded by the psychologists during both QSs.

It is observed in QS2, that the competitive environment of multiplayer gaming mode was building a peer pressure among the participants. Where the existence of this peer pressure in a competitive environment has already been acknowledged by the scientists (Brittain., 1963; Brown et al., 1986), there we also verbally reconfirmed about the observed phenomenon from the participants during a post-gameplay interview session (109 out of 117 agreed). Similar to the existing literature (Steinberg & Monahan., 2007; Mitchell & Kenneth., 2010), our observations also suggest that this peer pressure overall delivers a mixed-effect upon the audience; however, the effect is mostly positive. As the statements (e.g. n17 said "I will try my best" and n94 said "I will defiantly win this game") of many of the recruited participants indicated that the peer pressure is fruitful since it produces an impulse to compete and win. Moreover, aggression (e.g. n41 said "I will never let him win {screaming}") as well as nervousness (e.g. n74 said "I knew this answer! Oh I forgot {whispering with sad face}") among few participants are also recorded as a negative effect of this phenomenon. Similarly, the overall preceding CP trend suggests that the competitive environment of multiplayer gaming mode mostly accelerates the CP (see Figure. 3). This includes minor arousal in the efficiency, but extreme arousal in the accuracy of the participants during a memorization-and-recalling gaming activity. Plus, extreme arousal in the participants' efficiency as well as accuracy during the visualization-and-searching gaming activity. Conversely, a moderate level of distraction in the efficiency of the participants during the analytical gaming activity; however, their accuracy still holds a moderate level of arousal (see analysis summary in Table 1).

In continuation to the above discussed observational and quantitative findings, the results of the statistical analysis also support the multiplayer BGs environment. As both the components of CP in QS2 are reported as positively correlated, whereas in QS1 it is rather contrary. It seems as initially on each attempt, in a competitive environment of multiplayer BGs play, the peer pressure positively assists to sustain high CP rate. However, in case of delay in decision making, "nervousness" takes charge and that causes an erroneous response. Nonetheless, this needs further investigation on behavioral grounds; however, it was out of the scope of current research efforts.

Table 1. QSs-oriented conclusive remarks

Cognitive Performance (CP)											
Memory				Vision				Analytics			
QS$_1$		QS$_2$		QS$_1$		QS$_2$		QS$_1$		QS$_2$	
Efficiency	Accuracy	Efficiency	Accuracy	Efficiency	Accuracy	Efficiency	Accuracy	Efficiency	Accuracy	Efficiency	Accuracy
✗ *	✗ ***	✓ *	✓ ***	✗ ***	✗ ***	✓ ***	✓ ***	✓ **	✗ **	✗ **	✓ **

✗ *Distraction* ✓ *Arousal*
*[1% ≤ Minor ≤ 15%]**[15% < Moderate ≤ 30%]***[30% < Extreme ≤ 100%]

5. CONCLUSION

An impact of the different gaming modes upon the players' CP was previously fuzzy. Besides, the means to accelerate the process of CP improvement with relatively fewer BGs playing sessions were also previously unaddressed. In view of the cited literature, we constructed two independent hypotheses. Since CP is a multidimensional construct that mainly encompasses the components associated with memory, vision, and analytics. Therefore, the result of the presented QSs doesn't completely accept/reject any of the constructed hypothesis as H1 is absolutely correct for the memory and vision-related gaming activities, whereas both the hypotheses are partially correct for analytics-related gaming activities (i.e. H1 an$_d$ H2, b$_o$th are absolutely correct for analytical accuracy and efficiency, respectively).

5.1. Ethical Approval

All procedures performed in presented studies involving human participants were in accordance with the ethical standards of the institutional and/or national research committee and with the 1964 Helsinki declaration and its later amendments or comparable ethical standards.

5.2. Informed Consent

Informed consent was obtained from the parent(s) of all individual participants included in the study.

5.3. Availability of Data and Material

The data and material shall be provided if requested.

REFERENCES

Vasconcelos, A. (2012). Designing Tablet-Based Games for Seniors: the example of CogniPlay, a cognitive gaming platform. *Proceedings of ACM International Conference on Fun and Games*, 1-10. 10.1145/2367616.2367617

Aison, A. (2002). *Appeal and Interest of Video Game Use Among the Elderly*. The Harvard Graduate School of Education.

Faizan, A. (2017). BrainStorm: A psychosocial game suite design for non-invasive cross-generational cognitive capabilities data collection. *Journal of Experimental & Theoretical Artificial Intelligence*. Advance online publication. doi:10.1080/0952813X.2017.1354079

Melenhorst, A. S. (2002). *Adopting communication technology in later life: The decisive role of benefits* (PhD Dissertation). Eindhoven: Technische Universiteit Eindhoven.

Pearce, A. (2008). The Truth about Baby Boomer Gamers: A Study of Over-Forty Computer Game Players. *Games and Culture*, *3*(2), 142–174. doi:10.1177/1555412008314132

Lowery, B. R., & Knirk, F. G. (1982). Micro-computer video games and spatial visualization acquisition. *Journal of Educational Technology Systems*, *11*(2), 155–166. doi:10.2190/3PAN-CHJM-RT0L-W6AC

Drew, B., & Waters, J. (1986). Video Games: Utilization of a novel strategy to improve perceptual motor skills and cognitive functioning in the noninstitutionalized elderly. *Cognitive Rehabilitiation*, *4*(2), 26–31.

Brittain, C. V. (1963). Adolescent choices and parent-peer cross pressures. *American Sociological Review*, *28*(3), 385–391. doi:10.2307/2090349

Brown, B. B., Clasen, D. R., & Eicher, S. A. (1986). Perceptions of peer pressure, peer conformity dispositions, and self-reported behavior among adolescents. *Developmental Psychology*, *22*(4), 521–530. doi:10.1037/0012-1649.22.4.521

Cohen, J. (1988). *Statistical power analysis for the behavioral sciencies*. Routledge.

O'Donovan, C., Hirsch, E., Holohan, E., McBride, I., McManus, R., & Hussey, J. (2012). Energy expended playing Xbox Kinect™ and Wii™ games: A preliminary study comparing single and multiplayer modes. *Physiotherapy*, *98*(3), 224–229. doi:10.1016/j.physio.2012.05.010 PMID:22898579

Diamond, A. (2013). Executive functions. *Annual Review of Psychology*, *64*, 135-168. doi:10.1146/annurev-psych-113011-143750

Esteban-Cornejo, I., Tejero-Gonzalez, C. M., Sallis, J. F., & Veiga, O. L. (2015). Physical activity and cognition in adolescents: A systematic review. *Journal of Science and Medicine in Sport/Sports Medicine Australia*, *18*(5), 534-539. .007 doi:10.1016/j.jsams.2014.07

Fati-Ashtiani, A., Ejei, J., Khodapanahi, M., & Tarkhorani, H. (2007). Relationship between self-concept, self-esteem, anxiety, depression and academic achievement in adolescents. *Journal of Applied Sciences*, *7*(7), 995-1000. doi:10.3923/jas.2007.995.1000

Matsushima, F., Vilar, R. G., Mitani, K., & Hoshino, Y. (2014). Touch Screen Rehabilitation System Prototype Based on Cognitive Exercise Therapy. *HCI International Communications in Computer and Information Science*, *435*, 361–365. doi:10.1007/978-3-319-07854-0_63

Gale, C. R., Hatch, S. L., Batty, G. D., & Deary, I. J. (2008). Intelligence in childhood and risk of psychological distress in adulthood: The 1958 national child development survey and the 1970 British cohort study. *Intelligence*, *37*, 592-599. .002 doi:10.1016/j.intell.2008.09

Gale, C. R., Deary, I. J., Cooper, C., & Batty, D. G. (2012). Intelligence in childhood and chronic widespread pain in middle age: The National Child Development Survey. *Pain, 153*(12), 2339-2344. . doi:10.1016/j.pain.2012.07.027

Yuji, H. (1996). Computer games and information-processing skills. *Perceptual and Motor Skills, 83*(2), 643–647. doi:10.2466/pms.1996.83.2.643 PMID:8902044

Roschelle, J. M., Pea, R. D., Hoadley, C. M., Gordin, D. N., & Means, B. M. (2000). Changing How and What Children Learn in School with Computer-Based Technologies. *The Future of Children, 10*(2), 76–100. doi:10.2307/1602690 PMID:11255710

Jaycox, L. H., Stein, B. D., Paddock, S., Miles, J. N. V., Chandra, A., & Meredith, L. S. (2009). Impact of teen depression on academic, social, and physical functioning. *Pediatrics, 124*(4), e596-e605. . doi:10.1542/peds.2008-3348

Navarro, J. (2013). Game Based Monitoring and Cognitive Therapy for Elderly. *Workshop Proceedings of the 9th International Conference on Intelligent Environments, 17*, 116-127.

Wuertz, J., Alharthi, S. A., Hamilton, W. A., Bateman, S., Gutwin, C., Tang, A., Toups, Z. O., & Hammer, J. (2018). A Design Framework for Awareness Cues in Distributed Multiplayer Games. *Proceedings of the SIGCHI Conference on Human Factors in Computing Systems (CHI '18)*. 10.1145/3173574.3173817

Subrahmanyam, K., & Greenfield, P. M. (1994). Effect of video game practice on spatial skills in girls and boys. *Journal of Applied Developmental Psychology, 15*(1), 13–32. doi:10.1016/0193-3973(94)90004-3

Klopfenstein, L. C., Delpriori, S., Paolini, B. D., & Bogliolo, A. (2018). Code Hunting Games: A Mixed Reality Multiplayer Treasure Hunt Through a Conversational Interface. In S. Diplaris, A. Satsiou, A. Følstad, M. Vafopoulos, & T. Vilarinho (Eds.), Lecture Notes in Computer Science: Vol. 10750. *Internet Science. INSCI 2017.* Springer. doi:10.1007/978-3-319-77547-0_14

Okagaki, L., & Frensch, P. A. (1994). Effects of video game playing on measures of spatial performance: Gender effects in late adolescence. *Journal of Applied Developmental Psychology, 15*(1), 33–58. doi:10.1016/0193-3973(94)90005-1

Lopez-Samaniego, L. (2014). Cognitive rehabilitation based on working brain reflexes using computer games over iPad. IEEE Computer Games: AI, Animation, Mobile, Multimedia, Educational and Serious Games (CGAMES), 1-4. doi:10.1109/CGames.2014.6934155

Dorval, M., & Pepin, M. (1986). Effect of playing a video game on a measure of spatial visualization. *Perceptual and Motor Skills, 62*(1), 159–162. doi:10.2466/pms.1986.62.1.159 PMID:3960656

Martin, L. T., Kubzansky, L. D., LeWinn, K. Z., Lipsitt, L. P., Satz, P., & Buka, S. L. (2007). Childhood cognitive performance and risk of generalized anxiety disorder. *International Journal of Epidemiology, 36*(4), 769-775. . doi:10.1093/ije/dym063

Foukarakis, M. (2011). An adaptable card game for older users. *Proceedings of the 4th International Conference on Pervasive Technologies Related to Assistive Environments (PETRA)*. 10.1145/2141622.2141655

Chen, Zhou, & Tomlin. (2016). Multiplayer Reach-Avoid Games via Pairwise Outcomes. *IEEE Transactions on Automatic Control.*

Marin, C., Cloquell, J., Luo, Y., & Estrany, B. (2017). A Multiplayer Game with Virtual Interfaces. In Y. Luo (Ed.), Lecture Notes in Computer Science: Vol. 10451. *Cooperative Design, Visualization, and Engineering. CDVE 2017*. Springer. doi:10.1007/978-3-319-66805-5_13

Dick, M., Wellnitz, O., & Wolf, L. (2005). Analysis of factors affecting players' performance and perception in multiplayer games. *Proceedings of 4th ACM SIGCOMM workshop on Network and system support for games*. 10.1145/1103599.1103624

Mitchell, J. (2010). *Prinstein and Kenneth A. Dodge*. Understanding Peer Influence in Children and Adolescents.

McClurg, P. A., & Chaille, C. (1987). Computer games: Environments for developing spatial cognition? *Journal of Educational Computing Research, 3*(1), 95–111. doi:10.2190/9N5U-P3E9-R1X8-0RQM

Greenfield, P. M., & ... . (1996). Action video games and informal education: Effects on strategies for dividing visual attention. *Interacting with Video, 11*, 187–205.

Belchior, P., Marsiske, M., Sisco, S. M., Yam, A., Bavelier, D., Ball, K., & Mann, W. C. (2013). Video game training to improve selective visual attention in older adults. *Computers in Human Behavior, 29*(4), 1318–1324. doi:10.1016/j.chb.2013.01.034 PMID:24003265

Dustman, R. E., Emmerson, R. Y., Steinhaus, L. A., Shearer, D. E., & Dustman, T. J. (1992). The effects of videogame playing on neuropsychological performance of elderly individuals. *Journal of Gerontology, 47*(3), 168–171. doi:10.1093/geronj/47.3.P168 PMID:1573200

Garris, R., Ahlers, R., & Driskell, J. E. (2002). Games, Motivation, and Learning: A Research and Practice Model. *Simulation & Gaming, 33*(4), 441–467. doi:10.1177/1046878102238607

Ruiz, J. R., Ortega, F. B., Castillo, R., Martín-Matillas, M., Kwak, L., & Vicente-Rodríguez, G. (2010). Physical activity, fitness, weight status, and cognitive performance in adolescents. *The Journal of Pediatrics, 157*(6), 917-922. . doi:10.1016/j.jpeds.2010.06.026

Rui, W. (2014). StudentLife: Assessing Mental Health, Academic Performance and Behav-ioral Trends of College Students using Smartphones. *Proceedings of the ACM Confer-ence on Ubiquitous Computing*.

Ruiz-Ariza, A., Grao-Cruces, A., Loureiro, N. E. M., & Martínez-Lopez, E. J. (2017). Influence of physical fitness on cognitive and academic performance in adolescents: A systematic review from 2005-2015. *International Review of Sport and Exercise Psychology, 10*(1), 108-133. . doi:10.1080/17 50984X.2016.1184699

Ryan, R. M., Rigby, C. S., & Przybylski, A. (2006). The motivational pull of video games: A self-determination theory approach. *Motivation and Emotion, 30*(4), 347–363. doi:10.100711031-006-9051-8

Eggermont, S., Vandebosch, H., & Steyaert, S. (2006). Towards the desired future of the elderly and ICT: Policy recommendations based on a dialogue with senior citizens. *Poiesis & Praxis: International Journal of Ethics of Science and Technology Assessment, 4*(3), 199–217. doi:10.100710202-005-0017-9

Byun, S., & Park, C. (2011). Serious Game for Cognitive Testing of Elderly. *Communications in Computer and Information Science HCI International, 173*, 354–357. doi:10.1007/978-3-642-22098-2_71

Cecilia, S. L., & ... . (2014). "Logical Blocks" Multimedia Game Development for Students with Intellectual Disabilities. HCI International Posters Part II. *Communications in Computer and Information Science*, *435*, 371–375. doi:10.1007/978-3-319-07854-0_65

Steinberg, L., & Monahan, K. C. (2007). Age differences in resistance to peer influence. *Developmental Psychology*, *43*(6), 1531–1543. doi:10.1037/0012-1649.43.6.1531 PMID:18020830

Chuang & Chen. (2009). Effect of Computer-Based Video Games on Children: An Experimental Study. *Educational Technology & Society, 12*(2), 1-10.

Ijsselsteijn, W. (2007). Digital Game Design for Elderly User. *Proceedings of the Conference on Future Play*, 17-22. 10.1145/1328202.1328206

This research was previously published in the International Journal of Game-Based Learning (IJGBL), 11(1); pages 67-76, copyright year 2021 by IGI Publishing (an imprint of IGI Global).

Chapter 68
The Significance of the Hermeneutics of Play for Gamification:
The Limits of Virtual and Real Gamification

Kosti Joensuu
University of Lapland, Rovaniemi, Finland

Sanna Ryynänen
University of Lapland, Rovaniemi, Finland

ABSTRACT

Games and play are increasingly significant in everyday life. Thus, a philosophical and theoretical consideration of these concepts is needed. This article uses phenomenological hermeneutics to discuss games, play, and gamification; it also addresses the development of gamifying planes within gamification studies. It hypothesizes that the academic discussion of gamification becomes more valid, ontologically, by focusing on the phenomenon and lived experience of play and playing from a phenomenological perspective. It presents an upcoming practical intervention, an empirical research design of case study of playing a virtual game, to demonstrate how the essence of play and the integrated spheres of virtual and real worlds could be approached. Thus, it could provide valuable information that is needed in the fast-developing domain of interventions in gamification and the game-business. On the basis of this study's theoretical findings, a broader ontological notion is suggested to overcome the subjectifying notion of player and the objectifying notion of games and play.

INTRODUCTION

Games and play have an increasingly significant role in many aspects of everyday life. Virtual computer and Internet-based games are very popular leisure time activities and hobbies enjoyed by children, youth, and adults; they also often include real possibilities for developing the methods used in teaching and

DOI: 10.4018/978-1-6684-7589-8.ch068

education, as well as specific work-related skills, management and leadership skills, sports skills, and so forth. It has become clear that games and play, overall, and especially computer- and Internet-based virtual games, are not merely entertainment or relaxing and enjoyable leisure time activities. Increasingly, they are a part of everyday work, learning, and personal development, and they have an impact on a variety of cognitive and embodied skills. Academic research has focused on this theme under the multidimensional concept of *gamification*. That concept has functioned well and has already become popular in academic discussions. In popular culture, gamification refers to a broad variety of practical interventions. The academic notion of gamification most often refers to the study and innovative development of gamifying practices that support and strengthen the practices of education or that enhance the effectiveness and well-being of daily work.

The concept of gamification emerged around 2010. Deterding (2011) defined it as "the use of game design elements in non-game contexts." Gamification includes elements of gamefulness, gameful interaction, and gameful design. Gamefulness refers to a player's lived experience, gameful interaction refers to the objects, tools, and contexts related to the experience of gamefulness, and gameful design consists of the practice of crafting a gameful experience. While the definitions and features of gamification have been criticized, the term has emerged as being related to the concepts of games (Seaborn & Fels, 2015). Gamification aims to apply features of games to real world contexts by using motivational factors (Deterding, 2011; Hamari, Koivisto, & Sarsa, 2014; Zichermann, 2011). This brings new elements to ordinary social situations, and makes them interesting, motivating, and entertaining in a different way (Seaborn & Fels, 2015; Johnson, et al., 2016). Sometimes it seems as if a game immerses its audience in the experience of playing it, and it keeps players in its bubble or in a "motivational pull" (Ryan, Rigby, & Przybylski, 2006). The people around the players may experience opposite feelings, such as worry, especially in relation to the young children who are playing the game (Ferguson & Colwell, 2016; Alehdet, 2018).

In terms of its practical emphasis and focus, the specific meaning of gamification is not always clear, at least from the scientific and philosophical perspective. Thus, there is a constant need to discuss the phenomenon of gamification and its core question of what is meant by the terms game and play. What is the actual essence or nature of the game and of play, itself? In this respect, empirical studies on gamification, which often aim at developing valuable interventions to enhance human skills or social interactions, always require theoretical and philosophical thematization of the concept.

In terms of its research design, this article applies an important theoretical perspective and utilizes a practical intervention (a case study) to investigate games and play, which are now fundamentally seen as playing a mediative role between virtual reality and the real world and that are an inextricable part of everyday life, including leisure time and work. This research design was used for two reasons. First, by using a philosophically-oriented conceptual discussion it is possible to address some important aspects when addressing and applying the notion of games and play in academic research. Second, from this theoretical perspective, the article proposes one possible empirical setting through which it seems to be possible to simultaneously study the phenomenon of virtual play and games in action, and, from this basis, to study the mediative role of virtual playing, or its relationship to real exercise or hobbies. The meta-theoretical intention of this paper is to offer a critical alternative for the traditional objectifying ideas of games and the notion of play, and to critically address the common view of playing, which has been broadly perceived as a subjective activity. This will shed light on the shared view that play and playing function immersively, as if constituting a playfulness "bubble". Using phenomenological hermeneutics, this article attempts to explicate what these phrases actually mean. It is possible to argue that the activity or agency of an individual subject who plays a game does not embody the essence of gamification; rather, gamification consists of the more complex world and universe of the game and play itself that are played by the participants. Metaphorically, it could be said that it is not primarily the subject who plays the game according to its rules (and purposes) but play itself, and its continuously constituted rules, that becomes real (presented) through the responding activity of the participants (world worlds [welt weltet] and play plays through us). This phenomenological perspective, which bridges the gap between the dualistic distinction between the game/play and the player, also offers more fundamental ground for fruitful conceptual distinctions, such as regulative and constitutive rules.

In this respect, this article aims to participate in the discussion about revising the research paradigm of gamification (within management, leadership, and leadership psychology studies).

BACKGROUND

The theoretical framework and conceptual perspective of the research design is the general notions of game and gamification within leadership studies and their critical analysis through the philosophical notions of play and games found in phenomenological hermeneutics. Because the notion of gamification has traditionally been built upon Immanuel Kant's philosophy, the notion of play, as well as the agency/subjectivity of play, has become subjectivized. Thus, the game, itself, has been conceived as an objective distinct entity with its own plane/structure and rules. An individual user (player) has been emphasized as the core active subject who plays the game. Lately, this theoretical perspective has been challenged by the more phenomenological notion of games, play, and subjectivity, especially in reference to Hans-George Gadamer's (2003) notion of play and playing thematized in his magnum opus *Truth and Method*. Gadamer (2003) relied on traditional phenomenology, and especially on Heidegger's idea of being-in-the-world (In-der-Welt-Sein), and the continuous process of understanding (verstand) through which his main intentions are to deconstruct the solipsistic subjectivity, agency, and to also see the game as being an intersubjectively constituted event. Thus, the main themes in the Gadamerian view of gamification are the problem of subjectivization and the un-subjectifying perspective in relation to games and the event of playing. This article relies on the Gadamerian notion of games, play, and playing, and it tries to elaborate that concept for general use in studies on gamification.

This article addresses a broader notion of games and play from the perspective of phenomenological hermeneutics in relation to discussions about gamification within leadership studies (Harter, 2012; Perryer, Celestine, Scott-Ladd, & Leighton, 2016; Cebulski, 2017; Goryunova & Jenkins, 2017). Thus, it is important to clarify and define the concepts of virtual-based playing, games, and play. It is also necessary to clearly identify the essence and fundamental character of social interaction, which plays a crucial role both in virtual- and Internet-based playing and in a real exercise or hobby. The article also addresses the role that social interaction plays in virtual games and it discusses the significance of inter-subjectivity in playing. With respect to the upcoming empirical case study discussed in this article, the main questions are: How does the digital-virtual plane of the game interact with real practical playing (ice hockey)? What role does virtual imaginative playing take in the experience of participating in the real exercise? The hypothesis is that playing in the digitalized virtual plane is not fully distinct from the temporal significance of the experience as it continues and expands through imaginative capability in the sphere of real-world, practical exercise and playing.

Games can be categorized in different ways, including role-playing games and strategy games. Gadamer (2003) uses the concepts of representative and non-representative games in which the subjectivist meaning of the term, play, is theorized at the meta level. Generally, the game theory approach consists of several theories, such as the Nash solution and the prisoner's dilemma (McAdams, 2014). These theories can be applied to different situations with their own theoretical concepts and rules about a solution for a game (Davis & Brams, 2018). The term, game, is idealized as a collective action that has a mathematic design. Players affect the final outcome of the game according to their interests. The interests are formed by the payoffs as a result of the outcomes. If the outcomes between the players' payoffs are similar, this can convey cooperation. Otherwise, differences could end in conflicts.

Most social situations are similar to situations in the game, including cooperation and conflict. Game theory contains different scenarios about behavior to interpret these kinds of situations (Carmichael, 2005). The players' strategies depend on the information they have. Games can be simply categorized as having complete or incomplete information. In a game with complete information, all the players know their own position and what kinds of agents are involved in the game (Davis & Brams, 2018). In a game with incomplete information, such as asymmetric information, the players either do not know each other's utility functions or the information could change during the game. Game theory offers a tool to observe and examine the meaning, causes, and consequences of a virtual game. Seaborn and Fels (2015) noted that rules, structure, voluntariness, uncertain outcome, conflict, representation, and resolution are the common features of a game. Together, they form a variety of combinations for games.

The results of the negative effects of video games are controversial (Ryan, Rigby, & Przybylski, 2006; Ferguson & Colwell, 2016). The common understanding is that violent video games do not cause violent behavior in children; they are only one reason or one of many reasons for that type of behavior (Ferguson & Colwell, 2016). Several other factors have an impact on violent behavior. National authorities and media have provided parents with recommendations for how often children should play video games, and what types of games are appropriate for them to play. According to one of these recommendations, a child should regularly engage in some kind of physical activity at school or participate in a sport in which he/she can have face-to-face encounters with other children instead of digital encounters or virtual encounters on the Internet (A-lehdet, 2018). Ferguson and Colwell's (2016) research results showed that playing a violent game did not correlate significantly with either antisocial or civic behaviors or attitudes. Their study showed that violent video games might only have a minimal relationship with adolescent behavior.

Virtual games may also have a positive impact on children's activities (Mäyrä, Karvinen, & Ermi, 2016). Studies on the positive effects of virtual games have shown that perceived in-game autonomy and competence are associated with game enjoyment, preferences, and changes in well-being pre-to-post-play. Moreover, they are related to the intuitive nature of game controls and the sense of presence or immersion in the participants' game play experiences (Ryan et al., 2006).The results of Kovess-Masfety et al.'s (2016) large study showed that, during one week, over five hours of video game playing was significantly associated with higher intellectual functioning, increased academic achievement, a lower prevalence of peer relationship problems, and a lower prevalence of mental health difficulties. While the effects of playing video games could be positive, more investigation is needed to understand the mechanisms of video games that stimulate children (Kovess-Masfety et al., 2016). Ray et al.'s (2017) results have shown that the tasks of working memory and perceptual discrimination related to learning improved both in an action game and in a strategy game. Playing strategy games resulted in better performance on memory tasks, while playing action games, which stimulate the limbic area of the brain and affect emotions, might be useful for children with mood disorders (Ray et al., 2017). The effects of non-active video games on children's physical activity and psychosocial behavior need to be further researched (Baranowski, Baranowski, Thompson, & Buday, 2011). For example, added reality is an area of research that has not been fully investigated. Studies on game theory may reveal results that expand our perception of a child's virtual world and real world. Previous research has demonstrated a lack of knowledge about virtual games as an expansion of the real world.

GADAMER'S NOTION OF PLAY

Hans-George Gadamer was schooled in the neo-Kantia tradition, but he was later captivated by the promise of the phenomenological approach of Edmund Husserl and Martin Heidegger. In the field of philosophy, Gadamer became famous mainly due to his book, *Warheit und Methode* (*Truth and Method*), which was first published in 1960 (Moran & Mooney, 2004). Later, the phenomenological spirit of Gadamer's writings signified a holistic grasp of human situatedness within the lived cultural-historical world basically in a way that was similar to how his teacher and colleague, Heidegger, had thematized it in *Being and Time*, published in 1927, through the concept of Dasein and being-in-the-world. According to Moran and Mooney (2004, p. 311), in *Truth and Method* Gadamer (2003) argued "for the general point that we can talk of the truth of art and of cultural products in a genuine sense; not all truth is encaptulated in scientific method." Because Heiddeger's main intention was to thematize the question of understanding of being (Seinsverstandnis), and thus human existence, a new a-metaphysically—which signified a phenomenological grasp of historicity, subjectivity, and being-in-the-world (hermeneutics of facticity)—Gadamer shifted the Heideggerian phenomenological stance towards the question of historical understanding and the method used in humanistic sciences. This signified a new approach to human historicity and the hermeneutic method, which overcame the subjectivist notion of man and the objectivistic approach to history and human culture and artifacts. Toward that end, Gadamer presented his analysis of the aesthetic experience of art as a heuristic phenomenological view on the process of understanding, as such, which became crucially important in historical research and in explaining the meaning of human experience. Within this analysis Gadamer elaborated upon his phenomenological notion of games and play as components of the core of aesthetic experience and historical understanding.

In this context, it is important to ask how Gadamer defined the phenomenon of play and to determine if his definition could be applicable to the present day discussion about gamification. Gadamer (2003, pp. 101–134) discussed several aspects of the phenomenon of play: play as the mode of being that intertwines the game and the player, the unique kind of seriousness of play, play as an interpretation and fusion of horizons, and play as self-representation. This section will address the aspects of Gadamer's analysis that are important to the discussion about gamification. As will be seen later, Gadamer's notions of games and play are also applicable to the context of gamification.

Gadamer based his analysis on Heidegger's insight in *Being and Time* (1927, pp. 32–34), which posits that understanding (Verstehen) is the central mode of humans 'being-in-the-world', a world encountered and inhabited in and through language (Moran & Mooney, 2004, p. 311). For Heidegger, understanding is not merely a subjectivist cognitive faculty of humans; more fundamentally, it is the existential-ontological structure of human existence. According to Heidegger, understanding is the main existential-ontological structure of the revealedness of being-in-the-world, similar to mood (befindlickeit der stimmung) and language; when humans find themselves in the world they have "always already" viewed their embodied intentional relation to the world and their entire existence through understanding. Heidegger's hermeneutics of facticity states that understanding and continuous interpretation is a fundamental structure of a human being's orientation towards the world and the future. For Gadamer, hermeneutics signified this ongoing, never completely achieved process of understanding due to human finitude and human 'linguisticality' (Sprachlichkeit). As Gadamer (2003, p. 101) stated in *Truth and Method*, "language is the medium of the hermeneutic experience." Given this understanding of hermeneutics, for Gadamer, philosophy is an ongoing conversation that leads to mutual understanding (dialogue) in which phenomenology, and especially its focus on the experience of art, provides the best way to describe the experience of understanding (Moran & Mooney, 2004, p. 312).

Gadamer (2003, p. 101) stated that his intention was to free the concept of play from "the subjective meaning that it has in Kant and Schiller and that dominates the whole of modern aesthetics and philosophy of man." In addition to the subjectivist meaning of play as a process of interpretation and meaning, Gadamer addressed the traditional objectifying notion of understanding and a work of art. According to Gadamer (2003, p. 101), "aesthetic consciousness as something that confronts an object does not do justice to the real situation. This is why the concept of play is important in my exposition." Therefore, he saw a fruitful possibility in redefining the notion of play phenomenologically to provide a heuristic explanation of the continuous process of understanding and interpretation. Within the lived aesthetic experience of art, the work of art is not reducible to its objective constitutive aspects and structure, and the experiencing person or consciousness is not understood by his/her knowledge, capability of interpretation, etc. What the work of art actually *is* becomes revealed in the phenomenon of the flow and play of meanings in a person's genuine encounter with the work of art. Thus, the work of art—not the person viewing the art— redefines the meanings of the encounter. The meanings evoked by the work of art in experiencing subjectivity are always based on the unique situation and approach of the person who experiences the art; furthermore, this prejudicial starting point will be overcome by the new meanings made possible by the temporally continuous process of encounter with the art. This hermeneutic process of interpretation and understanding holistically reveals the meanings of the world anew and the experiencing person; thus, the self is revealed anew in an event of aesthetic experience. What is ontologically significant to note here is that within the aesthetic experience the work of art is essentially seen as a phenomenon of play, which deconstructs the dichotomy between the experiencing subject and the work of art. In other words, the work of art intertwines the subject and the object. The play of the constitution of meanings in the hermeneutic experience of art is philosophically based on the phenomenon that Heidegger described in *Being and Time* (vorhabe, vorsicht, vorgriff), which is generally known as a hermeneutic circle. In the wider context of historical interpretation, Gadamer's analysis highlights that understanding and interpretation always begin within the tradition; thus, they include prejudice (vorurteil) as a natural starting point. Prejudice is not a problem; rather, it is a necessary and positive starting point for genuine understanding and interpretation. Prejudice is the historical everyday being-in-the-world (Gadamer, 2003) upon which all understanding is grounded. Without an individual's unique, local lingual cultural-historical world, there is no possibility of beginning to achieve a "better-understanding". Constitutive play of the meanings starts from and individual's unique and locally-lived world.

Even though play is commonly conceived as an attitude and notion that is the antithesis of seriousness, Gadamer (2003, p. 102) emphasized that play—whether one thinks of the aesthetic experience, children playing with toys or any imaginable event of play—has its own kind of seriousness. He referred to Aristotle's idea of play as being essentially "recreation." According to Gadamer, the seriousness associated with play is sacred, which seems to be connected to the recreational aspect and significance of play itself, and the reflective distance that play enables within the everyday world. Gadamer (2003, p. 102) wrote: "Yet, in playing, all those purposive relations that determine active and caring existence have not simply disappeared, but are curiously suspended." Thus, play functions in the everyday world as a natural occurrence of phenomenological reduction. Therefore, it is possible to think of the developmental and educative significance of playing—playing as well as the experience of art actually serves as a reflective distance to one's own existence and the more communal and social existence. (A temporary suspension of the real is actually an initial condition for what is "possible" and, thus, applicable to recreation.)

However, in addition to its seriousness, play, "exists in a world determined by the seriousness of purposes" (Gadamer, 2003, p. 102). It is precisely the intentional attitude of playing within which a player "loses himself in play" and play fulfil its purpose (Gadamer, 2003, p. 102). "Seriousness is not merely something that calls us away from play; rather, seriousness in playing is necessary to make play a wholly play". Gadamer (2003) noted that a person who does not take play seriously is a spoilsport.

According to Gadamer (2003, p. 102), "the mode of being of play does not allow the player to behave toward play as if toward an object." A player knows that play is "only a game"; however, he does not know what exactly he 'knows' in knowing that". These lines from Gadamer make it clear why it is impossible to sharply distinguish between "virtual" and "real" spheres within the lived experience (they are intertwined). Gadamer seems to think about the phenomenon of being absorbed into play, the player's unobjectifying intentional relation to play. From an ontological perspective, the meaning of play cannot be revealed by examining the player's subjective reflectivity. It can only be understood by carefully studying the mode of play and playing as a whole. Gadamer (2003, p. 102) stated that the object of the examination must be "the experience (Erfahrung) of art and thus the question of the mode of being of the work of art." The present study adopts Gadamer's perspective by stating that the mode of being of the game (and play) is the object of the research.

What is radical in Gadamer's view is that it turns the relationship between the game and the player around, and it deconstructs the subjective agency of the player in order to emphasize the *event* and phenomenon of play. As Gadamer (2003) noted: "Instead the work of art has its true being in the fact that it becomes an experience that changes the person who experiences it. The 'subject' of the experience of art, that which remains and endures, is not the subjectivity of the person who experiences it but the work itself. For play has its own essence, independent of the consciousness of those who play. The players are not the subjects of play; instead play merely reaches presentation (Darstellung) through the players".

Gadamer (2003, p. 103) also noted that: "The movement of playing has no goal that brings it to an end; rather, it renews itself in constant repetition. The movement backward and forward is obviously so central to the definition of play that it makes no difference who or what performs this movement".

According to Gadamer (2003, p. 103), play is the occurrence of movement; to exemplify that he noted the general play of colors. Play does not require someone to behave in a playful manner. "Rather, the primordial sense of playing is the medial one. Thus, we say that something is 'playing' (spielt) somewhere or at some time, that something is going on (im Spiele ist) or that something is happening (sich abspielt)". From this linguistic observation, Gadamer (2003, p. 104) concluded that "play is not to be understood as something a person does." He noted that the actual subject of play is not the subjectivity of an individual who, among other activities, also plays. Instead, the subject of play is play itself. Gadamer (2003,) tried to emphasize the independent essence of a play by also deconstructing the agency of subjectivity; he wrote: "It is part of the play that the movement is not only without goal or purpose but also without effort. It happens, as it were, by itself." This fundamental dwelling in the game or spirit of play is based on the phenomenon of being immersed in the sphere of play. "The structure of play absorbs the player into itself, and thus frees him from the burden of taking the initiative, which constitutes the actual strain of existence". In this sense, playing is not primarily an activity of an individual but a way of being actualized within the game and within the experience of play. This relative emphasis on passivity does not exclude the significance of individual playing, which always happens in response to another player or a behavior, action or event to which one can respond:

In order for there to be a game, there always has to be, not necessarily literally another player, but something else with which the player plays, and which automatically responds to his move with countermove. Thus, the cat at play chooses the ball of wool because it responds to play, and ball games will be with us forever because the ball is freely mobile in every direction, appearing to do surprising things of its own accord (Gadamer, 2003, p. 106).

The attractiveness of play depends on how it challenges the players, which, in turn, reveals how play itself is the subject of the game/play. As Gadamer (2003) noted: "This suggests general characteristics of the nature of play that is reflected in playing: all playing is a being-played. The attraction of a game, the fascination it exerts, consists precisely in the fact that the game masters the players. Even in the case of games in which one tries to perform tasks that one has set oneself, there is a risk that they will not 'work,' 'succeed,' or 'succeed again,' which is the attraction of the game. Whoever 'tries' is in fact the one who is tried. The real subject of the game (…) is not the player but instead the game itself. What holds the player in its spell, draws him into play, and keeps him there is the game itself".

It is important to overcome the subjectivist notion of play as well as its psychologized interpretations. Gadamer (2003, p. 107) wrote: "Apart from these general determining factors, it seems to me that the characteristics of human play indicate that a player plays *something*." This means that the "choice" and the will to play are more than doing something else. Gadamer (2003) stated: "Thus the child gives itself a task in playing with a ball, and such tasks are playful ones because the purpose of the game is not really solving the task, but ordering and shaping the movement of the game itself".

When the structures and rules of a game are too strict, the actualization of play is limited. While play limits itself to self-representation, self-presentation is the "universal ontological characteristic of nature" (Gadamer, 2003, p. 108). Therefore, Gadamer (2003) stated that: "Only because play is always presentation is human play able to make representation itself a task of a game. Thus, there are games which must be called representation games, either because, in their use of meaningful allusion, they have something about them of representation (say "Thinker, Tailor, Soldier, Sailor") or because the game itself consists in representing something (e.g., when children play cars)".

Every game has its own spirit. "This point shows the importance of defining play as a process that takes place 'in between'" (Gadamer, 2003, pp. 106–107). This implies that Gadamer (2003, p. 109) sees play as a fundamental social dwelling. Gadamer (2003) wrote: "We have seen that play does not have its being in the player's consciousness or attitude, but on the contrary play draws him into its domination and fills him with its spirit. The player experiences the game as a reality that surpasses him".

In summary, in the present study, Gadamer's notion of play is used to investigate the essence and fundamental character of social interaction, which plays a crucial role both in virtual- and Internet-based playing and a real-world exercise or hobby (ice hockey). Toward that end, this study aims to answer two questions: How does the digital-virtual plane of the game interact with real-world practical playing? What kind of a role does virtual imaginative playing take in the experience of a real-world exercise? The study hypothesizes that playing in the digitalized virtual plane is not fully distinct from the temporal significance of the experience as it continues and expands through imaginative capability in real-world practical exercise and play. The research phenomenon is examined through phenomenological hermeneutics to determine what these phrases actually refer to.

METHODS

Data for the study are collected using the case study method (Eriksson & Koistinen, 2005; Yin, 2014). The study participants consist of six to eight players, all of whom are 10 to 11-year-old boys. They regularly play ice hockey on the same team. The team aims to play at the competitive level of ice hockey in their age category. The physical demands for competitive sports are increasing every year. On the one hand, ice hockey is a team sport; on the other hand, players have clear individual roles in the game, such as attackers, defenders, and the goalkeeper. Usually, there is a good atmosphere among athletes in team sports, and the players are close. However, communication can vary based on usual social interactions (for example, similar to how a circle of friends interact when engaged in leisure time activities) (Uronen, 2003). The hockey players play intensely on their team. They meet several times each week and practice approximately 1–2 hours each time. They also play virtual games with each other about 3–4 times a week. In the present study, all of the team members also play virtual games at home against other players. The participants chosen NHL and Formula 1 games that they play on PlayStation. Data collection are carried out by videotaping one game or several games and recording the players' conversations during the game. The games and the players' conversations are saved to the PlayStation application. The data are analyzed using two different methods. The games are observed via videos and the players' conversations are qualitatively categorized using the NVivo software program. NVivo allows content analysis of the audio material from the tape without literation. Tones of voices, pauses, and ways of speaking are analyzed at the same time. The results of the analysis are investigated in further phase of this study according to the research design. In this article, the theoretical framework was determined and presented including the research phenomenon.

DISCUSSION: PLAY AS CONTINUOUS INTERPRETATION AND THE FUSION OF HORIZON

Regarding the present study's aims, Gadamer's (2003) approach to deconstructing the subjectivist notion of play and the objectifying notion of game is important: "When we speak of play in reference to the experience of art, this means neither the orientation nor even the state of mind of the creator or of those enjoying the work of art, nor the freedom of a subjectivity engaged in play, but the mode of being of the work of art itself."

In a similar way, it is possible to think of the mode of being of the game and playing the game itself. Instead of focusing on the outer characteristics, the type of games or the set of rules and possibilities of the game, the present study focused on the actual event or process that constitutes the essence of the game in the actual event or the process that constitutes the essence of game in the act of playing it. In turn, this study investigates how the experience of the game feels for the players. Thus, it is clear from the start that this study does not merely focus on the experience of a player (subject) or the structure and qualities of the game; rather, it focuses on the relationship between the player and game, which fundamentally constitutes the "how" of their being (mode and identity).

CONCLUSION

In conclusion, the hermeneutics of play, playing, and virtuality were defined by Hans-Georg Gadamer (2003). His analysis of the notion of play and playing in *Truth and Method* belongs to a broader context within which he elaborated upon his theory and the method used in humanistic sciences. Gadamer's philosophy relies strongly on Martin Heidegger's (1927) phenomenological hermeneutics (*Being and Time*). In regard to the notion of play and playing, Gadamer analyzed aesthetic consciousness and experience as an essential phenomenon to show how the experience of art functions as a heuristic example to overcome the subjectivistic notion of the aesthetic experience and the objectifying interpretation of a work of art. His main intention was to show how the work of art escapes the objectifying gaze and interpretation, and how the lived aesthetic experience deconstructs the misleading categorical distinction between the work of art and the experiencing subject. In the experience of art, the distinction between the experience and the experienced is overcome; the interpretative activity of the experiencer is not that of the subjectivity of the person having an experience, rather it is the activity of the work of art itself. Thus, Gadamer argued that the subject of art is not a human being, but the art itself. The event of experiencing a work of art is something that overcomes the experiencing subjectivity and deconstructs the identity of the subject and the whole world around it. Thus, it is the play of the meanings of art that envelops the interpretative subjectivity of the human being into the "world" or sphere of the work of art, and simultaneously reveals the world and the human in a new light or meaningful relationship. What art actually does for humans and the world is the proper ontological essence of play.

Furthermore, through this article's discussion and analysis, it seems plausible to interpret that the notion of aesthetic experience as play in the experience of art drawn by Gadamer is relatively applicable – if not analogical – to the experience of play in a gamified context of a virtual video game or other similar game. What is crucial is that the experience of play overcomes the solus ipse, the individual subjectivity and playing agency, and it deconstructs the identity of the players as well as the dichotomy between the game and the players within the experience of the game. Therefore, in this analysis, the notions of play and playing are approached in a phenomenological hermeneutic way that offers an alternative unobjectifying understanding of play and the game and an un-subjectivized interpretation of the player as experiencing "agency" while playing the game.

The phenomenological approach offers an alternative perspective to the practical and instrumental discussion about gamification. A more fundamental discussion about the phenomenon of play and the mode of being of the game is always needed because both are integral to human existence. Phenomenological perspective also enables us to see how virtual imaginative playing is ontologically related to non-virtual or real-world practical exercise or play, and furthermore, what is the holistic meaning of virtual to the real.

REFERENCES

A-lehdet. (2018, June 8). *Millaisia haittavaikutuksia videopeleillä on nuoriin?* Retrieved from http://www.terve.fi

Baranowski, T., Baranowski, J., Thompson, D., & Buday, R. (2011). Behavioral science in video games for children's diet and physical activity change: Key research needs. *Journal of Diabetes Science and Technology, 5*(2), 229–233. doi:10.1177/193229681100500204 PMID:21527086

Carmichael, F. (2005). *A guide to game theory*. Essex, UK: Pearson Education.

Cebulski, A. R. (2017). Utilizing gamification to foster leadership competency development. *New Directions for Student Leadership,* (156). doi:. doi:10.1002/yd.20272

Davis, M. D., & Brams, S.J. (2018, May 28). *Game theory*. Retrieved from http://www.britannica.com/game theory/mathematics

Deterding, S. (2011). Situated motivational affordances of game elements: a conceptual model. In *Gamification: Using Game Design Elements in Non-gaming Contexts, a Workshop at CHI*. Retrieved from http://www.quilageo.com/wp-content/uploads/2013/07/09-Deterding.pdf

Eriksson, P., & Koistinen, K. (2005). *Monenlainen tapaustutkimus*. Helsinki: Kuluttajantutkimuskeskus.

Ferguson, C. J., & Colwell, J. (2016). A meaner, more callous digital world for youth? The relationship between violent digital games, motivation, bullying, and civic behavior among children. *Psychology of Popular Media Culture, 18*(July). doi:10.1037/ppm0000128

Gadamer, H. G. (2003). *Truth and method* (Revised ed.) (J. Weinsheimer & D. G. Marshall, Trans.). New York: Continuum.

Goryunova, E., & Jenkins, D. M. (2017). Global leadership education: Upping the Game. *Journal of Leadership Education, 16*(October), 76–93. doi:10.12806/V16/I4/A1

Hamari, J., Koivisto, J., & Sarsa, H. (2014). Does Gamification Work? - A Literature Review of Empirical Studies on Gamification. In *47th Hawaii International Conference on System Science* (pp. 3025–3034). Waikoloa, HI: IEEE Computer Society.

Harter, N. (2012). Point of view: Leadership studies from different perspectives. *Journal of Leadership Education, 11*(2), 158–175. doi:10.12806/V11/I2/TF1

Johnson, D., Deterding, S., Kuhn, K.-A., Staneva, A., Stoyanov, S., & Hides, L. (2016). Gamification for health and wellbeing: A systematic review of literature. *Internet Interventions, 6*, 89–106. doi:10.1016/j.invent.2016.10.002 PMID:30135818

Kovess-Masfety, V., Keyes, K., Hamilton, A., Hanson, G., Bitfoi, A., Golitz, D., ... Pez, O. (2016). Is time spent playing video games associated with mental health, cognitive and social skills in young children? *Social Psychiatry and Psychiatric Epidemiology, 51*(3), 349–357. doi:10.100700127-016-1179-6 PMID:26846228

Mäyrä, F., Karvinen, J., & Ermi, L. (2016). *Pelaajabarometri 2015. TRIM Research Reports 21*. Tampere: Tampereen yliopisto.

McAdams, D. (2014). *Game-changer: game theory and the art of transforming strategic situations*. New York: W.W. Norton & Company.

Moran, D., & Mooney, T. (2004). Hans-Georg Gadamer - Introduction. In *The phenomenology reader* (pp. 311–313). London: Routledge.

Perryer, C., Celestine, N. A., Scott-Ladd, B., & Leighton, C. (2016). Enhancing workplace motivation through gamification: Transferrable lessons from pedagogy. *International Journal of Management Education*, *14*(3), 327–335. doi:10.1016/j.ijme.2016.07.001

Ray, N. R., O'Connell, M. A., Kaoru, N., Smith, E. T., Qin, S., & Basak, C. (2017). Evaluating the relationship between white matter integrity, cognition, and varieties of video game learning. *Restorative Neurology and Neuroscience*, *35*(5), 437–456. doi:10.3233/RNN-160716 PMID:28968249

Ryan, R. M., Rigby, C. S., & Przybylski, A. (2006). The motivational pull of video games: A self-determination theory approach. *Motivation and Emotion*, *30*(4), 344–360. doi:10.100711031-006-9051-8

Seaborn, K., & Fels, D. I. (2015). Gamification in theory and action: A survey. *International Journal of Human-Computer Studies*, *74*, 14–31. doi:10.1016/j.ijhcs.2014.09.006

Uronen, V. (2003). *Juniorijalkapalloilijoiden fyysinen aktiivisuus, urheilumotiivit ja kaverisuhteet kahden vuoden aikana*. Jyväskylä: Liikunnan ja kansanterveyden edistämissäätiö.

Yin, R. K. (2014). *Case study research: Design and methods*. Thousand Oaks, CA: Sage.

Zichermann, G. (2011, October 27). Intrinsic and Extrinsic Motivation in Gamification. *Gamification*. Retrieved from http://www.gamification.co/2011/10/27/intrinsic-and-extrinsic-motivation-in-gamification/

This research was previously published in the International Journal of Innovation in the Digital Economy (IJIDE), 10(3); pages 13-23, copyright year 2019 by IGI Publishing (an imprint of IGI Global).

Chapter 69
Playing With the Dead:
Transmedia Narratives and the Walking Dead Games

Iain Donald
Abertay University, UK

Hailey J. Austin
University of Dundee, UK

ABSTRACT

This chapter discusses the theory and practice of transmedia narratives within the storyworld created by Robert Kirkman, Tony Moore and Charlie Adlard's comics series The Walking Dead. It examines key aspects from the comics series and AMC's adaptive television franchise to consider how both have been utilized and adapted for games. Particular focus will be paid to Telltale Games' The Walking Dead, Gamagio's The Walking Dead Assault and Terminal Reality's The Walking Dead: Survival Instinct. The chapter explains the core concepts of transmedia narratives as they relate to The Walking Dead, places the games in the context of both the comics and television franchise, examines the significance of commercial and grassroot extensions and considers the role gaming and interactive narratives have within rich storyworlds. In examining The Walking Dead as a transmedia property, the authors demonstrate how vast narratives are adopted, modified and transformed in contemporary popular culture.

INTRODUCTION

This chapter will discuss the theory and practice of vast transmedia narratives focusing on the storyworld created by Robert Kirkman, Tony Moore and Charlie Adlard's comics series *The Walking Dead* and adapted by the AMC television series of the same name. The overall aim will be to examine key aspects from the comics series, with the television franchise and consider how both have been utilized and adopted for analogue and digital games. Particular focus will be paid to Telltale Games *The Walking Dead* (2012), Gamagio's *The Walking Dead Assault* (2012) and Terminal Reality's *The Walking*

DOI: 10.4018/978-1-6684-7589-8.ch069

Dead: *Survival Instinct* (2013). The chapter will explain the core concepts of transmedia narratives as they relate to *The Walking Dead*, place the games in the context of both the comics series and the television franchise, examine the significance of commercial and grassroots extensions and consider the role that gaming and interactive narratives have within rich storyworlds. In order to do so, the authors will examine key moments/characterizations and assess the extent to which they are depicted across different media. In examining *The Walking Dead* as a transmedia property, the authors will demonstrate how vast narratives are adopted, modified and transformed in contemporary popular culture. They will explain the core concepts of transmedia storytelling across media delivery channels, and consider how these vast narratives are created and modified. Finally, the authors will explore the creation process of these experiences, and highlight how there is an increasing reliance on user discovery, participation, and collaboration that blurs the distinction between producer and consumer.

The concept of transmedia storytelling itself is not a new one and the entertainment industry has a long history of developing licensed products across multiple media channels (Mittell, 2012). However, this often took the form of reproducing the same stories across different media formats. Films have always utilized fiction and non-fiction, and subsequently encouraged novelization where the source was not already published. With the increasing utilization of digital streaming and online content by broadcast media, the ground has shifted again. There are now multiple channels for delivering content and this expansion has coincided with an increasing array of tools allowing fans to participate in the storyworld. The acceptance of fan culture and increasing development of commercial and grassroots extensions to the original storyworld has resulted in a resurgence of story elements being conveyed systematically across multiple media platforms, each making their own unique contribution to the whole. *The Walking Dead,* with its roots in the comic book and commercial success of the television series, has now developed numerous videogames and other media in order to interact with the fan base. As a whole, *The Walking Dead* lends itself to the exploration of transmedial worlds, but the games allow an immersive experience not found in comics or television. Games can occupy the space between the linear storytelling of established canon and new expressions within the storyworld. Fundamentally they allow fans to play within the constructed universe but also open up the possibilities of the canon, allowing the player more control over the characters they portray or interact with and the narratives that they wish to explore.

BACKGROUND

Transmedia

Over the past decade, the multitude of media platforms and the accessibility of creating content has resulted in a resurgence in the popularity of transmedia storytelling. The concept of transmedia storytelling itself is not a new one and the entertainment industry has a long history of developing licensed products across multiple media channels. Previously this often took the form of reproducing the same stories across different media formats with prohibitive licensing agreements. Increasingly the control of the story has become less restrictive and the actuality of transmedia has gained significant traction in both the media industries and in academic circles. Henry Jenkins (2007) has defined 'transmedia storytelling' as:

...a process where integral elements of a fiction get dispersed systematically across multiple delivery channels for the purpose of creating a unified and coordinated entertainment experience. Ideally, each medium makes its own unique contribution to the unfolding of the story.

Transmedia storytelling necessitates the creation of 'vast narratives'. These can be recognized partly by their sustaining of open-ended narratives over long periods of time, and the creation of narrative universes across media relying less on one form being considered 'canonical' but on all elements functioning as part of a vast fictional quilt (Harrigan and Wardrup-Fruin, 2009). It is now possible for these vast narratives and distributed worlds to harness fans' encyclopedic impulses, encouraging them to journey across media channels in an attempt to completely know an imaginary world or story. Ultimately this proves impossible; for as transmedia experiences expand, 'gaps' open up in their fictional worlds that create spaces for creative participation by their intended 'audience'. Networked technology transforms consumers into producers who can then add and change meaning in these worlds more easily than ever. Through fan-fiction, machinima, game mods (modifications), social media and many other forms, what was once termed 'the audience' has turned co-creator, constantly evolving and growing fictional universes through grassroots participation. For today's audiences, transmedia storytelling is not only expected to be facilitated by 'media convergence' (Jenkins 2006) but also participatory (Rose, 2012) where fans can synergize with the brand (Jenkins, 2013).

User-Generated Content and Fandom

Indeed, part of the fundamental makeup of a transmedia storyworld is the accessibility of the world to the fanbase or fandom. According to Jenkins (2007), fandom is the active participation of users in the expansive process of the canon. Max Giovagnoli (2011) posits that, keeping in mind the foundational narrative as defined by Brenda Laurel (2004), the basic element of fandoms includes narrative voluntarism, strict internal rules (narratively, but also within keeping a brand image), anonymous and explicit testing, and opposition to external aggregation. Developing multiple extensions both commercially and through grassroots encourages the fanbase to expand and maintain an active interest in the storyworld while also deepening engagement through participation. For Lisbeth Klastrup and Susana Tosca (2004), what characterizes a transmedial world is that "audience and designers share a mental image of the 'worldness' (a number of distinguishing features of its universe)." However, alongside the need to share an image of the storyworld, is the need for the fans to create their own content. Jenkins has explained the correlation between transmedia storytelling and fan fiction as:

Fan fiction can be seen as an unauthorized expansion of these media franchises into new directions which reflect the reader's desire to 'fill in the gaps' they have discovered in the commercially produced material (Jenkins, 2007).

While the storyworld is agreed upon, often the storyline or vagueness of the story is not. Thus, fans create their own versions of what happened or what they believe could happen within the constraints of both the storyworld as well as the fandom itself. According to Giovagnoli (2011), fandom generated content (such as fanfiction, short films, cartoons and graphics) is the largest area in the creation of new transmedia narratives. Fundamental to their success is the use of open source publishing platforms, such as Tumblr, YouTube, Reddit or DeviantArt, which enables their fandom quick and easy access to the created content.

Storyworld and Canon

The Walking Dead storyworld has become increasingly accessible, composed of the universe created in the comics and expanded by the television series. Now populated with commercial extensions from additional TV spin-offs, videogames, mobile applications, board games, and novels all overseen or produced by Robert Kirkman. However, due to the differences between the storyline and characters in the comics and the television series, there has become a distinct separation between two canons. According to Julie Sanders (2006), "Adaptation both appears to require and to perpetuate the existence of canon, although it may in turn contribute to its ongoing reformulation and expansion." In this regard, AMC's *The Walking Dead* becomes an adaptation through which the storyworld's canon becomes convoluted. While the television series attempts to expand upon the original canonical universe, it simultaneously creates a canon of its own that perpetuates other transmedial expansions. The videogames, board games, mobile apps and novels must choose, then, between falling in line with the original canon of the comics or the newly adapted canon of the television series. Table 1 gives an overview of the number of new commercial extensions based upon the license holder and the year.

Table 1. Commercial Extensions and Licensor

Year	Total Commercial Extensions	AMC	Skybound
2010	2	2	1
2011	6	4	2
2012	7	4	3
2013	8	3	5
2014	4	2	2
2015	6	3	3
2016	5	1	4
2017*	2	*0*	2
2018*	2	*Not Known*	2

* Currently Announced

However, the franchise has found ways other than transmedial output in which to engage the readers/viewers of *The Walking Dead*. Utilizing social media platforms, such as Facebook and Twitter, the franchise is able to engage and record the interest of the consumers. For example, the official *Walking Dead* television series' Facebook page has been liked by over 36 million people (*The Walking Dead AMC*, 2017a), while it's official Twitter account has over 6 million followers (*The Walking Dead*, 2017b). These accounts allow the creators to share exclusive content and events to their followers. The characters in the show also have their own unofficial accounts where fans can pose as their favorite characters and tweet or post things they believe the character would. Comparatively, the companion series *Fear the Walking Dead* launched in 2015 has been liked by 3 million people on Facebook (*Fear the Walking Dead*, 2017) and has just over 250,000 followers on Twitter (*Fear TWD*, 2017). With regards to the games and their popularity, by 2015 Telltale announced they had sold some 44 million episodes and won over 90 Game of the Year awards. The success of the television series as well as the game establishes the universe as a cultural phenomenon. However, in order to understand how this success developed, the canon and its creation must be considered.

FLESHING OUT THE WALKING DEAD

Comics and Canons

Robert Kirkman, Tony Moore and Charlie Adlard's comics *The Walking Dead* (2003-present) follow Kentucky police officer Rick Grimes and his family as they meet other survivors and traverse rural and urban Georgia in an attempt to find food, shelter, and safety during the zombie apocalypse. The story arcs for each volume of the series show the survivors as they go from Atlanta, to a gated community, to a farm, to a prison, to a refuge town, and so on, in the hopes of finally finding a sustainable and safe place away from the 'walkers'. However, a major theme running across the comics is that the characters are forced from one place of refuge to another due to their human flaws, as opposed to the threat of the zombies or 'walkers'. Tensions build as Rick and others vie for a leadership position in the group, which leads to scheming, sex, and violence in nearly every issue.

Stylistically, the comics are drawn using a black and white color palette. This not only made *The Walking Dead* comics cheaper to produce, but also positioned the comics within and paid homage to the horror comics genre as well as the horror movie industry. One of the most dynamic parts unique to a comic book is the anticipation of the reader turning the page and being immediately surprised by what it reveals. *The Walking Dead* picks up on this and often builds tension on the right-hand page so that the reader is left questioning what will happen next and will turn the page. The comic book medium complicates the creation of horror, as it cannot rely on sound or jump scares, unlike film, television or videogames. Instead, *The Walking Dead* comics rely on a page turn to produce suspense and horror.

One of the most striking instances of this happens in the first issue after Rick wakes up in the hospital, an image that alludes to both Danny Boyle's *28 Days Later* (2002) as well as John Wyndham's classic *Day of the Triffids* (1951). After stumbling over a body in the elevator, the final panel of the comic page depicts Rick opening the doors to the cafeteria (Kirkman, 2003, Issue 1). Suspense and tension are created when the reader must physically turn the page in order to find out what happens next. Once they do, the design of the following splash page creates surprise, immersiveness, and horror. The lines created by the ceiling tiles as well as the turned tables lead the reader's eyes to a vantage point at the back of the cafeteria. However, there is a hulking zombie in the periphery of the page that startles the reader as their eyes are led to the back of the cafeteria. He takes up nearly a third of the page, creating an uncomfortable and claustrophobic sensation in the reader. The shading and black and white style mixed with the gore and surprise of the zombies creates a sense of suspense and horror in the comic. This technique is utilized multiple times throughout the rest of the on-going comics series. Unlike television or videogames, comics as a medium utilize the tactility of the page, alongside the compelling storyline, in order to create feelings of fear, suspense and horror.

With the continued success of the still ongoing comic, it was only natural to want to adapt it to the screen. This was largely possible due to Kirkman's publishing the comics through *Image Comics,* a company that unlike *Marvel* or *DC Comics,* gives the creator full licensing and rights over their characters. The comics created the original storyworld, but it was the expansion of the story through other media, and fundamentally the adaptation for the AMC television series *The Walking Dead* and later the companion television series *Fear the Walking Dead* that has established the franchise as a successful transmedia property. However, because they were created first, the comics series is often considered canon for *The Walking Dead* universe. Due to the adaptive nature of the television series, however, characters and storylines were changed. This has created two different kinds of canon in *The Walking Dead* franchise; one from the original comics and one from the television adaptation. The games, books, and apps that followed have had to choose to pull from either canon, thus, creating a two-pronged storyworld within *The Walking Dead* Universe. The differences between the two are too numerous to detail but have added to the sense that the Walking Dead is truly transmedial. There remains enough commonality that the TV series is clearly an adaptation, but enough difference that fans can engage with the comics at a different level. It is not simply the case of a rehashing of the established canon but an interpretation that fans can augment their detailed understanding of the universe by engaging in both mediums and canons.

Made for Television

Aptly, on 31 October 2010, Kirkman's comic series was adapted to television as AMC's *The Walking Dead*. While the main characters, ideas and threads were present from the first episode of the series, the television adaptation used the medium to its advantage, using lighting, music, and jump scares to create suspense and fear. As in the comics, the television series begins with Rick waking up in the hospital, and disorientated and alone he decides to leave to find his family. However, the scenes of him wandering the hallway utilize lighting and suspense that work better for television than in comics. Rather than take the elevator, he takes the fire escape stairs in the hospital. The cafeteria scene that was so pivotal in the comics is changed. Rather than open the door and reveal the zombies inside, Rick reads an inscription on the door saying, "Do not open, dead inside" and sees hands pushing through the gap in the doors. He chooses then to take the staircase leading outside of the hospital. Once he closes the door, he is completely shrouded in darkness. The viewer can hear his struggling, and then there is a close-up of Rick's hands as they light a match, relieving a bit of tension. The match does not last long, however, illuminating a medium shot of Rick just enough so that the viewer sees him attempt some of the stairs, it quickly goes out again leaving him immersed in darkness. Cutting back and forth between the dark and light, together with the perspective and size of the shot, not only produces a sense of fear in the viewer, but also mimics the uneasiness and incoherence Rick is feeling. Once Rick opens the emergency exit door, the whole shot is oversaturated in light, effectively blinding Rick and the viewer. The brightness makes it so that the background is completely saturated and indecipherable, creating an atmosphere that is suspenseful and disorienting. The television series manipulates the lighting in the frame in order to confuse the viewer as well as mimic the confusion of the main character. It then goes over the top creating too much light, which is just as blinding as the pitch black before. By taking away the sight of the viewer, the television series forces them to feel disoriented and confused like Rick. This would not work effectively in comics, as having an all-white or all-black panel does not create the same suspense in a purely visual medium.

Another device used in the television show is music or sound effects to induce suspense and fear. After Rick opens the door outside of the hospital, as mentioned in the previous paragraph, he walks through dozens of wrapped bodies lined up in rows. At first, the viewer hears the cicadas chirping in the background as well as Rick's feet hitting the ground. However, as he begins to realize the extent of the horror that he is witnessing, eerie violin music begins playing. It gets more and more intense as he walks past the bodies and climbs a hill outside the hospital. The music reaches a peak pitch and climax as a helicopter and the full extent of the scale of the disaster comes into focus. The cicadas' noise continues, blending with the music. The music is used to portray the horror Rick feels as he begins to figure out some sort of disaster has happened, but also prompts the viewer to feel the same way, as they are also experiencing the scale of the horror that happened in the hospital for the first time. The music adds suspense and leads the viewer to understand the scale of the horror of the zombie apocalypse in time with Rick's unfolding comprehension.

The television series also changes Rick's encounter with his former police partner, Shane. In the comics, Rick chases Shane after a member of their party is bitten by a walker (Kirkman, 2003, Issue 6). Shane pulls a gun on Rick and threatens to shoot him because Rick was not meant to survive in the hospital. As Rick is trying to calm his friend down, his son, Carl, comes out of the woods and shoots Shane through the neck (Kirkman, 2003, Issue 6). This scene plays out differently in the television series in that it happens in the twelfth episode of the second series rather than the sixth comic. The mood and tensions are different as well, as Shane lures Rick into the woods in order to kill him. Rick feigns surrender and then stabs Shane. Shane stands back up as a walker, and Carl shoots him before he can hurt his father. The television series keeps Shane in order to create more tension between he and Rick, but changes the timeline of the original canon. AMC's *The Walking Dead* adapts the comics not just into the television format, but changes the original canon of the storyworld in order to create its own. T.S. Eliot's (1921) delineation of the term "historical sense" suggests that meaning is created in the relationship between texts, a relationship that inherently encourages contrast and comparison. In this regard the relationship between the comics and television series, as an adaptation that came about seven years after the comics, encourages comparison. Adrienne Rich (1971) defines re-vision as "the act of looking back, of seeing with fresh eyes, of entering an old text from a new critical direction… We need to know the writing of the past and know it differently than we have ever known it; not to pass on a tradition but to break its hold over us." In this case, Kirkman has looked upon his first work, and the medium through which it was told, and is able to further manipulate the storyline and canon through its adaptation to the television series format. In doing so, Kirkman manipulates the idea of a canon and expands the storyworld to encompass not only other mediums, but also other versions of the storyline.

The television series continues to change the timeline by combining two major events and locations that are separate in the comics: the prison and Woodbury. In the comics, Rick and his group stumble upon a prison at the end of issue #12 (the end of volume 2) and attempt to use it as a safe house. Later, in issue 25 (volume 5), the characters encounter a crashed helicopter and follow the footprints to the Woodbury community ruled by a man called 'The Governor'. These two communities do not fully interact until the end of the 7th volume in issue #42 in which Woodbury attacks the prison. However, the television series conflates these two storylines, having them occur simultaneously throughout the third season. Characters' relationships with one another are changed, and AMC's version of Woodbury is much more idealistic than the way it is depicted in the comics. While these changes could constitute the television series as unfaithful to the comics, Julie Sanders argues that "it is usually at the very point of infidelity that the most creative acts of adaptation and appropriation take place" (Sanders, 2006). In this regard, the television series creatively adapts the comics through the conflation of these storylines, allowing it to become a canon in and of itself. In the television series, Kirkman is able to reimagine and re-characterize various comic characters, like Glenn and Michonne. In the comics, Glenn is a younger man who, as a skilled supply runner, is able to single-handedly save Rick in his first encounter with the dead in Atlanta (Kirkman, 2003, Issue #2). He is young and naive, but also strong and able. The television series characterizes him as older and less capable, as in the second episode of the first Season "Guts" (2010) he helps Rick, but is aided by other survivors. He is also given the last name "Rhee" in the television series, but remains without a second name in the comics. However, Glenn has become a fan favorite and is one of the only characters to appear in almost all forms of media, including the comics, television series, and various games including Telltale videogame, *Assault* mobile game, and *The Walking Dead* social game (*AMC The Walking Dead Social Game: Chronicles*, n.d.).

Other characters that are not present in the comics are introduced and fleshed out in the television show. The most notable added character, and fan favorite, is Daryl Dixon. The character won IGN's "Best TV Hero" award in 2012 and has the second highest number of appearances on the show, behind Rick (IGN, 2012). The character was created specifically for the actor Norman Reedus after his audition. This demonstrates the relationship between the franchise/author and the fans, the power of the fanbase has kept him as a main protagonist in the television series, even if Kirkman has stated that he will not bring the character into the comic (Johnson, 2013).

The success of the TV series has seen AMC expand upon its own offering of the universe with the creation of companion content that further develops Kirkman's storyworld. Most notably AMC created the television series AMC's *Fear the Walking Dead* (2015), which takes place within *The Walking Dead* universe as a prequel to the original, but remains separate from canonical characters in both the comics as well as the first television series. Both *Fear the Walking Dead* and *The Walking Dead* also have webisodes released exclusively on AMC.com that give background information and storylines to the characters within their respective series. They also air a talk show on AMC after each new episode, called *The Talking Dead,* in which the series actors are interviewed in order to get more details on the episode. Similarly, the Woodbury community as well as the Governor's backgrounds are more fully fleshed out in an ongoing series of novels created by Kirkman and Jay Bonansinga. However, the novels take the character as he is portrayed in the comics rather than the television series.

Films have always utilized fiction and non-fiction, and subsequently encouraged other novelization where the source was not already published. With the increasing utilization of digital streaming and online content by broadcast media, the ground has shifted again. We now have multiple channels for delivering content and this expansion has coincided with an increasing array of tools allowing fans to participate in the storyworld. The acceptance of fan culture and increasing development of commercial and grassroots extensions to the original storyworld has resulted in a resurgence of story elements being conveyed systematically across multiple media platforms, each making their own unique contribution to the whole. *The Walking Dead,* with its roots in the comic series and the commercial success of the television series, has now delivered a breadth of content that raises interesting questions about the development of brands, franchises and their correlation to the storyworld. Few contemporary television dramas exist solely on television; their worlds, characters and story arcs are distributed and added-to using other media such as online webisodes, digital games, animations, comics, social media, and much more. This goes for story experiences originating from any medium; they are soon augmented by content dispersed across multiple channels, often to a point where no one form can claim to be the definitive text. It is this opportunity to create and play with the storyworld that allows fans to connect and engage at different levels. Crucially, the number of entry points ensures fans can create their own stories within the established storyworld.

WE WALKING DEAD

The Walking Dead provides a rich source for the study of transmedia storytelling with over twenty commercial games having been created. There are multiple analogue versions (dice, card and board games) and digital offerings on multiple platforms. There now exist multiple narrative threads, and while the comic is technically canon, the popularity of the television series has resulted in parallel and overlapping storyworlds. The games that have developed provide different perspectives of these universes. Despite the inherent interactivity of the medium the story is still often largely directed, but the player is given the illusion of control. In examining the games, the focus of this chapter is on those digital versions that emerged after the initial success of the TV Series. These are Telltale Games' *The Walking Dead* (2012), Gamagio's *The Walking Dead Assault* (2012) and Terminal Reality's *The Walking Dead: Survival Instinct* (2013).

Telltale's *The Walking Dead* was episodic and first released for PC, Xbox 360 and PlayStation 3 in April 2012 and ported to mobile (iOS) in July. Over the next two years it was ported to multiple other platforms including PlayStation Vita, Amazon Fire, Android, PlayStation 4, Xbox One, OS X and Linux. Gamagio's *The Walking Dead Assault* was released for iOS in November 2012, and Android the following year. Despite initial success, only the first episode was ever released and it therefore provides an interesting contrast to Telltale's success. Activision published *The Walking Dead Survival Instinct* in March 2013 although critically panned it sold better than expected and again provides a different perspective to understanding the gaming contribution to the arching storyworld. Each of these games were part of the initial offerings licensed via Skybound Entertainment (Kirkman's production company) or AMC. Reflecting on these several years after release helps provide an insight into the role that games can play in transmedia franchises. With Skybound *The Walking Dead* games have always strived to demonstrate the power of the medium. This is unlike other franchises where games are often regarded as marketing extensions of the original comic or TV show. For Skybound, games have genuinely taken the series in different directions. Arguably, it is this uniqueness that games can provide the fan as both a familiar form and an opportunity for some creative freedom that has led to their success. Fans and players can find their own stories in the universe within carefully constructed metes and bounds. Since *The Walking Dead*, Telltale has continued to see further success with the franchise, but has also seen the success replicated in providing narrative-driven episodic gaming editions of *Game of Thrones*, *Batman*, *Guardians of the Galaxy* and the very meta game of a game with the storymode version of *Minecraft*, a game that established itself largely because of its embrace of creative freedom and complete lack of narrative. Telltale have clearly established themselves as the market leader in the genre, but multiple other gaming companies have built on the early successes and failures of the franchise to deliver a digitally-rich world for fans to embrace. It is worthwhile to consider how the varying range of quality and different commercial successes of *The Walking Dead* games impacts the overall storyworld.

From movies to digital games, theatre performances to LEGO, there is a distinct movement towards everything becoming transmedia, or at least aspiring towards it. Creators and producers increasingly conceive of a fictional world as transmedial from the outset. They seek to generate multiple interconnected texts that stitch together imaginary transmedia worlds that differ from traditional self-contained media entities by encompassing books, films, games, website, and even reference works like dictionaries, glossaries, atlases, encyclopedias and more (Wolf, 2012). It is not just imaginary worlds and storytelling that have become transmedia; Jenkins (2011) suggests "Transmedia storytelling describes one logic for thinking about the flow of content across media. We might also think about transmedia branding, transmedia performance, transmedia ritual, transmedia play, transmedia activism, and transmedia spectacle, as other logics". It is therefore essential to consider where brands, franchises and the storyworld differentiate. How the perceived gaps are filled and disconnects connected is of academic interest. For the fans the driving force for engagement with content would appear to be the perceived authenticity it holds with the rest of the franchise. Arguably, how *The Walking Dead* franchise has evolved as a commercial entity and its impact upon fan affiliation and the development of further extensions has been significant in shaping the rest of *The Walking Dead* universe. Games are both a potential driver of new narratives as well as retainers for fans of the existing narratives. The core text of the games (whether based on the comic or television narrative), as well as the type of game (adventure, strategy or first-person shooter) affects the overall narratives. Success or failure of the game in turn impacts fan engagement and potential future narratives. By having such a complex and interweaving narratives with multiple storylines and adaptations, *The Walking Dead* provides an excellent example of transmedial successes and failures.

Telltale Games' The Walking Dead

The first digital game release, *The Walking Dead* by Telltale Games, utilizes the universe of the comic book and delivered content over five episodes. The game was a considerable success for Telltale in terms of both sales and critical acclaim, and has been the recipient of over 90 Game of the Year awards (Telltale Games, n.d.). For a licensed property releasing in 2012, the game took the unusual step in that it was based off of the original comic book series, and not the hit TV series and, even then, used few characters from the comics. Whilst this could have had a significantly negative impact upon the reception, it allowed Telltale to hone a unique story. Within *The Walking Dead* storyworld, the game is located as a prequel with the events taking place during the period where Rick Grimes is still in a coma (Telltale Games, n.d.). Uniquely, it can be considered to be 'canonical' to the television series and the comic book, as Robert Kirkman was involved in the creation of the game events. Kirkman has subsequently spoken about how he got on board with the project after being informed of the gameplay's attempt to have a direct emotional impact. Specifically, it was the potential impact on the game player when they were faced with having to kill the protagonist's brother during the first episode (Workman, 2013). The events within the game and the design of the player interaction provide an intense user experience, yet the control mechanisms remain particularly player friendly. From the outset, Telltale placed the player at the core of the story and set out to allow the player to experience the tension within the storyworld.

You won't be mowing down hordes of the undead as a super-powered killing machine with unlimited ammo; ... When you do tangle with the undead, it's going to be harrowing (Telltale Games, 2012).

Telltale emphasized that players faced difficult situations and would be forced to make decisions that are not only hard but that require the player to make an almost immediate choice. There's no time to ponder what various outcomes might result in. Instead, the player must choose and those decisions impact later gameplay. These were brave decisions for the development team to make. Designing a multi-faceted experience, or the illusion of one, is not a straightforward task. However, it was immensely successful. As the review site Polygon stated

...if you care about games at all, where they're going, where they've been, you have to play The Walking Dead, ... Even If you couldn't care less, if you've never played a game before, then The Walking Dead is a wonderful place to start. (McElroy, 2012)

Polygon added that the reason that *The Walking Dead* succeeds is "by inventing an entirely new kind of game structure" (McElroy, 2012). It relies on the fact that it is a hybrid of game and story where "both of those facets are absolutely dependent on one another" (McElroy, 2012).

The game Telltale created fits almost seamlessly into the extant storyworld. It is a new experience with fresh characters but one that from the outset is familiar to fans. The art style is clearly influenced by the origin source: comics. Telltale cite the artistic style of the comic book artists as an influence, but crucially they also chose color palettes that immediately help audiences locate the game within the AMC franchise. From the narrative side, the main goal of the player is to take care of a little girl 'Clementine'. This makes the player feel a degree of guardianship or protective instinct. This is further exemplified by the ability to engage in more dialogue with Clementine than other characters. The player can also find food items and choose who gets them. Giving these to specific characters develops the player relationship with that character whilst hurting the development of other relationships.

The Walking Dead also makes the player feel a sense of horror that is inherent in the storyworld as well as a need to do 'what needs to be done' in order to survive. Yet, the violence is not gratuitous. One example of this is towards the end of the first episode where the protagonist, Lee, must kill his reanimated brother in order to progress. At this point, Lee has an axe as a weapon. In the process of acquiring this axe the player had to fight two enemies. Each of these enemies are dispatched in a single swing. In comparison, the player now called on to dispatch his brother faces a different gameplay situation: one that requires five individual axe swings to kill the zombified brother. In terms of gameplay this is a deliberate design to lengthen the scenario in order to get the player to empathize with the protagonist. This explanation appears even more likely as the protagonist's brother is pinned down and unable to move freely, therefore posing very little threat. The emphasis on making the player think about their actions reinforces engagement with the storyworld. It is this form of interaction, where there are no obvious forms of reward or penalty that makes the Telltale game a different type of gaming experience. The fact that the player is discovering the protagonist's backstory through play, and having to make grim decisions and experience harrowing events, adds comprehension of the transmedia storyworld and allows them to try and comprehend that world. The result is an absorbing and immersive experience.

Another significant element of *The Walking Dead* is the necessity of companionship throughout the story arc. The player meets several people in a similar situation also looking for help. The player then has the option to further develop relationships with these characters through various actions. The game makes use of these developments by informing the player that an action they have just performed 'has been remembered'. How and to what extent this may affect later events is left to the player to determine. For example, there are points where the player must choose between two companions to save. The first is less than thirty minutes in and a companion's child, a young boy, needs rescuing, as does an adult. No matter the actions of the player, the adult dies; the only difference is that by saving the child the player's relationship with the father develops. An example of the knock-on impact your decisions can have comes later in the final sections of the episode where the player is knocked down and needs rescue. The child's father comes to the protagonist's aid, but his reaction is dependent on whether the player chose to save the child earlier or not. It is these mechanics that make the game player feel more engaged and as a result the experience the game offers a more harrowing and reflective one. It stays with the player, and makes them question the decisions they have made. As many of these decisions have to be made quickly and are not always straightforward, the player can be left wondering how the decisions they have made might affect the game later. That sense of foreboding and need to understand decisions from all perspectives in a single game moment makes the experience emotionally powerful. The episodic release of the game content not only added to that sense of engagement from the player, but continued with the release of a specific downloadable content (DLC) pack "400 Days" and subsequent series. While much has been made about the idea that decisions made by the player affect the decisions in later episodes and even Telltale's subsequent sequels, the reality is slightly different. Certainly, the decisions made by the player affect the gameplay experience but not the narrative outcomes. In fact, one of the main criticisms leveled at the series is that choices are irrelevant and lead to the same end points. You can change the journey but not the destination. This brings us back to the central difficulty that games have in allowing players to modify the storyworld: allow too much and it breaks the narrative, immersion and desired endings, but allow too little and players feel aggrieved that their decisions do not matter. The phenomenal success of Telltales' game demonstrates that it got the balance commercially and critically correct. However, other games show that it is an incredibly difficult achievement.

Gamagio's The Walking Dead Assault

The Walking Dead Assault was a mobile and tablet game developed by Gamagio and published by Skybound Entertainment, Robert Kirkman's multiplatform entertainment company and the licensor holder for the comic. *Assault* is a top-down strategy game and in some ways stayed truer to the comic book counterpart. Like the comic and TV Show, the game begins with the iconic moment of Rick awakening from his coma in the hospital. Players can play through missions as their favorite characters from the storyworld – Rick, Glenn, Shane, Carl, Andrea, Lori and Michonne. Each event (or Chapter) is based around the events through Atlanta, ending with the camp invasion. The game's ability to look and feel like that of the comic was amplified by the hand-drawn art style, featuring a black and white palette with only occasional splashes of color for emphasis.

In terms of the story, *Assault* initially runs parallel to the comic books' story with the first mission to escape the hospital where Rick (the main protagonist) wakes up. Shortly after that, the story diverges through the introduction of characters and mission order. However, the final mission is the initial attack on the group's campsite; this mirrors events in Issue 5 of the comic series. The game clearly wants to appeal to new and old fans of the series, and the primary method of doing this is through the characters. From the outset, players can purchase additional characters, with the first available being Michonne who makes no appearance in the comics until Issue 19, and not until the Season 2 finale of the TV series (Michonne - Walking Dead Wiki, n.d.).

Assault capitalizes on the player's familiarity with *The Walking Dead* storyworld and characters by creating unique abilities based on the known character traits. For example, Rick has the in-game ability to deal substantially higher damage to enemies, while also improving his team members' accuracy and firepower, thus, typifying the leader role and 'rallying the troops'. Conversely, the character Shane is shown throughout *The Walking Dead* media to be less balanced, impulsive and reckless. His in-game ability is entitled 'Freakout', where for a short period he is restricted to melee weapons but his damage increases vastly. This ability parallels his actions both in the TV series and the comic series, although his story arc within the comics is much shorter. Certain aspects of *The Walking Dead Assault*, including character portrayals are considered canonical to the comics, with just some structural and order differences. One key difference is that due to the nature of the extension, it is a game and requires some risk/reward elements, the game design allows for characters to perish during missions. Thus, the game can allow for are non-canonical elements. It is this balance between canon and non-canon that has to be carefully designed in any transmedia gaming experience. The game has to feel that it belongs and works within the storyworld. To that end, *The Walking Dead Assault* places both storyline and artistic style in the context of the comic book series, closely mirroring it with some exceptions. The result is that the game is neither prequel nor extension, but more a parallel telling with a reasonable degree of canonicity. A review from Android Police sums up the game overall.

It's fun, challenging, and does The Walking Dead justice. The best part, however, it's that it's a good game overall – not just a good game for Walking Dead fans. I think that anyone who enjoys this type of game could pick it up and have a good time playing, though TWD fans are more likely to get into (and appreciate) the storyline since they're already familiar with the characters. (Summerson, 2013)

Assault was ranked as a number one Strategy game, was featured and rated as a Top 5 Paid App in 2012. It won praise for faithfully following several of the story arcs of the comic and for its overall capture of the tone and feel of the comic book. Yet, the game has simply vanished with no further episodes or announcements from either the developer or publisher. This is perhaps because it competed with Telltale's game on the same platforms or because top-down squad based strategy games are too niche that the games sales were insufficient to support further episodes. What is clear is that the game pushed the franchise in a different direction. Unlike the comics, TV series and Telltale's game, *Assault* was less narrative-focused as one review put it, "It isn't about the end of the world, it isn't about the horror of humanity stretched to its limits. It's about obliterating zombies and living to tell the tale" (Campbell, 2012). The question arises as to whether it is the narrative and immersion in the storyworld that then drives fans to the content.

Terminal Reality's The Walking Dead: Survival Instinct

If the first two Walking Dead games gave clear examples of adding to a transmedia experience, the final game, *The Walking Dead: Survival Instinct* developed by Terminal Reality, provides insight into the difficulty of managing a franchise and maintaining a coherent transmedia storyworld. The game was released for consoles in March 2013 and is a single-player first-person shooter game. On paper, it should be a perfect fit for adding to *The Walking Dead* universe. The game acts as a prequel to the TV series again set in the Georgia countryside, and focuses on the core TV series characters Daryl and Merle Dixon as they make their way to Atlanta during the early days of the zombie apocalypse. Unfortunately, the game's development suffered and the release was critically maligned (Stanton, 2013; McElroy, 2013; Hamilton, 2013; Metacritic, n.d.):

The Walking Dead: Survival Instinct is the exact sort of lazy, cheap cash-grab that gave licensed games a bad name in the first place... [It's like] listening to a roomful of barely competent musicians, each of whom is playing a completely different song. And every once in a while one kicks you in the groin. And you have sunburn (McElroy, 2013).

The *Polygon* reviewer, Justin McElroy, was the same person who reviewed Telltale's *The Walking Dead*. The criticism is primarily concerned with the gameplay and it is worth stating that for another developer to follow-up any game as successful as Telltale's success was always going to be a significant challenge. Viewed purely as an addition to the transmedia experience, there are a number of core elements that make *Survival Instinct* interesting. For example, the primary characters are Daryl and his brother Merle, characters that only exist in the TV series, and the game is therefore canonically tied to the TV series, whereas *Assault* is canonically tied to the comic. The differences in licensing are key. Kirkman is on record as saying that *Survival Instinct,* came out of "very unique licensing situation" (Crecente, 2015) where Skybound has licensing control of *The Walking Dead* outside of the television series and AMC has their own licensing division that can license additional properties from the television series.

For many fans the distinction between the comic and the TV series can be a difficult one to make and even within the merchandising it remains complicated. This may well be due to the success of *The Walking Dead* as a transmedia franchise. Another example of this diverging canonicity are the two board games, again one ties to the television series and features the actors and the other to the comic. The management of both and their respective storyworlds is undoubtedly impacted by the various licensing agreements. Development of a console tie-in is undoubtedly affected by these agreements and the budget. That the game was developed suggests that the story of the Dixon brothers was one that was worth telling. Daryl is one of the most popular characters from the television series, therefore an experience that acts as a prequel to his story might have been desired by the market. It is also uniquely an aspect that AMC controls more directly as the characters do not exist within the comic universe.

However, the execution of that story has meant the game has been a critical failure though commercially it sold reasonably well, with approximately over a million sales (VGChartz.com, 2017). The main criticisms are that the game is not developed to the standard that players would expect, whether as the result of a lack of time, limited budget or simply poor development is unknown. Core gameplay mechanics are often buggy, repetitive and lack innovative ideas. Where new ideas are attempted they are not implemented successfully. As such the poor critical reception resulted in the game being classified as a 'cash-grab' by reviewers. Many reviews actively encouraging fans to avoid playing for fear of tarnishing their own experience of *The Walking Dead* storyworld. This is particularly interesting to the transmedia scholar primarily because of the disconnect or perceived inauthenticity from the rest of the franchise. The prospect that this could potentially affect the continuing success of *The Walking Dead* as a transmedia storyworld and commercial entity, devaluing the 'brand' and reducing coherence seems misplaced. Although not successful, it has generally been regarded by the fanbase simply as an aberration. Indeed, conversely it may actually have strengthened fan affiliation to the rest of the canon and new game offerings.

Other Notable Games

Since that first digital game release, *The Walking Dead*, has witnessed a plethora of games. Telltale have had two additional full series, there are multiple mobile offerings including Next Games hugely successful *No Man's Land* (2015) with over 4 million downloads (Grothaus, 2015) and there is a new console game in the works. The gaming sphere of *The Walking Dead* universe has always been and remains split between those licensed from Skybound and those from AMC. Undoubtedly some confusion is inevitable. There is *The Walking Dead Board Game* (2011) and *The Walking Dead: The Board Game* (2011), there are further licensed versions in both analogue and digital format. You can play strategy game versions in analogue form, *Risk: The Walking Dead Survival Edition* (2013) or digital, *The Escapists* (2015). You can purchase the Atlanta Survival camp as a property in *The Walking Dead Monopoly* (2013) or defend it in *Assault* (2012). You can play as Glenn in *The Walking Dead: Atlanta Run* (2010) or more obviously as Michonne in *The Walking Dead: Michonne* (2016). More commonly you can join the comic or TV show and play alongside the characters you are familiar with. You can fight alongside your favorites or carve out your own stories and moments within the universe. The real strength of games is that they provide a bridge for players to interact with the universe and play with the storyworld without fear of impacting upon the canon. Whilst several games are no longer available the appetite of fans for new interactive experiences has not dimmed. There are at least three games due for launch in the next year, and these shadow the three discussed in this chapter. A new mobile offering *The Walking Dead: March to War* is due to launch this year with a new console game by the developer Overkill slated for 2018. Next year will also see the final series of Telltale's game offering. Each will be licensed from Skybound and borne from the comic canon, and with Skybound's commitment to allowing creators to maintain creative control, fans seem reassured that the integrity of Kirkman's vision is upheld.

Fandom and User-Generated Content

The vast and complex storyworld of *The Walking Dead* seeks to harness the encyclopedic impulse of its audience, but also, through leaving gaps and disconnects, leaves room for them to participate. The generated content exists in different forms: from the official *Walking Dead Wikipedia* boasting "every facet of *The Walking Dead* from the comic series, novels, videogames, and television show, including character statuses and current storyline plot-points" (Walking Dead Wiki, n.d.), to the forum *Roamersandlurkers.com*, to *fanfiction.net*, and *undeadfanstories*, the fan audience can share their own content with fellow fans of *The Walking Dead*. These extensions from the content itself provide multiple points of entry for the audience to discover the storyworld, or other aspects of the storyworld. For example, a viewer only familiar with the television series can discover the comics or vice versa. Each extension offers up a different selection of story and adaption for the audience to flesh out the fictional world and/ or enhance realism and depth.

If the commercial extensions have been largely successful, it is the grassroots extensions that have demonstrated the breadth of the storyworld. Grassroots extensions have expanded to focus on perceived gaps and are mainly categorized as knowledge production, social texts and creative works. The vast and complex fictional world of *The Walking Dead* both seeks to harness the encyclopedic impulse of its audience but also, through leaving gaps and disconnects, leaves room for them to participate. Examples of this participation are plentiful, and while it is not possible to provide a definitive list here, some key grassroots extensions are briefly described in this section.

The Walking Dead universe has found itself an expansive world for fans to fill in the gaps, and the examples are plentiful with fans elaborating on the world, characters and plot gaps for both the TV series and Games in fan fiction (fanfiction.net, n.d.; undeadfanstories, 2012). More visual expressions are video mashups and parodies combining multiple sources of videos, with very little or no relation with each other, to lampoon the various component sources. Mashups are increasing in popularity with the availability of source material and easy to use video editors. Some of the best examples for *The Walking Dead* are: *The Walking Dead 80's Sitcom Intro* (Matincomedy, 2013), *The Trotting Dead* – a mashup of My Little Pony and *The Walking Dead* (Birdy Love, n.d.), and *The Walking Dumb – a Dumb Ways to Die Parody* (Teddiefilms, 2012). Each of these provide a humorous take on the universe but there are multiple examples available on YouTube which can be used to demonstrate the expansive nature that fans are engaging with the content. To that extent, fan fiction and mashups may be considered 'transformative' of original content, and as such may find protection from copyright claims under the "fair use" doctrine of U.S. copyright law. From the gaming side, fans have created replicas of *The Walking Dead* prison in *Minecraft* and opened the level up for people to play (ZackScottGames, 2013). It is the wealth of tools available for fans to utilize that has enabled the breadth of content to be developed. The grassroots expansions of *The Walking Dead* demonstrate the increasing difficulty in differentiating between fan and consumer and demonstrate that traditional perceptions of each are blurring in today's increasingly 'participatory' media and entertainment landscape.

CONCLUSION

The Walking Dead provides an example of how games can evolve transmedia narratives beyond the established canon. They serve to provide fans the opportunity to create their own stories (within the carefully designed limits and bounds of the game world), play as their favorite character or to see the impact of their decisions upon the storyworld without directly affecting the canon. Games are increasingly pivotal to transmedia properties in that they provide an alternate but immediate form for fans to immerse themselves within the storyworld.

Arguably, it is this immersion level that separates games from the other forms of media. For fans, that ability to affect the world and narratives makes games an essential offering in any transmedia franchise. The significance of how the format is consumed is the defining factor. Games rely on active consumption. It does not matter how fantastic the writing is in a game if the experience is crafted in such a way that players can avoid it. In contrast the comics, television series, and novels rely upon passive consumption. The narrative is directed to the consumer through the carefully constructed linear story. However, for games to engage in the storyworld they need to rely fundamentally on good, intelligent, story-driven design for these to be successful. Telltale Games give just enough choice to the player for them to feel they are meaningfully contributing to the world and that it is a narrative that is directly affected by their own actions. In contrast, *The Walking Dead: Survival Instinct* through flaws in the design did not inspire players to engage with the prequel narrative and was marred by technical difficulties. If the gameplay does not bring the connection with immersion to the overarching storyworld then it damages the overall experience. Reviews of *Survival Instinct* frequently state not to play the game if you are a fan of *The Walking Dead*, surely the worst possible indictment a reviewer can give on a licensed game of a popular franchise.

An additional factor that games within a transmedia property have to navigate is the inherent challenge within the medium. For gamers, that challenge typically has to be scalable - one of the main criticisms of Telltale's games is that there is little challenge. Yet, for the fan and potentially non-gamer that challenge has to be balanced well enough that the maintain engagement in the storyworld. If the tasks or actions required are too challenging, then the fan has multiple other mediums in which to engage with and spend their time. Indeed, one of the fundamental differences about *The Walking Dead* games is that they often provide limited or carefully balanced challenge. There are multiple examples of games based on films and other media properties that add little to the narrative experience. However, what *The Walking Dead* has is a multitude of smaller experiences that each add a different form of engagement for the fan/player.

What Telltale does so well is in making an experience that adds to the world. The episodic content allows the fan and player to collect more of the wider storyworld experience, without significant challenge.

The Walking Dead provides a rich source for the study of transmedia storytelling. From the core comic book and TV series through the commercial and grassroots extensions there is a plethora of content for the reader, writer, teacher, academic and transmedia scholar to utilize. Examination of the transmedia content provides many interesting questions regarding the development of brands, franchises and their correlation to the storyworld. Given the wide range of quality within the transmedia content for *The Walking Dead* there are several questions to consider the ways in which content in one area or platform has the potential to affect future stories within this context. The overwhelming success of Telltale's *The Walking Dead* suggested that game offerings would be a particularly interesting platform for further development. In contrast the poor reception of Terminal Reality's *Survival Instinct* did result in a general backing away of specific console offerings. However, any suggestion that any game similar in 'goal' to *Survival Instinct* (i.e. looking at character back stories, canonically tied to TV series) might be potentially viewed with a sense of trepidation and wariness, seem to have passed.

However, with all of these various adaptations and transmedial worlds, the reader must keep in mind Sanders' suggestion that "while it may enrich and deepen our understanding of the new cultural product to be aware of its shaping intertext, it may not be entirely necessary to enjoy the work independently" (Sanders, 2006). Even amongst all of the various adaptations, spin offs, and transmedial sources, the viewer or reader is still able to enjoy the consumption of one part of the storyworld without having to be familiar with the other modes. A fan of AMC's *The Walking Dead* does not need the comics in order to enjoy or understand the show. A fan is able to delve into any part of *The Walking Dead* storyworld and understand the world with little to no background information. However, if their interest is piqued, the fan is able to explore multiple transmedial modes, canons, storylines and characters made by franchise and fan alike. As Carlos A. Scolari posits, "Two practices converge and, at the same time, challenge each other in transmedia storytelling: the strategies of the media industry and the tactics of users and fans" (Solari, 2014). It is important to consider where brands, franchises and the storyworld differentiate. How the perceived gaps are filled and disconnects connected is of particular interest. For the fans the driving force for engagement with content would appear to be the perceived authenticity it holds with rest of the franchise and for the transmedia scholar there remains a plethora of work to study within *The Walking Dead* storyworld. How the franchise evolves as a commercial entity and its impact upon fan affiliation and the development of further grassroots extensions continues to be significant in shaping the rest of *The Walking Dead* universe.

The complexity of developing and controlling a transmedia franchise, such as *The Walking Dead*, is undoubtedly challenging. Robert Kirkman continues to receive praise and criticism about the development of the storyworld and accused of cashing in on the various extensions of his creation. Historically, it was Hollywood (or rather films) that provided the backbone to transmedia franchises. Games, novels and comics were spun out from film and typically it was the content from the film that was replicated in other media, often using the same universe and characters from the core film-based narrative. The production pipelines for films were typically similar to games but as the game production started later and often had additional technical challenges licensed games were often poor additions to the storyworld universe when they were launched. Licenses were often prohibitively restrictive with the rights to the property often requiring separate negotiation with the actors. The result was for many years game production could simply not align itself in terms of time and information confidentiality with the core properties.

In many ways, the success (and failings) of *The Walking Dead* as a transmedia property comes down to the licensing agreements. Robert Kirkman set up Skybound within Image Comics prior to the launch of the television show. It is Skybound that retains the control of licensing *The Walking Dead* outside of the television show. In contrast, it is AMC that licenses the television show. How much control Robert Kirkman has over the licensing of the AMC franchise appears minimal, and Kirkman has been clear to distance himself and Skybound from any involvement with *Survival Instinct*. Kirkman's vision and ethos on allowing the medium creators more freedom is certainly a contributing factor to the transmedia success of *The Walking Dead*. It is this differentiation from other transmedia models and the element of control that Kirkman has been able to exert that is particularly appealing for fans and the storyworld.

This chapter illustrates the transmedial nature of Kirkman's *The Walking Dead* series, from comic to television series and the subsequent boom of other narratives through various mediums. The success of the games highlights the importance of fan culture and the ability of the audience to be fully immersed in the storyworld. This has led to an innumerable amount of fan generated content, attempting to further position themselves within Kirkman's storyworld. In this respect, Kirkman's vision allows, and encourages, creativity from his franchise partners as well as his fans within his carefully constructed world. He creates not only a storyworld, but a level of engagement that allows others to toy with his characters and play with the dead.

REFERENCES

Birdy Love. (n.d.). The trotting dead. *Fimfiction.net*. Retrieved 15 June 2017, from https://www.fimfiction.net/story/154968/the-trotting-dead

Boyle, D. (2003). *28 days later*. 20th Century Fox Home Entertainment, Inc.

Crecente, B. (2015). The Kirkman Effect: How an undead army may recreate entertainment. *Polygon*. Retrieved 3 August 2017, from https://www.polygon.com/features/2015/3/30/8311735/the-walking-dead-invincible-outcast-fear-the-walking-dead-interview-r
obert-kirkman

Cryptozoic Entertainment. (2011). *The walking dead board game* [Board game]. Lake Forest, CA: Cryptozoic Entertainment.

Eliot, T. S. (1921). The sacred wood: Essays on poetry and criticism. New York, NY: Bartleby.com.

Facebook. (n.d.). AMC The Walking Dead Social Game: Chronicles. Retrieved 15 June 2017, from https://www.facebook.com/AMCTheWalkingDeadGame/

FanFiction. (n.d.). *Walking Dead fan fiction archive*. Retrieved 15 June 2017, from https://www.fanfiction.net/tv/Walking-Dead/

Fear the Walking Dead. (2017). Facebook. Retrieved 12 August 2017, from https://www.facebook.com/FearTWD/

Fear TWD. (2017). Twitter. Retrieved 12 August 2017, from https://twitter.com/FearTWD

Gamagio. (2012). *The Walking Dead: Assault*. [Mobile game]. London, UK: Gamagio

Game Studio, M. P. (2010). *The Walking Dead: Atlanta Run* [Online game]. New York: AMC.

Giovagnoli, M., Vaglioni, P., & Montesano, F. (2011). *Transmedia storytelling: Imagery, shapes and techniques*. ETC Press.

Grothaus, M. (2015). How AMC and next games "The Walking Dead" is Killing The Licensed Gaming Competition. *Fast Company*. Retrieved 11 August 2017 from https://www.fastcompany.com/3053490/how-amc-and-next-games-are-killing-the-licensed-gaming-competition

Hamilton, K. (2013). The Walking Dead: Survival instinct is the worst game i've played this year. *Kotaku.com*. Retrieved 3 August 2017, from http://kotaku.com/5991559/the-walking-dead-survival-instinct-is-the-worst-game-ive-played-this-year

Harrigan, P., & Wardrip-Fruin, N. (2009). *Third Person: Authoring and Exploring Vast Narratives*. Cambridge, MA: MIT Press.

IGN. (2012). *Best TV hero - Best of 2012*. Retrieved 3 August 2017, from http://uk.ign.com/wikis/best-of-2012/Best_TV_Hero

Jenkins, H. (2006). *Convergence culture: Where old and new media collide*. New York, NY: New York University Press.

Jenkins, H. (2007). *Transmedia storytelling 101*. Retrieved 15 June 2017, from http://henryjenkins.org/2011/08/defining_transmedia_further_re.html

Jenkins, H. (2011). *Transmedia 202: Further reflections*. Retrieved 15 June 2017, from http://henryjenkins.org/2011/08/defining_transmedia_further_re.html

Jenkins, H. (2013). *Transmedia storytelling and entertainment: A new syllabus*. Retrieved 15 June 2017, from http://henryjenkins.org/2013/08/transmedia-storytelling-and-entertainment-a-new-syllabus.html

Johnson, S. (2013). Robert Kirkman says no Daryl Dixon in The Walking Dead Comic Book. *Comicbook.com*. Retrieved 15 June 2017, from http://comicbook.com/blog/2013/07/18/robert-kirkman-says-no-daryl-dixon-in-the-walking-dead-comic-book/

Kirkman, R., Adlard, C., & Moore, T. (2003). The Walking Dead #1-42. California, CA: Image Comics.

Klastrup, L., & Tosca, S. (2004). Transmedial worlds - Rethinking cyberworld design. In *Proceedings of The International Conference on Cyberworlds*. Los Alamitos, CA: IEEE Computer Society.

Laurel, B. (2004). *Design Research: Methods and Perspectives*. Cambridge, MA: MIT Press.

Matincomedy. (2013, February 1). *The Walking Dead 80's sitcom intro*. [Video file]. Retrieved 15 June 2017, from https://www.youtube.com/watch?v=VizlD3lW9Ow

McElroy, J. (2012). *The Walking Dead - Episode Five review: family ties. Polygon*. Retrieved 13 August 2017, from https://www.polygon.com/2012/11/20/3667966/the-walking-dead-episode-five-review

McElroy, J. (2013). The Walking Dead: Survival Instinct review: Human Suffering. *Polygon*. Retrieved 13 August 2017, from https://www.polygon.com/2013/3/19/4125248/the-walking-dead-survival-instinct-review

Metacritic. (n.d.) *The Walking Dead: Survival Instinct*. Retrieved 13 August 2017, from http://www.metacritic.com/game/xbox-360/the-walking-dead-survival-instinct

Mittell, J. (2015). *Complex TV: The poetics of contemporary television storytelling*. New York, NY: NYU Press.

Mouldy Toof Studios. (2015). *The Escapists: The Walking Dead* [Video game]. Wakefield: Team 17

Next Games. (2015). *The Walking Dead: No Man's Land* [Video game]. New York: AMC.

Rich, A. (1972). When We Dead Awaken: Writing as Re-Vision. *College English*, *34*(1), 18–30. doi:10.2307/375215

RoamersAndLurkers.com. (n.d.). *The Walking Dead Forum*. RoamersAndLurkers.com. Retrieved 15 June 2017, from http://www.roamersandlurkers.com/

Rose, F. (2012). *The Art of immersion: How the digital generation is remaking Hollywood, Madison Avenue, and the way we tell stories*. New York, NY: Norton.

Sanders, J. (2006). *Authorship and appropriation*. London, UK: Routledge.

Scolari, C. (2014). Don Quixote of La Mancha: Transmedia Storytelling in the Grey Zone. *International Journal of Communication*, *8*, 2382–2405. Retrieved from http://ijoc.org/index.php/ijoc/article/view/2576/1199

Stanton, R. (2013). The Walking Dead: Survival Instinct review. *Eurogamer.net*. Retrieved 3 August 2017, from http://www.eurogamer.net/articles/2013-04-03-the-walking-dead-survival-instinct-review

Summerson, C. (2013). The Walking Dead: Assault Review. *Android Police*. Retrieved 15 June 2017, from http://www.androidpolice.com/2013/07/30/the-walking-dead-assault-review-not-just-good-for-hardcore-twd-fans-but-a-pretty-solid-game-overall/

Teddiefilms. (2012, December 18). *The Walking Dumb – a Dumb Ways to Die Parody*. [Video file] Retrieved 3 August 2017 from: http://www.youtube.com/watch?v=xPbVR6TgO28

Telltale Games. (2012a). *The Walking Dead* [Video game]. San Rafael, CA: Telltale Games.

Telltale Games. (2012b). *The Walking Dead Game - FAQ and open discussion! Telltale Community*. Retrieved 13 August 2017, from https://telltale.com/community/discussion/28483/the-walking-dead-game-faq-and-open-discussion/p42

Telltale Games. (2013). *The Walking Dead: 400 Days DLC* [Video game]. San Rafael, CA: Telltale Games.

Telltale Games. (2016). *The Walking Dead: Michonne* [Video Game]. San Rafael, CA: Telltale Games.

Terminal Reality. (2013). *The Walking Dead: Survival Instinct* [Video game]. Santa Monica, CA: Activision.

The Walking Dead. (2017). *AMC*. Retrieved 15 June 2017, from http://www.amc.com/shows/the-walking-dead

The Walking Dead AMC. (2017a). *Facebook*. Retrieved 12 Aug 2017, from https://www.facebook.com/pg/TheWalkingDeadAMC/community

The Walking Dead AMC. (2017b). *Twitter*. Retrieved 12 August 2017, from https://twitter.com/WalkingDead_AMC

Undead Fan Stories Wiki. (2012). *Walking Dead: Requiem*. Retrieved 15 June 2017, from http://undead-fanstories.wikia.com/wiki/Walking_Dead:Requiem

USAopoly. (2013). *Risk: The Walking Dead Survival Edition* [Board game]. Pawtucket, R.I.: Hasbro.

USAopoly. (2013). *The Walking Dead Monopoly* [Board game]. Pawtucket, R.I.: Hasbro.

VGChartz.com. (n.d.). *VGChartz - Survival Instinct. Vgchartz.com*. Retrieved 13 August 2017, from http://www.vgchartz.com/gamedb/?name=survival+instinct

Walking Dead Wiki. (n.d.). *Michonne (Comic Series)*. Retrieved 15 June 2017, from http://walkingdead.wikia.com/wiki/Michonne_(Comic_Series)

Walking Dead Wiki. (n.d.). *Walkingdead.wikia.com*. Retrieved 15 June 2017, from http://walkingdead.wikia.com/wiki/The_Walking_Dead_Wiki

Wolf, M. (2012). *Building Imaginary Worlds: The Theory and History of Subcreation*. New York: Routledge.

Workman, R. (2013). SDCC: Robert Kirkman, telltale games spill secrets of "The Walking Dead". *CBR*. Retrieved 15 June 2017, from http://www.cbr.com/sdcc-robert-kirkman-telltale-games-spill-secrets-of-the-walking-dead/

Wyndham, J. (1954). *The day of the triffids*. Harmondsworth, UK: Penguin Books.

Z-Man Games. (2011). *The Walking Dead: The Board Game* [Board game]. Los Angeles, CA: Skybound Entertainment.

ZackScottGames. (2013). Minecraft - *The Walking Dead Prison* [Video file]. Retrieved 15 June 2017, from https://www.youtube.com/watch?v=GrH6jMv5Vrk

KEY TERMS AND DEFINITIONS

Canon: The material that is accepted as officially a part of an individual universe or story. In the case of *The Walking Dead*, the comics create the first official material while the television series creates its own material.

Fandom: A group of people who are fans of a particular person, character, or series. It is often considered a community with its own unique culture.

Franchise: A type of business that holds the rights to different properties.

Grassroot Extensions: The marketing of products to ordinary people who are regarded as the main focus of the franchise.

Storyworld: The shared universe in which the settings, characters, objects, event, and actions of one or more narratives exist.

Transmedia: The telling of a single story or experience across multiple platforms, mediums, and formats.

Webisode: An original episode derived from a television series that is made exclusively for online viewing.

This research was previously published in the Handbook of Research on Transmedia Storytelling and Narrative Strategies; pages 50-71, copyright year 2019 by Information Science Reference (an imprint of IGI Global).

Chapter 70

Digital Games and Orientalism:
A Look at Arab and Muslim Representation in Popular Digital Games

Fatih Söğüt
Kırklareli University, Turkey

ABSTRACT

The cultural and ideological tools that enable the West to maintain the imperial and colonial rule over the East have been varied. With the help of Western-based digital technologies and communication tools, it is possible to produce, publish, and distribute all kinds of information easily and quickly. The western and Western perspective is also reflected in the media content, and all kinds of popular media texts such as films, music, newspapers, magazines, toys are the bearers of the political social, cultural, and ideological structure of the West. Media texts produce discourses, especially about the 'East' and position the East as one other. In this context, digital games should not be considered independent of the political, social, cultural, and economic structure in which they exist. The aim of this study is to assess research studies focusing on the orientalist perspective in digital games. While examining the relationship between orientalism and digital games within the framework of the literature, especially the Muslim and Arab representations in the plays were examined.

INTRODUCTION

With the development of new communication technologies, human beings have had the opportunity to be more closely connected and to know each other than ever before. Nowadays, a person living on one side of the world can communicate with someone living in another part of the world, get education from him, trade, make friends, play games, gather around an idea and make their voices heard more. In addition to all these positive possibilities, human beings may fear each other and feel enmity to an extent that they have never experienced before, they can marginalize, beyond the conflict of opinion, maybe they can get into a fight with someone they can never come together with in life. Othering and hate speech have become a common occurrence with the dominance of new communication technologies in daily

DOI: 10.4018/978-1-6684-7589-8.ch070

life. "Islamophobia", which includes a discriminatory, marginalizing and even hostile attitude towards Islam and Muslims as a religion, is a phenomenon that this situation is frequently experienced.

The most important intellectual source of Islamophobia is orientalism. In this idea, first expressed by Edward Said, the West examines the East, changes it, and creates images aimed at the East. In this sense, the East is not a geographical place but an idea. It is possible to find the traces of orientalist thought in the Western media's view of Muslims.

Islamophobic content, which is frequently pumped by various news, TV series and movies in conventional media, appears sometimes as a video, sometimes as an article, and sometimes as a visual in media where new communication technologies are used. One of these new channels in which Islamophobia comes to life is digital games. Arcade-style games were first connected to television, followed by computers, and advanced game consoles and digital games are an entertainment commodity that is used extensively not only by children but also by adults.

Today, digital games have surpassed a format played against artificial intelligence in the game, and with internet technologies, it has become a format where people from all over the world can play games together or mutually. The technical devices on which the games are played have also changed, and it has become possible to play these games at any time, sometimes over a social media network, or as an application, without time and space restrictions with mobile phones and tablets. Even virtual and augmented reality technologies and digital games are still in a transformation. There are simulators in which people play as protagonists in the game today. However, it is not practical to be easily produced and put into service and has not yet been commercialized in terms of demand-cost relationship.

The most important feature that distinguishes the digital game from other channels of new media is that it includes the player in the game. In these games, the person does not just look at a photo or watch a video like on a social network site. He gets excited by playing the game himself, is happy when he succeeds in the game, gets sad when he is defeated, sometimes gets ambitious, sometimes he is angry enough to kick the device he is playing and throws it against the wall. The fact that people live and reflect digital games to their behavior in this way makes the content of these games important. These games, which have a lot of content from violence to racism, and from sexism to pornography, are subject to certain regulations from age restrictions to prohibition in most countries. However, it has not been possible to prevent these games from reaching millions in today's world where everyone has access to everything. Representations towards Muslims are processed directly in some of the digital games and indirectly in others, and an environment is prepared for the formation of an attitude or behavior in this direction in the masses who play. With this study, the results of research on this issue have been compiled to reveal a general situation of Muslim representation in digital games.

ORIENTALISM: A CONCEPTUAL INTRODUCTION

Orientalism means "science of the Eastern world", with the old word Orientalism (Derin, 2006). As for the word orientalist, it generally means Eastern languages and Eastern Sciences expert, and is used to mean a scientist who studies the history, religion, language, literature, culture, and some other points of Eastern communities. Orientalism, which emerged as a research method and discipline because of non-professional studies, has paved the way for studies in various fields over time. The term Orientalist originally had a rather different meaning than its present meaning. In 1683, the term orientalist means "a member of the Eastern or Greek Church"(Bulut, 2010).

According to the Oxford English Dictionary, orientalism was a concept associated with Eastern nations, identifying the work of academics who knew eastern languages and literature well. This definition of Oxford continued without much difference until the decolonization period following World War II. Nearly two decades later, the concepts of Orientalism and Orientalist underwent changes in meaning with new debates on the agenda. As a result of these discussions and studies, orientalism has been considered together with definitions such as an instrument of Western imperialism, a way of thinking, and the epistemological and ontological distinction between west and east. This change of definition has undoubtedly occurred with the contributions of important names. Deconstructive studies of names such as "Anouar Abdel Malek (Orientalism in Crisis), A. L. Tibawi (Critique of Englishspeaking Orientalists), Bryan Turner (Marxism and the end of Orientalism), Edward Said (Orientalism: Western Conceptions of the Orient) have brought about radical changes in the traditional references of the concept. The works written by these names have significantly shaken established perceptions that think of Orientalism only as a field of study and have treated Orientalism as a new type of racism (Macfie, 2002). The relationship of orientalist studies carried out since the middle of the 19th century with imperialism has been expressed through multiple perspectives (Aydın, 2005).

The present meaning of orientalism - especially after Edward Said's definition of orientalism - has evolved into a negative meaning. In his article evaluating Edward Said's work Orientalism, Bernard Lewis lamented the negative meaning that academic circles in America and Europe attribute to the Orientalist concept, claiming that the concept was contaminated. For this reason, the use of the orientalist concept was abandoned with a decision taken at the "International Congress of Orientalists" that convened in the summer of 1973 (Lewis, 1982). The negative connotation of the concept is undoubtedly due to the paradigm crisis created by Edward Said. While Lewis restricted orientalism to an academic endeavor, Said spread the concept of orientalism widely to include travel books and novels about the Orient, as well as reports from academics working under government administrators (Shah, 2011). The differing views of Orientalism in the work of these two names are indications of theoretical disagreement. However, in the following periods, Said's contribution to the field enabled post-colonial thought to question the orientalist accumulation, and this led to the termination of the concept.

In addition to providing an analysis, Said's micro/macro relations between Orientalist knowledge and power production opened the door to many important discussions. Doubts about the objectivity of the Western knowledge produced about the East began to be expressed more after Edward Said's studies. The prominent emphasis in Edward Said's work is the claim that there is a secret cooperation and logic integrity between the production of knowledge and the dominant power structure. According to Said, there is a close cooperation between the political experience of the imperialist era and the cultural reproduction processes, and whether conscious or not, this is a distinctive feature of the Western world of thought.

Orientalism, as Said points out, is a path found by Western societies that think about the orient, depict the orient, and act in the name of being its supervisor. The existence of a field such as Orientalism undoubtedly starts with thinking about the East. Orientalism has come to life based on a basic ontological pre - acceptance in the process of evolving from the discourse of everyday life to a literary and scientific discourse (Arlı, 2009). This pre-acceptance object is the East itself, on which information is produced and speculated in almost every field. In fact, terms such as "Eastern" and "Western" have metaphysical, ontological and essentialist connotations (Uluç, 2009).

Orientalist studies express the desire not only to understand the non-European, but also to control and manipulate the different. Orientalism, according to Said, thus created a particular Orient image of Europeans and later Americans or a "representation" of different parts of the world that was not really concerned with how they were actually defined, and pointed to all the texts, institutions, images and approaches they maintained (Lockmann, 2004). Therefore, unless we reveal the epistemological mind and discourse that established the East, we also accept the discourse that the West produces about the East as legitimate. The way to question the legitimacy of these discussions will undoubtedly be possible by following Edward Said's method. If Orientalism is not studied as a discourse, it will be impossible to understand the awesome discipline that allows European culture after enlightenment manage–or even produce - the East politically, sociologically, militarily, ideologically, scientifically (Said, 1978). Edward Said not only revealed the relationship of orientalism to imperialism, but also revealed the aims and methods of imperialism.

Said defines Orientalism as an academic discipline, a style of thought and a legal institution at three different levels. This approach draws our attention to the institutional and historical relationship between the information of Eastern societies and the imperialist Powers (Mutman, 1999). As various studies point out, Orientalist literature is not a direct academic discipline, but rather a collective effort to achieve certain goals. All these efforts pave the way for the systematic exploitation of the geography called the East.

DIGITAL GAMES

Before defining digital games, it is necessary to resolve the naming confusion for this concept. Three different names are preferred in the literature, namely "digital game", "video game" or "computer game". Game researcher Schell (2008) emphasizes in his work The Art of Game Design: A Book of Lenses that the term "digital game" is more valid because it is more inclusive and qualified. In this context, the term "digital game" was preferred in this study. Digital games can be handled in different ways, depending on where they are viewed, as a game, an interactive software, audio-visual representation tools, fictional works containing narratives or social media (Sezen, 2011).

According to Binark (2007), digital game is the act of playing games in virtual space. Binark also distinguishes the digital game from the classic game. According to her, digital games differ from classical games with their interactivity and multimedia features specific to new media. After the second half of the 20th century, games have been transferred to the electronic environment and thus digital games have entered our lives (Akbulut, 2009). One of the important differences that distinguishes the digital game from the classic game is that the digital game emerged with an industrial design. Digital game emerges because of an industrial production and the game itself carries a commodity value (Binark & Bayraktutan-Sütçü, 2008).

The limitations that digital games have can be seen as a break from reality due to order, rules, and temporal-spatial environment. However, the software and hardware that create the online world is an extension of the real world. In this context, it would not be correct to position digital games in contrast with reality. If we further expand the link with software and hardware, the worlds created in games reflect the real world economically and socially. The digital game offers a representation of reality in this context.

Pargman & Jakobsson (2008) investigated the relationship of digital games with reality in terms of individuals. According to the results of this research, it was revealed that the game is a routine activity for the players. The act of playing digital games is regarded by the players as a part of their daily lives, not as an action disconnected from the flow of their daily lives.

Just like in classic games, the player tries to overcome the obstacles and reach the goal in digital games. However, the only difference is to perform all these actions in a virtual and interactive environment. In digital games, players experience being someone else by virtually having a different identity and find the opportunity to be identified (Akbulut, 2009). In this context, digital games make it easier for the player to understand the world and society.

The player improves himself by learning the rules and situations he is not used to during the game. Features such as self-improvement, gaining new skills increase the player's commitment to the game by increasing the pleasure they receive from the game. Another factor affecting the commitment to the game for the players is that the game has a solid story, or rather a narrative. At this point, the narrative and story attract the player with elements of curiosity, conflict, and tension. Digital games are designed with features that can attract people of all ages. There are many variables in games that are interdependent or not. Basically, the features that can be accepted for all digital games are listed as follows in Juul's (2005) study named Half-Real: Video Games between Real Rules and Fictional Worlds:

- **The Rule:** The rule can be briefly expressed as the principle that must be followed. In this context, like every system, games also have a structure laid with rules. Rules are produced to restrict player movements. The rules in the game are clear and specific.
- **Variability:** Variability refers to measurable results. Games have measurable results.
- **Value:** Value emphasizes the importance of the outcome in the game. Results have positive or negative values. At the end of the game, the results gain value.
- **Player:** Player tries to fulfill his responsibility in line with the rules determined in the game. This responsibility creates an element of competition with the player's effort.
- **Player link:** Player link is the effect of the player on the result. The winning player is happy, the losing player is unhappy.
- **Adaptability:** Adaptive results are realized by the player in a variable way, again in accordance with the rules. The game can be played without considering the results.

The development of technology leads to the further expansion of digital environments, which have a wide range of software and hardware options. These innovations have increased the prevalence and use of digital games. In the historical process, digital games have experienced many turning points in the fields of economy, technology, and marketing.

CONCEPT OF REPRESENTATION

The concept of representation as it is used in Communication Studies describes the way social groups, different subcultures, professions, ages, social classes and places are shown in the media and how this way of showing is interpreted by the audience (Price, 1998). In other words, the concept of representation problematizes how people are presented to themselves and others in the mass media.

Representation, according to Hall (2003), is the fundamental point of the process of common meanings, the production and exchange of these meanings between individuals with a certain culture. Hall also approached the relationship of representation and meaning from a different perspective. According to him, representation should be considered as a structure that constructs meaning.

According to Edward Said (1978), the concept of representation is intertwined with the historical, cultural, and political context. Questioning the relationship of representation with truth and correct,

Said emphasizes that representation is constructed with many things next to truth or correct, which is "again a representation".

The concept of representation, which entered the agenda of media research for the first time in the 70's, has led to debates about the political nature of all representations regarding culture. Feminist, black, and gay movements that emerged in the 1960s opposed their representation in the media and initiated the process in which representations were opened for discussion. In this process, the research produced positive representations in the media of certain groups. Some other groups are offered to society in a negative way, thus serves the interests of dominant social groups is revealed. Accordingly, role models in the media have been interpreted as an effective force that determines gender identity, norms, values, appropriate and inappropriate behaviors (Durham & Kellner, 2006).

One of the important points when explaining the concept of representation is its effect on meanings. The mass media participate in representation systems not only by coding or reflecting the real world, but also by producing meaning and allowing the change of meanings (Çelenk, 2005). In Hall's words (1998), the media is the maker of signification. The media not only reproduces reality, but also defines it. Selected definitions of what is called 'real' are represented in the media. On the relationship between meaning and reality, Stephane Greco Larson said that the media re-present reality in a way that supports certain meanings and interpretations of the way the world works. According to Larson (2006), these representations are chosen and structured in a way that consistently supports the status quo, that is, certain beliefs, structures, and inequalities. The most concrete examples of structured meanings reach the masses through media contents. Certain types of people are constantly shown in certain roles in the media, and in this way, certain patterns about society are presented to the people who follow the media content. These patterns lead people to see both others and themselves in certain ways, teach whom and what to value, to whom and what to oppose, and therefore construct certain ways of seeing.

The claim that representations construct certain ways of seeing requires questioning the relation of representation to reality. Lawrence Grossberg (2006) Say that the word representation, which means "re-presentation," means to take something original, mediate it and "show it again". However, this process almost necessarily changes the authenticity of the original. Representation involves making a claim about reality; but it is not the same as reality. On the other hand, it is not just a matter of realistically constructing an imaginary world. In the process of representation, the creator of the text tries to maximize the effect and experience of the text on the audience by drawing the audience to the universe created by the text (Grossberg, 2006). At this point, Grossberg emphasizes a reality universe created by representation. This universe of reality created by representation should be made attractive to the viewer.

DIGITAL GAMES AND ORIENTALISM

With the development of technology and the entertainment industry over the years, digital games have become an effective tool in spreading cultural images. It has industrial practices in digital games like other popular culture products. Stories, heroes, characters, and environment have an important place in these industrial practices. Digital games provide a schematized view of the world by its very nature. Besides game heroes with certain personality traits, usually game characters are created with only a few distinctive features. Similarly, the in-game environment and venue are created by iterating a limited number of graphic elements.

In digital games, it is possible to find many popular examples of stories, especially from the Middle East. The examples such as *Prince of Persia* (Broderbund, 1989), *The Magic of Scheherazade* (Cultural Brain, 1989), *Arabian Nights* (Krisalis, 1995), *Al-Qadim: The Genie's Curse* (SSI, 1994), *Beyond Oasis* (Sega, 1995), *Persian Wars* (Cryo, 2001) and *Prince of Persia: The Two Thrones* (Ubisoft, 2005) examples have an important place in the game world with their stories and heroes unique to the Middle East.

According to Edward Said's interpretation, photography, and cinematography, which depict the Middle East with a naive and historicizing perspective, have deliberately marginalized the Middle Eastern culture. According to Sisler (2008), the visual indicators used by the plays to create the impression of "Middle East" are exactly compatible with Said's patterns. Symbols such as turban, machete, camels, desert, and exotic dancers used in the plays are presented among the patterns unique to the East. The games use different images, narratives, and gameplay which are mostly Oriental, whether fantasy or historical (Sisler, 2008). Digital games contain narrative. The narrative in digital games serves a broader purpose, unlike literature and cinema. Together with the narrative, graphics, and gameplay, it shapes the broader associative message of the game. In most digital games with the Middle East in the background, the plot begins with the kidnapping of a woman (princess, sister, girl) by an evil character (vizier, caliph, demon), and the protagonist's in-Game reason for existence is to save her and revenge. These frequently used plot patterns are also very common in medieval western civilizations but are presented as if they belong only to Middle Eastern culture.

Most digital games build a fantastic Middle East, using historical elements to impose an Orientalist view on the player. Several games such as *Age of Empires 2* (Microsoft, 1999) depict a Middle East in line with historical facts. This prevalent orientalist view in digital games stands out, overshadowing contemporary reality.

One of the game types in which the orientalist view is widely presented in games is action games. *War in the Gulf* (Empire, 1995), *Delta Force* (Nova Logic, 1998), *Conflict: Desert Storm* (SCi Games, 2002), *Full Spectrum Warrior* (THQ, 2004), *Kuma / War* (Kuma Reality Games, 2004) and Popular action games such as *Conflict: Global Terror* (SCi Games, 2005) take place in the Middle East, and the anti-hero imagery in these games is usually Middle Eastern characters.

AN ASSESSMENT OF ARAB AND MUSLIM REPRESENTATION IN DIGITAL GAMES

Digital games have positioned themselves as mainstream media that influence our understanding and worldview through various representations in the modern world. Muslim and Arab representation in digital games should be contextualized with Muslim representation in the media in general. Recent studies show that the image of Muslims in Europe and America is reduced to general stereotypes and clichés, and Muslims are marginalized by making a distinction between us and them (Yorulmaz, 2018). According to these studies, many people perceive Muslims as threats (Poole, 2006). For Westerners, Islam is probably associated with terrorism (Karim, 2006) and the average Muslim image has been marginalized in the media (Richardson, 2004). According to a study conducted by Jack Shaheen (2001) on 900 Muslim characters in American movies and TV series, only 12 of these characters have positive and 50 positive-negative representations, while the remaining characters are terrorist, barbarian, wild men or love presented as repressed women deprived of love.

Digital games also have the general attitude of the media mentioned above. However, since games are "neglected media", that is, they are generally considered outside of the general cultural discourse, they are neglected in academic studies and they are less subject to criticism in the media field, they can include cliche and stereotypes more openly and daring (Reichmuth & Werning, 2006).

In the recent "FPS-first person shooter" games, Muslims and Arabs have been defined as the other and shown as enemies to be killed. In FPS games, the goal is based on finding and destroying the enemy, and in these games, the enemies that must be destroyed are Muslims and Arabs. According to Sisler (2008), the player usually controls American soldiers in these games while enemy forces are controlled by a computer. In these games it is mostly impossible to play the enemy. It has schemes such as skullcaps, baggy dresses, dark skin color depicting hostile Arabs or Muslims, and in-game narratives are usually associated with Islamic radicalism or international terrorism. For example, the game *Delta Force: Land Warrior* contains a story about a Muslim terrorist group coming together from different countries trying to undermine the activities of the USA. *Full Spectrum Warrior* takes place in Tajikistan, defined as "a paradise for terrorists" (Leonard, 2004). While the US and coalition soldiers are presented at a humane temperature with their nicknames and special abilities, the enemy is typified and verbally dehumanized with definitions such as "various terrorist groups" and "marginal groups". At the same time, the courage, professionalism, moral duties of the US soldiers controlled by the player are emphasized verbally in the in-game narratives and it is stated that the enemy soldiers are not real soldiers (Machin & Suleiman, 2006). Computer-controlled enemy soldiers display undisciplined behavior, shout, raise weapons over their head, and laugh mockingly when they kill someone. Created for smartphones and tablets, Trigger Fist (Lake Effect, 2012) game takes this situation a step further and brings on the agenda modern Crusades. Players who are new to the game receive their training on a base with an emphasis on the cross, and battles take place in Islamic countries.

In *Command and Conquer- Generals*, it is possible to choose one of the US, Chinese and Arab "Global Liberation Army". But in the game, the US Army is an army that is well trained, armed with superior weapons, has self-repairing tools, and has the ability to instantly attack wherever it wants on the map due to its intelligence and competence. The Arab "Global Liberation Army" is depicted with terrorists, suicide bombers, explosive-laden vehicles, and angry Arab gangs, and stands apart from the rest (Chick, 2003). While choosing the US army in the game makes it easier to win the game, it is very difficult to win the game with the Arab army (Sisler, 2008). Therefore, this situation encourages the selection of the US military by the players.

In the free-to-download computer game *Muslim Massacre*, the player parachutes into the Middle East as a US hero. The aim of the player is to kill all Muslims who appear on the screen with weapons in their hands. Some of them are terrorists wearing suicide vests and some of them are civilian people. The producer of the game, Eric Vaughn, stated that he was happy to produce the game and that this game was a fun game (Reporter, 2008). Similarly, games such as *Whack the Hamas*, *Gaza Assault: Code Red* and *Bomb Gaza*, produced for smartphones and tablets, are also games that focus on the killing of Muslims in the Israeli-Palestinian conflict (Hallett, 2014).

In some digital games, it has also been seen that symbols belonging to Islam are identified with hostile people or groups in the game. For example, in *Resident Evil 4* (Capcom, 2005), protagonist Leon is given the task of rescuing the president's daughter from the hands of a mysterious religious organization called Los Illuminados. During the rescue operation, they enter a castle belonging to the organization. The gate of the castle belonging to this demonic organization has a very great resemblance to the gate of the Masjid-i-Nabawi. The only difference is that the symbol of the Los Illuminados organization is placed in the center of the door.

Similarly, the door cover of the Kaaba was used in *Devil May Cry 3* (Capcom, 2005). In the game there is a tower called Temen-Ni-Gru. According to the game, this tower, which is the place of transition between the realm of humans and the realm of Demons, was built by devil worshippers. People under the influence of Satan can climb this tower and worship the forces of the dark there. The main door of this devil temple is the same as the door cover of the Kaaba.

There are some games in the Western world that Muslims are not the othering. For example, in *Sid Meiers's Civilizations 3: Conquest* game, players can control any civilization they want, and one of these civilizations is the Islamic Civilization. The player can take develop this Middle East-based civilization from its birth and put it into a race with other civilizations. There is no superiority among civilizations in the game and encyclopedic information is given about civilizations (Sisler, 2008). Another similar game is *Age of Empires 2* (Ensemble, 1999). In this game, the player can control the army of Saladin and fight with rival states. In addition, in the story parts of the play, the attention is drawn to the positive perspective towards Saladin and Islamic Civilization (Yorulmaz, 2018).

A lot of research has been carried out so far on the presentation of Muslims in digital games. Sisler, in his 2006 study, concluded that Muslims are marginalized in digital games. Again, Sisler, in his 2008 study titled "Digital Arabs: Representation in video games", concluded that Muslims are uniformized and associated with terrorism in games produced by Western companies. 2008 study by Al-Rawi investigated how Iraqis are represented in American-made films and games. According to the results of Al-Rawi's research, Iraqis are presented with oriental motifs in parallel with the political climate of America in American-made digital games and movies. According to the results of a study conducted by Naji and Iwar in 2013, orientalist motifs predominate in the presentation of the Middle East and Muslims in digital games. In a study he conducted in 2014, Komel investigated the orientalist motifs in the first game of the *Assassin's Creed* series, produced by Ubisoft. Cox's study in 2016 investigated Muslim representation in strategy games. According to Cox's results, Muslims are mostly presented with a barbarian and invading identity in strategy games. According to a study conducted by Ibaid in 2019, many American-made digital games contain Islamophobic elements.

FUTURE RESEARCH DIRECTIONS

The impact of the games, which portray Muslims as terrorists, barbarians and enemies that need to be killed, and that offer players the opportunity to experience this on Muslim and non-Muslim players is one of the important issues to be investigated. What does a Muslim player who is identified with a US soldier and who kills Muslims feel? Does he regret his work or just see it as a game? Does it glorify the US military and the West it controls? Does it fall into inferiority complex? Or is his anger towards the West growing? On the other hand, does a non-Muslim's view change related with Muslims who play these games? Is the perception of the terrorist Muslim in the media consolidating or do the players perceive this experience as just a game?

CONCLUSION

There is also a dimension of digital games that are sometimes played to have fun, sometimes played to spend free time, and sometimes played to realize oneself, which prepares the ground for marginalization and hate speech in players. Many digital games in different categories are unfortunately racist, fascist, vandal, pornographic, etc. and many negative contents are encountered from racing to action, adventure to simulation.

This study examined research focusing on Arab and Muslim representation in digital games. According to the researchers' studies, the Middle East is typically marginalized by using "Orientalist" images and with an Islamophobic perspective in the analyzed digital games. Digital games present the Middle East in a non-contemporary and decidedly confrontational framework by schematizing or stereotyping Arabs and Muslims as enemies. In this respect, it is necessary to focus on the political and cultural consequences of this representation strategy. While making this assessment, especially Said's "other" identity and the concept of "orientalist" approach, which is a distinction between East and West, gains importance. Western countries have been trying to create Islamophobia in public opinion around the world and trying to recreate their own images of Islam and Islamic civilization using digital games.

The representation of Muslims in Western producers' plays is presented and identified with terrorism in parallel with the general attitude of the media. However, since games are "neglected media" - they are trivial and neglected and are not subject to academic research and debates enough - they can use anti-Islamic discourses and representations more boldly. Especially in FPS games, the Middle East is chosen as the location and the enemy is clearly determined as Muslims. Winning the game depends on the number of Muslims killed. In these games, the player usually plays US soldiers, identifies himself with US soldiers, and with a few exceptions, it is not possible to play a Muslim fighter. In many of the games that give the chance to choose Muslim soldiers, managing the army of Muslims makes it difficult to win the game. It should also be noted that games featuring positive Muslim representations are rarely encountered among Western digital games, the majority of which contain negative Muslim representations, there are rarely.

Today, we very much need a critical understanding of the symbolic and ideological dimensions of representation politics. Obviously, no factors lead to stereotyping. The most dangerous effect of stereotyping is that sometimes negative images are perceived as a true depiction of the other culture. This is mainly the case in the absence of positive images of some communities, especially when these schemes remain unchallenged. With a greater emphasis on other languages and cultural areas, systematic and well-researched academic reflection of representation in digital games is needed.

REFERENCES

Akbulut, H. (2009). Gelenekselden Dijitale, Mekândan Uzama Oyun Kültürü. In Dijital Oyun Rehberi içinde (pp. 25-82). İstanbul: Kalkedon.

Al-Rawi, A. (2008). Iraqi stereotypes in American culture: The case of video games and films. *International Journal of Contemporary Iraqi Studies*, 2(2), 225–249. doi:10.1386/ijcis.2.2.225_1

Arlı, A. (2003). Edward Said'in Mirası. *Divan, İlmi Araştırmalar, 15*, 175–185.

Aydın, C. (2005). Orientalism by the Orientals? The Japanese Empire and Islamic Studies. *İslam Araştırmaları Dergisi, 14*, 1-36.

Binark, M. (2007). Dijital Oyunlar, Sektör – İçerik ve Oyuncular. *Folklor ve Edebiyat. Sanal Ortamda Dijital Oyun Kültürü Sayısı, 50*, 11–23.

Binark, M. & Bayraktutan-Sütçü, G. (2008). Kültür Endüstrisi Ürünü Olarak Dijital Oyun. İstanbul: Kalkedon Yayınları.

Bulut, Y. (2010). *Oryantalizmin Kısa Tarihi*. Küre Yayınları.

Çelenk, S. (2005). *Televizyon, Temsil, Kültür: 90'lı Yıllarda Sosyokültürel İklim ve Televizyon İçerikleri.* Ütopya Yayınları.

Chick, T. (2003). *Command & Conquer Generals (PC)*. Retrieved from http://pc.gamespy. com/pc/command-conquer-generals/5617p1.html

Cox, R. J. (2016). *Crusades and Jihad: An Examination of Muslim Representation in Computer Strategy Games* (Master's Dissertation). Retrieved from: https://jewlscholar.mtsu.edu/handle/mtsu/5078

Durham, M. G., & Kellner, D. (2006). *Media and Cultural Studies: Keyworks*. Blackwell Publishing.

Grossberg, L. (2006). *Media Making: Mass Media in a Popular Culture*. Sage.

Hall, S. (1998). Anlamlandırma, Temsil, ideoloji, Althusser ve Postyapısalcı Tartışmalar. In E. Mutlu (Eds.), Kitle iletişim Kuramları içinde (pp. 359-394). Ankara: Ankara Üniversitesi İletişim Fakültesi Yayınları.

Hall, S. (2003). İdeolojinin Yeniden Keşfi: Medya Çalışmalarında Baskı Altında Tutulanın Geri Dönüşü. In M. Küçük (Eds.), Medya, İktidar, İdeoloji içinde (pp. 77-126). Ankara: Ark Yayınları.

Hallett, N. (2014, August 5). *'Whack the Hamas': Gaza Bombing Games Branded 'Disgusting'*. Breitbart. Retrieved from: https://www.breitbart.com/london/2014/08/05/whack-the-hamas-gaza-bombing-games-branded-disgusting/

Ibaid, T. (2019). *The Waging of a Virtual War against Islam: An Assessment of How Post-9/11 War-themed Video Games Stereotype Muslims* (Master's Dissertation). Retrieved from: https://ir.library.dc-uoit.ca/bitstream/10155/1023/1/Ibaid_Taha.pdf

Juul, J. (2005). *Half-Real: Video Games Between Real Rules and Fictional Worlds*. MIT Press.

Karim, H. (2006). American Media's Coverage of Muslims: The Historical Roots of Contemporary Portrayals. In Muslims and the New Media (pp. 116-127). London: I.B. Tauris.

Komel, M. (2014). Orientalism in Assassin's Creed: Self-orientalizing the assassins from forerunners of modern terrorism into occidentalized heroes. *Teorija in Praksa, 51*(1), 72–90.

Larson, S. (2006). *Media & Minorities: The Politics of Race in News and Entertainment*. Rowman & Littlefield.

Leonard, D. (2004). Unsettling the Military Entertainment Complex- Video Games and a Pedagogy of Peace. *Studies in Media and Information Literacy Education*. Retrieved from http://utpjournals.metapress.com/content/4lu7213r34740854/

Lewis, B. (1982). *The Question of orientalism*. The New York Review of Books.

Lockman, Z. (2004). *Contending Visions of the Middle East: The History and The Politics of Orientalism*. Cambridge University Press. doi:10.1017/CBO9780511606786

Macfie, A. L. (2002). *Orientalism*. Pearson Education Press.

Machin, D., & Suleiman, U. (2006). Arab and American Computer War Games: The Influence of a Global Technology on Discourse. *Critical Discourse Studies*, *3*(1), 1–22. doi:10.1080/17405900600591362

Mutman, M. (1999). Oryantalizmin Gölgesi Altında: Batı'ya Karşı İslam. In Oryantalizm, Hegemonya, Kültürel Fark içinde (pp. 25-71). İstanbul: İletişim Yayınları.

Naji, J., & Iwar, M. (2013). Simulated stereotypes turning the unreal real: An analysis of representations of the 'Other' in traditional media forms and digital games. *Journal of Arab & Muslim Media Research*, *6*(2-3), 115–131. doi:10.1386/jammr.6.2-3.115_1

Pargman, D., & Jakobsson, P. (2008). Do You Believe in Magic? Computer Games in Everyday Life. *European Journal of Cultural Studies*, *11*(2), 225–244. doi:10.1177/1367549407088335

Poole, E. (2006). The Effects of September 2011 and the War in Irak on British Newspaper Coverage. In Muslims and the New in Media (pp. 89-102). London: I.B. Tauris.

Price, J. (1998). *Advanced Studies in Media*. Nelson Thornes.

Reichmuth, P., & Werning, S. (2006). *Pixel Pashas Digital Djinns*. ISIM Reviews.

Richardson, J. E. (2004). *(Mis)representing Islam: The Racism and Rhetoric of British Broadsheet Newspapers*. J. Benjamins. doi:10.1075/dapsac.9

Said, E. (1978). *Orientalism*. Pantheon Books.

Sezen, T. İ. (2011). Dijital Oyunları Anlamak: Oyun, Anlatı, Yazılım ve Platform Perspektiflerinden Dijital Oyunlar. In Dijital Oyunlar içinde (pp. 119-148). İstanbul: Derin.

Shah, M. H. (2011). Edward Said and Bernard Lewis On the Question of Orientalism: A Clash Of Paradigm. In Orientalism and Conspiracy, Politics and Conspiracy Theory in The İslamic World (pp. 45-70). London: I.B. Tauris.

Shaheen, J. (2001). *Reel Bad Arabs: How Hollywood Vilifies a People*. Olive Branch Press.

Sisler, V. (2006). Representation and self-representation: Arabs and Muslims in digital games. In Gaming realities: A challenge for digital culture (pp. 85-92). Athens: Fournos.

Sisler, V. (2008). Digital Arabs: Representation in video games. *European Journal of Cultural Studies*, *11*(2), 203–220.

Uluç, G. (2009). *Medya ve Oryantalizm, Yabancı, Farklı ve Garip*. Anahtar Kitaplar Yayınevi.

Yorulmaz, B. (2018). Representation of Muslims in Digital Games. *Journal of Media and Religion Studies, 1*(2), 275–286.

ADDITIONAL READING

Campbell, H., & Grieve, G. (Eds.). (2014). *Playing with Religion in Digital Games*. Indiana University Press.

Chapman, A. (2016). *Digital games as history: How videogames represent the past and offer access to historical practice*. Routledge. doi:10.4324/9781315732060

Malkowski, J., & Russworm, T. (Eds.). (2017). *Gaming Representation: Race, Gender, and Sexuality in Video Games*. Indiana University Press. doi:10.2307/j.ctt2005rgq

Rutter, J., & Bryce, J. (Eds.). (2006). *Understanding digital games*. Sage.

KEY TERMS AND DEFINITIONS

Digital Games: A digital game is an interactive program for one or more players, meant to provide entertainment at the least, and quite possibly more.

Game Studies: Game studies, or ludology, is the study of games, the act of playing them, and the players and cultures surrounding them.

Hate Speech: Public speech that expresses hate or encourages violence towards a person or group based on something such as race, religion, sex, or sexual orientation.

Islamophobia: It means hatred, discrimination, hostility, and hatred towards Muslims.

Literature Review: A literature review is a search and evaluation of the available literature in your given subject or chosen topic area.

Orientalism: Orientalism is the name given to all the Western-based research areas in which Near Eastern and Far Eastern societies, cultures, languages, and peoples are examined.

Othering: To make a person or group of people seem different, or to consider them to be different.

Representation: The fact of including different types of people, for example in films, politics, or media, so that all different groups are represented.

This research was previously published in the Handbook of Research on Contemporary Approaches to Orientalism in Media and Beyond; pages 717-729, copyright year 2021 by Information Science Reference (an imprint of IGI Global).

Chapter 71

The Cyber Awareness of Online Video Game Players:
An Examination of Their Online Safety Practices and Exposure to Threats

Soonhwa Seok
Korea University, Seoul, South Korea

Boaventura DaCosta
Solers Research Group, FL, USA

ABSTRACT

The cyber awareness of online video game players (n = 183) was investigated by examining their online safety practices and the degree to which they were exposed to threats. With findings revealing that gamers engaged in poor online practices, despite expressing concern for their safety, this investigation supports the view that gamers are unaware of the possible consequences of their online actions, and/or continue to show resistance to cybersecurity practices perceived to hinder gameplay. While the findings should be regarded as preliminary, game developers and publishers, policymakers, and researchers may find them valuable in obtaining a clearer understanding of gamers' cyber awareness and online practices. Coupled with ongoing research, these findings may also prove valuable for the identification of strategies that may be used to curb risky online behavior.

INTRODUCTION

Video gameplay has become an everyday activity, available on a multitude of platforms, from computers to mobile devices. While these games can offer rich interactive experiences, their connectivity raises concern about safety. Massively multiplayer online role-playing games (MMORPGs), for example, have been described as breeding grounds for hackers and cybercriminals. Further, mobile games are believed to expose gamers to cyber threats through vulnerabilities that, when coupled with granted permissions, can create opportunities for unintentional access to device features. With video games anticipated to

DOI: 10.4018/978-1-6684-7589-8.ch071

grow in popularity and sophistication, it is important to understand the cybersecurity risks associated with this form of entertainment.

This study investigated the cyber awareness of online video game players (hereafter referred to as "gamers") by examining their online safety practices and the degree to which they were exposed to online dangers. With findings revealing that gamers engage in poor online practices, despite concern for their safety, this investigation offers empirical data in preliminary support of the argument that gamers are unaware of the possible consequences of their online actions and/or continue to show resistance towards cybersecurity practices perceived to hinder gameplay.

BACKGROUND

Cybersecurity Gaming Threats

Although cybersecurity-related gaming threats are not new (Cook, 2016; Dickson, 2016), the popularity and growth of online games have created new opportunities for cybercriminals (Dickson, 2016), who see these games as a way to make money using a variety of methods. For example, data breaches have seen yearly growth that is not confined to a particular sector, but targeting everything from retail to government. The video game industry has not been excluded from this trend, with large breaches reported in just the past few years. One of the most noteworthy was the PlayStation Network breach in 2011, which resulted in 77 million accounts being compromised (Paganini, 2016). In addition, Valve revealed in 2015 that 77,000 Steam accounts were hacked for months (Dickson, 2016; Makuch, 2015) using malware that is readily available on black markets for as little as US$3 (Dickson, 2016).

Such breaches often result in compromised gamer accounts that can be looted for personally identifiable information and sold to other cybercriminals (Rashid, 2013; Trend Micro, 2015, 2016) for the purposes of identity theft or fraud (Trend Micro, 2015, 2016). Gaming accounts typically include name, birth year, mailing address, email, mobile number, payment information, and even social networking data (Trend Micro, 2015, 2016). With the average gamer's age 18 to 30 years old, these accounts are attractive to cybercriminals (Rashid, 2013) with far-reaching implications, particularly for those who use the same password for their email, social media, and banking. Furthermore, data found in compromised accounts may be mined beyond financial gain, putting lives at risk. For example, social engineering tactics might be employed to determine if account owners hold significant positions or have access to important information, such as U.S. intelligence (Rashid, 2013).

Money may also be made through the sale of virtual goods. For example, some online games are intensely played (Cimpanu, 2016; Cook, 2016) to amass in-game items (e.g., weapons, armor) or currency that can be sold for real-world money (Cook, 2016). A DFC Intelligence (2010) study in cooperation with Live Gamer helps illustrate the popularity of such sales. Of the 4,816 mostly male U.S. and European gamers surveyed, approximately 60% purchased in-game goods (that was not a full game), with nearly 50% specifically buying power-up items believed to offer a gameplay advantage. While the sale or trade of legitimately attained in-game items is not prohibited (although the practice is considered cheating by some and thus frowned upon), in-game goods associated with compromised and stolen accounts can be illegally sold or purchased with a linked credit card for subsequent sale (Trend Micro, 2015, 2016). This was the case with the aforementioned Steam data breach, where cybercriminals targeted assets to be resold on Steam Trade (Dickson, 2016). In fact, according to *The New York Times,* the sale of in-game items and currency is so profitable that in 2005 approximately 100,000 Chinese video game players were employed by gamers in other countries to farm popular role-playing games (Barboza, 2005). Sweatshops have also reportedly emerged forcing laborers to farm game currency for long hours with little pay under poor working conditions (Cybrary, 2016). For example, China has been accused of using labor camp inmates to mine in-game items (Moore, 2011) for sale to gamers (John, 2016), with proceeds going to the prisons (Vincent, 2011).

What is perhaps more troubling is that the earnings gained from these types of sales may become part of real-world money laundering schemes (Solon, 2013), with proceeds converted to other forms of virtual currency, such as Bitcoin, to elude detection (Osborne, 2016). This claim is supported by the 2013 report released by the United Nations Office on Drugs and Crime that found MMORPGs were among the successful ways in which cybercriminals launder money, made possible because of the growth in virtual currency systems and economies in online games (Richet, 2013). These funds are then used to fuel other forms of illegal online activities, such as distributed-denial-of-service (DDoS) attacks. The Lizard Squad attack on Christmas day of 2015, which took the PlayStation Network and Xbox Live offline, preventing thousands of gamers from accessing either service (Paganini, 2016), has been cited as one such example (Cybrary, 2016). Even worse, it has been claimed that this laundering platform is used by terrorist groups (Kish, 2017).

Cybersecurity, the Video Game Industry, and Gamers

The video game industry is believed not to have fully grasped that it has become the target of cybercriminals, who exploit server vulnerabilities for DDoS attacks, in-game glitches to steal goods (Cimpanu, 2016), or use gaming economies to fuel other illicit activities. Duping, for example, is said to be one of the more popular practices of exploiting bugs to illegally duplicate in-game items or currency for later sale (Cimpanu, 2016). In addition, cybercriminals are using financial sector hacking (Cook, 2016) and social engineering techniques (Rashid, 2013), to include email and spear phishing practices, to steal login credentials (Trend Micro, 2015, 2016). It has been contended that game developers and publishers continue to focus on the hardening of code to prevent piracy and reverse engineering (Dickson, 2016). Given that the size of the gaming industry rivals that of film in the context of money, and hacking techniques are only anticipated to grow in sophistication, this has created a serious problem (Cook, 2016, 2017).

This is not to suggest that game developers and publishers are not doing anything about cybersecurity or that they are solely responsible. Blizzard, for example, closed the Diablo auction houses, citing that although they offered a convenient and secure system for trading, they also undermined the game's core play (Atherton, 2015). Furthermore, Valve has also taken steps to implement new security features. Nevertheless, accounts continue to be compromised, in part, because gamers are not taking advantage of new capabilities (Makuch, 2015). For example, because antivirus and related security apps slow down computers, resulting in lost frame rates and consequently diminishing the gaming experience, gamers are known to disable or remove security software altogether (Dickson, 2016). This attitude is reflected in a Google Consumer Survey that polled 500 gamers, which found that 52% did not use security software on their gaming computers, with 36% actively turning this software off if it slowed down their systems (Abel, 2016).

This suggests that gamers are partly responsible for the increase in cybercrime, to include losses of in-game goods, by not only showing continued resistance to cybersecurity practices that are viewed as gaming hindrances (Cybrary, 2016) but by also purchasing and possibly selling what may be illegally attained in-game items and currency to fuel their competitive need for quick game advancement (Trend Micro, 2015, 2016). Moreover, gamers may not realize that their behavior is problematic, leading to criminal activity (or worse, cybercrime), seeing their activities as nothing more than an extension of regular game play (Trend Micro, 2016). It is difficult to conceive that stealing a virtual melee weapon from another gamer in a MMORPG could result in criminal charges. It is this mindset, however, that has contributed to a lack of regulation on the matter and the difficulty of imposing real-world legislation on activities that take place in a virtual world (Jiang, 2011).

Game developers and publishers are no less assisting in prosecuting gamers. Blizzard, for example, helped convict two gamers responsible for the fencing of stolen in-game goods from Diablo II, which was viewed by the courts as felony-level theft (Atherton, 2015). In Japan, Nexon cooperated with authorities in the arrests of three gamers for obstruction of business due to their role in creating and selling 37 kinds of cheats for Sudden Attack, allegedly netting US$78,621 (Ashcraft, 2014). South Korea has also recently criminalized the creation and use of online game cheats, with those convicted facing up to five years in prison and $43,000 in fines (Chalk, 2016).

Regrettably, gamers continue to be unaware of the possible consequences of their online behavior, raising serious concern because the Internet and related technologies have created environments that force young people to make decisions about situations that they are not developmentally ready to make (Miller, Thompson, & Franz, 2009). This is despite the expectation that they can circumnavigate today's technology-rich world almost instinctively. Compounding matters, young people are thought to be one of the fastest adopters of the Internet (Marcum, Ricketts, & Higgens, 2010). Thus, this lack of understanding, coupled with a growing online presence, has left young people predisposed to online dangers. These fears are not unfounded, but supported by empirical data showing an increasing pattern of harm against young people in the form of disclosure of personal information; cyberbullying and stalking; and exposure to sexually explicit and violent material, inappropriate solicitations, and harassment (Marcum et al., 2010). The purpose of this study is borne from these concerns, examining the cyber awareness of online gamers, their online practices, and their exposure to online threats.

METHOD

Setting

The study was conducted at four vocational-track high schools in and near Seoul, South Korea. Chosen for its high broadband penetration rate and leadership role in technological advancement, South Korea offered a well-suited population from which to sample online gamers.

Participants

Of the 1,092 participating students, 58% ($n = 638$) were 18-20 years old, and 41.5% ($n = 454$) 17 years old and younger; 53% ($n = 575$) were male, and 47% ($n = 517$) were female; 35% ($n = 378$) lived in households earning a gross annual income of US$20,000-$39,999, and 32% ($n = 348$) earned US$40,000-$59,999; finally, 28% ($n = 303$) were students of the visual and performing arts, 9% ($n = 94$) studied computer science and information technology, and 8.5% ($n = 93$) studied engineering.

Instrumentation

A 51-item survey developed by the authors was used to collect data on young people's overall cyber awareness. Items focused on technology ownership, online activity, and threat exposure. Part of a larger body of research focused on youth cyber awareness, safety, and education, only a subset of the survey items was used in this investigation concentrated on gaming.

Procedure

Permission to conduct the study was obtained from school officials. Students were invited to volunteer to participate, with parental consent obtained for students 17 years old and younger. School staff administered the survey, which was presented in Korean. The students could answer the items in any order, skip items, and withdraw from the study altogether. A Korean-English speaking expert translated the data for statistical analysis and reporting.

RESULTS AND DISCUSSION

Of the 1,092 participating students, a total of 16.7% ($n = 183$) reported principally playing online video games, in favor of common and everyday online activities (i.e., social media; streaming music, movies, and/or television; schoolwork). It is these gamers that the following statistical analysis and discussion is focused on.

As shown in Table 1, these gamers were 20 years old or younger, but mostly 18-20 (57%, $n = 104$); were overwhelmingly male (79%, $n = 144$); played 3-6 hours per week (28%, $n = 51$); mostly used personal computers (93%, $n = 171$) and mobile phones (91%, $n = 167$); played free games (96%, $n = 176$); lived in homes comprising four people (57%, $n = 104$) with a family gross income of US$20,000-59,999 (66%, $n = 121$); and predominantly studied the visual and performing arts (17.5%, $n = 32$), followed by computer science and information technology (13%, $n = 24$).

Table 1. Gamer demographics

Item		Frequency
Age	17 and younger	79 (43.2%)
	18-20	104 (56.8%)
Gender	Male	144 (78.7%)
	Female	39 (21.3%)

continues on following page

Table 1. Continued

Item		Frequency
Gameplay per week (hrs.)	Less than 1	3 (1.6%)
	1-3	28 (15.3%)
	3-6	51 (27.9%)
	6-10	21 (11.5%)
	10-15	24 (13.1%)
	15-20	13 (7.1%)
	20-30	22 (12%)
	More than 30	21 (11.5%)
Game device	PC	171 (93.4%)
	Console	32 (17.5%)
	Handheld	60 (32.8%)
	Mobile phone	167 (91.3%)
Type of online gaming	Free	176 (96.2%)
	Subscription-based	7 (3.8%)
People living in household	1	1 (.5%)
	2	10 (5.5%)
	3	29 (15.8%)
	4	104 (56.8%)
	5 or more	39 (21.3%)
Family gross income	$0-19,999	36 (19.7%)
	$20,000-39,999	65 (35.5%)
	$40,000-59,999	56 (30.6%)
	$60,000-99,999	17 (9.3%)
	$100,000 and over	9 (4.9%)
Primary area of study	Architecture/Drafting	12 (6.6%)
	Biological and Biomedical Sciences	2 (1.1%)
	Business	2 (1.1%)
	Communications and Journalism	15 (8.2%)
	Computer Sciences and Information Technology	24 (13.1%)
	Culinary Arts and Personal Services	11 (6.0%)
	Education	1 (.5%)
	Engineering	14 (7.7%)
	Game Development	1 (.5%)
	Liberal Arts and Humanities	2 (1.1%)
	Mechanic and Repair Technologies	17 (9.3%)
	Military	1 (.5%)
	Physical Science	2 (1.1%)
	Visual and Performing Arts	32 (17.5%)
	Other	47 (25.7%)

Online Safety Practices

The findings revealed that although 48.1% ($n = 88$) of the gamers ($n = 183$) reported that they were sometimes concerned about their online safety, 33.3% ($n = 61$) indicated that they never were, with only 18.6% ($n = 34$) noting that they were always worried. These percentages are aligned with the finding regarding the gamers' use of security measures to protect themselves from cybercriminals. That is, while 48.6% ($n = 89$) reported that they sometimes took necessary action, 32.8% ($n = 60$) never did, and only 18.6% ($n = 34$) indicated that they always safeguarded themselves while online.

Further analysis revealed poor online security practices, even among those who reported that they always (18.6%, $n = 34$) took steps to protect themselves while online. Among these who always took steps, 58.8% ($n = 20$) used the same password across all their accounts, with 38.2% ($n = 13$) responding that they never use the same passwords. This is a dangerous practice as cybercriminals may try the compromised password with the victim's other accounts (assuming the username(s) are also known), to include email, banking, and social media. Compounding matters, of the gamers who reported that they always protected themselves while online, 32.4% ($n = 11$) acknowledged that they never and only sometimes used complex passwords (comprising letters, numbers, and special characters), with 35.3% ($n = 12$) reporting that they only sometimes updated their anti-malware (i.e., anti-virus, anti-spam, anti-spyware) software. Such practices make it easier for cybercriminals not only to ascertain passwords but also to infect computers and software, to include browsers. Finally, among the total number of gamers ($n = 183$), 60.1% ($n = 110$) admittedly used public Wi-Fi hotspots. This is also a dangerous practice, and one that is often frowned upon by security experts, who typically view these wireless networks as open and unsecure, and a favorite way for cybercriminals to sniff for unencrypted traffic.

Altogether, these findings show that the gamers engaged in poor online practices, including those who expressed concern for their safety. This suggests that either they were not worried enough about their online safety to make the necessary adjustments to their online behavior and/or they did not understand how to protect themselves from online predators. The former adds credence to reports that gamers are not taking advantage of online security (Makuch, 2015) but are making conscious decisions to disregard safeguards that hinder their gaming (Dickson, 2016). While the latter might also be the case, in that the gamers may not have the knowledge to protect themselves while online. However, almost all the gamers understood the cybersecurity terms used in the survey, with a very small percentage acknowledging they did not understand the terms malware or phishing ($n = 1$), or identity theft or Wi-Fi hotspot ($n = 4$).

Online Victimization

Among all the gamers ($n = 183$), few reported having had been infected with malware (13.7%, $n = 25$) in the past six months, falling prey to phishing (3.3%, $n = 6$), or becoming a victim of identity theft (1.6%, $n = 3$). Given the participants' online practices, more cases of victimization would have been expected, particularly given these are some of the more popular online methods used by cybercriminals in targeting gamers.

Additionally, those who said they always acted to safeguard themselves ($n = 34$) would be expected to encounter fewer occurrences of online victimization than those who reported that they never took any measures at all. This was indeed the case regarding phishing and identity theft. Those who took no action at all reported a higher percentage of victimization in the contexts of phishing (14.7%, $n = 5$) and identity theft (8.8%, $n = 3$) than those who always protected themselves (2.9%, $n = 1$; 0%, respectively).

However, the same was not the case for malware. Those who always safeguarded themselves were infected more (41.1%, $n = 14$) than those who did not take any steps at all (32.4%, $n = 11$). There may be numerous explanations for this; for example, the gamers who always safeguarded themselves may have taken more risks while online, feeling confident in that they were protected by their anti-malware software. Issues of bias associated with self-reported data may also have played a factor in this finding. That is, the participants may have responded based on what they felt others wanted to hear or what they felt was socially acceptable. Thus, it is unknown if the participants took the appropriate steps to safeguard themselves, given their responses regarding the use of the same passwords for all accounts, the use of complex passwords, updating anti-malware software, and the use of Wi-Fi hotspots.

LIMITATIONS AND FUTURE RESEARCH

Caution is warranted in interpreting these findings, as several areas of this study may be viewed as limitations. First, as mentioned, there are always validity challenges associated with self-reported data. Although it is assumed the participants responded truthfully, it is conceivable that some of them did not want to admit that they had been victims. Second, the participants were not asked if they had been exposed to cyber awareness interventions and training, thus limiting the findings. Future studies, therefore, should take into consideration exposure to classes and training that teach online safety. Third, is the method of online access; this was not taken into consideration and may have had a significant impact on the online activities reported or the victimization rates. For example, accessing the Internet via school or home networks is generally perceived as being safer than public Wi-Fi. Malware, for instance, is presumed to be more prevalent on open networks. Therefore, it is conceivable that the participants might have taken different risks depending on how they connected. Thus, future study should take method of access into consideration. Finally, even though South Korea was explicitly chosen as the site of this study because of its advanced technological thinking, Asian countries are remarkably different from other parts of the world. Thus, future study should continue to examine the cyber awareness of youth from Eastern countries, but Western countries as well.

CONCLUSION

The cyber awareness of online gamers was explored in the contexts of the online safety practices they exhibited and the degree to which they had been exposed to online threats. Overall, the findings revealed that the gamers exhibited poor online behaviors, offering credence to the suppositions that gamers do not understand the ramifications of their online actions and/or are not interested in cybersecurity practices that may interfere with their gameplay.

These findings should be regarded as preliminary, however, with further careful examination warranted before conclusions can be safely drawn. Nevertheless, game developers and publishers, policymakers, and researchers may find these findings valuable for gaining a clearer understanding of the cyber awareness and online practices of gamers. Coupled with ongoing research, the findings may also be helpful in the subsequent identification of strategies that may be used to curb risky online behavior.

REFERENCES

Abel, R. (2016, September). Study finds gamer cyber hygiene stinks. *SC Media US*. Retrieved from https://www.scmagazine.com/study-gamers-actively-shut-off-security-software-if-it-inhibits-game-play/article/530161/

Ashcraft, B. (2014, June). Gamers hit with criminal charges allegedly made tons of money. *Kotaku*. Retrieved from http://kotaku.com/gamers-hit-with-criminal-charges-apparently-made-tons-o-1596352729

Atherton, K. D. (2015, May). When virtual crimes get prosecuted in real life. A dungeon dive into Diablo's in-game crime spree. *Popular Science*. Retrieved from http://www.popsci.com/no-sanctuary-diablos-game-thieves

Barboza, D. (2005, December). Ogre to slay? Outsource it to Chinese. *The New York Times*. Retrieved from http://www.nytimes.com/2005/12/09/technology/ogre-to-slay-outsource-it-to-chinese.html

Chalk, A. (2016, December). Creating hacks for online games could now earn you jail time in South Korea. *PCGamer*. Retrieved from http://www.pcgamer.com/south-korea-makes-cheating-in-online-games-an-actual-crime/

Cimpanu, C. (2016, October). Online gaming currencies used to launder money for cyber-criminals. *Softpedia News*. Retrieved from http://news.softpedia.com/news/online-gaming-currencies-used-to-launder-money-for-cyber-criminals-509177.shtml

Cook, M. (2016, May). Why online video gaming will be the next industry under cyber attack. *Dark Reading*. Retrieved from http://www.darkreading.com/vulnerabilities---threats/why-online-video-gaming-will-be-the-next-industry-under-cyber-attack-/a/d-id/1325519

Cook, M. (2017, January). What to expect – Video game cybersecurity in 2017. *Gamasutra*. Retrieved from http://www.gamasutra.com/blogs/MatthewCook/20170112/289076/What_To_Expect__Video_Game_Cybersecurity_In_2017.php

Cybrary. (2016, October). *Cybercrime and the gaming industry*. Retrieved from https://www.cybrary.it/2016/10/cybercrime-gaming-industry/

Dickson, B. (2016, June). The gaming industry can become the next big target of cybercrime. *Crunch Network*. Retrieved from https://techcrunch.com/2016/06/08/the-gaming-industry-can-become-the-next-big-target-of-cybercrime/

DFC Intelligence. (2010, March). *Consumers & downloadable items*. Retrieved from http://www.dfcint.com/dossier/consumers-downloadable-items/

Jiang, D. (2011). Security issues in massively multiplayer online games. *ACC 626 Research Paper*. Retrieved from http://uwcisa.uwaterloo.ca/Biblio2/Topic/ACC626%20Security%20Issues%20in%20Massively%20Multiplayer%20Online%20Games%20X%20Jiang.pdf

John, R. (2016, March). Outsourcing fun: Gold farming & the rise of digital sweatshops. *The Online Economy*. Retrieved from https://onlineeconomy.hbs.org/submission/outsourcing-fun-gold-farming-the-rise-of-digital-sweatshops/

Kish, S. (2017, May). Massively multiplayer games a platform for terrorism? *Intelligencer*. Retrieved from http://phcintelligencer.com/2017/05/15/massive-multiplayer-games-a-platform-for-terrorism-2/

Makuch, E. (2015, December). 77,000 Steam accounts hacked every month, new security measures deployed. *Gamespot*. Retrieved from http://www.gamespot.com/articles/77000-steam-accounts-hacked-every-month-new-securi/1100-6433003/

Marcum, C. D., Ricketts, M. L., & Higgens, G. E. (2010). Assessing sex experiences of online victimization: An examination of adolescent online behaviors using Routine Activity Theory. *Criminal Justice Review*, *35*(4), 412–437. doi:10.1177/0734016809360331

Miller, N. C., Thompson, N. L., & Franz, D. P. (2009). Proactive strategies to safeguard young adolescents in the cyberage. *Middle School Journal*, *41*(1), 28–34. doi:10.1080/00940771.2009.11461701

Moore, M. (2011, May). Chinese labour camp prisoners forced to play online games. *The Telegraph*. Retrieved from http://www.telegraph.co.uk/technology/news/8537467/Chinese-labour-camp-prisoners-forced-to-play-online-games.html

Osborne, C. (2016, October). Business is booming: How online gaming fuels cybercrime. *ZDNet*. Retrieved from http://www.zdnet.com/article/business-is-booming-how-online-gaming-fuels-cybercrime/

Paganini, P. (2016, May). The lucrative but vulnerable gaming industry is ripe for cyberattacks. *Security Affairs*. Retrieved from http://securityaffairs.co/wordpress/47376/cyber-crime/gaming-industry.html

Rashid, F. Y. (2013, July). Why video game companies are lucrative targets for hackers. *Security Week*. Retrieved from http://www.securityweek.com/why-video-game-companies-are-lucrative-targets-hackers

Richet, J.-L. (2013, June). Laundering money online: A review of cybercriminals' methods. *Tools and Resources for Anti-Corruption Knowledge – United Nations Office on Drugs and Crime (UNODC)*. Retrieved from https://arxiv.org/ftp/arxiv/papers/1310/1310.2368.pdf

Solon, O. (2013, October). Cybercriminals launder money using in-game currencies. *Wired*. Retrieved from http://www.wired.co.uk/article/money-laundering-online

Trend Micro. (2015, January). *Data privacy and online gaming: Why gamers make for ideal targets*. Retrieved from http://www.trendmicro.com/vinfo/us/security/news/online-privacy/data-privacy-and-online-gaming-why-gamers-make-for-ideal-targets

Trend Micro. (2016, October). *The cybercriminal roots of selling online gaming currency*. Retrieved from https://www.trendmicro.com/vinfo/us/security/news/cybercrime-and-digital-threats/cybercriminal-roots-selling-online-gaming-currency

Vincent, D. (2011, May). China used prisoners in lucrative Internet gaming work. *The Guardian*. Retrieved from https://www.theguardian.com/world/2011/may/25/china-prisoners-internet-gaming-scam

This research was previously published in the International Journal of Cyber Research and Education (IJCRE), 1(1); pages 69-77, copyright year 2019 by IGI Publishing (an imprint of IGI Global).

Chapter 72
Behavioral and Physiological Responses to Computers in the Ultimatum Game

Aleksandra Swiderska

Department of Psychology, Warsaw University, Warsaw, Poland

Eva G. Krumhuber

Department of Experimental Psychology, University College London, London, UK

Arvid Kappas

Department of Psychology and Methods, Jacobs University Bremen, Bremen, Germany

ABSTRACT

This article describes how studies in the area of decision-making suggest clear differences in behavioral responses to humans versus computers. The current objective was to investigate decision-making in an economic game played only with computer partners. In Experiment 1, participants were engaged in the ultimatum game with computer agents and regular computers while their physiological responses were recorded. In Experiment 2, an identical setup of the game was used, but the ethnicity of the computer agents was manipulated. As expected, almost all equitable monetary splits offered by the computer were accepted. The acceptance rates gradually decreased when the splits became less fair. Although the obtained behavioral pattern implied a reaction to violation of the rule of fairness by the computer in the game, no evidence was found for participants' corresponding emotional involvement. The findings contribute to the body of research on human-computer interaction and suggest that social effects of computers can be attenuated.

DOI: 10.4018/978-1-6684-7589-8.ch072

INTRODUCTION

Humans have a natural tendency to perceive non-human and non-living entities in terms of human qualities – they readily attribute the power to act or to intentionally behave in a certain way to animals, natural forces, gods, and technological gadgets, and thus create human-like agents in the surrounding environment (Waytz, Epley, & Cacioppo, 2010). One of the most scrutinized inanimate social actors is the computer. In this context, experiments that investigated the mechanisms of human-human interactions (HHI) were systematically adapted to the study of human-computer interactions (HCI). Substituting participants' interaction partner with a regular computer, it was shown that people adhere to politeness norms when they respond to computers, apply gender stereotypes, and take part in mutual self-disclosure (e.g, Nass, Moon, & Carney, 1999; Nass, Moon, & Green, 1997). The term "media equation" was coined to refer to these effects (Reeves & Nass, 1996). Invoking the ethopoeia approach, they were explained to occur due to the mindlessness of the computer users who unconsciously implement accessible behavioral scripts suited for social exchange in settings that involve computers, even though social cues in such settings are sometimes minimal (Nass & Moon, 2000).

Computers with anthropomorphic characters as interfaces have been demonstrated to instantly evoke reactions normally reserved for humans (Yee, Bailenson, & Rickertsen, 2007). However, it is especially the plausibility of the characters' behavior that produces enough social cues to engender interpersonal dynamics (Tinwell, Grimshaw, Nabi, & Williams, 2011). Behavioral realism and agency are two crucial factors responsible for the meaningfulness of HCI within the Threshold Model of Social Influence, an alternative to the ethopoeia approach (Blascovich et al., 2002). Behavioral realism denotes the extent to which the computer-generated characters act in a manner consistent with the user's expectations shaped throughout socialization, so mainly in everyday face-to-face interactions. It is even thought to be more essential than anthropomorphic appearance itself, which primarily serves to aid perception of given behaviors. Agency refers to whether artificial characters are perceived to accurately depict real people in real time.

How agency afforded by avatars (virtual personifications of the users operating in real time) and agents (virtual characters driven by a computer algorithm) influences people's responses in HCI remains unclear. Ethopoeia presumes that if avatars and agents exhibit enough social cues, they will elicit comparable social responses. This is parallel to how people would be expected to respond to regular computers, as demonstrated by research described earlier. Conversely, the Threshold Model of Social Influence predicts that since avatars represent real humans, their perceived agency is always greater. Hence, their social impact should be more pronounced in comparison to the agents. An interesting line of research that accommodated the versatile comparison of reactions to avatars and agents on the one hand and to humans and regular computers on the other was founded on a simple social decision-making paradigm frequently used in psychological experiments – the ultimatum game.

Typically, the ultimatum game engages two players, called the proposer and the responder. They have an amount of money to split between themselves. The proposer offers a certain amount to the responder and the responder's task is to either accept or reject it. If the offer is accepted, the money is distributed as determined by the proposer. If it is rejected, neither of the players gets the money. From the standard economic decision-making point of view, the proposer should offer the smallest possible amount and the responder should always accept it. In such a scenario, the players would take the only rational course of action – they would make decisions to boost their monetary gains (Becker, 2013). Nevertheless, it appears that proposers are inclined to split the money fairly and offer respondents approximately 50%

of the amount at their disposal. Respondents frequently refuse lower offers and the rejection rates grow as the offers become less fair (Nowak, Page, & Sigmund, 2000).

Unfair offers elicit anger and disgust in the respondents – emotions that arise in reaction to the perceived violations of social rules (e.g., Chapman, Kim, Susskind, & Anderson, 2009). Rejection of the unfair offer is the means to punish the proposer for the social transgression and people tend to choose punishment even though it is paired with lack of financial gains for them as well (Fehr & Gächter, 2002). Emotional components of decisions concerning unjust offers have been tackled further in studies that incorporated physiological measurements. Elevated electrodermal response (activity of sweat glands in the skin) may indicate emotional arousal and personal implication, and accompanies both reception and refusal of unfair offers (van't Wout, Kahn, Sanfey, & Aleman, 2006). Activation of facial muscles at the site of *Corrugator Supercilii* (the muscle responsible for drawing the eyebrows to the middle and downward) has been linked to expressions of negative affect (visible as frowning), and together with the activation at other muscle sites has been associated respectively with anger (Cannon, Schnall, & White, 2011) and disgust (Krumhuber, Tsankova, & Kappas, 2016).

Notably, the full-fledged behavioral and emotional reactions take place particularly when people believe to play the game against another person. Unfair splits generated by a computer are accepted more willingly (Sanfey, Rilling, Aronson, Nystrom, & Cohen, 2003). Ethopoeia effects in tasks that directly compare responses to computers with responses to humans are thereby attenuated – the overall magnitude of socio-affective reactions to computers diminishes. In an iteration of a decision-making dilemma with avatars and agents, the patterns of participants' behavioral responses were analogous to the responses to humans and regular computers found in prior research (de Melo, Gratch, & Carnevale, 2013). This was interpreted as evidence in support of the importance of the agency component in HCI. However, the responses to avatars seemed to be addressed to the individuals behind them and responses to agents were really directed at an object. What would happen if human partners were removed from this equation?

OVERVIEW OF THE PRESENT RESEARCH

The overarching aim of the current research was to examine behavioral and emotional responses in the ultimatum game played exclusively with computer proposers. There were two types of computer proposers that varied with regard to the degree of their anthropomorphic appearance. Specifically, the proposers were represented either by photos of artificially-looking faces and labeled as "agents" (highly anthropomorphic appearance) or by photos of a regular computer (non-anthropomorphic appearance). Involvement of other people in the ultimatum game was not implied; in fact, all of the offers were delivered by the same software. Research participants were assigned the role of the responder in the game.

Based on ethopoeia and on the Threshold Model of Social Influence, two divergent hypotheses pertaining to the behavioral responses in the game were formulated. First, as asserted by ethopoeia, participants were expected to respond in an entirely social manner to both types of the proposers since both computer agents and regular computers engaged them in the same social task and thereby contributed social cues. Unfair offers should appear as violation of social norms and consequently, both types of proposers should be alike punished by the responders with a rejection. However, it is worth emphasizing that anthropomorphic appearance of the agents actually provided more social cues than non-anthropomorphic appearance of a regular computer. Hence, responses to the former should be more social. Second, according to the Threshold Model of Social Influence, participants' social responses might be overall undermined because the agency of both types of the proposers was low (that is, none of them represented a real human being). Participants should be thus ready to accept unfair offers to maximize their own financial gains. Anthropomorphic appearance need not play a role as it is behavioral realism that produces the most salient social cues.

Physiological measures could be useful to further determine the nature of responses to the proposers. In line with previous findings, unfair offers from the computer agents were expected to be associated with increased activity of the *Corrugator Supercilii* and *Levator Labii* facial muscles (associated with expressions of anger and disgust) as well as with heightened skin conductance responses (SCR), which reflects more pronounced emotional engagement in the game and indicates a more social response to the agents in comparison to a regular computer. This would suggest that agency is not crucial for people to accept objects as legitimate social partners. Alternatively, if the agents were treated similarly to the computer, no changes in the activity of facial muscles and skin responses would occur after receiving unfair offers from the two types of proposers. This in turn would support the claim that entities of low agency are not recognized as proper social partners in an interaction.

The present setting, in which research participants played with multiple agents and one regular computer, corresponded to the earlier setups of the game employed in various studies, played with different humans and a single computer (Sanfey et al., 2003). It has been thereby established that reactions to unfair offers from humans, but not from the computer, were characterized by elevated electrodermal activation (van't Wout et al., 2006). Nevertheless, with a new human proposer in each round of the game and repetitive presentation of the same computer, previous research might have demonstrated an evaluative response to novelty, as this physiological measure is linked to it as well (see Bradley, Lang, & Cuthbert, 1993). In order to address this probable shortcoming, an independent group of participants was engaged in a version of the ultimatum game played with multiple agents and multiple regular computers.

EXPERIMENT 1

The main purpose of the first experiment was to compare participants' behavioral and emotional responses to computer agents versus a regular computer in the ultimatum game. Additionally, another group of participants played the ultimatum game with computer agents and many regular computers.

Method

Participants. 52 students (16 men), ranging in age from 18 to 25 years ($M = 19.79$, $SD = 1.26$), at Jacobs University Bremen, Germany, participated in this study on a voluntary basis. They were recruited via e-mail and received 10% of the amount earned in the ultimatum game and a partial course credit as compensation. All participants were Caucasian and proficient English language users. Data of four participants were excluded from the analyses (one due to computer malfunction, three reported extensive knowledge of the ultimatum game in the debriefing session). The final sample comprised 48 participants.

Materials. Images of the proposers depicted 10 faces of Caucasian males obtained from the Center for Vital Longevity Face Database (Minear & Park, 2004) and 11 computers, 10 of which were retrieved from the Internet and one was a photograph of a laboratory computer (see Figure 1). The faces were modified in Photoshop (CS3-ME, Adobe Systems Inc., 2007) to render them artificial (see Krumhuber, Swiderska, Tsankova, Kamble, & Kappas, 2015). The images of faces and of the laboratory computer measured 473 x 586 pixels and were displayed vertically. The rest of the images of computers included monitors and other pieces of equipment (e.g., keyboards, mice), measured 660 x 586 pixels, and were displayed horizontally.

Figure 1. Examples of stimuli used as visual representations of the two types of proposers in Experiment 1: A facial image representing one of the computer "agents" and a regular computer

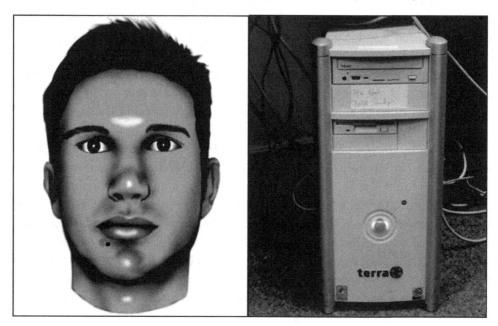

Procedure. Participants played 20 rounds of the ultimatum game, always in the role of the responder. In 10 rounds, the proposers were computer agents, represented by 10 pictures of artificial faces. In another 10 rounds, the proposer was a regular computer, represented by a single picture of a laboratory computer in one version of the game, or by 10 pictures of different computers in the additional setup. The versions differed only with respect to whether the proposer in the computer rounds was symbolized by always the same computer or by a different computer in every trial.

Computer and agent rounds were presented randomly. Each time, the amount of 10 € was divided. In each 10 rounds of the game, the proposers' offers were fair three times (5/5), and unfair 7 times (once 6/4, three times 7/3, twice 8/2, once 9/1). The rounds begun with a fixation point presented for a varying interval of 3, 6, or 9 seconds. Next, a picture of a proposer was displayed for 6 seconds, followed by an offer, displayed for 6 seconds as well, and lastly, a decision phase with no time limit. Participants' task was to either accept or reject the offers (see Figure 2).

Apparatus and Physiological Recordings

Participants were tested individually. They were seated in a reclining chair in a dimly lit sound-absorbent booth in front of a computer monitor, on which the experimental task was delivered by MediaLab software (V. 2010, Empirisoft Co., NYC, USA). Activity of facial muscles was recorded with three pairs of 11 mm Ag/AgCl (*DM-Davis*) miniature surface electrodes attached at the sites of *Corrugator Supercili* (associated with expressions of negative affect, e.g., frowning in anger), *Levator Labii* (associated with the expression of disgust), and additionally, *Zygomaticus Major* (as the activity of this muscle is associated with the expression of positive affect – smiling, it was measured here for the purpose of comparison with negative affect measures). One 20 mm Ag/AgCl electrode served as a ground reference. The placement of the electrodes adhered to the guidelines by Fridlund and Cacioppo (1986). Electrodermal activity was recorded with a pair of 8 mm Ag/AgCl electrodes attached to the distal phalanges of the index and middle finger of the non-dominant hand, as recommended by Boucsein and colleagues (2012). Data were acquired via MPR-150 *BIOPAC* system with three EMG-modules and one GSR-module, working with *AcqKnowledge* (*V.* 4.1; *BIOPAC Systems Inc.*) software, and filtered through a 50 Hz notch filter to reduce electrical noise.

Figure 2. Schematic representation of a single round of the ultimatum game in Experiment 1

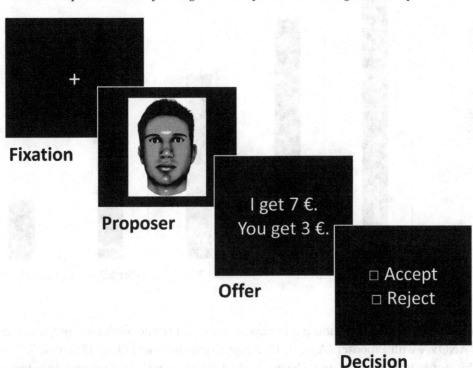

Results

Behavioral responses. Percentages of accepted offers coming from the agents and the regular computer are shown in Figure 3. To test whether the acceptance rates differed depending on the type of the proposer and the type of the offer, a repeated-measures analysis of variance (ANOVA) was conducted with Proposer (Agents, Single Computer) and Offer (5/5, 6/4, 7/3, 8/2, 9/1) as within-subjects factors. The main effect of Proposer was significant, $F(1, 23) = 7.32$, $p = .013$, $\eta_p^2 = .24$. The main effect of Offer was also significant, $F(4, 20) = 27.73$, $p < .001$, $\eta_p^2 = .85$. However, the interaction between Proposer and Offer did not reach significance ($p > .05$).

Pairwise comparisons revealed that participants were more likely to accept offers from the computer than the agents ($M = .62$ vs. $M = .52$, respectively). Furthermore, acceptance rates decreased with lower offers, with significant differences occurring between offers 7/3, 8/2, and 9/1 ($ps < .05$) and between the fair and least unfair offers (5/5 and 6/6) and the other three types of unfair offers ($ps < .05$).

Figure 3. Percentages of accepted offers in the ultimatum game played with 10 different agents and a single computer in Experiment 1

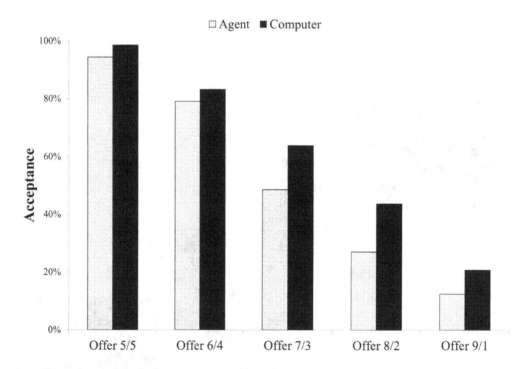

For the version of the ultimatum game played with agents and multiple computers, a repeated-measures ANOVA with Proposer (Agents, Different Computers) and Offer (5/5, 6/4, 7/3, 8/2, 9/1) as within-subjects factors was conducted. The main effect of Proposer and the interaction between Proposer and Offer turned out to be non-significant ($p > .05$). The main effect of Offer was again significant, $F(1, 23) = 27.48$, $p < .001$, $\eta_p^2 = .85$, showing that the acceptance rates significantly differed between the fair and least unfair offers and other unfair offers ($ps < .05$).

Physiological responses. The activities of *Corrugator Supercilii*, *Levator Labii*, and *Zygomaticus Major* as well as Skin Conductance Responses (SCR) were calculated separately for the two types of events in the ultimatum game: a) when the offers were made by the computer agents or regular computer, b) when the participant made the accept/reject decision. ANOVAs were conducted on four measures (activities of *Corrugator Supercilii*, *Levator Labii*, *Zygomaticus Major*, and SCR) for each of the 5 types of offers.

Results revealed significant differences in the context of the game played with agents versus a single computer. The main effect of Proposer was significant for *Levator* during presentation of Offer 6/4,

$F(1, 23) = 5.43$, $p = .029$, $\eta_p^2 = .19$, and Offer 9/1, $F(1, 23) = 6.86$, $p = .015$, $\eta_p^2 = .23$. Specifically, activity of the *Levator* muscle (involved in disgust expressions) was higher when Offer 6/4 came from the computer than the agents ($M = .63$ vs. $M = .31$, respectively). The reverse was true for Offer 9/1 ($M = .11$ vs. $M = .40$; see Figure 4A). For *Zygomaticus*, the main effect of Proposer was significant again for Offer 6/4, $F(1, 23) = 4.48$, $p = .045$, $\eta_p^2 = .16$, and Offer 7/3, $F(1, 23) = 5.80$, $p = .024$, $\eta_p^2 = .20$. Activity of *Zygomaticus* (involved in smiling) was higher when both Offer 6/4 and Offer 7/3 came from the computer than when it came from the agents ($M = .09$ vs. $M = -.10$ and $M = .05$ vs. $M = -.10$; see Figure 4B). No significant results emerged during presentation of offers in the setup of the game played with agents versus multiple computers.

*Figure 4. Mean difference scores of Levator Labii (**A**) and Zygomaticus Major (**B**) muscles' activities, and SCR (**C**) to the presentation of the offers and response phases of the ultimatum game played with the agents and a single computer in Experiment 1. The difference scores were calculated relative to 150-second baseline preceding the game. Error bars denote +SE. The marked differences are significant at *p < .05*

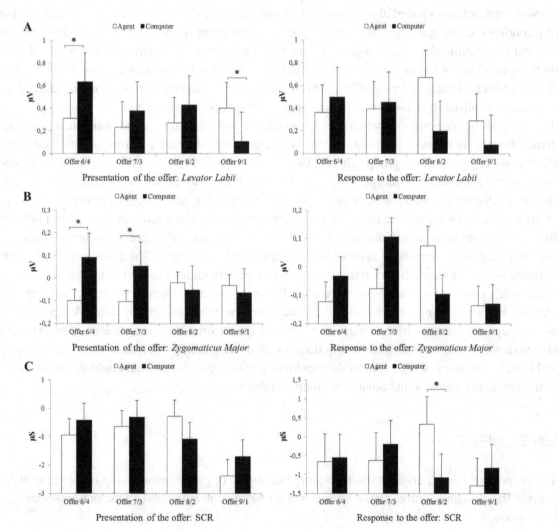

Considering physiological activity during the accept/reject decision phase of the game played with agents and a single computer, the only significant effect occurred for Offer 8/2, $F(1, 14) = 6.87$, $p = .02$, $\eta_p^2 = .33$, whereby SCR was higher in reaction to the agents than the computer ($M = .33$ vs. $M = -1.08$, respectively; see Figure 4C). In the case of the game played with agents and multiple computers, a significant effect occurred for Offer 6/4, $F(1, 20) = 5.67$, $p = .027$, $\eta_p^2 = .22$, when the activity of Zygomaticus was greater while responding to the offer from agents than computers ($M = -.12$ vs. $M = -.32$). This singular result did not allow for drawing any firm conclusions and will not be discussed any further.

Discussion

In line with previous research that employed the ultimatum game, almost all fair offers were accepted. As the offers became less fair, the acceptance rates decreased for both the offers generated by the agents and the regular computer. The unfair offers made by the agents were accepted less often compared to the unfair offers from the regular computer. Therefore, on the behavioral level, participants seemed to differentiate between the two types of the proposers. Analyses of data obtained from the recordings of participants' physiological activity yielded highly inconsistent results, which did not allow us to ascertain the pattern of physiological changes dependent on the type of the proposer or the offer. In the additional setup of the ultimatum game played with agents and multiple computers, the behavioral differences depending on the type of the proposer vanished, suggesting that certain outcomes of the game might be due to a clear contrast between pondering offers from distinct proposers and repetitively from the same proposer.

Group membership is another factor shown to exert complex influence on the process of economic decision making. For example, when people can choose how to distribute the available resources, they divide them fairly between in-group and out-group, but when they are confronted with predetermined allotments, they favor the in-group (Mullen, Brown, & Smith, 1992). When the decisions entail personal costs, as in the ultimatum game, people become less equitable and less rational (Kubota, Li, Bar-David, Banaji, & Phelps, 2013). That is, at the expense of prospective earnings, they generally reject unfair offers and further discriminate based on race of the proposers, being more prone to reject offers from Blacks compared to Whites (Kubota et al., 2013). In Experiment 1, all participants were Caucasian and they were exposed to computer agents symbolized by Caucasian faces. The faces were thus presumed to function as a representation of participants' in-group. Although compared to the regular computers, unfair splits proposed by the agents were then dismissed more frequently, this effect warrants further scrutiny. In the following Experiment 2, the Caucasian faces were replaced by South Asian faces, which were to represent an out-group to participants drawn again from Caucasian students. The experiment's objective was to test whether such manipulation would strengthen participants' reactions to the agents and increase the rates of rejections of different unfair offers, parallel to what could be predicted for the ultimatum game played with human out-group members.

EXPERIMENT 2

The purpose of this experiment was to explore the impact of group membership on participants' decisions in the ultimatum game, played with computer agents that embodied ethnic out-group and regular computers.

Method

Participants. 21 students (9 men), ranging in age from 18 to 22 years ($M = 19.90$, $SD = 1.18$), at Jacobs University Bremen, Germany, participated in the experiment on a voluntary basis. They were recruited via e-mail and received 10% of the amount earned in the ultimatum game and a course credit as compensation. All participants were Caucasian and fluent in English.

Materials. Images of the proposers included 10 faces of South Asian (Indian) males obtained from the Center for Vital Longevity Face Database (Minear & Park, 2004) and one photograph of a laboratory computer. As in Experiment 1, the faces were modified in Photoshop (CS3-ME, Adobe Systems Inc., 2007) in order to make them appear artificial. The images of South Asian faces and of the laboratory computer (same as in Experiment 1) measured 473 x 586 pixels and were displayed vertically on a black screen.

Procedure. The procedure closely followed that employed in Experiment 1 in the setup of the game played with computer agents and a single regular computer. Participants were to either accept or reject offers coming in 10 trials from agents, represented by images of 10 different South Asian faces, and in another 10 trials, from a computer, represented by a picture of a laboratory computer. The offers were the same as in Experiment 1. Physiological activity was not recorded.

Results

Percentages of accepted offers in the current experiment are displayed in Figure 5. A repeated-measures ANOVA was conducted with Proposer (Agents, Single Computer) and Offer (5/5, 6/4, 7/3, 8/2, 9/1) as the two within-subjects factors. The main effects were significant, both for Proposer, $F(1, 20) = 6.99$, $p = .016$, $\eta_p^2 = .26$, and Offer, $F(4, 17) = 25.23$, $p < .001$, $\eta_p^2 = .86$. These main effects were qualified by a significant interaction, $F(4, 17) = 4.42$, $p = .012$, $\eta_p^2 = .51$. Overall, participants accepted Offers 7/3 and 9/1 more often when they came from a regular computer ($M_{7/3} = .65$ and $M_{9/1} = .29$) than from computer agents ($M_{7/3} = .51$ and $M_{9/1} = .10$; $ps < .05$).

Data from Experiment 2 were compared with those from Experiment 1 (version with a single computer) to test for the effect of the agents' Ethnicity (Caucasian, South Asian) on participants' decisions. A repeated-measures ANOVA with Offer as within-subjects factor and Ethnicity as between-subjects factor showed that the main effect of Ethnicity was not significant ($p > .05$).

Discussion

The behavioral results adhered to the pattern obtained in Experiment 1 in that the unjust splits were accepted less often when proposed by the agents compared to the regular computer. Contrary to the hypothesis, ethnicity of the agents did not induce definitive changes in participants' decisions in the game.

CONCLUSION

Prior research has found people to consistently arrive at different decisions with regard to the same monetary incentives offered by another human compared to a computer. The latter are more likely to be accepted even when they are unfair. The present research focused on the investigation of the behavioral and emotional components of reactions to computers in the context of the ultimatum game. Unlike in

Figure 5. Percentages of accepted offers in Experiment 2. Marked differences are significant at *p < .05

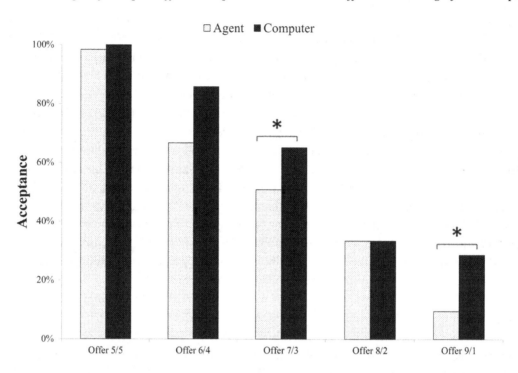

the earlier studies, participants' choices were not contrasted with their reactions to human partners. By avoiding the potential confound of an interaction with both another human and an object, the magnitude of social responses to computers was explored. On the behavioral level, in Experiments 1 and 2 almost all fair and the least unfair splits were accepted. As expected, the acceptance rates declined as the splits became more unequal and they varied as a function of the partner's anthropomorphic appearance. Unfair offers from non-anthropomorphic, regular computer were accepted more often than the offers from highly anthropomorphic computer agents. In general, both types of computers' representations elicited social responses analogous to responses to humans in that participants seemed to have perceived the unjust behaviors in terms of a transgression, for which the computer deserved a symbolic punishment. This phenomenon was stronger for the computers represented by facial images.

In Experiment 1, participants' physiological responses did not fluctuate consistently depending on the type of the proposer in the game or the presented offer. Lack of evidence for the expected emotional reactions to the unfairness of the computer indicates that its role as a social partner was limited to how it shaped the relevant behaviors. Further demonstration of the diminished social function of the computer was the absence of the predicted influence of the computer agents that embodied an ethnic out-group to participants in Experiment 2. The ethnicity of the computer, similarly symbolized by faces, has been previously shown to have a strong effect on participants in the human-computer interaction, just like an actual human in a human-human interaction. However, this concerned a slightly different evaluation task that did not directly affect participants' own outcomes (Nass & Moon, 2000). Although the proposition of an inequitable split in the ultimatum game was an instance of a violation of social norms, tangible in terms of financial losses, and people are typically more receptive of transgressions by out-group members (Valdesolo & DeSteno, 2007), reactions to the out-group computer agents appeared not to be clearly more negative than to the in-group agents.

These results may be interpreted in support of the ethopoeia approach. Ethopoeia puts an emphasis on the mindless execution of familiar behavioral scripts, attributed in turn to automatic cognitive processing that does not reach conscious awareness. It argues that even minimal social cues provided by a computer are sufficient for it to temporarily become a fellow human and the virtual world to become real to participants (Reeves & Nass, 1996). The more human-like characteristics the computer manifests, the more pronounced its social impact is (Nass & Moon, 2000). Nonetheless, the realization of behavioral scripts alone cannot fully explain decisions to reject concrete offers in the ultimatum game. These derive from negative emotions (e.g., anger, as well as wounded pride and spite; Straub & Murnighan, 1995). In the current setting, the emotional reactions might have been too subtle to capture.

Although human game partners were excluded from the interaction, with the focus of the present research on the interaction with objects, inclusion of highly realistic artificial faces to represent a proposer still constituted a stark contrast to a regular computer as proposer. Future studies could address this issue by improving the stimulus material. For example, the faces may be shown together with a background as part of an interface displayed on a monitor to reinforce the idea that they are computer-based entities. In addition, the faces could be animated to display emotional expressions dependent on participants' responses (de Melo et al., 2013). This would serve as another strong social cue more likely to elicit emotional responses, which were very limited in the present context. Moreover, the computer's subsequent offers could be contingent on participants' decisions (e.g., increasing when preceded by a rejection of a low offer). The computer could also take on the role of the responder with participants acting as proposers (Nouri & Traum, 2013). If participants would offer the computer fair or almost fair monetary splits, this would be evidence for a social interaction with an object coming about.

The advancement of ethopoeia approaches and the research it inspired have reflected a steady improvement in the quality of HCI, partly because regular computers with text or audio output evolved into machines that incorporate anthropomorphic interfaces (Reeves & Nass, 1996). The Threshold Model of Social Influence contributed to better understanding of interactions with avatars and agents (e.g., Von der Pütten, Krämer, Gratch, & Kang, 2010). An essential commonality of the two approaches is that they seek to elucidate the interplay of people and a variety of computer-generated entities. In doing so, they tend to center on human-like appearance and behavior, which augment social cues and are seen as advantageous for HCI by making it more natural and intuitive, and akin to HHI (Breazeal, 2002). While the computers began to fulfill roles once reserved for humans (Küster, Krumhuber, & Kappas, 2014), the range of the users' responses expanded from mainly task-oriented to emotional engagement. Some applications (e.g., educational programs) actually require the user to be emotionally involved for the intervention to be successful. Moreover, emotions are associated with reactions to moral violations, as in the ultimatum game, and this opens up the possibility for the computer to become a partner with moral obligations. Taken together, it seems that ethopoeia and the Threshold Model of Social Influence may not cover all of the intricacies of the HCI.

ACKNOWLEDGMENT

This research was supported by a grant from the EU FP7 project eCUTE (ICT-5-4.2 257666) to Arvid Kappas. Correspondence concerning this article should be addressed to Aleksandra Swiderska, Department of Psychology, Warsaw University, ul. Stawki 5/7, 00-183 Warsaw, Poland. E-mail: aleksandra.swiderska@psych.uw.edu.pl, Tel.: +48 22 55 49 811, Fax: +48 22 635 79 91.

REFERENCES

Becker, G. S. (2013). *The economic approach to human behavior*. Chicago, IL: University of Chicago Press.

Blascovich, J., Loomis, J., Beall, A. C., Swinth, K. R., Hoyt, C. L., & Bailenson, J. N. (2002). Immersive virtual environment technology as a methodological tool for social psychology. *Psychological Inquiry*, *13*(2), 103–124. doi:10.1207/S15327965PLI1302_01

Boucsein, W., Fowles, D. C., Grimnes, S., Ben-Shakhar, G., Roth, W. T., Dawson, M. E., & Filion, D. L. (2012). Publication recommendations for electrodermal measurements. *Psychophysiology*, *49*(8), 1017–1034. doi:10.1111/j.1469-8986.2012.01384.x PMID:22680988

Bradley, M. M., Lang, P. J., & Cuthbert, B. N. (1993). Emotion, novelty, and the startle reflex: Habituation in humans. *Behavioral Neuroscience*, *107*(6), 970–980. doi:10.1037/0735-7044.107.6.970 PMID:8136072

Breazeal, C. L. (2002). *Designing sociable robots*. Cambridge, MA: MIT Press.

Cannon, P. R., Schnall, S., & White, M. (2011). Transgressions and expressions: Affective facial muscle activity predicts moral judgments. *Social Psychological & Personality Science*, *2*(3), 325–331. doi:10.1177/1948550610390525

Chapman, H. A., Kim, D. A., Susskind, J. M., & Anderson, A. K. (2009). In bad taste: Evidence for the oral origins for moral disgust. *Science*, *27*(5918), 1222–1226. doi:10.1126cience.1165565 PMID:19251631

de Melo, C., Gratch, J., & Carnevale, P. (2013). The effect of agency on the impact of emotion expressions on people's decision making. In *Proceedings of the 5th Humaine Association Conference on Affective Computing and Intelligent Interaction (ACII)* (pp. 546-551). 10.1109/ACII.2013.96

Fehr, E., & Gächter, S. (2002). Altruistic punishment in humans. *Nature*, *415*(6868), 137–140. doi:10.1038/415137a PMID:11805825

Fridlund, A. J., & Cacioppo, J. T. (1986). Guidelines for human electromyographic research. *Psychophysiology*, *23*(5), 567–589. doi:10.1111/j.1469-8986.1986.tb00676.x PMID:3809364

Krumhuber, E., Tsankova, E., & Kappas, A. (2016). Examining subjective and physiological responses to norm violation using text-based vignettes. *International Journal of Psychology*. doi:10.1002/ijop.12253 PMID:26762218

Krumhuber, E. G., Swiderska, A., Tsankova, E., Kamble, S. V., & Kappas, A. (2015). Real or artificial? Intergroup biases in mind perception in a cross-cultural perspective. *PLoS One*, *10*(9), e0137840. doi:10.1371/journal.pone.0137840 PMID:26360588

Kubota, J. T., Li, J., Bar-David, E., Banaji, M. R., & Phelps, E. A. (2013). The price of racial bias: Intergroup negotiations in the Ultimatum Game. *Psychological Science*, *24*(12), 2498–2504. doi:10.1177/0956797613496435 PMID:24121413

Küster, D., Krumhuber, E., & Kappas, A. (2014). Nonverbal behavior online: A focus on interactions with and via artificial agents and avatars. In A. Kostic & D. Chadee (Eds.), *Social Psychology of Nonverbal Communications* (pp. 272–302). New York, NY: Palgrave Macmillan.

Minear, M., & Park, D. C. (2004). A lifespan database of adult facial stimuli. *Behavior Research Methods, Instruments, & Computers*, *36*(4), 630–633. doi:10.3758/BF03206543 PMID:15641408

Mullen, B., Brown, R., & Smith, C. (1992). Ingroup bias as a function of salience, relevance, and status: An integration. *European Journal of Social Psychology*, *22*(2), 103–122. doi:10.1002/ejsp.2420220202

Nass, C., & Moon, Y. (2000). Machines and mindlessness: Social responses to computers. *The Journal of Social Issues*, *56*(1), 81–103. doi:10.1111/0022-4537.00153

Nass, C., Moon, Y., & Carney, P. (1999). Are respondents polite to computers? Social desirability and direct responses to computers. *Journal of Applied Social Psychology*, *29*, 1093–1110. doi:10.1111/j.1559-1816.1999.tb00142.x

Nass, C., Moon, Y., & Green, N. (1997). Are computers gender-neutral? Social desirability and direct responses to computers. *Journal of Applied Social Psychology*, *27*, 864–876. doi:10.1111/j.1559-1816.1997.tb00275.x

Nouri, E., & Traum, D. (2013). A cross-cultural study of playing simple economic games online with humans and virtual humans. In M. Kurosu (Ed.), *Human-Computer Interaction. Applications and Services. HCI 2013*, LNCS (Vol. 8005, pp. 266–275). Berlin, Germany: Springer. doi:10.1007/978-3-642-39262-7_30

Nowak, M. A., Page, K. M., & Sigmund, K. (2000). Fairness versus reason in the Ultimatum Game. *Science*, *289*(5485), 1773–1775. doi:10.1126cience.289.5485.1773 PMID:10976075

Reeves, B., & Nass, C. (1996). *The media equation: How people treat computers, television, and new media like real people and places*. New York, NY: Cambridge University Press.

Sanfey, A. G., Rilling, J. K., Aronson, J. A., Nystrom, L. E., & Cohen, J. D. (2003). The neural basis of economic decision-making in the Ultimatum Game. *Science*, *300*(5626), 1755–1758. doi:10.1126cience.1082976 PMID:12805551

Straub, P., & Murnighan, J. K. (1995). An experimental investigation of ultimatum games: Information, fairness, expectations, and lowest acceptable offers. *Journal of Economic Behavior & Organization*, *27*(3), 345–364. doi:10.1016/0167-2681(94)00072-M

Tinwell, A., Grimshaw, M., Nabi, D. A., & Williams, A. (2011). Facial expression of emotion and perception of the Uncanny Valley in virtual characters. *Computers in Human Behavior*, *27*(2), 741–749. doi:10.1016/j.chb.2010.10.018

Valdesolo, P., & DeSteno, D. (2007). Moral hypocrisy: Social groups and the flexibility of virtue. *Psychological Science*, *18*(8), 689–690. doi:10.1111/j.1467-9280.2007.01961.x PMID:17680939

van't Wout, M., Kahn, R. S., Sanfey, A. G., & Aleman, A. (2006). Affective state and decision making in the Ultimatum Game. *Experimental Brain Research*, *169*(4), 564–568. doi:10.100700221-006-0346-5 PMID:16489438

Von der Pütten, A. M., Krämer, N. C., Gratch, J., & Kang, S. H. (2010). "It doesn't matter what you are!": Explaining social effects of agents and avatars. *Computers in Human Behavior*, *26*(6), 1641–1650. doi:10.1016/j.chb.2010.06.012

Waytz, A., Epley, N., & Cacioppo, J. T. (2010). Social cognition unbound: Insights into anthropomorphism and dehumanization. *Current Directions in Psychological Science*, *19*(1), 58–62. doi:10.1177/0963721409359302 PMID:24839358

Yee, N., Bailenson, J. N., & Rickertsen, K. (2007). A meta-analysis of the impact of the inclusion and realism of human-like faces on user experiences in interfaces. In *Proceedings of the SIGCHI conference on human factors in computing systems*. New York, NY: ACM. 10.1145/1240624.1240626

This research was previously published in the International Journal of Technology and Human Interaction (IJTHI), 15(1); pages 33-45, copyright year 2019 by IGI Publishing (an imprint of IGI Global).

Index

3D Graphics 63, 680, 688, 959
3D Models 460, 481, 1632
3D Serious Games 1621
3D Snake 644, 646, 649, 651-657, 661

A

ABM 732, 735, 738, 740, 745, 749, 755, 757, 759
Abstraction 15, 104, 135, 214, 217, 485, 493, 509-511, 944, 949, 956, 1363, 1731, 1855-1856
Academic Game Studios 1358
Academic Performance 460, 523, 708, 710, 1073-1075, 1083, 1117, 1265, 1299, 1421, 1562-1563, 1576, 1704-1707, 1711-1716, 1718-1719, 1736, 1751, 1886
Acquisition Strategies 287, 306
Action Game Semantics 345
Action Painting 1362-1364, 1367, 1374, 1385
Active Learning Methodologies 1891
Actor-Network Theory 187-188, 192-193, 195, 644, 646, 649-651, 659-661, 1910
Advanced Learning Technologies 411, 425, 427, 731, 1177, 1277, 1637
Advergames 52, 105-109, 117, 119, 1495-1497, 1499-1500, 1509-1514, 1533, 1554, 1556, 1798
Aestheticization 1640, 1660, 1756, 1771-1772, 1780
Aesthetics 4, 201, 203, 374, 386, 399, 413, 537, 542, 546, 563, 594, 645, 698-699, 737, 739, 744-746, 754-755, 759, 765, 876, 1041, 1187, 1222-1224, 1226-1229, 1231, 1233-1234, 1237, 1372, 1387-1388, 1408-1410, 1428, 1521, 1543, 1657, 1756, 1758-1759, 1766-1771, 1778-1779, 1836-1838, 1855, 1872-1873, 1878-1879, 1881, 1936
Affective Loop 383-384, 390
Affinity Spaces 895, 912-913
Agenda Setting 1304-1313, 1315, 1317-1319, 1723, 1732
Agile Development 259, 263, 284, 585, 587, 591-592, 596, 621

Algorithmic Thinking 509, 511-512, 527, 529
AMC 1435, 1438, 1440-1443, 1445, 1448, 1451-1455
Analog Prototyping 585, 587-588, 590-594, 596
Analysis Review 391
Ancient Game 1321
Animation Design 423, 680, 688-690
Anthropomorphism 1480, 1494
Anxiety Disorders 732-735, 762-765, 768, 770, 1013, 1263, 1265, 1277-1283
Application Programming Interface 12
Applied Learning 310, 1285, 1289
Appraisal Variables 376, 390
Apps Integration 716
Arousal 32, 368, 376-377, 531, 534, 539, 547-548, 551, 562, 564-565, 568, 576, 579, 740, 761, 957, 1040, 1043, 1045-1047, 1049-1051, 1185-1186, 1194, 1196, 1199, 1251, 1412, 1417-1418, 1482, 1495-1500, 1507, 1509, 1512, 1515, 1540-1541, 1553, 1556, 1734, 1748, 1782, 1790
Artificial Intelligence 14-15, 17-18, 28-30, 121-122, 141, 197, 235, 237, 240-241, 243-244, 256-257, 360, 362, 370, 387, 426, 582, 714, 941, 947, 953-956, 963, 991, 1181, 1237, 1239, 1271, 1273, 1279-1280, 1343-1344, 1347, 1419, 1458, 1618, 1620, 1892, 1940, 1984
Artificial Neural Networks 956
Asychronous Learning 1303
Attitude Change 96, 1253, 1956-1972, 1975
Attribute Agenda-Setting 1727-1728
Audio Games 644-649, 651-653, 655-661
Auditory Environment 644, 653, 656
Augmented Reality 55, 121-143, 392, 458, 460-461, 477-481, 545, 549, 601, 616, 713, 770, 839, 866, 870-871, 1101, 1119, 1278, 1458, 1522, 1536, 1561, 1566, 1572-1573, 1576, 1644, 1658, 1815-1816, 1887, 1889-1890, 1922
Authentic Projects 1358
Avatars 73, 88, 147, 414, 416, 424, 436, 451, 538, 541, 550, 564, 574, 576-577, 727, 744, 906, 1240,

1246-1248, 1250, 1272-1273, 1292, 1481-1482, 1491, 1493-1494, 1583-1584, 1586, 1617, 1620, 1839, 1856-1857, 1860, 1873, 1877-1880, 1882, 1884-1885, 1938-1944, 1947-1952, 1954

B

Backend as a Service 8, 10, 12
Baudrillard 1581-1583, 1616-1617, 1767-1768, 1773, 1776
Behavior Intention 785, 789, 791, 793, 798-800, 1965
Benchmarking 585-587, 590-594, 596, 598
Big Five 803, 1558, 1562, 1564-1565, 1567, 1569, 1572, 1574-1578, 1755
Biofeedback 59, 187-196, 604, 616, 1280
B-Learning 839, 842, 844, 871
Board Games 19, 483, 501, 590, 970, 1068, 1322-1323, 1343, 1438, 1443, 1448, 1805, 1923, 1925-1926, 1928-1930, 1933-1935, 1940
Body Image 1938, 1943, 1950, 1953-1954
Brain-Computer Interfacing (BCI) 599-603, 605, 613, 616
Brand Attitude 119, 555, 1495-1496, 1498-1500, 1502-1503, 1509, 1513, 1515
Brand Recall 119, 1495-1500, 1502, 1504-1510, 1515
Branded Entertainment 1496-1497, 1500, 1513

C

Car Racing 27, 1183, 1192, 1541
CBT 732, 734-735, 749, 757, 759, 1268, 1272, 1279
Challenge Based Learning 1891, 1893, 1900, 1905-1906
Character Modeling 366, 1620
Choose-Your-Own-Adventure 777
Civil Servant 1956, 1961
Co-Development 240, 994
Coding 201, 247-249, 271, 276, 310, 387, 492, 509, 529, 539, 577, 756, 774, 778, 892, 900, 1209, 1211, 1308, 1462, 1575, 1686, 1946, 1985
Cognitive behavior therapy 1155, 1263, 1281, 1284
Co-Located Opponents 1193, 1553
Comics 416, 454, 892, 898, 902, 1228, 1235, 1435-1436, 1438-1442, 1444-1447, 1449-1453, 1455, 1585, 1617
Commercial Videogames 67, 73, 83
Competition 2, 6, 88, 122, 124-125, 160, 162, 199, 291-292, 297, 300, 308-310, 375, 496-497, 515, 517, 521, 523, 525, 545, 588-589, 615, 663-664, 699, 701, 712, 744, 770, 816, 818, 823, 826, 835, 871, 1002, 1031, 1033-1036, 1038-1040, 1122,

1144, 1184-1186, 1188, 1194, 1196-1197, 1200, 1213-1214, 1244, 1247, 1270, 1349, 1352, 1453, 1461, 1539-1541, 1543, 1554, 1556-1557, 1607, 1645, 1684, 1750, 1774, 1800-1801, 1838-1839, 1853-1855, 1859-1860, 1863, 1866, 1872-1873, 1877, 1879, 1881
complementary innovators 1351-1352
Components Of Gamification 705-706, 1855, 1857, 1859-1861, 1867
Computational Cognitive Psychology 365-367, 376, 386, 390
computational models of emotion 365
Computational Thinking 507, 509-513, 524-529, 1926, 1934
Computer Games 30, 56, 60, 100, 121, 134, 142-143, 255, 307-308, 369, 386, 392-393, 404, 408, 455, 480, 499-500, 511, 513, 521, 523, 526, 566, 598, 645, 650, 657-658, 706, 729-730, 765, 767, 769, 783-784, 803, 807, 842, 868, 887-889, 940, 947, 957, 1014, 1031, 1042, 1054, 1057, 1078, 1082, 1116, 1180-1181, 1197-1202, 1206, 1213, 1215, 1217, 1220, 1321, 1383, 1420-1421, 1468, 1514, 1556, 1562, 1564, 1581, 1583, 1586, 1601, 1603, 1609, 1618, 1634-1637, 1659, 1679, 1698, 1702, 1733, 1750-1752, 1778, 1833, 1847, 1887, 1905-1906, 1910, 1953, 1973-1974, 1977, 1982, 1984, 1986, 1990-1991
Computer Programming 1, 6, 8, 12, 310, 361, 510, 512-513, 526-528, 843, 869, 1163, 1180, 1715, 1753, 1844, 1851
Computer Science Education 1, 11, 256, 525-527, 993, 1118, 1381-1383, 1907
Computer-Based Testing 774
Computer-Mediated Communication 119, 142, 678, 1216, 1318-1319, 1535, 1537, 1664, 1674, 1698, 1732, 1751, 1814, 1954
Continue To Use 59, 1803, 1808
COVID-19 85, 126, 198, 209-210, 995, 998, 1010, 1012, 1015, 1017, 1141, 1832-1833
Creativity 3, 87, 161, 210, 320, 339, 396, 434, 438, 447, 461, 523, 590, 603, 623, 629, 658, 701, 714, 786, 908, 947, 951, 956, 961, 1121-1138, 1346, 1348, 1354, 1361, 1367, 1381, 1386, 1388-1390, 1402, 1406, 1452, 1635, 1733, 1737, 1751, 1799, 1856, 1891-1892, 1897-1898, 1901, 1905-1906, 1923, 1926-1927, 1930, 1932-1933, 1936, 1979-1981, 1983, 1986, 1989
Critical Thinking 507, 527, 894, 949, 1056, 1141-1142, 1285, 1287, 1290, 1299, 1388, 1392, 1410, 1778, 1894, 1989
Cross-Literacy Schema 73

Crowdfunding 198-201, 203-204, 206-211, 1664, 1674
Crowdsourcing 200, 209, 531-532, 537, 552, 1240-1242, 1244, 1246, 1251, 1257-1258, 1260, 1262, 1836, 1849-1850, 1864, 1874, 1880, 1886, 1888, 1890
Current Motivation 1558, 1560, 1563-1565, 1569-1574, 1579-1580
Cyber Awareness 1470-1471, 1473-1474, 1477
Cybersecurity Practices 1470-1472, 1477

D

Data Analytics 838, 1162, 1166
Dbscan 341, 354, 357
Decision-Making 24, 109, 213-216, 220, 222, 230-231, 235, 237, 239, 371, 509, 710, 837, 891-892, 898, 928, 988, 1056, 1285, 1290, 1294, 1296, 1299, 1301, 1329, 1347, 1395, 1480-1482, 1493, 1516, 1559, 1564, 1578, 1733, 1831, 1834, 1921, 1957-1958, 1966, 1974
Declarative Knowledge 1818, 1820, 1824-1827, 1829-1830, 1832
Dennis Dutton 1756
Desensitization therapy 1263, 1267, 1274
Design Principles 128, 170-171, 182, 201, 246, 384, 409, 414, 872, 877, 1112, 1117, 1120, 1182, 1270, 1622, 1855, 1888
Design Process 14, 145-146, 152, 156, 161, 170, 177, 180, 207, 304, 335-336, 394, 482-483, 513, 558, 560, 577, 587, 589-590, 617-619, 621, 624, 626-628, 872, 875-877, 879-881, 883, 885, 897, 899-900, 945, 951, 1370, 1586, 1856, 1891, 1893, 1898-1900, 1909
Design Thinking Development 258
Desktop 32, 34, 53-54, 58, 169-170, 172, 176, 689, 748, 1000, 1002, 1044, 1086, 1198, 1201-1202, 1204, 1206, 1211-1212
Detachment From Other Activities 1678, 1680, 1684-1686, 1688, 1690, 1692-1694
Developing Countries 85, 92, 98, 1836, 1838, 1840-1843, 1845-1847, 1973, 1975, 1982
Digital Composing 891, 894
Digital Games 10, 29, 46, 71, 76, 81-82, 92-93, 108-110, 115, 183, 203, 240, 242, 246, 306, 322, 329, 361, 363, 392-393, 404, 456-457, 481, 500-501, 503, 513, 526, 560, 589-590, 603, 634, 644-647, 649, 653, 655-660, 716-717, 725-726, 728, 731, 766, 843, 874, 886, 889, 908, 956, 958-959, 996, 1014-1015, 1078, 1084, 1121-1122, 1126, 1129, 1137, 1178, 1194, 1215, 1234, 1237, 1349, 1370, 1382-1383, 1387-1388, 1392-1393, 1409, 1433,

1435, 1442-1443, 1457-1458, 1460-1466, 1468-1469, 1495, 1554, 1581, 1583-1585, 1616-1618, 1620, 1622, 1635, 1643-1644, 1659, 1677, 1748-1749, 1756-1757, 1762-1763, 1766-1770, 1772, 1775, 1778, 1780, 1922, 1952, 1974, 1978-1979, 1984-1985, 1987-1988, 1990-1992
Digital Interventions 732-734, 1011
Digital Literacy 508, 529, 1287, 1290, 1300, 1679, 1695, 1716
Digital Tools 65, 71, 891-893, 896, 898, 900-901, 908
Digital Transformation 122, 198, 1301, 1346, 1353, 1766, 1888
Disaster Preparedness 1818-1819, 1822-1824
Discourse Analysis 909, 1309, 1667-1668
Discriminant Analysis 342, 1678, 1686, 1688, 1690-1691, 1697
Dispositif 631, 1640-1641
Dr. Preety Khatri 14
Driving Game 1192, 1538, 1551

E

Educational Game 246, 254, 391-392, 396, 408-409, 411-412, 416, 423-424, 426, 475, 477-478, 515, 517, 522-523, 605, 625-626, 875, 877, 880-881, 885, 887, 889, 994, 997, 1008, 1177, 1182, 1358-1359, 1362, 1370-1371, 1624, 1637, 1899, 1975
Educational Robotics 507-508, 510-511, 521, 523-525, 527, 529
Educational Technology 58, 81-82, 197, 210, 255-256, 393, 409, 425, 430, 453, 456, 499-500, 502, 507, 524, 579, 707-708, 722, 730, 806-807, 869-871, 886-887, 889, 958-959, 961, 992-993, 1177, 1180, 1195, 1218, 1301-1303, 1409-1410, 1419, 1422, 1512, 1555, 1634-1636, 1638, 1718, 1833, 1867-1868, 1886
Educational Videogames 83, 1099
EEG or Electroencephalogram 602, 616
E-Government 1956, 1976
Ehealth 93, 95, 103, 733-734, 743, 772, 999, 1016
E-Learning 12, 35-36, 52, 57, 59, 236, 285, 428, 480, 499, 527, 540, 552, 582, 614, 706-708, 710-712, 714, 722, 784, 803, 839, 842, 844, 868-869, 871, 940, 1079, 1277, 1634, 1803, 1815, 1844, 1848-1849
Ellen Dissanayake 1756-1758
Embodied learning 1097, 1099-1100, 1117-1119
Emergency and Disaster Management 1285-1286, 1289-1294, 1296, 1298-1300, 1303
emotion architectures 365
Emotion Model 365-367, 369, 372, 375-377, 379-386,

390, 415

Emotional Agents 411, 413, 416, 424, 427

Emotional Dependence 1678, 1680, 1682-1686, 1688, 1690, 1692-1694, 1700

Emotions 4, 17, 64, 77, 84, 88, 104, 129, 187-189, 191, 202, 246, 310, 366-371, 373, 375-378, 385, 388-390, 394, 411-413, 415-417, 420, 422-429, 441-443, 453, 531, 533-535, 547, 549, 551, 568, 586, 663-664, 714, 764, 767, 918, 997, 1045, 1047, 1124, 1156, 1165-1166, 1177, 1180-1181, 1183, 1186, 1189, 1193, 1195, 1198, 1201, 1204-1206, 1208-1214, 1220, 1223, 1227, 1237, 1258, 1268, 1273-1275, 1282, 1306, 1313, 1427, 1482, 1491, 1509, 1513-1514, 1521, 1541-1542, 1544-1545, 1551-1552, 1555, 1562, 1564, 1571-1572, 1589, 1610, 1614, 1646, 1660, 1714, 1759, 1765, 1775, 1782, 1789, 1873, 1884, 1928

Energy Transition 482-483, 486, 491, 495, 498

Engineering Practicals 839-842, 849, 854

Entrepreneurial Self 1640, 1642, 1659

Entrepreneurship 198, 200, 209-210, 283, 1125, 1350, 1352, 1356, 1577, 1975

ERP or Event-Related Potential 603, 616

E-servicescape 546, 557, 562-565, 567, 572, 574, 576, 580-581

Essence of Play 1423, 1432

Ethnography 269-270, 272, 276, 282-284, 1390, 1409-1410, 1667-1668

Ethopoeia 1480-1482, 1491

Evaluation Study 391, 393, 402, 406

Evaluative Measures 307

Evolutionary Prototyping 883, 889

Exergames 53, 101, 103, 551, 702, 1016, 1888

Expected Utility 207, 988, 993

Experiential Learning 428, 437-438, 454, 607, 612-613, 622, 730, 874, 1165, 1285-1287, 1289, 1291, 1299-1301, 1303, 1371, 1908, 1910-1911, 1916-1917, 1921, 1957, 1959, 1966-1967, 1971-1972, 1975

Experimental Research 412, 988, 1214, 1923

Experimentation 172, 212, 237, 261, 385, 492, 495, 589-590, 607, 613, 893, 895, 901, 913, 944, 949, 956, 1056, 1233, 1347, 1352-1353, 1398, 1632, 1915, 1958

Exposure therapy 1263, 1267, 1269, 1271, 1274, 1277-1278, 1281-1284

Extrinsic Motivation 3, 9, 36, 52, 87, 146, 167, 257, 699-700, 705, 1183-1184, 1186-1187, 1189, 1191-1193, 1242, 1244, 1434, 1538-1539, 1541-1542, 1544, 1547, 1549-1553, 1854, 1867

F

Fan Culture 1436, 1442, 1452, 1661, 1663-1665, 1671

Fandom 1304-1306, 1314-1315, 1320, 1437-1438, 1449, 1456, 1662, 1664, 1675, 1677

Fantasy 67, 210, 414, 485, 493, 636, 663, 719, 730, 734, 766, 783, 873-874, 878, 946, 953, 955, 1032, 1040, 1043-1047, 1049, 1051, 1067, 1071, 1127, 1230, 1237, 1248, 1250, 1367, 1391, 1463, 1585, 1605, 1609, 1611, 1661-1664, 1667-1671, 1673-1674, 1676-1677, 1702, 1737, 1750, 1754, 1756, 1794, 1815, 1872, 1879, 1881

Fear of Missing Out (FoMO) 1661, 1666, 1676

Fear of Missing Out (FoMO) theory 1661, 1666

Feeling of Pride 105, 116

Fidelity 32-33, 55, 241-253, 255-256, 261, 281-282, 497, 589, 595, 889, 920, 1415, 1632, 1971

Fiero 79, 307-320, 1924

First-Person Shooter 32, 811, 1052, 1058, 1071, 1330, 1343, 1444, 1447, 1736, 1781, 1785-1787, 1789-1790, 1987

Flipped Classroom 839-840, 843, 869-871, 1900, 1907

Flow Experience 53, 58, 60, 117, 256, 396, 409, 789, 798, 805, 961, 1140, 1143-1144, 1148, 1153, 1155, 1157, 1163, 1165, 1182, 1195, 1496-1497, 1509-1512, 1516-1523, 1528-1531, 1533-1534, 1536, 1554-1555, 1635, 1796, 1799, 1801, 1815-1816, 1840, 1933

Flow State 37, 52, 105, 108, 115, 119, 131, 310, 396, 577, 692, 743, 1034, 1126, 1135, 1156, 1255, 1495-1496, 1498-1500, 1518, 1522, 1541

Flow Theory 31, 33-34, 45, 47, 49, 53, 805, 807, 961, 1157, 1165, 1253-1255, 1257, 1513, 1516-1519, 1528, 1530, 1702, 1719, 1795, 1797, 1800, 1840

FMP 170, 186

Franchise 811, 1187, 1316, 1435-1436, 1438, 1440, 1442-1445, 1447-1448, 1450-1452, 1456, 1543, 1585, 1667

Free-To-Play 286-287, 300, 304-306, 1071, 1535, 1663, 1676-1677, 1707, 1709

Free-To-Play Games 305-306, 1663, 1709

Functional Fidelity 240-241, 244, 248, 251-252

Functional Magnetic Resonance Imaging or fMRI 602, 616

G

Gadamer 1423, 1425-1434

Gamagio 1435, 1443, 1446, 1452

Game Characters 368, 375, 388-389, 400, 955, 1183, 1185, 1187-1188, 1192-1193, 1462, 1538-1540,

1543-1544, 1547, 1549, 1551, 1553, 1611, 1769

Game Console 788, 1034, 1066, 1978, 1995

Game Design 2, 4, 11, 14-15, 70, 87, 90-92, 95-96, 98-99, 101, 103, 107, 117, 122, 142, 146, 150, 155, 159, 166, 169-171, 173-177, 180, 182, 184, 196, 198-199, 202, 207-208, 210-211, 214, 216, 219, 232, 236-239, 276, 278, 286-287, 296, 298, 300, 304-306, 329, 341, 359, 366, 385, 389-394, 396-397, 399, 408-409, 411-413, 415, 417-419, 421, 424, 429-430, 456, 458-459, 462-463, 467, 482-483, 491, 497, 502, 513, 525, 548, 550, 553, 557-561, 580, 582, 585-588, 590, 592, 595-598, 605, 608, 611, 617-622, 624-625, 627-631, 646, 659, 666, 691, 699, 708, 710, 712, 716, 718-719, 723, 728, 730, 735, 743, 746-747, 752, 758, 762, 768, 771, 777, 786, 788, 872-881, 883, 885, 887-892, 897, 899-902, 906, 908-909, 911, 914, 916-918, 928, 941, 959-960, 963, 1014, 1078, 1080, 1083-1084, 1098, 1101, 1106, 1112, 1120, 1164-1165, 1181-1182, 1215, 1222-1237, 1239, 1246-1248, 1261, 1270, 1282, 1289, 1346, 1348-1349, 1353, 1356, 1358-1361, 1366, 1379-1380, 1382, 1385, 1387-1388, 1409, 1422, 1424, 1433, 1447, 1460, 1578, 1622-1623, 1636, 1644, 1778, 1798, 1812, 1814, 1836-1840, 1842, 1844, 1846, 1851, 1855-1856, 1867, 1885-1887, 1889, 1891-1893, 1895-1900, 1903-1907, 1909, 1935, 1956, 1963, 1970, 1972, 1974-1975

Game Design and Development Programs 1359-1360, 1379, 1385

game design documents 872, 883, 885

Game Design Fundamentals 211, 306, 429, 771, 872, 875, 877, 881, 887-889, 911, 1778

Game Design Process 170, 304, 394, 482, 590, 627-628, 872, 876-877, 880-881, 883, 899, 1893, 1898-1899, 1909

Game Design Schema 889

Game Design Thinking 1891-1893, 1895-1896, 1898, 1900

Game Development 8, 29-30, 95, 170, 198, 200-202, 208-209, 211, 236, 239, 259, 261, 278, 281-282, 286-287, 295, 300, 306-307, 319, 323, 376, 459, 475, 477-478, 586-588, 590-593, 596-598, 612, 719, 742, 786, 881, 891-892, 896-898, 900-907, 917, 938, 941, 1177, 1222-1223, 1227, 1237, 1348, 1358, 1360, 1377, 1380, 1383-1385, 1422, 1623, 1780, 1797-1798, 1834, 1891, 1895-1896, 1899-1900

Game Elements 8, 90, 94, 97-98, 125, 144-145, 150, 159-162, 242, 286-287, 300, 344, 350, 483-484, 490, 515, 532, 538, 551, 558-559, 565, 568, 577,

873, 881, 1014, 1098, 1165, 1239, 1246, 1248, 1257, 1433, 1498, 1624, 1837, 1840, 1850, 1873, 1885, 1888, 1957

Game Engagement 57, 202, 499, 807, 1031, 1033-1036, 1038-1040, 1043-1052, 1154, 1517, 1562, 1753

Game Entertainment Goals 1385

Game Environment 173, 177, 260, 297, 346, 379, 478, 526, 541, 544, 566, 606-607, 742, 880, 889, 936, 940, 942, 945, 1002, 1143, 1163, 1246-1247, 1388, 1498, 1509, 1622-1623, 1643, 1820, 1941

Game Genre 175-176, 201, 246, 593, 596, 650, 878, 900-901, 903, 947, 1054-1055, 1057-1058, 1064, 1077-1079, 1081-1084, 1250, 1387, 1530

Game Habit 1140-1146, 1148-1150, 1152-1153

Game Intensity 1140

Game Interest 1056, 1187, 1538-1539, 1542-1543, 1549-1551

Game Learning Outcome 1385

Game Mechanics 1, 6-7, 88-89, 91-92, 97, 103, 107, 118-119, 122-123, 163, 166, 178, 199, 213, 219-220, 230, 234, 261-262, 278, 280, 290, 293, 401, 413, 418, 424, 482-485, 490, 492, 494-500, 504, 524, 530, 532, 559, 570, 580, 582, 590, 592, 615, 646-647, 718-719, 721, 728, 873-874, 878-879, 886-887, 889, 901, 914, 917, 938-940, 949-950, 1057, 1077, 1133, 1226, 1230-1231, 1233, 1236, 1270, 1348-1350, 1388, 1390, 1831, 1837, 1851, 1853, 1869-1873, 1883, 1925, 1935

Game Production 211, 304, 365, 897, 1228, 1358, 1360, 1373, 1381, 1385-1386, 1451

Game Sound 240, 254, 644, 657, 1833

Game Studies 93, 107, 502, 561, 631, 644, 646, 650, 658-660, 876, 962, 1078, 1083, 1193, 1215, 1387, 1469, 1552-1553, 1575, 1643, 1659, 1775, 1778, 1820, 1934

Game Transfer Phenomenon 121, 137-138

Game Type 346, 402, 1621, 1632-1633, 1707, 1987

Game-Based Approaches 84, 87, 92, 95, 97-99, 103, 426, 1912

Game-Based Learning 52, 70-71, 83, 101, 143, 239-241, 243, 254-257, 285, 340, 392, 395, 409, 411-412, 425-430, 433, 437-438, 461-462, 481-483, 497, 499-502, 504, 524, 528, 632, 707-708, 711-713, 728, 731, 784, 869, 872, 874, 878, 880, 886-888, 941, 943, 958-959, 991-992, 996, 1013, 1054, 1078-1080, 1082, 1084, 1118, 1165, 1179, 1181, 1302-1303, 1387, 1392, 1408, 1422, 1532-1533, 1580, 1624, 1632-1634, 1636-1638, 1815, 1817, 1833, 1840, 1842, 1844, 1847-1848, 1868, 1922, 1934, 1937, 1975, 1977

Gamefulness 90, 92, 98-99, 101, 104, 117, 142, 166,

1356, 1424, 1867, 1974

Gameplay 27, 47, 56, 76, 91-92, 101, 171, 174-176, 178, 180, 202-203, 205-207, 237-238, 240-242, 244-249, 251, 254-256, 287, 291, 294, 299, 308, 310, 313, 315-317, 321, 360, 367-368, 390, 393, 396-397, 399-405, 408, 411-412, 416, 418-424, 449-450, 483-485, 489-490, 492, 496-499, 586, 588, 591, 593-596, 605-606, 609, 613, 620-621, 632, 644, 646-656, 660-661, 663-664, 674-675, 719, 726, 741-742, 755, 757, 774, 776, 778-779, 788, 808, 810, 812, 877, 880, 889, 906, 918, 920-921, 927, 938, 952, 955, 993, 996-997, 1002, 1031-1032, 1041, 1043-1044, 1050-1051, 1055, 1057-1058, 1064, 1066-1068, 1073, 1077, 1083-1084, 1098-1099, 1103, 1109-1112, 1114-1115, 1120, 1155, 1163-1165, 1200, 1212, 1225-1227, 1233-1234, 1247-1248, 1250, 1348, 1363-1364, 1366-1369, 1371-1373, 1377, 1390-1391, 1395-1397, 1411, 1413, 1444-1446, 1448, 1450, 1463, 1470-1471, 1477, 1501-1502, 1509, 1515, 1549, 1576, 1621, 1623, 1625, 1632, 1657, 1661, 1669, 1709, 1737, 1754, 1778, 1820, 1825, 1828-1829, 1831, 1844, 1846, 1855, 1862-1863, 1898-1899, 1926, 1930-1931, 1944-1945, 1952, 1955, 1959, 1966, 1971, 1984

Gameplay Evidence 774, 776

Game-Playing Experience 1621-1622, 1624, 1627-1633

Gamers 62-65, 67, 69, 71-72, 74, 76-77, 79, 83, 94, 106, 121-122, 124, 131, 138, 145, 241, 247, 249, 308, 310-311, 404-405, 436, 453, 490, 603, 605, 634, 663, 676, 691, 789, 808, 945, 950, 996, 1015, 1031-1036, 1044-1047, 1053, 1066, 1068-1069, 1071, 1078-1079, 1083, 1141, 1143-1147, 1153-1155, 1157, 1188, 1196, 1212-1213, 1315, 1392, 1419, 1450, 1470-1474, 1476-1479, 1508-1509, 1516-1517, 1524, 1534, 1536-1537, 1543-1544, 1556, 1561, 1581, 1630, 1632-1633, 1637, 1662, 1678-1681, 1683-1685, 1688, 1692-1698, 1700, 1706-1707, 1711-1713, 1719, 1732-1733, 1735-1739, 1741-1743, 1746-1749, 1752-1753, 1795-1801, 1803, 1805, 1809-1812, 1814, 1820, 1844, 1890, 1941-1943, 1947-1951, 1954

Games Education 1358

Games For Health 57, 84, 92-94, 99-103, 257, 458-459, 480, 678, 743, 763, 766, 771, 1011-1012, 1118, 1260, 1283, 1379, 1383, 1833, 1974

Gamification Components 97, 695, 1852-1853, 1857, 1860-1861, 1863-1864, 1866-1867

Gamification Contexts 539, 1852

Gamification Framework 2-4, 102, 168, 711, 714, 1349,

1845, 1867, 1869

Gamification toolbox 84, 88

Gamified Activities 1852-1867

Gamified Systems 33, 87, 93, 97, 664, 678, 705, 1236, 1246, 1250, 1836-1837, 1840, 1845-1846, 1867

Gaming Addiction 94, 666, 677, 805, 808, 1154, 1673, 1678-1679, 1681, 1683-1686, 1695-1696, 1698-1699, 1701-1702, 1707, 1715, 1717, 1719, 1813, 1815

Gaming Disorder 94, 666, 675, 1042, 1079, 1680-1681, 1694, 1696, 1698, 1701, 1704, 1706-1707, 1709-1713, 1716-1719, 1736, 1752, 1934

Gaming Engagement 307, 311-313, 319, 1153

Gaming Motivation 36, 662-664, 674-675, 677

Gaming Player Types 662

Gaming Studies 1457

Generic Model 380, 617, 622, 626-630

Genetic Algorithm 1321, 1323, 1329-1330, 1342-1344

Grassroot Extensions 1435, 1456

Gulf-Arab Women 1538

H

Hand Detection and Tracking 1086, 1096

Haptic Technology 66, 79, 83

Hate Speech 1457, 1466, 1469

Hearing Aids 129, 324, 338-340

Hearing Loss 323-324, 337-340

Henry Jenkins 1436

Heterogeneous Wireless Networks 814-817, 835-838

Heuristic User Evaluation 240

High Resolution Animation 368, 374, 390

High School 60, 70, 254, 256, 410, 433, 528, 905-906, 1055, 1065, 1074-1077, 1102, 1117-1118, 1127, 1305, 1309, 1388, 1516, 1558, 1564-1565, 1571, 1702, 1706, 1719, 1727, 1740

Higher Education 82, 169, 241, 256, 427, 502-503, 557-559, 579, 701, 708, 713-714, 768, 842, 869, 871, 887, 889, 899, 909, 957, 961, 1014, 1118, 1177, 1222, 1285-1287, 1289, 1293, 1301-1303, 1371, 1382, 1575, 1577, 1621, 1623-1624, 1636-1638, 1705, 1713-1720, 1776, 1833, 1886, 1888, 1892, 1899, 1921-1922, 1984

History Learning 391, 393, 406, 408-410

HMD 138, 186, 1201-1202, 1205-1206

Homo Aestheticus 1756-1760, 1769, 1775, 1777, 1780

Hot Wash 1303

Human-Centered Design 144

Human-Computer Interaction 49, 51-52, 56, 58-59, 82, 118, 122, 191, 209, 338, 340, 481, 499, 527, 579, 582, 603, 614, 657-658, 782, 806, 940, 957, 960,

1085, 1087, 1096, 1156, 1177, 1179, 1219-1220, 1254, 1411, 1480, 1490, 1493, 1511, 1530, 1578, 1801, 1847-1848, 1975
Hunicke 4, 11, 199, 201, 210, 216, 237, 484, 502, 537, 550, 698-699, 710, 1222-1224, 1226-1228, 1235, 1387, 1409, 1872-1873, 1887, 1898, 1906

I

ICT Skills 1624, 1626-1633
Identification Process 1581-1582, 1584, 1620
Identification With Avatar 1582, 1584, 1620
Immersive Environments 72, 187-193, 195-196, 1118, 1211, 1261
Immersive Experiences 176, 1198, 1201, 1214, 1889
Improved Learning Strategy 1411
IMS 14, 193-195, 843, 869
in process data 1097
Indie Game Studio 963
Industry Advisory Council (IAC) 1286, 1303
Influence Factors 1795, 1969
Information System Design 212, 218
In-Game Guidance 1818-1819, 1822, 1825-1832
In-Game Purchase Intention 1516-1519, 1522, 1528-1531
Instructional Design 255, 269, 412, 434, 452, 527, 718-720, 722, 730, 843, 869-871, 889, 1164, 1410
Intelligent Agents 654, 1321
Intelligent Algorithm 680, 688
Intensity 92, 189-191, 195, 307-314, 317-320, 374-376, 530, 535, 543, 1140, 1143, 1146, 1148-1150, 1152-1153, 1157, 1264, 1269, 1274, 1497, 1534, 1561, 1605, 1706, 1800, 1854
Interaction Fidelity 32, 55, 240, 242, 256
Interactive Dashboard 1162, 1164, 1174, 1176, 1182
Interactive Virtual Anatomy 456
Interdependent Self-View 1031, 1035-1037, 1039-1040, 1046, 1049-1050
Intrinsic Engagement 1183-1187, 1189, 1191-1193, 1538-1542, 1544, 1546-1553
Inverted Gatekeeping 1665, 1676
Islamophobia 1457-1458, 1466, 1469
Iterative Design 268, 510, 876, 879, 883, 897, 1407-1408, 1895

J

Javascript 7, 463, 1090, 1121, 1129, 1138
Johnson-Glenberg 1097-1098, 1100-1101, 1112-1113, 1115, 1117-1118

K

Kinect sensor 1097, 1100, 1104, 1111, 1113, 1115, 1118
K-Means Clustering 341-342, 353
Knowledge Co-Construction 433-434, 445-446, 451, 455
Knowledge Transfer 213, 363, 716-718, 721, 723, 725-728
KWS Method 926, 943

L

Latent Dirichlet Allocation 341-342, 345, 357, 359-360, 362-363
Latent Semantic Analysis 341-343, 360-364
Lean Process 258-259, 262-263, 265, 267-268, 282
Leap Motion 177, 186, 1087, 1113
Learning Events 438, 482-485, 490, 492-493, 495-498, 502
Learning Experience 77, 125, 391, 393, 396-397, 400, 402-404, 406-408, 438, 457, 479, 483-484, 491-493, 497, 508, 567, 718, 742, 757, 843, 871, 873, 875, 878, 915, 925, 1081, 1166, 1292, 1300, 1363, 1388-1389, 1623, 1635, 1815, 1911
Learning Language through Simulation 433
Learning Standards 12
Learning-Play Integration 482
Leblanc 4, 11, 199, 201, 210, 216-217, 236-237, 484, 502, 550, 698, 710, 1222-1224, 1235, 1387, 1409, 1872, 1887, 1906
Literacy-first Activity 891, 893, 895, 900, 912
Literature Review 2, 11, 55, 57, 102, 118, 164, 210, 241, 244, 247, 255, 295, 362, 391, 393, 408, 427, 453, 502, 521, 535, 537, 549, 551-552, 579, 581, 618, 629, 666, 706-707, 712, 729, 767, 769, 803, 868, 870-871, 886-888, 961, 992, 1016, 1054, 1064, 1081-1082, 1086, 1116, 1141, 1164, 1202, 1258, 1260, 1286, 1300, 1303, 1433, 1457, 1469, 1523, 1528, 1623, 1635, 1637-1638, 1662, 1664, 1719, 1722, 1784, 1797, 1836, 1850, 1853, 1870, 1873-1874, 1876-1877, 1880, 1883-1884, 1888, 1956, 1958-1960, 1972-1976, 1988
Live-Action Simulation Game 1558, 1570, 1573
LMS 7, 558-559, 565-567, 573, 576, 578, 851, 1842
LookAt 172-174, 179, 183-184, 186
Loot Box 1663, 1671, 1676-1677

M

Machine Learning 122, 255, 275, 341, 348, 360-361, 363, 385-386, 706, 938, 952, 961, 1164, 1166,

1168, 1170, 1172, 1176-1177, 1180, 1182, 1343

MAGIC 24, 875, 883, 947, 953, 1232, 1236, 1347, 1361-1362, 1367, 1375, 1378, 1381, 1386, 1463, 1468, 1513, 1535, 1585, 1589, 1595, 1613

Massive Multiplayer Online Role-Playing Videogames (MMORPG) 83

Massively Multiplayer Online Games 662, 1478, 1696, 1748, 1754, 1941

Mathematics Games 411

Mechanics 1, 4, 6-8, 88-89, 91-92, 97, 103, 107, 118-119, 122-123, 125, 163, 166, 170, 177-178, 199, 201-203, 213, 215, 219-220, 230, 234, 246, 261-262, 278, 280, 289-290, 292-293, 296, 305, 397, 401, 413, 418, 424, 482-486, 490, 492-500, 504, 513-514, 524, 530, 532-533, 537-546, 549, 559, 570, 580, 582, 585-587, 589-590, 592-596, 605-606, 615, 646-648, 651-652, 655, 661, 663, 692, 699-700, 702, 707, 714, 718-719, 721, 728, 740, 745, 747, 873-874, 876, 878-879, 886-889, 901, 914, 917, 938-940, 947, 949-950, 953, 999, 1002, 1009, 1033, 1057, 1077, 1104, 1115, 1133, 1187, 1222-1234, 1236-1237, 1270, 1301, 1307, 1348-1350, 1388, 1390, 1445, 1448, 1543, 1624, 1632, 1637, 1667, 1684, 1820, 1831, 1836-1838, 1851, 1853, 1855-1857, 1860, 1867, 1869, 1871-1885, 1892, 1898, 1903, 1905, 1925-1926, 1929-1930, 1933, 1935, 1958

Media Literacy 484, 1305, 1307, 1318-1319, 1512

Meditation 599-601, 604-614, 616, 1014, 1268, 1594, 1696

Mental Health 96-97, 101, 142, 187, 197, 600-601, 616, 732-734, 742, 765-769, 773, 805, 808, 994-995, 997, 1014-1015, 1017, 1079, 1081, 1121, 1154-1155, 1215-1216, 1218, 1263-1265, 1267-1268, 1271, 1278-1284, 1370, 1421, 1426, 1433, 1675, 1679-1680, 1695-1696, 1698-1702, 1705, 1713, 1715, 1717, 1719, 1736, 1751, 1784, 1799, 1833

Mental Illness 599, 602, 764-765, 768, 1014, 1381, 1659

Metacognition 943, 1575, 1631, 1818, 1821, 1825, 1831-1832

Mhealth 92-93, 104, 772, 1014, 1016, 1283, 1888

MhIST 994-995, 997-998, 1001, 1005-1006, 1010-1011, 1020-1021, 1025

Minecraft 40, 433-438, 441-444, 450-454, 657, 1383, 1388-1393, 1395-1398, 1401, 1403, 1405-1410, 1443, 1450, 1455, 1988-1989, 1991, 1994

Mixed Approaches 603, 616

mixed reality 1097-1098, 1101, 1112, 1117-1118, 1383, 1420

Mobile Advergames 1495-1497, 1514

Mobile Game Applications 391, 399-400, 406, 1516, 1799

Mobile Games 29, 34, 60, 127, 286-288, 293, 295-296, 298, 300-301, 304-306, 391, 393, 397-398, 402, 404, 408, 508, 529, 736, 787, 790, 805-806, 953, 1055-1058, 1064-1065, 1077-1079, 1081-1083, 1156, 1247, 1470, 1498-1500, 1502, 1510-1513, 1517, 1529-1530, 1536-1537, 1640-1644, 1656-1657, 1662-1663, 1667, 1671, 1673, 1694, 1795-1801, 1803-1805, 1809-1812, 1814, 1816, 1984, 1987

Mobile Gaming 806, 1054, 1077, 1144, 1154, 1498-1500, 1506-1507, 1509-1510, 1512, 1516-1517, 1519, 1522-1525, 1528-1531, 1661-1662, 1667-1668, 1670, 1672, 1676-1677, 1679, 1705, 1795, 1799, 1805, 1813-1814, 1816

Mobile Phone 111, 651, 815, 847, 1014, 1055, 1065-1066, 1079-1080, 1083, 1273, 1496, 1662, 1673

Model-Driven Engineering 213, 890

Modeling Language 9, 11, 13, 166, 213, 220, 235, 238-239, 879

Monetization 29, 286-288, 291, 293-294, 296, 298, 300, 305-306, 586, 593, 595, 1347, 1536, 1675

Monetization Strategies 287, 306

Monte Carlo Method 976, 993

Mood Repair 1198-1206, 1208-1215, 1218

Multimodal Literacies 62, 71, 73, 907-908

Multimodality 65, 81, 891-893, 896-897, 900, 908-909, 911-913, 1966

Multiplayer Online Battle Arena (MOBA) 785-786, 788, 802

Multiprofessional approach 84

N

Narrative Learning 914

Nash Equilibrium 818, 822-823, 828-829

Natural Risks Management 212

Need For Cognition 539, 554, 1558, 1563-1565, 1569-1570, 1572, 1574-1575, 1578-1579, 1798, 1816

Need for Orientation 1313, 1319

Negotiation Of Meaning 433, 445-446, 448, 451, 455, 1353

Network Externality 1140, 1145-1146, 1149-1150, 1154

Network Selection 814-815, 817-820, 827, 835-838

Networked Publics 893, 913

Networked Society 891, 895

Neural Network 26-28, 243, 360, 380, 382, 681, 820, 952, 1086, 1168-1170, 1172-1174, 1182

Neurofeedback 187-188, 196, 604-607, 609, 611-616, 771, 1284

Noida 14, 1678
Non-Cooperative Game 814, 816-818, 821-824, 826-828, 835, 837-838
Non-Player Character (NPC) 241, 390
Non-Violent Video Games 1735, 1782, 1788, 1792
non-virtual reality 633
NPC 175, 186, 241, 243-245, 247, 251, 253, 365-370, 372-373, 375-376, 378-380, 384-386, 390, 439, 442, 446, 1184, 1620, 1823, 1966
Nursing 258-259, 266, 276, 280-281, 459, 708, 769, 1214, 1281, 1286, 1298, 1302, 1716

O

Online Actions 1470-1471, 1477
Online Advergames 1495-1496, 1500, 1512, 1533, 1554
Online Competitive Gaming 307-309, 319-320
Online Gaming 53, 106, 309, 322, 554, 662-663, 676-677, 679, 806, 808, 968, 1041, 1082, 1141, 1143, 1153-1155, 1157, 1221, 1224, 1478-1479, 1498-1500, 1506, 1510, 1516-1518, 1522, 1525, 1535, 1624, 1657, 1664, 1679-1687, 1694-1700, 1702, 1709, 1717-1718, 1815-1816, 1938, 1945, 1951
Online Learning 722, 959, 1300, 1302, 1531, 1887
Online Player Type Scale 662, 667-668, 673-674
Online Safety Practices 1470-1471, 1476-1477
Online Social Game 1140
Online Strategic Video Games 785-789, 791, 793, 798-799, 802
Online Threats 1473, 1477
Orientalism 1457-1460, 1462, 1467-1469
Othering 1465, 1469
Ottomentality 1640, 1645-1647, 1656-1658, 1660
Ottomentality Subjectivity 1640

P

Pakistani Children 1781, 1783-1784
Participatory Culture 453, 891, 895, 909, 913, 1317, 1675-1676
Perceived Learning Effectiveness 1621-1622, 1625-1633
Perceived Risk 53, 105, 111, 116, 119, 1799
performance theories 365, 376, 386
Performative Mediation 375, 390
Persona 5 1304-1309, 1311-1312, 1315-1316, 1318-1319
Personality Traits 100, 372, 387, 783, 1122, 1156, 1199, 1220, 1462, 1530, 1534, 1558, 1562-1565, 1569, 1571-1572, 1574-1577, 1580, 1681, 1739, 1782, 1801, 1814, 1939

Personas 30, 269, 327-328, 338-339, 1305, 1319, 1897
Persona-Scenario 323, 326-330, 332-333, 335-336
Persuasive Technology 144, 161, 729, 767, 1270, 1643, 1658, 1974
Phantom Thieves 1305-1306, 1308-1315, 1319-1320
Phenomenological Hermeneutics 1423-1425, 1431-1432
Physical Fidelity 251
Play-Centric Account 890
Player Acceptance 31, 1816
Player Character 14, 173, 175, 366, 390, 594, 767, 810, 955
Player Modeling 341-342, 347, 359-363
Player Perception 31, 314, 1556
Playfulness 34, 36, 90-92, 98-99, 104, 108, 115, 145, 209, 707, 1158, 1424, 1502, 1512, 1555, 1803, 1838, 1879, 1954, 1991
Playography 78, 83
Positive Emotions 84, 104, 420, 568, 1198, 1201, 1204, 1206, 1208-1214, 1509, 1562, 1564, 1572, 1714
Postsecondary Education 1075, 1704
Problem Solving 269, 283, 342, 362, 416, 429, 435, 461, 484, 509-510, 526, 776, 781, 784, 914, 926, 939, 1117-1118, 1122, 1126, 1128, 1136-1137, 1163, 1237, 1257, 1285, 1353, 1389, 1398, 1402, 1406-1410, 1561, 1572-1573, 1575, 1579, 1610, 1738, 1820-1821, 1832, 1936
Procedural Content Generation 244, 944-945, 950-952, 956, 958-963
Procedural Knowledge 1398, 1407, 1818, 1820-1822, 1824-1825, 1827-1830, 1832
Procedural Rhetoric 266, 1307, 1317, 1319, 1965
Production Experience 1358, 1360-1363, 1369-1372, 1374-1376, 1378, 1381, 1386
Program Director 1286, 1289-1292, 1303
Proposer 1480-1491
Prototyping 307, 319, 394, 585-594, 596-598, 626, 734, 872, 874, 876-877, 881-885, 888-890, 1373, 1892, 1895, 1898-1899
Pseudo-Event 1665, 1670, 1676-1677
Psychological Fidelity 241, 244, 253
Psychometric Testing 674
Psychophysiology 196, 615-616, 764, 1195, 1480, 1492, 1555, 1753
Public Relations 1317, 1661-1676

R

Rapid Throwaway Prototyping 890
Real-Time 8, 19, 24, 26-28, 30, 32, 83, 128, 130, 134, 143, 180, 187-190, 193, 196, 213, 238, 271, 308,

338, 370, 394, 436, 452, 461, 599, 750, 776, 786, 788, 815, 915, 929, 959, 1085-1088, 1096, 1146, 1284, 1300, 1303, 1497, 1603, 1667, 1769, 1875

Reception Analysis 1766, 1780

Reception Study 1756

reflection-in-action 1388-1389, 1391, 1393, 1398-1399, 1406-1408

Rehabilitation 33, 49-50, 54, 57-58, 93, 102, 325, 459, 714, 764, 769-770, 1015, 1042, 1079, 1219, 1263, 1271, 1273, 1278, 1412, 1419-1420

Relative Performance 1538, 1540, 1545, 1548, 1550-1552, 1866

Reliability Testing 662, 674

Replayability 248-249, 944-945, 951, 957, 963, 999, 1002

Restriction 727, 1121, 1126, 1138, 1876

RETAIN Model 201, 207, 210, 716-721, 723-726, 728-731

Retention Strategies 287, 306, 439

Risky Online Behavior 1470, 1477

Robert Kirkman 1435, 1438-1439, 1444, 1446, 1451-1453, 1455

Robotics 30, 507-508, 510-511, 513, 521, 523-525, 527, 529, 1119, 1344

Role Play 455, 649, 1276, 1302, 1773, 1781, 1785-1787, 1789-1790

Role Playing 321, 409, 434-436, 664, 950, 959, 964, 1017, 1304, 1577, 1583, 1585, 1620, 1700, 1816

Role-Playing Videogames (RPG) 62, 944-945, 947-948, 950, 953, 955-956, 1319

S

Schell 91, 570, 582, 586, 588-589, 598, 734, 771, 873-876, 880-883, 888-889, 1223, 1228-1229, 1236, 1385, 1460, 1872, 1889

Scientific Background 1621-1624, 1626-1627, 1630, 1633

Secondary Education 507-508, 511, 514, 521-522, 1080, 1815

Self-Determination Theory 31, 33, 36, 38, 45-47, 49, 52-57, 59-60, 102, 124, 278, 280, 538, 579, 582, 678, 699, 735, 742, 761, 771, 1010, 1016, 1196, 1218, 1421, 1434, 1555, 1754, 1840

Self-Efficacy 49, 91, 257, 387, 776, 803, 997, 1113, 1140, 1145, 1148, 1153-1154, 1156, 1199, 1216, 1251, 1281, 1287, 1300, 1532, 1576, 1631-1632, 1636, 1638, 1736, 1799, 1928, 1933, 1968, 1973

Self-Esteem 997, 1265, 1270, 1412, 1419, 1681, 1683-1684, 1715-1716, 1729, 1735, 1738-1739, 1741-1744, 1746, 1749, 1751, 1753-1755, 1791,

1978, 1995

Self-Identity 1031-1032, 1034, 1039-1040, 1050-1051

Self-Presentation 210, 1430, 1698, 1773, 1938-1940, 1952, 1954

Sensory Theory 62, 64, 77-79

Sentiment Analytics 1162, 1164, 1166-1168, 1170, 1172-1174, 1176, 1178, 1180, 1182

Serious Games 9-11, 58, 80, 88, 96, 103, 124-125, 142, 145-146, 150, 156, 158, 163, 165, 167, 188, 198-201, 203-204, 207-220, 222, 226, 235-244, 247-248, 251-261, 268-269, 323, 339, 359, 392, 394, 408-409, 414, 425-426, 456-459, 461, 475, 477-484, 489, 491, 495, 497-504, 507-508, 511-513, 515, 521, 523-525, 527, 529, 549, 559, 599-601, 604-605, 607-609, 613-618, 620-623, 625-631, 678, 716-717, 719, 723, 725, 729-731, 733-734, 763-764, 766, 783, 803, 839-843, 845, 868, 870, 879-880, 886-889, 914-917, 938-943, 960-962, 994, 996-997, 1009, 1012-1014, 1078-1079, 1083, 1098, 1116, 1119, 1126, 1137-1138, 1162, 1164, 1175, 1177-1182, 1250, 1270, 1280, 1282, 1300-1301, 1381, 1383, 1420, 1621-1623, 1633-1638, 1818-1823, 1829-1834, 1844, 1846, 1868, 1888, 1890, 1899, 1902, 1908, 1919, 1934, 1958, 1965, 1972-1974

Service-Dominant Logic 1238, 1243, 1256-1257, 1261

Servicescape 106, 116, 118, 530-531, 533-536, 540-546, 549-551, 557-558, 561-568, 570, 572, 574, 576-578, 580-582

Shmup 1362, 1366, 1381, 1384, 1386

Similarity Index 1821, 1825, 1832

Simulation Design 433, 1288

Simulation Game 241, 244, 433-439, 441-445, 447, 449-452, 455, 842, 1128, 1178, 1185, 1247, 1255, 1539-1540, 1558-1567, 1569-1574, 1576-1577, 1580, 1816

Simulation Theory 1581, 1620

Simulation-Based Learning 433, 1302

Simulations 22-23, 60, 76, 88, 121, 123, 137, 140, 199, 215, 253, 269, 283, 285, 320, 322, 338, 364, 392, 441, 453, 455, 499, 504, 512, 618, 632, 690, 772, 784, 817, 830-831, 842, 871, 886, 915, 935, 942-943, 948, 950, 957, 959, 961, 976, 983, 1054, 1073, 1098, 1101, 1119-1120, 1178, 1180, 1197, 1221, 1230, 1285-1295, 1298-1303, 1341, 1344, 1410, 1557, 1559, 1577, 1579, 1582, 1617, 1638, 1732, 1748, 1755, 1834, 1853, 1908-1909, 1912, 1915, 1919, 1925, 1959, 1963, 1972

Situation-Congruent 1870-1871

Skill and Challenge 1253, 1255, 1495-1496, 1498, 1500, 1517-1519, 1522, 1528, 1530

Skyfall 1085, 1088-1090, 1092-1095
Social Attention 1183
Social Development 57, 102, 579, 678, 771, 1016, 1218, 1346-1347
Social Distance 1040, 1043, 1051
Social Environment 563, 691-692, 694-697, 705, 1122, 1125, 1354-1355, 1695, 1845, 1978, 1986, 1991
Social Facilitation 767, 1183-1185, 1191-1193, 1196-1197, 1538-1540, 1545, 1547, 1551-1553, 1556-1557
Social Game 1140, 1142, 1145, 1321, 1354, 1442, 1452, 1800, 1814, 1987
Social Information Processing 774-776, 781
Social Interaction 38, 54, 89, 98, 128, 394, 435, 455, 496, 534, 663, 665, 702, 769, 785-787, 789-791, 793, 797-802, 876, 1011, 1031, 1034-1036, 1038-1040, 1051-1052, 1159, 1185, 1266, 1269, 1273-1274, 1277, 1280, 1287, 1407, 1425, 1430, 1491, 1497, 1520, 1540, 1545, 1683-1684, 1693, 1762, 1794, 1801, 1840, 1858-1859, 1863, 1865, 1879, 1940-1941, 1943
Social Learning 484, 501, 503-504, 695, 700, 702-703, 705-707, 709, 1287, 1781, 1791, 1978, 1985
Social Phobia 187, 733, 770, 773, 1263-1269, 1271-1275, 1278, 1280-1281, 1684, 1702, 1738
Social Science Education 1558-1559, 1562-1563
Social Withdrawal 1678, 1680, 1683-1686, 1688, 1690, 1692-1694
Socializing Feeling 105, 119
Sociocultural Theory 891, 893-895, 911-913
Software Design 875, 883, 887, 1907
S-O-R 533-536, 543, 562
State Hostility 1184-1186, 1188, 1190-1192, 1196, 1538-1542, 1544, 1546, 1549-1552, 1556
STEM 91, 241, 244, 437, 507-510, 522, 528-529, 778, 839-840, 843-844, 866-868, 870, 914-915, 918, 1097-1099, 1101, 1116, 1222
STEM Education 507, 509-510, 528-529, 1097
Storyworld 1435-1438, 1440-1452, 1456
Strategic Communication 512, 1661, 1666
Structural Equation Modeling 31, 43, 53-54, 58, 676-678, 768, 785, 794, 807, 1140, 1148, 1153, 1155, 1157, 1259, 1555, 1696
Student Engagement 1, 62, 66, 68, 210, 273, 394, 510, 559, 579, 708, 726, 900, 940, 1054, 1635, 1704-1708, 1710-1720, 1907
Subconscious 443, 530, 543
Subject Matter Expert (SME) 1303
Sunk Cost Bias 968, 993
Supervised Learning 27-28, 1168-1169, 1182
Support for Regulation 1721-1723

Susan Sontag 1756
Sustainable City 917-918, 943
System Thinking 944, 949, 956, 984
System Usability Scale (SUS) 616

T

Targeted Affect 1183-1186, 1189-1190, 1192-1193, 1538-1539, 1541, 1544, 1546, 1552
Teaching And Learning 67, 71, 393, 477-478, 508, 511-512, 521, 525-526, 717-718, 728, 893, 1162, 1386, 1624, 1713, 1846, 1894, 1899-1900, 1920
Technical Fidelity 248, 252
Techniques Video Game 169
Technology Acceptance Model (TAM) 31, 33, 45, 49-55, 57, 59-60, 741, 743, 757, 785-787, 789-791, 796-797, 801, 803, 805-808, 1530, 1795, 1797, 1801, 1816
Technology of Self 1640, 1660
Telepresence 35, 51-52, 56, 105-106, 111, 115, 119, 143, 787, 789-790, 1143, 1215, 1219, 1497, 1502, 1504-1505, 1507, 1511, 1513, 1515, 1517-1519, 1522-1523, 1528, 1530, 1532, 1535, 1812
Telepresence Experience 105-106, 119, 1497
Telltale Games 1435, 1443-1444, 1450, 1454-1455
Tensorflow 1085-1086, 1088-1090, 1095
Terminal Reality 1435, 1443, 1447, 1451, 1455
The Advergame 105-107, 110-111, 114-116, 119, 1495, 1502
The Telepresence Experience 119, 1497
The Walking Dead 1435-1436, 1438-1455
The Witcher 3: Wild Hunt 1581-1582, 1585-1586, 1588, 1594-1595, 1603-1606, 1611-1614, 1616, 1619-1620
Theory vs Practice 84, 95
therapeutic games 732, 734-735, 742, 744, 746-748, 758, 762, 994
Therapeutic Gaming 732
Third-Person Effect 1721-1726, 1728-1732
Threshold Model of Social Influence 1481-1482, 1491
Time Distortion 119, 396, 1143, 1495-1496, 1499-1500, 1507-1510, 1515
Traceability 212-220, 223, 225-226, 231, 234-235, 237, 239
Traditional Games 947, 1921, 1978, 1981, 1985, 1990, 1995
transformation processes 1346
Transformative Learning 609, 918, 940, 943
Transmedia 409, 892, 898, 902, 1435-1437, 1440, 1443-1445, 1447-1448, 1450-1454, 1456, 1575, 1581-1584, 1617-1618, 1620

Transmediatic Storytelling 1583, 1620
True Folk Culture 1646, 1660
Tutorial 291, 416, 479, 566-568, 576, 709, 836, 838, 919, 949, 1104-1105, 1114-1115, 1214, 1829
Typology 366, 369, 389, 503, 664, 674, 1078, 1351, 1850, 1908, 1912

U

UML Profile 212, 214, 217, 219-228, 236
Unique Mechanics 1870, 1880, 1882-1883
University Students 246, 792, 842, 848, 1017, 1040, 1051, 1621-1623, 1704, 1706-1707, 1712, 1716, 1840, 1847-1848, 1889
Unreal Engine 170, 185-186
User Experience (UX) 159, 391, 393-395
User Preferences 814-815, 817-819, 826, 835, 837
User Satisfaction 32, 815, 873, 1516-1523, 1528-1531, 1868
User-Evaluation 735, 748, 762, 1003
User-Requirements 323, 326, 328-337

V

Validity Testing 667
Value Co-creation 1238-1245, 1247-1249, 1251, 1253, 1255-1256, 1258, 1260-1261, 1351
Vertical Handoff 814-820, 830-831, 835-837
Video Game Addiction 803, 808, 1701, 1706, 1714, 1719
Video Game Genre 903, 947, 1054, 1064, 1077-1079, 1082-1084
Video Game Journalism 1665, 1677
Video Game Players 664, 786, 792, 935, 1071, 1079, 1194, 1470-1472, 1554, 1638, 1666, 1674
Video Games 9, 23-24, 27, 30, 34, 37-38, 40, 45, 51, 53-54, 57, 62, 71, 80-82, 84, 99, 107-108, 121, 131, 142, 161, 171, 210, 243, 254, 256-257, 260, 283-284, 288, 308, 313, 320, 365-369, 374, 385, 388, 391-392, 397, 411-413, 418, 427-428, 437, 500-504, 512, 526, 528, 603, 614, 617, 623-626, 629, 641, 646, 648, 655-660, 674, 678, 730, 733-734, 763-765, 767, 769-771, 774-775, 782-783, 785-789, 791, 793, 798-799, 802-805, 807, 839, 843, 847, 857-858, 866-867, 869-871, 876, 889, 897, 903, 909, 912, 917, 941, 944-953, 955-962, 965, 996, 998, 1001, 1006, 1008, 1014-1016, 1018, 1031-1033, 1041-1042, 1044, 1052-1058, 1067, 1077-1084, 1086, 1117-1118, 1154, 1181, 1183-1185, 1187-1188, 1193-1194, 1196, 1201-1202, 1211, 1215-1219, 1223, 1225, 1233, 1237, 1251, 1256, 1259, 1304, 1307, 1316-1319, 1348, 1370, 1381-1382, 1409-1410, 1419, 1421-1422, 1426-1427, 1433-1434, 1461, 1465-1470, 1474, 1498, 1512, 1536, 1538-1540, 1544, 1552-1556, 1562, 1575, 1578, 1618, 1630, 1635-1636, 1662-1663, 1667, 1676, 1680-1681, 1697, 1699, 1701, 1706-1707, 1712-1713, 1719, 1721-1744, 1746-1754, 1756, 1761, 1767, 1776-1777, 1781-1794, 1833, 1853-1854, 1869, 1934, 1938, 1945, 1950, 1973, 1975, 1984, 1986-1987, 1989-1990, 1994-1995
Violent Video Games 782-783, 788, 804, 957, 1014, 1426, 1721-1723, 1725-1734, 1736-1739, 1741-1744, 1746, 1748-1752, 1754, 1767, 1781-1793, 1994
Virtual Agents 365, 369-373, 376, 384, 386, 388-390, 1272
Virtual Anatomy Learning 456
Virtual Goods 8, 88, 162, 166, 293, 580, 1471, 1516-1517, 1531, 1533, 1800, 1814, 1859, 1865, 1873
Virtual Learning Environments 53, 199, 842, 871
Virtual Reality (VR) 31-35, 38, 45, 48-60, 102, 122, 126-127, 131, 135, 137, 142-143, 169, 185-187, 255-257, 340, 392, 460-461, 480-481, 529, 548, 599, 604, 633, 636, 681, 686, 688-690, 769, 843, 871, 941-942, 962, 1015, 1042, 1117, 1119, 1198-1199, 1214-1215, 1219-1220, 1261, 1267, 1269, 1271-1275, 1277-1284, 1424, 1561, 1582-1584, 1620, 1637-1638, 1756, 1768, 1884, 1939, 1973, 1978
Visual Reality 1581
Vocational 1065, 1074-1075, 1077

W

Web Services 750
Web3d 456, 458, 462-463, 477, 481, 690
Webisode 1456
Wellbeing 54, 102, 167, 245, 324, 580, 599, 601-602, 733-734, 742-743, 758, 943, 994-1002, 1004-1018, 1020-1025, 1029-1030, 1138, 1281, 1433

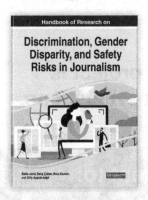

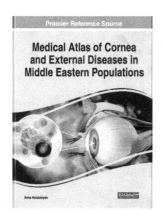
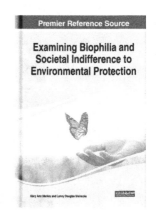
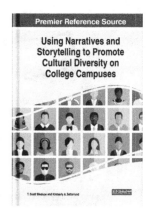

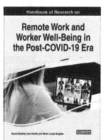

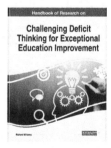

Printed in the United States
by Baker & Taylor Publisher Services

Printed in the United States
by Baker & Taylor Publisher Services